Hazard Branch Library
1620 W. Genesee St.
Syracuse, N.Y. 13204

Explore Korea

Essence of Culture and Tourism

How to Use This Book

Cover

Daedongyeojido, which is a map of Korea drawn by the cartographer Kim Jeongho in 1861, is used as the design for this book's cover. It is by far the most accurate and detailed map made during the Joseon Dynasty (1392-1910).
Hunminjeongeum is the earliest form of Hangeul, the Korean alphabet. It can be seen on the upper-left part of the cover.
Hunminjeongeum was designated as a 'Memory of the World' by UNESCO. Daedongyeojido and Hangeul are part of the rich heritage of Korea.

Introduction

'Explore Korea: Essence of Culture and Tourism,' provides information and detailed explanations concerning Korean culture and tourism resources.
This book also furnishes accurate and detailed location information on tourist resources in the regional sections. It includes maps of 7 metropolitan cities and 9 provinces, area maps and walking tour maps. Information on cultural experiences in Korea can be found in the theme sections.
Various important information, such as the use of public facilities, accommodations, transportation, and basic Korean phrases, can be found in the appendix section.

Romanization

The Korean government standardized the form of spelling according to the Romanization system in 2000. Tourist signboards, guidebooks and maps using the 1984 system will be gradually changed over the next few years.

	1984	2000
Vowels	ŏ Kyŏngju ŭ Kŭmgangsan	→ eo Gyeongju → eu Geumgangsan
Consonants	p Pusan t Taegu k Kangnŭng ch Cheju p' P'unggi t' T'ohamsan k' K'ok'ŭnijae ch' Ch'ungju	→ b Busan → d Daegu → g Gangneung → j Jeju → p Punggi → t Tohamsan → k Kokeunijae → ch Chungju

Name of Noteworthy Attractions

Introduction to Noteworthy Attractions

Image of Attractions

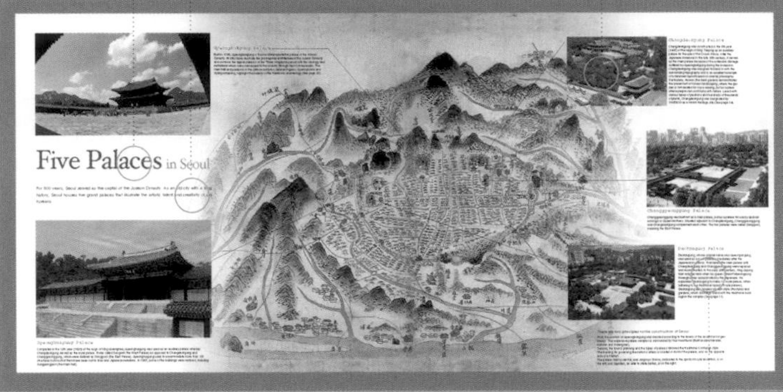

Explanation of Attractions

Noteworthy Attractions

Information on noteworthy Attractions in each region is introduced on double-faced pages with relevant photos.

Name of the City / Province

Grid for Locations

Locator Map of the City / Province in Korea

Index of Locations

City Map / Province Map

Main tourist resources are shown with an illustrated image which marks their location. Road information and administrative district names are also noted on the maps. Areas where there are concentrations of tourism resources are noted with enlarged box-type maps. There are indicated page numbers in the area boxes which link readers to detailed area maps in other parts of the atlas.
Index information, which includes main tourism resources, accommodation and shopping areas, is listed on the right side of the map.

Seoul

Area of Major Attractions

Page Number for the Detailed Area Map

Map Legend

Web Address & Tourist Information

Each Area is Color-coded.

Name of Area with Major Attractions

Number Linking Written Information to Location on the Map

Illustrated Image

Name of Attractions

Serial Number of Attractions on the Map

Photo Caption

GWANGHWAMUN AREA

Areas of Major Attractions

The name of the area is shown on the upper portion of the map.
Main tourist attractions are represented by an illustrated image and a number code on the detailed area map, which allows tourists to find locations and further information.
Special tourist attractions are introduced with more detailed information and photos (for example: Gyeongbokgung Palace).
Web addresses, which are given in English, are located at the end of the column.

The Inmyeon munwon wadang is placed at the left and right ends of the pages. It is a symbol which was made between A.D. 668 and A.D. 935 for the eaves of houses. It depicts a Korean smile. A depiction of a courageous hunter can be seen at the upper end of the pages as a decoration . It is part of Suryepdo (a painting of a hunting scene) in a tomb called Muyongchong (the tomb of the dancer). The tomb dates from the Goguryeo Kingdom (B.C. 37- A.D. 668) and is located in China's Jilin Province. These designs show some of the aesthetic beauty created in Korean artwork.

Walking Tour Map

This map provides detailed information and close-up views of special tourist locations and tourist attractions. It is very useful for those touring by foot.

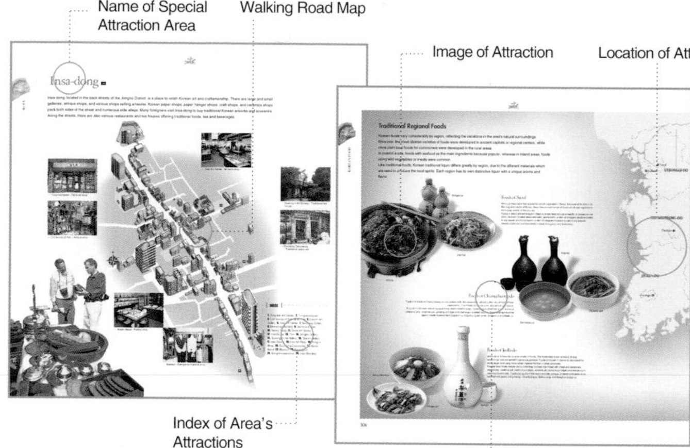

Maps of Thematic Attraction

Maps contain various information about the location of traditional foods, clothes, houses, interesting museums, cultural experiences, festivals, eco-tours and shopping.

Legend

Transportation & Public Facilities

- Expressway
- Interchange / Toll Road (Toll Gate)
- National Road
- Local Road
- City Expressway
- Other Roads
- Railroad Line (Train Station)
- Metro Station Number (Metro Station)
- Transfer Station (Metro Station)
- Tourist Special Area (Tourist Street/Cultural Street)
- Boundary of Province
- Boundary of City, gu & gun
- Boundary of Town & eup
- Boundary of National & Provincial Park
- Seat of Metropolitan & Provincial Government
- Seat of City, gu & gun Office
- Seat of Town & eup Office
- Dam
- Railroad Station
- Airport
- Port
- Bus Terminal
- Metro Line
- Cable Car Platform
- Rest Area
- Parking Area
- Yacht Club
- Hospital
- Police Station
- Embassy
- Post Office
- Tourist Information Center
- University or School
- Library
- Broadcasting Station

Cultural Attractions

- Museum
- Gallery · Exhibition
- Theater
- World Heritage Site
- Prehistoric Relics Site
- Tomb
- Fortress
- Temple
- Site of Buddhist Artifacts
- Church
- Traditional Building
- Traditional Pavilion
- Battlefield
- Korean War Historical Site
- Movie Theater
- Cultural Experience Area

Natural Attractions & Leisure Facilities

- Falls or Valley
- Cave
- Beach
- Ski Resort
- Golf Course
- Horse Track
- Hot Spring or Spa
- National or Pronvincial Park
- Scenic Area
- Amusement Park
- Migratory Birds' Sanctuary
- Zoo
- Natural Recreation Forest
- Arboretum
- Botanical Garden
- Mountain
- Stadium
- Other Tourist Attractions

Accommodations & Shopping

- Hotel
- Condominium
- Youth Hostel
- Department Store or Market
- Duty Free Shop
- Reference Point

※ Location which helps visitors determine where they are.

Specific symbols are used in this book in order to help readers better understand the maps.
Most symbols adopt internationally recognized pictograms, although some symbols are newly designed in order to indicate tourist resources which are unique to Korea.
These symbols are divided into four types: Transportation & Public Facilities, Cultural Attractions, Natural & Leisure Facilities, and Accommodations & Shopping.
Tourists may notice that many geographical locations are designated with Korean words like: 'do, si, gu, gun, eup, myeon, ri, and dong.' Please refer to these meanings: -do (Province), -si (City), -gu, -gun (County), -eup (Town), -myeon (Village), -ri/dong (District)

Explore Korea

Essence of Culture and Tourism

CONTENTS

Introducing Dynamic Korea

Location

Korea lies in the northeastern part of the Asian continent. It is located between 33 degrees and 43 degrees in Northern Latitude, and 124 degrees and 132 degrees in Eastern Longitude. China, Russia and Japan are adjacent to Korea. Local time is nine hours ahead of GMT.

Climate

Korea's climate is regarded as a continental climate from a temperate standpoint and a monsoon climate from a precipitation standpoint.
The climate of Korea is characterized by four distinct seasons: spring, summer, fall and winter.
Spring lasts from late March to May and is warm. Various flowers, including the picturesque cherry blossom, cover the nation's mountains and fields during this time.
Summer lasts from June to early September. It is a hot and humid time of the year. Autumn lasts from September to November, and produces mild weather. It is the best season for visiting Korea.
Winter lasts from December to mid-March. It can be bitterly cold during this time due to the influx of cold Siberian air. Heavy snow in the northern and eastern parts of Korea makes favorable skiing conditions.

National Flag of Korea : the Taegeukgi

The Korean flag's design symbolizes the principles of yin and yang in oriental philosophy. Note that the circle in the center of the flag is divided into two equal parts. The upper red section represents the positive cosmic forces of yang. The lower blue section represents the negative cosmic forces of yin. Four trigrams are located in each corner. Each trigram symbolizes one of four universal elements: heaven, earth, fire and water.

National Flower of Korea : the Mugunghwa (the Rose of Sharon)

This flower symbolizes 'mugung,' meaning immortality.

Mt. Seoraksan

Administration

South Korea's official name is the Republic of Korea (ROK). It is also sometimes referred to as Daehanminguk in Korean.

Changgyeonggung Palace

The capital city is Seoul. Korea consists of 7 metropolitan cities and 9 provinces.
Korea is a democratic republic with its power centralized in an executive president.
Promulgated on July 17, 1948, the Korean constitution guarantees individual rights and calls for three independent branches of government: legislative, judicial and administrative.
Regional autonomy was established in 1995.
Administrative districts include the capital city: Seoul; 6 metropolitan cities: Busan, Daegu, Incheon, Daejeon, Gwangju and Ulsan; and 9 provinces: Gangwon-do, Gyeonggi-do, Chungcheongbuk-do, Chungcheongnam-do, Jeollabuk-do, Jeollanam-do, Gyeongsangbuk-do, Gyeongsangnam-do and Jeju-do.

The Korean Language: Hangeul

Hangeul was invented in 1443, during the reign of King Sejong.
It is composed of 10 vowels and 14 consonants. Hangeul has 11 complex vowels, 5 glottalized sounds, and 24 basic Hangeul letters.
The chart below represents the 24 Hangeul letters and their romanized equivalents.
'The Hunminjeongeum,' a historical document which provides instructions to educate people using Hangeul, is registered with UNESCO.
UNESCO awards a 'King Sejong Literacy Prize,' every year in memory of the inventor of Hangeul.

Hangeul is written in syllabic units made up of two, three, or four letters.

The Korean Alphabet

Consonants

ㄱ	g, k	ㅂ	b, p	ㅋ	k
ㄴ	n	ㅅ	s	ㅌ	t
ㄷ	d, t	ㅇ	ng, silent	ㅍ	p
ㄹ	r, l	ㅈ	j	ㅎ	h
ㅁ	m	ㅊ	ch		

Vowels

ㅏ	a	ㅗ	o	ㅠ	yu
ㅑ	ya	ㅛ	yo	ㅡ	eu
ㅓ	eo	ㅜ	u	ㅣ	i
ㅕ	yeo				

Dynamic Korea

Co-hosting the 2002 FIFA World Cup

As Korea prepares to co-host the 2002 FIFA World Cup with Japan, the Korean government has made strenuous efforts to improve the tourist reception systems. These efforts have resulted in upgraded facilities and service quality of the tourism industry. The 2002 FIFA World Cup shows Korea's cordial welcome and warm hospitality to international visitors all over the world.

Korean Cultural Assets

Korean culture has an ancient history. Though influenced by other Asian cultures, Korea has a unique culture and has invented some of the great masterpieces of civilization. One of them is the world's oldest movable metal type which predate that of Gutenberg. Other examples are the 'turtle ship,' which was the world's first ironclad battleship, and Korea's alphabet, Hangeul, which was devised by the great King Sejong in the Joseon Dynasty.

There are seven World Heritage Sites in Korea that have been designated by the UNESCO, including Jongmyo Shrine, Changdeokgung Palace, Bulguksa Temple and Seokguram Grotto, the Tripitaka Koreana woodblocks (at Haeinsa), Suwon Hwaseong Fortress, the Dolmen sites (Gochang, Hwasun and Ganghwa) and the Gyeongju historic area.

Shopping in Korea

Korea's shops and department stores are numerous and varied, and satisfy even seasoned shoppers, whether they are looking for traditional art objects, handcrafts or state-of-the-art electronic goods.

Goods include clothing, leather goods, furs, jewelry, suitcases & handbags, celadons, antique reproductions, watches and accessories, sports equipment and electronic merchandise. Native products, such as traditional liquors, lacquerware, dried seaweed, dolls, fans, kites, paper masks, bamboo, embroidery and traditional macrame are also very popular with visitors. These items represent the unique cultural and artistic traits of Korea. Ginseng is well known all over the world for its healing properties and beneficial side effects. It has become the most popular item for foreign shoppers. Kimchi is one of the most well-known traditional Korean foods. There are at least 40 kinds of kimchi. Kimchi typically consists of a fermented mixture of radish or cabbage with hot pepper powder, green onions, garlic and salt. It has a unique spicy taste. It is believed that more than 30% of foreign tourists purchase Kimchi while in Korea.

Visitors Looking at Antiques in Insa-dong

Red Devils, the Supporters of the Korean World Cup Team

Suryeopdo, the mural in the tomb of the dancers of the Goguryeo Kingdom, vividly depicts a hunting scene.

Hansandaecheopdo, Joseon Dynasty

Independence Movement, March 1. 1919

History

The Prehistoric Age

Archaeological findings have indicated that the first settlements on the Korean Peninsula occurred 700,000 years ago.

Go-Joseon (B.C. 2333～B.C. 108)

According to legend, the mythical figure Dan-gun founded Go-Joseon, the first Korean Kingdom, in 2333 B.C. Subsequently, several tribes moved from the southern part of Manchuria to the Korean Peninsula.

The Three Kingdoms Period (B.C. 57～A.D. 676)

The three kingdoms, Goguryeo, Baekje and Silla, were established in the 1st century A.D. During this period, the kingdoms' political systems, religions (Buddhism and Confucianism), and cultures developed.

The Unified Silla Kingdom (676～935)

The Unified Silla Kingdom promoted the development of culture and arts, and the popularity of Buddhism reached its peak during this period. The Unified Silla Kingdom declined because of contention for supremacy among the noble classess, and was annexed by Goryeo in 935.

The Goryeo Dynasty (918～1392)

The Goryeo Dynasty was established in 918. Buddhism became the state religion during this time and greatly influenced politics and culture. Famous items produced during this time include Goryeo celadon and the Tripitaka Koreana. During the Goryeo Dynasty, Jikji was invented. Jikji is the world's oldest movable metal type. It was invented a full 78 years before the German movable metal type created by Gutenburg.
The Goryeo Dynasty's strength decreased gradually in the latter half of the 14th century.

The Joseon Dynasty (1392～1910)

The Joseon Dynasty was formed at the end of the 14th century. Confucianism became the state ideology and exerted a massive influence over the whole of society. The Joseon Dynasty produced Hangeul, the Korean alphabet, which was invented in 1443, during the reign of King Sejong. The dynasty's power declined sharply later because of foreign invasions, beginning with the Japanese invasion of 1592.

The Japanese Colonial Period (1910-1945)

In 1876, the Joseon Dynasty was forced to adopt an open-door policy regarding Japan. The Japanese annexation of Korea was concluded in 1910, and Korean people had to accept Japanese colonial rule until the surrender of Japan which ended World War Ⅱ.

The Republic of Korea (1945-Present)

In 1945, Japan surrendered to the Allies and withdrew from the Korean Peninsula. The Korean Peninsula was then divided into two zones, South and North Korea. The Korean War broke out on June 25, 1950 and fighting ended when an armistice was signed on July 27, 1953.
In 2000, an historic summit took place between South and North Korea in Pyeongyang, the capital of North Korea.

Traditional Art

Traditional Dance

Korea's traditional dance, like its music, can be classified into either court dances or folk dances. The slow, gracious movements of the court dances reflect the beauty of moderation and the subdued emotions formed as a result of the strong influence of Confucian philosophy. In contrast, the folk dances, mirroring the life, work and religion of common people, are exciting and romantic, and aptly portray the free and spontaneous emotions of the Korean people.
Court dances are called 'jeongjae,' and include hwagwanmu (a flower crown dance), geommu (a sword dance), cheoyongmu, mugo, suyeonjang and gainjeonmokdan. Folk dances include talchum (a mask dance), seungmu (a monk dance) and salpuri.

Hwagwanmu (Flower Crown Dance)

Traditional Music

Traditional music can be divided into two types: jeongak, or the music of the royal family and the upper classes, and minsogak, or folk music. Jeongak has a slow, solemn and complicated melody, while minsogak is fast and vigorous.
Jeongak is divided

Gayageum, 12-stringed Zither

into two types: yeomillak and sujecheon. Minsogak is also divided into two types: seongak, which includes pansori, minyo and gagok, and giak, which includes the sanjo and samullori styles.
The first noteworthy characteristic of Korean court music is its leisurely tempo. As a result, the mood of this music is meditative and reposeful.
The reason for this slow tempo is related to Koreans' concept of the importance of breath. Whereas Western music is based on the tempo of the heartbeat, and can be as lively, energetic and dynamic as the pounding of the heart, Korean court music is based on the rhythm of breathing, and takes on the attributes of a long breath: tranquility, meditation and contemplation.

Traditional Paintings

From the murals of ancient tombs to the paintings of the Joseon Dynasty (1392-1910), there are a number of indigenous Korean styles. Korean artists have an inclination toward naturalism, in which subjects such as landscapes, flowers or birds are rendered in ink and colored pigments on mulberry paper or silk. In the middle Joseon Dynasty, new techniques were established in Korean painting by noble artists. Folk Paintings which described the joys and sorrows of people's lives became popular.

'Painting of Mt. Inwangsan after Rain' by Jeong Seon

Religion

Buddhism

Buddhism first arrived in Korea in the 2nd year (A.D. 372) of the reign of King Sosurim of the Goguryeo Kingdom. After its introduction, Buddhism exerted a powerful influence in the Baekje Kingdom and Silla Kingdom. Bulguksa Temple and Seokguram Grotto, which are designated as World Heritage Sites by UNESCO, are Buddhist creations from the Silla Kingdom.
Buddhism has exercised a far-reaching influence on Korean culture throughout its long history. The nation's invaluable Buddhist heritage abides in buildings, sculptures, paintings and handicrafts.

Protestantism & Catholicism

Protestantism came to Korea after the signing of the Korean-American Treaty in 1882. Because Christianity challenged the basic values of Joseon society, its believers were subject to persecution in the early years, but as Christians took an increasingly active role in the anti-colonial struggle against the Japanese and churches promoted more educational opportunities, Christianity gained acceptance. Today Korean churches evangelize abroad, and approximately twenty five percent of the Korean population is Christian. Catholicism first came to Korea as a western scholarly pursuit. Korean tributary missions to the imperial court of China took an interest in Jesuit missionary books and brought them back to Korea. In 1784 the first Korean was baptized in Beijing and returned to Korea to set up a house of worship. Despite considerable persecution by the government, numerous people joined the Catholic Church. Presently, over two million people belong to the church.

Myeongdong Cathedral

Jikjisa Temple

'A Threshing' (from a genre painting album) by Kim Hong-do

The gut is a rite in which a shaman offers a sacrifice to the spirits and, through singing and dancing, begs them to intercede in the fortunes of the human world.

Confucianism

Confucianism became a common philosophy in ancient Korea. When it came into contact with fundamental Korean sentiments, Confucianism brought about profound changes and exerted considerable influence on the Korean people. It has been an indispensable component of the Korean moral system, way of life and national laws.

Confucianism, which was the major philosophy of the Joseon Dynasty, eventually gave rise to Silhak, or practical learning. Confucianism has deeply permeated the consciousness of Korean people and can be seen today in many forms, including in these ceremonies that continue to day: Jongmyo Jerye, the royal ancestral service at Jongmyo Shrine and Seokjeon Daeje, and the worship rites at the Seonggyungwan in honor of Confucius, his disciples, and other celebrated Chinese and Korean Confucian scholars.

Shamanism

Various shamanistic practices are deeply ensconced in Korean life. Shamanism has deep roots in folk beliefs from ancient times. It is closely related to the primitive cults which practiced communal rites for the gods of heaven, and which were uninfluenced by Buddhist tradition. One distinguishing characteristic of Korean shamanism is that it seeks to solve human problems through a meeting between humans and the spirits. This can be seen in the various types of shamanistic rites which are still widely practiced even today.

Major Holidays

The Korean lunar calendar has seasonal divisions of 24 jeolgi, each one lasting about 15 days. In an agrarian society, seasonal festivals naturally evolved on the cycle of the lunar calender. New Year's Day, the first full moon day, Dano and Chuseok (Thanksgiving) are all examples of festivals related to the seasons.

New Year's Day

This time of year is called 'Seollal,' which means the first day of the year. During

Jongmyo Jerye

Seollal, Koreans make an ancestral offering at a ritual table set with offerings of foods and drinks as they pray for the well-being of their family. After the service, younger family members bow to their elders and exchange New Year's greetings with them.

The most common food eaten on this day is tteokguk (rice cake soup). It is said that one cannot become a year older without eating a bowl of tteokguk on New Year's Day.

People also engage in traditional games and activities, like 'yut' (a game using wooden sticks as dice), 'neolttwigi' (a kind of traditional seesaw) and kite-flying on Seollal.

Neolttwigi

First Full Moon Day

The day of the first full moon of the new year is the time to perform rites to help avert disasters and bad luck. At dawn, people eat walnuts, chestnuts or peanuts and sip rice wine, praying for good health during the year.

Typical dishes eaten on this day include ogokbap (rice cooked with four other grains: red beans, kidney beans and two kinds of millet) and mugeun namul (made of 9 to 12 different dried vegetables). Diverse folk games are held to encourage communal peace, health, and abundance. For example, a bridge-crossing game (dari balkki) involves crossing a bridge a number of times equal to one's age under the first full moon, in the belief that this will ward off leg pain and promote a person's health until the year's end.

Traditional Fire Twirling

Dano

During the spring festival of Dano, on the 5th day of the 5th month of the lunar calendar, people make amulets with charms and post them above their doors believing that they will keep out evil spirits. Traditionally, people thought the amulet would work best on that day because it was the day which represented full male vitality.

On Dano, some men participate in wrestling tournaments, or ssireum, while women wash their hair with an iris extract.

Chuseok

The harvest festival, Chuseok, is held on the 15th day of the 8th month of the lunar calendar. It is another family-oriented occasion, equal to New Year's Day in importance. An ancestral rite is held with freshly harvested fruits and vegetables.

Special foods for Chuseok include songpyeon (crescent-shaped rice cakes) and torantang (taro soup). Songpyeon is hand-filled with beans, chestnuts, jujubes or sweetened sesame seeds, and steamed with pine needles.

Along with freshly-picked fruits, these foods are presented at an altar for ancestral memorial services.

On Chuseok games such as 'sajanori,' 'ganggangsullae,' and 'juldarigi' are played.

Ssireum

Samullori

Percussion Instruments, (clockwise from upper left: Jing, Buk, Kkwaenggwari)

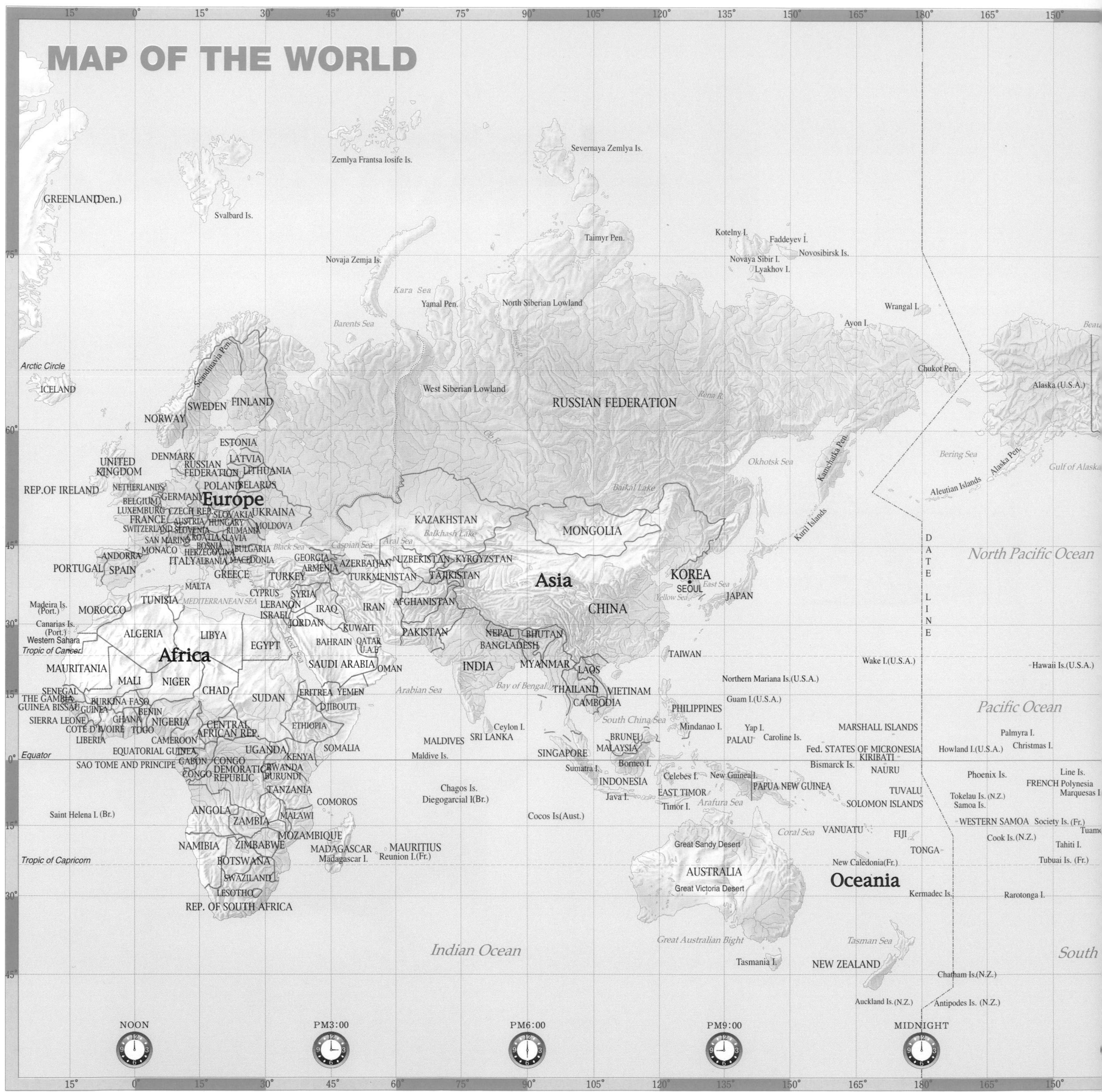
MAP OF THE WORLD
15° 0° 15° 30° 45° 60° 75° 90° 105° 120° 135° 150° 165° 180° 165° 150°
75° 60° 45° 30° 15° 0° 15° 30° 45°
GREENLAND(Den.)
Svalbard Is.
Zemlya Frantsa Iosife Is.
Severnaya Zemlya Is.
Taimyr Pen.
Kotelny I.
Faddeyev I.
Novaya Sibir I.
Novosibirsk Is.
Lyakhov I.
Novaja Zemja Is.
Kara Sea
Yamal Pen.
North Siberian Lowland
Wrangal I.
Ayon I.
Barents Sea
Arctic Circle
ICELAND
Scandinavia Pen.
Chukot Pen.
Alaska (U.S.A.)
West Siberian Lowland
RUSSIAN FEDERATION
Rena R.
SWEDEN
FINLAND
NORWAY
Ob R.
ESTONIA
UNITED KINGDOM
DENMARK
RUSSIAN FEDERATION
LATVIA
LITHUANIA
Okhotsk Sea
Kamchatka Pen.
Bering Sea
Alaska Pen.
Gulf of Alaska
REP.OF IRELAND
NETHERLANDS
BELGIUM
GERMANY
POLAND
BELARUS
Europe
LUXEMBURG
CZECH REP.
SLOVAKIA
UKRAINA
FRANCE
AUSTRIA
HUNGARY
SWITZERLAND
SLOVENIA
RUMANIA
MOLDOVA
SAN MARINO
CROATIA
SLAVIA
BOSNIA HERZEGOVINA
MONACO
BULGARIA
ANDORRA
ITALY
ALBANIA
MACEDONIA
PORTUGAL
SPAIN
GREECE
TURKEY
Baikal Lake
Aleutian Islands
Kuril Islands
KAZAKHSTAN
Balkhash Lake
MONGOLIA
Black Sea
Caspian Sea
Aral Sea
GEORGIA
ARMENIA
AZERBAIJAN
UZBEKISTAN
KYRGYZSTAN
TURKMENISTAN
TAJIKISTAN
Asia
KOREA
SEOUL
East Sea
Yellow Sea
JAPAN
North Pacific Ocean
DATE LINE
MALTA
TUNISIA
MEDITERRANEAN SEA
CYPRUS
SYRIA
LEBANON
ISRAEL
IRAQ
IRAN
AFGHANISTAN
CHINA
Madeira Is. (Port.)
MOROCCO
Canarias Is. (Port.)
Western Sahara
Tropic of Cancer
ALGERIA
LIBYA
EGYPT
JORDAN
KUWAIT
BAHRAIN
QATAR
U.A.E
PAKISTAN
NEPAL
BHUTAN
BANGLADESH
TAIWAN
Africa
Red Sea
SAUDI ARABIA
OMAN
INDIA
MYANMAR
LAOS
Wake I.(U.S.A.)
Hawaii Is.(U.S.A.)
MAURITANIA
MALI
NIGER
CHAD
SUDAN
ERITREA
YEMEN
Arabian Sea
Bay of Bengal
THAILAND
VIETINAM
Northern Mariana Is.(U.S.A.)
SENEGAL
THE GAMBIA
GUINEA BISSAU
GUINEA
BURKINA FASO
BENIN
DJIBOUTI
CAMBODIA
Guam I.(U.S.A.)
PHILIPPINES
Pacific Ocean
SIERRA LEONE
GHANA
TOGO
NIGERIA
COTE D'IVOIRE
LIBERIA
CAMEROON
CENTRAL AFRICAN REP.
ETHIOPIA
Ceylon I.
South China Sea
Mindanao I.
Yap I.
MARSHALL ISLANDS
Palmyra I.
SRI LANKA
MALDIVES
BRUNEI
PALAU
Caroline Is.
Christmas I.
EQUATORIAL GUINEA
UGANDA
SOMALIA
Fed. STATES OF MICRONESIA
Howland I.(U.S.A.)
Equator
SAO TOME AND PRINCIPE
GABON
CONGO
KENYA
Maldive Is.
SINGAPORE
MALAYSIA
KIRIBATI
CONGO DEMORATIC REPUBLIC
RWANDA
BURUNDI
Sumatra I.
Borneo I.
Bismarck Is.
NAURU
Line Is.
Phoenix Is.
FRENCH Polynesia
Marquesas I.
INDONESIA
Celebes I.
New Guinea I.
PAPUA NEW GUINEA
Chagos Is.
Diegogarcial I(Br.)
TANZANIA
COMOROS
Java I.
EAST TIMOR
TUVALU
Tokelau Is. (N.Z.)
Samoa Is.
Timor I.
Arafura Sea
SOLOMON ISLANDS
Saint Helena I. (Br.)
ANGOLA
MALAWI
ZAMBIA
Cocos Is(Aust.)
WESTERN SAMOA
Society Is. (Fr.)
Coral Sea
VANUATU
FIJI
MOZAMBIQUE
NAMIBIA
ZIMBABWE
MADAGASCAR
MAURITIUS
Great Sandy Desert
Cook Is.(N.Z.)
Tahiti I.
TONGA
Tropic of Capricorn
BOTSWANA
Madagascar I.
Reunion I.(Fr.)
New Caledonia(Fr.)
Tubuai Is. (Fr.)
SWAZILAND
AUSTRALIA
Oceania
LESOTHO
Great Victoria Desert
Kermadec Is.
Rarotonga I.
REP. OF SOUTH AFRICA
Indian Ocean
Great Australian Bight
Tasman Sea
South
Tasmania I.
NEW ZEALAND
Chatham Is.(N.Z.)
Auckland Is.(N.Z.)
Antipodes Is. (N.Z.)
NOON
PM3:00
PM6:00
PM9:00
MIDNIGHT

Routes to Korea

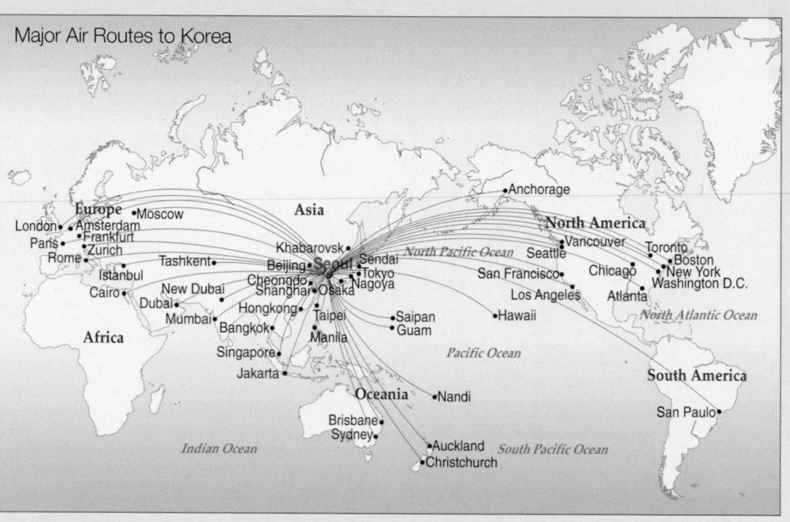

INTERNATIONAL AIRLINES

Airline	Phone	Airline	Phone
Korean Air	82-32-742-5175	Siberia Airlines	82-2-501-6277
Asiana Airlines	82-32-744-2626	Khabarovsk Airlines	82-32-744-8672/4
Northwest Airlines	82-32-744-6300	Uzbekistan Airways	82-2-722-6856
United Airlines	82-32-744-6666	Air Kazakstan	82-2-775-0047
Japan Airlines	82-32-744-3600/11	Cathay Pacific Airways	82-32-744-6777
Japan Air System	82-32-744-3330/1	Singapore Airlines	82-32-744-6500/2
All Nippon Airways	82-32-744-3200	Air Macau	82-2-3442-4200
Air China	82-32-744-3250/68	Thai Airways	82-32-744-3571/2
China Eastern Airways	82-32-744-3780/8	Philippine Airlines	82-32-744-3720/3
China Southern Airlines	82-32-744-0270/9	Garuda Indonesia Airways	82-32-744-1990/9
China Northern Airlines	82-32-744-3455/60	Vietnam Airlines	82-2-663-6648
China Northwest Airlines	82-32-744-6900	Malaysia Airlines	82-32-744-3500/2
China Southwest Airlines	82-2-310-9988	Mongolian Airlines	82-2-756-9761
China Yunnan Airlines	82-2-777-7779	Turkish Airlines	82-32-744-3737/8
Vladivostok Air	82-2-733-2920	Air France	82-32-744-4900/9
Shkhalinsk Airlines	82-2-318-7033	Air Canada	82-32-744-0898/9
Aeroflot Russian Int'l	82-32-744-8672/3	KLM Royal Dutch Airlines	82-32-744-6700/9
Krasnoyarsk Airlines	82-2-777-6399	Lufthansa Airlines	82-32-744-3411/9

ESTIMATED FLYING TIME

ROUTE	DURATION	ROUTE	DURATION
Seoul - Tokyo	02:10	Seoul - Sao Paulo	23:30
Seoul - Osaka	01:40	Seoul - Toronto	14:50
Seoul - Beijing	02:10	Seoul - Vancouver	09:50
Seoul - Hongkong	04:00	Seoul - Sydney	10:00
Seoul - Bangkok	06:10	Seoul - Guam	04:20
Seoul - Singapore	06:40	Seoul - Amsterdam	11:45
Seoul - Taipei	02:40	Seoul - Frankfurt	11:55
Seoul - Moscow	09:55	Seoul - London	12:35
Seoul - Los Angeles	10:50	Seoul - Paris	12:15
Seoul - New York	13:50	Seoul - Roma	15:10
Seoul - San Francisco	10:15	Seoul - Zurich	12:00
Seoul - Chicago	12:35	Seoul - Tehran	15:30

MAP OF KOREA

Sea Routes to Korea

CHINA
RUSSIA
JAPAN
KOREA
Changchun
Vladivostok
Sapporo
Shenyang
Baekdusan
Cheongjin
Beijing
Dandong
Manpo
Aomori
Tianjin
Dalian
Sinuiju
Wonsan
Sendai
Pyeongyang
Sokcho
Yantai
Seoul
Niigata
Weihai
Incheon
Qingdao
Tokyo
Gunsan
Busan
Nagoya
Hiroshima
Osaka
Shimonoseki
Jeju
Fukuoka (Hakata)
Shanghai

Baekdusan

Baekdusan
CHEONJI

124° 125° 126° 127° 128° 129° 130° 131° 132°
43° 42° 41° 40° 39° 38° 37°

RUSSIA
DUMANGAN
AMNOKGANG
Hoeryeong
Najin
Hamgyeongbuk-do
Cheongjin
Hyesan
Yanggang-do
Manpo
Ganggye
Janggang-do
Seongjin
Dancheon
Hamgyeongnam-do
Sinuiju
Guseong
Huicheon
Sinpo
Pyeonganbuk-do
Hamheung
Deokcheon
Gaecheon
Jeongju
Anju
DONGHANMAN BAY
Pyeongseong
Pyeongannam-do
SEOHANMAN BAY
Wonsan
Pyeongyang
Nampo
Songnim
Sariwon
Hwanghaebuk-do
Goseong
Demilitarized Zone
East Sea
Sokcho
Hwanghaenam-do
Cheorwon
Hwacheon
SEORAKSAN NAT'L PARK
Haeju
Yeoncheon
Yanggu
Inje
Yangyang
Baengnyeongdo
Gaeseong
Gangwon-do
Daecheongdo
Socheongdo
Dongducheon
Paju
Gapyeong
Chuncheon
ODAESAN NAT'L PARK
Gangneung
Ganghwa
Goyang
Uijeongbu
Sunwido
BUKHANSAN NAT'L PARK
Daeyeonpyeongdo
Gimpo
Namyangju
Hongcheon
Ganghwado
Guri
Yeongjongdo
Seoul
Hanam
Ulleung
Ulleungdo
Donghae
GYEONGGIMAN BAY
Incheon
Bucheon
Seongnam
Yangpyeong
Hoengseong
Samcheok
Muuido
Anyang
Gwangju
Wonju
Pyeongchang
Ansan
Uiwang
Gyeonggi-do
CHIAKSAN NAT'L PARK
Yeongheungdo
Jeongseon
Dokdo
Deokjeokdo
Suwon
Icheon
Yeoju
Hwaseong
Yeongwol
Taebaek
Osan
Yongin
Seongapdo
Daenanjido
Anseong
Jecheon
SOBAEKSAN NAT'L PARK
Pyeongtaek
Jincheon
Chungju
Danyang
Uljin
Eumseong
WORAKSAN NAT'L PARK
Bonghwa
Dangjin
Seosan
Cheonan
Taean
Asan
Chungcheongbuk-do
Yeongju
TAEAN COASTAL NAT'L PARK
Yesan
Cheongju
Yeongyang

Domestic Air & Sea Routes

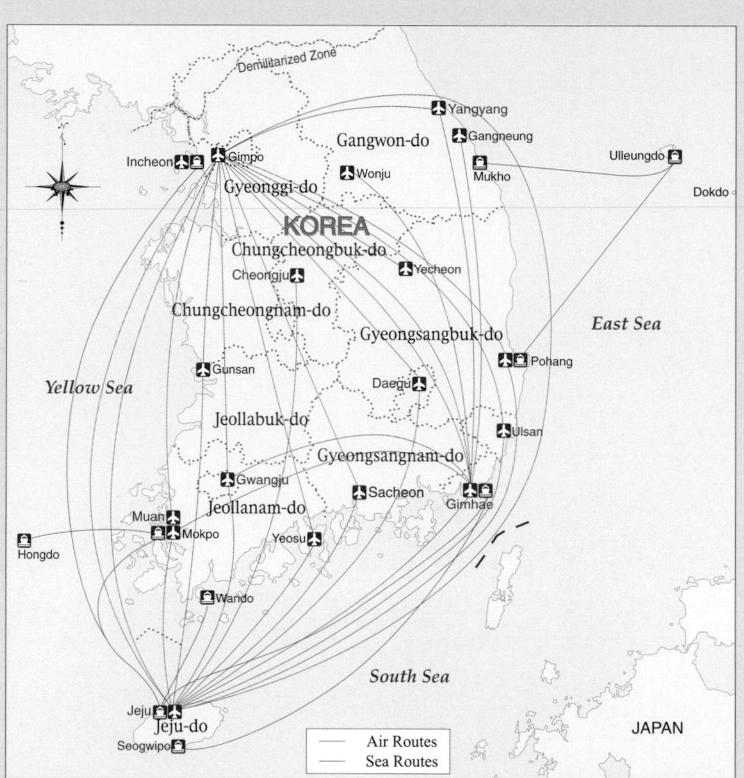

DOMESTIC & INTERNATIONAL AIRPORTS IN KOREA

Airport	Phone	Airport	Phone
Incheon International Airport	82-32-741-0104	Sacheon Airport	82-55-852-0768
Gangneung Airport	82-33-648-2391	Yeosu Airport	82-61-683-7997
Gwangju International Airport	82-62-940-0323	Yecheon Airport	82-54-653-9301
Gunsan Airport	82-63-471-5051	Ulsan Airport	82-52-288-7012
Gimpo Airport	82-2-660-2114	Jeju International Airport	82-64-742-3011
Gimhae International Airport	82-51-972-3010	Pohang Airport	82-54-284-4767
Daegu International Airport	82-53-982-1459	Cheongju International Airport	82-43-210-6114
Mokpo Airport	82-61-471-0085~7	Yangyang International Airport	82-33-670-7114

ESTIMATED FLYING TIME

ROUTE	DURATION (Mins.)	ROUTE	DURATION (Mins.)
Seoul - Gimhae	60	Seoul - Yeosu	60
Seoul - Jeju	65	Seoul - Sokcho	50
Seoul - Daegu	50	Seoul - Yecheon	45
Seoul - Ulsan	55	Seoul - Gangneung	50
Seoul - Pohang	50	Seoul - Mokpo	60
Seoul - Sacheon	60	Seoul - Gunsan	50
Seoul - Gwangju	50	Seoul - Yangyang	50

Korean Air 82-2656-2000 Asiana Airlines 82-2669-4000

Regional Attractions

Seoul

The word 'Seoul' is derived from the ancient word 'Seorabeol' or 'Seobeol', meaning 'capital.' Seoul is a megalopolis with more than 10 million citizens, but it is also a human-oriented city with more than 600 years of history. Seoul is a unique place where the modern age is harmonized with the past. Here skyscrapers, cultural heritage and historical sites, such as ancient palaces, coexist. It is always bustling with exciting events and has many cultural facilities, including plenty of museums and galleries. Seoul was host of the Olympic Games in 1988 and co-hosts the 2002 World Cup. With its brisk political and economic activities, Seoul is a city filled with great energy and vitality. The official flower of Seoul is the forsythia and the official bird is the magpie.

Five Palaces in Seoul

For 500 years, Seoul served as the capital of the Joseon Dynasty. The city houses five grand palaces which illustrate the artistic talent and creativity of Koreans throughout the city's history.

Gyeonghuigung Palace

Completed in the 12th year (1620) of the reign of King Gwanghae, Gyeonghuigung was used as an auxiliary palace whereas Changdeokgung served as the royal palace. It was called Seogwol (the West Palace) while Changdeokgung and Changgyeonggung were dubbed as Donggwol (the East Palace).

Gyeongbokgung Palace

Built in 1395, Gyeongbokgung is the most representative palace of the Joseon Dynasty. The main hall and pavilions in the palace complex; Geunjeongjeon, Gyeonghoeru and Hyangwonjeong, highlight the beauty of the traditional architecture (See page 28).

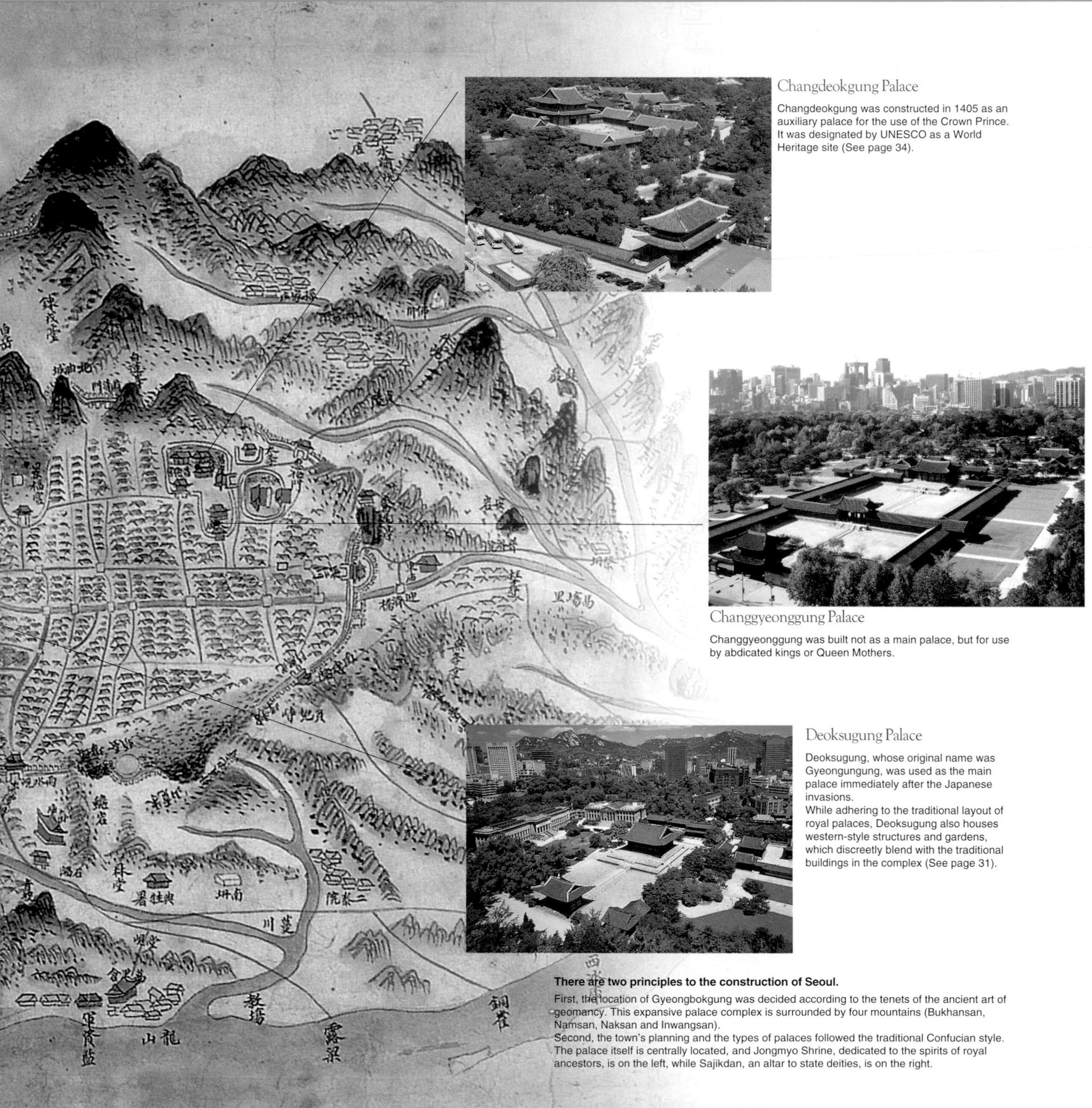

Changdeokgung Palace

Changdeokgung was constructed in 1405 as an auxiliary palace for the use of the Crown Prince. It was designated by UNESCO as a World Heritage site (See page 34).

Changgyeonggung Palace

Changgyeonggung was built not as a main palace, but for use by abdicated kings or Queen Mothers.

Deoksugung Palace

Deoksugung, whose original name was Gyeongungung, was used as the main palace immediately after the Japanese invasions.

While adhering to the traditional layout of royal palaces, Deoksugung also houses western-style structures and gardens, which discreetly blend with the traditional buildings in the complex (See page 31).

There are two principles to the construction of Seoul.

First, the location of Gyeongbokgung was decided according to the tenets of the ancient art of geomancy. This expansive palace complex is surrounded by four mountains (Bukhansan, Namsan, Naksan and Inwangsan).

Second, the town's planning and the types of palaces followed the traditional Confucian style. The palace itself is centrally located, and Jongmyo Shrine, dedicated to the spirits of royal ancestors, is on the left, while Sajikdan, an altar to state deities, is on the right.

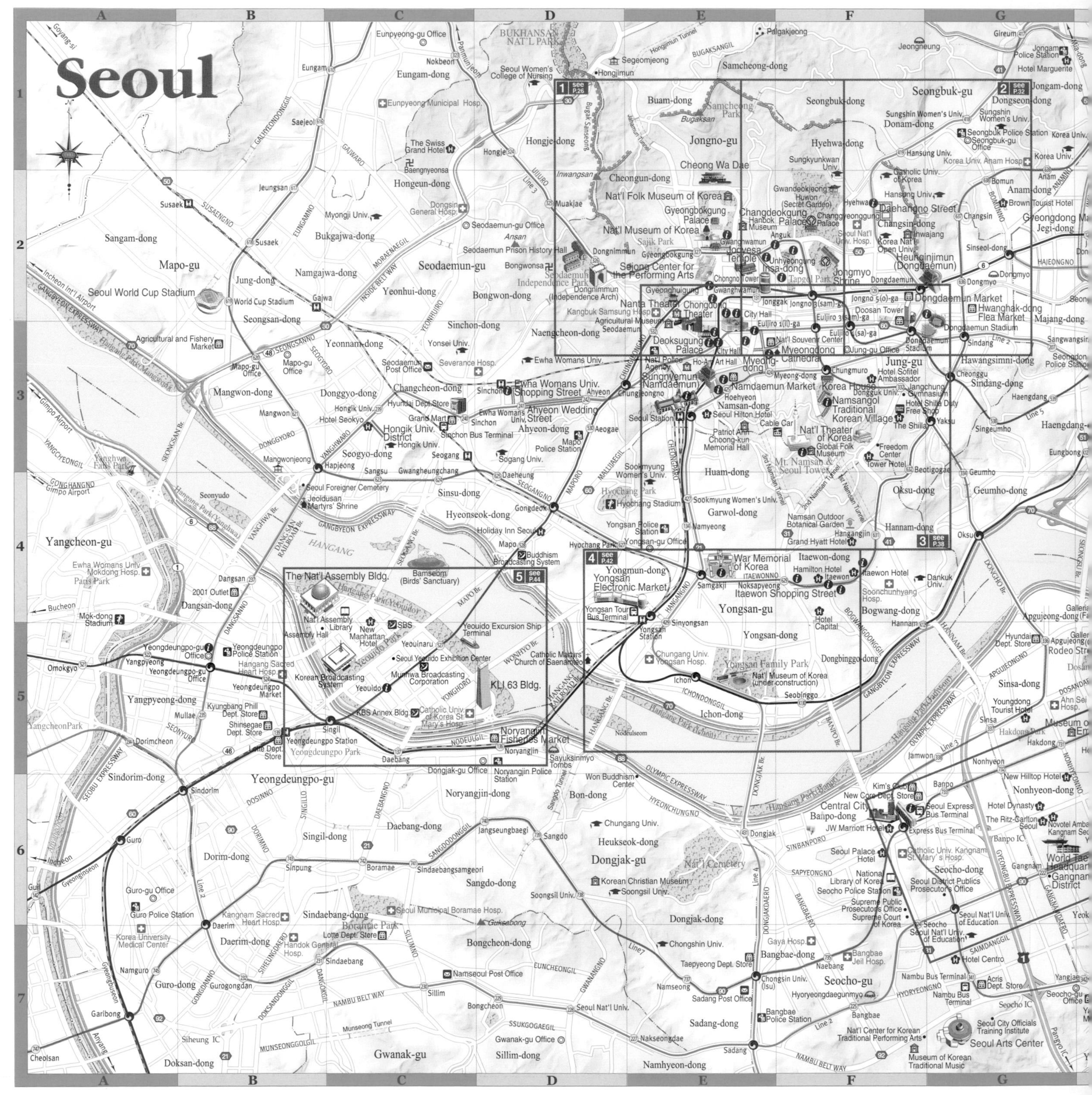

Seoul
A
B
C
D
E
F
G
1
2
3
4
5
6
7
Goyang-si
Eunpyeong-gu Office
BUKHANSAN NAT'L PARK
Hongjimun Tunnel
Palgakjeong
Jeongneung
Gireum
Jongam Police Station
Hotel Marguerite
Eungam
Eungam-dong
Nokbeon
Seoul Women's College of Nursing
Segeomjeong
Hongjimun
BUGAKSANGIL
Samcheong-dong
Eunpyeong Municipal Hosp.
Saejeol
Buam-dong
Samcheong Park
Bugaksan
Seongbuk-dong
Seongbuk-gu
Jongam-dong
Dongseon-dong
Sungshin Women's Univ.
Donam-dong
Seongbuk Police Station
Seongbuk-gu Office
Korea Univ.
The Swiss Grand Hotel
Baengnyeonsa
Hongeun-dong
Hongje
Hongje-dong
Jongno-gu
Hyehwa-dong
Sungkyunkwan Univ.
Hansung Univ.
Korea Univ. Anam Hosp.
Inwangsan
Cheong Wa Dae
Cheongun-dong
Nat'l Folk Museum of Korea
Gwandeokjeong
Huwon (Secret Garden)
Catholic Univ. of Korea
Anam
Anam-dong
Bomun
Brown Tourist Hotel
Jeungsan
Susaek
SUSAENGNO
Myongji Univ.
Dongsin General Hosp.
Seodaemun-gu Office
Ansan
Muakjae
Gyeongbokgung Palace
Changdeokgung Palace
Changgyeonggung Palace
Hanbok Museum
Hyehwa
Daehangno Street
Changsin-dong
Changsin
Gyeongdong Market
Jegi-dong
Sangam-dong
Mapo-gu
Susaek
Bukgajwa-dong
Seodaemun Prison History Hall
Nat'l Museum of Korea
Sajik Park
Gwanghwamun
Anguk
Seoul Nat'l Univ. Hosp.
Korea Nat'l Open Univ.
Ihwajang
Heunginjimun (Dongdaemun)
Sinseol-dong
Jung-dong
Namgajwa-dong
Seodaemun-gu
Bongwonsa
Dongnimmun
Gyeongbokgung
Jogyesa Temple
Insa-dong
Unhyeongung
Tapgol Park
Jongmyo Shrine
Dongmyo
Incheon Int'l Airport
GANGBYEON EXPRESSWAY
Seoul World Cup Stadium
World Cup Stadium
Gajwa
Yeonhui-dong
Seodaemun Independence Park
Dongnimmun (Independence Arch)
Sejong Center for the Performing Arts
Bongwon-dong
Gyeonghuigung
Chongno Tower
Jongno 3(sam)-ga
Jongno 5(o)-ga
Dongdaemun Market
Seongsan-dong
Kangbuk Samsung Hosp.
Nanta Theater
Chongdong Theater
Jonggak
Doosan Tower
Hwanghak-dong Flea Market
Majang-dong
Sinchon-dong
Agricultural Museum
City Hall
Euljiro 1(il)-ga
Euljiro 3(sam)-ga
Euljiro 4(sa)-ga
Dongdaemun Stadium
Agricultural and Fishery Market
Yeonnam-dong
Yonsei Univ.
Naengcheon-dong
Seodaemun
Deoksugung Palace
Nat'l Souvenir Center
Myeongdong Cathedral
Jung-gu Office
Sindang
Sangwangsimni
Mapo-gu Office
Mangwon-dong
Seodaemun Post Office
Severance Hosp.
Ewha Womans Univ.
Nat'l Police Agency
Ho-Am Art Hall
Myeong-dong
Myeong-dong
Chungmuro
Jung-gu
Hwangsimni-dong
Seongdong Police Station
Donggyo-dong
Changcheon-dong
Sinchon
Ewha Womans Univ. Shopping Street
Ahyeon
Chungjeongno
Sungnyemun (Namdaemun)
Namdaemun Market
Korea House
Hotel Sofitel Ambassador
Cheonggu
Sindang-dong
Hoehyeon
Dongguk Univ.
Jangchung Gymnasium
Hongik Univ.
Hotel Seokyo
Hyundai Dept. Store
Mangwon
Namsan-dong
Namsangol Traditional Korean Village
Hotel Shilla Duty Free Shop
Haengdang
Grand Mart
Ewha Womans Univ.
Ahyeon Wedding Street
Seoul Station
Seoul Hilton Hotel
Cable Car
Yaksu
The Shilla
Singeumho
Haengdang-dong
Hongik Univ. District
Sinchon Bus Terminal
Ahyeon-dong
Aegogae
Patriot Ahn Choong-kun Memorial Hall
Nat'l Theater of Korea
Global Folk Museum
Mapo Police Station
Seogang
Sogang Univ.
Freedom Center
Tower Hotel
Eungbong
Mangwonjeong
Seogyo-dong
Hapjeong
Mt. Namsan & Seoul Tower
Yanghwa Falls Park
Sangsu
Gwangheungchang
Daeheung
Sookmyung Women's Univ.
Huam-dong
Beotigogae
Geumho
Gimpo Airport
Seoul Foreigner Cemetery
Sinsu-dong
Hyochang Park
Oksu-dong
Geumho-dong
Seonyudo
Jeoldusan Martyrs' Shrine
Gongdeok
Hyochang Stadium
Sookmyung Women's Univ.
Garwol-dong
Hyeonseok-dong
Namsan Outdoor Botanical Garden
Yangcheon-gu
Holiday Inn Seoul
Yongsan Police Station
Namyeong
Hannam-dong
Mapo
Hyochang Park
Yongsan-gu Office
Hangangjin
Grand Hyatt Hotel
Oksu
HANGANG
Buddhism Broadcasting System
War Memorial of Korea
Itaewon-dong
Ewha Womans Univ. Mokdong Hosp.
Paris Park
The Nat'l Assembly Bldg.
Bamseom (Birds' Sanctuary)
Yongmun-dong
Yongsan Electronic Market
Hamilton Hotel
Itaewon
Itaewon Hotel
Dankuk Univ.
Dangsan
Samgakji
ITAEWONNO
Noksapyeong
Itaewon Shopping Street
Soonchunhyang Hosp.
2001 Outlet
Dangsan-dong
Bucheon
Mok-dong Stadium
Nat'l Assembly Library
New Manhattan Hotel
SBS
Yeouido Excursion Ship Terminal
Yongsan Tour Bus Terminal
Yongsan-gu
Hotel Capital
Bogwang-dong
Hannam
Apgujeong-dong
Assembly Hall
Yeouido Park
Yeouinaru
Yongsan Station
Sinyongsan
Yongsan-dong
Hyundai Dept. Store
Apgujeong
Rodeo Street
Yeongdeungpo-gu Office
Yeongdeungpo Police Station
Yangpyeong
Omokgyo
Hangang Sacred Heart Hosp.
Yeongdeungpo-gu Office
Seoul Yeouido Exhibition Center
Catholic Martyrs' Church of Saenamteo
Chungang Univ. Yongsan Hosp.
Yongsan Family Park
Dongbinggo-dong
Yeongdeungpo Market
Korean Broadcasting System
Munhwa Broadcasting Corporation
Yeouido
KLI 63 Bldg.
Ichon
Nat'l Museum of Korea (under construction)
Seobinggo
Sinsa-dong
Yangpyeong-dong
Mullae
Kyungbang Phill Dept. Store
Shinsegae Dept. Store
Singil
KBS Annex Bldg.
Catholic Univ. of Korea St. Mary's Hosp.
Ichon-dong
Youngdong Tourist Hotel
Sinsa
Ahn Sei Hosp.
YangcheonPark
Dorimcheon
Yeongdeungpo Station
Yeongdeungpo Park
Lotte Dept. Store
Noryangjin Fisheries Market
Noryangjin
Nodeulseom
Hakdong Park
Hakdong
Museum of
Jamwon
Nonhyeon
Sindorim-dong
Yeongdeungpo-gu
Daebang
Dongjak-gu Office
Noryangjin Police Station
Sayuksinmyo Tombs
Won Buddhism Center
Bon-dong
OLYMPIC EXPRESSWAY
New Hilltop Hotel
Nonhyeon-dong
Kim's Club
New Core Dept. Store
Central City
Banpo
Sindorim
Noryangjin-dong
Banpo-dong
Seoul Express Bus Terminal
Hotel Dynasty
The Ritz-Carlton Seoul
Novotel Ambassador Kangnam
Daebang-dong
Chungang Univ.
JW Marriott Hotel
Express Bus Terminal
Guro
Singil-dong
Jangseungbaegi
Sangdo
Heukseok-dong
Dongjak
Banpo IC
Dorim-dong
Sinpung
Boramae
Sindaebangsamgeori
Dongjak-gu
Nat'l Cemetery
Seoul Palace Hotel
Catholic Univ. Kangnam St. Mary's Hosp.
Seocho-dong
Gangnam
World Trade Headquarters
Gangnam District
Guil
Sangdo-dong
Korean Christian Museum
Soongsil Univ.
National Library of Korea
Seocho Police Station
Seoul District Publics Prosecutor's Office
Guro-gu Office
Guro Police Station
Kangnam Sacred Heart Hosp.
Sindaebang-dong
Seoul Municipal Boramae Hosp.
Soongsil Univ.
Dongjak-dong
Supreme Public Prosecutors Office
Supreme Court of Korea
Seoul Nat'l Univ. of Education
Korea University Medical Center
Daerim
Daerim-dong
Handok General Hosp.
Lotte Dept. Store
Boramae Park
Gwanaksan
Bongcheon-dong
Chongshin Univ.
Gaya Hosp.
Seocho
Seoul Nat'l Univ. of Education
Hotel Centro
Namguro
Sindaebang
EUNCHEONGIL
Taepyeong Dept. Store
Bangbae-dong
Bangbae Jeil Hosp.
Naebang
Seocho-gu
Guro-dong
Gurogongdan
Namseoul Post Office
Sillim
Namseong
Chongsin Univ. (Isu)
Sadang Post Office
Hyoryeongdaegunmyo
Nambu Bus Terminal
Acris Dept. Store
Yangjae
Garibong
Bongcheon
Seoul Nat'l Univ.
Bangbae Police Station
Bangbae
Seocho IC
Seocho-gu Office
NAMBU BELT WAY
Munseong Tunnel
SSUKGOGAEGIL
Sadang-dong
Nat'l Center for Korean Traditional Performing Arts
Seoul City Officials Training Institute
Seoul Arts Center
Siheung IC
Gwanak-gu Office
Nakseongdae
Sadang
Cheolsan
Gwanak-gu
Sillim-dong
Namhyeon-dong
Museum of Korean Traditional Music
Doksan-dong

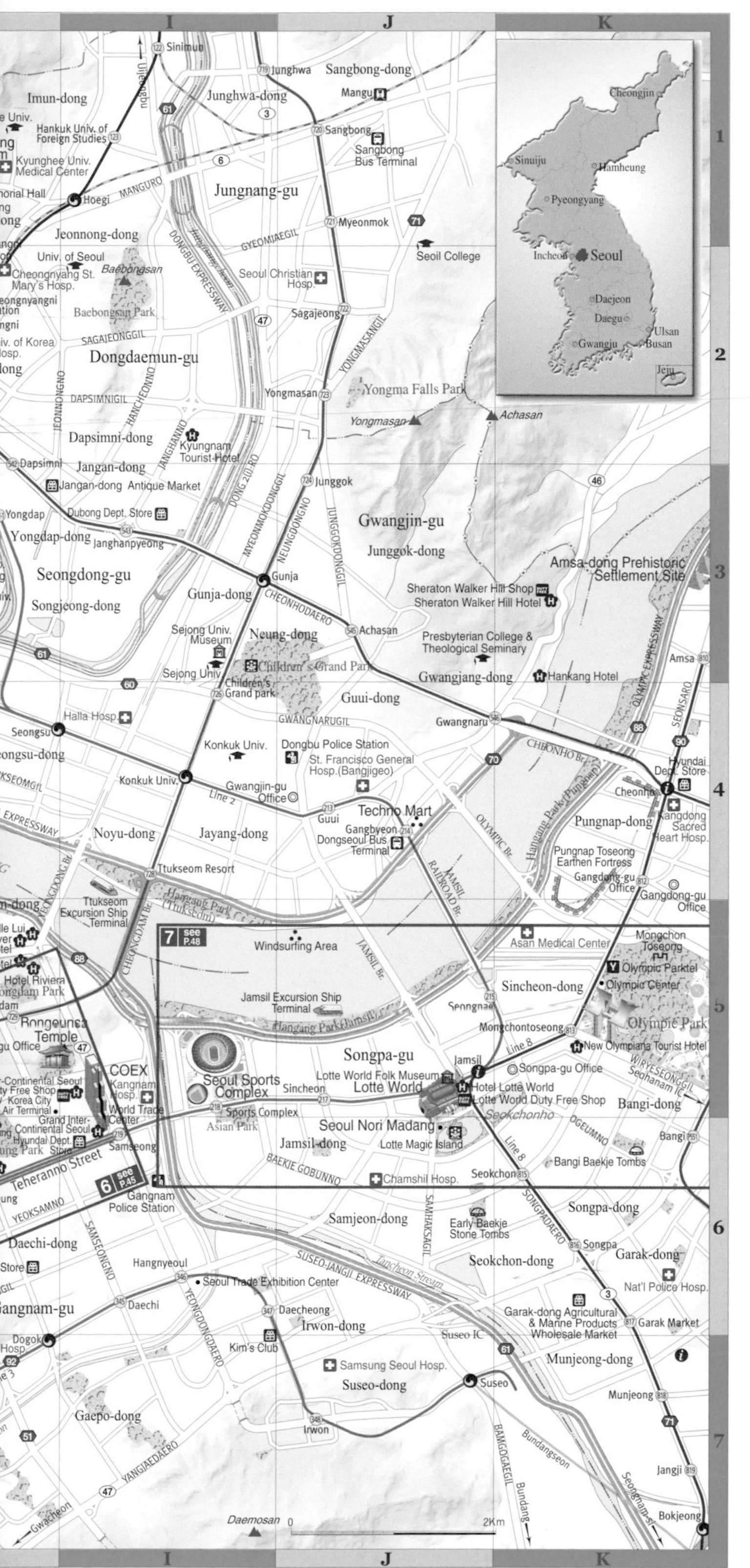

7 see P.48
6 see P.45

INDEX

Cultural Relics

Natural Attractions

Museums & Theaters

Places of Interest

Accommodations

Transportation

Tourist Information

Seoul Tourist Information Center 82-2-731-6337
www.metro.seoul.kr

LEGEND

- Railroad Station
- Bus Terminal
- Metro Line
- Cable Car Platform
- Hospital
- Police Station
- Post Office
- Tourist Information Center
- University or School
- Library
- Broadcasting Station
- City Expressway
- Museum
- Gallery
- Theater
- World Heritage Site
- Tomb
- Fortress
- Temple
- Church
- Traditional Building
- Traditional Pavilion
- Falls or Valley
- Transfer Station
- Golf Course
- Park
- Amusement Park
- Arboretum
- Mountain
- Stadium
- Other Tourist Attractions
- Hotel
- Youth Hostel
- Department Store or Market
- Duty Free Shop
- Reference Point
- Metro Station Number

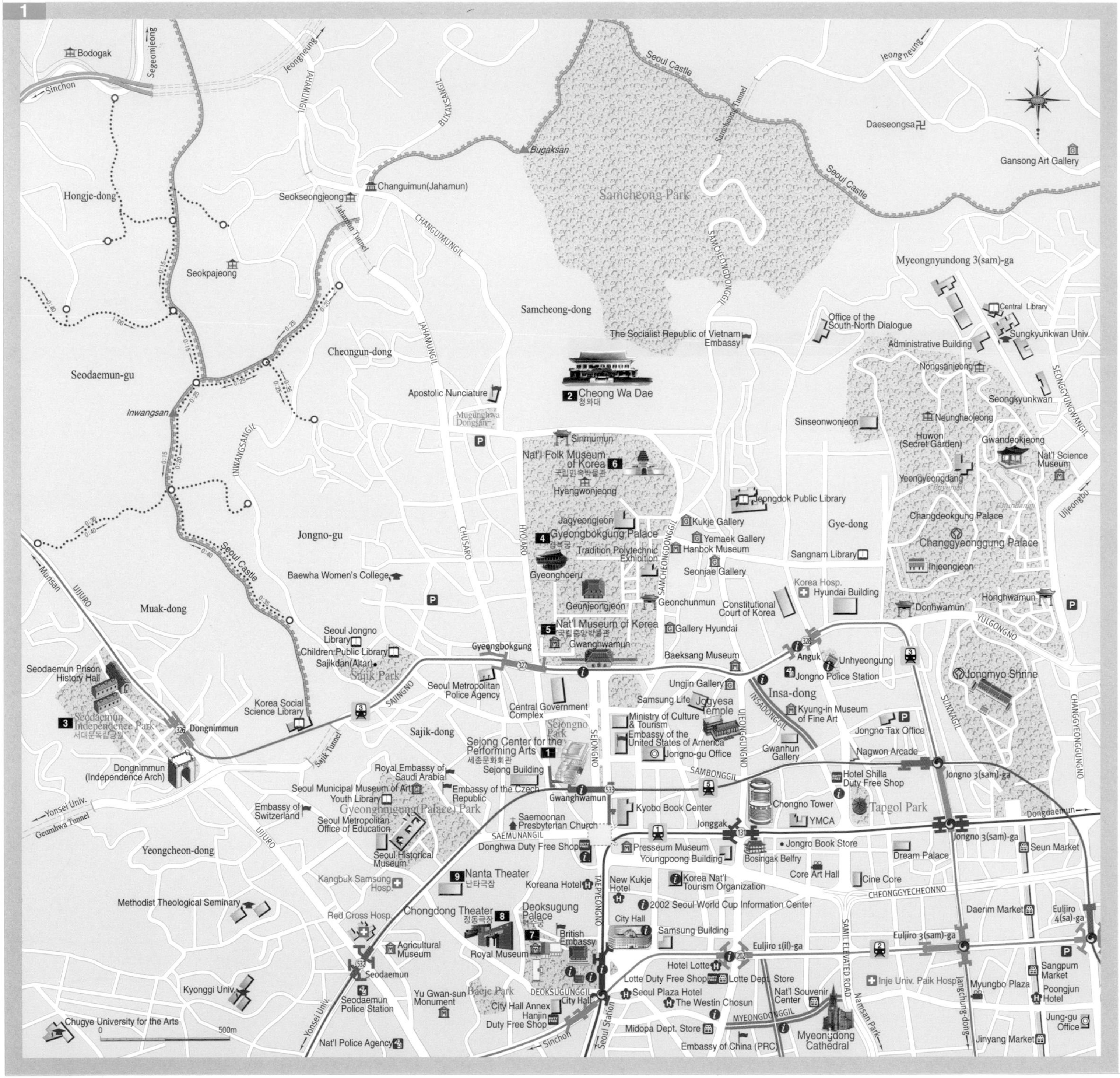

GWANGHWAMUN AREA

1

Bodogak
Segeomjeong
Sinchon
Jeongneung
JAHAMUNGIL
BUKAKSANGIL
Seoul Castle
Samcheong Tunnel
Jeongneung
Daeseongsa
Gansong Art Gallery
Bugaksan
Hongje-dong
Seokseongjeong
Changuimun(Jahamun)
Jahamun Tunnel
CHANGUIMUNGIL
Samcheong Park
Seoul Castle
SAMCHEONGDONGGIL
Myeongnyundong 3(sam)-ga
Seokpajeong
Samcheong-dong
Central Library
Office of the South-North Dialogue
Sungkyunkwan Univ.
The Socialist Republic of Vietnam Embassy
Administrative Building
Cheongun-dong
JAHAMUNGIL
Nongsanjeong
Seodaemun-gu
Apostolic Nunciature
Cheong Wa Dae
청와대
Seongkyunkwan
SEONGGYUNGWANGIL
Inwangsan
Mugunghwa Dongsan
Sinseonwonjeon
Neungheoleong
Sinmumun
Huwon (Secret Garden)
Gwandeokjeong
Nat'l Folk Museum of Korea
국립민속박물관
Nat'l Science Museum
INWANGSANGIL
Hyangwonjeong
Yeongyeongdang
Jeongdok Public Library
Uijeongbu
Jagyeongjeon
Kukje Gallery
Gye-dong
Changdeokgung Palace
Jongno-gu
Gyeongbokgung Palace
경복궁
Yemaek Gallery
Changgyeonggung Palace
Tradition Polytechnic Exhibition
Hanbok Museum
Sangnam Library
Gyeonghoeru
Seonjae Gallery
Injeongjeon
Munsan
UIJIURO
Baewha Women's College
CHUSARO
HYOJARO
SAMCHEONGDONGGIL
Korea Hosp.
Hyundai Building
Muak-dong
Seoul Castle
Geunjeongjeon
Geonchunmun
Constitutional Court of Korea
Honghwamun
Donhwamun
Nat'l Museum of Korea
국립중앙박물관
Gallery Hyundai
YULGONGNO
Seoul Jongno Library
Gwanghwamun
Children Public Library
Gyeongbokgung
Baeksang Museum
Anguk
Unhyeongung
Seodaemun Prison History Hall
Sajikdan(Altar)
Sajik Park
Jongno Police Station
Jongmyo Shrine
SAJIKNO
Seoul Metropolitan Police Agency
Ungjin Gallery
Insa-dong
Korea Social Science Library
Samsung Life
Jogyesa Temple
Kyung-in Museum of Fine Art
Seodaemun Independence Park
서대문독립공원
Dongnimmun
Central Government Complex
Sejongno Park
Ministry of Culture & Tourism
Jongno Tax Office
Sajik-dong
Embassy of the United States of America
INSADONGGIL
SUNNAEGIL
CHANGGYEONGGUNGNO
Sajik Tunnel
SEJONGNO
Sejong Center for the Performing Arts
세종문화회관
Jongno-gu Office
UJEONGGUKNO
Gwanhun Gallery
Nagwon Arcade
Dongnimmun (Independence Arch)
Royal Embassy of Saudi Arabia
Sejong Building
SAMBONGGIL
Hotel Shilla Duty Free Shop
Jongno 3(sam)-ga
Yonsei Univ.
Seoul Municipal Museum of Art
Embassy of the Czech Republic
Youth Library
Gwanghwamun
Kyobo Book Center
Chongno Tower
Tapgol Park
Geumhwa Tunnel
Embassy of Switzerland
Gyeonghuigung(Palace) Park
Seoul Metropolitan Office of Education
Saemoonan Presbyterian Church
YMCA
Dongdaemun
UIJURO
SAEMUNANGIL
Jonggak
Jongno 3(sam)-ga
Yeongcheon-dong
Donghwa Duty Free Shop
Presseum Museum
Jongro Book Store
Seun Market
Seoul Historical Museum
Youngpoong Building
Bosingak Belfry
Dream Palace
Nanta Theater
난타극장
Core Art Hall
Kangbuk Samsung Hosp.
Koreana Hotel
New Kukje Hotel
Korea Nat'l Tourism Organization
Cine Core
TAEPYEONGNO
CHEONGGYECHEONNO
Methodist Theological Seminary
2002 Seoul World Cup Information Center
Daerim Market
Euljiro 4(sa)-ga
Red Cross Hosp.
Chongdong Theater
정동극장
Deoksugung Palace
덕수궁
City Hall
Samsung Building
British Embassy
SAMIL ELEVATED ROAD
Euljiro 3(sam)-ga
Agricultural Museum
Royal Museum
Euljiro 1(il)-ga
Seodaemun
Hotel Lotte
Sangpum Market
Lotte Duty Free Shop
Lotte Dept. Store
Inje Univ. Paik Hosp.
Myungbo Plaza
Poongjun Hotel
Kyonggi Univ.
Seodaemun Police Station
Yu Gwan-sun Monument
Baeje Park
DEOKSUGUNGGIL
City Hall
Seoul Plaza Hotel
Nat'l Souvenir Center
The Westin Chosun
Namsan Park
Jangchung-dong
City Hall Annex
Jung-gu Office
Chugye University for the Arts
Hanjin Duty Free Shop
MYEONGDONGGIL
0 500m
Yonsei Univ.
Sinchon
Seoul Station
Midopa Dept. Store
Myeongdong Cathedral
Jinyang Market
Nat'l Police Agency
Embassy of China (PRC)

Gwanghwamun is the center of the historical section of Seoul and serves as the civic center of metropolitan Seoul, which developed mostly in the late 1900's. Gwanghwamun Gate, a landmark here, is located at the north end of Sejongno. It served as the main gate of Gyeongbokgung Palace, the national seat of government during the Joseon Dynasty.

Sejongno, the main street of the Gwanghwamun area

In this area there are many cultural relics, museums and other items of interest, including Gyeongbokgung Palace, Deoksugung Palace, Seodaemun Independence Park, Dongnimmun Gate, the National Museum and the National Folk Museum.

Gwanghwamun

Gwanghwamun is the main gate to Gyeongbokgung Palace and is embellished with many stone carvings on its eaves. Its roof is painted in exquisite colors.

Sejong Center for the Performing Arts 1

The Sejong Center for the Performing Arts not only boasts a grandiose building, but also serves as a cultural center where people can enjoy a wide variety of events. It hosts various performances year round, and its traditional performances are a must for foreigners who want to experience Korean culture.

www.sejongpac.or.kr

Cheong Wa Dae 2

Cheong Wa Dae (the Blue House) contains the residence and offices of the President of the Republic of Korea. Cheong Wa Dae was given its current name because of its traditional blue roof tiles. Cheong Wa Dae is open to the general public for tours. The Hyoja-dong Sarangbang, situated adjacent to Cheong Wa Dae, is a place where a variety of

gifts received by Korean presidents from heads of states and other foreign guests are exhibited.

www.cwd.go.kr/English

Seodaemun Independence Park 3

Built in 1908, the Seodaemun Prison symbolizes the brutal oppression during the period of Japanese colonial rule. Numerous patriots fighting for independence were imprisoned, tortured and executed or left to die in the prison until the country regained its independence on August 15, 1945. Afterwards, it continued use as a prison until the facilities were relocated to Gyeonggi-do in 1987. The old prison complex was transformed into the Seodaemun Independence Park, which houses the Seodaemun Prison History Hall, Dongnimmun (Independence Arch) and the March 1st Independence Movement Tower. The Seodaemun Prison History Hall holds the Prison History Room, the Prison Life Room, the Provisional Detention Room and the Torture Room. The prison building, execution site, watchtower and sigumun (a passage used for secretly moving dead bodies) are all well preserved.

Dongnimmun

Dongnimmun was modeled after the Arc de Triomphe of Paris and built in 1897.
It was constructed with 1,850 pieces of white granite.

Gyeongbokgung Palace 4

Built in the 4th year (1395) of the reign of King Taejo, Gyeongbokgung was the primary palace of the Joseon Dynasty.
Numerous cultural assets are found in the complex. In particular, Geunjeongjeon, Hyangwonjeong and Amisan Garden are preserved intact, showing the unique charm and beauty of traditional Korean design and architecture.

Gyeonghoeru

Constructed in the 12th year (1412) of the reign of King Taejong, Gyeonghoeru was a hall where the king held receptions and parties. Gyeonghoeru is the epitome of old Korean pavilions. It stands on stone supports in a square lotus pond, looking as if it were floating on water.

Gyotaejeon

Gyotaejeon housed the queen's sleeping quarters. This building is notable for its absence of ridge roof beams, which is characteristic of buildings that contained the bedrooms of royal monarchs.

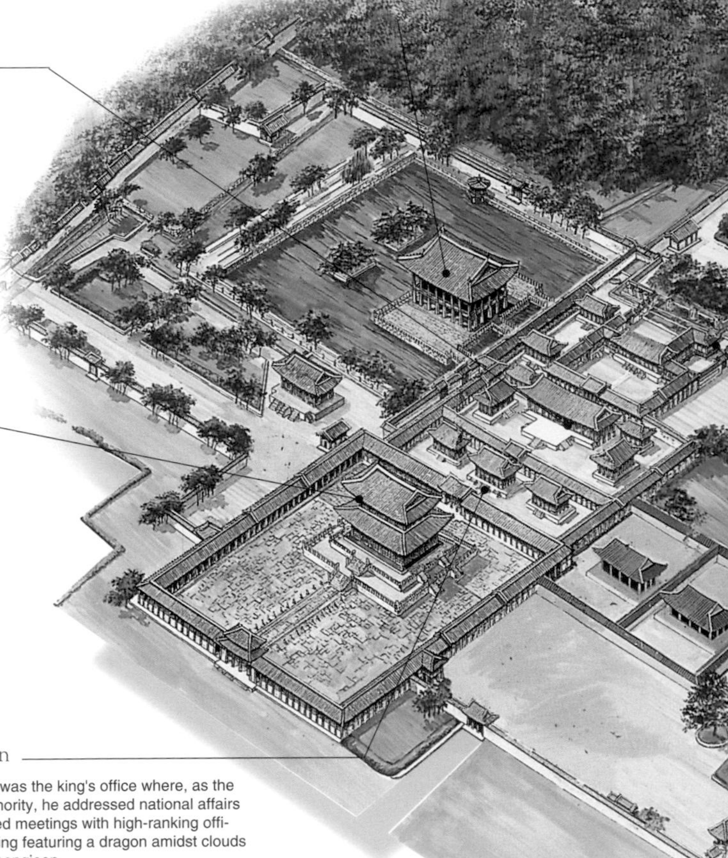

Geunjeongjeon

Geunjeongjeon is the main hall of Gyeongbokgung, where civil and military officials administered national functions. It has a two-tiered stone stairway, decorated with sophisticated patterns, and two-tier roofs, augmenting its elegance and majesty.
The walls of the buildings are painted in a series of colorful designs, highlighting the overall architectural beauty of these structures.

Sajeongjeon

Sajeongjeon was the king's office where, as the supreme authority, he addressed national affairs and conducted meetings with high-ranking officials. A painting featuring a dragon amidst clouds hangs in Sajeongjeon.

Seoksu

The animal sculptures of Geunjeongjeon were said to be charged with protecting the building. They are categorized into two types. The first type represents the guardian spirits which were responsible for guarding each of the four directions: a blue dragon for the east, a white tiger for the west, a phoenix for the south and a turtle for the north.
The second type is the twelve zodiac animals, namely the rat, cow, tiger, hare, dragon, snake, horse, sheep, monkey, cock, dog and pig.

Hyangwonjeong

Hyangwonjeong is a hexagonal pavilion constructed on an isle in the pond. Hyangwonjeong is generally considered to be two-stories in height, but when taking into account the structure under its floor, it is actually three stories.

Jagyeongjeon

Jagyeongjeon, which was designed as the women's private quarters, is the only bedroom chamber that has survived, with the exception of bedroom chambers built for the king and queen. Characters inscribed on the wall express the wish for longevity, while flowers symbolize good fortune.

The Wall of the Jagyeongjeon

The National Folk Museum (See page 30)

Amisan Garden

Amisan is a uniquely designed garden which looks as if a small mountain was moved to the palace complex. The chimneys in Amisan are regarded as the most beautiful chimneys in Korea.

The layout of the palace was designed in accordance with the principles of feng shui, the ancient practice of positioning objects especially buildings. Feng shui is said to be based on a belief in the patterns of Yin and Yang and the flow of chi, which can have positive and negative effects on a space.

National Museum of Korea 5

National Museum of Korea (currently under construction)

As Korea's depository for national treasures, the National Museum of Korea displays a wide range of materials related to Korea's history, archeology, art and tradition. It is a world-class museum with 135,000 artifacts, 5000 of which are permanently displayed.The museum has 18 galleries, in addition to several movie rooms and audio guide equipment is available for self tours.

On the second floor of the museum are the Prehistoric Gallery, Proto Three Kingdoms Gallery, Goguryeo Gallery, Baekje Gallery, Gaya Gallery and Silla Gallery. Ceramic-related materials and artifacts can be found on the first floor in the Goryeo Celadon Gallery, the Joseon Buncheong ware Gallery, and the Joseon White Porcelain Gallery. The Buddhist Relics Gallery, the Metal Works Gallery, the Art Gallery and the Historical Material Gallery are all located on the first level of the basement.

The building which originally housed the National Museum of Korea, and the former offices of the Japanese governor-general, was demolished on August 15, 1993. A new museum building is now under construction at Yongsan Family Park. As a center for the artifacts of Korea's 5000-year history and cultural heritage, the new National Museum of Korea will serve as a site for various functions, including exhibitions, historical and cultural research, and public education.

www.museum.go.kr

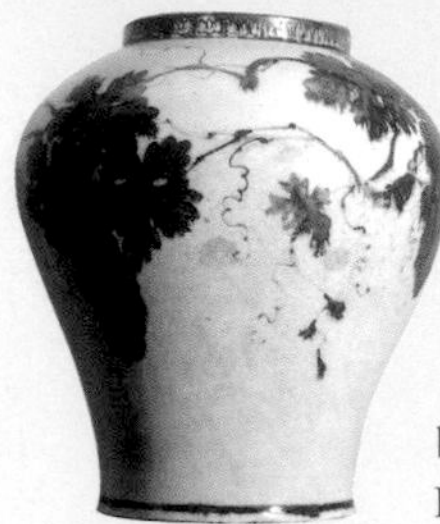
White Porcelain Jar with an Underglazed Iron-painted Grapevine Design (National Treasure No. 93)

National Folk Museum of Korea 6

Located in Gyeongbokgung Palace, the National Folk Museum of Korea features aspects of both the traditional folk culture of ordinary people and the culture of the aristocracy, centering on the Joseon Dynasty. The buildings of the museum follow traditional Korean architectural designs. The middle facade of the main building was designed to resemble two of Korea's most beautiful bridges, the Bridge of Azure Clouds and the Bridge of White Clouds of Bulguksa Temple. The five-story main building was modeled on Palsangjeon Hall at Beopjusa Temple. The three-story building to the east of the main building and the two-story building to the left of the main building were modeled after Mireukjeon Hall at Geumsansa Temple and Gakhwangjeon Hall, respectively.

www.nfm.go.kr

Traditional Wedding

Gilt-bronze Maitreya in Meditation (National Treasure No. 78)

Pottery Vessel in the Form of a Mounted Warrior (National Treasure No. 91)

Celadon Gourd-shaped Ewer with an Inlaid Peony-scroll Design (National Treasure No. 116)

Gold Earrings with Large Bells (National Treasure No. 90)

Seokjojeon in the Deoksugung Palace

Deoksugung Palace 7

Deoksugung was not originally planned as a palace but after King Seonjo used it as a temporary residence, it attained the status of a palace.
Deoksugung witnessed tumultuous changes at the end of the Joseon Dynasty. The palace complex contains several western style buildings, such as Seokjojeon. Seokjojeon was designed in the neo-classical style that prevailed in the early 19th century in the West. Currently it houses the Deoksugung Art Museum and the Royal Museum.
The area fronting Seokjojeon contains the nation's first European style garden. It is symmetrical with a fountain and a pond in the center.
In front of Daehanmun Gate, the main gate of Deoksugung, visitors can witness the ceremony of the Royal Guard change at the gate. This is a re-enactment of the ritual of keeping watch over the royal gate during the Joseon Dynasty.

Ceremony of the Royal Guard Shift

Place: Daehanmun, Main Gate of Deoksugung Palace
Performance schedule:
Mar. ~ Jun. Sept. ~ Dec. 14:00 ~ 15:30
Jul. ~ Aug. 15:00 ~ 16:30
Closed: Monday
Fee: Free of charge

Chongdong Theater 8

The Chongdong Theater traces its origins to Wongaksa, founded in 1908 as the nation's first modern theater. The theater has evolved to host a wide variety of art performances and cultural programs and provides entertainment year round.
www.chongdong.com

Nanta Theater 9

Nanta, meaning 'reckless punching,' is the nation's most well-known non-verbal performance. Nanta integrates traditional Korean percussion tempos with western performance styles. Although the setting is a common kitchen, dramatic elements are added to the performance, engaging and delighting the audience.
www.nanta.co.kr

JONGNO

2

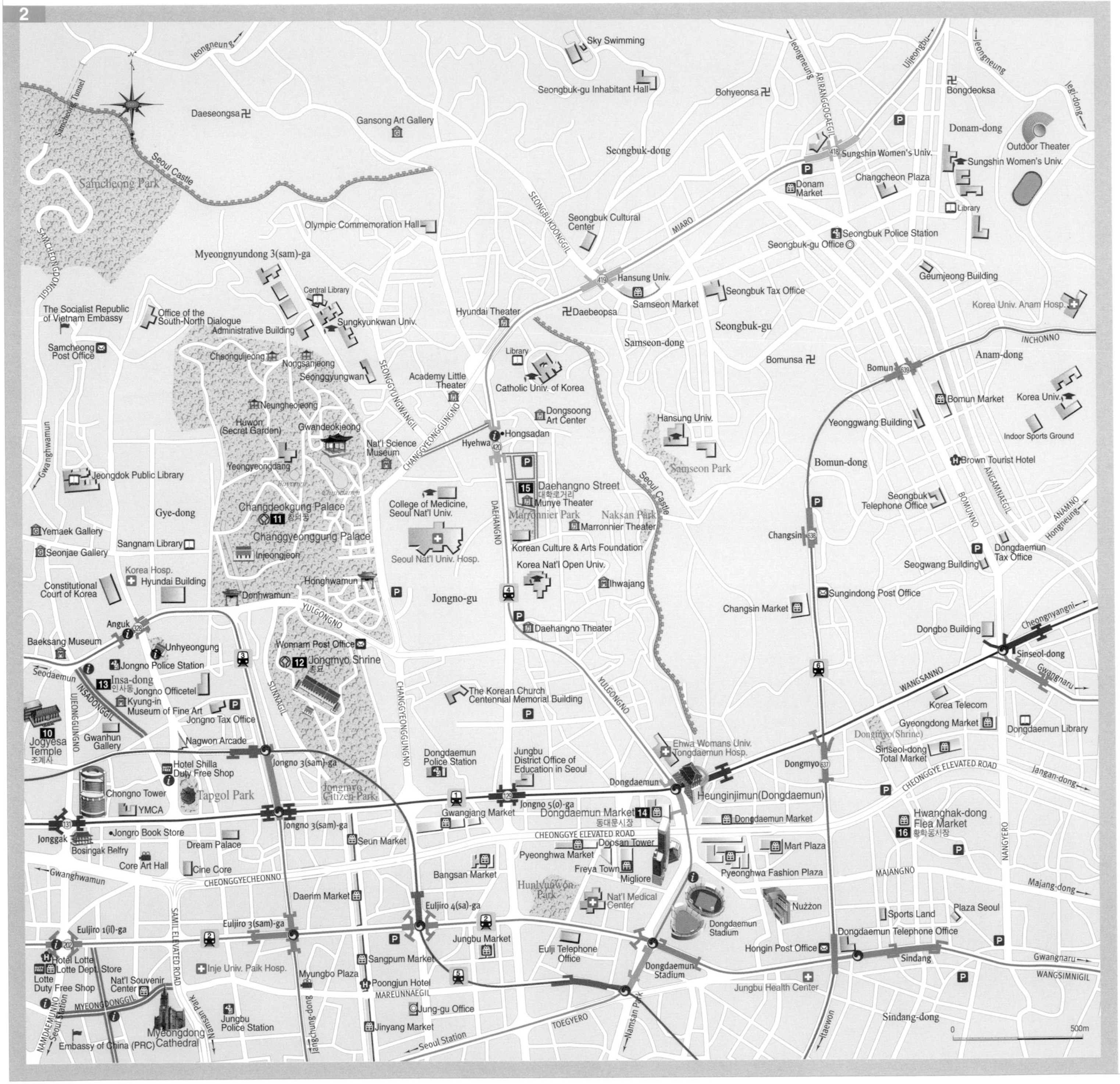

Sky Swimming
Jeongneung
Seongbuk-gu Inhabitant Hall
Bohyeonsa
Jeongneung
Uijeongbu
Jeongneung
Bongdeoksa
Jegi-dong
Samcheong Tunnel
Daeseongsa
Gansong Art Gallery
Donam-dong
Outdoor Theater
Seoul Castle
Samcheong Park
Seongbuk-dong
ARIRANGGOGAEGIL
Sungshin Women's Univ.
Sungshin Women's Univ.
Donam Market
Changcheon Plaza
Library
SEONGBUKDONGGIL
Seongbuk Cultural Center
MIARO
Seongbuk Police Station
Seongbuk-gu Office
Olympic Commemoration Hall
SAMCHEONGDONGGIL
Myeongnyundong 3(sam)-ga
Hansung Univ.
Geumjeong Building
Central Library
Seongbuk Tax Office
Samseon Market
Korea Univ. Anam Hosp.
The Socialist Republic of Vietnam Embassy
Office of the South-North Dialogue
Administrative Building
Sungkyunkwan Univ.
Hyundai Theater
Daebeopsa
Seongbuk-gu
INCHONNO
Samseon-dong
Samcheong Post Office
Library
Anam-dong
Cheongujeong
Nongsanjeong
Bomunsa
Bomun
Seonggyungwan
SEONGGYUNGWANGIL
Academy Little Theater
Catholic Univ. of Korea
Bomun Market
Korea Univ.
Neungheojeong
Dongsoong Art Center
Hansung Univ.
Yeonggwang Building
Huwon (Secret Garden)
Gwandeokjeong
Hyehwa
Hongsadan
Indoor Sports Ground
Gwanghwamun
Nat'l Science Museum
CHANGGYEONGGUNGNO
Brown Tourist Hotel
Jeongdok Public Library
Yeongyeongdang
Bomun-dong
Samseon Park
Daehangno Street
대학로거리
College of Medicine, Seoul Nat'l Univ.
Munye Theater
Seongbuk Telephone Office
Gye-dong
Changdeokgung Palace
창덕궁
DAEHANGNO
Marronnier Park
Naksan Park
ANGAMNAEGIL
BOMUNNO
ANAMNO
Hongneung
Yemaek Gallery
Changgyeonggung Palace
Marronnier Theater
Changsin
Seonjae Gallery
Sangnam Library
Injeongjeon
Seoul Nat'l Univ. Hosp.
Korean Culture & Arts Foundation
Dongdaemun Tax Office
Korea Hosp.
Korea Nat'l Open Univ.
Seogwang Building
Constitutional Court of Korea
Hyundai Building
Honghwamun
Ihwajang
Donhwamun
Jongno-gu
Sungindong Post Office
YULGONGNO
Changsin Market
Anguk
Daehangno Theater
Dongbo Building
Cheongnyangni
Baeksang Museum
Unhyeongung
Wonnam Post Office
Jongmyo Shrine
종묘
Sinseol-dong
Jongno Police Station
Seodaemun
Insa-dong
인사동
Jongno Officetel
SUNNAEGIL
YULGONGNO
Gwangnaru
INSADONGGIL
UIJEONGBUNGNO
Kyung-in Museum of Fine Art
The Korean Church Centennial Memorial Building
WANGSANNO
Korea Telecom
Jongno Tax Office
Jogyesa Temple
조계사
Gwanhun Gallery
CHANGGYEONGGUNGNO
Gyeongdong Market
Dongdaemun Library
Nagwon Arcade
Ehwa Womans Univ. Dongdaemun Hosp.
Dongmyo (Shrine)
Hotel Shilla Duty Free Shop
Jongno 3(sam)-ga
Dongdaemun Police Station
Jungbu District Office of Education in Seoul
Sinseol-dong Total Market
Dongmyo
CHEONGGYE ELEVATED ROAD
Jangan-dong
Chongno Tower
Tapgol Park
Jongmyo Citizen Park
Dongdaemun
Heunginjimun(Dongdaemun)
YMCA
Jongno 5(o)-ga
Gwangjang Market
Dongdaemun Market
동대문시장
Hwanghak-dong Flea Market
황학동시장
Jonggak
Jongro Book Store
Jongno 3(sam)-ga
Dongdaemun Market
NANGYERO
Bosingak Belfry
Dream Palace
Seun Market
CHEONGGYE ELEVATED ROAD
Doosan Tower
Mart Plaza
Core Art Hall
Cine Core
Pyeonghwa Market
Freya Town
Pyeonghwa Fashion Plaza
MAJANGNO
Gwanghwamun
CHEONGGYECHEONNO
Bangsan Market
Migliore
Hunlyunwon Park
Majang-dong
Daerim Market
Nat'l Medical Center
Nuzzon
Eulijiro 4(sa)-ga
Sports Land
Plaza Seoul
Euljiro 1(il)-ga
Euljiro 3(sam)-ga
SAMIL ELEVATED ROAD
Jungbu Market
Dongdaemun Stadium
Dongdaemun Telephone Office
Eulji Telephone Office
Hongin Post Office
Sindang
Hotel Lotte
Lotte Dept. Store
Lotte Duty Free Shop
Nat'l Souvenir Center
Inje Univ. Paik Hosp.
Sangpum Market
Dongdaemun Stadium
Gwangnaru
WANGSIMNIGIL
Myungbo Plaza
Poongjun Hotel
MAREUNNAEGIL
Jungbu Health Center
MYEONGDONGGIL
Namsan Park
Jungbu Police Station
Jung-gu Office
Sindang-dong
NAMDAEMUNNO
Seoul Station
Myeongdong Cathedral
Jangchung-dong
Jinyang Market
TOEGYERO
Namsan Park
Itaewon
0
500m
Embassy of China (PRC)
Seoul Station

Jongno

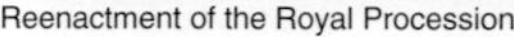

Reenactment of the Royal Procession

Jongno is in the heart of modern Seoul. The Sejongno intersection at the north-east end of Jongno is the starting point from which all national roads originate, hence, this district is known as the nucleus of Korea.

Because it is home to many bookstores, educational institutes, movie theaters, restaurants and bars, Jongno is a popular hangout with youngsters. Tapgol Park and Jongmyo Shrine blend the urban landscape with natural settings.

Jongmyo was once a ceremonial place for kings of the Joseon Dynasty. This area is recognized as one of the World Heritages Sites by UNESCO. There are many cultural relics, including Changdeokgung Palace and Changgyeonggung Palace.

In addition, there are jewelry shops in Yeji-dong, a traditional market in Dongdaemun, Buddhist supply shops in Ujeonggungno and antique shops in Insa-dong.

Chongno Tower, One of the Landmarks in Jongno

Jogyesa Temple

Jogyesa Temple 10

Jogyesa was the only major temple within the old city walls of Seoul. Built in 1910, the temple was first called Gakhwangsa, but the name was changed to Teagosa in 1936. During this time, the temple became the main temple of Korean Buddhism. In 1954, after a great movement to rid the country of any vestiges of the Japanese occupation, the temple came to be called Jogyesa. The temple holds a wide array of Buddhist shrines, including Daeungjeon and Deogwangjeon, and it also contains a 500-year-old pine tree and a 400-year-old pagoda tree. Jogyesa runs a program that helps foreigners experience Korean Buddhism.

A large number of shops carrying all kinds of clothing, goods and gifts related to Buddhist activities and traditional Korean arts can be found on either side of the main entrance to the temple compound.

www.ijogyesa.net

Buddhist Drum in Jogyesa

Child Monks in Lantern Parade

Changdeokgung Palace 11

Changdeokgung was built in 1405 as a villa palace. It was also used as a main palace where several kings conducted state affairs. The layout of Changdeokgung was designed to be in harmony with the surrounding terrain. Huwon, the back garden of Changdeokgung epitomizes traditional landscaping, with the garden designed not merely for viewing, but as a place where people could go to commune with nature. Changdeokgung was added to the UNESCO's World Heritage Site list in December 1997.

Ongnyucheon Stream

Ongnyucheon is a stream that flows through the most inner part of the back of Changdeokgung. The man-made stream was built by excavating natural rocks.

Buyongji Pond and Buyongjeong Pavilion

Buyongji is a rectangular pond (symbolizing the earth) with a round island (symbolizing the sky) in its center. It was built based on the Yin and Yang philosophy that stresses the concept of round sky and square earth. The Buyongjeong pavilion stands next to the pond. One pillar of the pavilion is embedded in the pond, so the pavilion looks as if it were floating on the pond.

Hwagye

Hwagye is a flower garden built on a hill in the rear of Daejojeon, the queen's living quarters.

Daejojeon

Daejojeon is a mid-sized hall which included the queen's living quarters. The building was moved to its current site in 1920 during restoration work. Like other living quarters of the queen, its roof has no ridge on top.

Gwallamjeong Pavilion

Gwallamjeong stands at the edge of a pond called Bandoji. Its uniqueness derives from its fan-shaped floor and roof.

Yeongyeongdang House

Yeongyeongdang is the only non-royal style building in Changdeokgung. It is modeled after the Korean gentry' s houses, the 99 kan (unit of measure between pillars) building.

Bullomun Gate

Bullomun is a gate carved out of stone where kings prayed for long life as they entered.

Juhamnu Pavilion

The first floor was used as a gyujanggak, where books were preserved, and the second floor was used as a place for reading.

Injeongjeon

Injeongjeon is the main hall of Changdeokgung, where kings conducted affairs of state and held official functions. The canopy over the throne is carved with bonghwang (mythical birds) and yeouiju (magical beads of a dragon), symbols of regal grandeur and dignity.

Jongmyo Jerye Ritual

Jongmyo Shrine 12

Jongmyo is a shrine where the tablets of kings and queens were preserved and memorial services for deceased kings and queens were performed based on the Confucian practices of the Joseon Dynasty. The king, after building up the nation, constructed the Jongmyo and Sajik to preserve and perpetuate the royal line and traditions. The Joseon Dynasty designated Seoul as the nation' s capital and built Jongmyo and Sajik on the left and right of Gyeongbokgung palace, respectively.

The Jongmyo Jerye (Jongmyo Ritual) refers to a memorial service performed by the king, his crown prince, his relatives, and high civil and military officials. The Jongmyo Ritual was performed in the first month of each new season and whenever auspicious or ominous events took place. Jongmyo was registered on the UNESCO' s World Heritage list in 1995 and is one of the nation' s most precious cultural properties.

Jongmyo Jeryeak (ritual music)

Insa-dong 13

Insa-dong, located in the back streets of the Jongno District, is a place to relish Korean art and craftsmanship. There are galleries of all size, antique shops, and shops selling artworks. Korean paper shops, paper hanger shops, craft shops, and ceramic shops pack both sides of the street and numerous side alleys. Many foreigners visit Insa-dong to buy traditional Korean artworks and souvenirs. Along the streets, there are also various restaurants and tea houses offering traditional foods, tea and beverages. On weekends the streets are usually closed to traffic and frequent street festivals are often packed with all kinds of performers and vendors selling traditional snacks, candies and gifts.

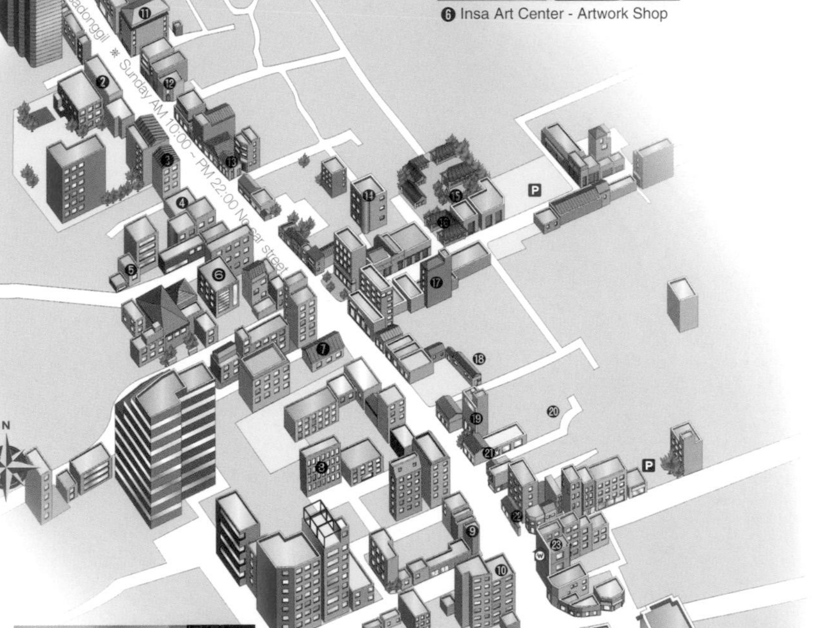

❻ Insa Art Center - Artwork Shop

❷ Tongmoongwan - Old and Rare Books Store

❸ Old Goods of Toto - Antique Shop

⓯ Gyeong-in Art Gallery - Traditional Tea House

⓴ Eoureong Deoureong - Traditional Restaurant

㉑ Atelier Seoul - Pottery Shop

㉒ Baeteul - Saengwhal Hanbok Shop

INDEX

1. Dongduk Art Gallery **2.** Tongmoongwan **3.** Old Goods of Toto **4.** Artside **5.** Daerim Art Gallery **6.** Insa Art Center **7.** Seobong Gallery **8.** Baeksang Building **9.** Jeonbuk Paper **10.** Gallery Sang **11.** Gana Art Gallery **12.** HakGoJae **13.** Toin **14.** Jongno Gallery **15.** Gyeong-in Art Gallery **16.** Gaeam Gallery **17.** Insa Gallery **18.** Insa Art Plaza **19.** Tong-in Shop **20.** Eoureong Deoureong **21.** Atelier Seoul **22.** Baeteul **23.** Kwangjuyo **24.** Songcheonseohoe **25.** Daeil Building

Dongdaemun Market 14

Dongdaemun Market is the nation's busiest shopping area. Traditional open-air markets stand alongside modern shopping malls. You can find almost everything you need at Dongdaemun Market. The market is full of shoppers year round and is open all night long, enabling people to enjoy both shopping and other cultural activities at any time of the day or night.

⑩ Shoe Shop in Dongdaemun Shoe Market

❶ Korean Traditional Fashion Store in the Hanbok Market

❷ Casual Fashion Store in Doota

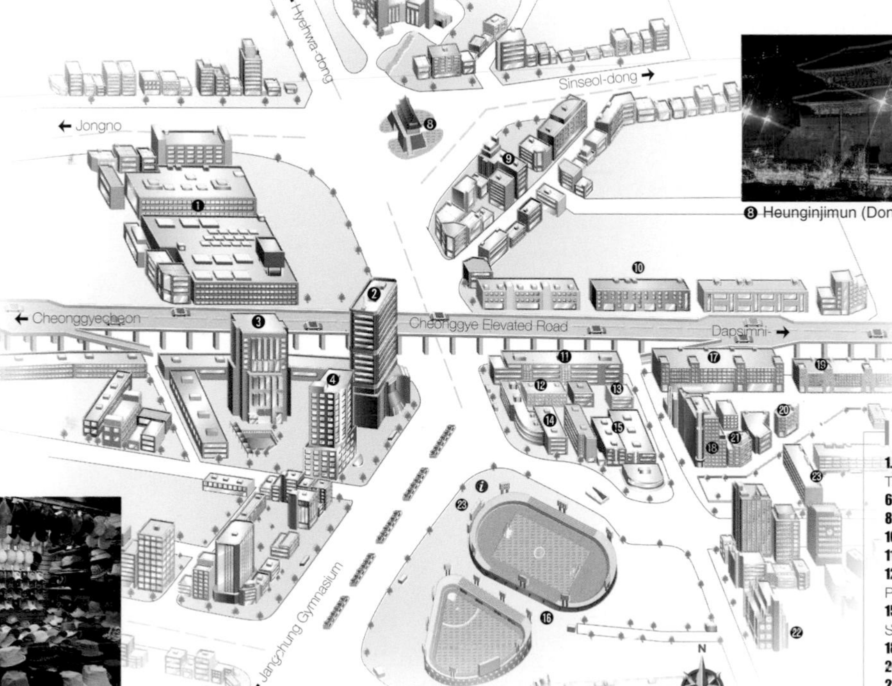

⑧ Heunginjimun (Dongdaemun)

⑬ Fashion Store in Gwanghui Fashion Town

❹ Fashion Accessory Shop in Freya Town

INDEX

1. Dongdaemun Chain Store **2.** Doota **3.** Freya Town **4.** Migliore **5.** Pyeonghwa Fashion Plaza **6.** Tongil Market **7.** Dae Hwa Tourist Hotel **8.** Heunginjimun (Dongdaemun) **9.** Eastern Hotel **10.** Dongdaemun Shoes Market **11.** Sinpyeonghwa Fashion Town **12.** Nampyeonghwa Plaza **13.** Gwanghui Fashion Plaza **14.** Heungin Market **15.** Jeil Pyeonghwa Market **16.** Dongdaemun Stadium **17.** Dongpyeonghwa Market **18.** Uno Core **19.** Cheongpyeonghwa Market **20.** Ambassador Roberta **21.** MC Plaza **22.** Nuzzon **23.** Sports Shop

Daehangno Street 15

Daehangno, College Street

Daehangno is a street dedicated to youthful energy and culture, where plays and concerts are performed every day. Exhibition halls, small theaters, and unique restaurants occupy every corner in the area.

Hwanghak-dong Flea Market 16

Hwanghak-dong Flea Market

One can find almost anything at Hwanghak-dong Flea Market, which sells a huge assortment of second-hand articles. The market stretches along the back alleys of Dongdaemun Market, and consists of approximately 500 shops. Rare and precious items from traditional Korean houses and various antiques, such as liquor bottles, lamps, gas burners, small speakers and watches can be found here.

MYEONG-DONG/NAMDAEMUN

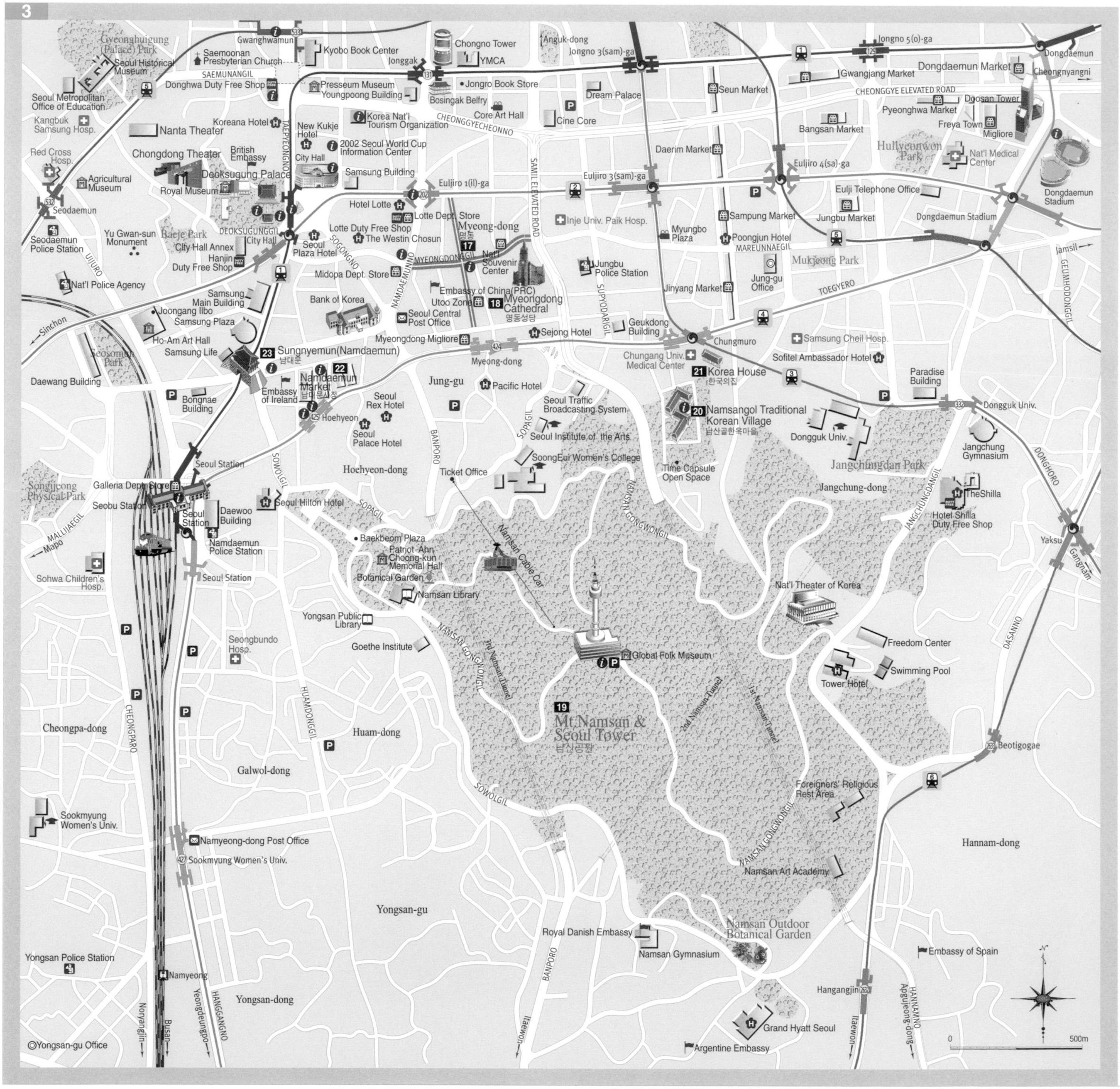

3

Gyeonghuigung (Palace) Park
Gwanghwamun
Kyobo Book Center
Chongno Tower
YMCA
Anguk-dong
Jongno 3(sam)-ga
Jongno 5(o)-ga
Dongdaemun
Saemoonan Presbyterian Church
Seoul Historical Museum
SAEMUNANGIL
Jonggak
Donghwa Duty Free Shop
Presseum Museum
Youngpoong Building
Jongro Book Store
Bosingak Belfry
Dream Palace
Seun Market
Gwangjang Market
Dongdaemun Market
Cheongnyangni
Seoul Metropolitan Office of Education
CHEONGGYE ELEVATED ROAD
Dgosan Tower
Kangbuk Samsung Hosp.
Koreana Hotel
Korea Nat'l Tourism Organization
Core Art Hall
Cine Core
Pyeonghwa Market
Nanta Theater
New Kukje Hotel
CHEONGGYECHEONNO
Bangsan Market
Freya Town
Migliore
Red Cross Hosp.
British Embassy
2002 Seoul World Cup Information Center
Daerim Market
Hullyeonwon Park
Nat'l Medical Center
Chongdong Theater
City Hall
SAMIL ELEVATED ROAD
Euljiro 4(sa)-ga
Agricultural Museum
Deoksugung Palace
Samsung Building
Euljiro 3(sam)-ga
Royal Museum
Euljiro 1(il)-ga
Eulji Telephone Office
Dongdaemun Stadium
TAEPYEONGNO
Seodaemun
Hotel Lotte
Lotte Dept. Store
Sampung Market
Jungbu Market
Dongdaemun Stadium
Myeong-dong
명동
Inje Univ. Paik Hosp.
Myungbo Plaza
Poongjun Hotel
Yu Gwan-sun Monument
Baeje Park
DEOKSUGUNGGIL
City Hall
Lotte Duty Free Shop
The Westin Chosun
MAREUNNAEGIL
Seodaemun Police Station
City Hall Annex
Seoul Plaza Hotel
SOGONGNO
17
Nat'l Souvenir Center
Jamsil
Hanjin Duty Free Shop
MYEONGDONGGIL
Jungbu Police Station
Mukjeong Park
UIJURO
Midopa Dept. Store
Jung-gu Office
Nat'l Police Agency
Samsung Main Building
Embassy of China(PRC)
Utoo Zone
18 Myeongdong Cathedral
명동성당
Jinyang Market
TOEGYERO
GEUMHODONGGIL
Joongang Ilbo
Bank of Korea
NAMDAEMUNNO
SUPYODARIGIL
Samsung Plaza
Seoul Central Post Office
Geukdong Building
Sinchon
Ho-Am Art Hall
Myeongdong Migliore
Sejong Hotel
Chungmuro
Samsung Cheil Hosp.
Samsung Life
23 Sungnyemun(Namdaemun)
남대문
Myeong-dong
Chungang Univ. Medical Center
Sofitel Ambassador Hotel
Seosomun Park
22 Namdaemun Market
남대문시장
21 Korea House
한국의집
Paradise Building
Daewang Building
Jung-gu
Pacific Hotel
Bongnae Building
Embassy of Ireland
Seoul Rex Hotel
Seoul Traffic Broadcasting System
Hoehyeon
20 Namsangol Traditional Korean Village
남산골한옥마을
Dongguk Univ.
SOPAGIL
Seoul Institute of the Arts
Dongguk Univ.
Seoul Palace Hotel
BANPORO
Jangchung Gymnasium
Hochyeon-dong
SoongEui Women's College
Jangchungdan Park
Seoul Station
SOWOLGIL
Time Capsule Open Space
Jangchung-dong
DONGHORO
Galleria Dept. Store
Ticket Office
Songjijeong Physical Park
Seobu Station
Seoul Station
Daewoo Building
Seoul Hilton Hotel
SOPAGIL
NAMSAN GONGWONGIL
JANGCHUNGDANGIL
TheShilla
Hotel Shilla Duty Free Shop
MALLIJAEGIL
Mapo
Namdaemun Police Station
Baekbeom Plaza
Patriot Ahn Choong-kun Memorial Hall
Namsan Cable Car
Yaksu
Gangnam
Sohwa Children's Hosp.
Seoul Station
Botanical Garden
Namsan Library
Nat'l Theater of Korea
Yongsan Public Library
NAMSAN GONGWONGIL
3rd Namsan Tunnel
Freedom Center
Goethe Institute
Seongbundo Hosp.
Global Folk Museum
Swimming Pool
Tower Hotel
DASANNO
HUAMDONGGIL
2nd Namsan Tunnel
1st Namsan Tunnel
19 Mt.Namsan & Seoul Tower
남산공원
Cheongpa-dong
CHEONGPARO
Huam-dong
Beotigogae
Galwol-dong
SOWOLGIL
Foreigners' Religious Rest Area
Sookmyung Women's Univ.
NAMSAN GONGWONGIL
Hannam-dong
Namyeong-dong Post Office
Sookmyung Women's Univ.
Namsan Art Academy
Yongsan-gu
Namsan Outdoor Botanical Garden
Royal Danish Embassy
Namsan Gymnasium
Yongsan Police Station
Embassy of Spain
Namyeong
BANPORO
Hangangjin
Yongsan-dong
HANNAMNO
Apgujeong-dong
Noryangjin
Busan
Yeongdeungpo
HANGGANGNO
Itaewon
Itaewon
Grand Hyatt Seoul
Argentine Embassy
Yongsan-gu Office
0
500m

Myeong-dong 17

Myeong-dong, a financial district which plays a pivotal role in the Korean economy, has recently earned the reputation of being a center of fashion. There are many luxurious boutiques, live music cafes, as well as restaurants for every taste.

The Myeong-dong Festival is held here every spring and autumn. The festival begins with an opening parade, followed by a wide range of events, such as the Miss Myeong-dong Beauty Pageant, traditional Korean games, traditional wedding ceremonies, Korean music performances, fashion shows and make-up shows.

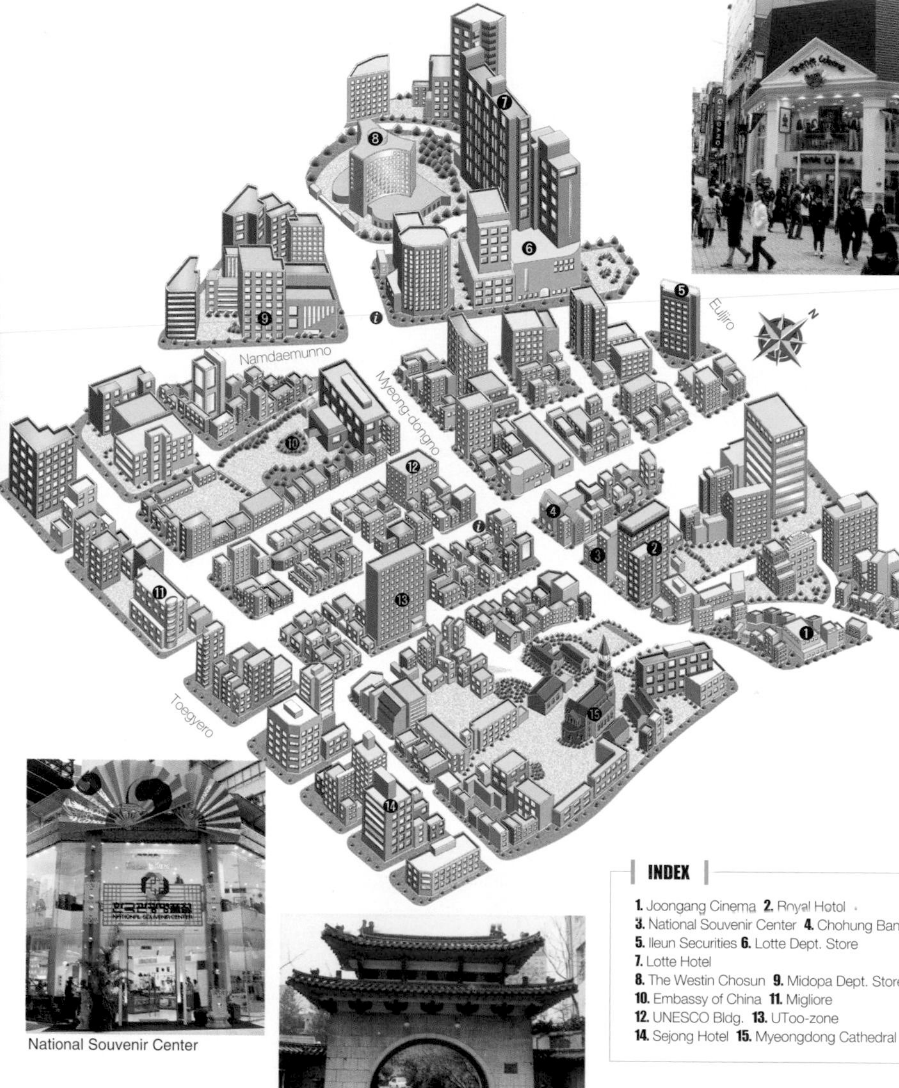

INDEX

1. Joongang Cinema **2.** Royal Hotel
3. National Souvenir Center **4.** Chohung Bank
5. Ileun Securities **6.** Lotte Dept. Store
7. Lotte Hotel
8. The Westin Chosun **9.** Midopa Dept. Store
10. Embassy of China **11.** Migliore
12. UNESCO Bldg. **13.** UToo-zone
14. Sejong Hotel **15.** Myeongdong Cathedral

National Souvenir Center

Embassy of China

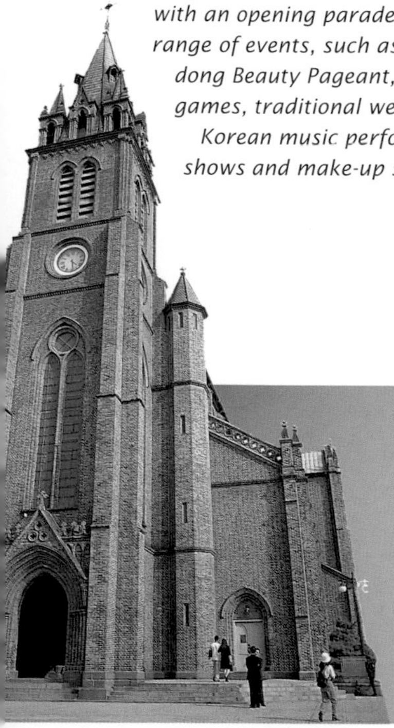

Myeongdong Cathedral 18

Myeongdong Cathedral is a Gothic-style cathedral which was completed in 1898, making it the nation's first great church. It is the administrative seat of the Catholic church in Korea. At the time its construction was completed, the cathedral was dubbed the 'Steeple House' and it became one of the most notable attractions in Seoul. The location of Myeongdong Cathedral is historically significant since it was where the Joseon Catholic Church was built in 1784.

Myeongdong Cathedral

Mt. Namsan & Seoul Tower 19

The 262m-high Namsan stands at the center of Seoul. With the Seoul Tower at its summit, the mountain serves as a symbol of Seoul. At Namsan, visitors can stop at the Seoul Tower Observatory for a spectacular view of Seoul and surrounding mountains, go to the botanical garden or ride a cable car up and down the mountain. The outdoor botanical garden is becoming a favorite tourist attraction in Seoul. In the immediate vicinity of Namsan are world-class hotels, including the Hilton, Hyatt, Shilla and Tower Hotels. Also, located here are the Namsan Gymnasium, the Freedom House and the Namsangol Traditional Korean Village.

Observatory on Seoul Tower (top)
Outdoor Botanical Garden (bottom)

Namsangol Traditional Korean Village 20

Namsangol Traditional Korean Village was created by restoring and relocating five traditional houses and gardens, which were scattered across Seoul. Inside the houses, household items of all kinds are preserved. Visitors can learn and experience Korea's traditional culture and lifestyle at the village through interactive courses in traditional etiquette, calligraphy, music (using Gayageum, a traditional Korean instrument), and bamboo craft.

Korea House 21

Korea House, in the vicinity of the Namsangol Traditional Korean Village, was built to introduce traditional culture and customs of Korea. Visitors can taste many courses of Korean Court Cuisine. The spacious yet cozy Folk Theater (1989 seats) provides visitors various performance by Korean top traditional dancers and traditional classical musicians.
www.koreahouse.or.kr

Traditional Wedding

Namdaemun Market 22

Namdaemun Market is the nation' s largest and most prominent conventional open market. It is widely acknowledged as one of the country's best tourist attractions. Unlike other marketplaces, Namdaemun Market is more vibrant and bustling at night than during the day. Clothing malls take up the biggest share of the market. Besides clothing, visitors can shop at large specialized areas for items such as fashion accessories, kitchenware, flowers, embroideries, and handbags. Traditional oriental foods and medicine, such as ginseng are also popular items here.

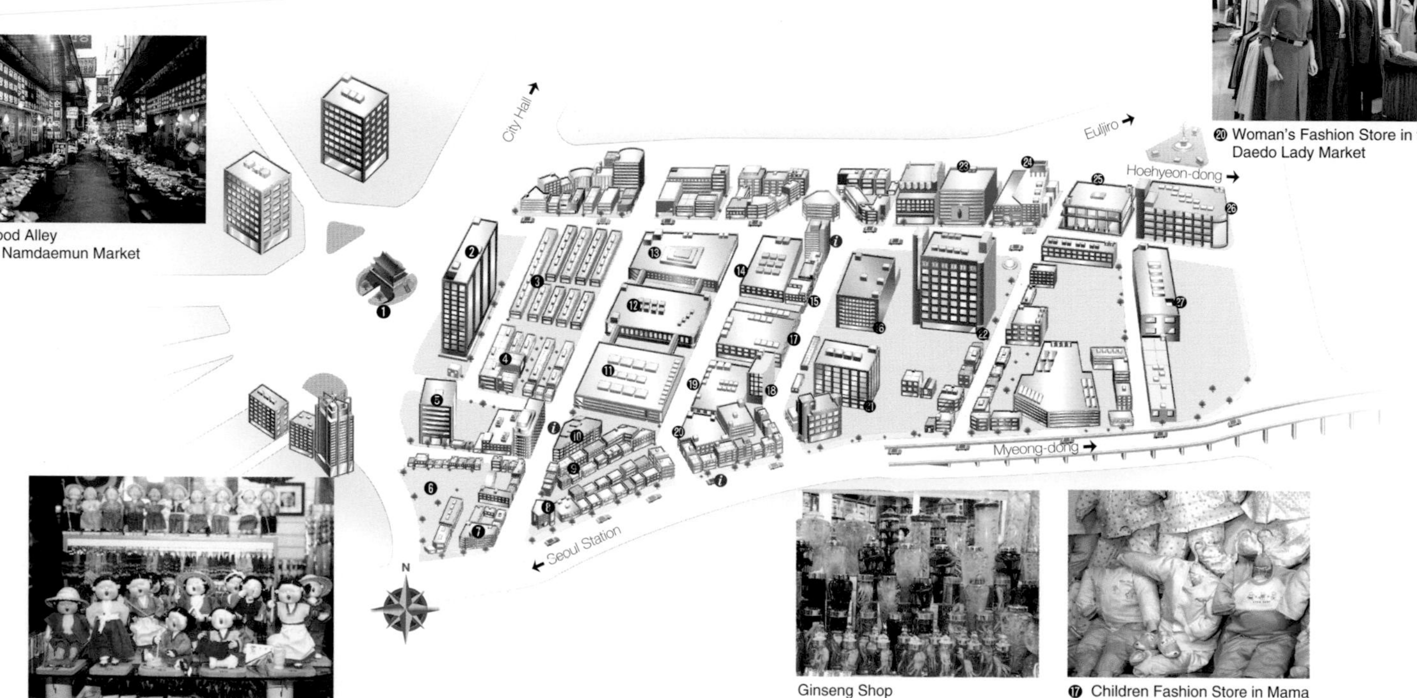

⓴ Woman's Fashion Store in the Daedo Lady Market

㉘ Food Alley in Namdaemun Market

Ginseng Shop

⓱ Children Fashion Store in Mama Children's Wear Arcade

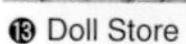

⓭ Doll Store

Sungnyemun (Namdaemun) 23

Sungnyemun (Namdaemun), National Treasure No. 1, was built in 1396 when King Taejo of the Joseon Dynasty moved the capital from Songdo (now called Gaeseong) to Hanyang (now called Seoul).

It served as the main gate through the fortress walls surrounding the capital. The Sungnyemun structure itself is the largest gate among those which remain in Seoul.

It is one of the structures which is most representative of the early Joseon architecture.

INDEX

1. Sungnyemun (Namgdaemun) **2.** Daehan Fire & Marine Insurance **3.** Bondong Arcade **4.** Namdaemun Arcade **5.** Namdo Imported Goods Arcade **6.** Yuseong Arcade **7.** Young Chang Accessories **8.** All-star Plaza **9.** Kennedy Arcade **10.** Cheongja Arcade **11.** Daedo Arcade, Men Course Arcade **12.** Daedo Jonghap Arcade Second Floor **13.** Jungang Arcade C-dong **14.** Daedo Eunnam Arcade **15.** Daedo Market **16.** Samik Shopping Town **17.** Mama Children' s Wear Arcade **18.** Daedo Arcade Market **19.** Wings Town **20.** Daedo Lady Market **21.** Common Plaza **22.** MESA **23.** Good & Good **24.** Road Town **25.** Korea First Bank **26.** Shinsegae Dept. Store **27.** Shinsegae Dept. Store Annex

4

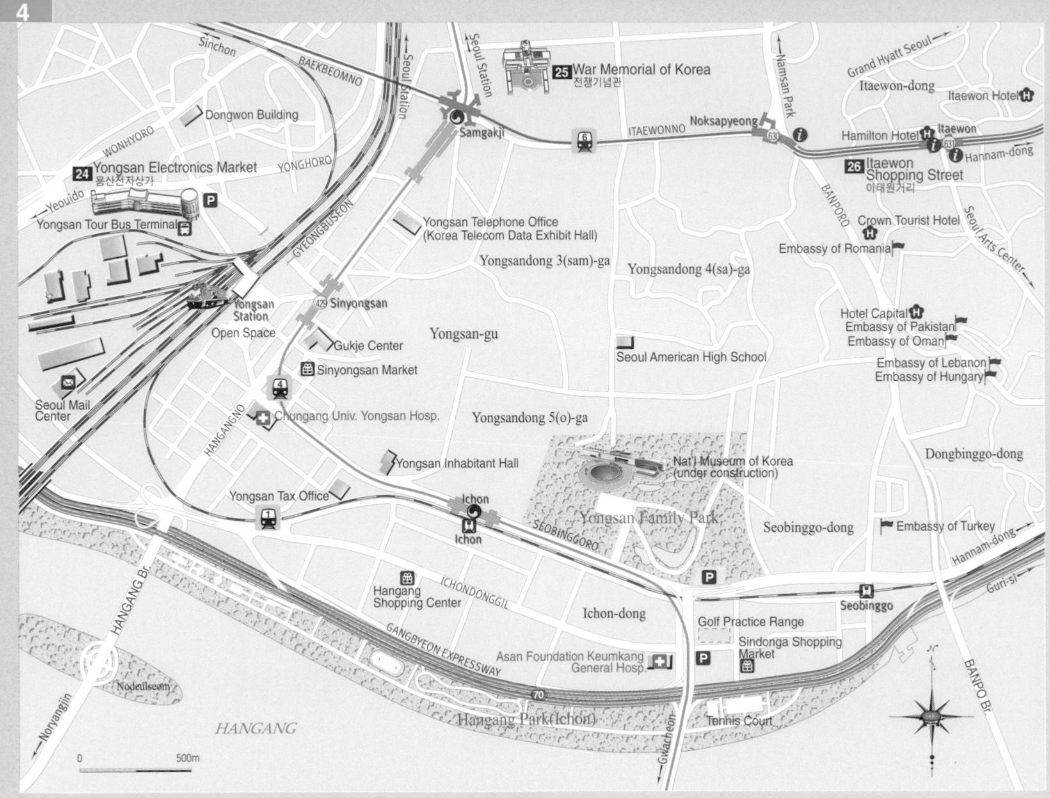

Yongsan Electronics Market 24

Yongsan Electronics Market specializes in electronic goods ranging from 1.6-inch mini TVs to computers, telephones and home appliances. It consists of 24 large-scale buildings and as many as 7,000 stores selling specialized products.

It attracts people because of the diversity of items and low prices. Because goods here are sold at lower prices than in retail stores, both Koreans and foreigners frequently visit Yongsan Electronics Market.

War Memorial of Korea 25

View of the War Memorial

Developed to promote peace on the Korean Peninsula and to educate future generations about the Korean war, the War Memorial of Korea was opened in June 1994.

In the center of the plaza in the museum complex stands the Statue of Two Brothers. The elder of the two is a South Korean soldier, and the younger a North Korean soldier. This statue symbolizes the confrontational history and tragic national division of the North and South.

Six exhibition rooms display about 8,500 war related materials and records, while strategic bombers, fighter jets, tanks, missiles and other large-scale weapons and equipment attract the visitor's attention in the outdoor exhibition area.

Honor guard ceremonies and music performances by military bands are featured at 10:00 am every Friday.

www.warmemo.co.kr

Aircraft Exhibit of the War Memorial

Itaewon Shopping Street 26

Itaewon is a major shopping district which is located in the Yongsan area and caters to the tastes of foreign shoppers. It is crowded with around 2,000 shops of all kinds, which sell shoes, clothes, bags and many other items. There are a wide range of accommodations, restaurants, entertainment establishments, hotels and health clinics. Boasting many ethnic restaurants, Itaewon is the best place for those who wish to try delicacies from countries around the world. Restaurants serving traditional German, Italian, Indian, Pakistani, Swiss and Thai foods are concentrated in Itaewon. This concentration of such a diverse range of ethnic restaurants is rare in Korea. Visitors to Itaewon can also enjoy tasty and traditional Korean, Chinese and Japanese foods.

Tourists at Itaewon Shopping Street

❸ Harubang Gift, an Antique Shop

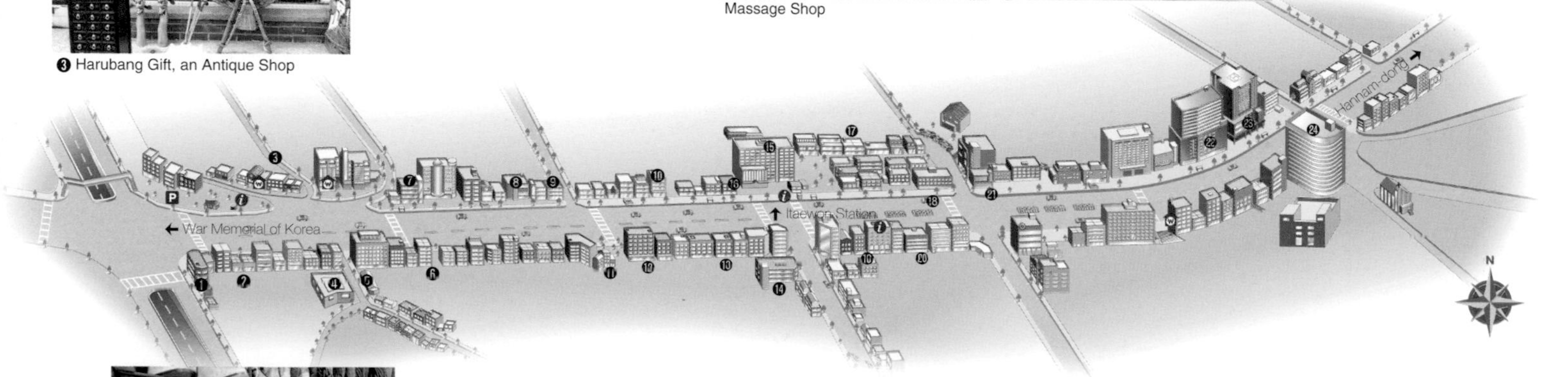

Street Stall

Massage Shop

← War Memorial of Korea

↑ Itaewon Station

Hannam-dong →

N

❺ Shoes Park, Shoe Shop

Street Arcade

Western-style Bar

INDEX

1. Supreme Optical **2.** Victory Town **3.** Harubang Gift
4. Itaewon Market **5.** Shoes Park **6.** Pony Town
7. Korea Exchange Bank **8.** Gapbu Town
9. Academy Hong Kong Jewelry Shop
10. Hit Town Shopping
11. OK Shopping Center **12.** Popeye Shopping Center
13. Bandolino Shoes **14.** Yuyong Plaza
15. Hamilton Hotel **16.** Hamilton Shopping Center
17. Korea Garden **18.** Grand Town **19.** Kookmin Bank
20. Ostrich House **21.** Joseon Antique
22. Seoul Shopping **23.** Itaewon Hotel
24. Cheil Communications

KLI 63 Building 27

Near the southern bank of the Hangang is the Korea Life Insurance Co. Building (also known as the 63 Building), with 60 stories above ground and 3 basement floors. This towering structure, reaching higher than any other buildings in Seoul, offers a wide variety of services for business persons and visitors. The first and second levels of the basements contain 63 Sea World, a popular aquarium, and the ground floor features an I-MAX theater.

On the top floor is the 63 Golden Tower, an observation deck commanding an impressive view of the whole city.

www.63city.co.kr

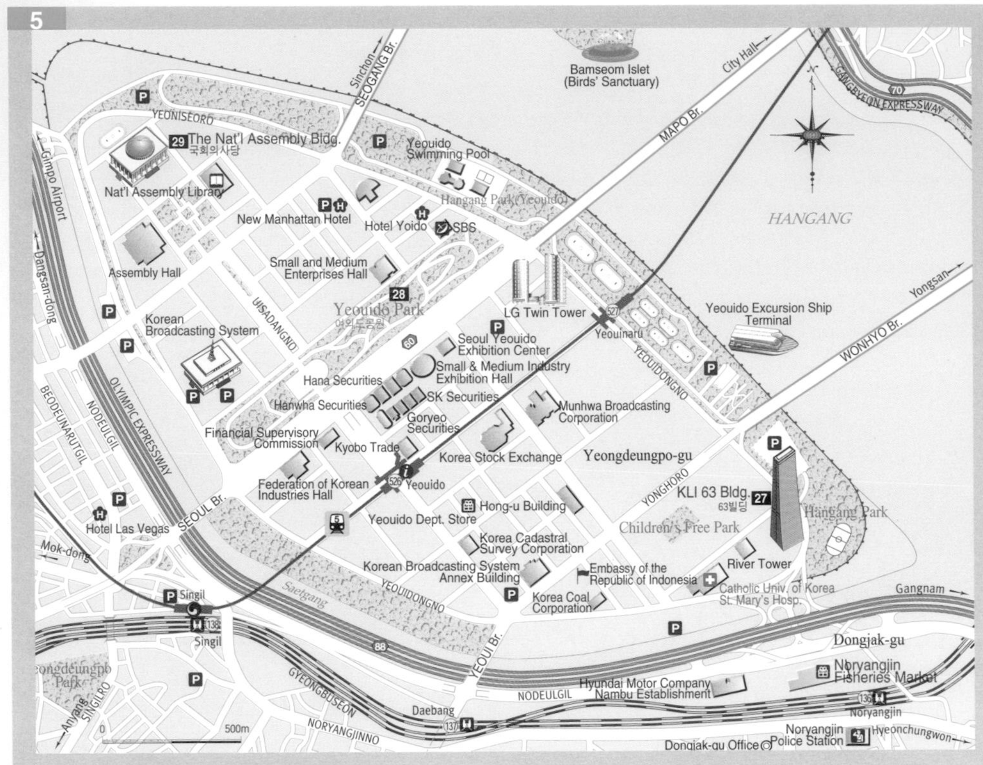

Yeouido Park 28

Yeouido Park

Yeouido Park consists of four areas: a traditional Korean pond in the shape of Seoul, a wooded area where people can enjoy nature, grassy lawns with winding paths where people can enjoy bicycling or skating, and the Yard of Culture, where a variety of cultural events such as concerts, music performances, and contests are held.

www.parks.seoul.kr/youido

The National Assembly Building 29

National Assembly Bldg.

The National Assembly Building is where lawmakers carry out their responsibilities, including enacting legislation under the parliamentary system.

Twenty four square granite pillars support the building and the roof of the building is domed.

www.assembly.go.kr

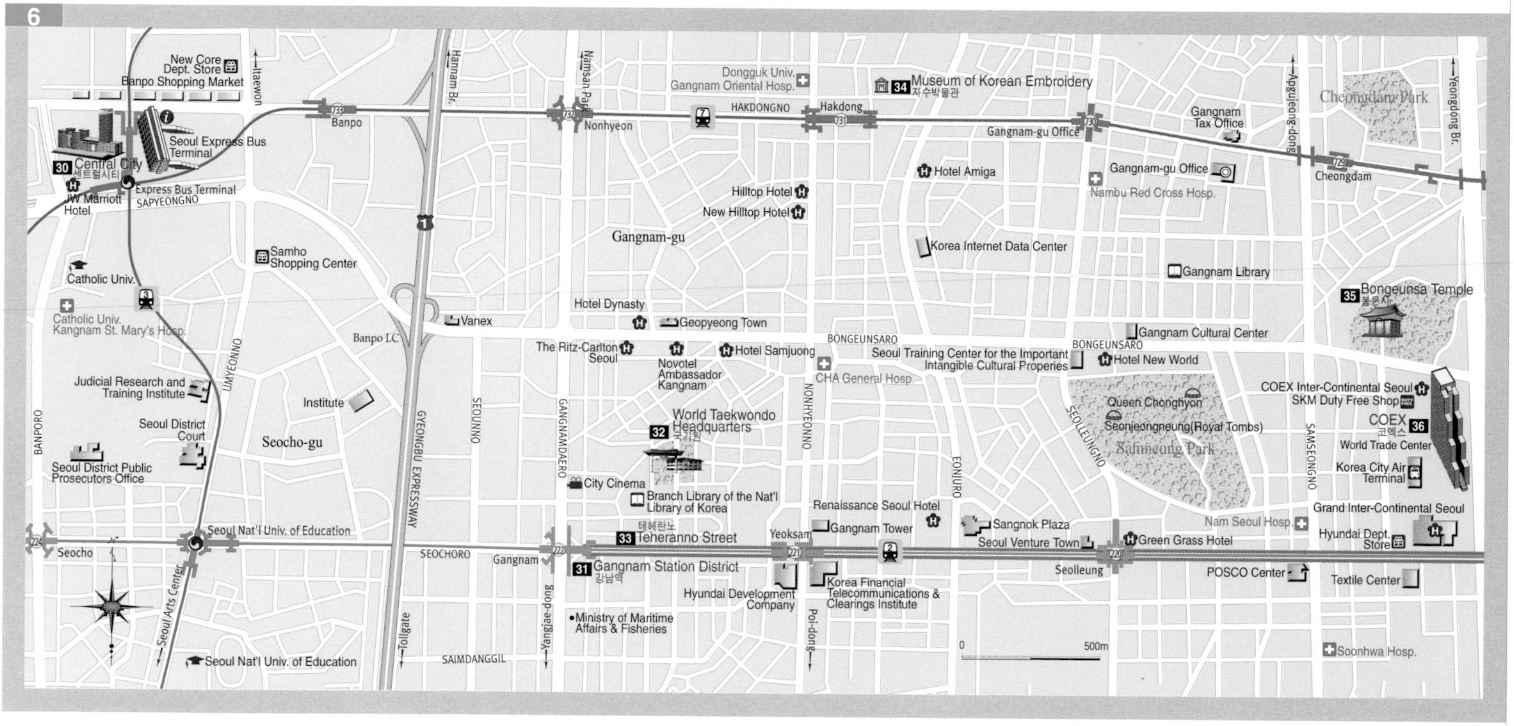

6

Central City 30

Central City is located in the Express Bus Terminal, a national transportation hub in the Gangnam area. It is a newly-built complex of shops that serves as a 'small city.' More than 50,000 people visit this shopping area daily. Many of the area's finest stores are located here, including the largest department store in Korea, renowned fashion boutiques and a large bookstore.
It also houses a world class hotel with 500 rooms and various other facilities.

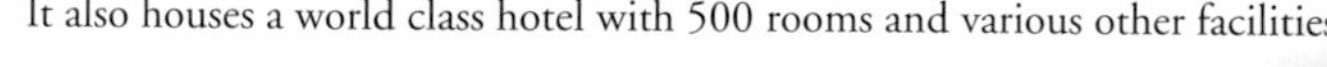

Marques Mall

Express Bus Terminal

View of Central City

Gangnam Station District, 'Street of Youth'

Gangnam Station District 31

The Gangnam area went through a period of rapid development and modernization in the late 1970s and now competes with Jongno and Myeong-dong as a bustling district popular with youngsters.
The area is packed with educational institutes, theaters, bookstores, record shops, restaurants, cafes and bars, and is crowded with young people, day and night. The area's neon signs keep the area brilliantly illuminated throughout the night and always a feeling of youthful passion and enthusiasm fills the air.

World Taekwondo Headquarters 32

The World Taekwondo Headquarters, established in 1972, is the primary center of Taekwondo, Korea's main traditional martial art. Taekwondo originated from the practice of Taekgyeon during the Three Kingdoms period. It has developed into the most widely studied form of Oriental martial art in the world. The World Taekwondo Headquarters is used as both the central Taekwondo Hall and as a testing site. Since Taekwondo has formally been adopted as a medal sport by the Olympic Games, the World Taekwondo Headquarters has emerged as an important place for Taekwondo.

Taekwondo

Teheranno Street 33

Teheranno was named after Teheran, the capital of Iran, to promote friendship between Korea and Iran. Teheranno contains hundreds of venture firms, forming a modern day venture town. It is also called Teheran Valley.
Teheran Valley, along with Daedeok Valley in Daejeon, make up the two pillars of the nation's venture industry. Teheranno has sophisticated optical communications networks, essential to the high-tech corporate environment dominated by the internet and IT networks.

Museum of Korean Embroidery 34

The Museum exhibits approximately 3,000 pieces of embroidery and women's crafts, much of which was produced in women's living quarters during the Joseon Dynasty. The museum also displays 'Jasusagyebungyeongdo,' which was produced in the 13th-14th century and is Korea's finest existing example of an embroidered folding screen (Treasure No. 653). Other folding screens, Buddhist embroidery works, embroidered ornaments and precious relics are on display.

Bongeunsa Temple 35

Bongeunsa was built by Yeonheoguksa, one of the highest-ranking Buddhist priests of the time in the 10th year (794) of King Wonseong's reign during the Silla Kingdom. Since then, it has served as one of the nation's leading Buddhist seminaries. The temple houses the Seonbuldang, a unique wooden structure, and the Panjeon, a hanging plaque with calligraphy written by Chusa Kim Jeong-hee, a renowned Korean calligrapher. The 3,175 pieces of the first edition of Daebanggwanbul Hwaeomgyeong Susoyeon, the Avatamska Sutra, are also preserved at the temple.

Monk's Procession around the Pagoda

COEX

Convention and Exhibition Center 36

COEX is the nation's largest exhibition center. On the 36,300㎡ site, 150 specialized exhibitions and other events are held annually. COEX is comprised of four exhibition areas.

www.coex.co.kr

COEX Mall

The COEX Mall houses world-class recreational facilities, famous brand name stores, and a wide range of restaurants from traditional Korean food to fast food and family restaurants.

Convention Auditorium

Convention Hall

Lobby in the ASEM Hall

Coffee Shop

ASEM Hall

Multi Complex Cinema

Exhibit of the Kimchi Museum

Kimchi Museum

The Kimchi Museum is dedicated to kimchi, the most popular food in Korea. It displays the various types of regional kimchi in visual images. Visitors can examine artifacts related to kimchi's history, different types of kimchi, kimchi recipes, processes of making kimchi, and techniques of fermenting kimchi.

COEX Aquarium

The COEX Aquarium is Korea's largest aquarium and serves as an ecological exhibition center for a wide variety of sea creatures. The aquarium exhibits 40,000 sea animals of 500 species. It houses the Sea Water Exhibition Hall, Fresh Water Exhibition Hall, exhibition halls by region and a special exhibition hall.

JAMSIL AREA

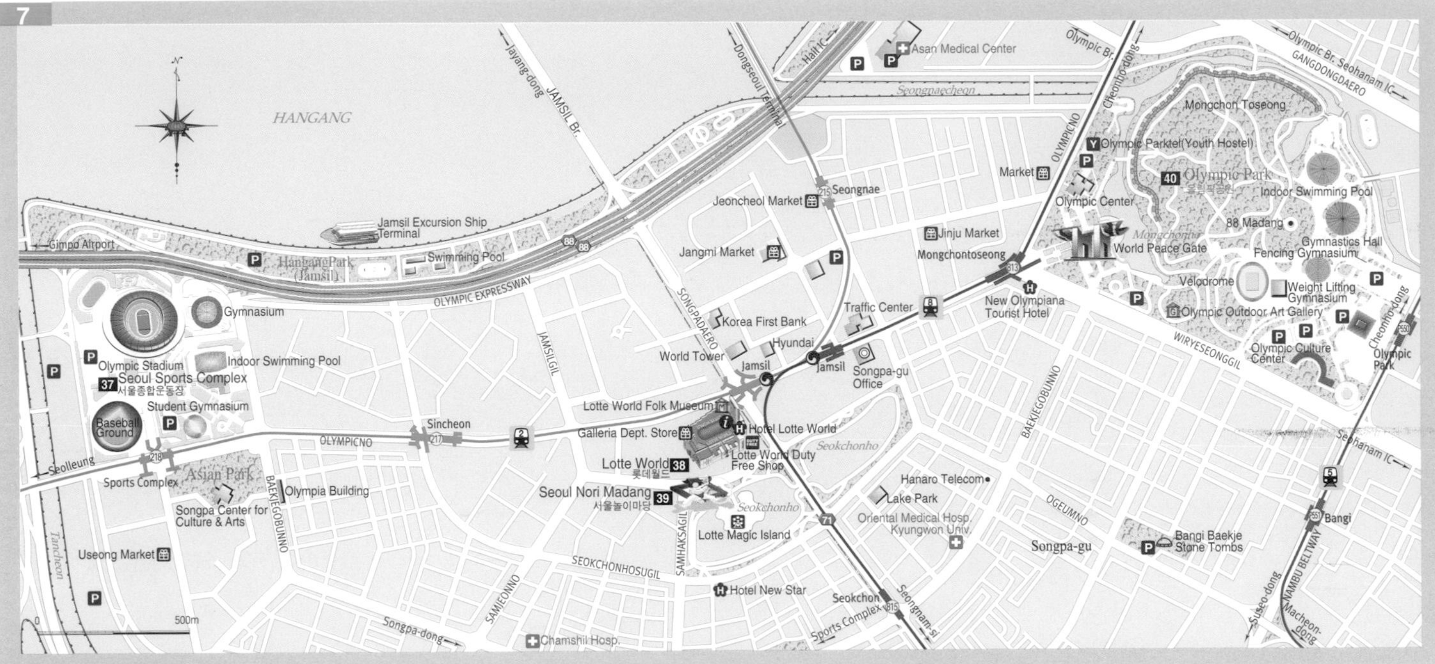

Aerial View of the Seoul Sports Complex

Seoul Sports Complex 37

The Seoul Sports Complex contains such sports facilities as the Olympic Stadium, a baseball stadium, a swimming arena and an indoor gymnasium. The Olympic Stadium is historically significant because it is where the opening and closing ceremonies, and other events were held during the 1986 Asian Games and the 1988 Seoul Olympic Games. The Olympic Exhibition Hall, on the south side of the Seoul Sports Complex, displays various information about the Olympic Games, ranging from the origin, past sites and mascots of the Olympic Games through the years to the events of the 1988 Seoul Olympic Games.

Lotte World 38

Lotte World Adventure is an indoor, glass domed amusement park where people can enjoy fun and excitement in any season or weather. Magic Island, located in the adjacent Lake Park, has a beautiful fairy tale theme. The glittering lights of Magic Island provide a scenic view at night. In addition, Lotte World offers its visitors world-class shopping in adjoining shopping malls, as well as a broad range of cultural activities, sports facilities, a cinema multiplex, and a folk museum that features displays on Korea's history and culture.
www.lotteworld.com

Lotte World Ice Rink

Seoul Nori Madang 39

Seoul Nori Madang, adjacent to Lotte World, stages traditional Korean performances, including traditional music, dances, and songs. Artists designated as intangible cultural assets perform at Seoul Nori Madang every Saturday and Sunday. On traditional holidays, visitors can play a

Seoul Nori Madang

wide range of folk games, such as seesaw, giant swings, foot shuttlecock and 'yut,' a kind of board game with four sticks used as dice.

Olympic Park 40

Olympic Park was completed in 1986 in commemoration of the 1986 Asian Games and in anticipation of the 1988 Seoul Olympic Games. On the 1,419,000㎡ site are symbolic structures and sculptures designed to harmonize with the landscaping. Mongchon Toseong, a historical mud fortification, is located across the lake in the park, enabling visitors to enjoy both a full day of sightseeing as well as a cultural and historical experience. The 200 sculptures scattered across the park were donated by 155 artists from the 66 countries that participated in the 1988 Seoul Olympic Games. They give the park a multi-national refinement. Major sculptures include 'The Thumb' by Cesar of France, 'Dialogue' by Amara of Algeria and the '1988 Seoul Olympic Games' by Staccioli of Italy.

World Peace Gate in Olympic Park

'Dialogue' by Amara of Algeria

Cafe near Hongik Univ.

Clothing Shops near Ewha Womans Univ.

Body Painting on Rodeo Street

Hongik Univ. District C3

The Hongik University district is known for its underground culture. The district has emerged as a center of pop culture, with its rock clubs, techno bars, specialized record shops and galleries, all densely packed into this area.

Many buildings with distinctive facades, including Mexican motifs and medieval European castles, can be seen throughout the area.

Ahyeon Wedding Street D3

The Ahyeon-dong area is adjacent to Ewha Womans University. It is one of the world's largest wedding-dress shop districts. More than 200 specialized wedding dress shops here cater to more than 50% of Korea's domestic demand.

Ewha Womans Univ. Shopping District D3

The Ewha Womans University shopping district is a young people's shopping paradise. Hip-hop clothing shops, accessory shops, cafes and beauty salons fill the small streets. There are a number of private brand clothing shops, as well as boutiques and other small shops with unique and individualized items to satisfy the most finicky fashion demands of the younger generation.

Rodeo Street H5

Located in Apgujeong-dong, Rodeo Street is one of the most bustling areas in Seoul and leads the nation's fashion trends. A wide variety of exclusive boutiques and other shops line both sides of the street. Regardless of what they sell, shops in Rodeo Street are known for their distinctive and individualistic interior designs, creating the so-called 'Apgujeong Culture' and attracting numerous people of distinctive styles and tastes.

Cheongdam-dong District H5

Cheongdam-dong is a high-end fashion area, filled with boutiques, luxurious fashion shops and designer goods shops, many of which feature distinctive architectural styles.

Cheongdam-dong contains the Galleria Designer Product Hall, Hak-dong intersection and Cheongdam-dong intersection.

Rodeo Street

Noryangjin Fisheries Market D5

Noryangjin Fisheries Market is a large-scale wholesale seafood market, serving an average of about 15,000 customers every day. All kinds of fresh fish caught off the coast of Korea or brought in from deep-sea fishing vessels are sold here at both retail and wholesale. The market is packed year round with people who want to buy and taste the freshest seafood at a reasonable price.

Noryangjin Fisheries Market

Techno Mart J4

Techno Mart is a state-of-the-art multiplex where all kinds of electronics and IT products are found. A visit to Techno Mart provides an opportunity to catch a glimpse of the current status of the latest technology of Korea's IT products.
Each floor is specialized and there are about 2,500 stores selling electronic goods.
Techno Mart is a one-stop electronics shopping center in the truest sense, as it is equipped with a shopping mall, a discount store and other facilities for the convenience

CGV, Multiplex Cinema

of shoppers. Visitors can also take advantage of a multi-screen cineplex and a fitness club.

Seoul Arts Center G7

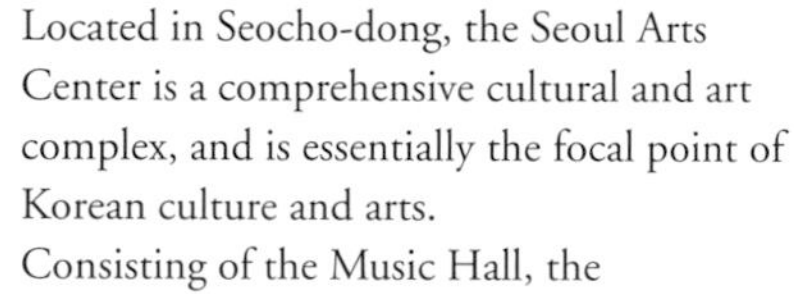

Located in Seocho-dong, the Seoul Arts Center is a comprehensive cultural and art complex, and is essentially the focal point of Korean culture and arts.
Consisting of the Music Hall, the Calligraphy Hall, the Hangaram Art Gallery, the Arts Library and the Opera House, the complex presents concerts and exhibitions of all genres.
In the Korean Garden and Symbolic Plaza, outdoor performances are held, enabling visitors to enjoy sophisticated culture and arts in a natural setting.
www.sac.or.kr

Seoul Arts Center, the Showcase of Korean Culture and Arts

Insubong, the Gigantic Granite Peak of Mt. Bukhansan

Bukhansan National Park D1

Located in the northern section of Seoul, Bukhansan National Park provides Seoul citizens with a tranquil retreat near the city. Featuring beautiful scenery and lush forests, it offers much-needed 'green space' to urban dwellers.

Between gigantic granite peaks lie deep valleys and pure streams, creating scenery reminiscent of a beautiful and serene Oriental painting. The park is home to 1,300 kinds of plants and animals, as well as abundant historical and cultural assets.

Hongneung Arboretum H1

Korea's indigenous plants and those from countries around the world have been transported and planted here in the Hongneung Arboretum, making it home to approximately 40,000 trees of 2,000 different species. Visitors have a great opportunity to see rare Korean plants.

Amsa-dong Prehistoric Settlement Site

Amsa-dong Prehistoric Settlement Site K3

The Amsa-dong Prehistoric Settlement Site is the largest Neolithic habitation site ever found in Korea. It dates back to around 3,000-4,000 B.C. and contains remains from the New Stone Age. Visitors can view earthenware with comb-teeth patterns, the most distinctive feature of the New Stone Age, and stoneware which includes stone points, stone axes, pounders, scratchers, sharpening plates and sharpening stones. These precious artifacts provide a glimpse into the lifestyle and agricultural culture during the Neolithic Age.

Gyeongdong Herbal Medicine Market

Gyeongdong Market H2

Gyeongdong Market is Korea's most popular herbal medicine market, where over 70% of Seoul's oriental medicine is bought and sold. It is crammed with nearly 1,000 oriental health clinics, herbal drugstores and pharmaceutical shops.

Visitors to Gyeongdong Market will experience the unique scent of oriental medicine as soon as they set foot in the entrance of the market. Each store is filled with huge stocks of oriental medicine, offering visitors a chance to see an endless variety of remedies.

Unlike modern shopping facilities, Gyeongdong Market has retained the traditional aspects of a Korean marketplace. Scenes of merchants selling herbal medicine, customers haggling over prices and people hawking their wares to attract customers' attention leave a lasting impression on visitors.

Seoul World Cup Stadium B2

Seoul World Cup Stadium is located in Sangam-dong and is the center of much attention due to its unique design.
Seen from above, the outline of the stadium resembles a huge rectangular shield kite, a type of traditional Korean kite. The shape, which resembles a kite soaring in the sky, symbolizes the Korean people's aspirations for a victory in the World Cup Games and their wish to enhance the nation's image in the eyes of the world. It is also a symbol of the hopes of the Korean people for national unification and world peace in the 21st century.
The stadium will be the venue to showcase Korea's cordial welcome and warm hospitality to international visitors.
The curved lines of the stadium roof and its linear splendor utilize cutting-edge construction technology, while symbolizing the lines found in the roofs and eaves of traditional Korean houses.
www.2002worldcupkorea.org
worldcup.metro.seoul.kr

'The Red Devils', the Korean Football Team Supporters

Hangang River

The Hangang River is the main source of water for Seoul and its surrounding vicinity, and is important to the city as both a natural resource and a recreational resource. Two branches of the river converge and flow through Seoul, separating the city into southern and northern halves. The banks of the Hangang not only offer recreational spaces for citizens but are also becoming thriving tourist attractions thanks to the unique features of each district along the river. Each section of the river presents a unique scenic attraction. Taking a river cruise offers visitors a fine view of the multi-faceted nature of Seoul, and an evening cruise presents a particularly dramatic view of the night skyline.

www.hangang.seoul.kr

Jeoldusan Holy Martyrs' Shrine

Ecology

The Hangang is home to all kinds of fauna and flora, with more than 580 species of 106 flora families and 54 species of aquatic insects. About 35 kinds of migratory birds can be seen along the Hangang, including wild ducks, spotbill ducks, mandarin ducks, whooper swans, white-tailed sea eagles, and kestrels.

Kestrel

Bamseom

Located adjacent to Yeouido, Bamseom is the nation's largest sanctuary for mig ry birds and one can view flocks of birds flying through a telescope at the Yeouid lookout.

Bamseom

Hwangpo Sailing Boat

Seoul World Cup Stadium

Swimming Pool

There are outdoor public pools in seven districts of the Hangang Parks. These facilities are used as swimming pools in the summer, rollerskating rinks in the spring and fall, and ice-skating rinks in the winter.

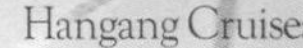

Hangang Cruises

A cruise between Yeouido and Jamsil is sure to leave a long-lasting memory. The evening cruise provides a glittering view of Seoul' s nightscape.

Hangang Cruise Information

One way trip

Yeouido – Jamsil: 7,000 won
Jamsil – Yeouido: 7,000 won

Round trip

Yeouido – Hangang bridge – Yanghwa – Yeouido: 7,000 won
Yanghwa – Yeouido – Hangang Bridge – Yanghwa: 7,000 won
Jamsil – Hannam Bridge – Jamsil: 7,000 won

KLI 63 Building Aquarium

Leisure activities on the Hangang

A variety of recreational and leisure activities can be enjoyed along the Hangang riverside. Divided into 13 areas, the riverside enables people to enjoy jogging, riding bicycles and roller-skating, as well as playing soccer, basketball, volleyball and badminton. Water sports such as windsurfing, water skiing, boating and ski jets are also available.

Bicycle Trail

Visitors can enjoy a bike ride along the Hangang bicycle trail. The trail spans 36.9 km from the Yanghwa region to Gwangnaru region. The trail winds along side the river, through grasslands and various parks offering natural scenery and great views of Seoul.

an & Seoul Tower

Seoul Sports Complex

Seoul City Tour Bus

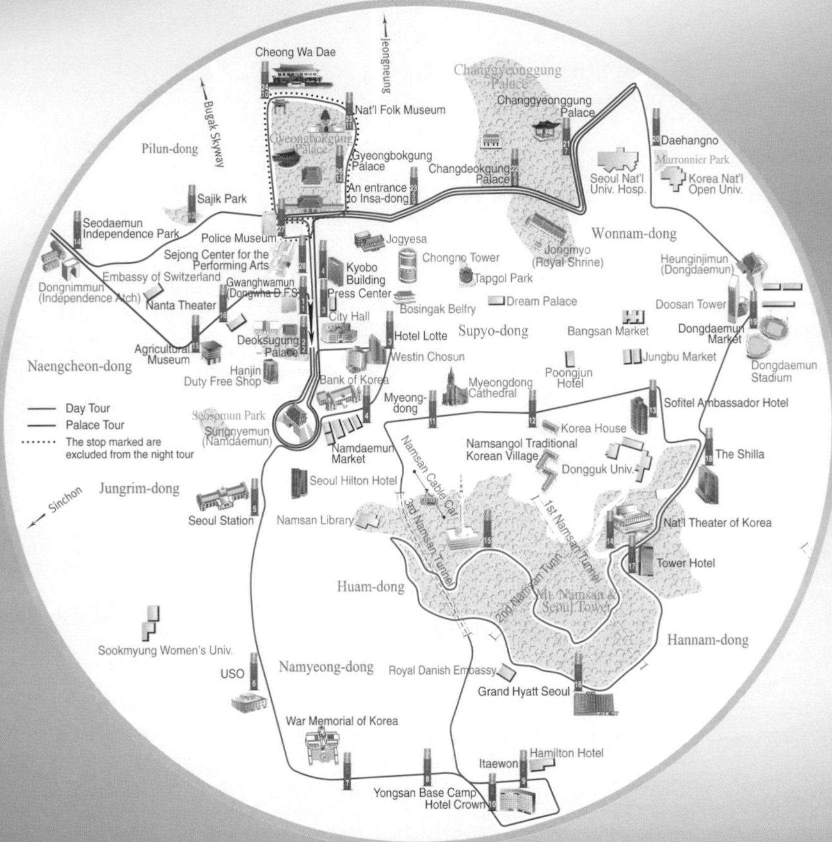

"Meet Seoul's Past and Present with Seoul City Tour Bus for Only Five Dollars"

Specifically designed for touring Seoul, these 35-seat luxury buses ensure passengers a comfortable ride with spacious, reclining seats. Expert tour guides who can speak Korean, English, Japanese, or Chinese accompany each tour. As a bus approaches each tourist attraction, a recorded description of the site, in Korean, English, Japanese, and Chinese can be heard.

All bus drivers are veterans with more than 15 years of driving experience.

Tours begin every 30 minutes at the bus stop in front of the Dongwha Duty Free Shop. Tourists with a day ticket can get on and off different tour buses at any time at any of the designated tour-bus stops. The Seoul City Tour Bus runs year round and costs about $5.00/US.

Tour Routes

Day Tour

Gwanghwamun (Dongwha D.F.S.) – Deoksugung Palace – Lotte Hotel – Namdaemun Market (Main bldg. of the Bank of Korea) – Seoul Station – USO (United Service Organization) – War Memorial – U.S. Army Post – Itaewon – Crown Hotel – Myeong-dong (Next to Prince Hotel) – Namsan Traditional Korean Village – Sofitel Ambassador Hotel – National Theater of Korea – Namsan Seoul Tower – Grand Hyatt Hotel – Tower Hotel – Shilla Hotel – Dongdaemun Market – Daehangno – Changgyeonggung Palace – Changdeokgung Palace – Insa-dong – Cheong Wa Dae – National Folk Museum – Gyeongbokgung Palace – Police Museum – Sejong Center for the Performing Arts – Gwanghwamun

Night Tour

Gwanghwamun (Dongwha D.F.S.) – Deoksugung Palace – Lotte Hotel – Namdaemun Market (Main Bldg. of the Bank of Korea) – Seoul Station – USO (United Service Organization) – War Memorial – U.S. Army Post – Itaewon – Crown Hotel – Myeong-dong (Next to Prince Hotel) – Namsan Traditional Korean Village – Sofitel Ambassador Hotel – National Theater of Korea – Namsan Seoul Tower – Grand Hyatt – Hotel Tower Hotel – Shilla Hotel – Dongdaemun Market – Daehangno – Insa-dong – Sejong Center for the Performing Arts – Gwanghwamun

Palace Tour

Gwanghwamun – Deoksugung Palace – Press Center – Kyobo Building – An entrance to Insa-dong – Changdeokgung Palace – Changgyeonggung Palace – Changdeokgung Palace – An entrance to Insa-dong – Cheong Wa Dae – National Folk Museum – Gyeongbokgung Palace – Sajik Park – Independence Park – Agricultural Museum – Nanta Theater – Gwanghwamun

World Cup Tour

Gwanghwamun - Deoksugung Palace - Ahyeondong Wedding Street - Ewha Womans Univ. Vicinity - Hong Ik Univ. Vicinity - Jeoldusan Martyrs' Shrine - Seoul World Cup Stadium - National Assembly - Yeouido Park - Yeouido Excursion Ship Terminal - KLI 63 Building - Yongsan Electronics Market - War Memorial of Korea - Seoul Station - Namdaemun Market - Sejong Center for the Performing Arts

Seoul City Tour Bus Information

Hours of Operation

- Day Tour: (09:00am ~ 6:00pm) Tour takes 2 hours 30 minutes
- Night Tour: (18:00am ~ 11:00pm) Tour takes 2 hours
- All Day Tour: Full Time

Fares

- Day Tour or Night Tour: $ 5
- Full or All Day Ticket: $ 8

www.seoulcitytourbus.com

Busan

Busan is the second largest city in Korea, with a population of four million. Busan is proud to be playing a major role on the world stage by hosting the 2002 Asian Games and its participation in the 2002 FIFA World Cup Korea/Japan.

Its deep harbor and gentle tides have allowed it to grow into the largest container handling port in the country and the fourth largest in the world, with the potential for continued growth. Busan is a beautiful port city that has a bustling urban energy. Its geography includes a coastline with fine beaches, scenic cliffs, a wide river, tall mountains, and hot springs. Its natural environment and rich history have resulted in Busan's increasingly good reputation as a world class city.

The logo of PIFF was adopted from calligraphy contained in the Tripitaka Koreana. Hundreds of years ago, the Tripitaka Koreana was carved as an entreaty to Buddha to protect the Goryeo Dynasty against the Mongolian invasions. It took 16 years of labor to complete the work which was registered as a world heritage item by UNESCO in 1995.
The PIFF logo was made from the seal of a traditional oriental painting.

*Pusan International Film Festival (PIFF)

Catalyst for Asian Cinema

A Scene from Yim Kwon-taek's Film 'Chunhyangjeon'

Outdoor Movie Screen at the Yachting Center

Ever since its inauguration in September 1996, the Pusan International Film Festival (PIFF) has been held annually, providing movie lovers with the opportunity to enjoy a selection of celebrated international films in a wide range of genres. Despite its short history, it has grown into one of the most influential film festivals in Asia, crowding Busan with famous film makers, actors, critics, fans and huge audiences.
While PIFF places its primary focus on Asian films, the festival screens films from all over the world, including North America and Europe. This enables movie fans to gain a comprehensive perspective of the current trends in both Asian and world movies. The PPP (Pusan Promotion Plan) has been implemented since the 3rd PIFF to promote international exchanges among international movie circles, thereby expanding the market for Asian films and supporting the Asian film industry.
PIFF is composed of seven categories: 1) *A Window on Asian Cinema* which screens new films by Asian directors; 2) *New and Current* screens debut films or second efforts by new directors; 3) *World Cinema* screens films from outside Asia; 4) *Korean Panorama* showcases Korean films; 5) *Wide Angle* provides screenings of short, animated and documentary films; 6) *Open* offers screenings of controversial new films by world famous directors; and 7) *Special Programs in Focus* screen Special and retrospective movies.
The films are screened at numerous movie theaters on the Nampo-dong Street area, at the Cinema Hall in Millak-dong and on a giant outdoor screen at Suyeongman Bay.

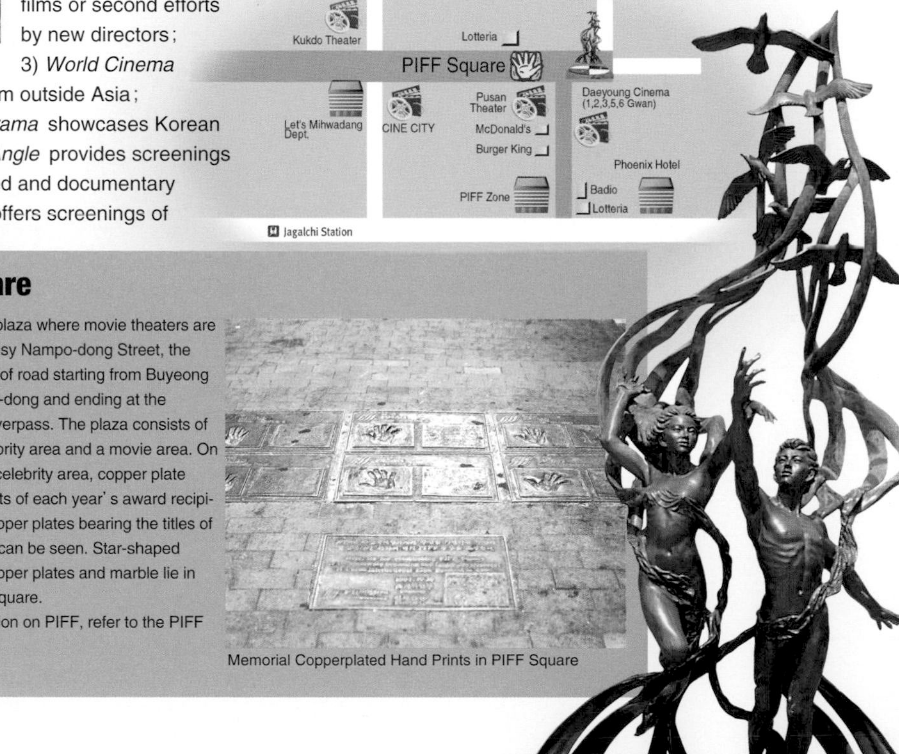

PIFF Square

PIFF Square is a plaza where movie theaters are clustered along busy Nampo-dong Street, the 400-meter stretch of road starting from Buyeong Cinema in Nampo-dong and ending at the Chungmu-dong overpass. The plaza consists of two areas : a celebrity area and a movie area. On the square of the celebrity area, copper plate hand and foot prints of each year's award recipients as well as copper plates bearing the titles of participating films can be seen. Star-shaped granite stones, copper plates and marble lie in the center of the square.
For more information on PIFF, refer to the PIFF website.
www.piff.org

Memorial Copperplated Hand Prints in PIFF Square

A Sculpture Commemorating PIFF in PIFF Square

*Pusan is the former name of Busan (Under the previous romanization system)

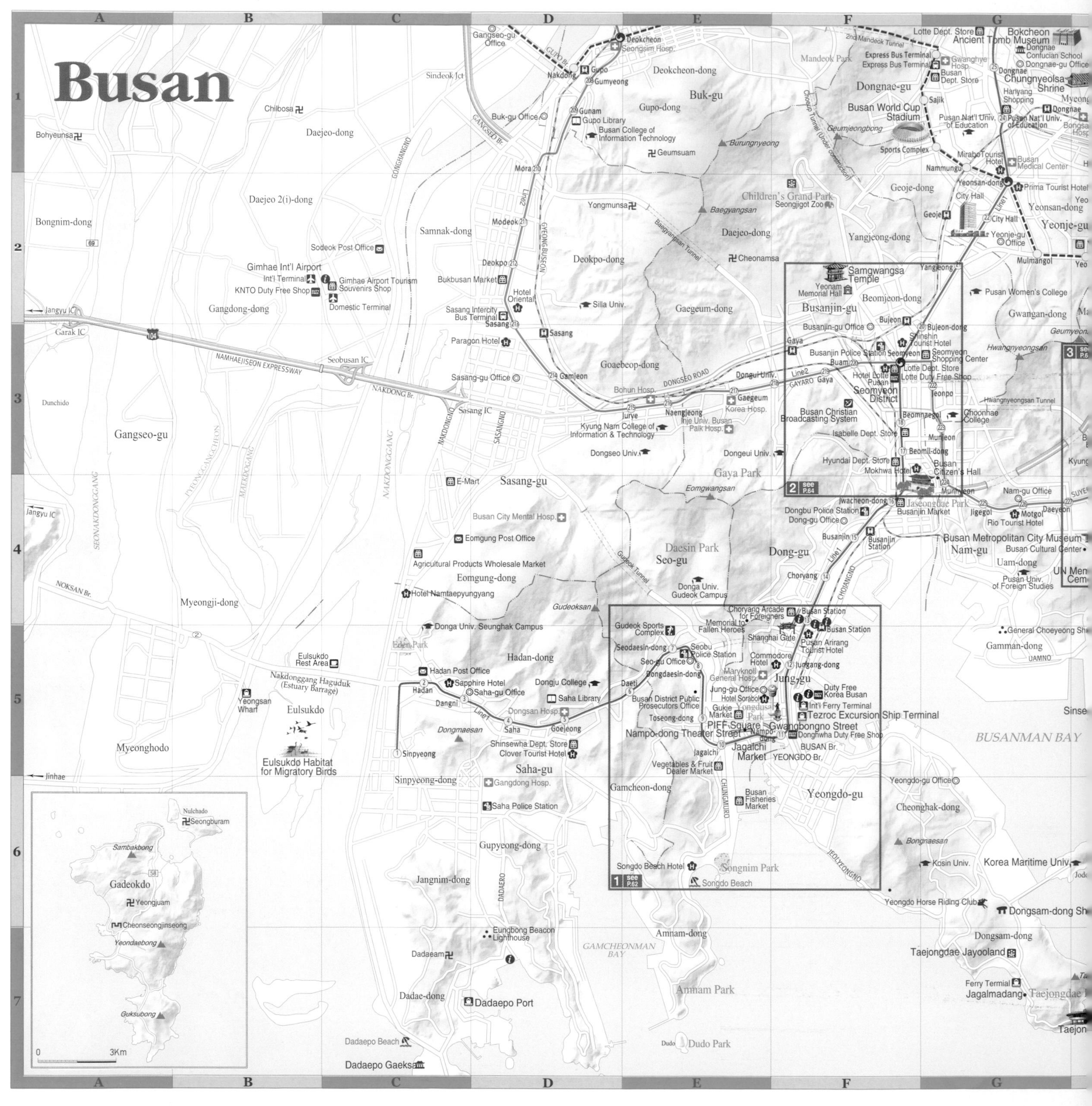

Busan
A
B
C
D
E
F
G
1
2
3
4
5
6
7
Bohyeunsa
Chilbosa
Daejeo-dong
Sindeok Jct
Gangseo-gu Office
Deokcheon
Seongsim Hosp.
Gupo
Nakdong
Gumyeong
Deokcheon-dong
Buk-gu
Gupo-dong
Gunam
Gupo Library
Busan College of Information Technology
Geumsuam
Buk-gu Office
Burungnyeong
Mandeok Park
2nd Mandeok Tunnel
Lotte Dept. Store
Express Bus Terminal
Express Bus Terminal
Gwanghye Hosp.
Busan Dept. Store
Dongnae-gu
Bokcheon Ancient Tomb Museum
Dongnae Confucian School
Dongnae-gu Office
Dongnae
Chungnyeolsa Shrine
Hanyang Shopping
Dongnae
Myeong
Sajik
Busan World Cup Stadium
Geumjeongbong
Pusan Nat'l Univ. of Education
Pusan Nat'l Univ. of Education
Sports Complex
Mirabo Tourist Hotel
Busan Medical Center
Nammungu
Yeonsan-dong
Prima Tourist Hotel
Daejeo 2(i)-dong
Bongnim-dong
69
Samnak-dong
Mora
Modeok
Line2
Gyeongbuseon
Yongmunsa
Baegyangsan
Children's Grand Park
Seongjigot Zoo
Geoje-dong
City Hall
Geoje
City Hall
Yeonsan-dong
Yeonje-gu
Yeonje-gu Office
Yangjeong-dong
Sodeok Post Office
Gimhae Int'l Airport
Int'l Terminal
Gimhae Airport Tourism Souvenirs Shop
KNTO Duty Free Shop
Domestic Terminal
Deokpo
Deokpo-dong
Baegyangsan Tunnel
Daejeo-dong
Cheonamsa
Mulmangol
Yangjeong
Samgwangsa Temple
Yeonam Memorial Hall
Beomjeon-dong
Pusan Women's College
Bukbusan Market
Hotel Oriental
Sasang Intercity Bus Terminal
Sasang
Silla Univ.
Gaegeum-dong
Busanjin-gu
Bujeon
Bujeon-dong
Gwangan-dong
Jangyu IC
Garak IC
Gangdong-dong
104
Sasang
Busanjin-gu Office
Shinshin Tourist Hotel
Geumyeonsan
Paragon Hotel
Gaya
Busanjin Police Station
Seomyeon
Seomyeon Shopping Center
Hwangnyeongsan
3 see P.6
NAMHAEJISEON EXPRESSWAY
Seobusan IC
Goaebeop-dong
Buam
Lotte Dept. Store
Lotte Duty Free Shop
Sasang-gu Office
Gamjeon
DONGSEO ROAD
Dongui Univ.
Line2
GAYARO
Gaya
Hotel Lotte Pusan
Seomyeon District
Jeonpo
Hwangnyeongsan Tunnel
NAKDONG Br.
Dunchido
Sasang IC
Bohun Hosp.
Jurye
Naengjeong
Gaegeum
Korea Hosp.
Busan Christian Broadcasting System
Beomnaegol
Choonhae College
Gangseo-gu
Kyung Nam College of Information & Technology
Inje Univ. Busan Paik Hosp.
Isabelle Dept. Store
Munhyeon
Dongseo Univ.
Dongeui Univ.
Beomil-dong
Hyundai Dept. Store
Mokhwa Hotel
Busan Citizen's Hall
Gaya Park
E-Mart
Sasang-gu
Emgwangsan
2 see P.64
Munhyeon
Jwacheon-dong
Jaseongdae Park
Nam-gu Office
Jigegol
Motgol
Daeyeon
Rio Tourist Hotel
Busanjin Market
Dongbu Police Station
Dong-gu Office
Jangyu IC
Busan City Mental Hosp.
Eomgung Post Office
Busanjin
Busanjin Station
Busan Metropolitan City Museum
Nam-gu
Busan Cultural Center
Daesin Park
Seo-gu
Dong-gu
Uam-dong
Agricultural Products Wholesale Market
Gudeok Tunnel
Chorycang
Line1
CHOJANGRO
Pusan Univ. of Foreign Studies
UN Mem Cem
NOKSAN Br.
Eomgung-dong
Myeongji-dong
Hotel Namtaepyungyang
Donga Univ. Gudeok Campus
Gudeoksan
Chorycang Arcade for Foreigners
Busan Station
Memorial to Fallen Heroes
Busan Station
Gudeok Sports Complex
Shanghai Gate
Pusan Arirang Tourist Hotel
General Choeyeong Sh
Donga Univ. Seunghak Campus
Eden Park
Gamman-dong
UAMNO
Eulsukdo Rest Area
Hadan-dong
Seodaesin-dong
Seobu Police Station
Seo-gu Office
Commodore Hotel
Jungang-dong
Hadan Post Office
Maryknoll General Hosp.
Dongdaesin-dong
Nakdonggang Haguduk (Estuary Barrage)
Sapphire Hotel
Dongju College
Daeti
Jung-gu
Hadan
Saha-gu Office
Jung-gu Office
Duty Free Korea Busan
Yeongsan Wharf
Eulsukdo
Dangni
Saha Library
Busan District Public Prosecutors Office
Hotel Sorabol
Int'l Ferry Terminal
Tezroc Excursion Ship Terminal
Line1
Dongsan Hosp.
Gukje Market
Yongdusan Park
Sinse
Toseong-dong
Dongmaesan
Saha
Goejeong
PIFF Square
Gwangbongno Street
Nampo-dong Theater Street
Nampo
Donghwa Duty Free Shop
BUSANMAN BAY
Myeonghodo
Shinsewha Dept. Store
Clover Tourist Hotel
Jagalchi
Jagalchi Market
BUSAN Br.
YEONGDO Br.
Sinpyeong
Eulsukdo Habitat for Migratory Birds
Vegetables & Fruit Dealer Market
Jinhae
Sinpyeong-dong
Saha-gu
Gangdong Hosp.
Gamcheon-dong
CHUNGMURO
Yeongdo-gu
Yeongdo-gu Office
Busan Fisheries Market
Nulchado
Seongburam
Saha Police Station
Cheonghak-dong
Sambakbong
58
Gupyeong-dong
Bongnaesan
Gadeokdo
Songdo Beach Hotel
Songnim Park
Kosin Univ.
Korea Maritime Univ.
Yeongjuam
Jangnim-dong
DADAERO
1 see P.62
Songdo Beach
JEOLYEONGRO
Cheonseongjinseong
Yeongdo Horse Riding Club
Dongsam-dong Sh
Yeondaebong
Eungbong Beacon Lighthouse
Amnam-dong
Dongsam-dong
GAMCHEONMAN BAY
Dadaeam
Taejongdae Jayooland
Ferry Terminal
Amnam Park
Jagalmadang
Taejongdae
Dadae-dong
Dadaepo Port
Guksubong
Dadaepo Beach
Dudo
Dudo Park
Taejon
0
3Km
Dadaepo Gaeksa

INDEX

Cultural Relics

Natural Attractions

Museums & Theaters

Places of Interest

Accommodations

Transportation

Tourist Information

Busan Tourism Promotion Division 82-51-888-3501
Busan Tourist Information 82-51-441-3121
www.metro.pusan.kr

LEGEND

- Railroad Station
- Airport
- Port
- Bus Terminal
- Metro Line
- Rest Area
- Hospital
- Police Station
- Post Office
- Tourist Information Center
- University or School
- Library
- Broadcasting Station
- Museum
- Prehistoric Relic Site
- Fortress
- Temple
- Traditional Building
- Movie Theater
- Falls or Valley
- Beach
- Horse Track
- Hot Spring or Spa
- Park
- Scenic Area
- Amusement Park
- Zoo
- Mountain
- Stadium
- Other Tourist Attractions
- Hotel
- Condominium
- Department Store or Market
- Duty Free Shop
- Reference Point
- Transfer Station
- Metro Station Number

NAMPO-DONG AREA

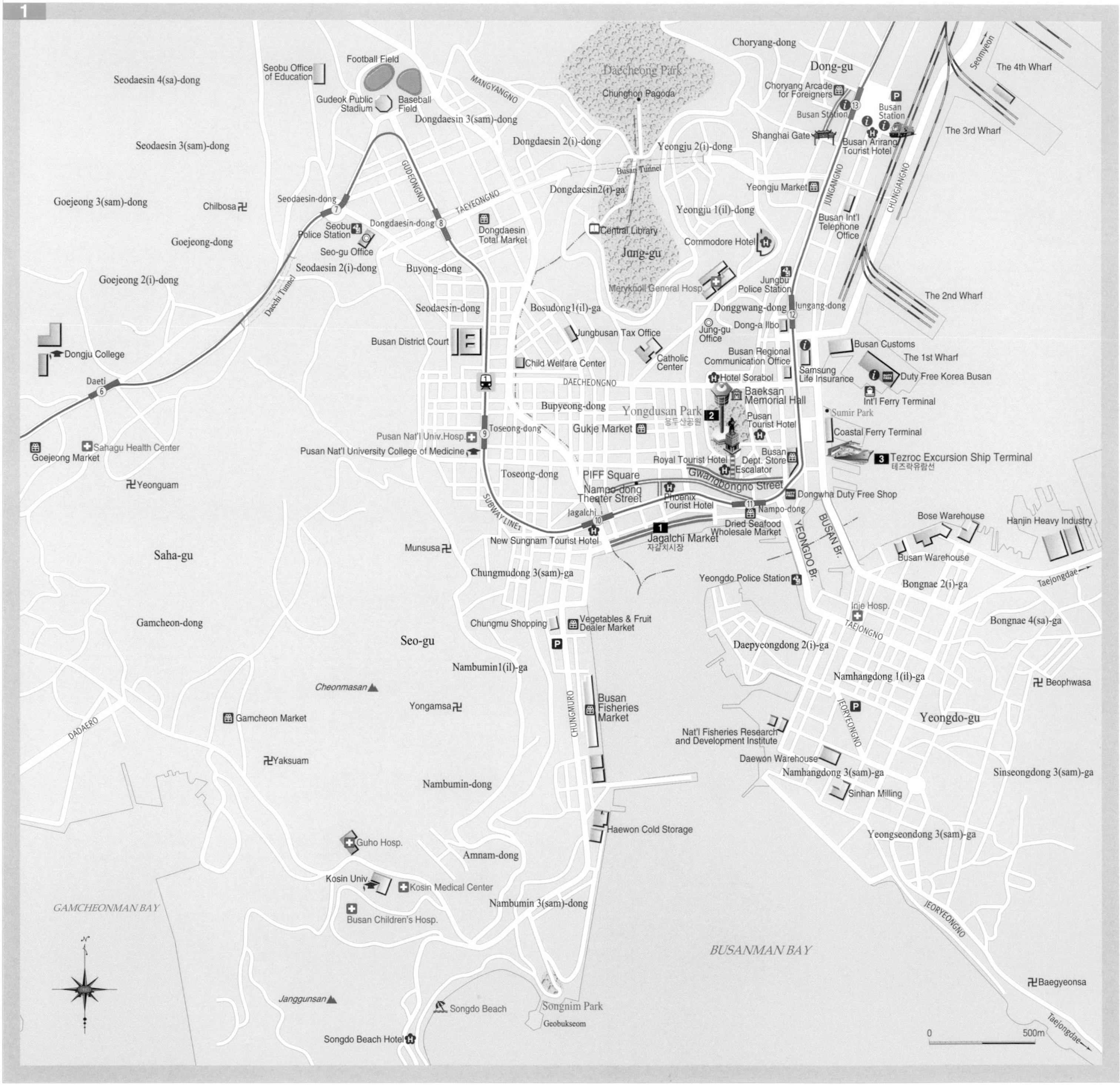

1

Choryang-dong
Dong-gu
Seomyeon
The 4th Wharf
Daecheong Park
Chunghon Pagoda
Choryang Arcade for Foreigners
Busan Station
Busan Station
Shanghai Gate
Busan Arirang Tourist Hotel
The 3rd Wharf
Seobu Office of Education
Football Field
Gudeok Public Stadium
Baseball Field
MANGYANGNO
Dongdaesin 3(sam)-dong
Seodaesin 4(sa)-dong
Seodaesin 3(sam)-dong
Dongdaesin 2(i)-dong
Yeongju 2(i)-dong
Busan Tunnel
GUDEONGNO
TAEYEONGNO
Dongdaesin2(i)-ga
Yeongju Market
JUNGANGNO
CHUNGJANGNO
Goejeong 3(sam)-dong
Chilbosa
Seodaesin-dong
Yeongju 1(il)-dong
Busan Int'l Telephone Office
Seobu Police Station
Dongdaesin-dong
Dongdaesin Total Market
Central Library
Commodore Hotel
Goejeong-dong
Seo-gu Office
Jung-gu
Seodaesin 2(i)-dong
Buyong-dong
Goejeong 2(i)-dong
Daechi Tunnel
Merykholl General Hosp.
Jungbu Police Station
The 2nd Wharf
Seodaesin-dong
Bosudong1(il)-ga
Donggwang-dong
Jungang-dong
Jung-gu Office
Dong-a Ilbo
Jungbusan Tax Office
Busan District Court
Dongju College
Busan Customs
Catholic Center
Busan Regional Communication Office
The 1st Wharf
Child Welfare Center
Samsung Life Insurance
Duty Free Korea Busan
Daeti
DAECHEONGNO
Hotel Sorabol
Baeksan Memorial Hall
Int'l Ferry Terminal
Bupyeong-dong
Yongdusan Park
용두산공원
Sumir Park
Pusan Tourist Hotel
Toseong-dong
Gukje Market
Pusan Nat'l Univ.Hosp.
Coastal Ferry Terminal
Sahagu Health Center
Goejeong Market
Pusan Nat'l University College of Medicine
Royal Tourist Hotel
Busan Dept. Store
Escalator
Tezroc Excursion Ship Terminal
테즈락유람선
Toseong-dong
PIFF Square
Gwangbongno Street
Yeonguam
Nampo-dong Theater Street
Phoenix Tourist Hotel
Dongwha Duty Free Shop
SUBWAY LINE 1
Jagalchi
Nampo-dong
Bose Warehouse
Hanjin Heavy Industry
Dried Seafood Wholesale Market
BUSAN Br.
Jagalchi Market
자갈치시장
New Sungnam Tourist Hotel
Munsusa
YEONGDO Br.
Busan Warehouse
Saha-gu
Chungmudong 3(sam)-ga
Yeongdo Police Station
Bongnae 2(i)-ga
Taejongdae
Inje Hosp.
TAEJONGNO
Gamcheon-dong
Chungmu Shopping
Vegetables & Fruit Dealer Market
Bongnae 4(sa)-ga
Seo-gu
Daepyeongdong 2(i)-ga
Nambumin1(il)-ga
Namhangdong 1(il)-ga
Beophwasa
Cheonmasan
Yongamsa
Busan Fisheries Market
CHUNGMURO
JEORYEONGNO
Yeongdo-gu
Gamcheon Market
DADAERO
Nat'l Fisheries Research and Development Institute
Yaksuam
Daewon Warehouse
Namhangdong 3(sam)-ga
Sinseongdong 3(sam)-ga
Nambumin-dong
Sinhan Milling
Haewon Cold Storage
Guho Hosp.
Yeongseondong 3(sam)-ga
Amnam-dong
Kosin Univ.
Kosin Medical Center
GAMCHEONMAN BAY
Nambumin 3(sam)-dong
Busan Children's Hosp.
JEORYEONGNO
BUSANMAN BAY
Janggunsan
Songdo Beach
Songnim Park
Geobukseom
Baegyeonsa
Songdo Beach Hotel
0
500m
Taejongdae

Jagalchi Market

Jagalchi Market 1

Jagalchi Market is one of the most popular attractions in Busan. The market has a wide variety of fish, such as sea bream, flatfish, octopus, and abalone, to name just a few. One big draw of this market is its flexible pricing system. Since a wide array of foods from the sea sold here do not have fixed prices, visitors are free to haggle over what they expect to pay.
Furthermore, Jagalchi Market plays host to the Jagalchi Festival held every fall.
Near the market is Gwangbongno, Busan's fashion street. Plenty of large brand name shops offer wares such as luxurious adult and childrens' clothing, furs, formal wear and cosmetics.

Gwangbongno

Yongdusan Park 2

'Yong' means dragon in Korean, while 'du' means head. The name of this park originates from the fact that the shape of the mountain within the park resembles a dragon head soaring into the sky from the sea.
The 120m high Busan Tower is located in the park and its observatory deck commands a panoramic view of the cityscape and the sea. The spectacular ocean scenery that surrounds Busan fills visitors' senses during the day, while the glittering view of the city at night is dazzling.

Busan Tower

In the middle of the park square stands the statue of the national hero, Admiral Yi Sun-shin. His heroic figure gazes out into the sea. Adjacent to the statue is the Memorial Monument, dedicated to those who played a role in bringing democracy to Korea during the April 19th Democratization Uprising.

Tezroc Excursion Ship Terminal 3

Tezroc Excursion Ship Terminal

While the panorama of the ocean scenery from land is spectacular, a Tezroc excursion provides an even closer view of Taejongdae, the pebble beach, Saengdo Island, Oryukdo Islets and the dazzling Busan skyline.
The Tezroc excursion ships depart from the Coastal Passenger Terminal located near Sumir Park, and pass by famous areas around Busan, including Oryukdo, Gwangalli Beach and Taejongdae Beach.

Tezroc Excursion Ship Information	
Tour Frequency - Weekdays: 2 Times - Weekends: 3 Times **Tour Length** - 1 hour 10 minutes - 1 hour 40 minutes (Operation frequency may change during the peak season)	**Fares**: - Lunch Cruise: ₩ 30,000 - Sunset Cruise: ₩ 15,000 - Dinner Cruise: ₩ 30,000 **Reservations**: 82-51-463-7680

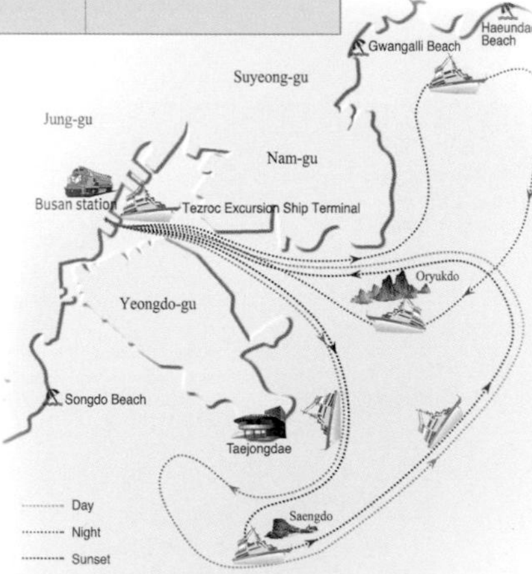

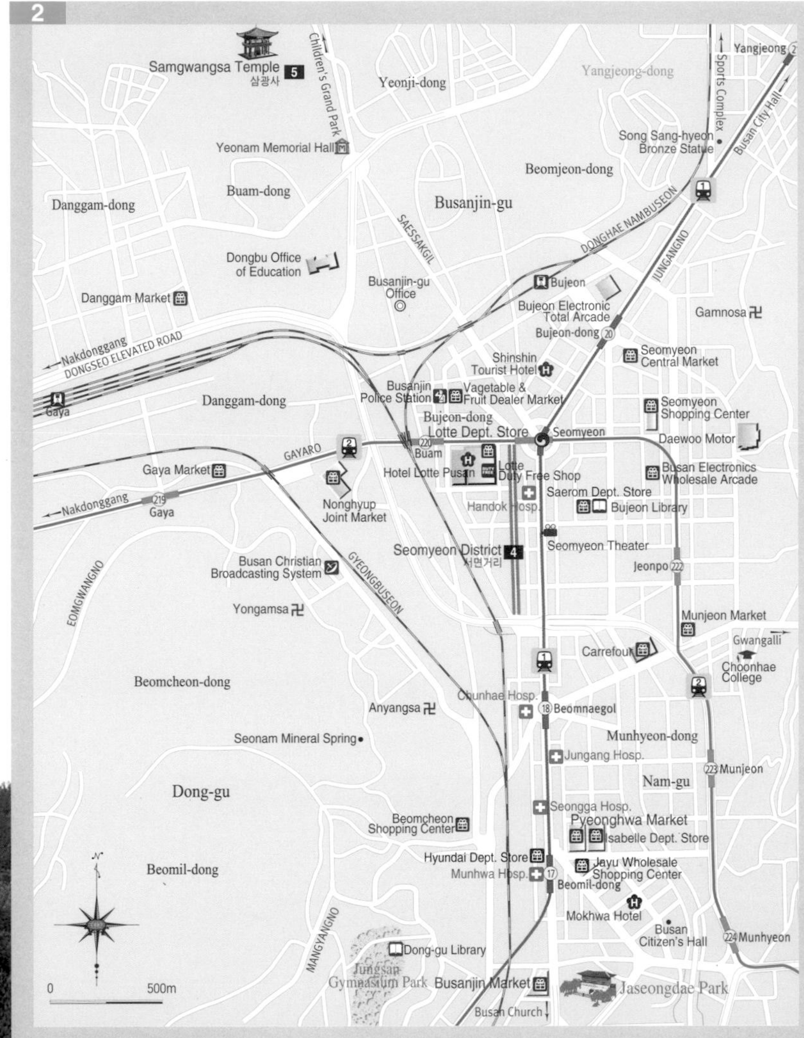

Seomyeon District 4

Underground Shopping Center in the Seomyeon District

Seomyeon District is the largest commercial district in Busan. It serves as the city's financial and distribution center, as well as a central shopping district. With the Seomyeon Rotary at its center, large stores are densely concentrated in the area.

Seomyeon District also offers two large underground shopping complexes. The Daehyeon Underground Shopping Mall stretches to the south from the Seomyeon subway station, and the Seomyeon Underground Shopping Mall stretches from the Seomyeon subway station to the Yangjeong area. Seomyeon Market and Bujeon Market, traditional open-air markets, are filled with shops containing everthing from bargain clothes and accessories to housewares.

Samgwangsa Temple 5

Located about half way up Mt. Baegyangsan, Samgwangsa Temple is the center of the Buddhist culture in Busan. Along with Daeungjeon, the main hall, there is Jigwanjeon Hall, a huge Buddhist hall that can accommodate up to 10,000 people at a time, the Beophwa Samaedang Pavilion, the largest pavilion in Korea, and the nine-story Dabotap Pagoda. As a center of Buddhist culture and arts, Samgwangsa hosts a wide range of Buddhism-related events year round.

Samgwangsa Temple

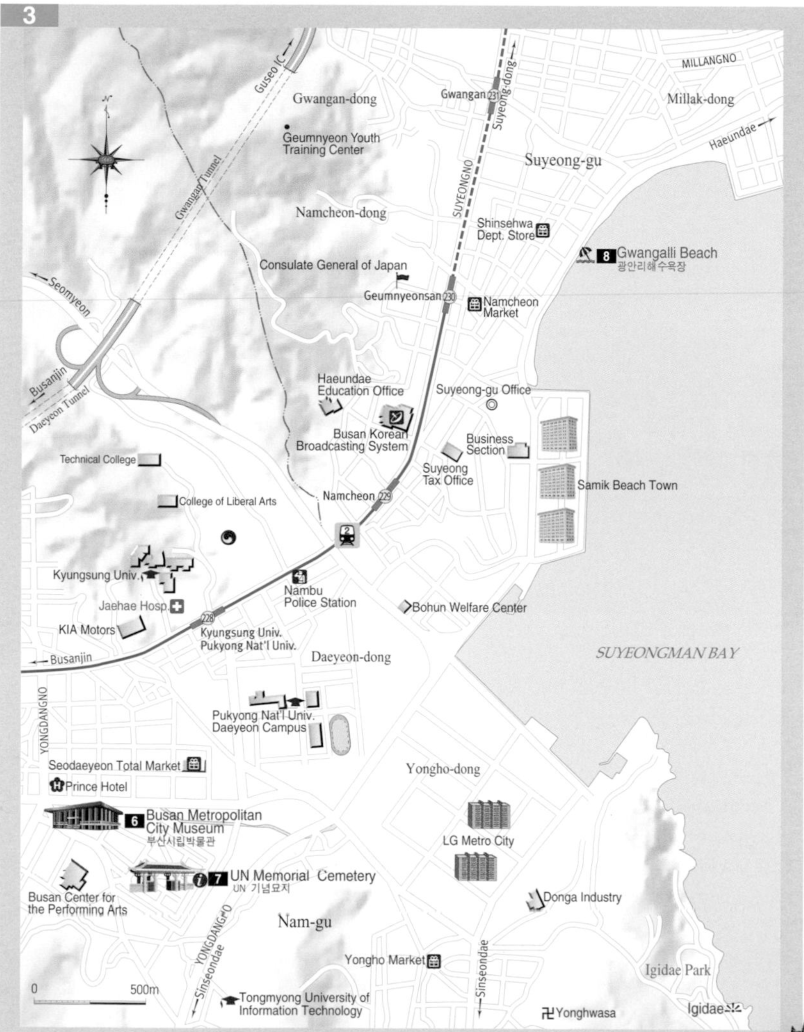

Busan Metropolitan City Museum

Busan Metropolitan City Museum 6

Standing Gilt-bronze Bodhisattva Statue (National Treasure No. 200)

The Busan Metropolitan City Museum is located in Daeyeon-dong. The museum houses seven exhibition halls, which feature everything from prehistoric relics to folk artifacts.

Other items exhibited at the museum include artifacts unearthed from tombs, ceramics, calligraphy works from the late Joseon Dynasty, Buddhist statues, metal works, relics from the New Stone Age and Bronze Age, and artifacts from the Joseon Dynasty.

They are displayed in various exhibition halls arranged by time period. The Special Exhibition Hall features remains of kilns, such as the Busanduk Kiln, as well as a variety of stone artifacts and tombstones.

The Bokcheon Museum, which is annexed to the Busan Metropolitan City Museum, was built next to the Bokcheondong tombs from the Three Kingdoms Period. Through excavation and research, the Bokcheon Museum successfully recreated aspects of Busan's ancient culture. It is currently specializing in the research of buried cultural assets.

The memorial hall commemorating Busan's status as a temporary capital during the Korean War belongs to the Busan Metropolitan City Museum located in Bumin-dong, Seo-gu.

Articles from the Korean War give visitors a better understanding of life in Korea during the war.

Agalmatolite Jar with Inscription (National Treasure No. 233)

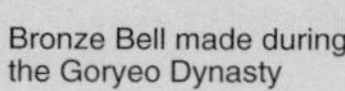
Bronze Bell made during the Goryeo Dynasty

Monument to UN Forces in Korea

UN Memorial Cemetery 7

The UN Memorial Cemetery was established in 1951 and is dedicated to the soldiers and medical staff from 16 UN allied countries and five other countries that sent troops and medical personnel to Korea during the Korean War.

The gravestones and remains of 2,282 war dead from the United States, the UK, Turkey, Canada, Australia, Holland, France, New Zealand, South Africa, and Norway, as well as a number from the Republic of Korea, are preserved here. A total of 11,000 gravestones marking the war dead from 16 allied countries were earlier kept here. The number decreased as Ethiopia, Thailand, Greece, Luxemburg, and Colombia transferred the remains of their servicemen to their home countries.

The cemetery is divided into 20 sections and each section is dedicated to an allied country that participated in the Korean War. The national flag of each country flies above each section.

The cemetery also houses the UN Memorial Tower. Details about combat equipment, the size of the forces mobilized, and the soldiers' names are inscribed on a bronze plaque on the tower in both Korean and English.

Restaurants at Gwangalli Beach

Gwangalli Beach 8

Gwangalli Beach is one of the most renowned beaches in Korea and has a 1.4km long and 64m wide strip of sand that is shaped like a half moon.

The beach has recently been transformed into a bustling tourist beach resort. As many as 300 different restaurants, cafes, galleries, small theaters, and performance halls line its main street.

In early August the Busan Sea Festival is held at the beach, providing vacationers and tourists with an opportunity to participate in a number of activities.

UN Memorial Cemetery

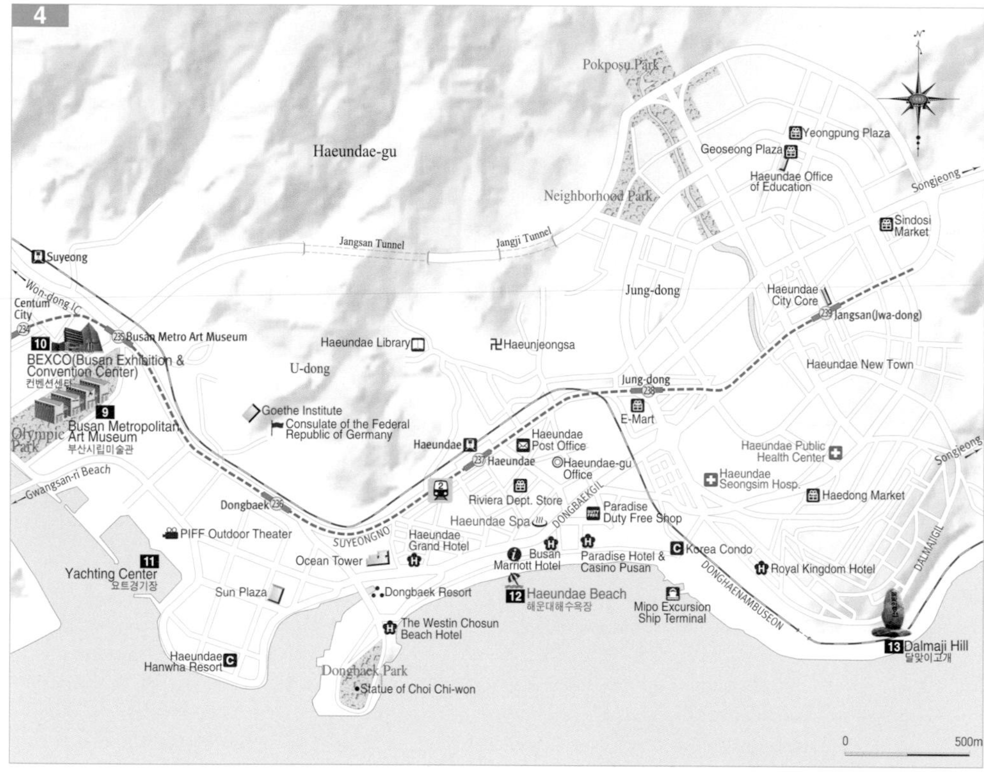

Busan Metropolitan Art Museum 9

The Busan Metropolitan Art Museum, located in the Olympic Park at Haeundae-gu, is Busan's comprehensive cultural and high-tech art center. This art museum is laid out in a unique design and features a vast collection of modern art. Its total indoor exhibition space is approximately 6,600㎡, and includes exhibition halls foyers and an outdoor sculpture park. Events hosted by the museum include the Busan Biennale, the International Art Festival, modern art exhibitions and outdoor sculpture symposiums.

BEXCO (Busan Exhibition & Convention Center) 10

BEXCO is an exhibition and convention facility in 'Centum City,' a future-oriented, high-tech complex.
'Centum City' is scheduled to be completed in 2010. In addition to its already completed convention center, 'Centum City' will house an international business district, an urban entertainment center, a digital media zone, commercial distribution facilities, public buildings, a theme park, and a waterfront.
The BEXCO Exhibition Hall is a single-storied structure without pillars, the only structure of its type in Korea
The BEXCO Convention Center, which is equipped with advanced audio/visual presentation equipment, can accommodate as many as 2,800 guests. As added attractions, BEXCO offers auxiliary facilities such as a business center and a shopping mall.

Entrance to the Busan Metropolitan Art Museum

General View of BEXCO

BEXCO Conference Room

Yachting Center 11

The Yachting Center is located in Suyeongman Bay, which is situated between Gwangalli and Haeundae Beach. During the 1986 Asian Games and the 1988 Seoul Olympic Games, yachting events were held at the center.

The favorable weather conditions in the area provide an optimum environment for yachting and windsurfing and diving courses are also offered.

In fall, the Yachting Center is transformed into an outdoor theater during the Pusan International Film Festival (PIFF). Opening and closing ceremonies are held at the center where a six-story gigantic movie screen features a variety of international films.

Haeundae Beach 12

Coastline at Haeundae Beach

Haeundae Beach has been designated as one of the eight most scenic places in Korea. Haeundae's soft white sand stretches 1.5km along a beautifully curved coastline. The 1m-deep water has an average water temperature of 22.5 degrees Celsius in the summer and is ideal for swimming.

Besides swimming and sun bathing, other activities are also available as a number of tourist attractions are situated in the vicinity of Haeundae Beach. They include tours of Dongbaekseom Island, spas, excursion ships, Mipo Raw Fish Town, Dalmaji Hill, Olympic Park and the Yachting Center.

The annual 'Polar Bear Swimming Contest' is a winter event where participants swim in sub-zero degree water every January. In early August the 'Busan Sea Festival' is held at Haeundae Beach.

Dalmaji Hill 13

Dalmaji Hill is situated between Mipo and Songjeong. The hill has 15 winding paths and from the hill, the moon over Haeundae Beach makes a fantastic view. The hill is one of the area's favorite places for a drive.

The Dongsanbi Monument stands where the sunrise and moon can most clearly be seen from the hill. Haewoljeong, located adjacent to the monument, is a pavilion where many people come to view the first full moon of the year.

Dalmaji Hill offers abundant sights and delicious cuisine for tourists. There are cultural attractions such as the Mystery Literature Center and Dongbaek Art Center and some of Busan's most celebrated restaurants. Another tourist attraction on the hill is the Tower Clock, which was erected in January 2000 to celebrate the new millennium.

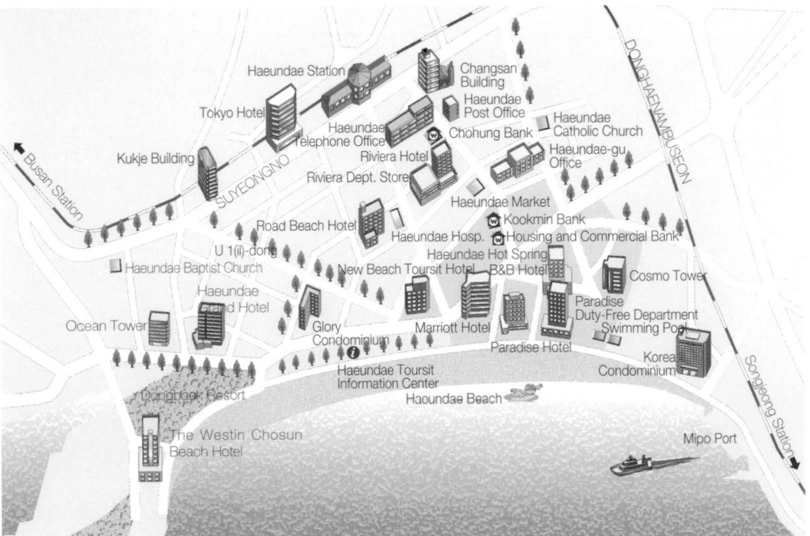

Haewoljeong, Dalmaji Hill

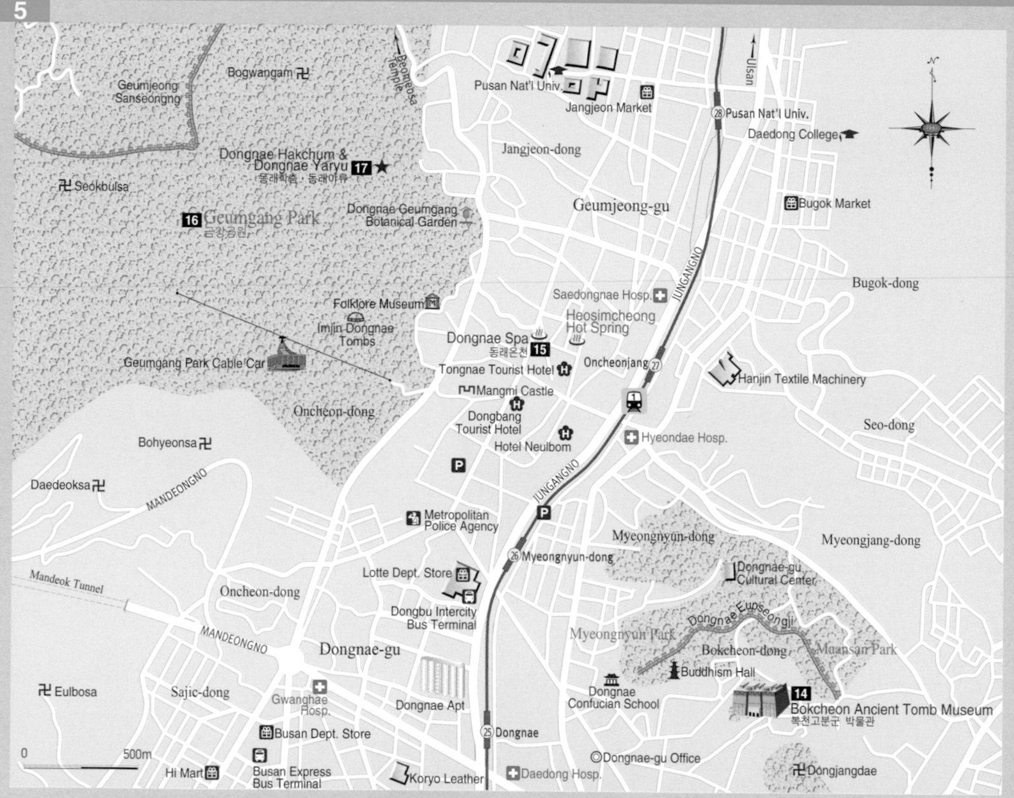

Gilt Bronze Crown

Pottery Jar with a Stand

Bokcheon Ancient Tomb Museum 14

The Bokcheon Ancient Tomb Museum was constructed in 1996 after a group of tombs dating back to the 4th and 5th centuries were excavated. On display at the museum are historic artifacts excavated from the tombs, and relics of Gaya, an ancient kingdom that thrived in adjacent areas and Japan.

A visit to the museum offers a rare opportunity to learn about the history of the Gaya Kingdom and the relationship between Korea and Japan in ancient times. The museum features a tomb park where an outdoor exhibit is located.

Armor, Excavated from Bokcheon-dong Tomb

Bokcheon Ancient Tomb Museum

Dongnae Spa 15

Dongnae spa was developed in 1691 during the 17th year of the reign of King Sukjong of the Joseon Dynasty. The area's large hot spring resort, which is called Husimcheong, is a popular destination with tourists. Husimcheong can accommodate up to 1,500 guests at a time and is equipped with an indoor swimming pool and around 40 distinctive large bathtubs.

Geumgang Park 16

Located on the southern ridge of Mt. Geumjeongsan, this park is surrounded by 100-year old pine trees and strangely-shaped rocks and cliffs. Cable cars operate from the entrance to the summit of Mt. Geumjeongsan (1,260m), for the convenience of park visitors. Popular tourist attractions here include the Busan Marine Museum, the Folk Art Gallery, a zoo, and a botanical garden.

Dongnae Hakchum & Dongnae Yaryu 17

Dongnae Yaryu

The movements of the Dongnae Hakchum (the crane dance) conjure an image of the graceful motions of a crane. The Dongnae Hakchum features willowy body movements combined with spontaneous movements unique to each dancer, creating a beautiful and free dancing style.
From ancient times, the Dongnae area has been famous as a habitat for a large number of cranes. Geographically, its shape also resembles a crane. The best place to enjoy the Dongnae Hakchum is at the folk performance stage located in Geumgang Park in Dongnae. A performance is held on the 2nd and 4th Sundays of every month.
The Dongnae Yaryu is a mask dance which has been handed down and performed in the Dongnae area. It was traditionally performed every January 15th of the lunar calendar. The mask dance features an interesting character called Maldduk whose role is to poke fun at the Yangban (the upper class). As mockery of the Yangban was taboo in old times, this humorous mask dance served as an outlet for ordinary citizens to express their complaints about the rich and powerful.

INDEX

1. Main Entrance 2. Citizens Athletic Park
3. Amusement Park 4. Geumeosa Temple 5. Cable Car
6. Dongnae Dokjin Daeamun Gate 7. Hyujeongam Temple
8. Yaksuam Temple 9. Chilseongam Temple
10. Cheongyongsa Temple 11. Sorimsa Temple
12. Geumgang Gymnasium 13. Geumjeongsa Temple
14. Imjin Dongnae Tombs 15. Folk Art Gallery
16. Amusement Park 17. Busan Marine Museum
18. Zoo 19. Youth Hostel 20. Geumgangsa Temple
21. Botanical Garden

Beomeosa Temple

Beomeosa, a large temple situated on the eastern slopes of Mt. Geumjeongsan, is one of the three most famous temples in Gyeongsangnam-do Province, along with Tongdosa Temple and Haeinsa Temple. It is said that Uisangdaesa, a famous Buddhist monk during the Silla Kingdom, established Beomeosa in the 18th year (678) of the reign of King Munmu, the 30th king of the Silla Kingdom.

Beomeosa is known for the numerous historical cultural assets in its compound, and also for the quiet and picturesque landscape surrounding the temple. Inside the temple are a broad range of cultural and natural assets, including a grove of Japanese wisteria, a three-storied stone pagoda, Daeungjeon Hall and Beomeosa Iljumun (Busan City's Tangible Cultural Properties No. 2), the front gate of Beomeosa.

Beomeosa Monastery

Taejongdae H7

Lighthouse at Taejongdae

Taejongdae, located to the southeast of Yeongdo Island, has the most scenic rocky coastline around Busan. The unusual rocks harmonizing with a lush forest and surging waves here offer a splendid view. On a clear day, the Japanese island of Daemado can be seen from Taejongdae.

Taejongdae was reportedly named after King Taejong of the Silla Kingdom who rested here. He was impressed by its scenic view during his national tour after achieving the unification of the Three Kingdoms.

Well known spots around Taejongdae include Sinseonbawi Rock, Jagalmadang (a pebble field), and Mangbuseok, a legendary stone on which a faithful wife is said to have stood waiting for her lost husband until she perished.

One of the most exciting things to do at Taejongdae is to take a boat ride to the open sea to have a closer look at the lighthouse, Jasalbawi (Suicide Rock), Sinseonbawi (a rock where Sinseon, a legendary hermit with supernatural powers, is said to appear), Mangbuseok and Achiseom Island.

Chungnyeolsa Shrine H1

Located in Allak-dong, Dongnae-gu, Chungnyeolsa is a site commemorating the patriotic spirit of those who sacrificed their lives in defense of the nation against the Japanese Invasion. Aside from the main hall, there are ten buildings where the memorial tablets of 91 patriots hailing from the Busan region are preserved. In the exhibition room, visitors can view large war paintings. Every May 25th memorial services are held here by the Busan Metropolitan Government.

Food Made in Beomeosa Temple

Chungnyeolsa

Eulsukdo Habitat for Migratory Birds B5

Eulsukdo island, located at the mouth of the Nakdonggang River is an internationally renowned habitat for migratory birds. Grassy, reed-filled deltas occupy the area making Eulsukdo the optimum environment for birds.
The sea converges with the river, forming a large silt field where birds can find plentiful prey. It also has weather conditions (a cool summer and mild winter), favorable for birds to breed and spend the winter.
As many as 100,000 migratory birds of 10 families and 50 species visit Eulsukdo between October and March every year, covering the river and deltas. Watching birds feeding in the river and the deltas and soaring into the sky is a magnificent sight. Eulsukdo is regarded as a haven for rare migratory birds, such as white-naped cranes, blackfaced spoonbills and white-taled sea eagles, all of which can be seen here during the winter.

Eulsukdo, Habitat for Migratory Birds

Busan World Cup Stadium F1

The Busan World Cup Stadium is a comprehensive stadium suitable for competitive sports and field and track events. The 54,534-seat main stadium can accommodate 70,000 people and has an open roof that covers almost every seat, enabling all-weather matches.
The architectural concept of the stadium expresses the rising spirit of Busan and the world in the new millennium, with its sphere-shaped stadium imitating the morning sun rising above the horizon.
The 48 pillars and 72 entrances and exits within the structure symbolize roads in all directions. No walls were constructed, giving the stadium an openness to breathe in the 'chi' (natural energy of the world and universe).
Curved lines maximize harmony and accentuate the beauty of the stadium, while the rippled roof was designed to resemble the waves of the East Sea.

www.2002worldcupkorea.org
www.busanworldcup.net

Incheon

Incheon is a major port city in western Korea and is gaining international status with the opening of the Incheon International Airport. It lies in a strategically important position for trade and cultural exchange with ferry links to nearby Chinese cities and sea routes connecting Korea to Asia and the rest of the world. Located to the west of Seoul, Incheon is part of a large metropolitan area where tourists can enjoy many places of interest.

The official bird of Incheon is the crane due to the abundance of migrating cranes in the area. The official city flower is the rose. Roses are found all over the city and are said to reflect the active and enthusiastic nature of Incheon citizens.

Baengnyeongdo Island

Baengnyeongdo is located 222.2km northwest of Incheon. Situated just 15km away from the North Korean territory of Jangsangot, Hwanghae-do, it is the nearest island to North Korea. The island is a key military point, requiring a relatively complicated process to enter. But any visitor to the island is sure to fall in love with its splendid beauty. Baengnyeongdo is considered a storehouse of natural treasures.

Ocean and Seaside Tour

Incheon is adjacent to the West Sea which is dotted with numerous islands and islets. Deokjeokdo Island is one of the most pleasant tourist destinations in the western sea. Yeongjongdo Island is home to Incheon International Airport. Baengnyeongdo island is located not very far from North Korea and is well known for its clean environment. Yeonpyeongdo Island and Daecheongdo Island are also popular. Sindo Island, Sido Island and Modo Island enable visitors to directly experience a natural eco-system. During weekends, the islands attract many visitors from metropolitan areas, including Seoul, who want to enjoy the beautiful scenery and dine the freshest sushi.

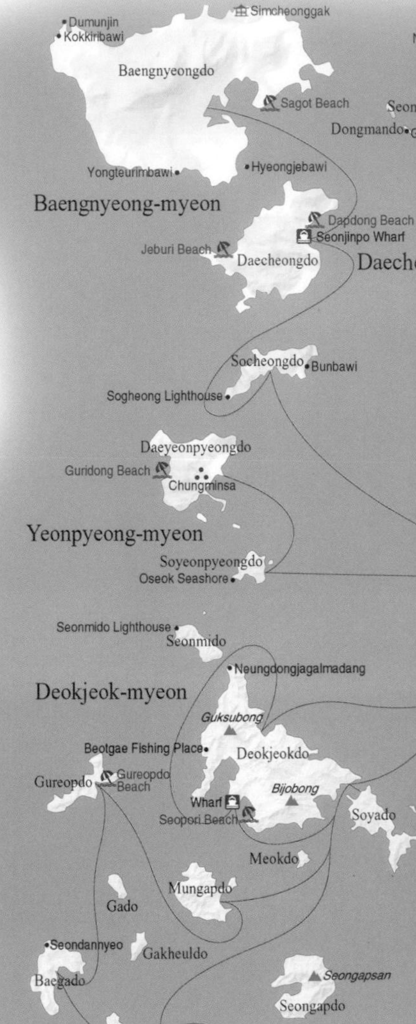

Papillon Cliff

Yeonpyeongdo Island

Visitors see that most of the mountains, the sea and cliffs here have managed to keep their natural bcauty froe of pollution. But tourists feel the greatest joy visiting 'Papillon Cliff' with a spectcular view that makes visitors forget hectic city life for a while.

Deokjeokdo Island Sunset

Deokjeokdo Island

This island has a 292-meter tall peak called Bijobong and beautiful sandy beaches along its coast. Unique rock formations and ancient pines harmonize here to offer one of the best tourist spots on the west coast. Deokjeokdo is famous for its Seopo-ri and Batjireum beaches, which boast the finest quality sand. Eight kilometers north is a reed field with great views of reeds and unusual rock formations. The nearby sea is rich with various species of fish and attracts many fishermen.

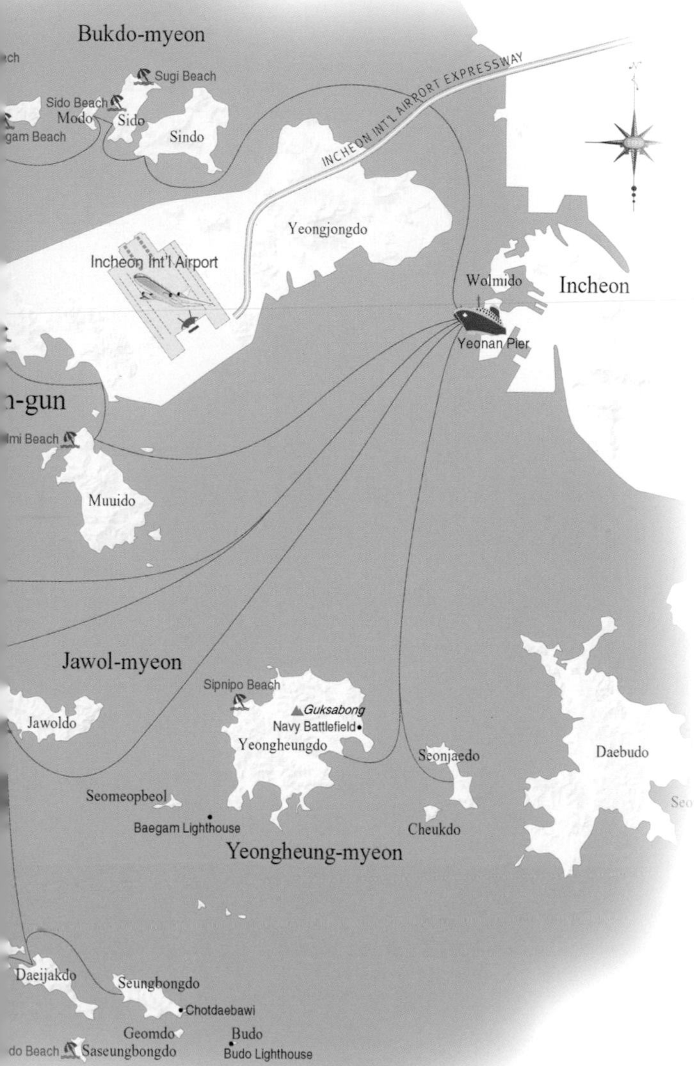

Wetlands

Ganghwado' s wetlands are known as one of the five most fertile in the world, along with the Eastern coast of Canada, the Eastern coast of the US, the coastal area of the North Sea, and the Amazon area. Stretching from Janggot Dondae to Dongmak-ri, they are characterized by expansive mudflats to the south of Ganghwado which are over-looked by green, forested mountains. The spring tidal range averages over 9 meters, one of the largest tidal ranges anywhere in the world, and results in exposure of many kilometers of mud.

Most tidal flats are full of life because they retain rain-washed nutrients from the mountains and plains, and the nutrients are concentrated in a narrow zone of deposits. Visitors can enjoy the unique experience of catching lugworms, clams, crabs, and shrimp as well as receiving an invigorating mudpack here.

Birds such as oyster catchers and yellow-billed egrets are known to stop here as they migrate. Wetlands are extremely important for migratory birds. They support many migrant shorebirds, cranes and a few globally-endangered species of waterbirds known to nest only in this region. Large numbers of shorebirds also pass through the region, including the endangered Juasae. Presently, a total of only 530 birds of this species remain in the world and the Korean government has designated it as a protected species.

www.wetland.co.kr
www.janghwari.org

Marine Ecology Park

The Marine Ecology Park is a natural ecosystem located in Namdong-gu. It was built around natural silt banks (called gaetbeol) and salt ponds, to provide visitors with a nature-friendly park. Bio-colonies, migratory bird habitats and reed fields have been restored for this purpose. Over 191 species of fresh water, salt water and swamp plants, as well as 11 different species of silt organisms, live in the area. There are seven species of fish, five species of amphibians and reptiles, and 71 species of birds. The Ecosystem Exhibit Hall features photographs of various salt-water plants, salt farmers processing salt under the scorching sun, and the sights of Sorae Inlet. The nearby salt ponds are dotted with water mills which salt farmers in straw hats used to produce salt. Visitors can have a hands-on experience working in traditional Korean salt ponds. There is also a small 4,000 sq. yd. silt bank located beside the salt ponds.

Sindo Island' s breeding ground for seagulls

Sindo Island, Modo Island and Jangbongdo Island

People call Sindo Island the island of birds, Sido Island the island of fine sand, Modo Island the island of shellfish and Jangbongdo Island the island of mermaids. The extensive tidal flats around these islands are inhabited by a variety of shellfish and small octopuses, thus providing a direct contact between sea animals and humans.

Yongudo Island' s Eulwang-ri Sunset

Yeongjongdo Island, Yongyudo Island and Muuido Island

On Yeongjong Island, students can explore tidal flats at an ocean study center. And Yeongjong Sky Park, the largest Korean flight test center, teaches anyone how to operate an ultralight plane.

Yongyudo Island' s Eulwang-ri swimming beach is well known for its 200-meter wide sands being fully revealed at low tide, and its magnificent sunset. At one end of the beach tourists can ride jet skis and banana boats or try other sports.

A beautiful pine forest surrounds Muuido Island. The island' s name Muui (dancer' s dress) is attributed to the fact that the island looks like an ancient dancer wearing a general' s horse riding uniform.

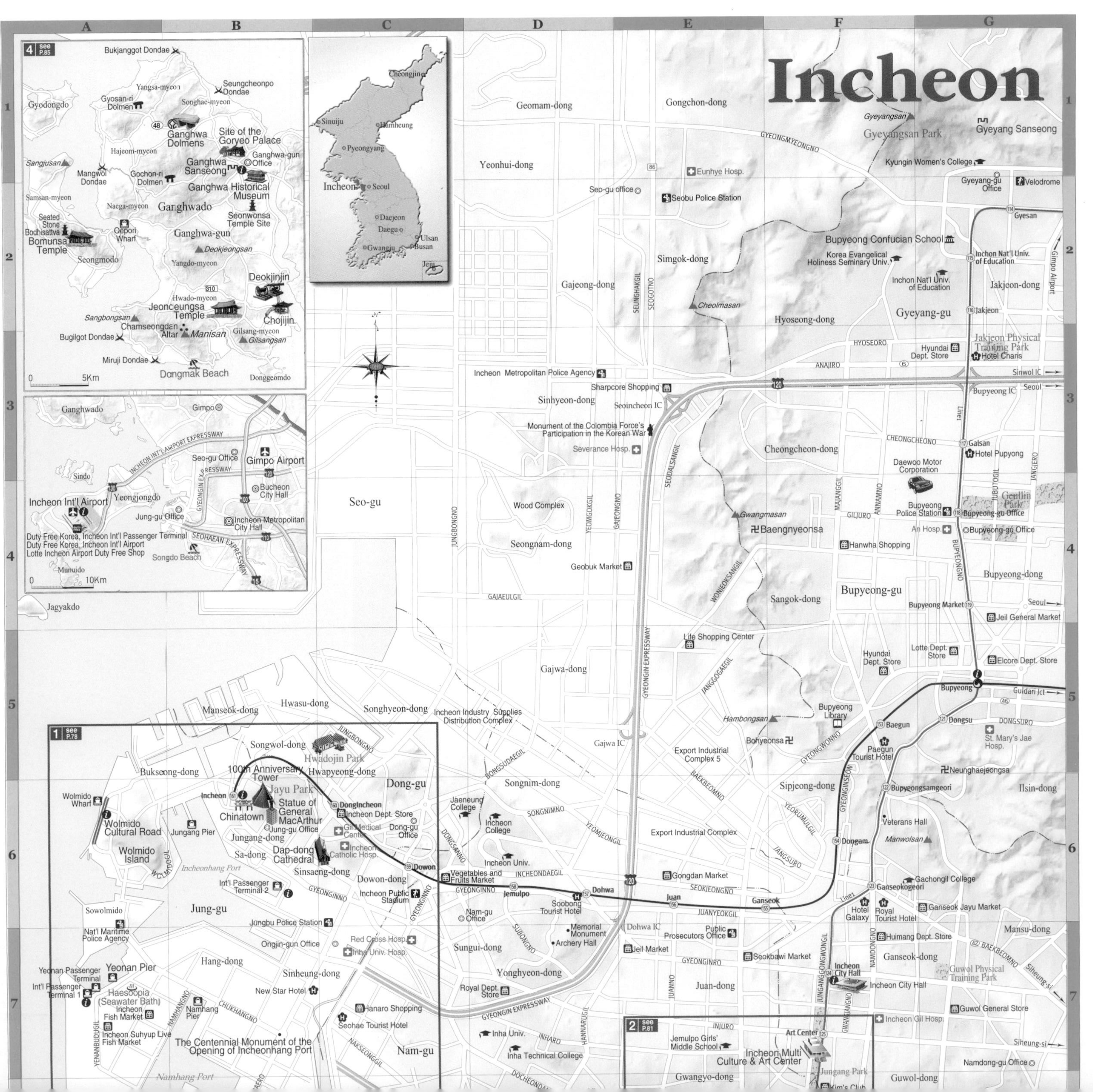

Incheon
A
B
C
D
E
F
G
1
2
3
4
5
6
7
4 see P.85
Bukjanggot Dondae
Yangsa-myeon
Seungcheonpo Dondae
Songhae-myeon
Gyodongdo
Gyosan-ri Dolmen
Ganghwa Dolmens
Site of the Goryeo Palace
Ganghwa-gun Office
Hajeom-myeon
Sangjusan
Mangwol Dondae
Gochon-ri Dolmen
Ganghwa Sanseong
Ganghwa Historical Museum
Samsan-myeon
Naega-myeon
Ganghwado
Seonwonsa Temple Site
Seated Stone Bodhisattva
Bomunsa Temple
Oepori Wharf
Ganghwa-gun
Deokjeongsan
Seongmodo
Yangdo-myeon
Deokjinjin
Hwado-myeon
Jeonceungsa Temple
Sangbongsan
Chamseongdan Altar
Manisan
Chojijin
Gilsang-myeon
Gilsangsan
Bugilgot Dondae
Miruji Dondae
Dongmak Beach
Donggeomdo
0
5Km
Cheongjin
Sinuiju
Hamheung
Pyeongyang
Incheon
Seoul
Daejeon
Daegu
Ulsan
Busan
Gwangju
Jeju
Ganghwado
Gimpo
INCHEON INT'L AIRPORT EXPRESSWAY
Seo-gu Office
Gimpo Airport
Sindo
Bucheon City Hall
Incheon Int'l Airport
Yeongjongdo
Jung-gu Office
Incheon Metropolitan City Hall
Duty Free Korea, Incheon Int'l Passenger Terminal
Duty Free Korea, Incheon Int'l Airport
Lotte Incheon Airport Duty Free Shop
SEOHAEAN EXPRESSWAY
Songdo Beach
Muuido
0
10Km
Jagyakdo
Geomam-dong
Gongchon-dong
Gyeyangsan
Gyeyangsan Park
Gyeyang Sanseong
GYEONGMYEONGNO
Yeonhui-dong
Kyungin Women's College
Eunhye Hosp.
Gyeyang-gu Office
Velodrome
Seo-gu office
Seobu Police Station
Gyesan
Bupyeong Confucian School
Korea Evangelical Holiness Seminary Univ.
Inchon Nat'l Univ. of Education
Gimpo Airport
Simgok-dong
Gajeong-dong
SEUNGHAKGIL
SEOGOTNO
Inchon Nat'l Univ. of Education
Jakjeon-dong
Cheolmasan
Gyeyang-gu
Jakjeon
Hyoseong-dong
HYOSEORO
Jakjeon Physical Training Park
Hyundai Dept. Store
Hotel Charis
ANAJIRO
Sinwol IC
Incheon Metropolitan Police Agency
Sharpcore Shopping
Sinhyeon-dong
Seoincheon IC
Bupyeong IC
Seoul
Monument of the Colombia Force's Participation in the Korean War
CHEONGCHEONO
Galsan
Hotel Pupyong
Severance Hosp.
SEODALSANGIL
Cheongcheon-dong
Daewoo Motor Corporation
JANGJERO
Seo-gu
Wood Complex
Line1
Geullin Park
Bupyeong Police Station
Bupyeong-gu Office
Gwangmasan
Baengnyeonsa
MAJANGGIL
GILJURO
ANNAMNO
An Hosp.
Bupyeong-gu Office
JUNGBONGNO
YEOMGOKGIL
GAJEONGNO
Seongnam-dong
Hanwha Shopping
BUPYEONGNO
WONJEOKSANGIL
Geobuk Market
Bupyeong-dong
GAJAEULGIL
Sangok-dong
Bupyeong-gu
Bupyeong Market
Seoul
Jeil General Market
GYEONGIN EXPRESSWAY
Life Shopping Center
Lotte Dept. Store
Hyundai Dept. Store
Elcore Dept. Store
Gajwa-dong
JANGGOGAGIL
Bupyeong
Guldari jct
Manseok-dong
Hwasu-dong
Songhyeon-dong
Incheon Industry Supplies Distribution Complex
Hambongsan
Bupyeong Library
Baegun
Dongsu
DONGSURO
1 see P.78
JUNGBONGNO
Songwol-dong
Hwadojin Park
Gajwa IC
Bohyeonsa
Export Industrial Complex 5
GYEONGWONNO
Paegun Tourist Hotel
St. Mary's Jae Hosp.
Buksceong-dong
100th Anniversary Tower
Hwapyeong-dong
BONGSUDAEGIL
Songnim-dong
BAEKBEOMNO
Neunghaejeongsa
Jayu Park
Dong-gu
Sipjeong-dong
Bupyeongsamgeori
Ilsin-dong
Wolmido Wharf
Incheon
DongIncheon
Jaeneung College
SONGNIMNO
YEORUMULGIL
GYEONGINSEON
Statue of General MacArthur
Chinatown
Incheon Dept. Store
Wolmido Cultural Road
Jungang Pier
Jung-gu Office
Gil Medical Center
Dong-gu Office
Incheon College
YEOMJEONGIL
Veterans Hall
Jungang-dong
Export Industrial Complex
Dongam
Manwolsan
Wolmido Island
Sa-dong
Dap-dong Cathedral
Incheon Catholic Hosp.
DONGSANNO
Incheon Univ.
JANGSURO
WOLMIDOGIL
Incheonhang Port
Sinsaeng-dong
Dowon
Vegetables and Fruits Market
INCHEONDAEGIL
Gongdan Market
Gachongil College
Int'l Passenger Terminal 2
Dowon-dong
GYEONGINNO
Jemulpo
Dohwa
SEOKJEONGNO
Ganseokogeori
Incheon Public Stadium
Juan
Ganseok
Hotel Galaxy
Sowolmido
Jung-gu
Nam-gu Office
Soobong Tourist Hotel
JUANYEOKGIL
Royal Tourist Hotel
Ganseok Jayu Market
Nat'l Maritime Police Agency
Jungbu Police Station
Memorial Monument
Dohwa IC
Public Prosecutors Office
Mansu-dong
Ongjin-gun Office
Red Cross Hosp.
Sungui-dong
Archery Hall
Huimang Dept. Store
Hang-dong
Inha Univ. Hosp.
SUBONGNO
Jeil Market
BAEKBEOMNO
Sinheung-dong
Seokbawi Market
Ganseok-dong
Yeonan Passenger Terminal
Yeonan Pier
Yonghyeon-dong
GYEONGINRO
Guwol Physical Training Park
Int'l Passenger Terminal 1
Haesoopia (Seawater Bath)
New Star Hotel
Royal Dept. Store
Juan-dong
Incheon City Hall
Incheon City Hall
Siheung-si
Incheon Fish Market
Namhang Pier
CHUKHANGNO
Hanaro Shopping
GYEONGIN EXPRESSWAY
NAMDONGNO
JUANNO
Guwol General Store
Seohae Tourist Hotel
HANNARUGIL
2 see P.81
Incheon Gil Hosp.
Incheon Suhyup Live Fish Market
The Centennial Monument of the Opening of Incheonhang Port
Inha Univ.
INHARO
INJURO
Art Center
Siheung-si
YENANBUDUGIL
NAMHANGNO
NAKSEONGGIL
Nam-gu
Inha Technical College
Jemulpo Girls' Middle School
Incheon Multi Culture & Art Center
JUNGANGGONGWONGIL
GWANGYANGNO
Namdong-gu Office
Namhang Port
DOCHEONGNO
Gwangyo-dong
Jungang Park
Guwol-dong
Kim's Club

INDEX

Tourist Information

Incheon Tourism Promotion Division 82-32-440-3310
Incheon Tourist Information Center 82-32-421-5628
www.inpia.net.

LEGEND

- Airport
- Port
- Bus Terminal
- Metro Line
- Hospital
- Police Station
- Post Office
- Tourist Information Center
- University or School
- Library
- Broadcasting Station
- Museum
- World Heritage Site
- Prehistoric Relic Site
- Fortress
- Temple
- Site of Buddhist Artifacts
- Traditional Building
- Traditional Pavilion
- Battlefield
- Korean War Historical Site
- Beach
- Hot Spring or Spa
- Park
- Amusement Park
- Mountain
- Stadium
- Other Tourist Attractions
- Hotel
- Department Store or Market
- Duty Free Shop
- Reference Point
- Transfer Station
- Metro Station Number

1

Taesung Wood Ind.Corp.
Korea Silo
Dong-il Group
Hwasu -dong
Wolmido
JUNGBONGNO
Gimpo
Dongkuk Steel
Manseok-dong
BANWOLLO
Hwadojin Park
Hwapyeong-dong
ELEVATED ROAD
Songwol-dong
CHAMOEJEON STREET
HWADOJINGIL
SONGHYEONNO
Hanyang Industry
Bukseong-dong
Jeon-dong
Jeongboksa卍
Sunchang Corporation
TS Corporation
Incheon Aviation Weather Office
Chinatown
차이나타운
100th Anniversary Tower
Songhyeon-dong
Dong-gu
Gajwa IC
Raw Fish Town
Passenger Terminal
Jungang Wharf
Incheon
161
2
3
Jayu Park
자유공원
New Core Dept. Store
Jayu Market
Dong Incheon
160
Songhak-dong
Incheon Dept. Store
SONGNIMGIL
Paradise Olympos Hotel
Statue of General MacArthur
Inhyeon-dong
GYEONGINSEON
Dong-gu Office
Wolmido Cultural Road
WOLMIDOGIL
Wolmido Island
월미도
1
Christian Memorial Hall
Jung-gu Office
Gil Medical Center
Yong-dong
Dongbu Police Station
Songnim Market
Sinpo-dong
Incheon Open Port District
5
개항거리
WOLMIDOGIL
Incheon Daily News
UHYEONNO
Incheon Catholic Hosp.
Incheon Tax Office
SETGOLGIL
Bukseong-dong
JUNGBONGNO
Dap-dong Cathedral
City Library
CHAMOEJEONGIL
WOLMIDOGIL
JEMULNYANGGIL
Dowon
159
Incheon Nat'l Maritime High School
Jungang-dong
Int'l Passenger Terminal 2
Sinsaeng-dong
SEOHAERO
Baseball Field
Dohwa IC
Incheonhang Port
Indoor Swimming Pool
Football Field
Sa-dong
Incheon Maritime Police Station
Korea Cadastral Survey Corporation
Suin Market
GYEONGINNO
GYEONGINNO
Sowolmido
Jungbu Police Station
The 3rd Wharf
Namincheon Tax Office
Hyeondae Hosp.
Nat'l Maritime Police Agency
Jung-gu
Incheon Immigration Office
Ongjin-gun Office
Nat'l Incheon Quarantine Station
SINHYEONNO
Korea Express Co.,Ltd.
Hanjin Transportation Co., Ltd.
The 4th Wharf
Incheon Regional Maritime Affairs and Fisheries Office
Incheon City Hall
Inha Univ. Hosp.
Nat'l Federation of Fisheries Cooperatives
Samsung Corporation Logistics Center
Yeonan-dong
Incheon Customs
Incheon IC
Yonghyeon-dong
Seongyeong Cold-Storage Company
GYEONGIN EXPRESSWAY
Kyungin Machinery
Myeongjin Seawater Public Bath
Yeonan Pier
4
연안부두
YEONAN BUDU GIL
New Star Tourist Hotel
Life Shopping Center
Hanaro Shopping
Yeonan Passenger Terminal
Incheon Fish Market
Heung-A Shipping Co., Ltd.
120
Seoul
Int'l Passenger Terminal 1
Goryeo Public Bath
CHUKHANGNO
Seohae Tourist Hotel
Gungjeon Seawater Public Bath
Namhang Pier
Namhae Public Bath
Dongbu Steel
Mirabo Plaza
Dongbang Container
Yonghyeon 5(o)-dong
Incheon Suhyup Live Fish Market
Hangdong 7(chil)-ga
RAW FISH CENTER AREA
Life Beach Apt.
EOSIANGGIL
NAMHANGNO
The Centennial Monument of the Opening of Incheonhang Port
Yeonan Apt.
Nam-gu
AAMNO
Heungguk Sangsa
NAKSEOMGIL
Incheon Raw Fish Center
Sinheungdong 3(sam)-ga
Daewoo Electronics Co.,Ltd.
Gyeongin Cold-Storage Company
THE SECOND GYEONGIN EXPRESSWAY
Namhang Port
Yeonan Warehouse
SEOHAERO
Halla Heavy Industry
Ssangyong Timber Terminal
Sorae Inlet
110
Seochang IC
0
500m

Wolmido Amusement Park

Wolmido Island 1

Wolmido Island is the most popular tourist attraction in Incheon. Located 1km west of Incheon Station, it is known for its beautiful sunsets and its scenic view of the West Sea. Originally an island, Wolmido was connected to the mainland in a land reclamation project. Numerous cafes and restaurants allow visitors to enjoy refreshments and dining while enjoying the beauty of the West Sea. Wolmido offers a wide selection of restaurants specializing in raw fish (Sassimi).

Wolmido has long been a coastal tourist attraction but its popularity has grown since 1989 when one of its areas was designated as a 'Cultural Road,' a special zone where people can enjoy art performances and cultural activities.

This 840m long street is divided into four sections: a meeting area; a performance area; a culture and art area; and a folk music performance area.

Every October Wolmido hosts the Wolmi Festival during which participants can engage in traditional Korean dancing and singing, and watch a sea parade. Wolmido is also a good place to go sightseeing by ferry. Ferries offer visitors a unique opportunity to view the western coast from the water.

Ferry Tours

Ships: Cosmos, Harmony
Departure Time: Hourly
From 11:00 am to 8:00 pm
Time Required: 1 hour
Fare: ₩ 7,000 for Adults

Chinatown 2

Incheon's Chinatown was developed in the late 19th century when Incheonhang Port(called Jemulpohang) opened to the outside world. Shortly after the opening of the harbor, numerous Chinese immigrated to Incheon and formed this community and the Chinese Consulate was established a year later. Until the 1940s, Chinatown was one of the largest and most

dynamic commercial areas in Incheon. The Chinese trading houses here dealt in everything from Chinese silk to Oriental medicinal herbs. Chinatown also became known for its authentic Chinese cuisine.

Chinatown is smaller these days but its Chinese characteristics and the aura of its heyday are still preserved. Chinatown is currently being renovated by Incheon City.

Incheon Zhonghua Christian Church established in 1971, Uiseondang (a Buddhist temple for Chinese and once a Kungfu training center) and Oriental medicine shops still operate here. In addition, you can find a number of Chinese restaurants including Jageumseong, Pungmi, Daechang Banjeom, and Bokraechun. At Jageumseong, you will see that the main entrance is held up by two Chinese-style, thick reddish pillars and decorated with colorful ornaments and displays. Chinese-style buildings on the sides of the small alley leading to the Chinese Korean Association and a school for Chinese-Koreans give the impression that they have been designed to accommodate the Korean lifestyle.

Jayu Park 3

Jayu Park was the first Western-style park in Korea. It was built to commemorate the fifth anniversary of the opening of Incheonhang Port to the western world. The park, located on Mt. Eungbongsan, boasts a scenic view of downtown Incheon and the Incheonhang areas. Visitors can also see two historical landmarks. The first is the statue of General MacArthur which was erected to commemorate his heroic efforts as the commander in chief of the United Nations forces in Korea during the Korean War.
The second monument, which was built in 1982 to celebrate the 100th anniversary of the signing of the 1882 Korea-U.S. Security and Trade Treaty, commemorates 100 years of diplomatic relations between Korea and the United States.

Yeonan Pier 4

Yeonan Pier services passenger ships sailing to islands on the West Sea. It also has a seafood market, raw fish restaurants and the Namhang Pier, a popular spot for fishing. The Yeonan Passenger Terminal connects passengers to various islands around the west coast, and is used by both island residents and tourists. The seafood market is renowned for its blue crabs, mussels, hard-shell rockfish, red snappers and other seafood that is caught daily and sold at reasonable prices. There are over 600 stalls located in the market. Outdoor stalls, called Pojangmachas, are located on the sidewalk and offer drinks and snacks throughout the night.

Centennial Monument Commemorating Korea and U.S. Diplomatic Relations

Yeonan Pier

Incheon Open Port District 5

By visiting Incheon, one can see the changes of the past hundred years by looking at Gothic- and Renaissance-style structures built during the early period of Korea' s modernization. In Sinheung-dong, visitors can tour a warehouse district used in the past to transport rice to Japan, Incheon Girls' Commercial High School bearing the remnants of Dong Park where Japanese people once paid homage to their ancestors in a palace, Haegwang Temple constructed by the Japanese in 1910, as well as Japanese-style houses. Among all remaining Japanese-style structures, one that grabs most attention is the old Incheon City Library building. The building has managed to keep its original form and the traces of traditional Japanese gardens are still visible.
Moreover, buildings used by Japanese banks long ago are still sitting on a street that was called 'Bonjeongtong' during the Japanese colonial period. They include the building that Nagasaki-based 18th Japan Bank began using in 1890 and the building that 58th Japan Bank occupied. The building previously used as a branch for 58th Bank has been designated as the Tangible Cultural Asset No. 19 by the city of Incheon and now used by the Jung-gu Food Industry Association. The bank, which had its head office in Osaka, built a two-story building and began using it in 1892. The (old) Korea First Bank branch (Tangible Cultural Asset No. 7 of Incheon) is also reminiscent of the early period of Korea' s modernization.

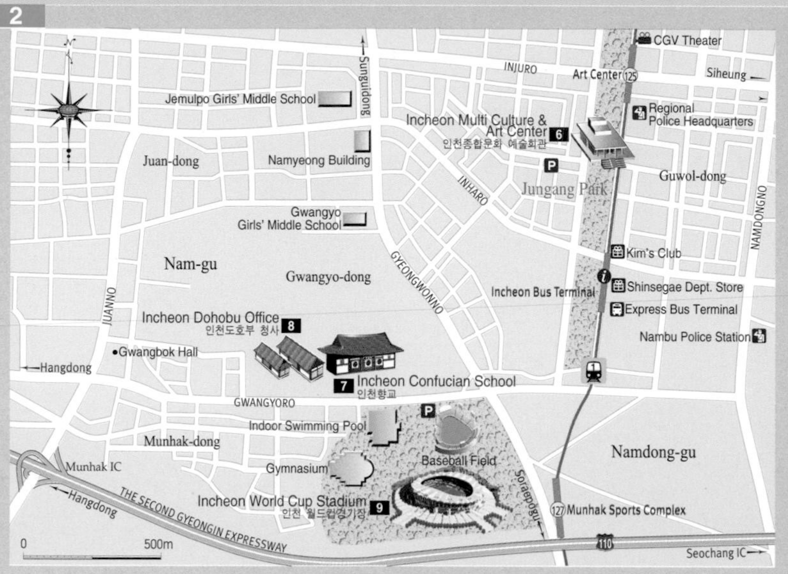

Incheon Multi Culture & Art Center 6

Incheon Multi Culture & Art Center includes a theater, outdoor stage, recreation area, exhibit halls, and a variety of other facilities. Performances and exhibitions held throughout the year make the center a focal point for regional arts.

Incheon Multi Culture & Art Center

Incheon Confucian School 7

The Incheon Confucian School, established during the early Joseon Dynasty, is a traditional Confucian learning complex that also houses ancestral shrines in honor of Confucius and other sages. The complex contains a grand shrine where the mortuary tablet of Confucius is housed, Dongmu and Seomu (the east & west lecture halls), which contain the mortuary tablets of Korean and Chinese sages, a student lecture hall called Myeongnyundang, and student residence halls called Dongjae and Seojae (the east & west residence halls).

Daeseongjeon of the Incheon Confucian School

Incheon Dohobu Office 8

The Incheon Dohobu Office was constructed early in the Joseon Dynasty for use as a city hall. Originally there were several structures but most have been lost, with the exception of the guest rooms and part of the public affairs building.

Incheon Dohobu Office

Incheon World Cup Stadium 9

The Incheon World Cup Stadium is Incheon's newest sports facility. The Stadium is situated at the foot of Mt. Munhaksan. Its design is based on an architectural motif of a ship sailing the seas. It is designed to highlight Incheon's regional identity as a gateway to the West Coast and a hub of international trade. The roof of the Incheon World Cup Stadium was built in the image of sails and masts. The 52,179 seat stadium will be transformed into a cultural center, sports facilities, multi-purpose event hall, business center and outdoor theater after the 2002 World Cup.

www.2002worldcupkorea.org
www.worldcup.inpia.net

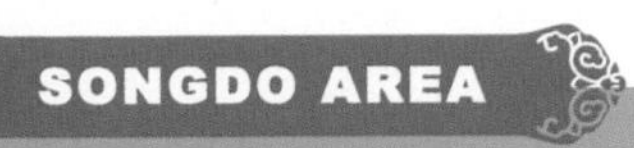

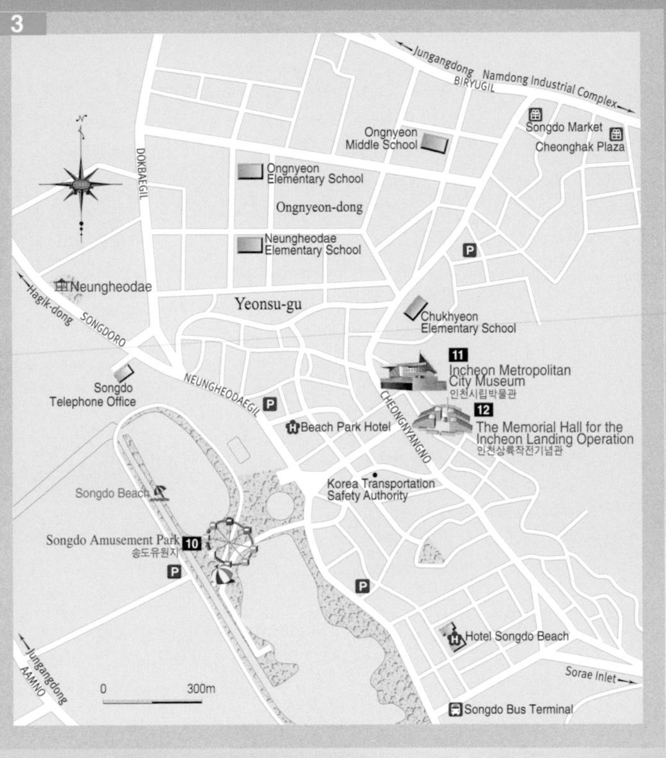

Songdo is being remodeled into a world-class information-oriented city with a business park, media park and convention park. The business park will be the center of trading, finance and new technology and will feature intelligent buildings. The media park will concentrate on fostering the telecommunications and multimedia industries. The convention park will house such amenities as an international exhibition hall, sports center, department store and hotels that will be vital to the area's increasing international trade.

Songdo Amusement Park 10

Songdo Amusement Park is a year-round recreation center located near Mt. Cheongnyangsan. It has more than 20 arttractions including a bungee-jump tower, beach, pool, boat pier, golf course and slopes for sledding. Its favorable location and diverse facilities make the park a popular site for family outings with Incheon residents and residents from neighboring metropolitan areas. Adjacent to the amusement park are over 200 restaurants and cafes that are sure to satisfy any palate. They offer western, Japanese, Korean and Chinese foods and specialties like shabu shabu, hot plate dishes and steaks.

Songdo Amusement Park

Incheon Metropolitan City Museum 11

The Incheon Metropolitan City Museum, which opened in 1946, is Korea's first municipal museum and its collection spans from prehistoric to modern times, with 4,700 artifacts displayed in circular exhibits. The first exhibit room displays cultural relics from prehistoric, Three Kingdom, Silla Kingdom and Goryeo Dynasty periods, as well as cultural assets excavated from the Incheon area. The second room features pottery and folk craftwork of the Joseon Dynasty, and remnants of the Sino-Japanese and Russo-Japanese wars. The third room holds paintings and records from the Joseon Dynasty.

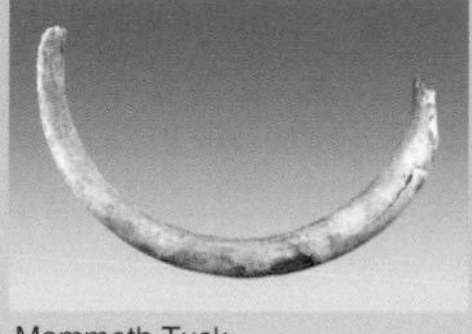

Mammoth Tusk

Red Earthenware Jar with Handle

Memorial Hall for the Incheon Landing Operation

Memorial Hall for the Incheon Landing Operation 12

This war memorial was established to commemorate the successful Incheon landing by the commander-in-chief of the UN forces, General MacArthur, during the Korean War (1950). The exhibit halls feature North and South Korean weapons and uniforms used in the war and dioramas explaining the Incheon landing. There is also an outdoor exhibit center, an outdoor performance hall, an audiovisual room that contains DVDs on the Incheon landing, lounges, an observatory and small parks. Visitors can view photographs and 825 objects from the Incheon landing in the first exhibit hall. The second hall offers a comparative display of necessities and personal items which were used in North and South Korea during the war. The large-screen audiovisual room runs films on the outbreak of the war, which occurred on June 25, 1950, the Incheon landing of September 15, 1950, and the development of Incheon after the war. Tanks, landing craft, machine guns, and naval guns are displayed in the outdoor exhibit center.

The Incheon Landing Operation

Outdoor Exhibition Hall

In 1950 during the Korean War, South Korean forces, having retreated all the way to the edge of the Korean Peninsula, were in a precarious situation. With the help of UN forces, they were able to push the invading force back north but North and South Korean forces were locked in a long confrontation on the battlefront along the Nakdonggang River. To break the gridlock, General MacArthur decided to penetrate the mid-point of the Korean Peninsula on the west coast to cut the supply line of North Korea and turn the tide of the war.
Thus the Incheon landing plan was hatched and the strategy succeeded. The allied forces were able to recapture Seoul and were provided with a crucial opportunity to win the war. In the first phase of the Incheon landing, South Korean and US marines landed on Wolmido Island on September 15, 1950, and successfully established a beachhead in just two hours. In the second phase, four South Korean marine battalions, the US 7th Infantry Division and the 1st Marine Division launched a surprise attack to capture Incheon, Gimpo Airfield and Suwon, thus securing the Incheon. The third and last phase involved two South Korean marine battalions and the US 1st Marine Division crossing the Hangang River on the 19th of September, the main force crossing the river on the 20th, and the successful completion of the Incheon landing strategy with the hoisting of the South Korean flag at Jungangcheong in Seoul at noon on the 26th of September.

Ganghwado Island holds special archeological and historical significance. People have inhabited the area since prehistoric times, as evidenced by the excavation of numerous artifacts from the Bronze Age, including a large number of megalithic tombs.
Ganghwa also played an important role in Korea's history. During the Mongolian invasion of the 13th Century, Ganghwa was the site of anti-Mongolian resistance by the Goryeo Dynasty. During the latter half of the 19th Century, the island became a symbol of the Joseon Dynasty's defense against foreign encroachment following victories in battles against French forces in 1866 and American forces in 1887.

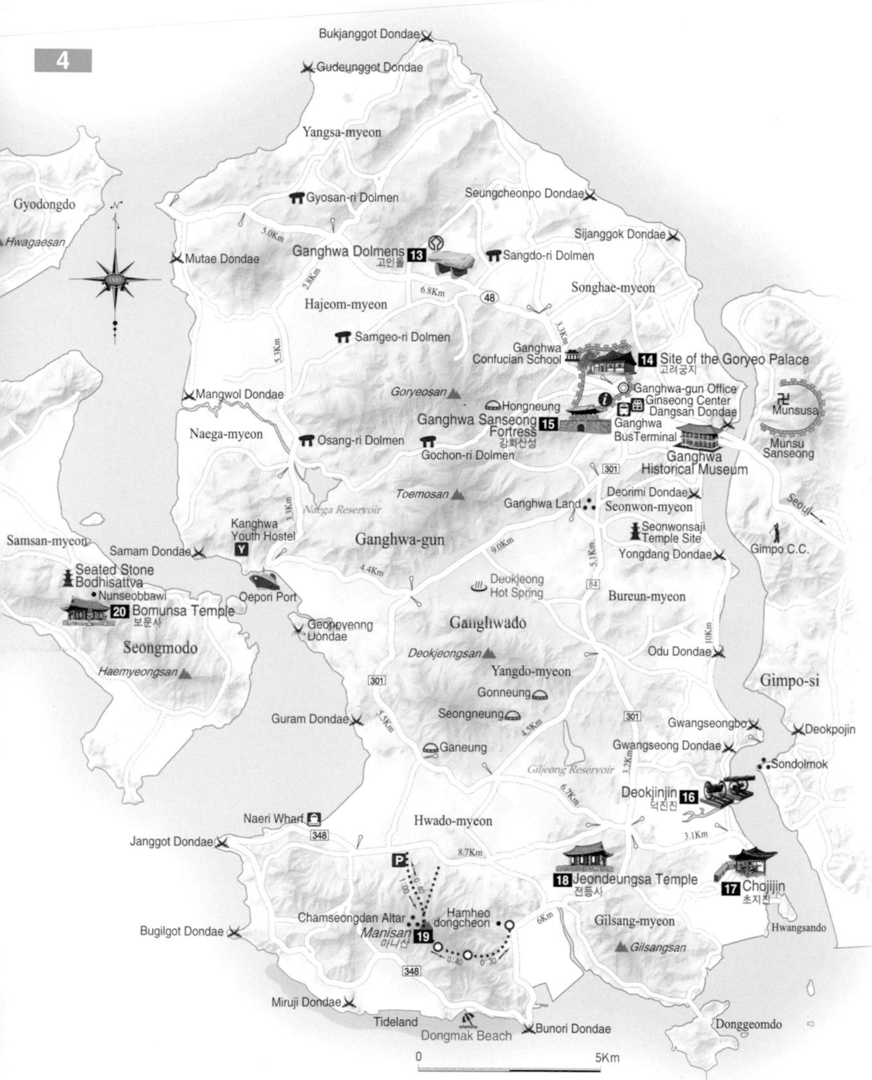

Ganghwa Dolmens 13

Ganghwa Historical Museum

Ganghwa is famous for its dolmens, which are simple megalithic burial chambers with three or more upright stones and one or more capstones. Approximately 130 dolmens have been found in Ganghwa. The most well-known dolmen in Korea is the Bugeun-ri dolmen, located 6km west of central Ganghwa. Shaped like a table, a prototypical northern dolmen is constructed with five stone plates: two main supporting prop stones, two end (head and tail) stones, and one large capstone. As the largest in Korea, the Bugeun-ri dolmen is characterized by an immense capstone which is 7.1m long and 5.5m wide, weighs about 50 tons, and has two supporting prop stones which are 2.6m high. Ganghwa dolmens have special archeological significance in that they are located near the southernmost boundary in the global distribution of dolmens. The Dolmen Festival is held in Ganghwa every summer.
Ganghwa dolmens were registered as a World Heritage site by UNESCO.

Ganghwa Dolmen

Ganghwa Battlefields

Ganghwado, having served as a strategic point in national defense against foreign incursions, almost always had military troops stationed there. It is known to have had at least 70 defensive posts with contingents of troops at crucial locations. Historical strongholds in Ganghwado include Chojijin, Deokjinjin and Gwangseongbo, which were all built in the mid-17th century. Chojijin was the site of fierce battles during the French incursion of 1866, the US incursion of 1871, and the Japanese warship attack during the early Joseon Dynasty.

Old Site of Goryeo Palace

Site of the Goryeo Palace 14

This area was the transient palace site during a 39-year long resistance against a Mongolian invasion. In 1232, King Gojong of the Goryeo Dynasty decided to defend the nation's sovereignty and transferred the capital to Ganghwado. The palace and government offices were newly built in 1234. With the concluding of peace with Mongolia in 1270, the capital was transferred back to Gaeseong. Most of the palace structures had been lost during the numerous battles. Only the public affairs and personnel buildings remain today.

Deokjinjin

Ganghwa Sanseong Fortress 15

The Ganghwa Sanseong Fortress is an expansive earthen fortification built by King Gojong of the Goryeo Dynasty. The original fortress, which extended around Ganghwa-eup and Seonwon-myeon, was dismantled at the insistence of the Mongolians. It was re-built as a stone fortress in the early Joseon Dynasty. The Ganghwa fortress has 1,813 battlements, 4 major gates, 4 minor gates, and 4 gate stations.

Deokjinjin 16

Deokjinjin served as a strategic point in the outer fortification that protected the Ganghwa Strait during the Goryeo Dynasty. The Yongdu Dondae, Deokjin Dondae, Deokjin Podae, and Namjang Podae, all built during the 5th year of King Sukjong's rule, are parts of Deokjinjin. This was the site of heavy fighting during the French Indochina fleet incursion of 1866 and the US Asian fleet incursion of 1871. The castle walls and the upper story of the gate, which had deteriorated with time, were restored to their original form in 1976.

Chojijin 17

The Chojijin was built to ward off foreign naval invasions in the 7th year of the reign of the Joseon Dynasty's King Hyojong. It was the site of fierce battles against the French Indochina fleet led by Admiral Rose, who

Canons at Gwangseongbo

Chojijin

HWAMUNSEOK

Hwamunseok is a flowery mat made from pure white sedge plants. It is a representative product of Ganghwado and was originally made as an all-white mat during the Goryeo Dynasty. About a hundred years ago, the royal family of the Joseon Dynasty commanded that flowery designs be etched on the mat, thus giving birth to the ornate mat that exists today. Hwamunseok is a high quality indoor ornament, with elaborate designs and graceful, detailed craftsmanship. The mat is also practical in that it helps to keep floors cool during summer, blocks out the cold during winter, and will not lose its luster or break easily. Aside from on mats, the Hwamunseok design is also used in other handicrafts such as baskets and cushions.

attacked in response to the persecution of Catholics, the US Asian Fleet led by Admiral Rogers, who sought to open trade relations by force, and the Japanese warship, Unyang. All of this occurred during the rule of King Gojong of the Joseon Dynasty.

Jeondeungsa Temple 18

One of the major tourist attractions on Mt. Manisan is Jeondeungsa, located within the Samnangseong Fortress, which is believed to have been built by the three sons of Dangun, the legendary founder of the first Korean Kingdom. Its present name was acquired in 1282 when Queen Jeonghwa of Goryeo Dynasty made an offering of a jade lamp oil container to the temple.

The grounds of Jeondeungsa house numerous national treasures, such as the Daeungjeon (its main hall), Yaksajeon, and Beomjong (an iron bell). Furthermore, visitors can see Jangsagakji, where the Sillok (the Goryeo Dynasty chronicles) are preserved, and Seonwonbogakji, which preserves the Jokbo (the genealogical records of the Joseon Dynasty), and where the world renowned Tripitaka Koreana was engraved and enshrined.

· Jeondeungsa (left)
· A picture of the manufacturing of the Tripitaka Koreana tablets (upper right)
· Daeungjeon in Jeondeungsa (bottom right)

Mt. Manisan 19

Southwest of Ganghwado and 468m above sea level, Mt. Manisan is said to be the site where Dangun, the legendary founder of the first Korean Kingdom, descended from the heavens 5,000 years ago. The Chamseongdan Altar on its peak is believed to be the site which was used by Dangun to pay tribute to the heavens for the prosperity of the Korean people. The tradition of paying tribute at this altar continues to this day, with Koreans holding worship ceremonies here as part of the celebrations for National Foundation Day every October 3rd. The torch for the National Athletic Games, the most prestigious sports event in Korea, is lit here by seven young maidens.

Mt. Manisan is also famous for its magnificent sunrises.

Early morning visitors can experience the gradual appearance of the sun from behind the mountains.

Bomunsa Temple 20

Bomunsa is a Buddhist temple located on Seongmodo Island, west of Ganghwado. Visitors can take a boat to this beautiful island in the West Sea. The temple is known for Seoksil, a stone chamber housing the image of Buddha, and Maaeseokbul, a grand stone carving of Buddha. The temple compound also contains a 600-year old Chinese juniper tree (Monument No. 17). Behind the tree is Seoksil, which contains statues of the 23 disciples of Buddha. The main shrine, the Shrine of the Three Sages, and the Shrine of Ten Kings can also be found on the temple grounds. Maae seokbul is located just 8 minutes walking distance from the grounds. Its image of Buddha is carved on a stone 10 meters high and 3 meters wide.

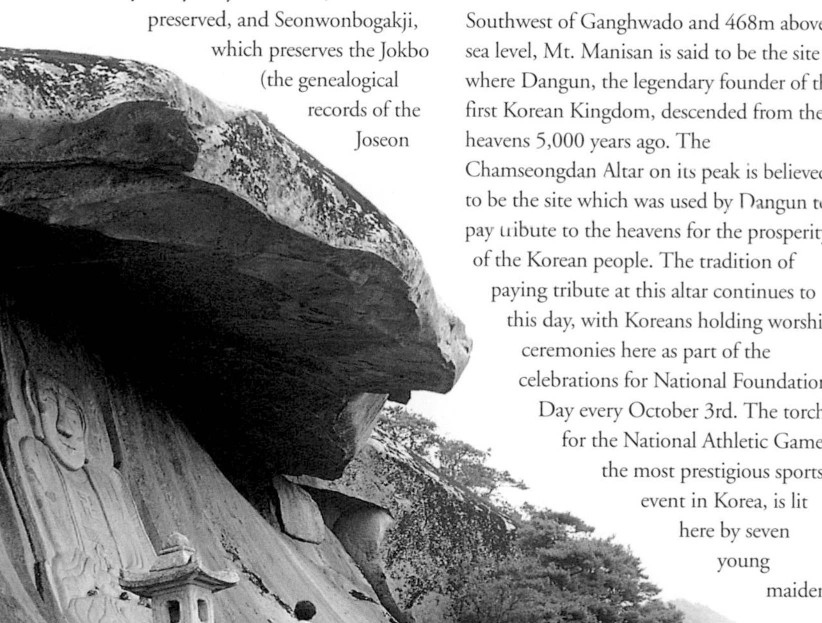

Maae seokbul

Sorae Inlet

Sorae Inlet

This inlet is a popular tourist site where visitors can buy blue crabs, shrimp, croaker, flounder, hard-shell rockfish, and other delicacies caught in nearby waters. There are open-air, raw fish restaurants throughout the local seafood market that can readily serve fresh, affordable fish prepared in a variety of ways.

Haesoopia (Seawater Bath) A7

Haesoopia had its origin in the ancient wisdom that helped many people cure their diseases with the help of seawater around 100 years ago. Originally begun in a small fishing town of Hanpyeong, Jeollanam-do Province, Haesoopia has now become a famous local tourist attraction by recently opening a branch easily accessible by city-dwellers. Seawater has long been known to be effective in preventing a variety of diseases, including arteriosclerosis, hypertension, diabetes, arthritis, lumbago, dermatitis, women' s diseases, athlete' s foot and eczema, and especially good for skincare (which is why it is so popular with young women) as it contains more than 100 minerals. The seawater bath, which is located near the wharf has a pump that goes deep down underground to get clean water.

Inside Haesoopia

Gas Science Museum D10

The museum is located inside the Incheon production center of Korea Gas Corporation. It is composed of several sections that help ordinary people understand how natural gas is created, liquefied, transported, distributed, delivered and used, and provides an opportunity for a hands-on experience with energy. Visitors should make a reservation for guided tours provided by the museum.

A step into the space station-like museum opens the door to an exciting journey. First comes the tour of geologic formations created and changed through events since the birth of our globe 4.6 billion years ago. Next is the 'Ice Land' where visitors get to know about the lifecycle of liquefied natural gas (LNG) in a setting designed to resemble ice walls and a forest. In addition, the tour leads visitors to other sections like 'Birth of Energy', 'Let's Study Energy', 'Thoughts on Energy' and 'LNG Story'.

The museum provides a valuable chance for anyone, regardless of age, to learn all about energy through easy-to-understand explanations and interesting experiments.

Gas Science Museum

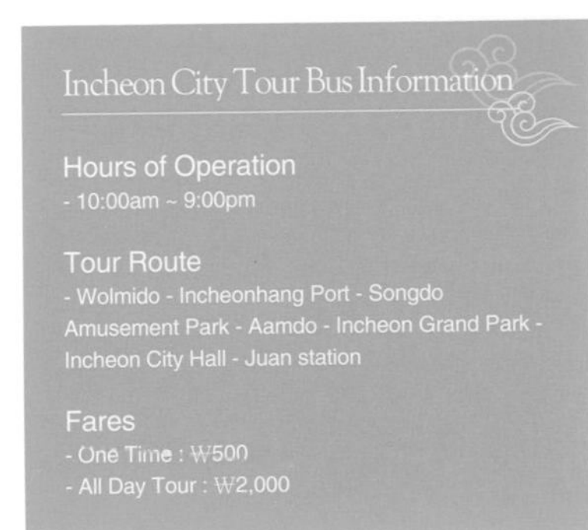

Incheon City Tour Bus Information

Hours of Operation
- 10:00am ~ 9:00pm

Tour Route
- Wolmido - Incheonhang Port - Songdo Amusement Park - Aamdo - Incheon Grand Park - Incheon City Hall - Juan station

Fares
- One Time : ₩500
- All Day Tour : ₩2,000

Daegu

Daegu is Korea's third largest city, with a population of 2.5 million people, and is located in the southeastern part of the Korean Peninsula. Daegu sits in a basin surrounded by mountains on all sides and a river runs through the city. Daegu is a product of the rich cultural heritage of Silla and Gaya Kingdoms. This city is home to countless cultural and historic relics and sites and is a prime destination for those interested in Korea's history.

Daegu is now the political, economic, and cultural heart of the southeastern region of Korea. It is especially well-developed in such industries as textiles and machinery.

Textile & Fashion

Along with Gyeongsangbuk-do, Daegu is the biggest textile producer in Korea, housing 18.9% of the nation' s textile companies, employing 22.2% of textile workers, and accounts for 27.8% of the total national production and 23.3% of textile exports. In the past, the focus of Daegu' s industrial development was on spun thread and weaving and dyeing industries, but the recently implemented Milano Project aspires to transform Daegu' s textile industrial structure.

In accordance with this ambitious goal, a total of 17 projects are scheduled to be launched in four areas : 1) creation of sophisticated textile products ; 2) revitalization of the fashion design industry ; 3) establishment of a textile industry infrastructure ; and 4) concentration on R&D and enhancement of productivity.

Hanbok Fashion Show of Korean Traditional Clothes

Daegu Textile Fashion Festival

This biannual festival, held every May and October, promotes the city of Daegu and its textile industry. A wide range of events are held every May, including the rendezvous of the textile and fashion industries, sewing contests, traditional embroidery contests, the Daegu International Textile Design Exchange Fair, fashion shows, and the Daegu Collection and Hanbok (traditional Korean apparel) Fashion Show.

The October festival is held simultaneously with the Dalgubeol Festival and is closely linked with the Milano Project in that it serves as a venue for attracting foreign buyers to promote locally produced textile goods.

EXCO Daegu

Daegu International Exhibition & Convention Center is a five-story complex accommodating a shopping mall, four exhibition rooms and an international convention hall. Its unique design, cutting-edge facilities, and natural lighting system distinguish it from other exhibition centers.
As the center for the implementation of Daegu Metropolitan Government's Milano Project, the new EXCO plays a pivotal role in displaying and promoting the city's textile industry.
www.excodaegu.co.kr

EXCO (Daegu Exhibition & Convention Center)

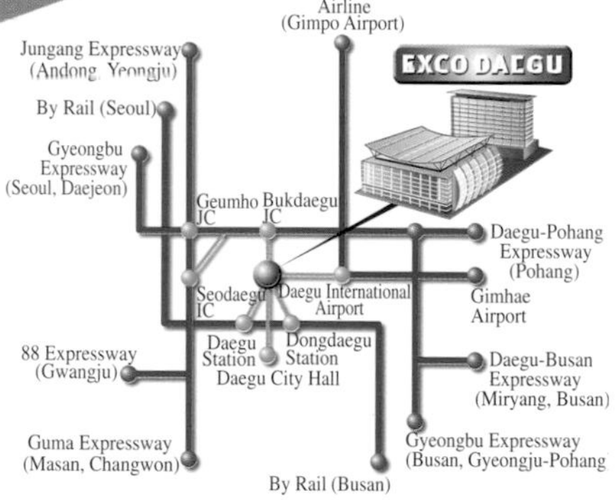

Convention Hall

Exhibition Hall

Conference Room

Open Air Stage

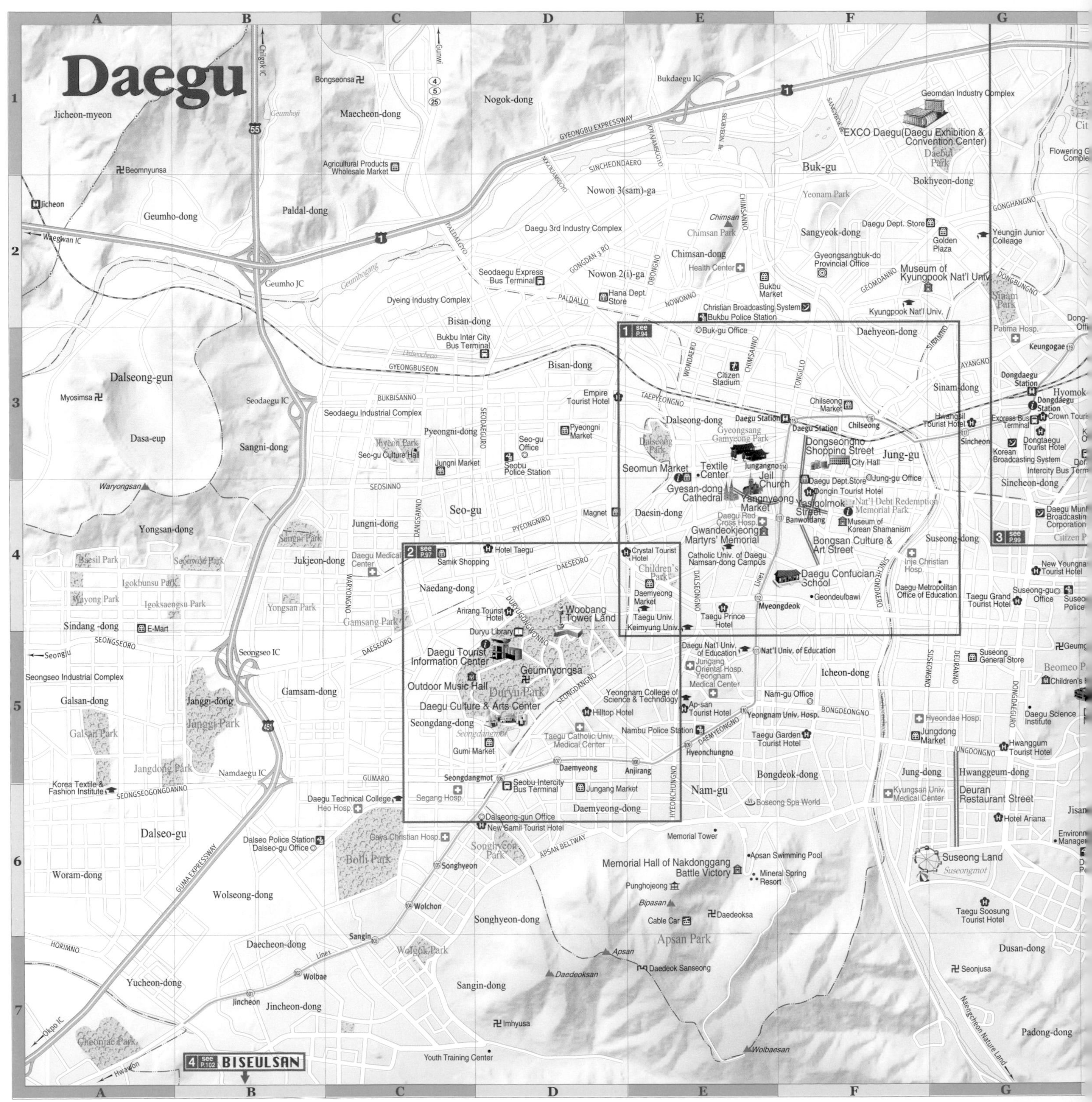
Daegu
Jicheon-myeon
Bongseonsa
Maecheon-dong
Nogok-dong
Bukdaegu IC
Geomdan Industry Complex
EXCO Daegu(Daegu Exhibition & Convention Center)
Buk-gu
Bokhyeon-dong
Agricultural Products Wholesale Market
Beomnyunsa
Paldal-dong
Geumho-dong
Nowon 3(sam)-ga
Daegu 3rd Industry Complex
Chimsan Park
Sangyeok-dong
Daegu Dept. Store
Golden Plaza
Yeungjin Junior Colleage
Chimsan-dong
Gyeongsangbuk-do Provincial Office
Museum of Kyungpook Nat'l Univ.
Geumho JC
Seodaegu Express Bus Terminal
Nowon 2(i)-ga
Hana Dept. Store
Bukbu Market
Dyeing Industry Complex
Christian Broadcasting System
Bukbu Police Station
Kyungpook Nat'l Univ.
Bisan-dong
Buk-gu Office
Daehyeon-dong
Bukbu Inter City Bus Terminal
Citizen Stadium
Dalseong-gun
Myosimsa
Seodaegu IC
Seodaegu Industrial Complex
Empire Tourist Hotel
Sinam-dong
Dongdaegu Station
Dasa-eup
Sangni-dong
Pyeongni-dong
Pyeongni Market
Dalseong-dong
Daegu Station
Chilseong Market
Chilseong
Seo-gu Culture Hall
Seo-gu Office
Gyeongsang Gamyeong Park
Dongseongno Shopping Street
Jung-gu
Jungni Market
Seobu Police Station
Seomun Market
Textile Center
Jeil Church
City Hall
Jung-gu Office
Sincheon-dong
Waryongsan
Gyesan-dong Cathedral
Yangnyeong Market
Daegu Dept. Store
Dongin Tourist Hotel
Yasigolmok Street
Nat'l Debt Redemption Memorial Park
Yongsan-dong
Jungni-dong
Seo-gu
Magnet
Daesin-dong
Museum of Korean Shamanism
Gwandeokjeong Martyrs' Memorial
Bongsan Culture & Art Street
Suseong-dong
Jukjeon-dong
Daegu Medical Center
Hotel Taegu
Crystal Tourist Hotel
Catholic Univ. of Daegu Namsan-dong Campus
Daegu Confucian School
Samik Shopping
Naedang-dong
Daemyeong Market
Daegu Metropolitan Office of Education
Taegu Grand Tourist Hotel
Myeongdeok
Geondeulbawi
Woobang Tower Land
Taegu Prince Hotel
Sindang -dong
E-Mart
Arirang Tourist Hotel
Duryu Library
Taegu Univ. Keimyung Univ.
Seongseo IC
Daegu Tourist Information Center
Daegu Nat'l Univ. of Education
Nat'l Univ. of Education
Icheon-dong
Seongseo Industrial Complex
Geumnyongsa
Outdoor Music Hall
Duryu Park
Gamsam-dong
Galsan-dong
Janggi-dong
Daegu Culture & Arts Center
Yeongnam College of Science & Technology
Nam-gu Office
Seongdang-dong
Hilltop Hotel
Ap-san Tourist Hotel
Yeongnam Univ. Hosp.
Daegu Science Institute
Taegu Catholic Univ. Medical Center
Nambu Police Station
Taegu Garden Tourist Hotel
Jungdong Market
Hwanggum Tourist Hotel
Gumi Market
Daemyeong
Anjirang
Bongdeok-dong
Jung-dong
Hwanggeum-dong
Korea Textile & Fashion Institute
Namdaegu IC
Seongdangmot
Seobu Intercity Bus Terminal
Jungang Market
Nam-gu
Daegu Technical College
Deuran Restaurant Street
Daemyeong-dong
Dalseong-gun Office
New Samil Tourist Hotel
Hotel Ariana
Dalseo-gu
Dalseo Police Station
Dalseo-gu Office
Gaya Christian Hosp.
Memorial Tower
Apsan Swimming Pool
Suseong Land
Woram-dong
Songhyeon
Memorial Hall of Nakdonggang Battle Victory
Mineral Spring Resort
Wolseong-dong
Punghojeong
Wolchon
Songhyeon-dong
Cable Car
Daedeoksa
Taegu Soosung Tourist Hotel
Apsan Park
Daecheon-dong
Sangin
Dusan-dong
Wolbae
Apsan
Daedeok Sanseong
Seonjusa
Yucheon-dong
Daedeoksan
Sangin-dong
Jincheon
Jincheon-dong
Imhyusa
Padong-dong
Okpo IC
Wolbaesan
Youth Training Center
4 see P.102 BISEULSAN
GYEONGBU EXPRESSWAY
GUMA EXPRESSWAY
APSAN BELTWAY

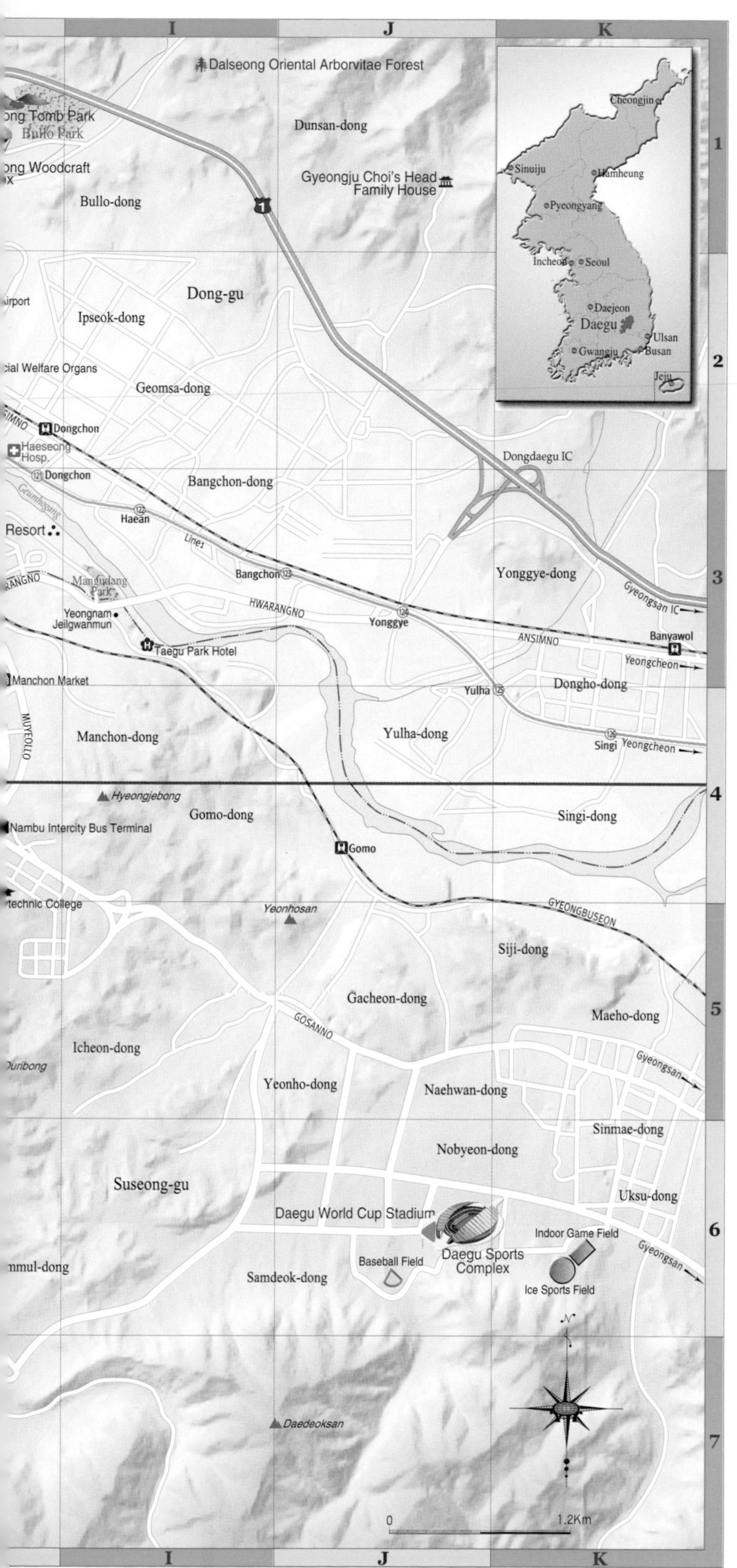

INDEX

Cultural Relics

Bullo-dong Tomb Park H1
Daegu Confucian School F4
Geumnyongsa Temple D5
Gwandeokjeong
Martyrs' Memorial E4
Gyeongju Choi's Head
Family House J1
Gyeongsang
Gamyeong Park E3
Gyesan-dong Cathedral E4
Jeil Church E4
Nat'l Debt Redemption
Memorial Park F4

Natural Attractions

Apsan Park E7
Dalseong Oriental
Arborvitae Forest I1
Dalseong Park E3
Duryu Park D5

Museums & Theaters

Daegu Culture &
Arts Center D5
Daegu Nat'l Museum H5
Memorial Hall of
Nakdonggang
Battle Victory E6
Museum of Kyungpook
Nat'l Univ. G2
Outdoor Music Hall C5

Places of Interest

Bongsan Culture &
Art Street F4
Boseong Spa World E6
Bullo-dong Woodcraft
Complex H1
Daegu Sports Complex J6
Daegu Tourist
Information Center D5
Daegu World Cup Stadium J6
Deuran Restaurant Street G6
Dongchon Resort H3
Dongseongno
Shopping Street F3
EXCO Daegu (Daegu Exhibition
& Convention Center) G1
Seomun Market E3
Suseong Land G6
Textile Center E3
Woobang Tower Land D4
Yangnyeong Market E4
Yasigolmok Street F4

Accommodations

Crown Tourist Hotel G3
Crystal Tourist Hotel E4
Dongin Tourist Hotel F4
Dongtaegu Tourist Hotel G3
Hotel Ariana G6
Hotel Taegu D4
Hwanggum Tourist Hotel G5
Hwangsil Tourist Hotel G3
New Samil Tourist Hotel D6
New Youngnam
Tourist Hotel G4
Taegu Garden Tourist Hotel F5
Taegu Grand Tourist Hotel G4
Taegu Park Hotel I3
Taegu Prince Hotel E4
Taegu Soosung
Tourist Hotel G6

Transportation

Daegu Int'l Airport H2
Daegu Station F3
Dongdaegu Station G3
Express Bus Terminal G3
Seodaegu Express Bus
Terminal D2

Tourist Information

Daegu Division of Tourism 82-53-429-3331
Daegu Tourist Information Center 82-53-627-8900
www.daegu.go.kr

LEGEND

- Railroad Station
- Airport
- Bus Terminal
- Metro Line
- Cable Car Platform
- Hospital
- Police Station
- Post Office
- Tourist Information Center
- University or School
- Library
- Broadcasting Station
- Museum
- Theater
- Fortress
- Temple
- Traditional Pavilion
- Park
- Amusement Park
- Arboretum
- Mountain
- Stadium
- Other Tourist Attractions
- Hotel
- Department Store or Market
- Reference Point
- Metro Station Number

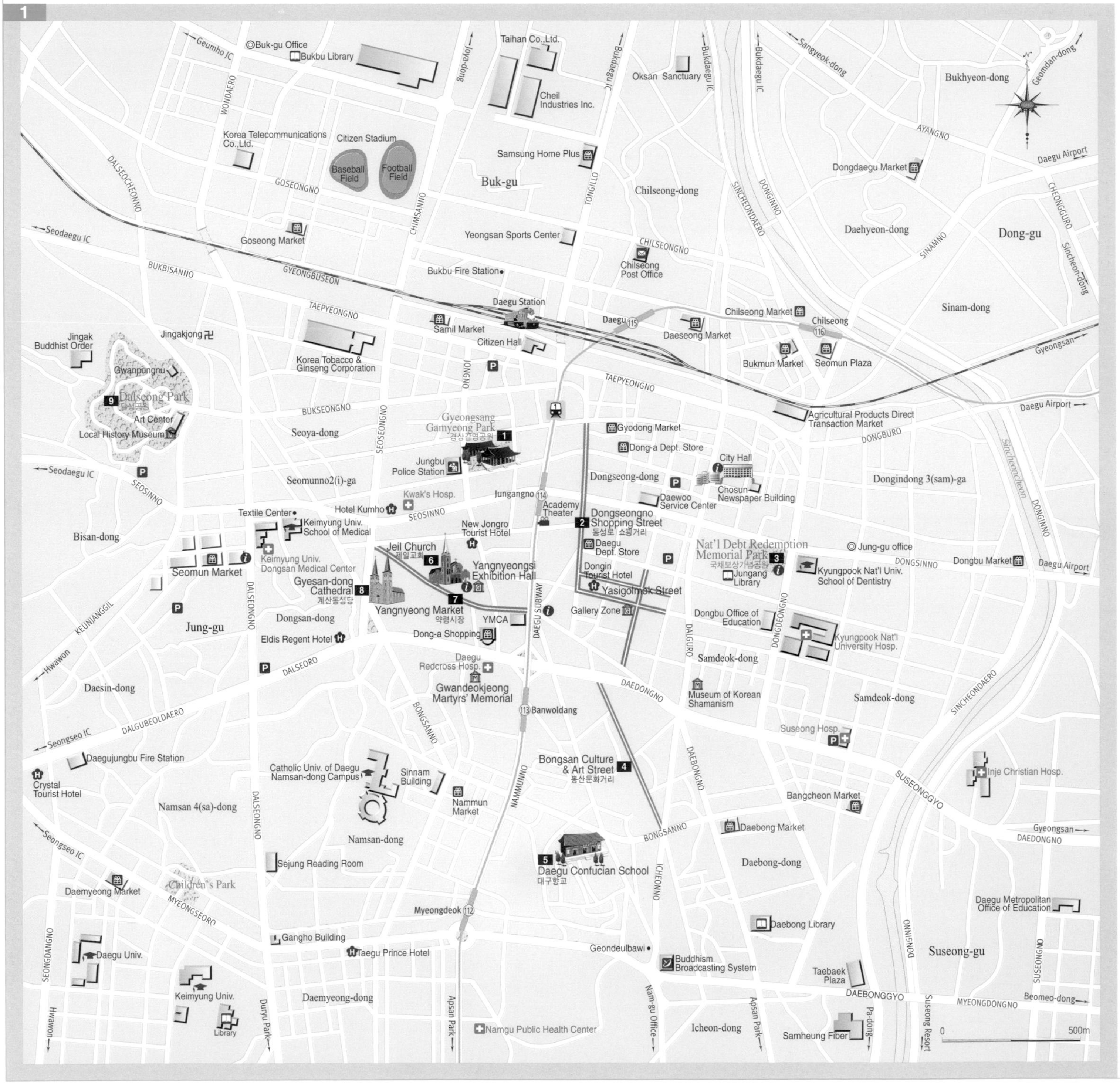

1

Geumho IC
Buk-gu Office
Bukbu Library
Ioya-dong
Taihan Co.,Ltd.
Bukdaegu IC
Oksan Sanctuary
Bukdaegu IC
Bukdaegu IC
Sangyeok-dong
Geomdan-dong
Bukhyeon-dong
WONDAERO
Cheil Industries Inc.
AYANGNO
Daegu Airport
Korea Telecommunications Co.,Ltd.
Citizen Stadium
Baseball Field
Football Field
Samsung Home Plus
Dongdaegu Market
DALSEOCHEONNO
GOSEONGNO
Buk-gu
TONGILLO
Chilseong-dong
SINCHEONDAERO
DONGBUNO
CHEONGGURO
Daehyeon-dong
Dong-gu
Seodaegu IC
Goseong Market
CHIMSANNO
Yeongsan Sports Center
CHILSEONGNO
SINAMNO
Sincheon-dong
BUKBISANNO
GYEONGBUSEON
Bukbu Fire Station
Chilseong Post Office
Daegu Station
TAEPYEONGNO
Samil Market
Daegu 115
Daeseong Market
Chilseong Market
Chilseong 116
Sinam-dong
Jingak Buddhist Order
Jingakjong
Korea Tobacco & Ginseng Corporation
Citizen Hall
Bukmun Market
Seomun Plaza
Gyeongsan
Gwanpungnu
JONGNO
TAEPYEONGNO
Dalseong Park
달성공원
Art Center
Local History Museum
BUKSEONGNO
Seoya-dong
SEOSEONGNO
Gyeongsang Gamyeong Park
경상감영공원
Gyodong Market
Agricultural Products Direct Transaction Market
Daegu Airport
DONGBURO
Sincheoncheon
Dong-a Dept. Store
Jungbu Police Station
City Hall
Seodaegu IC
SEOSINNO
Seomunno2(i)-ga
Dongseong-dong
Chosun Newspaper Building
Dongindong 3(sam)-ga
Kwak's Hosp.
Jungangno 114
Daewoo Service Center
Textile Center
Hotel Kumho
SEOSINNO
Academy Theater
Dongseongno Shopping Street
동성로 쇼핑거리
Keimyung Univ. School of Medical
New Jongro Tourist Hotel
Bisan-dong
Jeil Church
제일교회
Daegu Dept. Store
Nat'l Debt Redemption Memorial Park
국채보상기념공원
Jung-gu office
DONGSINNO
Dongbu Market
Daegu Airport
DONGINNO
Seomun Market
Keimyung Univ. Dongsan Medical Center
Yangnyeongsi Exhibition Hall
Dongin Tourist Hotel
Jungang Library
Kyungpook Nat'l Univ. School of Dentistry
Gyesan-dong Cathedral
계산동성당
Yasigolmok Street
KEUNJANGGIL
DALSEONGNO
Yangnyeong Market
약령시장
DAEGU SUBWAY
Gallery Zone
Dongbu Office of Education
DONGDEOKRO
Jung-gu
Dongsan-dong
YMCA
DALGURO
Kyungpook Nat'l University Hosp.
Eldis Regent Hotel
Dong-a Shopping
Samdeok-dong
Hwawon
DALSEORO
Daegu Redcross Hosp.
DAEDONGNO
Daesin-dong
Gwandeokjeong Martyrs' Memorial
Museum of Korean Shamanism
Samdeok-dong
SINCHEONDAERO
BONGSANNO
113 Banwoldang
DALGUBEOLDAERO
Seongseo IC
Suseong Hosp.
Daegujungbu Fire Station
Bongsan Culture & Art Street
봉산문화거리
DAEBONGNO
Crystal Tourist Hotel
Catholic Univ. of Daegu Namsan-dong Campus
Sinnam Building
Inje Christian Hosp.
SUSEONGGYO
Namsan 4(sa)-dong
DALSEONGNO
Nammun Market
NAMMUNNO
Bangcheon Market
Seongseo IC
Namsan-dong
BONGSANNO
Daebong Market
Gyeongsan
DAEDONGNO
Sejung Reading Room
Daegu Confucian School
대구향교
Daebong-dong
Children's Park
Daemyeong Market
MYEONGSEORO
ICHEONNO
Myeongdeok 112
Daegu Metropolitan Office of Education
Daebong Library
Gangho Building
SEONGDANGNO
Daegu Univ.
Taegu Prince Hotel
Geondeulbawi
Buddhism Broadcasting System
DONGSINNO
Suseong-gu
SUSEONGNO
Taebaek Plaza
Keimyung Univ.
Library
Daemyeong-dong
DAEBONGGYO
MYEONGDONGNO
Beomeo-dong
Hwawon
Duryu Park
Apsan Park
Namgu Public Health Center
Nam-gu Office
Icheon-dong
Apsan Park
Samheung Fiber
Pa-dong
Suseong Resort
0 500m

Gyeongsang Gamyeong Park 1

This small park is located in the center of downtown Daegu. It is a popular resting spot for those working in the area. The park opened in 1970 to preserve the historical area of Daegu. Two old buildings on the premises exemplify the grandeur of the old governor' s office. Seonhwadang (Daegu Tangible Cultural Asset No.1) was the governor' s office and Jingcheonggak (Daegu Tangible Cultural Asset No. 2) was the residential hall of the governor.

Dongseongno Shopping Street 2

Dongseongno is one of the busiest streets in Daegu. A multitude of department stores, shopping malls and smaller shops pack both sides of the street. The street is always bustling with people. Movie theaters, bookstores, cafes, restaurants and coffee shops also abound.

Dongseongno Shopping Street

Nat'l Debt Redemption Memorial Park 3

Nat'l Debt Redemption Memorial Park

This park was formed in remembrance of the national debt repayment movement which started in Daegu in 1907. Visitors can enjoy the serene atmosphere of the park by walking along a 255 meter path lined with black oak trees and a path dotted with monuments inscribed with poems of local poets. There is also the path where sages inscribed words of wisdom on monuments. The park contains water fountains and the Dalgubeol Grand Bell, which weighs 22.5 tons.

Bongsan Culture & Art Street 4

Bongsan Culture & Art Street Festival

Bongsan Street is the center of Daegu' s culture and art, with over 20 galleries. In October, during the Bongsan Art Festival, the area features art exhibitions, Pungmullori traditional music performances, outdoor concerts, writer's lectures, performance art shows and sculpture exhibits.

Gyeongsang Gamyeong Park

Daegu Confucian School

Daegu Confucian School 5

The Daegu Confucian School contains Myeongnyundang, which was used as a classroom, the Nagyukje Pavilion, and Daeseongjeon Hall, which was built during the Joseon Dynasty. Korean and Chinese ancestral tablets are preserved inside Daeseongjeon. Stone monuments commemorating the virtuous deeds of various governors of Gyeongsang-do are also found in the front lawn.
Currently the Confucian School provides education in subjects such as Chinese classic literature and social etiquette.
Myeongnyundang is also used as a traditional wedding hall.

Jeil Church 6

Traditional Medical Books (Donguibogam)

Jeil Church was the first Protestant church founded in Daegu, and is located in the Yangnyeong Market. It was first constructed in 1897, and was expanded through reconstruction in 1933.
The church is a two-story building with red brick walls and its design is a mixture of traditional Korean and Western styles. Due to its unique architecture, which reflects the Gothic style, Jeil Church is an important building in the study of modern architectural history in the Daegu region.

Yangnyeong Market 7

In Yangnyeong Market, oriental medical clinics, herb shops, ginseng stores, and natural food restaurants are packed along Namseong Street. The market traces its origin to a medicinal herb fair first held during the Joseon Dynasty. The market hosts the Yangnyeongsi Festival every year to preserve and hand down oriental medical culture. The festival offers diverse events, including a herb-chopping contest, exhibitions of herb flowers and herbal food,

Oriental Medicine Shop in Yangnyeong Market

and demonstrations of oriental medical techniques.
The Oriental Medicine Exhibition Hall, located in the market, displays over 1,000 items and materials related to oriental medicine, such as rare medicinal herbs, old oriental medical books, old medical tools, and raw herbs.

Gyesan-dong Cathedral 8

Gyesan-dong Cathedral is a historic building representing the propagation of Catholicism in Korea. It was first built in a Korean style, but the original structure was lost in a fire in 1902. The current building is in the Gothic style, with a blend of red and black bricks, and the exterior is in the shape of a Latin cross.

Gyesan-dong Cathedral

Adjacent to Gyesan-dong lies Namsan-dong, the birthplace of Catholicism in Daegu. Namsan-dong has a huge Catholic community, accommodating a Catholic university, a parish, a convent and St. Mary' s Cathedral.

Dalseong Park 9

Dalseong Park, one of the oldest parks in Korea, is where Dalgubeol, an ancient tribal nation which thrived in the region, constructed a clay fortress called 'Dalseong'.
Lush carpets of grasss, flowers of all colors, and elm, zelkova, fringe and other trees adorn the landscape of the park.
The park' s zoo is the most popular attraction, while other attractions include statues of historic figures hailing from Daegu, poem tablet monuments, the Gwanpungnu (the front gate) of the provincial governor' s building (Gyeongsang Gamyeong), and a cultural center.

DURYU PARK

Daegu Culture and Arts Center 10

Opened in 1991 as Daegu's cultural center, the Daegu Culture and Arts Center has modern performance halls, exhibition halls, and an outdoor performance stage, which host a variety of performances and exhibitions year round.

Daegu Culture and Arts Center

Daegu Tourist Information Center

Information Hall

Daegu Tourist Information Center 11

The Daegu Tourist Information Center is located in Duryu Park. This center provides tourist information on Daegu and adjacent tourist attractions, including Gyeongju, Andong and Hapcheon.
Interpretation services are offered and airplane and train tickets can be booked here. Additionally, tourists can make reservations for city bus tours departing from the center.
The center has a tourist information room, archive room, video room, and a souvenir shop. A lounge and Sarangbang allow tourists a chance to relax.

· Tourist Information Room

The tourist information room introduces Daegu's history, culture, festivals, and tourist attractions. Interpreters provide tourist information services for foreign visitors.

· Archive Room

The archive room has 800 domestic and foreign tourist guidebooks as well as computers connected to the Internet for those searching for tourist information.

· Video Room

The video room, which holds 102 seats, screens PR films on the history, culture and tourist attractions of Daegu City and Gyeongsangbuk-do.

· Daegu City Tour Bus Information

Frequency: 4 times a week
(Tue., Thurs., Sat. & Sun.)

Tour length:
One day: 7 hours
Half day: 4 hours

Types of tours: 7 regular tours and 1 special tour (for foreign tourists)

Reservations: 82-53-627-8900

Tour Route:

One day: Daegu Confucian School – Daegu National Museum – Gyeongju Choi's Head Family House – Donghwasa Temple – Daegu Tourist Information Center
Half day : Yangnyeongsi Exhibition Hall – Nat'l Debt Redemption Memorial Park – Seomun Market – Daegu Tourist Information Center

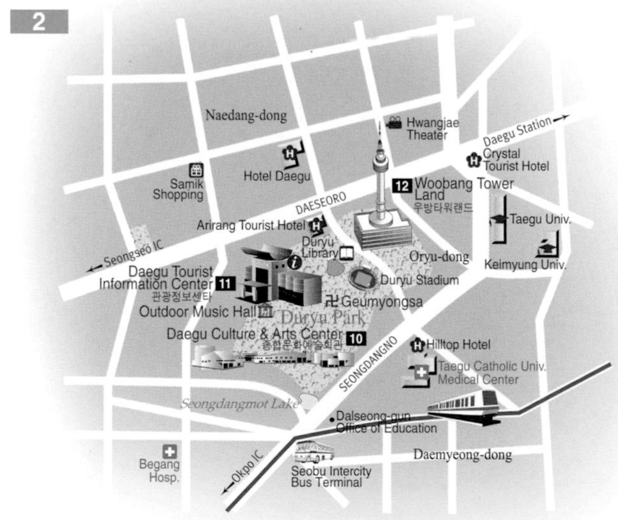

Woobang Tower Land 12

Woobang Tower Land is a theme park with one of Daegu' s major landmarks, Daegu Tower, standing at its center. Woobang Tower Land has over 30 amusement rides and a cable car ride, all integrated into a lush forest setting. The 202m high octagonal Daegu Tower, which is Korea's tallest, was designed after the Dabotap (Pagoda) of the Silla Kingdom. It houses an observation deck, a science hall, a small performance hall, among other features. The night view from the observation deck is especially impressive.

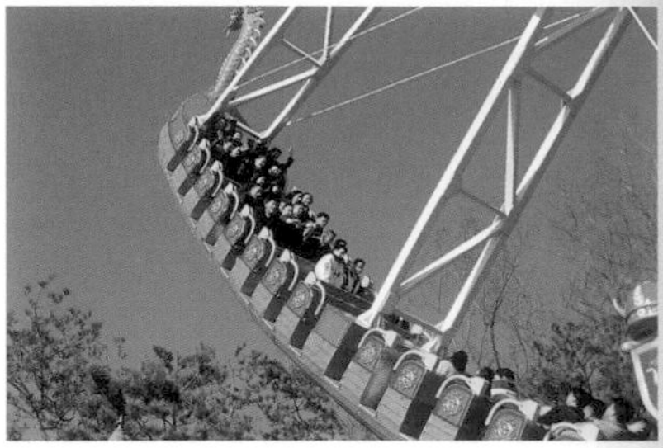

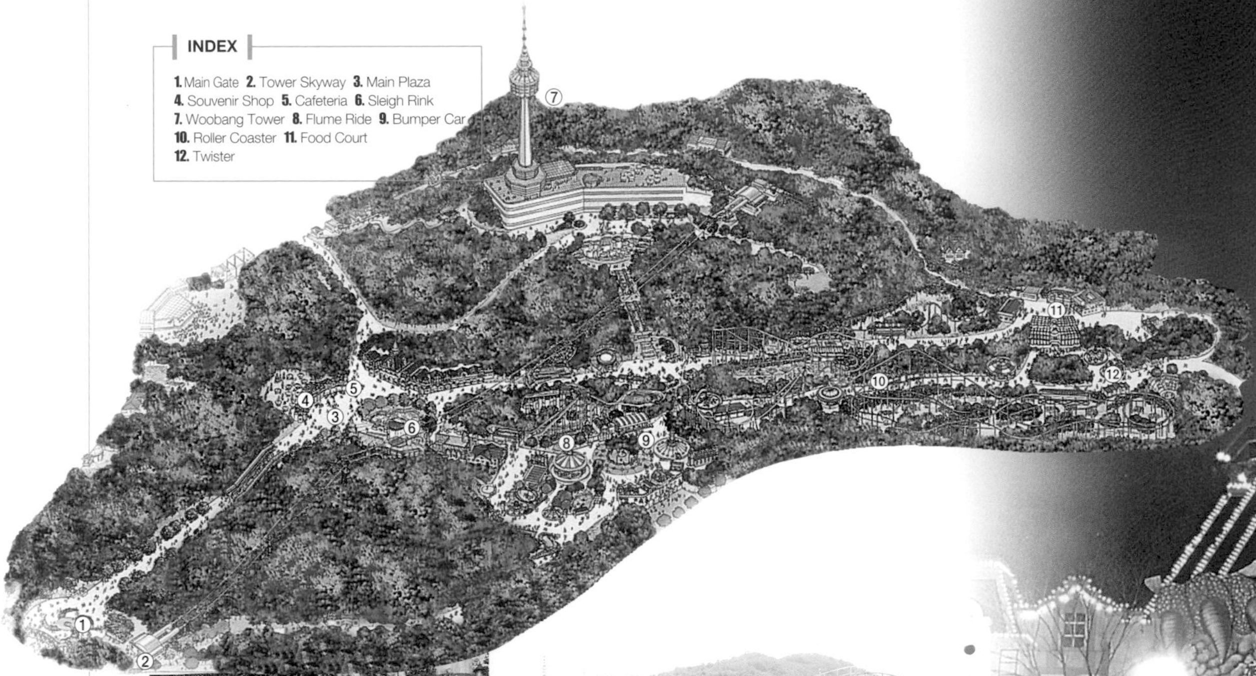

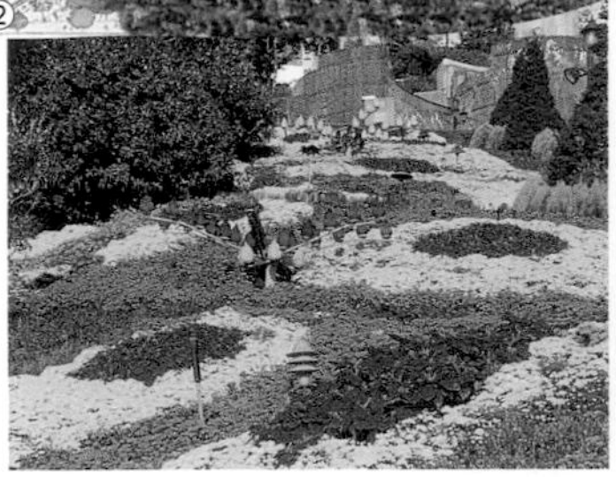

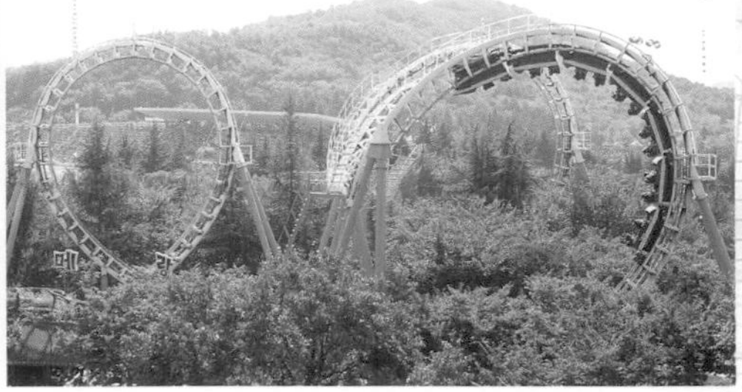

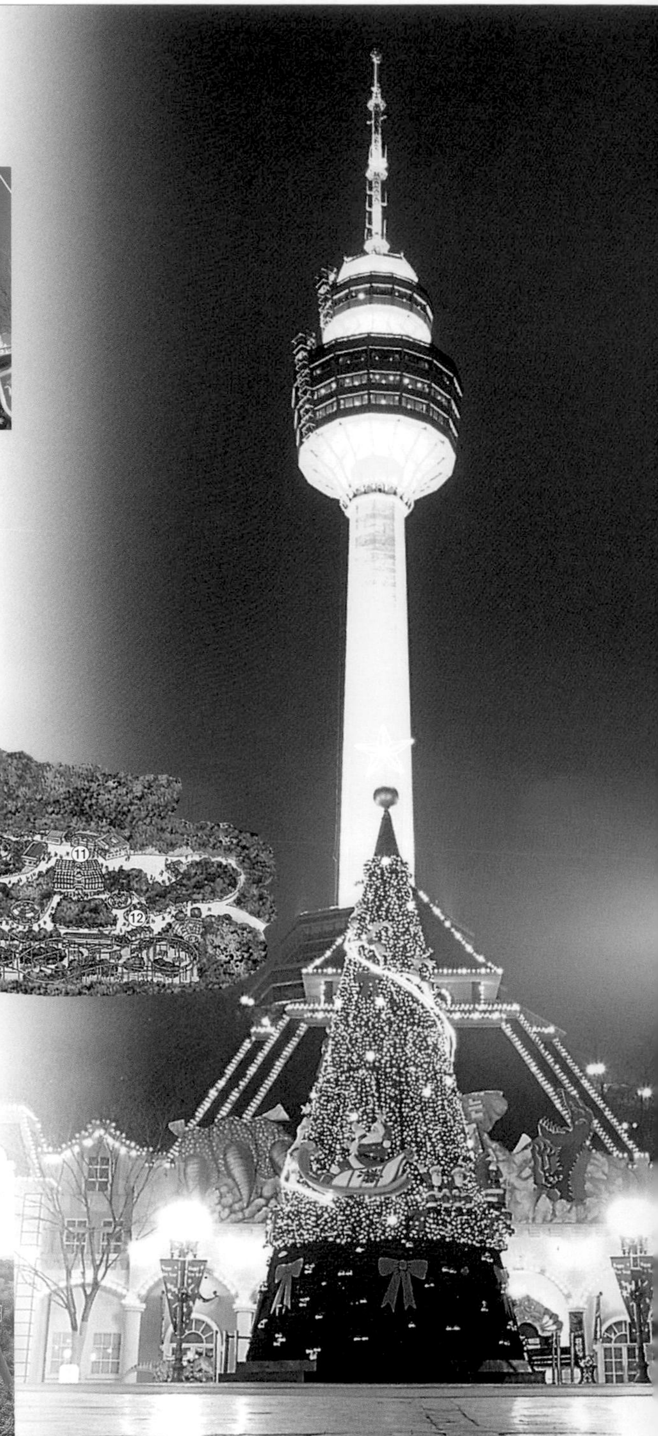

INDEX

1. Main Gate **2.** Tower Skyway **3.** Main Plaza
4. Souvenir Shop **5.** Cafeteria **6.** Sleigh Rink
7. Woobang Tower **8.** Flume Ride **9.** Bumper Car
10. Roller Coaster **11.** Food Court
12. Twister

Tower in Duryu Park

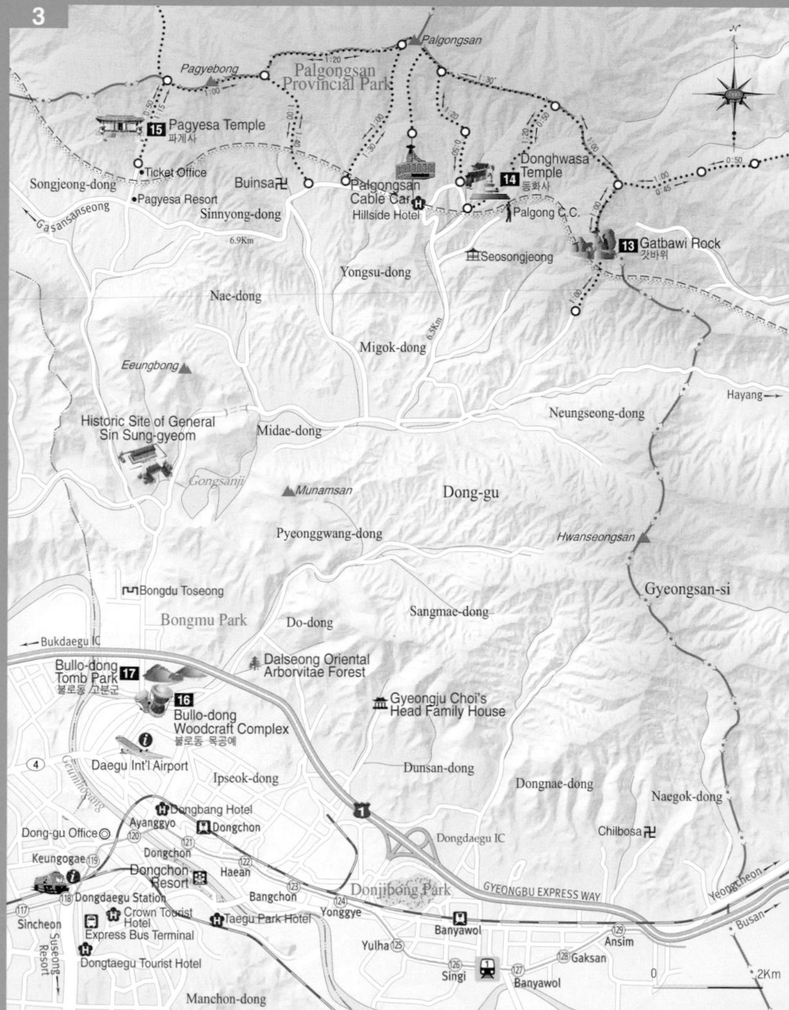

Mt. Palgongsan, rising 1,192m above sea level, has been considered sacred from ancient times and is an important Buddhist site due to its many temples, Buddhist statues, pagodas and Buddhist images. Palgongsan Skyline cable cars carry passengers from Donghwasa Temple to the 820m-high peak. The trail from Donghwasa to Sutaegol Valley is popular with hikers.

Cable Cars on Mt. Palgongsan

Gatbawi

Gatbawi Rock 13

Gatbawi is a huge Buddha sitting on 850m Gwanbong peak and is representative of Silla Kingdom art.

The official name of the four-meter tall statue is Gwanbong Seokjo Yeorae Jwasang (Gwanbong Sitting Stone Buddha). It is also called Gatbawi ('Gat' is a traditional Korean hat and 'bawi' means 'rock') because the statue has a 15cm-thick hat-like flat stone on its head. Many people visit Gatbawi believing that their prayers are answered when they pray before this Buddha.

Donghwasa Temple, Mt. Palgongsan

Donghwasa Temple 14

Donghwasa was constructed in 493. Its main worship hall, Daeungjeon, has pillars made of a naturally twisted tree. The Tongil Yaksayeorae (Great Pharmaceutical Stone Buddha for Unification) measures 33m in height and 16.5m in circumference and symbolizes a longing for national unification.

Donghwasa also holds such national treasures as Maaebul Jwasang, a seated rock-relief Buddha (Treasure No. 243), Birojanabul jwasang, a seated stone Vairocana Buddha (Treasure No. 244), and a three-storied pagoda (Treasure No. 247).

Tongil Yaksayeorae (Great Pharmaceutical Stone Buddha for Unification)

Wontongjeon, Main Worship Hall of Pagyesa

Woodcraft Shop in Bullo-dong

Pagyesa Temple 15

Pagyesa, a temple situated at Mt. Palgongsan, was established in 804, during the reign of King Aejang of the Silla Kingdom. The temple is surrounded by lush forests and crystal-clear streams, offering a perfect place for prayer and meditation.
Four structures, Wontongjeon, Jindongnu Tower, Seolseondang and Jeongmukdang, are arranged to form a square. In Wontongjeon sits Mokgwaneumbosal Jwasang, a seated wooden Avalokitesvara Bodhisattva (Treasure No. 992).

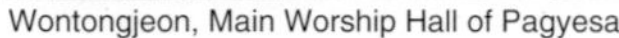

Mokgwaneumbosal Jwasang

Bullo-dong Woodcraft Complex 16

Bullo-dong Woodcraft Complex contains more than 70 woodcraft shops. Most of the woodcrafts are handmade and feature distinctive artistry. The woodcrafts produced here are supplied to every corner of Korea and some are exported.
The different types of woodcrafts produced here include blocks (which are struck by monks creating the distintive woodblock sound heard in temples throughout Korea), Buddhist rosaries, tea tables, side tables, bowls, wares used for ancestor memorial services, and mortuary tablets.

Bullo-dong Tomb Park 17

In the hills of Bullo-dong, there are more than 200 ancient burial sites dating back to around the 5th or 6th century in the Three Kingdoms period. These tombs were constructed by piling stones and then topping them with a large flat capstone. The tombs have small stone chambers from which gold and gold plated copper accessories, iron weapons and earthenware have been excavated.

Bullo-dong Tomb Park

Mt. BISEULSAN AREA

4

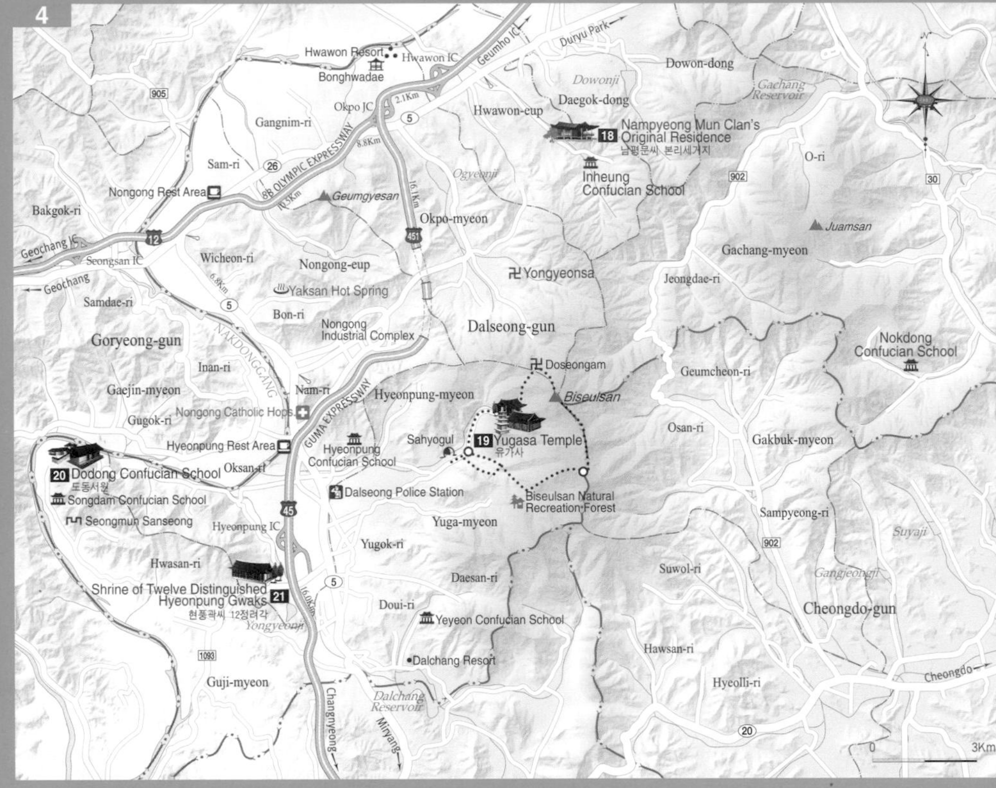

Mountain Reeds on Mt. Biseulsan

Biseulsan mountain is in the area bordering Dalseong-gun and Cheongdo-gun. The main peak, Daegyeonbong (1,083.58m) is at the center, and two peaks, Johwabong (1,058m) and Gwangibong (990m), are within easy hiking distance. The beauty of nature reaches its peak in the spring when royal azaleas embroider the mountain and in the fall when a multitude of eulalias cover the mountain. There are a number of hermitages and temples on the mountain, including Yugasa Temple, Yongmunsa Temple, Sojaesa Temple and Yongyeonsa Temple.

Nampyeong Mun Clan's Original Residence 18

Nampyeong Mun Clan' s Original Residence

Located in Bon-ri, this collective settlement of the Nampyeong Mun clan was founded by Mun Gyeong-ho, an 18th generation descendent of Mun Ik-jeom (pen name - Samudang), one of the royal literati of the Goryeo Dynasty. In the complex are nine traditional gentry houses and two pavilions, featuring the architecture of the late Joseon Dynasty. In order to build the complex, Mun Gyeong-ho arranged the land in accordance with Jeongjeonbeop (ancient regulations for land usage) and constructed roads before building the houses. This residence area remains almost intact, allowing visitors to learn about the style of traditional villages. Representative buildings in the complex are Subongjeongsa, Gwanggeodang and Insumungo. Standing at the entrance of the village, Subongjeongsa Pavilion is where the Mun clan received guests or held meetings. Gwanggeodang is a lecture hall which was used as a children's school. Insumungo was the clan' s library, with more than 10,000 old books, including those listed in the Gyujanggak (the central library of the Joseon Dynasty).

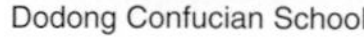
Dodong Confucian School

Roofs with the Yin and Yang Precepts

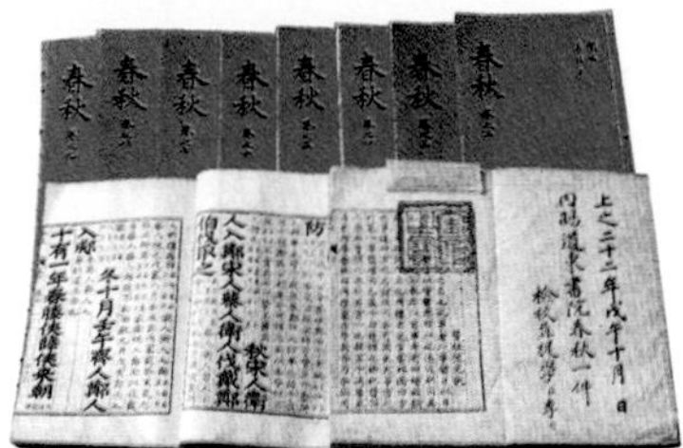
Chunchu at the Dodong Confucian School

Yugasa Temple 19

Deep in the valley of Biseulsan, Yugasa is said to have been established by teacher monk Doseonguksa in the 2nd year (827) of the reign of King Heungdeok.
The temple is a perfect setting for meditation since it is located deep in the mountains and visited by few people.
Behind the temple, mountain peaks of different colors unfold like a traditional painted screen (Byeongpung).

Dodong Confucian School 20

The Dodong Confucian School commands a panoramic view, with a river that runs in front of it and a mountain behind it. The school is historically significant since it enshrines the great teacher Kim Goeng-pil (pen name - Hanhwondang), one of the five great sages of the Joseon Dynasty.
The roof is decorated with female-shaped roof tiles and male-shaped roof ends, which were layered alternately based on the yin and yang precepts.

Shrine of Tweleve Distinguished Hyeonpung Gwaks 21

This building holds the Jeongnyeo citations given to 12 members of the Hyeonpung Gwak clan during the period between the 31st year (1598) of the reign of King Seonjo and the reign of King Yeongjo.
Jeongnyeo was an honor awarded for exemplary deeds, such as extraordinary loyalty, filial piety or faithfulness to one's husband. It was extremely rare for one clan to receive as many as 12 Jeongnyeo.

Daeungjeon in Yugasa

Shrine of Tweleve Distinguished Hyeonpung Gwaks

Daegu National Museum H5

In Daegu National Museum, many cultural assets of Daegu and Gyeongsangbuk-do are on display.
About 1,300 historical relics of the Gyeongsang-do region are displayed, in the Archeology Hall Art Works Hall and in the Folklore Hall, in chronological order. The Folklore Hall features replicas of houses and representations of the lifestyle and religion of the region. In the Art Work Hall, Buddhist art works, including Buddhist images and traditional bells, as well as ceramics of the Goryeo and Joseon Dynasty, are displayed. Artifacts excavated throughout the Gyeongsang-do region are also displayed here.

Daegu National Museum Display

Daegu National Museum

Standing Gilt-bronze Bodhisattva (National Treasure No. 183)

Daegu World Cup Stadium J6

Daegu World Cup Stadium

As one of the host stadiums for the 2002 World Cup Games, the Daegu World Cup Stadium has about 66,000 seats and occupies $512,479m^2$. 74% of the seats in the stadium are covered.
The architectural concept of the stadium aims to bring together people from all over the world under the stadium' s roof. The stadium's design reflects the area's mountainous topography and draws from the linear beauty of traditional houses. After the World Cup Games, the stadium will be transformed into a theme park complex.
www.2002worldcupkorea.org
www.worldcup.daegu.kr

Gwangju

Located in the southwestern corner of the Korean Peninsula, Gwangju is Korea's fifth largest city and has a population of 1.3 million. Gwangju has long been well known for its beautiful landscape and warm-hearted people. Gwangju is sometimes called 'Ye-Hyang,' which means a city of arts and culture. The Gwangju Biennale, a festival of international arts and exhibitions, is held here as a testament to the area's artistic heritage.

Soswaewon

Soswaewon is a famed traditional garden. It served as a hermitage for the scholar Yang San-bo in the Joseon Dynasty, after he retired from his government post. The garden represents the sentiment of the Joseon people who found contentment in poverty and delight in the Taoist way.

Chwigajeong

The name Chwigajeong, the Pavillion of a Poem of Drunkenness, originated from the poem, Chwiga, which Gwon Pil wrote after he saw a drunken General Kim Deok-ryeong in his dream. General Kim had previously been killed on unjust grounds.

Gasa Literature

Lyric Literature of the Joseon Dynasty

Gwangju has long been acclaimed for its natural setting. Gwangjuho Lake, at the foot of Mt. Mudeungsan, was a popular site for celebrated poets in the Joseon Dynasty, who immersed themselves in the beauty and tranquility of nature as inspiration for their poetic creations. The pavilions around the lake were the birthplace of the 'Gasa ' literary style which flourished around that time. It reflected the spiritual deliberations of intellectuals. Song Sun's 'Myeonangjeongga,' and Jeong Cheol's 'Seongsanbyeolgok' and 'Samiingok,' the representative poetry of 16th century Korea, originated in the Gwangju area.

The philosophical background of this literature was Taoism, the nature-based philosophy which seeks an accord between human beings and nature. Full appreciation and enjoyment of nature were poignantly expressed in the literature of the time, which eventually exerted a great influence upon ensuing Korean literature.

Sigyeongjeong

Sigyeongjeong, called the pavillion where even the shadow can rest, is located on top of a hill overlooking Mt. Mudeungsan. The pavilion was built next to the Seohadang building in 1560. At the entrance stands a monument inscribed with the 'Seongsanbyeolgok' poem.

Doksujeong

Doksujeong is the place where Jeon Sin-min retired from his political career at the end of the Goryeo Dynasty. The pavilion is surrounded with red pine trees and a variety of plants, like roses, maehwa (a kind of an apricot tree) and ginkgo trees.

Myeonangjeong

Surrounded by thick woods, Myeonangjeong is a perfect place for philosophical meditation. Although the architecture itself is simple, the pavilion is preserved for its historical significance.

Songgangjeong

Songgangjeong is in a thick pine forest on a hill past the Gwangju dam and Goseo Interchange. In this pavilion Jeong wrote the famed poems 'Samiingok' and 'Songmiingok'. Beside the pavilion is a monument inscribed with the 'Samiingok' poem.

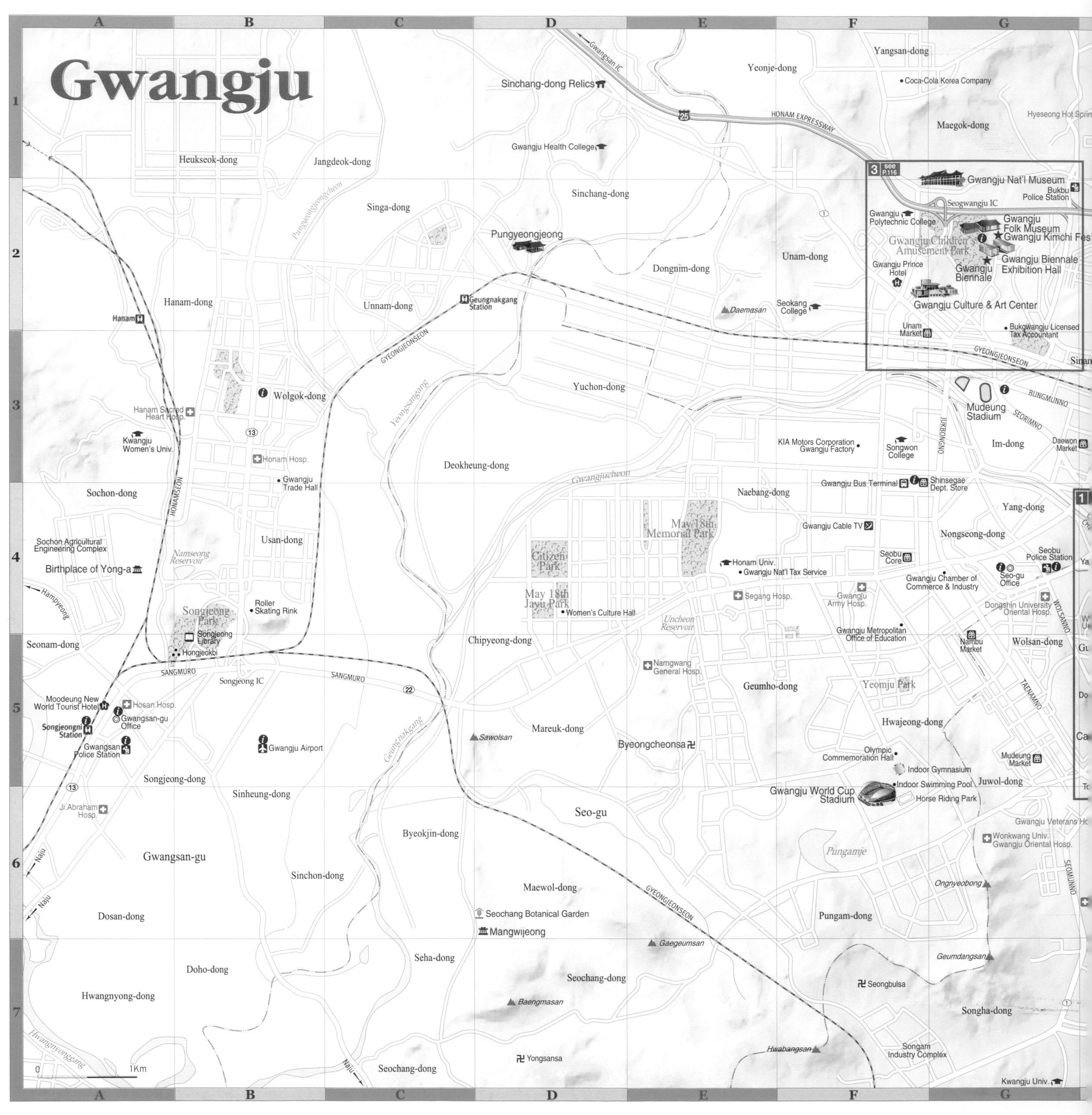

Gwangju
A
B
C
D
E
F
G
1
2
3
4
5
6
7
Sinchang-dong Relics
Gwangsan IC
25
HONAM EXPRESSWAY
Yeonje-dong
Yangsan-dong
Coca-Cola Korea Company
Hyeseong Hot Sprin
Maegok-dong
Heukseok-dong
Jangdeok-dong
Gwangju Health College
Pungyeongjeongcheon
Singa-dong
Sinchang-dong
3 see P.116
Gwangju Nat'l Museum
Bukbu Police Station
Seogwangju IC
Gwangju Polytechnic College
Gwangju Folk Museum
Gwangju Kimchi Fes
Gwangju Children's Amusement Park
Gwangju Prince Hotel
Gwangju Biennale
Gwangju Biennale Exhibition Hall
Gwangju Culture & Art Center
Unam Market
Bukgwangju Licensed Tax Accountant
GYEONGJEONSEON
Sinan
Pungyeongjeong
Dongnim-dong
Unam-dong
Hanam-dong
Hanam
Unnam-dong
Geungnakgang Station
Daemasan
Seokang College
GYEONGJEONSEON
Yeongsangang
Wolgok-dong
Yuchon-dong
Hanam Sacred Heart Hosp.
13
Kwangju Women's Univ.
Honam Hosp.
Gwangju Trade Hall
Deokheung-dong
Mudeung Stadium
BUNGMUNNO
SEORIMNO
JUKBONGNO
Im-dong
Daewon Market
KIA Motors Corporation Gwangju Factory
Songwon College
Gwangjucheon
Gwangju Bus Terminal
Shinsegae Dept. Store
Sochon-dong
HONAMSEON
Naebang-dong
Yang-dong
May 18th Memorial Park
Gwangju Cable TV
Nongseong-dong
Sochon Agricultural Engineering Complex
Namseong Reservoir
Usan-dong
Citizen Park
Seobu Core
Seobu Police Station
Birthplace of Yong-a
Honam Univ.
Gwangju Nat'l Tax Service
Gwangju Chamber of Commerce & Industry
Seo-gu Office
Hampyeong
May 18th Jayu Park
Women's Culture Hall
Segang Hosp.
Gwangju Army Hosp.
Dongshin University Oriental Hosp.
WOLSANNO
Songjeong Park
Roller Skating Rink
Uncheon Reservoir
Songjeong Library
Hongjeokbi
Chipyeong-dong
Gwangju Metropolitan Office of Education
Nambu Market
Wolsan-dong
Seonam-dong
SANGMURO
Songjeong IC
SANGMURO
22
Namgwang General Hosp.
Geumho-dong
Yeomju Park
TAENAMNO
Moodeung New World Tourist Hotel
Hosan Hosp.
Gwangsan-gu Office
Songjeongni Station
Geungnakgang
Mareuk-dong
Hwajeong-dong
Sawolsan
Gwangsan Police Station
Gwangju Airport
Byeongcheonsa
Olympic Commemoration Hall
Mudeung Market
Indoor Gymnasium
Songjeong-dong
Sinheung-dong
Indoor Swimming Pool
Juwol-dong
Gwangju World Cup Stadium
Horse Riding Park
Ji.Abraham Hosp.
Seo-gu
Gwangju Veterans Ho
Byeokjin-dong
Wonkwang Univ. Gwangju Oriental Hosp.
Pungamje
Naju
Gwangsan-gu
Sinchon-dong
Ongnyeobong
SEOMUNNO
Maewol-dong
GYEONGJEONSEON
Naju
Dosan-dong
Seochang Botanical Garden
Mangwijeong
Pungam-dong
Gaegeumsan
Doho-dong
Seha-dong
Gumdangsan
Seochang-dong
Seongbulsa
Hwangnyong-dong
Baengmasan
Songha-dong
Hwangnyonggang
Hwabangsan
Songam Industry Complex
0
1Km
Naju
Yongsansa
Seochang-dong
Kwangju Univ.

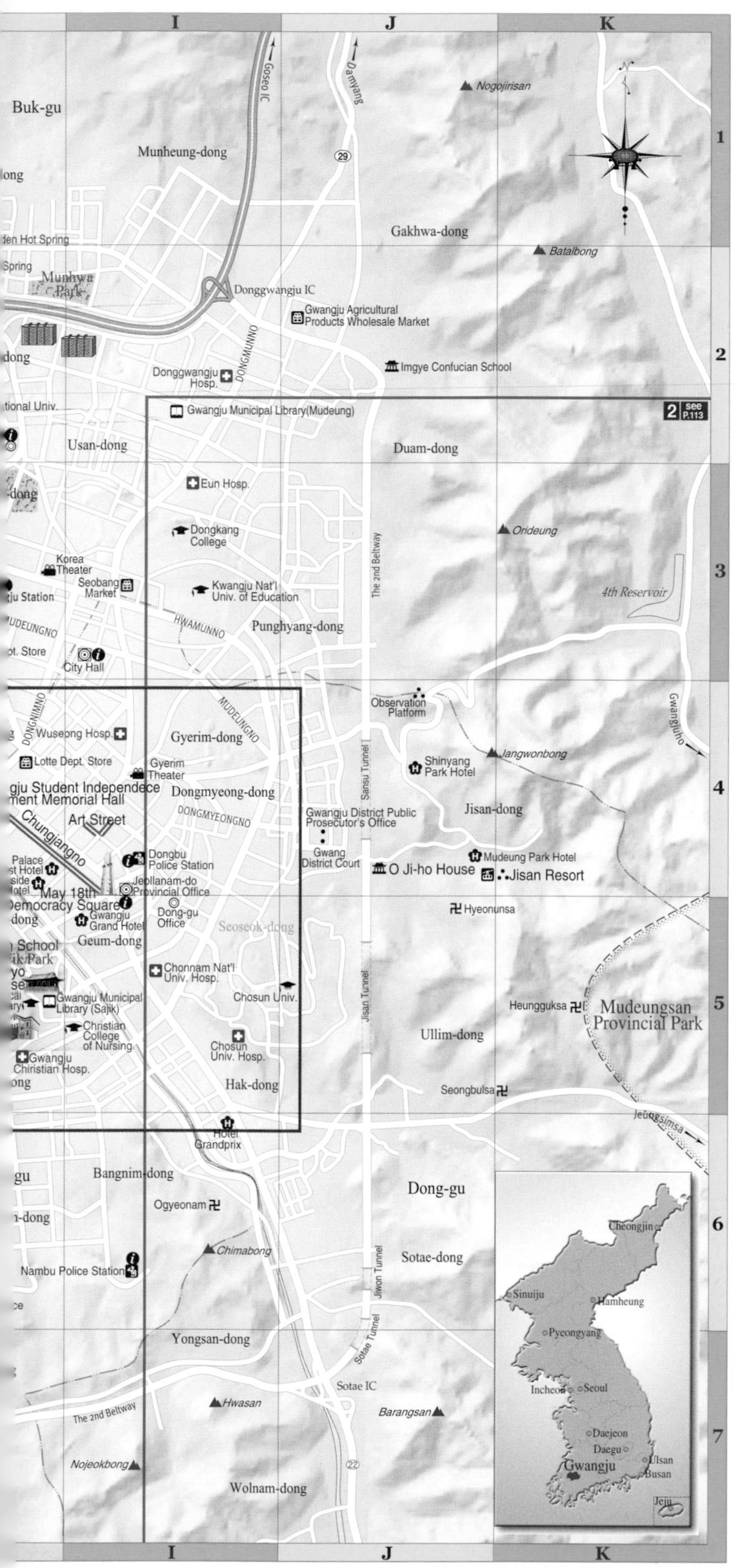

INDEX

Tourist Information

Gwangju Dept. of Tourism 82-62-225-0101
Gwangju Tourist Information Center 82-62-525-9370
www.metro.gwangju.kr

LEGEND

- Railroad Station
- Airport
- Bus Terminal
- Cable Car Platform
- Hospital
- Police Station
- Post Office
- Tourist Information Center
- University or School
- Library
- Broadcasting Station
- Prehistoric Relic Site
- Temple
- Traditional Building
- Cultural Experience Area
- Movie Theater
- Hot Spring or Spa
- Park
- Amusement Park
- Botanical Garden
- Mountain
- Other Tourist Attractions
- Hotel
- Department Store or Market
- Reference Point

CENTRAL GWANGJU

1

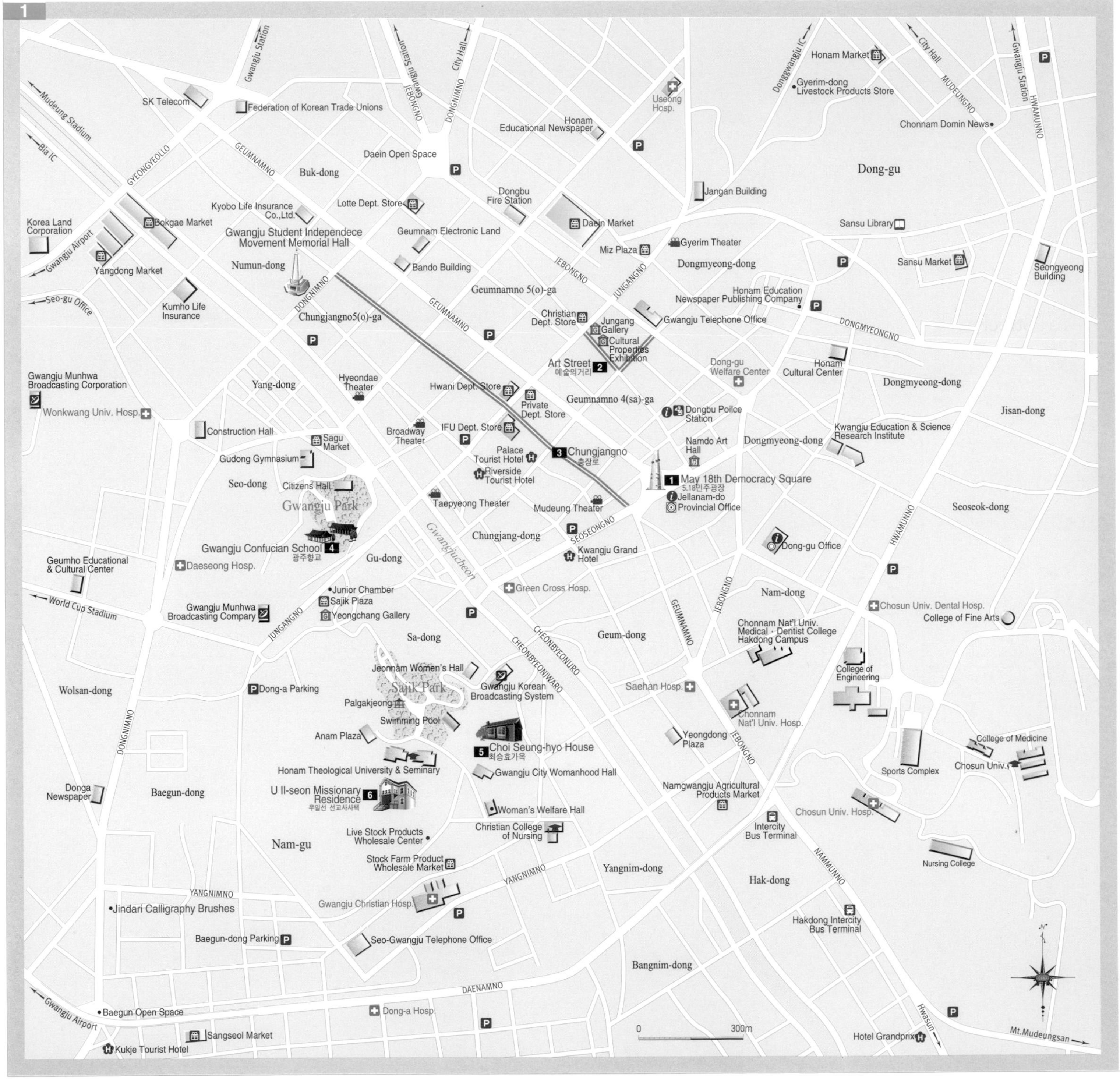

Gwangju Station
Jebongno
City Hall
Dongnimno
Dongggwangju IC
Honam Market
City Hall
Gwangju Station
Hwamunno
Mudeungno
Mudeung Stadium
Bia IC
SK Telecom
Federation of Korean Trade Unions
Useong Hosp.
Gyerim-dong Livestock Products Store
Honam Educational Newspaper
Chonnam Domin News
Gyeongyeollo
Geumnamno
Daein Open Space
Buk-dong
Dong-gu
Dongbu Fire Station
Lotte Dept. Store
Kyobo Life Insurance Co.,Ltd.
Jangan Building
Korea Land Corporation
Bokgae Market
Daein Market
Sansu Library
Gwangju Student Independece Movement Memorial Hall
Geumnam Electronic Land
Gwangju Airport
Gyerim Theater
Miz Plaza
Yangdong Market
Numun-dong
Bando Building
Jebongno
Jungangno
Dongmyeong-dong
Sansu Market
Seongyeong Building
Seo-gu Office
Kumho Life Insurance
Dongnimno
Geumnamno 5(o)-ga
Honam Education Newspaper Publishing Company
Christian Dept. Store
Jungang Gallery
Gwangju Telephone Office
Chungjangno5(o)-ga
Geumnamno
Dongmyeongno
Cultural Properties Exhibition
Art Street 2
예술의거리
Dong-gu Welfare Center
Honam Cultural Center
Gwangju Munhwa Broadcasting Corporation
Yang-dong
Hyeondae Theater
Hwani Dept. Store
Private Dept. Store
Geumnamno 4(sa)-ga
Dongmyeong-dong
Wonkwang Univ. Hosp.
Dongbu Poilce Station
Jisan-dong
Kwangju Education & Science Research Institute
Construction Hall
Broadway Theater
IFU Dept. Store
Sagu Market
Namdo Art Hall
Dongmyeong-dong
Gudong Gymnasium
Palace Tourist Hotel
3 Chungjangno
충장로
Riverside Tourist Hotel
1 May 18th Democracy Square
5.18민주광장
Seo-dong
Citizens Hall
Jellanam-do Provincial Office
Gwangju Park
Taepyeong Theater
Mudeung Theater
Seoseok-dong
Gwangjucheon
Seoseongno
Chungjang-dong
Hwamunno
Gwangju Confucian School 4
광주향교
Dong-gu Office
Kwangju Grand Hotel
Geumho Educational & Cultural Center
Daeseong Hosp.
Gu-dong
Green Cross Hosp.
Nam-dong
Junior Chamber
World Cup Stadium
Gwangju Munhwa Broadcasting Company
Sajik Plaza
Yeongchang Gallery
Chosun Univ. Dental Hosp.
College of Fine Arts
Jungangno
Sa-dong
Cheonbyeonuro
Geum-dong
Geumnamno
Jebongno
Chonnam Nat'l Univ. Medical · Dentist College Hakdong Campus
Cheonbyeonjwaro
Jeonnam Women's Hall
Wolsan-dong
Dong-a Parking
Sajik Park
Gwangju Korean Broadcasting System
Saehan Hosp.
College of Engineering
Palgakjeong
Swimming Pool
Chonnam Nat'l Univ. Hosp.
Anam Plaza
Choi Seung-hyo House 5
최승효가옥
Yeongdong Plaza
Jebongno
College of Medicine
Dongnimno
Honam Theological University & Seminary
Gwangju City Womanhood Hall
Sports Complex
Chosun Univ.
Donga Newspaper
Baegun-dong
U Il-seon Missionary Residence 6
우일선 선교사사택
Namgwangju Agricultural Products Market
Woman's Welfare Hall
Chosun Univ. Hosp.
Christian College of Nursing
Live Stock Products Wholesale Center
Intercity Bus Terminal
Nam-gu
Nursing College
Stock Farm Product Wholesale Market
Yangnim-dong
Nammunno
Yangnimno
Hak-dong
Yangnimno
Jindari Calligraphy Brushes
Gwangju Christian Hosp.
Hakdong Intercity Bus Terminal
Baegun-dong Parking
Seo-Gwangju Telephone Office
Bangnim-dong
Daenamno
Gwangju Airport
Baegun Open Space
Dong-a Hosp.
Hwasun
0 300m
Hotel Grandprix
Sangseol Market
Mt.Mudeungsan
Kukje Tourist Hotel
N

May 18th Democracy Square 1

The May 18th Democracy Square is in front of the Jeollanam-do provincial office. The square, which has been the venue of historic movements for independence and democracy, such as the March 1st Independence Movement, the Gwangju Students' Independence Movement, the April 19th Democratic Movement and the May 18th Democratic Movement, symbolizes a spirit of democracy and independence.

Art Street 2

Art Street is a cornucopia of galleries, exhibition halls, art schools, and art shops. All genres of art, from the old to the contemporary, are exhibited and sold here. On weekends there is an open air antique market near Art Street where one can find

Antique Shop on Art Street

antique paintings, sculpture, jewelry, books and household wares.

Chungjangno 3

Chungjangno is a street that is crowded with department stores, shops and restaurants. Much like Myeong-dong in Seoul in its display of new fashion trends, Chungjangno is also permeated with the traditional touches of the Gwangju area. It is bustling seven days a week with Gwangju's youth.

Chungjangno, Gwangju's Main Shopping Street

May 18th Democracy Square

Gwangju Confucian School

Choi Seung-hyo House

U Il-seon Missionary Residence

Gwangju Confucian School 4

The Gwangju Confucian School consists of a group of typical Korean tile-roofed houses. It is one of the national schools built during the Goryeo and Joseon Dynasties to teach the principles of Confucianism. The school consists of the Myeongnyundang, Dongseomu, Dongseojae, Nae/oesammun and Bigak. Currently, the Confucian school no longer serves as an educational institute, but it is still a shrine to Confucius and contains a library of Confucian teachings and literature, providing a rich resource for research of local history. It is often also used for traditional weddings.

Choi Seung-hyo House 5

Originally the home of Choi Sang-hyeon, an independence fighter against Japanese colonialism, the Choi Seung-hyo House is a typical traditional house in a straight-line design. Standing on a slope, the house is unique in that it is half underground. All of its rooms have lofts, in which independence fighters took refuge from the Japanese police. The house showcases the design of traditional Korean houses in the 1920s.

U Il-seon Missionary Residence 6

The U Il-seon Missionary Residence was built by an American missionary named Wilson in the 1920s. Located at the foot of Mt. Yangnimsan, it is the oldest western-style house in Gwangju. Built of gray bricks in the Dutch style, the house has a living room, a family room, a storage room, a kitchen and a bathroom on the first floor, a cellar and boiler storage underground, and bedrooms on the second floor.

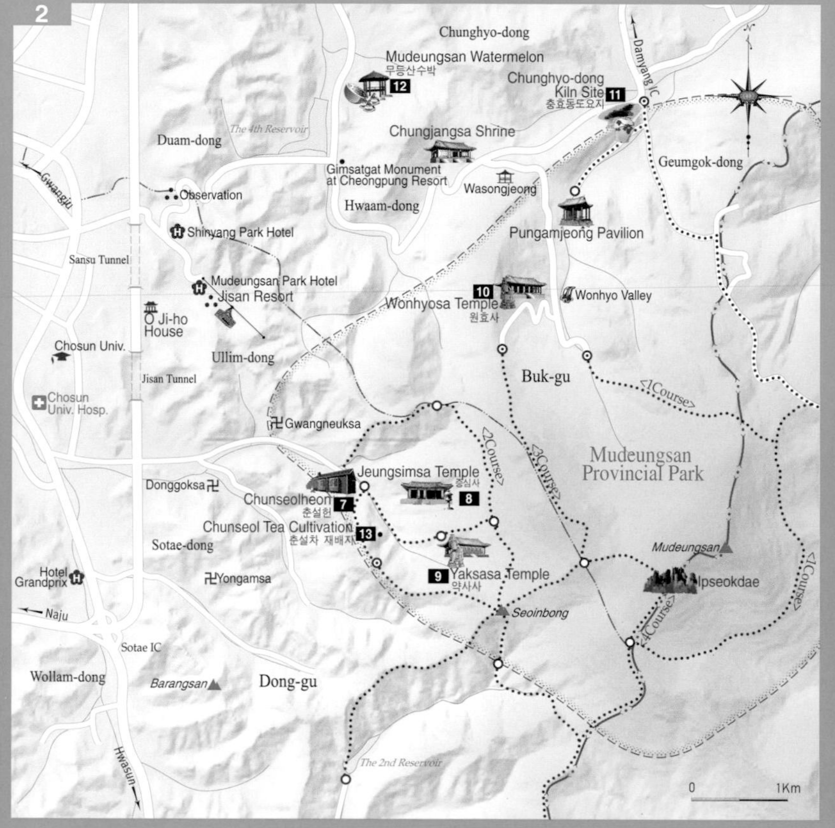

Mt. Mudeungsan is a spiritual symbol of the Gwangju region, a cradle of southern culture and an excellent place to retreat into nature. Majestically rising 1,187 meters above sea level, the mountain boasts spectacular scenery and imposing rock formations. At the foot of the mountain there are Buddhist temples: Jeungsimsa, Wonhyosa, Yaksaam and Gyubongam. On the northern side of the mountain, there are various pavilions; Hwanbyeokdang, Sigyeongjeong and Soswaewon, where scholars in the olden times wrote lyrical literature and polished their scholarly skills. The great artist Heo Baek-ryeon brought his artistic genius to this mountain, in addition to using his time for teaching students.

Chunseolheon Gallery & Tea House

Chunseolheon 7

Chunseolheon refers to the gallery and house where the great painter Heo Baek-ryeon lived and worked from 1946 until 1977. A descendant of Heo Ryeon, the master of Korean Namjonghwa painting in the late Joseon Dynasty, Heo Baek-ryeon devoted himself to traditional Korean painting and educating others on the subject. He also built the Samae School to foster leaders in the field of agriculture, and grew and distributed Chunseol green tea from Chunseol Dawon on Mt. Mudeungsan. In 1950 the house was renovated to its present condition.

Daeungjeon in Jeungsimsa (left)
Wonhyosa (below)

Obaekjeon in Jeungsimsa

Jeungsimsa Temple 8

Jeungsimsa, built in 860 during the Silla Kingdom era by the Buddhist monk Cheolgamseonsa, is the prominent Buddhist seminary of the region. Obaekjeon at Jeungsimsa is the oldest of all of the temples on Mt. Mudeungsan. Obaekjeon houses various valuable treasures, such as a golden statue of Buddha, a representation of the 500 Arhans who collected Buddha's teachings to fashion them into a scripture, and representations of Buddha's 10 disciples. Other valuable cultural treasures of Jeunsimsa include the Seated Iron Vairocana Buddha (Treasure No. 131) in Birojeon (or Saseongjeon), a three-storied stone pagoda from the late Silla Kingdom, the Pavilion of the Buddhist Bell, and a seven-tiered stone pagoda with the Chinese character for 'beom' inscribed on all sides of it.

Seokjo Yeorae Jwasang in Yaksasa
(Treasure No. 600)

Yaksasa Temple 9

Yaksasa was built by Cheolgamseonsa before Jeungsimsa. The treasures it holds include Seokjo Yeorae Jwasang (the Seated Granite Buddha, National Treasure No. 600) and a three-storied stone pagoda which dates back to the first half of the 9th century.

Wonhyosa Temple 10

Located on the northern slope of Mt. Mudeungsan, Wonhyosa was built by the Buddhist monk Wonhyo during the Silla Kingdom. It houses such valuable cultural treasures as the Wonhyosa Dongbudo (East Sarinar Stupa) and the Mansusa Buddhist Bell. The Wonhyosa Dongbudo represents the most outstanding sculptural technique of all existing sarina stupas in Korea, and its humorous animal sculptures on all four sides add a unique element to it.
Various treasures were excavated during the renovation of the main temple in May 1980, such as the standing copper Buddha, a copper mirror, and various little Buddhas (over 100 pieces). These items date over a wide span of time, from the late United Silla to the Joseon Dynasty, signifying the ancient history of the Wonhyosa.

Chunghyo-dong Doyoji Museum

Chunseol Tea Plants on Mt. Mudeungsan

Mudeungsan Watermelon

Celadon Artist at Work

Chunghyo-dong Doyoji 11

Chunghyo-dong Doyoji refers to the extensive porcelain kilns throughout the valley to the north of Mt. Mudeungsan. Excavations in the area found such artifacts as porcelain, waste from kilns, pottery tools and broken kilns between the sediment layers. Most of the excavated articles were Buncheong ware, white porcelain and a few pieces of blue porcelain.

This kiln site, which was in operation from the late Goryeo to the early Joseon Dynasty, is a significant historic relic that marks the passage from the late Goryeo's blue celadon to Buncheong ware to Joseon's white porcelain. The secret of the Goryeo Celadon's mysterious colors was once lost due to the passage of time until the renowned celadon artist Jo Gi-jeong, who is designated as Local Cultural Treasure No. 5, revived 90% of the crafts past quality. Mr. Jo runs the Mudeung Pottery Craft Studio in Yonsan-dong, Gwangsan-gu, which is dedicated to experimental pottery craft. Visitors are welcome to come and witness the methods used in making blue porcelain.

Buncheongsagi Maebyeong (right)
Buncheongsagi Janggunbyeong (left)

Mudeungsan Watermelon 12

The popularity of Mudeungsan mountain watermelon dates back to when it was presented to kings as a tribute. The melons are grown in the fertile soil formed by the mulch of fallen leaves in ideal conditions. Compared with other watermelons, Mudeungsan watermelons are dark green with no stripes and generally larger. They are normally 4 to 5kg in weight, but some grow to weigh as much as 30kg.

Chunseol tea 13

Chunseol tea was first grown and drunk by the great artist Heo Baek-ryeon (Uijae), the creator of the Namjonghwa paintings. It is made with leaves picked from late April to early May from tea plants grown at the 200m altitude of Mt. Mudeungsan. This area is subject to frequent mists and cloud cover, with substantial differences between the lows and highs of daily temperature. Fresh taste and gentle fragrance are typical of the tea. The Chunseol Tea Festival is held in the region every May.

JUNGWOE PARK

3

INDEX

1. Gwangju Art Museum **2.** Gwangju Culture & Art Center
3. Rainbow Bridge **4.** Jungwoe Park **5.** North Korean Hall
6. Education and PR Hall **7.** Yongbong Reservoir
8. Gwangju Kimchi Festival **9.** Gwangju Biennale Exhibition Hall

Jungwoe Park, located in the north of Gwangju, is near the access road to the West Gwangju highway.
The Park is a cultural area that serves as the venue for the Gwangju Biennale. One of its unique features is its North Korean Hall.
Many recreational facilities, such as the Children's Theme Park, the Olympic Park, the Olympic Monument, and the Rainbow Bridge, built for the first Biennale, are in the park. Gwangju National Museum, Gwangju Culture & Art Center, and Gwangju Folk Museum are also near the park.

Gwangju National Museum 14

The Gwangju National Museum is where one can trace the culture of the Jeolla region from prehistoric to contemporary times. Outside the museum are replicas of stone pagodas, dolmens, and Gangjin blue celadon kilns. The museum exhibits relics from the Chinese Sung and Won Dynasties. The relics were raised from the sea at Sinan.

Twin Lion Stone Lantern
(National Treasure No. 103)

Gwangju Folk Museum

Gwangju Folk Museum 15

The Gwangju Folk Museum features displays of folk life in the region, spanning the 2,000 years since the Mahan Age. Insights can be attained here into the daily lives, the agriculture and crafts, and the spiritual, social and cultural lives of the people traced from birth to death.

The Sipsinsaji Stone Pagoda (Local Tangible Cultural Asset No. 2) and Stone Monument (Local Tangible Cultural Asset No. 3) are exhibited in an outdoor exhibition space with stone folklore relics displayed around them.

Robes of General Jeong Ji (Treasure No. 336)

Spinning Wheel (left)
Funeral Bier (right)

Gwangju Biennale

Gwangju Biennale Exhibition Hall

Conceived as an international festival for contemporary art which contributes to the cultural enrichment of humankind, the Gwangju Biennale was launched in 1995 with the theme : 'Beyond the Borders,' which was followed by the second Biennale : 'Blank Space of the Earth,' and the third Biennale : 'Human + Beings.' As a voice of the global village, it made remarkable artistic achievements and emerged as a bona fide international artistic festival on equal footing with such noted festivals as the Venice Biennale and the San Paolo Biennale. Various exhibitions and cultural events seek to display trends in contemporary art during the biennale.

Emblem of the Gwangju Biennale

The official emblem of the Gwangju Biennale was designed with the motifs of Gwangju, the City of Light, as well as Mt. Mudeungsan and features of that mountain. The Korean logo reflects traditional woodblock printing that was used in the southern region during the late Joseon Dynasty. The English logo is Stone Sans typeset, which harmonizes with Korean characters.

Exhibits at the Gwangju Biennale

May 18th Memorial Park E4

The May 18 Memorial Park is the sanctuary of Korean democracy, where victims of the May 18 Democratic Movement lay in rest. Located in Unjeong-dong, Buk-gu, and with Mt. Mudeungsan as a backdrop, the cemetery contains the Gate of Democracy, the Gate of History, Sungmo Pavilion, and the Gate of Mourning. Annual rites of mourning are held on May 16, when various performances are held, starting with a symbolic road paving. This is followed by concerts, dances and a shaman ritual to console the victimized souls. This educational site and monument to democracy welcomes visitors all year.

5.18 Memorial Tower in the May 18 Memorial Park

Gwangju World Cup Stadium F6

Gwangju World Cup Stadium

The Gwangju World Cup Stadium was built exclusively for soccer, with a seating capacity of 42,000. Facilities at the stadium include a media center and advanced telecommunication and medical facilities. The concept of the stadium design is reflected in the roof, which is shaped in the image of Mt. Mudeungsan. The design of the entrance and the field, as well as the decorative arrangements of numerous objects, focus light within the circular stadium. This is especially fitting for a city with the nickname 'the City of Light.'

www.2002worldcupkorea.org
2002.gjcity.net

Gossaumnori in Chilseok-dong

Kimchi Making Contest for Foreigners

An Jong-seon, Maker of Jindari Calligraphy Brushes

The Gossaumnori

The Gossaumnori is a traditional folk performance of the southern region of Korea which takes place from January 10 through February 1 on the lunar calendar. Currently, it is held in Chilseok-dong, Nam-gu, in April. Designated as Important Intangible Cultural Properties No. 33, it received worldwide recognition when performed under the name of Go Game during the Seoul Olympic Games in 1988. The Gossaumnori is one of the most masculine and physical folk games in Korea, and it involves two teams of young men supporting an individual who rides on the Go head. The teams clash and try to unseat their opponent. It requires the close cooperation of team members to win and was believed to contribute to collaboration and cooperation amongst townspeople. To commemorate the handing down of this traditional game through the generations, the Inheritance Hall in Chilseok-dong now serves as a setting in which young people are trained in various programs that emphasize cooperation.

Gwangju Kimchi Festival G2

The Jeolla-do region, rich with agricultural products from its fields and seafood from the western and southern seas, has produced a wide range of tasty foods. In celebration of its tradition as the city with the best Korean cuisine, Gwangju has hosted an annual Kimchi Festival since 1994. This festival takes place in October and provides a special occasion for people to enjoy both Korean culture and various local varieties of kimchi.

Jindari Calligraphy Brushes H5

One of the most highly regarded craft specialties in Gwangju are Jindari calligraphy brushes. Jindari refers to the old name of Baegun-dong, which attained fame when the grandfather of An Jong-seon, an intangible cultural treasure, settled in Gwangju and crafted the celebrated calligraphy brushes. An Jong-seon is now the fourth generation of this brush artisan family. The Jindari brush is made of whiskers from the Siberian mink's tail and lamb's wool and is reputed to be one of the best quality brushes among calligraphers.

FOODS

As the city known for having some of the most delicious food in Korea, Gwangju has a variety of special local dishes.

Tteokgalbi

Tteokgalbi is made from beef carved from rib bones, which is then chopped, seasoned and charcoal broiled. Its name is similar to the word used for traditional Korean rice cakes, and this is because its shape is reminiscent of a rice cake. Mild in flavor, Tteokgalbi is a tender and enjoyable food.

Hanjeongsik

Hanjeongsik refers to the entree course which was served in the royal court of the Joseon Dynasty. The recipes for these dishes were retained and handed down in the Jeolla-do region, but they have been made famous throughout the country. Hanjeongsik consists of Korean side dishes and over 20 special course items. For those who wish to enjoy traditional Korean food, eating Hanjeongsik is a must.

Daejeon

Daejeon, located in the heart of the Korean Peninsula, has long been a transportation hub where railway lines, national roads, and expressways merge. While hosting the Daejeon Expo in 1993, Daejeon transformed itself into a world-class exposition site. The site plays a major role as a center for advanced science and technology in Korea. The city is the nation's second administrative capital, behind Seoul. Daejeon is also known as a city with a splendid culture and old traditions. The official bird of Daejeon is the Korean magpie. According to Korean legend, it is said to bring close friends and good news if it sings in the morning. Daejeon's city flower is the white magnolia, which represents friendship.

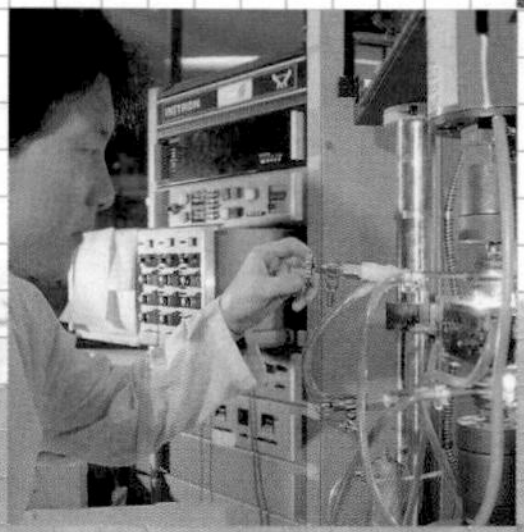

Expo Science Park

Hanbit Tower

The Expo Science Park is located in Doryong-dong, Yuseong-gu, where the 1993 International Expo was held. This science theme park carries on the spirit of the 1993 Expo, which was themed 'The Challenge of a New Road to Development'. The park is on a 627,000㎡ site and consists of five separate complexes and 18 exhibition pavilions and other public facilities. The exhibition pavilions inside the park include the Material Pavilion, Hanbit Tower, Earth Pavilion, Technopia Pavilion, Hanvit Pavilion, Energy Pavilion, and Expo Pavilion, as well as others. Each pavilion displays various high-tech presentations in accordance with its respective theme.

Technopia Pavilion

Materials Pavilion

Imagination Pavilion

Earthscape Pavilion

Auxiliary facilities include monorails, the 1,100-seat Expo Art Hall, where a variety of performances and events are held, and an international convention center equipped with facilities for simultaneous interpretation of up to 12 languages. The landmark Hanbit Tower stands tall in the center of Expo Science Park. The Hanbit Tower symbolizes a ray of light that links the present with the future, based on the wisdom of the past. A 40m high observatory tower commands a panoramic vista of Daejeon and allows visitors to feel as if they are in a space station.

Expo Science Park Information

Entrance fee: 3,000 won
Big 3: 7,000won
Big 5: 9,000won
Individual tour coupon 2,500won
Hours : 09:30 ~ 18:00 (Winter)
09:30 ~ 19:00 (Summer)

Observatory of Hanbit Tower

Nature & Life Pavilion

Starquest Pavilion

Hanbit Tower Nightscape

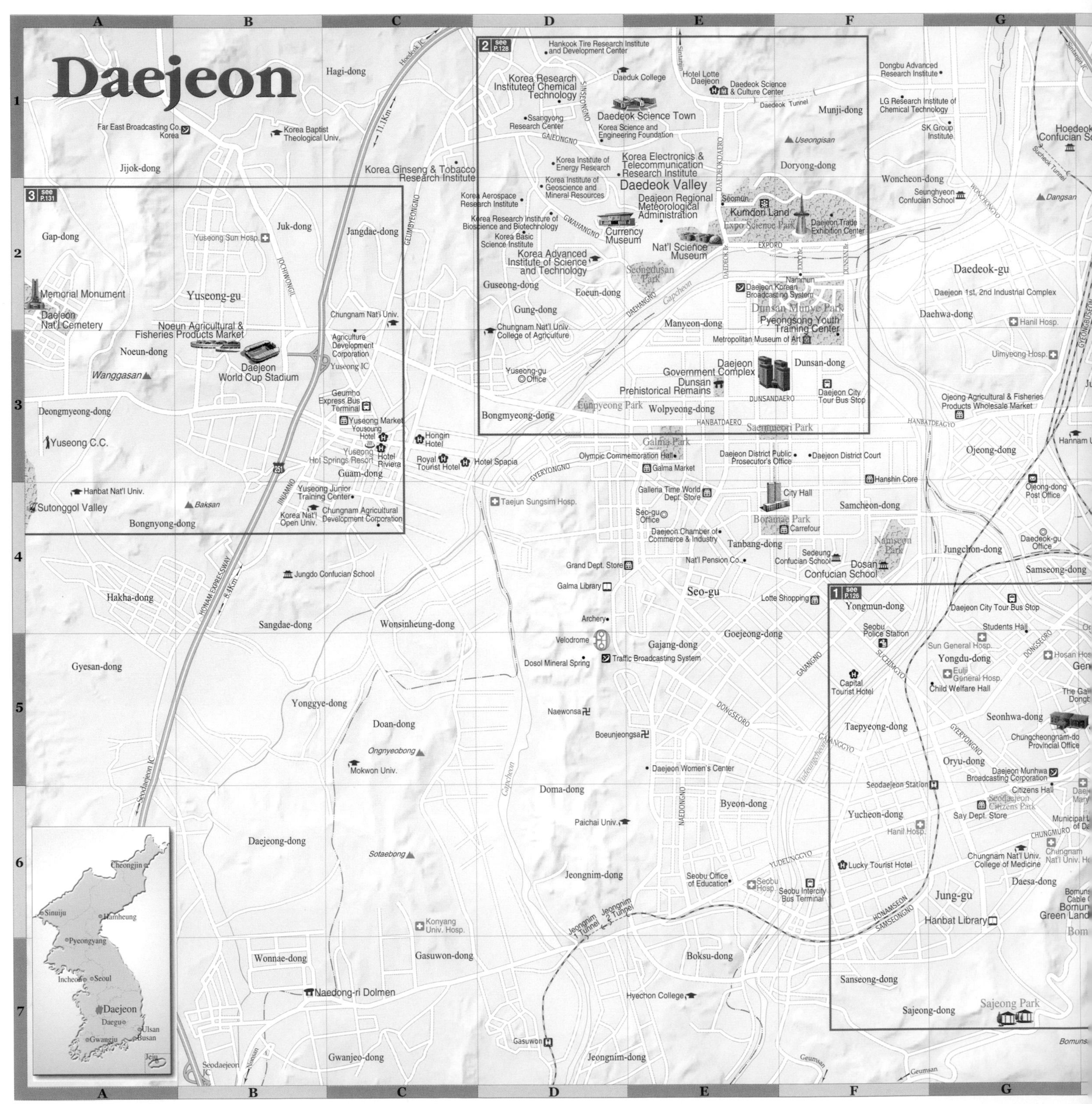

Daejeon
A
B
C
D
E
F
G
1
2
3
4
5
6
7
Hagi-dong
Far East Broadcasting Co. Korea
Korea Baptist Theological Univ.
Jijok-dong
Hoedeok IC
11.1Km
Korea Ginseng & Tobacco Research Institute
2 see P.128
Hankook Tire Research Institute and Development Center
Daeduk College
Korea Research Institute of Chemical Technology
Ssangyong Research Center
Daedeok Science Town
Korea Science and Engineering Foundation
GAJEONGNO
SINSEONGNO
Sintanjin
Hotel Lotte Daejeon
Daedeok Science & Culture Center
Daedeok Tunnel
Munji-dong
Useongisan
Doryong-dong
Korea Institute of Energy Research
Korea Electronics & Telecommunication Research Institute
Korea Institute of Geoscience and Mineral Resources
Daedeok Valley
Korea Aerospace Research Institute
Deajeon Regional Meteorological Administration
Korea Research Institute of Bioscience and Biotechnology
Korea Basic Science Institute
GWAHANGNO
Currency Museum
Korea Advanced Institute of Science and Technology
Nat'l Science Museum
Seongdusan Park
Seomun
Kumdori Land
Expo Science Park
Daejeon Trade Exhibition Center
EXPORO
DAEDEOKDAERO
Guseong-dong
Eoeun-dong
Gung-dong
Chungnam Nat'l Univ. College of Agriculture
DAEHANGNO
Gapcheon
Daejeon Korean Broadcasting System
Nammun
Dunsan Munye Park
Manyeon-dong
Pyeongsong Youth Training Center
Metropolitan Museum of Art
Yuseong-gu Office
Daejeon Government Complex
Dunsan-dong
Dunsan Prehistorical Remains
Daejeon City Tour Bus Stop
DUNSANDAERO
Bongmyeong-dong
Eunpyeong Park
Wolpyeong-dong
HANBATDAERO
Saemmeori Park
3 see P.131
Gap-dong
Juk-dong
Jangdae-dong
Yuseong Sun Hosp.
JOCHIWONGIL
GEUMBYEONGNO
Memorial Monument
Daejeon Nat'l Cemetery
Yuseong-gu
Chungnam Nat'l Univ.
Noeun Agricultural & Fisheries Products Market
Agriculture Development Corporation
Noeun-dong
Daejeon World Cup Stadium
Yuseong IC
Wanggasan
Geumho Express Bus Terminal
Deongmyeong-dong
Yuseong Market
Yousoung Hotel
Hongin Hotel
Yuseong C.C.
Yuseong Hot Springs Resort
Hotel Riviera
Royal Tourist Hotel
Hotel Spapia
Guam-dong
Hanbat Nat'l Univ.
Yuseong Junior Training Center
Sutonggol Valley
Baksan
Korea Nat'l Open Univ.
Chungnam Agricultural Development Corporation
Bongnyong-dong
JINJAMNO
HONAM EXPRESSWAY
8.4Km
Dongbu Advanced Research Institute
LG Research Institute of Chemical Technology
SK Group Institute
Hoedeok Confucian School
Sucheok Tunnel
Woncheon-dong
Seunghyeon Confucian School
WONCHONGYO
Dangsan
Daedeok-gu
Daejeon 1st, 2nd Industrial Complex
Daehwa-dong
Hanil Hosp.
Uimyeong Hosp.
Ojeong Agricultural & Fisheries Products Wholesale Market
HANBATDAEGYO
Hannam Univ.
Ojeong-dong
Galma Park
Olympic Commemoration Hall
Daejeon District Public Prosecutor's Office
Daejeon District Court
GYERYONGNO
Galma Market
Hanshin Core
Ojeong-dong Post Office
Galleria Time World Dept. Store
City Hall
Taejun Sungsim Hosp.
Samcheon-dong
Seo-gu Office
Boramae Park
Carrefour
Daejeon Chamber of Commerce & Industry
Tanbang-dong
Sedeung Confucian School
Namseon Park
Jungchon-dong
Daedeok-gu Office
Nat'l Pension Co.
Dosan Confucian School
Samseong-dong
Grand Dept. Store
Jungdo Confucian School
Galma Library
Seo-gu
Lotte Shopping
1 see P.126
Yongmun-dong
Daejeon City Tour Bus Stop
Hakha-dong
Archery
Students Hall
Sangdae-dong
Wonsinheung-dong
Seobu Police Station
Goejeong-dong
Velodrome
Gajang-dong
Sun General Hosp.
DONGSEORO
Hosan Hosp.
Gyesan-dong
Dosol Mineral Spring
Traffic Broadcasting System
Yongdu-dong
GAJANGNO
SUCHIMGYO
Capital Tourist Hotel
Eulji General Hosp.
Child Welfare Hall
Yonggye-dong
Naewonsa
DONGSEORO
Seonhwa-dong
Doan-dong
Taepyeong-dong
Boeunjeongsa
GYERYONGNO
Chungcheongnam-do Provincial Office
Ongnyeobong
GAJANGGYO
Oryu-dong
Mokwon Univ.
Daejeon Women's Center
Yudeungcheon
Daejeon Munhwa Broadcasting Corporation
Seodaejeon Station
Doma-dong
Byeon-dong
Citizens Hall
Seodaejeon Citizens Park
Gapcheon
NAEDONGNO
Yucheon-dong
Say Dept. Store
Paichai Univ.
Hanil Hosp.
CHUNGMURO
Daejeong-dong
Sotaebong
YUDEUNGGYO
Chungnam Nat'l Univ. College of Medicine
Chungnam Nat'l Univ. Hosp.
Jeongnim-dong
Lucky Tourist Hotel
Daesa-dong
Seobu Office of Education
Seobu Hosp.
Seobu Intercity Bus Terminal
Jung-gu
HONAMSEONNO
SAMSEONGNO
Konyang Univ. Hosp.
Jeongnim 1 Tunnel
Jeongnim 2 Tunnel
Hanbat Library
Bomun Green Land
Wonnae-dong
Gasuwon-dong
Boksu-dong
Sanseong-dong
Naedong-ri Dolmen
Hyechon College
Sajeong-dong
Sajeong Park
Gasuwon
Jeongnim-dong
Gwanjeo-dong
Seodaejeon IC
Nonsan
Geumsan
Cheongjin
Sinuiju
Hamheung
Pyeongyang
Incheon
Seoul
Daejeon
Daegu
Ulsan
Gwangju
Busan
Jeju

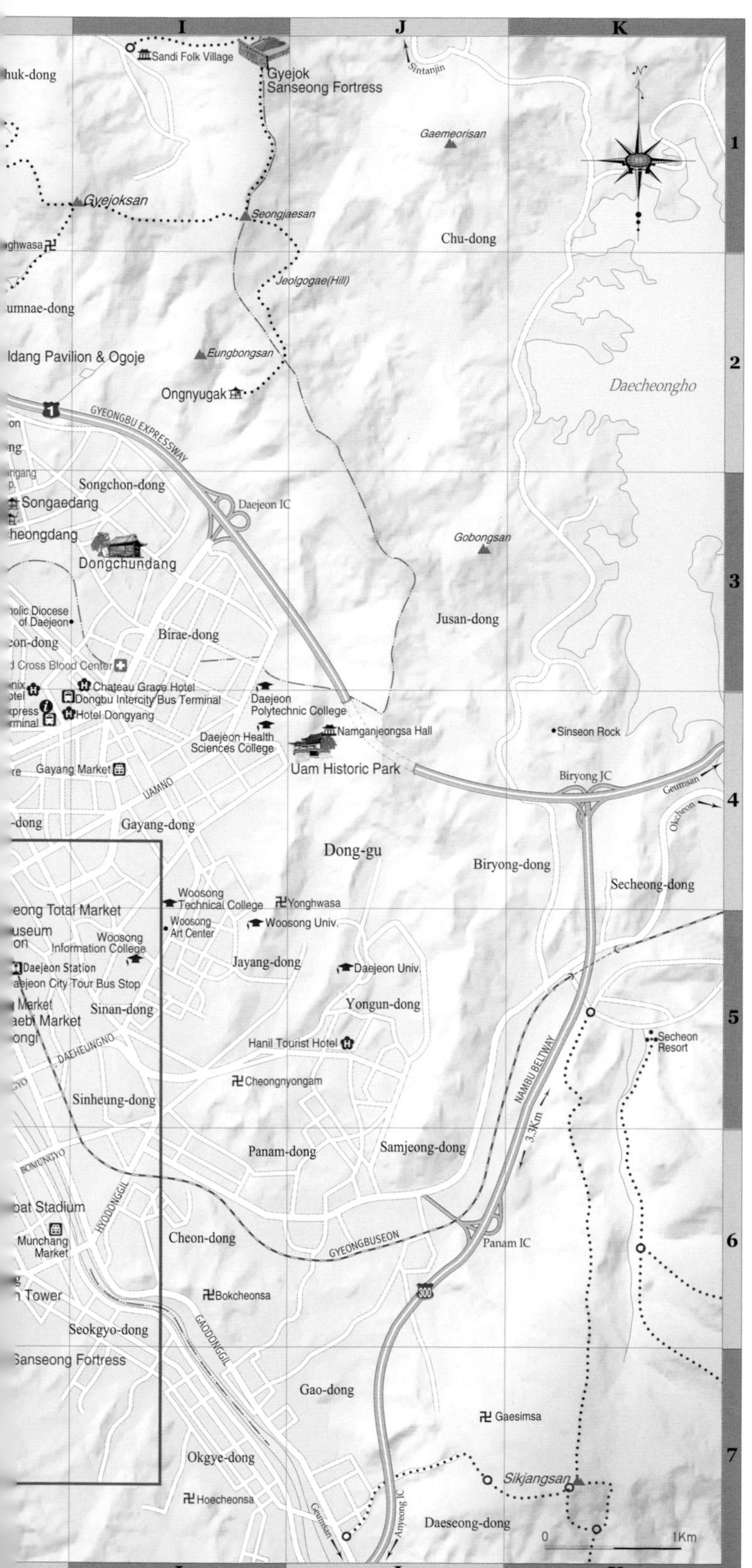

INDEX

Tourist Information

Daejeon Division of Tourism 82-42-600-3114
www.metro.daejeon.kr

LEGEND

- Railroad Station
- Bus Terminal
- Cable Car Platform
- Hospital
- Police Station
- Post Office
- Tourist Information Center
- University or School
- Library
- Broadcasting Station
- Museum
- Gallery
- Theater
- Prehistoric Relic Site
- Temple
- Traditional Building
- Traditional Pavilion
- Golf Course
- Hot Spring or Spa
- Park
- Amusement Park
- Mountain
- Other Tourist Attractions
- Hotel
- Department Store or Market
- Reference Point

Mt. BOMUNSAN AREA

1

Expo Park
Daejeon City Tour Bus Stop
Daejeon IC
Hanbat Nat'l Univ.
Daejeon Industrial Complex
SAMSEONGNO
Daesung Industry
UAMNO
Daejeon IC
Singayang Total Market
Gayang-dong
Tanbang-dong
Jungchon-dong
Daejeoncheon
Seodaejeon IC
Mok-dong
Freedom Hall
Students' Hall
Taejon Oriental Hosp.
Samseong Total Market
Soje-dong
Seobu Police Station
Daejeon Immigration Office
Hanbat Museum of Education
Seo-gu
Heungnyongsa
Sun General Hosp.
Hosan Hosp.
Korea Tobacco & Ginseng Corp.
Woosong Technical College
Yudeungcheon
SUCHIMGYO
Genealogical Museum
Nat'l Agricultural Cooperative Federation
Dong-gu
Capital Tourist Hotel
Child Welfare Center
Seonhwa-dong
DAEJONGNO
Life Tourist Hotel
Woosong Information College
Eulji General Hosp.
Daejeon Tax Office
Jung-dong
Jungbu Market
Seodaejeon IC
DONGSEORO
Daejeon Station
Yongdu-dong Intercity Bus Terminal
Daejeon City Tour Bus Stop
Daejeon IC
Dalim Tourist Hotel
Jung-gu
Melleo Dept. Store
Eunhaeng-dong
Jungang Market
Sinan-dong
Taepyeong-dong
Hongmyeong Market
Lachangte Dept. Store
Yongdu-dong
The Galleria Dongbaek Dept. Store
Dokkaebi Market
Daedong Market
Taepyeong Total Market
Dongah Life
1 Euneungjeongi Street
DAEHEUNGNO
Chungcheongnam-do Provincial Police Agency
JUNGANGNO
Jung-gu Office
Dong-gu Office
Chungcheongnam-do Provincial Office
Prince Tourist Hotel
Daejeon Post Office
Korea Express Co.,Ltd
Yuseong
Jungbu Police Station
GYERYONGNO
Oryu-dong
Kyobo Building
INHYORO
Taepyeong-dong Post Office
Yeongyeol Tower
Daejeon Telephone Office
INCHANGGYO
Sinheung-dong
Daejeon Munhwa Broadcasting Corporation
Korea Hosp.
Mugunghwa Dept. Store
Jeil Furniture Plaza
Daejeon St. Mary's Hosp.
Seodaejeon Station
Chungnam Ilbo
Citizens Hall
Daejeon Market
Seodaejeon Citizens Park
Jisan Building
Daeheung-dong
Seongnam Corporation
Gwanam IC
JUNGANGNO
Say Dept. Store
BOMUNGYO
GYEONGBUSEON
Daejeon Ilbo
BOMUNRO
Taemr Park
Byeksan Plaza
Daeheung Market
Cheongjin Library
Hanil Hosp.
Municipal Library of Daejeon
In-dong
HONAMSEON
Munchang-dong
HYODONGGIL
Daejeon Customs
Munhwa1(il)-dong
CHUNGMURO
Gasuwon
Chungnam Nat'l Univ. Hosp.
Chungmu Gymnasium
Yucheon Market
Chungnam Nat'l Univ. College of Medicine
Baseball Field
Sports Complex
Cheon-dong
Indoor Swimming Pool
Lucky Tourist Hotel
Chungcheongnam-do Office of Education
Gwangbok Hall
Hanbat Stadium
Munchang Market
MUNHANGNO
Science Pavilion
MUNCHANGGYO
Taejon Broadcasting
Yucheon-dong
Chinese School
Seobuseongmo Hosp.
Daesa-dong
Indansan
Bomunsan Cable Car
Insam Dept. Store
Daechang Market
Geumsan
Bomunsan Tower
Mt.Daedunsan
Munhwa-dong
Busa-dong
OKGYERO
SAMSEONGNO
Hanbat Library
Bomun Green Land
Namdaecheon
Gasuwon
Sanseong-dong
Seokgyo-dong
Outdoor Concert Hall
2 Bomunsan Park
Secheonam
Peace Pagoda
Gasuwon
3 Bomun Sanseong Fortress
Sajeong-dong
0 500m
Sajeong Park 4
Geumsan

Euneungjeongi Street 1

Euneungjeongi Street Cultural Festival

Euneungjeongi Street is renowned for its youthful fashion and culture. As is hinted by its nickname 'Fashion Street', Euneungjeongi Street is lined with fashion boutiques and bustling with youngsters day and night. Cars are prohibited and pedestrians freely roam and explore.
In addition to being the center of local culture, Euneungjeongi Street hosts a cultural festival every May for the enjoyment of locals and tourists alike.

Observation Tower on Mt. Bomunsan

Bomunsan Park 2

Bomunsan Park is Daejeon's biggest park and is situated next to 457m Mt. Bomunsan. Located in a forest, it has many attractions, such as an outdoor music hall, an observatory, various entertainment facilities, a botanical garden, sports facilities, an outdoor swimming pool, a monument commemorating the Battle of Daejeon, a pagoda dedicated to the war dead, and a world peace pagoda.
The outdoor music hall hosts a variety of music concerts and cultural events, while the observatory provides visitors with a panoramic view of all of Daejeon.
Cable cars are also operated for the convenience of park visitors.
Beautiful azaleas and cherry blossoms abound in the spring and the changing leaves make it special in the fall.

Bomun Sanseong Fortress 3

Bomun Sanseong Fortress was built along the ridgeline leading up to the summit of Mt. Bomunsan during the Three Kingdoms period. The fortress wall was constructed with simple layers of square-shaped stones, with thicker stones used on the outer wall for sturdiness. No wall is found on the east and north

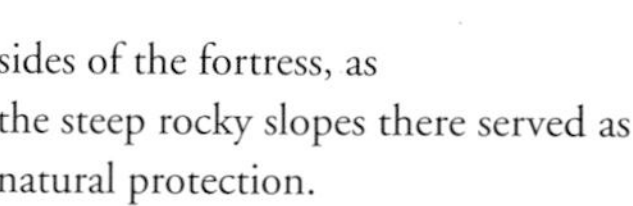

sides of the fortress, as the steep rocky slopes there served as natural protection.
Bomun Sanseong Fortress, built during the height of the hostilities between the Silla Kingdom and Baekje Kingdom, is believed to have been constructed to enable easier communications with fortresses nearby.

Sajeong Park 4

Located in Mt. Bomunsan, Sajeong Park is both a recreational and sports park, equipped with diverse sports facilities and a huge grassy square. The site is both educational and suitable for family recreation thanks to its numerous attractions: monuments to poets Han Yong-un and Kim Gwan-sik, a commemorative monument honoring the academic achievements of Changam Ji Heon-young, a monument for anti-communist youth martyrs, the tombs of patriots, and other notable attractions.

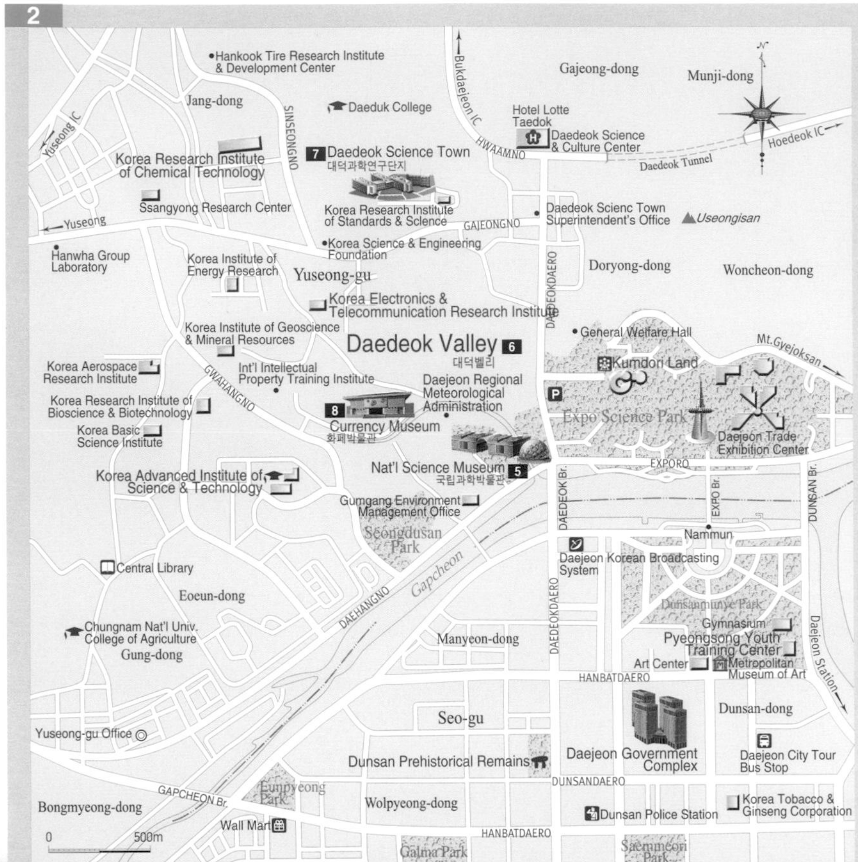

National Science Museum 5

Exhibit at the National Science Museum

The National Science Museum is located to the east of Daedeok Science Town, along Gapcheon stream. It is built on a site measuring 165,000㎡. The motto of the museum is 'Harmony between nature, humanity and science'. At the museum, science-related materials are exhibited by themes such as nature in Korea, the history of Korean science, and the harmony between nature, humans and science. Approximately 6,000 items are displayed at the museum.

General view of the National Science Museum

Animal Robot

Daedeok Valley Observatory

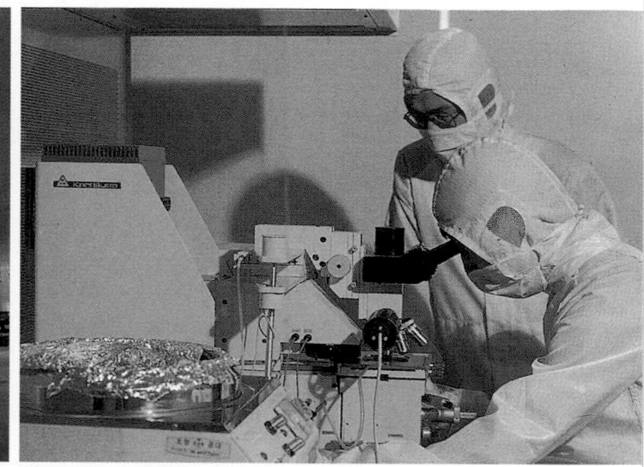

R&D in Daedeok Valley

Daedeok Valley 6

Daedeok Valley, the Silicon Valley of Korea, is where technology-related venture firms are concentrated.
Daedeok Valley has a venture industrial belt that links Daedeok Science Town, the Third and Fourth Industrial Complexes, Expo Science Park, Yuseong Spa and the newly-developed Dunsan downtown.
Daedeok Valley, with Daedeok Science Town located at its center, serves as one of the two major pillars of the nation's venture industry along with Teheran Valley, located in Seoul.
There are about 700 resident venture companies in the valley and 70% of these firms are located in Daedeok Science Town.

Daedeok Science Town 7

Over 100 research institutes are concentrated here in Daedeok Science Town, which is rapidly developing into a center for the nation's high-tech industry research.

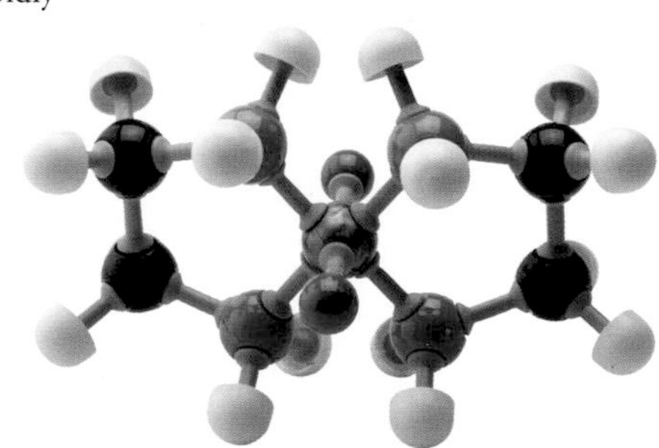

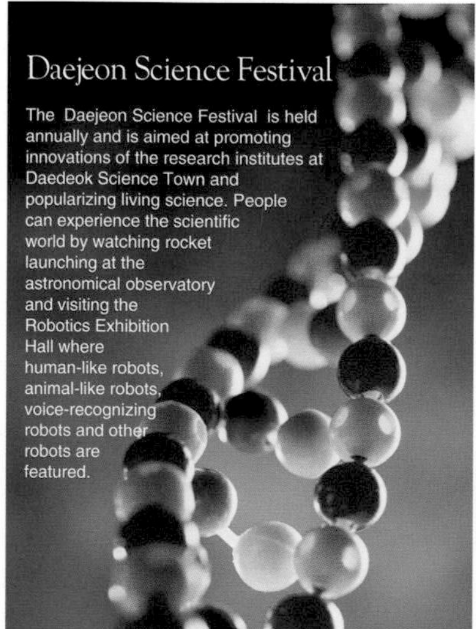

Daejeon Science Festival

The Daejeon Science Festival is held annually and is aimed at promoting innovations of the research institutes at Daedeok Science Town and popularizing living science. People can experience the scientific world by watching rocket launching at the astronomical observatory and visiting the Robotics Exhibition Hall where human-like robots, animal-like robots, voice-recognizing robots and other robots are featured.

Currency Museum

Yeolsoepae, An Item Used for Attaching Various Forms of Currency from the Late Period of the Joseon Dynasty

Currency Museum 8

Located in Daedeok Science Town, the Currency Museum is a Korean-style stone building with unique architectural features. The museum features minting machines of the past and present in actual size and in scale form. Exhibits related to the history of currencies of the East and the West, as well as that of Korea, and the history of paper notes and paper manufacturing can be viewed. Currencies, postage stamps, Christmas seals, medals and decorations from around the world are also on display here.

Eunbyeong, Currency from Goryeo Dynasty

5 Ryang Half Won, 1906

20 Whan Gold with a Plum Blossom Emblem, 1906

Joseontongbo, Currency from the Joseon Dynasty

Geonwonjungbo, the First Currency in Korea

Sangpyeongtongbo, Currency from the Joseon Dynasty

Buchaejeon, Currency from the Joseon Dynasty

Currency Note Exhibit

Brass Coin Exhibit

Currency Museum Exhibit

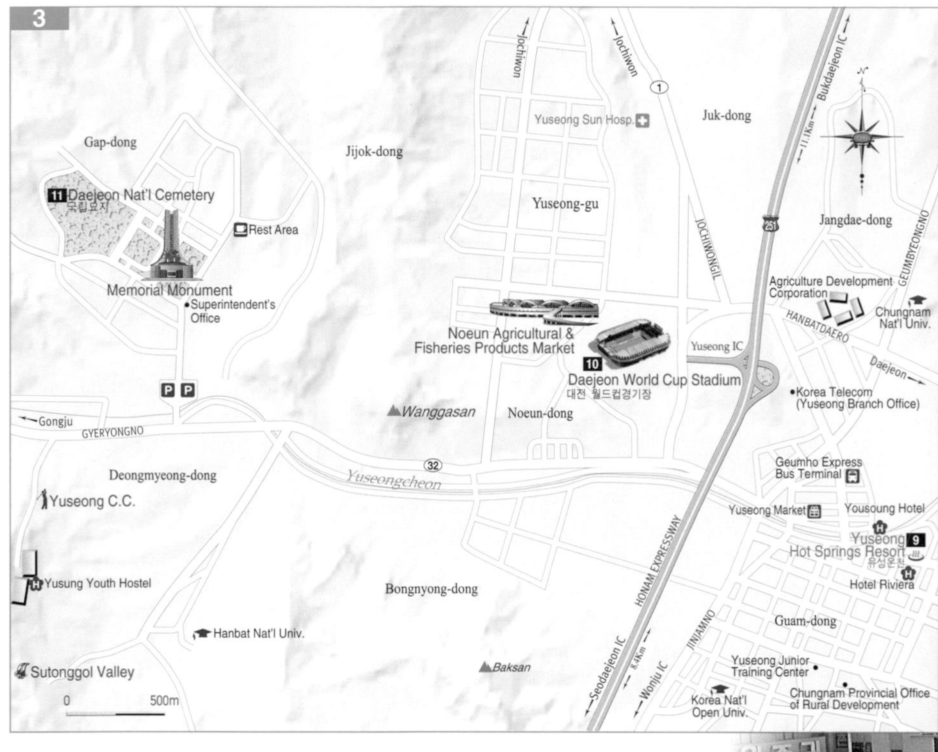

Open Air Hot Spring Pool in Yuseong

Night View of the Yuseong Hot Springs Resort

Yuseong Hot Springs Resort 9

Yuseong Hot Springs Resort is located about 11km west of downtown Daejeon. The spring' s water temperatures range from 42 to 55 degrees Celsius. The alkaline water of the hot springs has a pH-level of 8.4 due to large amounts of radium contained in the water.

The resort is one of the best hot spring destinations in Korea and a great number of people visit the area year round due to the therapeutic qualities of the water.

Yuseong Hot Springs Resort offers a spa park and a wide range of accommodations and restaurants. It is also close to other attractions, including the Yuseong Country Club and Expo Science Park.

The hot springs are believed to be effective in treating all sorts of ailments including depressions, diabetes, addictions, and gastric disorders and are thought to be especially good for the skin.

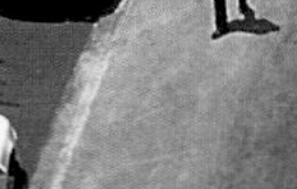

Daejeon World Cup Stadium 10

Daejeon World Cup Stadium

The Daejeon World Cup Stadium is located adjacent to the Yuseong IC, 5km from downtown Daejeon. The stadium's design focuses on a simplistic structure without any ostentatious embellishment. Its roof is retractable, making the stadium distinctive.

www.2002worldcupkorea.org

Daejeon National Cemetery 11

Tombstones, Daejeon National Cemetery

The Daejeon National Cemetery is a hallowed national site that serves as the final resting place for those who have died in defense of the nation. Major features of the National Cemetery, which stretches over approximately 3.3 million m² of land, include the commemorative gate, a pagoda and various tombs. There are also memorial and patriotic halls, as well as an outdoor exhibition where war equipment used during the Korean War is on display. A man-made waterfall, three reservoirs, a garden of Korea's traditional wildflowers and a wide variety of rare birds, grazing deer and other wildlife can be seen in the cemetery's memorial site.

Hyeonchungtap Monument, Daejeon National Cemetery

Daecheongho Lake

Daecheongho Lake K2

Daecheongho Lake is 80km-long and has the capacity to hold 1.5 billion tons of water. The length and height of its dam are 495m and 72m respectively. The man-made lake was created during the implementation of the Comprehensive Development Plan in the Geumgang Basin in 1980.

An observatory deck offers a great view of lake scenery. At the observatory deck is a water conservation exhibit with documents pertaining to the value of water conservation and dam construction. There is also an aquarium featuring the diverse varieties of fish found in the lake.

The scenery by the road alongside the lake makes it perfect for a drive in any season.

Jangtaesan Recreational Forest

Jangtaesan Recreational Forest is Korea's first ever privately formed recreational forest, contained in an area which stretches over 825,000㎡. Among the growth of the lush forest are metasequoia trees, chestnut, pine nut, ginkgo, pine, eucommia ulmoides, and other trees indigenous to Korea.

A lookout situated on twin rocks provides a great view of the sunset over the forest. Awaiting the forest's many visitors are various nature paths, campgrounds, bungalows, bird and animal farms and sports facilities.

Beautiful Scene at Mt. Jangtaesan

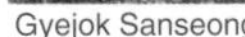

Gyejok Sanseong

Bonghwangjeong on the Gyejok Sanseong

Ppuri Park

Gyejok Sanseong Fortress J1

Gyejok Sanseong Fortress on Mt. Gyejoksan (429m) is assumed to have been built when the Baekje Kingdom moved its capital to Ungjin (now called Buyeo) in the 6th century. It is the largest stone fortress among the 30 or so Baekje forts in the Daejeon region. In the fortress, a number of Baekje-style roof tiles and earthenware were excavated, and pieces of Silla Kingdom earthenware and ceramics from the Goryeo and Joseon periods have also been found. It is believed that the fortress was in constant use up until the Goryeo and Joseon periods, well after the Baekje era had ended.

Donghaksa Temple

Situated in the eastern part of Mt. Gyeryongsan, Donghaksa was built in 724 during the Silla Kingdom, and is noted for being the oldest school in Korea for Buddhist monks. The temple is home to Daeungjeon, a main hall which enshrines a statue of Buddha, a three-storied stone pagoda, the Samseonggak Pavilion, Donggyesa, Sameungak Pavilion, Sungmojeon Hall and other historical sites.

Donghaksa is the most popular of Mt. Gyeryongsan's attraction's owing to its proximity to adjacent attractions, as well as being easily accessible. At the entry to the temple stands a string of cherry trees which have brilliant white blossoms in the springtime. A spring flower festival is held every April.

Donghaksa

Ppuri Park

Ppuri Park is a theme park focusing on extolling the virtues of filial piety. It also serves as a recreational area.

Ppuri Park consists of the following four parks: Educational Park, dedicated to promoting filial piety and patriotism; Family Park, which hosts a variety of family oriented events; Sports Park, which seeks to develop the minds and bodies of the young; and Nature Park, which displays the area's natural scenery.

Features within the park include the Ppuri Park Stone Monument, monuments explaining the origins of Korean surnames, sculptures depicting the origins of surnames, and 72 pieces of sculpture bearing each last name. In addition, the park has a water fountain decorated with the god of mortality and 12 zodiac animals, an octagonal pavilion, a grassy square, a straw-thatched cottage, nature paths and a rose tunnel.

Dosan Confucian School F4

The Dosan Confucian School was constructed in the 19th year (1693) of the reign of King Sukjong of the Joseon Dynasty, by Confucian scholars who wished to commemorate the scholarship and virtue of the great Confucian scholar Manhoe Kwon Deuk-gi and his son Tanong Kwon Si. It was granted the status of a government-sponsored Confucian academy by King Sukjong during the 37th year (1711) of his reign.
Originally, the school is believed to have had a total of 23 buildings including three sadang (the space used for holding memorial services), four auditoriums, three archives, four dormitories and three halls.

Dosan Confucian School

Dongchundang I3

Built by the famous Confucian scholar Dongchundang Song Jun-gil in the 4th year (1653) of the reign of King Hyojong of the Joseon Dynasty, Dongchundang is an annex pavilion and one of the important cultural assets of Daejeon. Dongchundang is the epitome of Korea's annex architecture, with its half-gabled and half-hipped roof in the shape of '八'. The Dongchundang Cultural Festival is held here every April.

Dongchundang

Daejeon City Tour Bus

The Daejeon City Tour Bus offers visitors an opportunity to visit the high-tech facilities that Daejeon is famous for and to see cultural relics and other tourist attractions in Chungcheong Province. The daily city tour is divided into two routes: the downtown route and an expanded route which is linked to adjacent tourist attractions.

Science course
Expo Science Park, National Science Museum, Currency Museum, KAIST (Korea Advanced Institute of Science & Technology), Electronics & Telecommunication Research Institute, Korea Institute of Geology Mining & Materials, Korea Basic Science Institute, Korea Institute of Machinery & Materials, Korea Atomic Energy Research Institute, Korea Institute of Ginseng & Tobacco Research, Korea Research Institute of Chemical Technology, Hanwha Group Materials, Regional Meteorological Office, Science Education Center

Cultural course
Uam Historic Park, The Birth Place of Shin Chae-ho, Dongchundang, Dunsan Prehistoric Site, Ppuri Park, Hanbat Education Museum, Dosan Confucian School, Yuheodang

Administration course
Wolpyeong Filtration Plant, Sewage Treatment Plant, Geumgodong Sanitary Landfill, Daejeon Metropolitan Museum of Art, Korean Folk Music Research Institute, Government Administrative Complex, Daejeon City Hall

Industry course
Yuhan Kimberly, Hansol Paper Co., KBS, Pacific Co. Kunyong Food Co., Industrial Materials Distribution Complex, Daecheong Dam, Lotte Co., Dongyang Gangchul, Korea Tobacco & Ginseng Corp.

Open: M - F (Except Holidays)
Operating hours: Individuals 08:30 ~ 16:00, 09:30 ~ 17:00, Group tour times can be arranged.
Tour Fees:
Downtown Daejeon - All day: 5,000 won
Expanded Route: 8,000 won
82-42-231-5451

Uam Historic Park

Uam Historic Park J4

Uam Historic Park is where the Confucian scholar Uam Song Si-yeol devoted himself to educating students and studying Confucianism during the reign of King Sukjong of the Joseon Dynasty (1674-1730). Covering an area of 52,800㎡, it has sixteen buildings, including Jangpangak, a depository for scholastic works.

The park also houses a portrait of Uam Song Si-yeol, the Namganjeongsa where Confucian scholars put forward an idea of northward advance during the reign of King Hyojong of the Joseon Dynasty, Gigukjeong Pavilion, Uam's collective writings (called Songjadaejeon), and many other items.

Gujeungmuk Village

The Gujeungmuk Village is noted for its traditional acorn-starch gelatin. The entire village is involved in making and selling acorn-starch gelatin which is made by grinding acorns and buckwheat using a traditional tool called a maetdol (stone grinder).

Aside from the acorn-starch gelatin, visitors can enjoy buckwheat jelly, mung-bean pancakes, chicken boiled with rice and locally brewed traditional liquors. Currently, around 30 restaurants serve acorn-starch jelly and other dishes in Gujeungmuk Village.

Namgangjeongsa Schoolhouse

Ulsan

Located on the southeastern coast of the Korean Peninsula, Ulsan is one of the largest cities in Korea. It has about one million inhabitants and takes up one thousand and fifty five square kilometers of total area. Since the 1960s, when the Korean government launched Korea's first and largest industrialization drive, Ulsan has grown dramatically. It has an extensive industrial infrastructure, which includes Hyundai Motor Company, Hyundai Heavy Industries, LG Chemical and other companies. Because of this Ulsan is a popular destination for industrial inspection tours in Korea. The city flower is a pear flower, which symbolizes noble mindedness, integrity and diligence. The city bird is a white heron, which symbolizes the harmony & unity of the citizens of Ulsan.

Bangudae Amgakhwa

The Bangudae Amgakhwa refers to prehistoric petroglyph which is presumed to have been made sometime during the Neolithic and Paleolithic eras. The Amgakhwa are mainly concentrated on one 6.5m-wide and 3m-high rock. About ten other rocks found nearby also have patterns engraved on them. The stone carvings are divided into two types: the first type has patterns which have chiseled inner sections, while the second type has patterns with chiseled outlines.
The Amgakhwa is designated as National Treasure No. 285.

Daegok-ri Valley

Bangudae Amgakhwa in Daegok-ri (National Treasure No. 285)

The patterns etched into the rocks range from ocean creatures and land animals such as whales, deers, tigers and bears, to human faces, whale hunters at sea and animal hunters with bows. Man-made items such as ships, fishing nets, animal traps, fences, harpoons and other fishing instruments are also drawn on the rocks. It appears that these stone carvings were used to teach hunting skills and were part of a religious offering asking for a bountiful fishing and hunting catch and the birth of healthy children. The detailed etchings are of great interest to visitors seeking information on Korea's prehistoric past.

Whale | Whale & Ship | Canoe | Turtle

Wild Boar | Tiger | Hunter | Wild Ox

Cheonjeon-ri Gakseok

Stone Carvings in Cheonjeon-ri (National Treasure No. 147)

Cheonjeon-ri Gakseok is prehistoric petroglyph which was inscribed on a flat rock (9.7m × 2.7m) in a valley in the mid-upper part of the Daegokcheon stream. The upper part of the rock features geometrical patterns, and human and animal images, and the lower part displays linear patterns and letters from the time of the Silla Kingdom. The geometrical patterns include diamond, ascidian, two-prong circles and egg, and plant shapes. A two-pronged circle symbolizes the sun, and the additional geometrical patterns signify that this was an altar where people of the Bronze Age held religious rituals to pray for agricultural abundance and the prosperity of their descendents. Other patterns, which feature people riding horses and a ship with a large sail, were inscribed by a man named Ipjonggalmunwang to commemorate his pilgrimage here during the 26th year of the reign of King Beopheung of the Silla Kingdom.

Cheonjeon-ri Dinosaur Footprints

The area surrounding Cheonjeon-ri is known for its rock drawings and fossils of dinosaur footprints. It appears that the footprints belong to medium or large sized dinosaurs that lived during the Cretaceous period about 1 billion years ago. They provide a valuable means to study the area' s natural history.

There are 200 dinosaur footprints in an area of 1,750 square meters. The footprints indicate that the dinosaurs were not traveling in any certain direction. Rather, they roamed around this area, which was their habitat. Given that dinosaurs lived in riverside savannahs with subtropical climates and alternating rainy and dry seasons, it is assumed that this area was once a savannah.

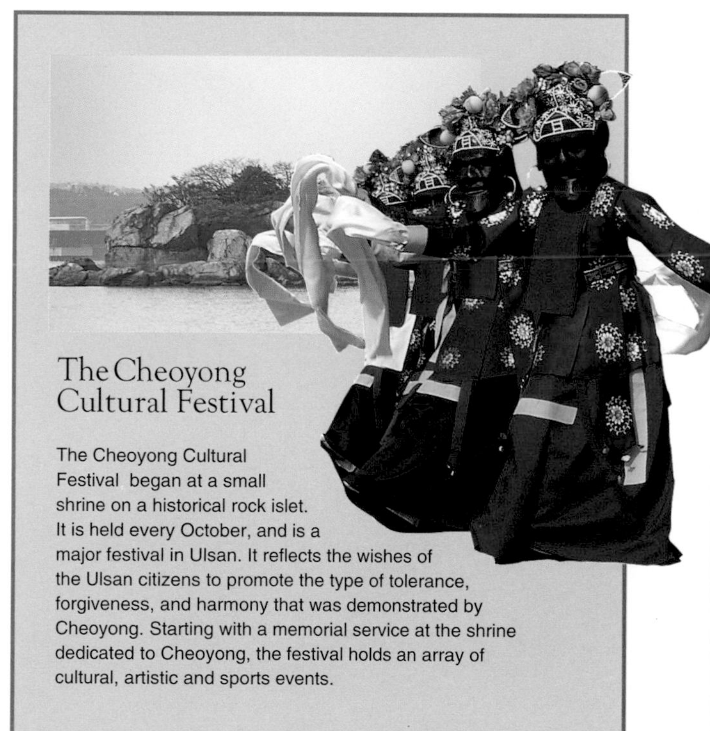

The Cheoyong Cultural Festival

The Cheoyong Cultural Festival began at a small shrine on a historical rock islet. It is held every October, and is a major festival in Ulsan. It reflects the wishes of the Ulsan citizens to promote the type of tolerance, forgiveness, and harmony that was demonstrated by Cheoyong. Starting with a memorial service at the shrine dedicated to Cheoyong, the festival holds an array of cultural, artistic and sports events.

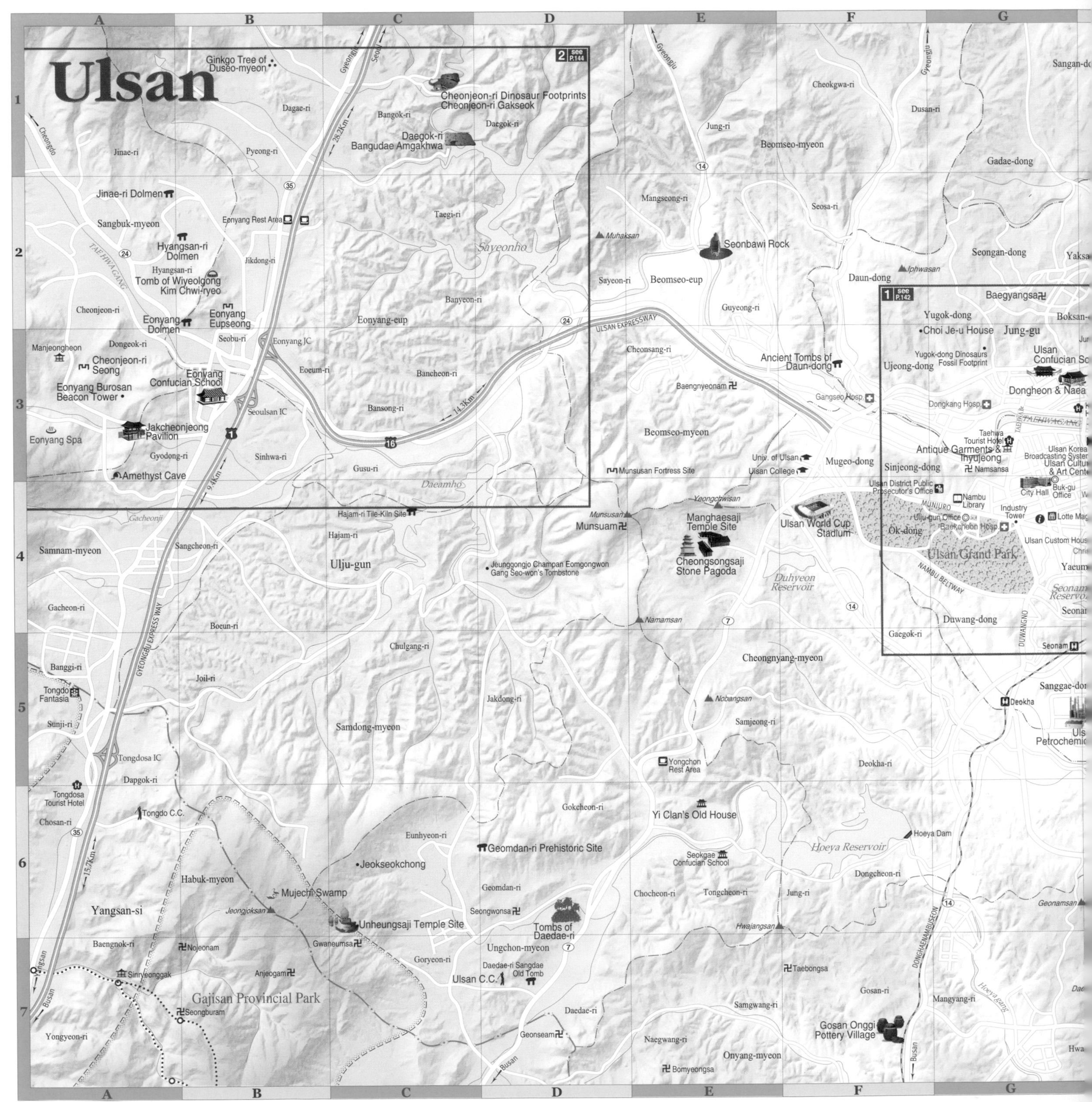

Ulsan
2 see P.144
1 see P.142
A
B
C
D
E
F
G
1
2
3
4
5
6
7
Ginkgo Tree of Duseo-myeon
Cheonjeon-ri Dinosaur Footprints
Cheonjeon-ri Gakseok
Dagae-ri
Bangok-ri
Daegok-ri
Daegok-ri Bangudae Amgakhwa
Cheongdo
Jinae-ri
Pyeong-ri
Gyeongju
Seoul
28.2Km
Jinae-ri Dolmen
Sangbuk-myeon
Eonyang Rest Area
Taegi-ri
Hyangsan-ri Dolmen
Hyangsan-ri
Tomb of Wiyeolgong Kim Chwi-ryeo
Jikdong-ri
Sayeonho
Taehwagang
Cheonjeon-ri
Eonyang Dolmen
Eonyang Eupseong
Banyeon-ri
Eonyang-eup
Manjeongheon
Dongeok-ri
Seobu-ri
Eonyang JC
Cheonjeon-ri Seong
Eoeum-ri
Bancheon-ri
Eonyang Confucian School
Eonyang Burosan Beacon Tower
Seoulsan IC
Bansong-ri
14.3Km
Eonyang Spa
Jakcheonjeong Pavilion
Gyodong-ri
Sinhwa-ri
Gusu-ri
Amethyst Cave
9.4Km
Daeamho
Gacheonji
Hajam-ri Tile-Kiln Site
Hajam-ri
Samnam-myeon
Sangcheon-ri
Ulju-gun
Jeunggongjo Champan Eomgongwon Gang Seo-won's Tombstone
Gacheon-ri
Boeun-ri
Gyeongbu Expressway
Chulgang-ri
Banggi-ri
Tongdo Fantasia
Joil-ri
Jakdong-ri
Sunji-ri
Samdong-myeon
Tongdosa IC
Dapgok-ri
Tongdosa Tourist Hotel
Tongdo C.C.
Chosan-ri
Gokcheon-ri
Eunhyeon-ri
Geomdan-ri Prehistoric Site
Jeokseokchong
15.7Km
Habuk-myeon
Geomdan-ri
Mujechi Swamp
Yangsan-si
Jeongjoksan
Seongwonsa
Unheungsaji Temple Site
Tombs of Daedae-ri
Baengnok-ri
Nojeonam
Gwaneumsa
Ungchon-myeon
Goryeon-ri
Daedae-ri Sangdae Old Tomb
Yangsan
Sinpyeonggak
Anjeogam
Ulsan C.C.
Gajisan Provincial Park
Seongburam
Daedae-ri
Busan
Yongyeon-ri
Geonseam
Jung-ri
Gyeongju
Cheokgwa-ri
Dusan-ri
Sangan-do
Beomseo-myeon
Gadae-dong
Mangseong-ri
Seosa-ri
Muhaksan
Seonbawi Rock
Seongan-dong
Yaksa
Iphwasan
Sayeon-ri
Beomseo-eup
Daun-dong
Baegyangsa
Guyeong-ri
Yugok-dong
Boksan
Ulsan Expressway
Choi Je-u House
Jung-gu
Cheonsang-ri
Yugok-dong Dinosaurs Fossil Footprint
Ulsan Confucian School
Ancient Tombs of Daun-dong
Ujeong-dong
Baengnyeonam
Dongheon & Naea
Gangseo Hosp.
Dongkang Hosp.
Taehwagang
Beomseo-myeon
Taehwa Tourist Hotel
Antique Garments & Ihyujeong
Ulsan Korea Broadcasting System
Univ. of Ulsan
Mugeo-dong
Sinjeong-dong
Namsansa
Ulsan Culture & Art Center
Munsusan Fortress Site
Ulsan College
Ulsan District Public Prosecutor's Office
City Hall
Buk-gu Office
Yeongchwisan
Nambu Library
Muniuro
Industry Tower
Munsusan
Manghaesaji Temple Site
Ulsan World Cup Stadium
Ulju-gun Office
Lotte Mag
Munsuam
Baekcheon Hosp.
Ok-dong
Ulsan Custom House
Cheongsongsaji Stone Pagoda
Ulsan Grand Park
Nambu Beltway
Yaeum
Duhyeon Reservoir
Seonam Reservoir
Namamsan
Duwang-dong
Seonam
Duwangno
Gaegok-ri
Cheongnyang-myeon
Sanggae-do
Nobangsan
Deokha
Samjeong-ri
Ulsan Petrochemic
Yongchon Rest Area
Deokha-ri
Yi Clan's Old House
Hoeya Dam
Hoeya Reservoir
Seokgae Confucian School
Dongcheon-ri
Chocheon-ri
Tongcheon-ri
Jung-ri
Geonamsan
Hwajangsan
Donghaenambuseon
Taebongsa
Gosan-ri
Mangyang-ri
Hoeyagang
Samgwang-ri
Gosan Onggi Pottery Village
Naegwang-ri
Onyang-myeon
Bomyeongsa
Hwa

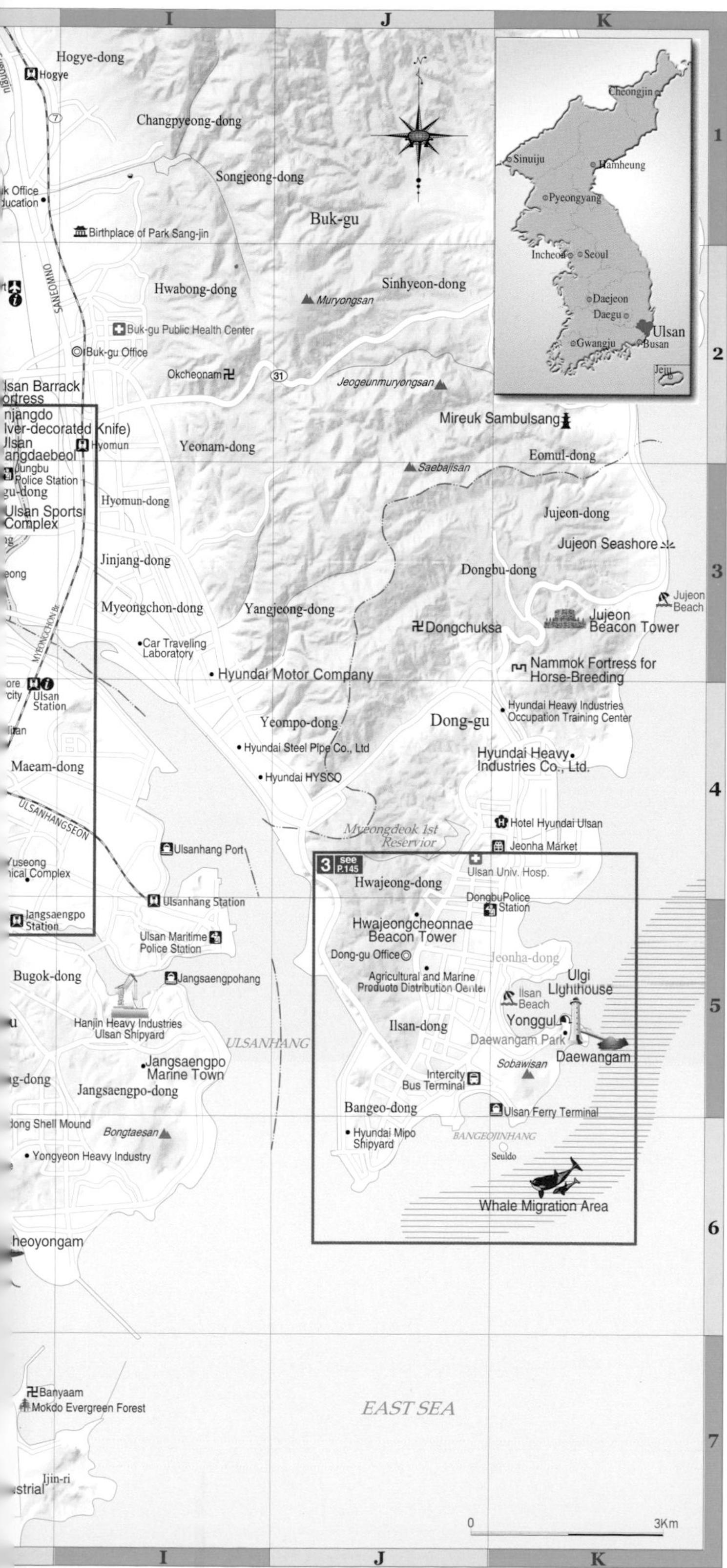

INDEX

Tourist Information

Ulsan Culture & Tourism Division 82-52-229-3713
www.metro.ulsan.kr

LEGEND

Railroad Station
Airport
Port
Bus Terminal
Rest Area
Hospital
Police Station
Post Office
Tourist Information Center
University or School
Library
Broadcasting Station
Theater
Prehistoric Relic Site
Tomb
Fortress
Temple
Site of Buddhist Artifacts
Traditional Building
Traditional Pavilion
Cave
Beach
Golf Course
Hot Spring or Spa
Park
Scenic Area
Amusement Park
Migratory Birds' Sanctuary
Arboretum
Mountain
Stadium
Other Tourist Attractions
Hotel
Department Store or Market
Reference Point

1

The Republic of Korea Nat'l Red Cross Ulsan Chapter
Yugok-dong
Choi Je-u House
Eunjangdo (Silver-decorated Knife) 3
병영은장도
Ulsan Jangdaebeol
Beonyeong Market
Hyomun
Ulsan Airport
Hwansaengsa
Jung-gu
Bukjeong-dong
Jung-gu Office
Jungbu Police Station
SANEOMNO
MYEONGNYUNNO
BEONYEONGNO
Bohyeonsa
Yugok-dong Dinosaurs Fossil Footprints
Daun-dong
Gyo-dong
Mosasa
Haksan-dong
Jeongun Market
Ulsan Sports Complex
Jinjang-dong
Taehwa Reservoir
Ujeong-dong
Ulsan Confucian School 2
울산향교
Weather Station
Boksan-dong
Ulsan Munhwa Broadcasting Corporation
Gymnasium
BUKBU BELTWAY
MYEONGNYUNNO
Pyeonghwa Market
Dongheon & Naea 1
동헌 및 내아
Vegetable and Fruit Dealer Market
Gilmen Hosp.
Buk-gu
Gwaneumsa
Hotel Juungang
Paul's Hosp.
Ulsan Waeseong
Hakseong Park
Dongcheongang
Myeongchon-dong
Ulsan Expressway
Hyundai Dept. Store
Okgyo-dong
12 Guardian-embossed Stupa at Taehwasa
Dongkang Hosp.
Koreana Hotel
Myeonghwa Theater
Hakseong-dong
Cheonggu Sports Plaza
TAEHWARO
GANGBYEONNO
Ulsan Univ.
TAEHWA Br.
ULSAN Br.
BEONYEONG Br.
TAEHWAGANG
HAKSEONG Br.
Outdoor Concert Hall
Taehwa Tourist Hotel
Modeuni Dept. Store
Jeil Hosp.
Dal-dong
Nambu Fire Station
MYEONGCHON Br.
MYEONGCHON RAILWAY Br.
Antique Garments & Ihyujeong
Moja Hosp.
PALDEUNGNO
Ulsan Hosp.
Ulsan Cultural Center
Samsan-dong
NAMSANNO
BONGWOLLO
GONGGORO
Korean Broadcasting System
Nam-gu Office
HAKSEONGNO
Jeongtosa
Namsansa
JUNGANGNO
Ulsan Metropolitan Office of Education
Ulsan Culture & Art Center
Boram Hosp.
Sinjeong Market
Korea Electric Power Corporation
Catholic Women Clinic
Ulsan District Public Prosecutor's Office
Sinjeong-dong
Labor Hall
HANJEONNO
BEONYEONGNO
Chamber of Commerce & Industry
Hyundai Dept. Store
Ulsan Agricultural & Marine Products Wholesale Market
Ulsan Station
Ulsan District Court
City Hall
Sinjeong Pyeonghwa Market
Gangnam Hosp.
Express Intercity Bus Termial
Ulsan Metropolitan Police Agency
Dotjilsan
SAMSANNO
World Cup Stadium
Nambu Library
Nambu Police Station
Daldong Market
Yeocheon-dong
MUNJURO
Keunbit Hosp.
New Olympia Tourist Hotel
Lotte Magnet Dept. Store
Nam-gu
Yeocheoncheon
Yaeum-dong
SANEOMNO
Ulju-gun Office
Industry Tower
YMCA Hall
Ulsan Tourist Hotel
Yaeum Park
Samsung Fine Chemicals Co.,Ltd.
Baekcheon Hosp.
Bogwang Co., Ltd.
Ulsan Custom House
Namgu Health Center
Christ Hosp.
SUAMNO
World Cup Stadium
Ok-dong
ULSAN HANGSEON
NAMBU BELTWAY
Ulsan Grand Park
Yaeum Market
Dongbu Chemical
DONGHAENAMBUSEON
Sinseonsa
Seonam-dong
Jinyang Co., Ltd.
Seonam Reservoir
JANGSAENGPORO
Sammi Co., Ltd.
Duwang-dong
DUWANGNO
Duwangcheon
Korea Flange
SK Co., Ltd.
Seonam Park
Yuseong Chemical Complex
Hamwolsan
Taehwa Industrial Co.
N
Seonam
Sanggae Park
SK
0
1Km
Busan
Busan
Jangsaengpo

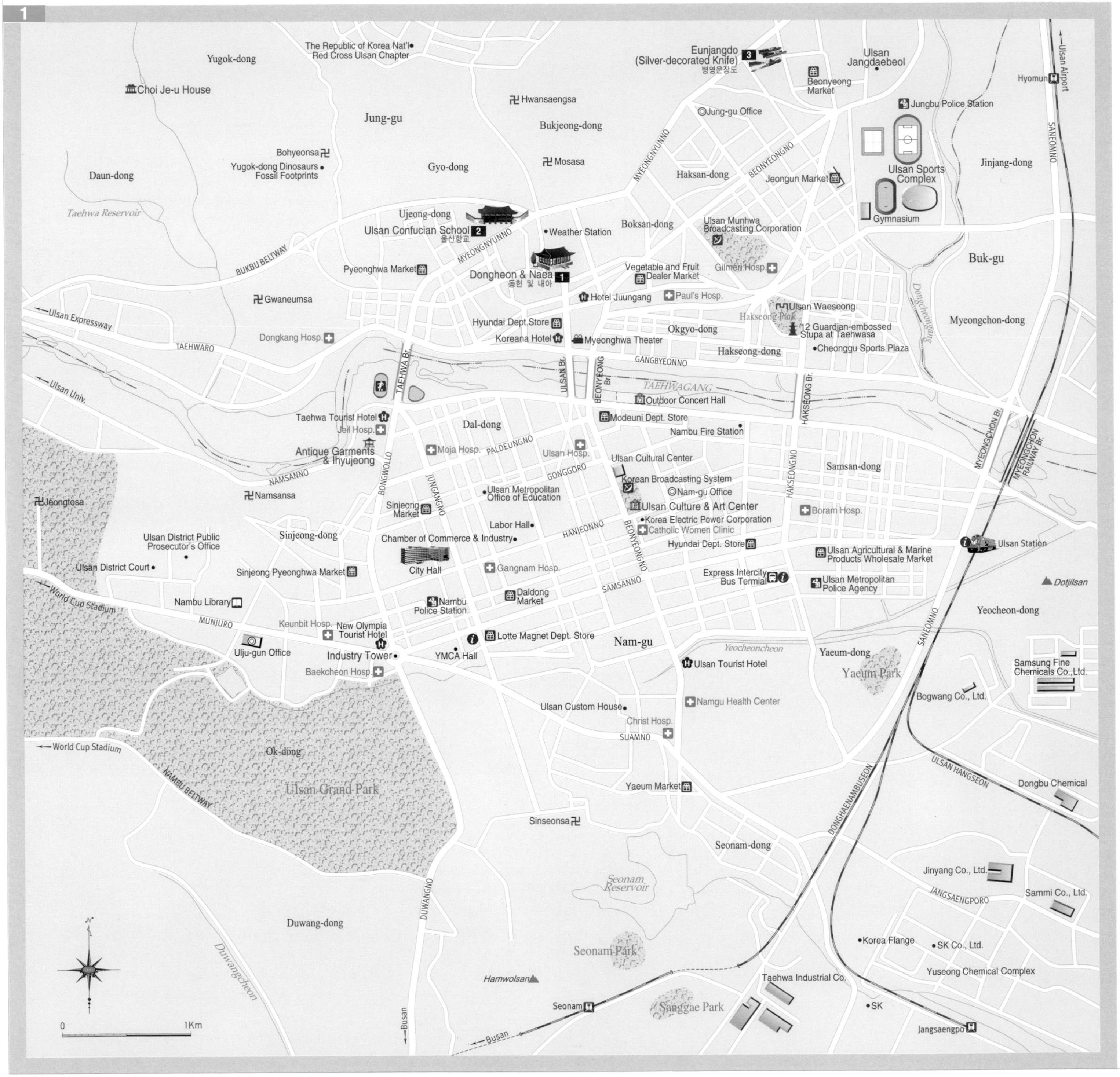

Dongheon & Naea

Ulsan Confucian School

Dongheon & Naea 1

Dongheon is the central structure of an ancient Ulsan citadel built by Kim Su-o, a local governor in the 7th year (1681) of the reign of King Sukjong. Another major structure of the citadel is Naea. Dongheon was where the governor of Ulsan attended to his official duties, while Naea served as his living quarters. Besides Dongheon and Naea, the citadel's other surviving structures include the Hakseonggwan Jongnu Pavilion and the Dochongso Osongjeong Pavilion.

Ulsan Confucian School 2

The Ulsan Confucian School was first built in the Gugyo village of Bangu-dong but was later reestablished at its current site in the 3rd year (1652) of the reign of King Hyojong, after the original building was destroyed during the 1592 Japanese invasion.

The structures of the school were arranged so that the buildings which run from south to north intersect the buildings which run from east to west, displaying traditional Confucian school architecture.

Eunjangdo (Silver-decorated Knife) 3

Nowadays, the Eunjangdo is used as a type of ornament. However, it was once considered a necessity for aristocratic men and women, who usually had one tied to

their hanbok (traditional Korean clothes) on a string or belt. The Eunjangdo could be used for protection and also used to detect poison in food. It was so expensive that it was almost impossible for ordinary laymen to even have a chance to glimpse it.

Ulsan was an area frequently invaded by Japan and consequently, there was a need to make various weapons. Gyeongsang Jwabyeongyeong (a military base in the western part of Gyeongsang-do) was established in the 17th year (1417) of the reign of King Taejong of the Joseon Dynasty. After the establishment of the military base, a metal-processing industry was developed here. Metal weapons and items for daily living were produced. Consequently, metal-processing experts began concentrating in this area, and they preserve the tradition of metallurgy to this day. Im Won-jung is currently the most well known metal-processing expert, and he produces elegant and sophisticated Eunjangdo. He has been designated as Intangible Cultural Properties No. 1 in Ulsan. Visitors can observe him making Eunjangdo at his shop and buy his works.

Eunjangdo

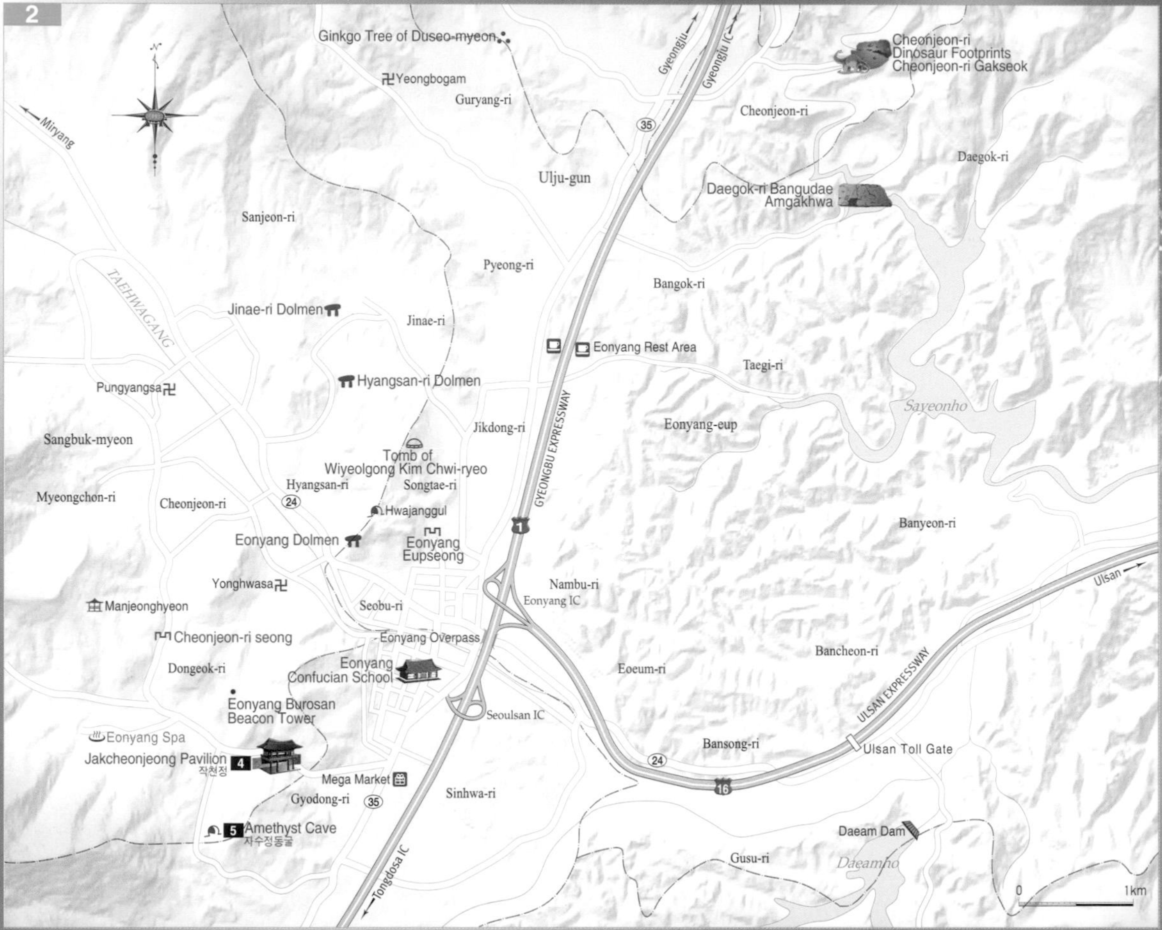

2

Ginkgo Tree of Duseo-myeon
Yeongbogam
Guryang-ri
Miryang
Gyeongju
Gyeongju IC
35
Cheonjeon-ri Dinosaur Footprints
Cheonjeon-ri Gakseok
Cheonjeon-ri
Daegok-ri
Ulju-gun
Daegok-ri Bangudae Amgakhwa
Sanjeon-ri
Pyeong-ri
Bangok-ri
TAEHWAGANG
Jinae-ri Dolmen
Jinae-ri
Eonyang Rest Area
Taegi-ri
Pungyangsa
Hyangsan-ri Dolmen
Sayeonho
Sangbuk-myeon
Jikdong-ri
Eonyang-eup
Tomb of Wiyeolgong Kim Chwi-ryeo
Hyangsan-ri
Songtae-ri
GYEONGBU EXPRESSWAY
Myeongchon-ri
Cheonjeon-ri
24
Hwajanggul
Banyeon-ri
Eonyang Dolmen
Eonyang Eupseong
1
Yonghwasa
Nambu-ri
Eonyang IC
Ulsan
Manjeonghyeon
Seobu-ri
Cheonjeon-ri seong
Eonyang Overpass
Bancheon-ri
Dongeok-ri
Eonyang Confucian School
Eoeum-ri
ULSAN EXPRESSWAY
Eonyang Burosan Beacon Tower
Seoulsan IC
Eonyang Spa
Bansong-ri
Ulsan Toll Gate
Jakcheonjeong Pavilion 4
작천정
24
Mega Market
16
Gyodong-ri
35
Sinhwa-ri
5 Amethyst Cave
자수정동굴
Daeam Dam
Gusu-ri
Daeamho
Tongdosa IC
0 1km

Jakcheonjeong Pavilion 4

Jakcheonjeong is a pavilion located in a valley in Samnam-myeon, Ulju-gun. In the spring, cherry blossoms decorate the entrance of the valley, and the hiking trails of Mt. Ganwolsan beckon visitors all year round.

Amethyst Cave 5

The Amethyst Cave is found at the entrance of Jakcheonjeong Valley. Before it was developed into a tourist site, it was used to mine amethyst ore, which is regarded as one of the five most precious gems, along with the diamond, ruby, emerald and sapphire. The 2.5km long cave has spacious chambers and many tunnels connected to each other.

The cave houses a mine vein exhibition hall, Dokdo Island Hall (where there is a replica of the island), a hall of human evolution, a primitive life hall and other interesting attractions. In addition, events are held inside the cave daily.

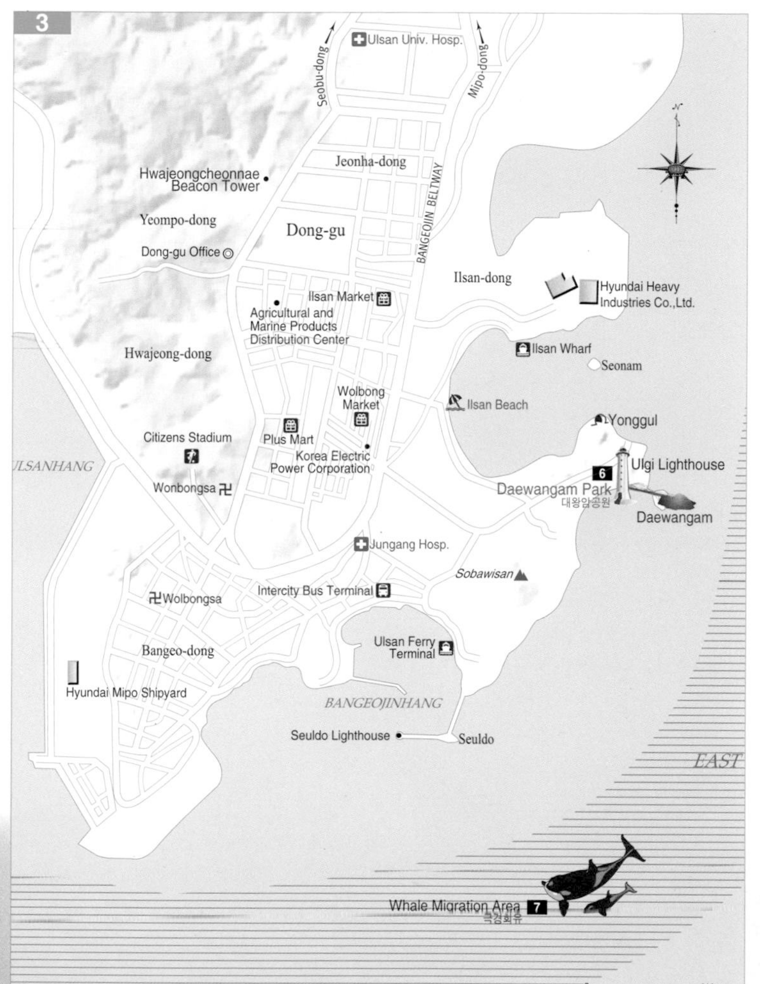

Daewangam Park 6

The Korean coastline protrudes out into the ocean about 2km east of Bangeojin, and Daewangam Park occupies this cape. The park has a beautiful forest of 15,000 seashore pine trees that are more than 100 years of age, and rocks such as the Daewangam, Nakhwaam and Tanggeunam, which stand next to seashore cliffs. These rocks have various legends surrounding them.

At the tip of the park is the large rock called Daewangam. Legend has it that Queen Munmu became a dragon and submerged herself under Daewangam to protect Korea. Originally Daewangam was isolated by the ocean, but a bridge was built to provide easier access to it.

Whale Migration Area 7

'Soegorae,' also known as 'Geukgyeong (gray whales),' are often seen off the coast of Ulsan. 'Soegorae', whose length can vary from 10 to 17m, live off the coast of the North Pole in the summer and migrate southward during the winter. Ulsan and whales have had a recationship since the prehistoric age, as is attested to by the whales which are depicted in the Bangudae Amgakhwa (rock drawings).

'Soegorae' swim as near as one or two miles from shore during their stay in the area, which lasts from December to January.

Gosan Onggi Pottery Village F7

The Gosan Onggi Pottery Village is a famous place where more than half of the villagers are pottery makers. In 1957, villagers began to make pottery using traditional methods, a practice which has continued to this day.

The traditional method requires about 8 to 10 days to bake pottery. A low-temperature fire and a high-temperature fire are alternated when baking in a traditional kiln. Nowadays, however, more environment-friendly modified kilns are used. Gosan-ri's rich, high-quality clay gives the area an advantage in its pottery materials.

Seongnamsa Temple

Seongnamsa is a temple which was established on Mt. Gajisan (1,240m). The great Buddhist monk Doui built the temple in the 16th year (824) of the reign of King Heondeok of the Silla Kingdom. Seongnamsa is known for its beautiful architecture, the exquisite harmony of its rocks and the clear valley water that flows through the temple complex.

Seongnamsa has a seminary for Buddhist nuns and houses the Daeungjeon, Geungnakjeon and Jonggak. It also houses such significant cultural assets as the stupa of the great Buddhist priest Doui, a three-storied pagoda and an ancient stone trough.

Seongnamsa

Gosan Onggi Pottery Village

Mujechi Swamp B6

Squarrose Gentian

Whitlow Grass

Korean Aster

Grass of Parnassus

Mujechi Swamp is a marsh that is home to countless wild plants, such as Drosera Rotundifolar, Lilium Concolar Var, Partheneion and Platanthera Logottis Maxim. It has a large variety of marshland plant species. Currently, around 260 kinds of wetland plants are found here.

This swamp is believed to have formed around 6,000 years ago, which means that it provides an excellent resource for learning about the evolutionary process of the ecosystem, changes in the habitats of wetland plants and animals and climatic changes in the southern part of the Korean Peninsula.

Mujechi Swamp

Seosaengpo Waeseong Fortress

Seosaengpo Waeseong is a fortress built by the Japanese General Kato Kiyomasa during the early days of the Japanese Invasion, from the 25th year (1592) of the reign of King Seonjo to the following year. It is a Japanese style tiered stone fortress and has a layered structure which runs from the top of the mountain to the bottom in a downward spiral. Because the fortress wall is highly slanted, it is regarded as a valuable asset in the study of Japanese forts which were constructed around the end of the 16th century.

Jinju Fortress, Korean Style Fortress

The main fortress is on the summit of the mountain, rising 200m above sea level, a second one is situated in the middle of the mountain, and a third further down. The wall of the fortress is 6m high and slanted 15 degrees.

Seosaengpo Waeseong, Japanese Style Fortress

Park Je-sang Remains

At its summit of Mt. Chisullyeong, there is a stone called Mangbuseok (the waiting widow stone), from which the legend about the allegiance of a loyal government official, Park Je-sang, and his wife, originated during the Silla Kingdom Period.

Park Je-sang, a loyal Silla official, went to Goguryeo and Japan to rescue two of King Nulji's brothers who had been taken hostage. After succeeding in getting Bokho, one of the king's brothers, out of Goguryeo, he went to Japan to free Misaheun, the king's other brother. Although he successfully brought the king's brothers back to Silla, Park Je-sang himself was captured by the Japanese and burnt to death after being severely tortured.

In the meantime, his wife Kim took her two daughters to Mt. Chisullyeong and waited for her husband. When she learned of her husband's tragic death, legend has it she died of grief and turned into Mangbuseok. Her spirit is said to have become a bird which hid behind this rock.

Out of gratitude, the king arranged a marriage between his brother Misaheun and Park Je-sang's daughter. He also awarded Park Je-sang a posthumous government post called Daeachan (the 5th grade of the 17 government ranks). Park Je-sang's wife also posthumously received the honorary post of Gukdaebuin. People of the area later built a shrine called Chisan Confucian School on the top of the mountain for performing memorial services dedicated to her.

Ulsan World Cup Stadium F4

Ulsan World Cup Stadium

Ulsan World Cup Stadium is located 10 minutes from the downtown area and is surrounded by a lake and thick forests. It has a seating capacity of 43,512 and the area contains a football field, an auxiliary stadium, an observation square, an open-air theater and quiet walking paths.

In accordance with its architectural concept, the stadium is crown-shaped to symbolize Ulsan's ambition to become the industrial capital of the Pacific Rim region in the 21st century. Its simple and bold structure is representative of Ulsan's image as an industrial center of Korea.

After the 2002 World Cup, there are plans to use the stadium as a comprehensive sports complex, with the additional construction of a baseball stadium, an indoor swimming pool and other facilities.

www.2002worldcupkorea.org
worldcup.metro.ulsan.kr

Gyeonggi-do

Centrally positioned on the Korean Peninsula, Gyeonggi-do has born witness to the country's 5,000-year history. It has some of the most interesting tourist resources around the region. Gyeonggi-do served as a capital during several Korean dynasties. Today, the province surrounds the capital city of Seoul and a part of it even extends into North Korea. Gyeonggi-do is a treasure trove of tourist destinations, which provide visitors with all kinds of attractions, such as mountains, temples, valleys, waterfalls, sea, rivers, beaches, cultural and historical sites, museums, galleries, resorts and parks, golf clubs and hot springs. The official flower of Gyeonggi-do is the golden bell, which signifies prosperity, friendly sentiment, nobility, and brightness.

Suwon Hwaseong Fortress

Hwaseong in Suwon is one of Korea's most notable cultural heritages. It boasts of both historical and architectural significance. Hwaseong represents the most advanced features of fortification available in the 18th century in Korea. The UNESCO World Heritage Committee designated Suwon Hwaseong as a World Heritage site in December 1997.
Hwaseong was originally built by King Jeongjo of the Joseon Dynasty to show his devotion to his deceased father. King Jeongjo transferred the grave of his father, Crown Prince Sado, from Yangju to Hwasan in Suwon in order to comfort his wandering spirit. As a newly-enthroned king, Jeongjo felt the need to consolidate his royal authority and decided to construct a new city to strengthen loyalty and cooperation among his supporters.
Jeong Yak-yong, a young scholar with the pen name of 'Dasan,' was commissioned by the king to build the Suwon Hwaseong. He researched extensively through materials in the royal library and consulted over 5,000 books from China before finalizing the design. Maps, building blueprints, a list of tools used, annex layouts, the names of carpenters, masons and painters, a list of materials used and other details on how the fortress was built can be found in the 'Exemplar of the Construction of Hwaseong Fortress.' Jeong also invented special carts for transporting construction materials and an advanced, stone-lifting pulley called 'Geojunggi.' Hwaseong envelops downtown Suwon in a huge ellipse running a total of 5.52km.

Seojangdae (Western Command Post) & Seonodae (Western Arrow Launching Platforms)

Jangdae can be found on both the east and west ends of the fortress.

Paldalmun (South Gate)

There are four gates in the fortress: the North Gate, Janganmun; the South Gate, Paldalmun; the West Gate, Hwaseomun; and the East Gate, Changnyongmun.

Bongdon (Beacon Tower)

The Hwaseong Fortress also has a communications post that was used for making emergency contact with nearby castles or military stations. The communications post used five smoke boxes, with varying smoke signals used to relay different messages.

Hwaseomun (West Gate) &
Seobuk Gongsimdon (Northwest Observation Tower)

Hwahongmun (North Floodgate)

Along the stream that flows from north to south, there are two stone sluices, or water gates.

Banghwa Suryujeong (Pavilion of the Northeast Angle Tower)

This pavilion was used for numerous purposes, including reconnoitering the enemy and resting. It has a traditional architectural beauty.

Dongbuk Gongsimdon (Northeast Observation Tower)

Sentinels tracked enemy movements and defended against assaults on the fortress from these platforms.

Reenactment of King Jeongjo's Procession to His Father's Tomb

Hwaseong Cultural Festival

About 200 years ago, King Jeongjo, the 22nd King of the Joseon Dynasty, used to parade to his father' s grave to show reverence. The parade is still reenacted in Suwon. The current reenactment is based on meticulous historical research and over 2,000 participants, dressed in the costumes of civil and military officials, court attendants, and guards, participate. The procession covers a distance of several kilometers. Watching the procession helps visitors understand the oriental concept of filial piety. The Yungneung Religious Rite, a memorial service performed here in honor of dead ancestors at the royal tomb, is also reenacted based on historical records.

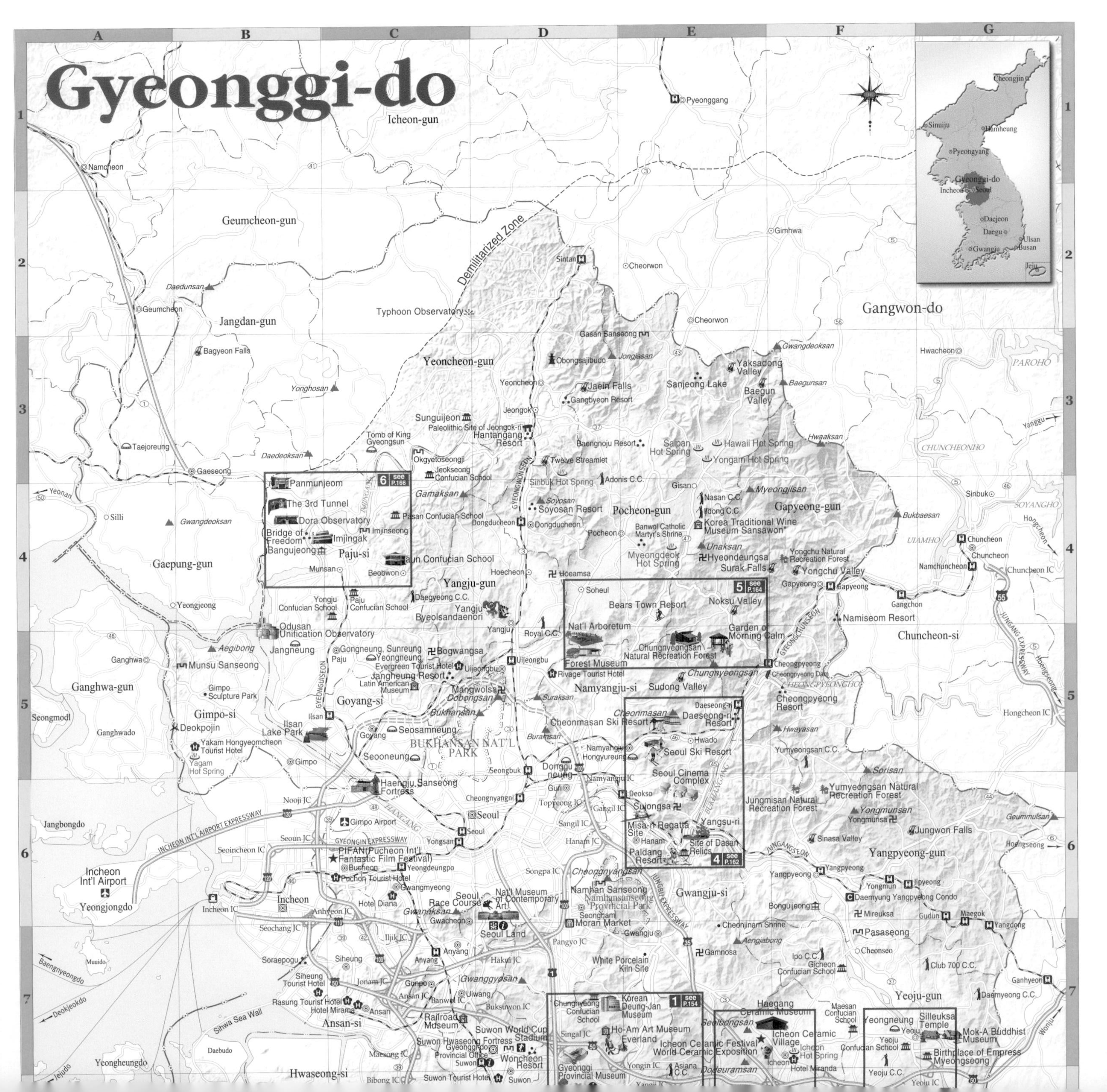

Gyeonggi-do
A
B
C
D
E
F
G
1
2
3
4
5
6
7
Cheongjin
Sinuiju
Hamheung
Pyeongyang
Gyeonggi-do
Incheon
Seoul
Daejeon
Daegu
Ulsan
Busan
Gwangju
Jeju
Icheon-gun
Pyeonggang
Namcheon
Geumcheon-gun
Gimhwa
Demilitarized Zone
Sintan
Cheorwon
Daedunsan
Geumcheon
Jangdan-gun
Typhoon Observatory
Gangwon-do
Bagyeon Falls
Gasan Sanseong
Obongsajibudo
Jongjasan
Gwangdeoksan
Yaksadong Valley
Hwacheon
PAROHO
Yeoncheon-gun
Yeoncheon
Jaein Falls
Sanjeong Lake
Baegun Valley
Baegunsan
Yonghosan
Gangbyeon Resort
Sunguijeon
Jeongok
Paleolithic Site of Jeongok-ri
Hantangang Resort
Tomb of King Gyeongsun
Yanggu
Taejoreung
Baengnoju Resort
Saipan Hot Spring
Hawaii Hot Spring
Hwaaksan
CHUNCHEONHO
Daedeoksan
Okgyetoseongji
Jeokseong Confucian School
Twelve Streamlet
Yongam Hot Spring
Gaeseong
Panmunjeom
Gamaksan
Sinbuk Hot Spring
Adonis C.C.
Gisan
Myeongjisan
Sinbuk
Yeonan
The 3rd Tunnel
Soyosan
Soyosan Resort
Nasan C.C.
Gapyeong-gun
SOYANGHO
Silli
Gwangdeoksan
Dora Observatory
Pasan Confucian School
Dongducheon
Pocheon-gun
Ildong C.C.
Bukbaesan
Hongcheon
Bridge of Freedom
Imjingak
Imjinseong
Banwol Catholic Martyr's Shrine
Pocheon
Korea Traditional Wine Museum Sansawon
UIAMHO
Chuncheon
Bangujeong
Paju-si
Myeongdeok Hot Spring
Unaksan
Hyeondeungsa
Yongchu Natural Recreation Forest
Gaepung-gun
Munsan
Jaun Confucian School
Hoecheon
Surak Falls
Yongchu Valley
Namchuncheon
Chuncheon IC
Beobwon
Hoeamsa
Gapyeong
Yangju-gun
Soheul
Bears Town Resort
Noksu Valley
Gangchon
Yeongjeong
Yongju Confucian School
Paju Confucian School
Daegyeong C.C.
Yangju Byeolsandaenori
Namiseom Resort
Odusan Unification Observatory
Yangju
Royal C.C.
Nat'l Arboretum
Garden of Morning Calm
Chuncheon-si
Aegibong
Jangneung
Gongneung, Sunreung
Bogwangsa
Chungnyeongsan Natural Recreation Forest
Ganghwa
Munsu Sanseong
Paju
Yeongneung
Uijeongbu
Forest Museum
Cheongpyeong
JUNGANG EXPRESSWAY
Evergreen Tourist Hotel
Rivage Tourist Hotel
Chungnyeongsan
Cheongpyeong Dam
Ganghwa-gun
Gimpo Sculpture Park
Jangheung Resort
Latin American Museum
Namyangju-si
Sudong Valley
CHEONGPYEONGHO
Goyang-si
Mangwolsa
Dobongsan
Suraksan
Cheongpyeong Resort
Hongcheon IC
Seongmodl
Gimpo-si
Ilsan
Bukhansan
Cheonmasan
Daeseong-ri Resort
Ganghwado
Deokpojin
Ilsan Lake Park
Goyang
Seosamneung
Cheonmasan Ski Resort
Hwayasan
Yakam Hongyeomcheon Tourist Hotel
BUKHANSAN NAT'L PARK
Buramsan
Hwado
Yagam Hot Spring
Gimpo
Seooneung
Seongbuk
Donggu neung
Namyangju
Hongyureung
Seoul Ski Resort
Yumyeongsan C.C.
Sorisan
Haengju Sanseong Fortress
Guri
Seoul Cinema Complex
Yumyeongsan Natural Recreation Forest
Nooji JC
Cheongnyangni
Namyangju IC
Deokso
Jungmisan Natural Recreation Forest
Jangbongdo
Gimpo Airport
Seoul
Topyeong IC
Gangil IC
Sujongsa
Yongmunsan
Gyeummulsan
INCHEON INT'L AIRPORT EXPRESSWAY
HANGANG
Yongmunsa
Seoun JC
GYEONGIN EXPRESSWAY
Yongsan
Sangil IC
Misa-ri Regatta Site
Yangsu-ri
Jungwon Falls
Seoincheon IC
PIFAN(Pucheon Int'l Fantastic Film Festival)
Hanam IC
Hanam
Site of Dasan Relics
Sinasa Valley
Incheon Int'l Airport
Bucheon
Yeongdeungpo
Paldang Resort
Hoengseong
Yangpyeong-gun
Pucheon Tourist Hotel
Songpa IC
Cheongnyangsan
Yangpyeong
Gwangmyeong
Seoul
Nat'l Museum of Contemporary Art
Namhan Sanseong
Namhansanseong Provincial Park
Gwangju-si
Yongmun
Jipyeong
Yeongjongdo
Incheon IC
Incheon
Hotel Diana
Race Course
Daemyung Yangpyeong Condo
Anhyeon JC
Gwanaksan
Seongnam
Bongujeong
Mireuksa
Gudun
Maegok
Seochang JC
Gwacheon
Moran Market
Gwangju
Chedinjinam Shrine
Yangdong
Seoul Land
Pasaseong
Ijik JC
Pangyo JC
Aengjabong
Cheonseo
Baengnyeongdo
Soraepogu
Siheung
Anyang
Hakui JC
Gamnosa
Ipo C.C.
Gicheon Confucian School
Muuido
White Porcelain Kiln Site
Club 700 C.C.
Siheung Tourist Hotel
Jonam JC
Gunpo
Gwanggyosan
Ganhyeon
Deokjeokdo
Ansan JC
Uiwang
Banwol IC
Chunghyeong Confucian School
Korean Deung-Jan Museum
Maesan Confucian School
Yeongneung
Silleuksa Temple
Yeoju-gun
Daemyeong C.C.
Rasung Tourist Hotel
Hotel Mirama
Ansan
Buksuwon IC
Haegang Ceramic Museum
Yeoju
Wonju
Sihwa Sea Wall
Ansan-si
Railroad Museum
Suwon World Cup Stadium
Singal JC
Ho-Am Art Museum
Seolbongsan
Icheon Ceramic Village
Mok-A Buddhist Museum
Daebudo
Suwon Hwaseong Fortress
Gyeonggi-do Provincial Office
Everland
Icheon Ceramic Festival
Confucian School
Birthplace of Empress Myeongseong
Jejudo
Yeongheungdo
Maesong IC
Suwon
Woncheon Resort
Yongin IC
World Ceramic Exposition
Icheon Hot Spring
Hwaseong-si
Bibong IC
Suwon Tourist Hotel
Suwon
Gyeonggi Provincial Museum
Asiana C.C.
Dodeuramsan
Icheon
Hotel Miranda
Yeoju C.C.
Yeoju IC
see P.166
see P.164
see P.162
see P.154

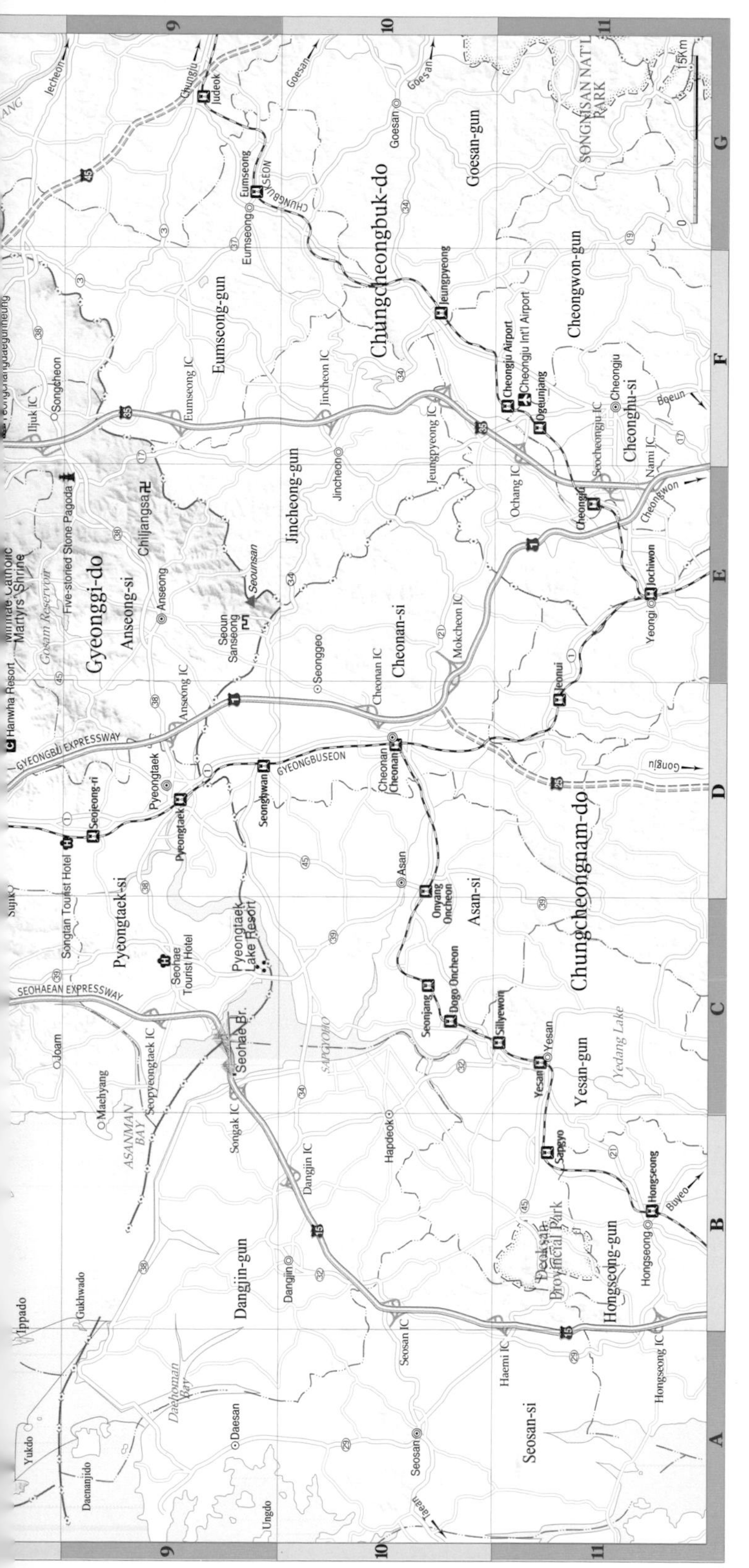

INDEX

Cultural Relics

Natural Attractions

Museums & Theaters

Places of Interest

Accommodations

Transportation

Tourist Information

Gyeonggi-do Tourist Information Center 82-31-228-2766
Gyeonggi-do Tourist Complaint Center 82-31-242-0101
www.provin.kyonggi.kr

LEGEND

- Railroad Station
- Tourist Information Center
- Museum
- Gallery
- Prehistoric Relic Site
- Tomb
- Fortress
- Temple
- Site of Buddhist Artifacts
- Traditional Building
- Traditional Pavilion
- Cultural Experience Area
- Battlefield
- Falls or Valley
- Beach
- Ski Resort
- Golf Course
- Horse Track
- Hot Spring or Spa
- Scenic Area
- Amusement Park
- Mountain
- Other Tourist Attractions
- Hotel
- Condominium
- Department Store or Market
- Reference Point

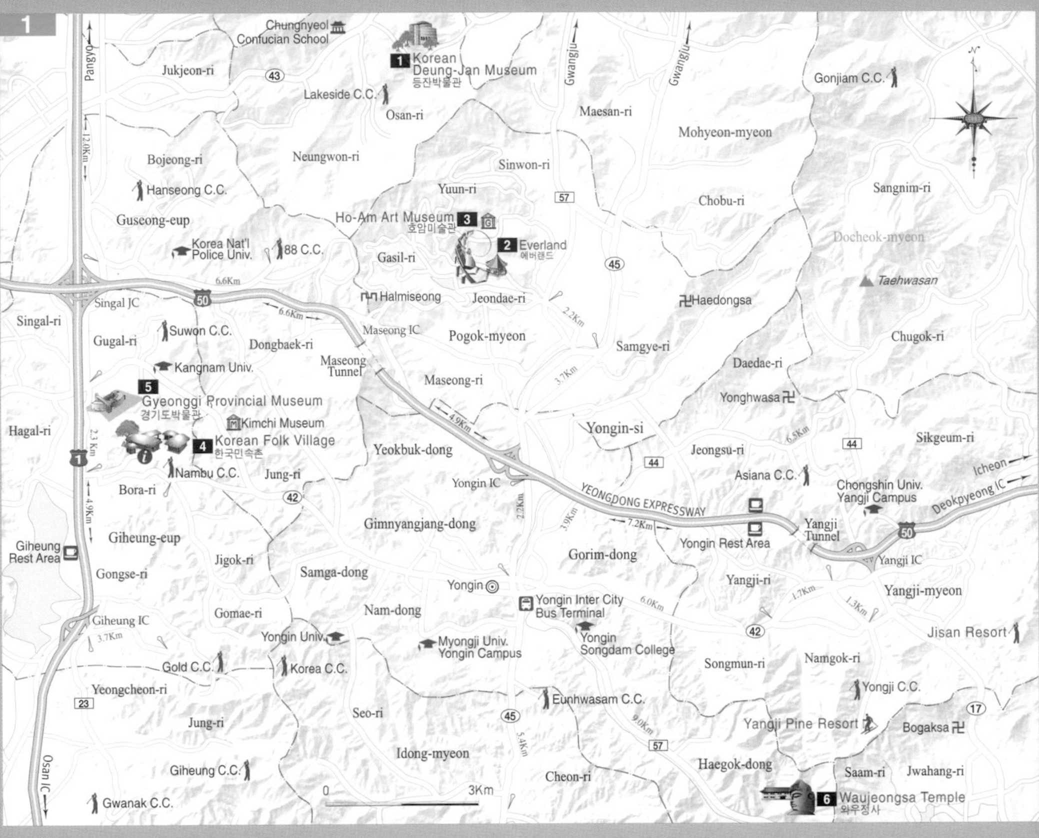

Yongin is in the middle of Gyeonggi-do, 40 km south of Seoul. It has a lush green environment and diverse cultural facilities. A convenient transit system provides easy access to the town.
Yongin offers visitors a variety of tours which allow them to visit any number of the cultural heritage and relics sites. Yongin's attractions include the Korean Folk Village, Gyeonggi Provincial Museum and a wide range of sports and leisure facilities, including golf courses, ski slopes and sledding courses.

Korean Deung-Jan Museum 1

Deung-Jan Museum Exhibit

The Korean Deung-Jan Museum is a private gallery which was established to preserve the history of traditional lamps. A Deung-Jan is a traditional lamp which was used to light houses at night. The museum's exhibit rooms are classified into 3 sections.

The first section introduces how traditional lamps were used in the lives of Koreans. The second section shows the history of lamps, from ancient to modern times. The third section displays various traditional lamps, which have designs ranging from very simple to highly intricate.

Deung-Jan, a Traditional Lamp

Safari World
Rose Garden

Caribbean Bay

Everland 2

Everland is an integrated theme park located in Pogok-myeon, Yongin. It is now the world's 7th most-visited theme park. It has a zoo, a children's park, sleigh slopes, an amusement park, and botanical gardens, all of which are located on 3,700 acres of land.
Currently, Everland consists of three theme parks: Festival World, Caribbean Bay and Speedway. Festival World is equipped with more than 40 attractions and a zoo. It offers various flower festivals and seasonal events. Caribbean Bay opened in July of 1996 and is the largest water-park in the world with both indoor and outdoor water facilities in year-round operation. Speedway is one of the best motor sport racetrack in Korea.

Ho-Am Art Museum 3

The Ho-Am Art Museum opened in 1982 with 1,167 artifacts and art objects donated to the Samsung Foundation of Culture by the late Lee Byung-chul, founder and former chairman of the Samsung Group.
Today it is a home to the collection of more than 15,000 items, including earthenware, metalworks, ancient books, paintings and porcelain.
Each year since its establishment, the museum has rotated its own collections and brought in various works from abroad.

Celadon Wine Pot with Lotus Design in Inlaid Copper (National Treasure No. 133)

Korean Folk Village 4

A Nobleman's House

The Korean Folk Village is one of five major outdoor folk museums in the world, and one of the most popular destination for foreign tourists in Korea.

A wide assortment of residential structures, from the straw-thatched cottages of commoners to the 99-room home of the noble class, have been re-created to help illustrate the diversity of traditional Korean culture.

Houses, oriental herbal medicine shops, schools, local weather stations, smith shops, brassware workshops, ceramic and iron pot factories, and markets which sell traditional food and housewares have also been re-created according to the particular styles of the northern, central, southern regions, Jeju, and Ulleungdo Island. The Korean Folk Village offers various performances as well, including folk music and dance, tightrope acrobatics, traditional weddings, traditional seesaw jumping, and seasonal cultural and art performances, as well as many other special events.

Weaving Bamboo Basketry

Wooden Bridge
Stepping Stone
Stone Bridge
Bridge Gate

INDEX

1. Main Gate **2.** Hangukkwan (Korean Restaurant) **3.** Souvenir Shop **4.** Seonangdang (Shrine of Village) **5.** Three Passage Gate **6.** Pottery Shop **7.** Yeonja banga (Mill stone) **8.** Farmer' s House In the Southern Region **9.** Manor House In the Southern Part **10.** Herbal Medicine Shop **11.** Farmer' s House In the Central Region **12.** Geumryeonsa Temple **13.** Provincial Governor' s Office **14.** Performing Area **15.** Seodang (Private School) **16.** Fortune Teller' s House **17.** Yangban (Nobleman' s House) **18.** House in the Northern Part **19.** Jangteo (Traditional Market) **20.** Folk Museum **21.** Art Museum **22.** Chunghyeon Confucian School **23.** Amusement Park

Korean Folk Village Information

Farmer' s Music and Dance
12:00 and 15:00 - Performing Arena

Tightrope Acrobatics
12:30 and 15:30 - Performing Arena

Traditional Wedding
13:00 and 16:00 - House No. 9

Entrance fee : 8,500 won

Hours
09:00 ~ 16:30 (Winter)
09:00 ~ 18:30 (Summer)

www.koreanfolk.co.kr

Korean Folk Village Pavilion

Gyeonggi Provincial Museum 5

Gyeonggi Provincial Museum

This museum is Korea's first provincial museum. It was established to preserve and display the local cultural heritage of Gyeonggi-do. The building's exterior is designed to resemble the shape of the Suwon Hwaseong Fortress. The museum includes a printing workshop as well as folk lifestyle, painting, calligraphy, natural history, ancient art, literature and record rooms.
www.musenet.or.kr

Geojunggi, a Stationary Hoist

Waujeongsa Temple 6

Waujeongsa is a Buddhist temple situated amidst the 48 peaks of Mt. Yeonhwasan. This is the head temple of the Yeolban (Nirvana) sect of Korean Buddhism. Among the three thousand Buddhist statues enshrined in Waujeongsa, the Buldu (Buddha head) and the Wabul (Reclining Buddha) are particularly well known. The eight-meter tall Buldu has been recorded as the world's largest image of Buddha by the Guinness Book of World Records. The Wabul, which is three meters tall and twelve meters long, and carved from a single juniper tree.
Other attractions include the Five Brass Buddhas, made from 30,000kg of brass over a ten-year period; the twelve-ton Unification Bell; and Korea's biggest bronze statue of a meditating Maitreya. Beside the steps leading to the Yeolbanjeon Shrine is a stone tower which was built using stones from various Buddhist holy sites around the world.

Jar, Featuring Comb-pattern Pottery

Slate Spear & Dagger

Wabul (the world' s largest wooden statue of a lying Buddha)

The Buldu Buddha Head

Five Brass Statues of Buddha

ICHEON

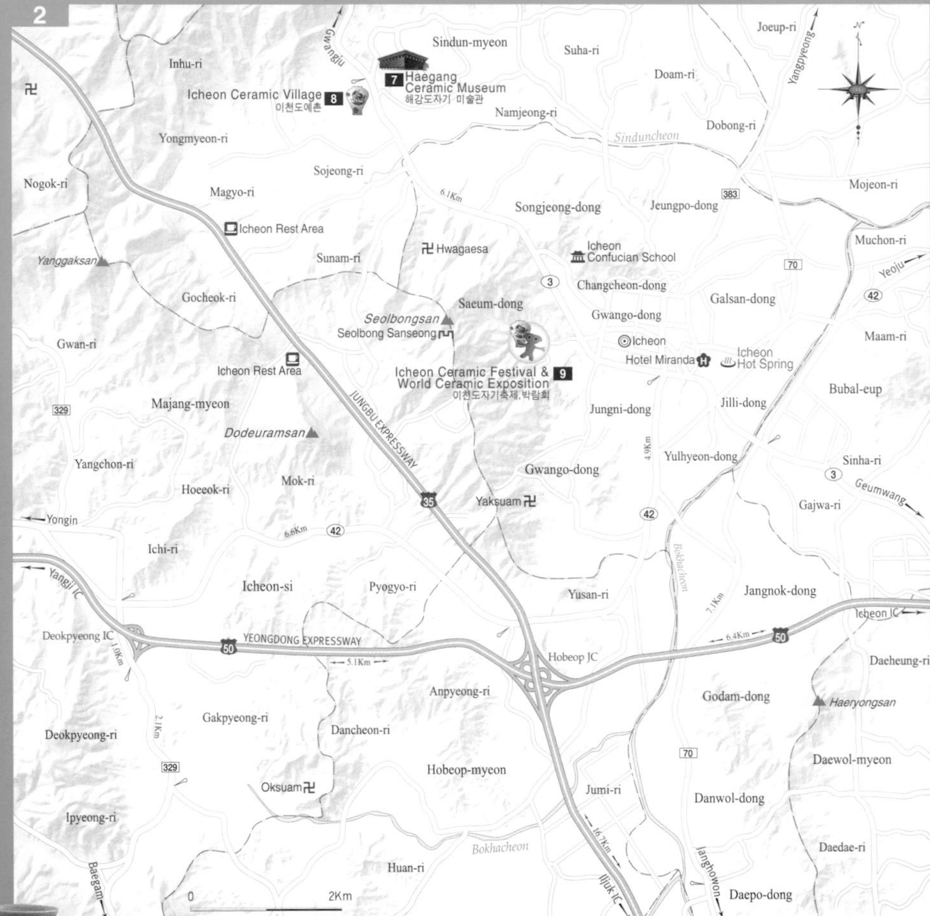

Icheon is located in the heart of southeastern Gyeonggi-do. It is surrounded by mountains and rice fields.
Icheon's artisans produce world-famous ceramic products using the city's rich soil, continuing a proud tradition which has endured for over a thousand years.
Icheon is also renowned for its natural hot springs, which flow from a source originating near Mt. Seolbongsan and Mt. Dodeuramsan. The city has many nearby tourist attractions, including Seolbong Fortress, Dokpyong Golf Club and Jisan Resort.

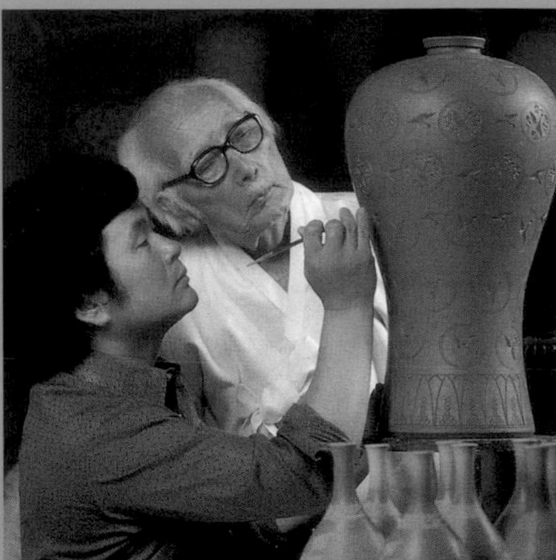

Haegang Ceramic Museum 7

The Haegang Ceramic Museum is an art gallery built specifically to promote Korea's celadon.
The ceramic culture room displays different classifications of pottery, pottery types, production processes, and design techniques. More than 1,400 items are displayed, including 12th century Goryeo celadon, Joseon white porcelain and grayish-green chinaware. The Haegang Memorial Center exhibits twenty masterpieces by the renowned artist Haegang. His exquisite works have a mystical blue hue, and their unique inlay and design carry on the rich tradition of world-renowned Goryeo porcelain.

Icheon Ceramic Village 8

Icheon has been known for earthenware craftsmanship since the Bronze Age. The area has many vestiges of earthenware culture in Korea. With the influence of Joseon Dynasty porcelain, which was introduced by neighboring Gwangju, Icheon has carried on the tradition of Korean porcelain making from generation to generation. It remains home to many ceramic artisans who strive to re-create the beauty of Goryeo celadon and Joseon white porcelain.
The Icheon Ceramic Village has evolved into the center of traditional Korean ceramics. There are approximately 350 pottery shops spread over the Saeum-dong and Sindun-myeon areas.

A Celadon Vase (left) and a White Porcelain (right)

Experience Time in the Icheon Ceramic Village

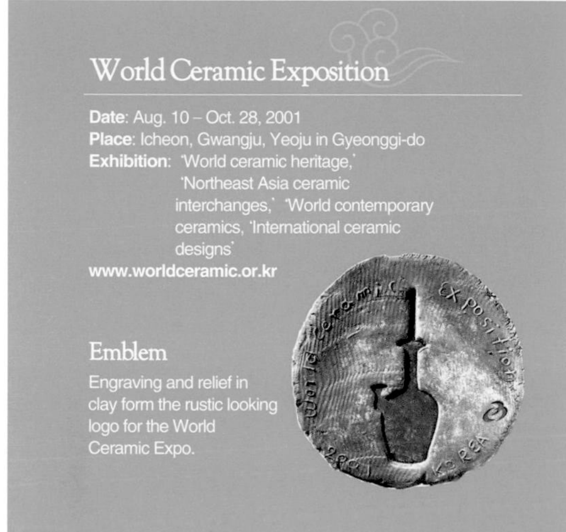

World Ceramic Exposition

Date: Aug. 10 – Oct. 28, 2001
Place: Icheon, Gwangju, Yeoju in Gyeonggi-do
Exhibition: 'World ceramic heritage,' 'Northeast Asia ceramic interchanges,' 'World contemporary ceramics, 'International ceramic designs'
www.worldceramic.or.kr

Emblem

Engraving and relief in clay form the rustic looking logo for the World Ceramic Expo.

Icheon Ceramic Festival 9

Korea's biggest ceramic festival is held in Icheon, Korea's ceramics center. There are about 250 kilns in this town and visitors can witness first-hand the process of creating some of the world's finest ceramics artwork. Festival-goers may also have the unique experience of creating their own celadon or white porcelain pieces.

The Process of Pottery-making

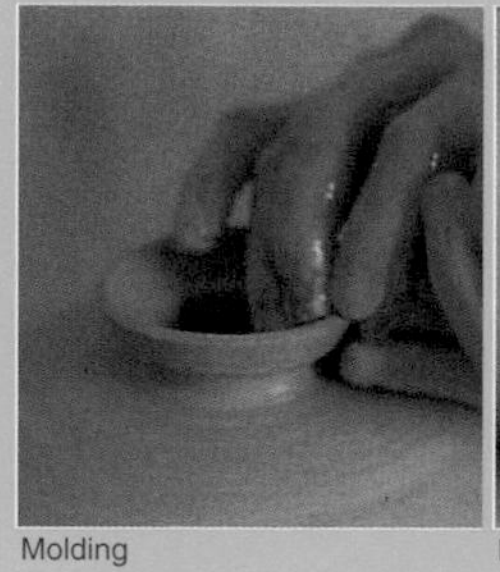
Molding

Marking

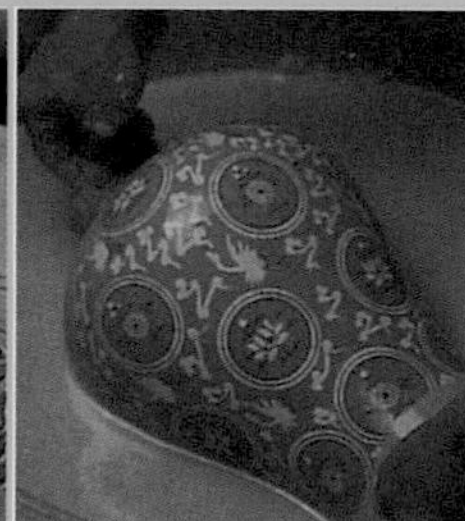
Glazing

Finished Pottery

Donghae Ceramic
82-31-634-4998

Gwangjuyo
82-31-632-7007

Goryo Ceramic
82-31-632-7009

Jigang Ceramic
82-31-638-5548

Joseon Ceramic
82-31-632-7034

Yewon Ceramic
82-31-634-2244

Haegang Ceramic Museum
82-31-634-2266

A Ceramist

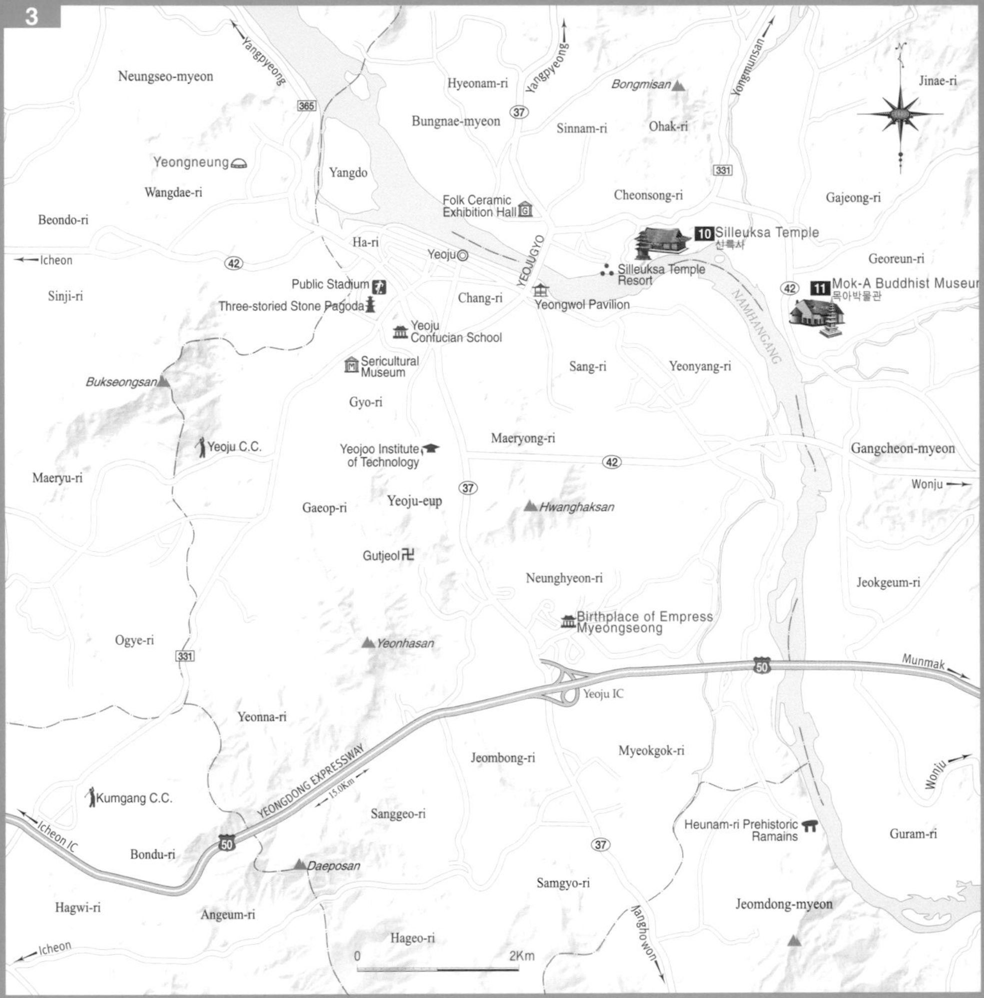

Yeoju is located close to Icheon in the southeast area of Gyeonggi-do and borders the Namhangang River.
This is the largest pottery village in Korea. Artisans here use traditional techniques to create Goryeo celadon and Joseon white porcelain.
The rice produced in the fertile soil of Yeoju is known for being of the highest quality in Korea.
Yeoju tourist destinations include Silleuksa Temple, the Mok-A Buddhist Museum, Yeongneung (the Tomb of King Sejong) and the birth place of Empress Myeongseong.

Gangweolheon Pavilion, Silleuksa Temple

Silleuksa Temple 10

Located in the foothills of Mt. Bongmisan, 2.5km from Yeoju, Silleuksa is said to have been founded by the great Buddhist monk Won-hyo of the Silla Kingdom. Nearby this historic temple flows the Namhangang River. In Korea, it is unusual for a temple to be situated so close to a river. The temple holds many important national treasures, like the Geungnakbojeon Hall, the Josadang Shrine (Treasure No. 180), a multi-storied stone pagoda (Treasure No. 225), a multi-storied brick pagoda (Treasure No. 226), and a stupa of Buddhist priest Bojejonja (Treasure No. 228).

Geungnakbojeon Hall

Mok-A Buddhist Museum

· Mireuk Samjonbul (Maitreya Triad) in the Outdoor Sculpture Park (top)
· Buddha Statue in the Mok-A Buddhist Museum (bottom)

Mok-A Buddhist Museum 11

Mok-A Buddhist Museum is a privately run museum specializing in Buddhist art. The museum's founder, Park Chan-soo, has been designated as a national human cultural asset. The museum contains a main exhibition hall and an outdoor sculpture park. The four-storied main exhibition hall preserves and exhibits over 6,000 Buddhist artifacts and pieces of artwork, including woodwork, statues, calligraphy and paintings. In the basement is a theater where a documentary film, 'the Wood that would like to become a Buddha' is shown. This film explains the development of Korean Buddhist images, the characteristics of each era, and the process of creating Buddhist sculptures. Visitors can also enjoy notable Buddhist sculptures such as the Mireuk samjonbul (Maitreya Triad), Bironajabul, and a three-storied stone pagoda.

www.moka.or.kr

Child Monks Crafted from Wood

Beopsang (the seat used by a Buddhist master when he preaches to the public)

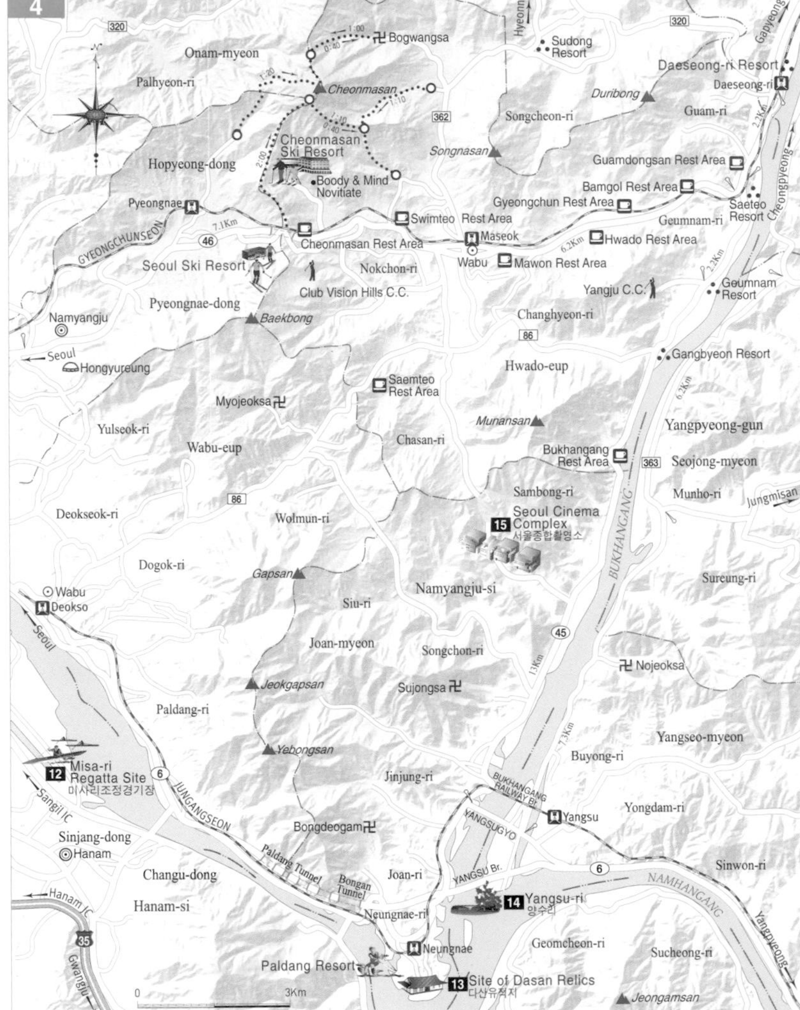

Misa-ri Regatta Site 12

This boat racing track was designed to meet international standards and was used during the '88 Seoul Olympics for boat racing and canoeing. The wide grassy areas and promenades bordering the water are often used for family picnics and walking. There are also cafes and restaurants on the lakeside.

Misa-ri Regatta

Birthplace of Dasan Jeong Yak-yong

Site of the Dasan Relics 13

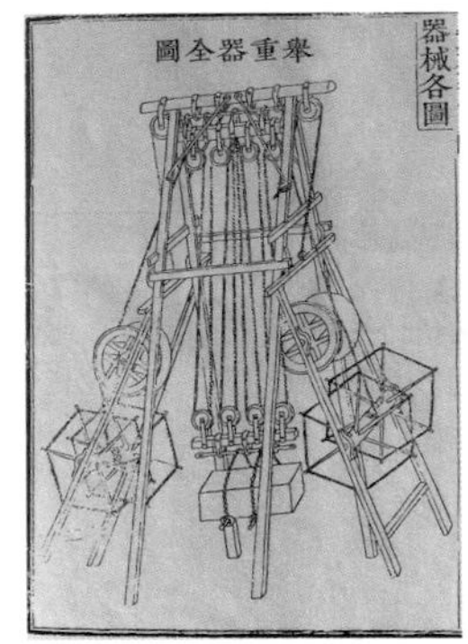

'Geojunggi,' a Stationary Hoist

The birthplace and burial site of 'Dasan' Jeong Yak-yong is in Namyangju-gun, Gyeonggi-do. Dasan was a renowned administrator, scientist, architect and philosopher during the late Joseon Dynasty. He was also a reform-minded scholar who led the Real Learning Movement, which emphasized practical and pragmatic learning. This site contains Dasan's birthplace, shrine, Memorial House and his burial place.

The relics and writings of Dasan are displayed at the Dasan Memorial Hall. This exhibit is organized according to the four major periods of his life.

There are more than 500 volumes of books written by Dasan, which are categorized by subject matter, showing the breadth of his work.

Among the exhibited materials are scale models of 'Geojunggi,' a stationary hoist, and 'Nongno,' a modern-day crane, which were both produced based on designs by Dasan. He designed these engineering devices to alleviate some of the toil of the workers building Suwon Hwaseong.

Portrait of Jeong Yak-yong

Yangsu-ri Riverside

· An Open Set of the Popular Korean Movie, 'JSA' (top)
· Undang was originally located in Jongno, Seoul. This the replica of Undang displays the features of a typical noble house from the Seoul/Gyeonggi area.(bottom)

Yangsu-ri 14

Yangsu-ri means the place that the Namhangang River and the Bukhangang River meet. Its scenery is similar to that of a landscape painting. Yangsu-ri is said to be the most beautiful at dawn. In the spring or fall, when there's a big difference in the temperatures of night and day, the morning fog shrouds the riverside reeds and forms a ethereal sight in the quiet of dawn.

Indoor Studio at the Seoul Cinema Complex

Seoul Cinema Complex 15

The Seoul Cinema Complex is situated near the Bukhangang and surrounded by a thick forest. Visitors can learn about the world of film-making through various exhibits and hands-on experiences.
The Visual Support Center displays various movie-related materials. Visitors who enter the Visual Experience Center can learn about movie production methods, state-of-the-art special effects and sound effect technologies. The Principles-of-Film Experience Hall introduces visitors to the world of editing, sound effects, lighting, image composition, and the basic technical aspects of film making. The Film & Culture Hall showcases still pictures, movie posters, movie models, movie-making equipment, and up-to-date video materials. The outdoor & indoor studios and the Prop and Wardrobe Center are also open to visitors.

Seoul Cinema Complex Information

Tour Course
An open set of the popular Korean movie 'JSA' – Small town set – Traditional Korean house 'Undang' – Visual Support Center – Visual Theater

Hours
10:00 ~ 17:00 (Mar. – Oct.)
10:00 ~ 16:00 (Nov. – Feb.)

www.kofic.or.kr

Garden of Morning Calm 16

The Garden of Morning Calm blends in naturally with its surroundings, forming a harmonious link with nearby Mt. Chungnyeongsan. The garden is composed of various theme gardens, such as the Korean Garden, the Bonsai Garden, the Wild Flower Garden, the Iris Garden, the Biblical Garden, the Morning Plaza, the Poets Trail, and the Rose of Sharon Hill. It also has a pine tree forest where visitors can engage in the ancient practice of meditative walking.

National Arboretum 17

The National Arboretum has been carefully managed for more than 500 years. It was designated as the Imperial Forest of the Joseon Dynasty. This dense forest is a part of the tomb site of King Sejo, the 7th King of the Joseon Dynasty.

This area is one of the most diverse ecosystems in Korea. It supports more than 1,900 native and 2,800 non-native species of plants. The arboretum consists of 15 special sections; wetland flora, alpine plants, aquatic plants, deciduous trees, conifer trees, ground cover plants, medicinal and edible herbs, subtropical plants, foreign flora, and botanical plants.

Due to its rich bio-diversity, the National Arboretum also serves as a natural habitat for such rare wild animals as the Korean woodpecker, the flying squirrel, the long-horned beetle and many others.

The arboretum is open for educational purposes on weekdays. To explore the arboretum, visitors must make reservations five days in advance.

www.foa.go.kr

Forest Museum 18

The Forest Museum in the National Arboretum displays various fauna and flora samples, arboriculture technology, natural resources and diverse products which have been made from wood. About 1,500 items are exhibited in this two-story building. The museum is designed in the style of a traditional Korean structure.

Forest Walking Path

▲ Bog Garden
◀ Water Lily

▲ Subtropical Botanical Garden
◀ Camellia Flower

▲ Aquatic and Wetland Garden
◀ Day Lily

▲ Blind Person Garden
◀ Japanese Spicebush

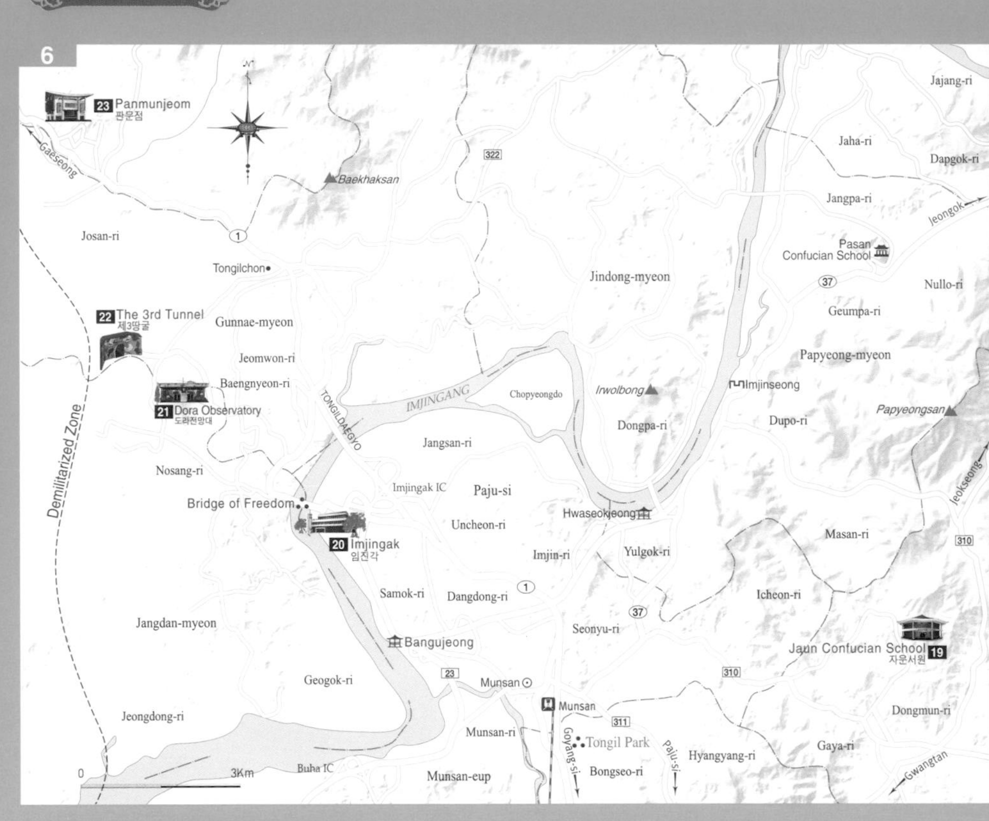

Paju is in the northwest part of the Gyeonggi-do, in the middle of the Korean Peninsula. It is located 30 minutes from Seoul by either the Jayuro, Tongillo or Gyeongui Railway Lines.

The military demarcation line, which extends 241 km, and the Joint Security Area in Panmunjeom, are well known tourist destinations. The DMZ (Demilitarized Zone) remains a unique place where ideologies from the Cold war still divide the country. Currently, access to the area is limited due to security reasons. Because it has been untouched and has remained an unspoiled natural ecosystem for the 50 years since Korean War, it will become an invaluable asset as a cultural and tourism attractions after the unification of the Korean Peninsula.

Jaun Confucian School 19

Jaun Confucian School

This school was originally built in 1615 in order to commemorate the scholarly attainments and virtues of Yulgok Yi Yi (1536-1584), a great scholar from that period. In front of the school is the Yulgok Training Center.

The Yulgok Culture Festival is held every October to commemorate his accomplishments.

Imjingak 20

This is a place where tourists contemplate the tragedy of the Korean War and the national division that followed. Built in 1972 to console those who had to leave their homes in the north, the building has a museum where various documents and about 400 pictures are displayed to provide a rare look at North Korea's military, politics and society. Outside, numerous tanks, airplanes and other forms of war weaponry are displayed.

Located nearby is the Bridge of Freedom, and the remnants of the Gyeongui Railway Line, which once ran into North Korea but which now is represented by a rusting locomative. Also here is the Mangbaedan Altar, which is a place where those who were displaced from their homes in the north gather to pray for their ancestors.

The Bridge of Freedom

· View of North Korea from the Dora Observatory (above left)
· Panmunjeom (above center)
· Inside the 3rd Tunnel (above)

Dora Observatory 21

The Dora Observatory was established in 1986. It is the most northern observatory for viewing of the life and environment of the people living in North Korea. There are 12 telescopes here and a viewing room with 500 seats.

From the observatory, visitors can see a good view of Mt. Songaksan, a statute of Kim Il-seong, Gaeseong-si, and other notable sites. Tourists need to get permission from the military to visit this observatory.

The 3rd Tunnel 22

The 3rd Underground Tunnel is a strategic military area which was excavated by North Korea in order to infiltrate the South. The tunnel was discovered on October 17, 1978, based on intelligence information given by a North Korean defector, Kim Bu-seong. It is located 44km north of Seoul, or approximately 45-minutes away by car. Though its size is similar to a tunnel which was previously discovered, because of its proximity to the Seoul metropolitan area, this tunnel is by far the most threatening secret passageway. The tunnel is arch-shaped and is 2m in width and height and 1,635m in length. It can allow the passage of an estimated ten thousand fully armed soldiers or thirty thousand unarmed soldiers per hour.

3rd Tunnel Entrance

Panmunjeom 23

Panmunjeom is the truce village where the Korean Armistice Agreement was signed on July 27, 1953, ending the fierce fighting of the Korean War (1950-53). It is now a Joint Security Area managed by the U.N. Command and North Korean guards and is beyond the administrative control of both South and North Korea. Panmunjeom is a living symbol of the tragedy of modern Korean history.

In the northern section of Panmunjeom stands the Bridge of No Return, the deserted Jangdan Station, and a railcar full of bullet-holes. Currently, Panmunjeom is the site of inter-Korean peace talks.

Mirinae Catholic Martyrs' Shrine

Yangju Byeolsandaenori D4

The traditional mask dance of this area is called 'Byeolsandaenori.' Yangju Byeolsandaenori embodies the humor and travails of the commoner's life. Korean mask dances served as an outlet for the general population to express their discontent against the ruling class through subtle and satirical songs and dance movements. Every Saturday, from April to October at 16:00, a one and a half hour performance is presented.

Byeolsandaenori performer

Mirinae Catholic Martyrs' Shrine E8

Mirinae is one of the regions in Korea where Catholicism first took root. Many early followers of the Catholic faith lived in hiding here during the persecutions of the Joseon Dynasty. The relics of Korea's first ordained priest, Kim Dae-geon, are enshrined here. In 1984, when the Pope visited Korea, 103 martyrs were canonized, including Kim Dae-geon. The cathedral was built to commemorate the canonization of these saints.

Mt. Yongmunsan F6

Mt. Yongmunsan has so much bedrock that it appears as though it is virtually covered with rocks. Yongmunsa Temple, which has a history of over a thousand years is located

Yongmunsa Temple

here. In front of Yongmunsa, a huge ginkgo tree is visible. This tree has a girth of 14m, a height of 60m, and is also said to be over one thousand years old.

Jebudo Island B8

This island is known for an unusual phenomenon; twice a day the sea divides in half, providing a Korean version of the biblical story where Moses parts the Red Sea. The island has a long coastal line at the end of a sand flat.

When the tide is out, a 3m-wide path appears, and on both sides of it a 500m flat area is exposed. The left side is primarily muddy, while the right side contains sand and gravel. As the tide comes in, the path and flat area are again covered by the sea. The tide remains high for about six hours a day, though the time changes depending on the day. Maebawi (the Hawk Rock), the fish market and the beach are a few of the more popular attractions.

Maebawi (the Hawk Rock) in Jebudo

Puchon International Fantastic Film Festival (PIFAN) C6

The PIFAN is a festival that features non-mainstream films, providing an alternative to commercial movies. Films that are imaginative and future-oriented take center stage at this annual gala. The PIFAN has become a venue for the introduction of various international fantasy films to Korean movie fans, as well as a means of introducing Korean movies to foreign film critics. The festival also promotes the production of fantasy films in Korea and assists in their international distribution.
www.pifan.com

National Museum of Contemporary Art D6

The National Museum of Contemporary Art (MOCA) exhibits a diverse range of 20th century Korean and international art work which reflects trends in modern art. The museum owns approximately 3,600 pieces of art from the modern period. The MOCA consists of six permanent exhibition halls which showcase traditional Korean paintings, western paintings, sculptures, crafts, calligraphy, and photography. There is also a hall for special exhibitions and an outdoor sculpture park. One of the most popular exhibits in the museum's permanent collection is a work of video art titled 'The More the Better' by the celebrated Paik Nam-jun.
www.moca.go.kr

National Museum of Contemporary Art

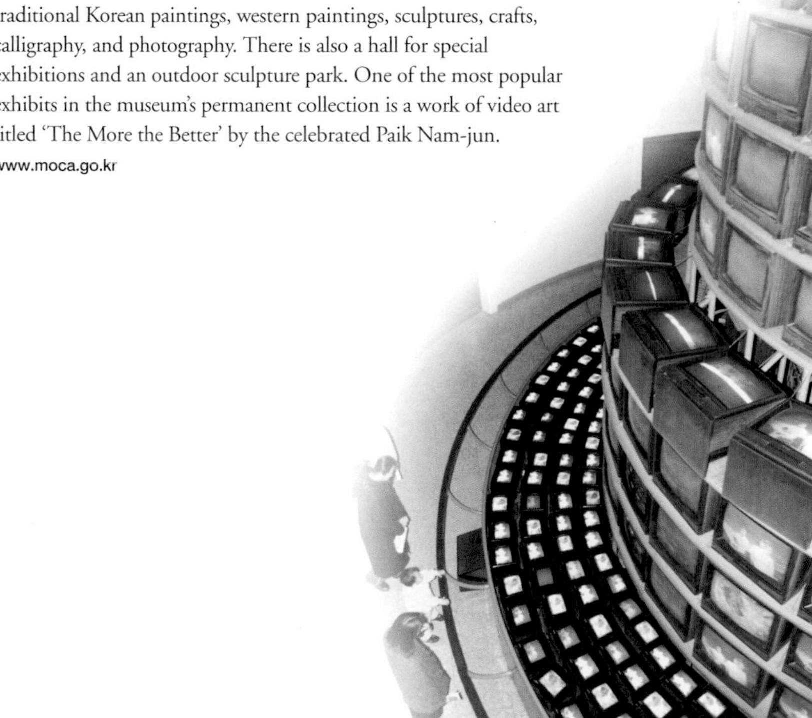
'The More the Better' by the Video Artist Paik Nam-Jun

Sanjeong Lake

Sanjeong Lake E3

The scenery of Sanjeong Lake is breathtaking with the surrounding mountains encircling the lake like a folding screen. The lake's name, Sanjeong, implies a sense of tranquility and peacefulness, as it means a spring between the mountains.

The mist that forms at dawn and dusk creates a mystical atmosphere and a boat ride on the lake at this time is recommended. There are also many facilities for tourists to enjoy, like the hiking trails, boat piers, bungalows and playgrounds. Jainsa Temple, Deungnyong Fall, Biseon Fall and numerous other tourist sights are located near the lake.

In 1996, Hanwha Condominium was opened, offering such facilities as swimming pools, bowling lanes and a sauna. Recently, a snow-sledding field and an ice-skating rink were added.

Pocheon Makgeolli (rice wine)

Pocheon Makgeolli has traditionally been one of the Pocheon area's special products.
Unlike other alcoholic drinks, makgeolli is rich in protein and vitamins. It is fermented from rice and has a thick, rough initial taste while leaving a mild after taste. Makgeolli is a popular drink with Koreans.

Suwon World Cup Stadium D7

Suwon World Cup Stadium

The Suwon World Cup Stadium will be used for soccer matches of the 2002 FIFA World Cup. It is equipped with ultramodern features and has a seating capacity for more than 40,000 people.

The design concept of the Suwon Stadium merges the past and future by harmonizing the historical background of old Suwon Hwaseong with cutting-edge architectural technology. The wing-shaped roof is said to symbolize the city soaring into a promising future.

www.2002worldcupkorea.org
www.2002suwon.net

Gangwon-do

Located in the mid-eastern part of the Korean Peninsula and flanked by the East Sea and the Taebaek Mountains, Gangwon-do is full of natural beauty. Thanks to its splendid landscape and thickly forested mountains, Gangwon-do is better suited for tourist attractions than for residential areas. Another feature of this area is the Tongil (Reunification) Observatory, from which visitors can enjoy a fantastic view of Mt. Geumgangsan, located in North Korea. Gangwon-do has a small population compared to its land size and has been slow to develop. Its official flower is the royal azalea and official bird is the crane. Cranes symbolize peace and unification because of their coming and going freely between South and North Korea.

Gwandongpalgyeong

The Eight Scenic Vistas of Gwandong

From olden times, Korean people have extolled the merits of scenic spots, representing each region of Gwandongpalgyeong with poems, songs, and drawings. Scenic places were often grouped into gyeong (scenic views). Gwandongpalgyeong refers to the eight most beautiful scenic spots in the Gwandong region, which is located east of Daegwallyeong Pass. The Gwandongpalgyeong are regarded as the most celebrated locations because of the stunning views from pavilions which were built on each of the eight spots.
The Gwandongpalgyeong includes Chongseokjeong in Tongcheon, Samilpo in Goseong, Cheongganjeong in Ganseong, Uisangdae in Yangyang, Gyeongpodae in Gangneung, Jukseoru in Samcheok, Mangyangjeong in Uljin and Wolsongjeong in Pyeonghae.

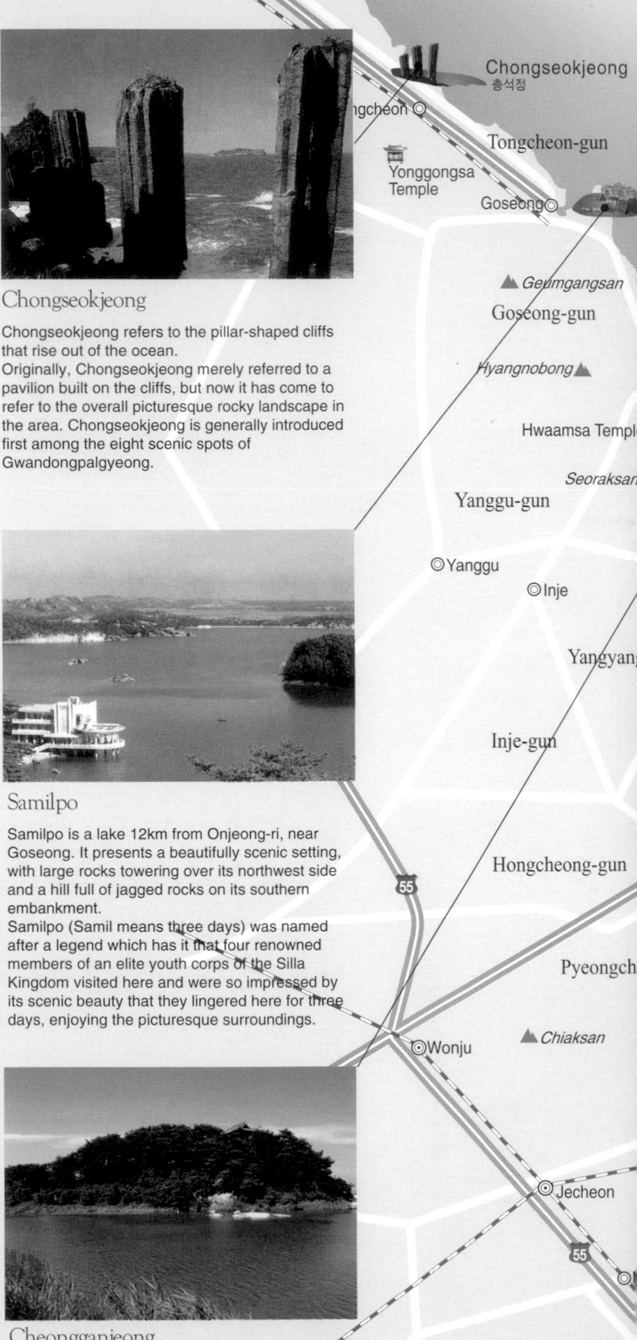

Chongseokjeong

Chongseokjeong refers to the pillar-shaped cliffs that rise out of the ocean.
Originally, Chongseokjeong merely referred to a pavilion built on the cliffs, but now it has come to refer to the overall picturesque rocky landscape in the area. Chongseokjeong is generally introduced first among the eight scenic spots of Gwandongpalgyeong.

Samilpo

Samilpo is a lake 12km from Onjeong-ri, near Goseong. It presents a beautifully scenic setting, with large rocks towering over its northwest side and a hill full of jagged rocks on its southern embankment.
Samilpo (Samil means three days) was named after a legend which has it that four renowned members of an elite youth corps of the Silla Kingdom visited here and were so impressed by its scenic beauty that they lingered here for three days, enjoying the picturesque surroundings.

Cheongganjeong

Cheonggangjeong, 7km to the north of the city of Sokcho, is a two-storied pavilion located on a cliff at Cheongganchean stream, which flows through the valleys of Mt. Seoraksan and cascades into the East Sea.
Traditionally, poets and artists frequented the pavilion to indulge themselves in music, drawing and poetry.

Uisangdae

Located on the coast north of Yangyang-gun, Uisangdae, is a pavilion built in the compound of Naksansa Temple. The pavilion offers an awesome view of the vast East Sea.
Uisangdae was named after the great Buddhist monk, Uisang, who would sit on this spot for hours at a time to meditate. The hexagonal pavilion, which sits on a hill on the shoreline, commands a spectacular view of the sunrise over the East Sea.

Gyeongpodae

The widely renowned Gyeongpodae is located on a hill situated to the west of Gyeongpoho, where fresh water and sea water converge along the sandy coast. This area is 6km northeast from Gangneung.
Gyeongpodae is famous for its magnificent views of sunrises and sunsets, which fill the sky with brilliant reddish colors.

ach
eongganjeong
정
okcho Beach
Uisangdae
의상대
Jumunjin
Gyeongpodae
경포대
Gangneung
Gangneung
65
Okgye
Balwangsan
Donghae
Samcheok
Jukseoru
죽서루
eongseon
Sabuk
Gosa
Taebaek
Wondeok
Taebaeksan
Uljin-gun
wa-gun
Seungbu
Uljin
Mangyangjeong
망양정
Bongseon
Wolsongjeong
월송정

Jukseoru

Jukseoru, located in Samcheok-si, is the only pavilion among the eight scenic spots of Gwandongpalgyeong to be situated along a river. The other Gwandongpalgyeong sites all overlook the sea.
It is named Jukseoru (juk and seo mean bamboo and west, respectively) as it is situated to the west of a bamboo field.
The pavilion is surrounded by the nearby Mt. Garyasan and Mt. Bonghwangsan, and in the distance are the grand Taebaek Mountains, which stretch extensively across the landscape like a folding screen.

Mangyangjeong

Mangyangjeong is a pavilion sitting on a coastal hill where the Buryeongcheon Stream in Gyeongsangbuk-do flows into the East Sea.
White sands stretch below a hill filled with pine trees, and the pavilion overlooks a vast expanse of the sea. Mangyangjeong has long been known for its scenic sunrise and moonlit view.

Wolsongjeong

Wolsongjeong is a pavilion located 4km north of Pyeonghae-eup. The pavilion overlooks the emerald colored East Sea and is surrounded by a forest of sea pines.

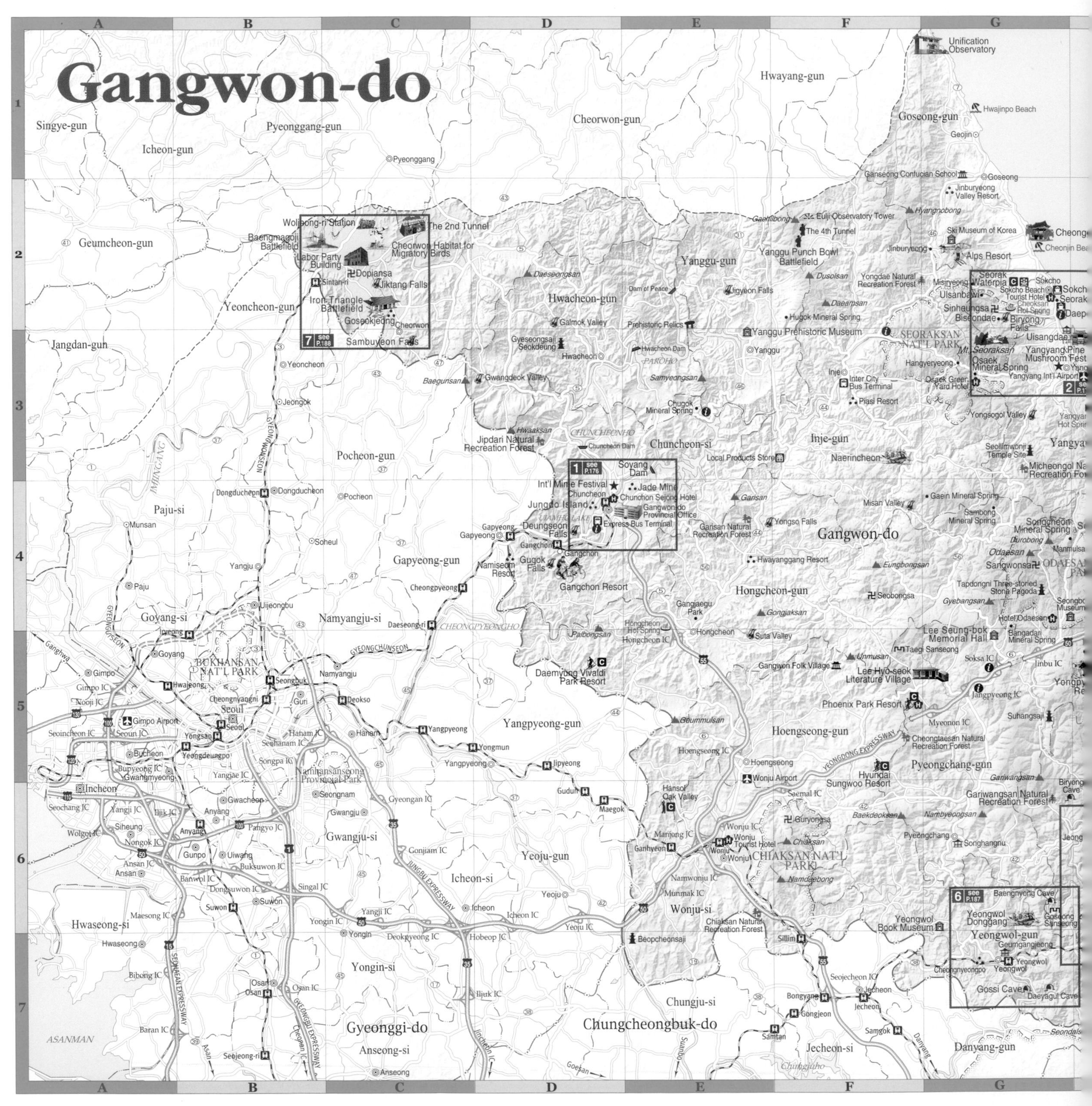

Gangwon-do
A
B
C
D
E
F
G
1
2
3
4
5
6
7
Unification Observatory
Hwayang-gun
Singye-gun
Icheon-gun
Pyeonggang-gun
Cheorwon-gun
Goseong-gun
Hwajinpo Beach
Geojin
Pyeonggang
Ganseong Confucian School
Goseong
Jinburyeong Valley Resort
Geumcheon-gun
Baengmagoji Battlefield
Woljeong-ri Station
The 2nd Tunnel
Labor Party Building
Cheorwon Habitat for Migratory Birds
Dopiansa
Sintan-ri
Jiktang Falls
Iron Triangle Battlefield
Goseokjeong
Cheorwon
Sambuyeon Falls
7 see P.188
Yeoncheon-gun
Jangdan-gun
Yeoncheon
Jeongok
Daeseongsan
Hwacheon-gun
Dam of Peace
Gaechilbong
Euiji Observatory Tower
The 4th Tunnel
Yanggu-gun
Yanggu Punch Bowl Battlefield
Hyangnobong
Ski Museum of Korea
Jinburyeong
Alps Resort
Cheongganjeong
Cheonjin Beach
Jigyeon Falls
Dusolsan
Yongdae Natural Recreation Forest
Misiryeong
Seorak Waterpia
Sokcho
Sokcho Beach
Tourist Hotel
Ulsanbawi
Cheoksan Hot Spring
Sinheungsa
Biseondae
Biryong Falls
Daeamsan
Hugok Mineral Spring
Galmok Valley
Prehistoric Relics
Yanggu Prehistoric Museum
SEORAKSAN NAT'L PARK
Mt. Seoraksan
Uisangdae
Yangyang Pine Mushroom Fest
Gyeseongsaji Seokdeung
Hwacheon Dam
Hwacheon
PAROHO
Yanggu
Samyeongsan
Inje
Inter City Bus Terminal
Hangyeryeong
Osaek Mineral Spring
Osaek Green Yard Hotel
Yangyang Int'l Airport
Baegunsan
Gwangdeok Valley
Chugok Mineral Spring
Pinasi Resort
Yongsogol Valley
Hwaaksan
CHUNCHEONHO
Chuncheon Dam
Chuncheon-si
Inje-gun
Jipdari Natural Recreation Forest
Pocheon-gun
Local Products Store
Naerincheon
Seollimwonji Temple Site
Micheongol Natural Recreation Forest
1 see P.176
Soyang Dam
Int'l Mime Festival
Jade Mine
Chuncheon
Chunchon Sejong Hotel
Jungdo Island
Gangwon-do Provincial Office
UIAMHO LAKE
Express Bus Terminal
Garisan
Misan Valley
Gaein Mineral Spring
Sambong Mineral Spring
Dongducheon
Pocheon
Munsan
Paju-si
IMJINGANG
GYEONGWONSEON
Gapyeong
Deungseon Falls
Garisan Natural Recreation Forest
Yongso Falls
Gangwon-do
Songcheon Mineral Spring
Durobong
Odaesan
Sangwonsa
ODAESAN NAT'L PARK
Soheul
Gapyeong-gun
Gangchon
Gugok Falls
Namiseom Resort
Hwayanggang Resort
Eungbongsan
Yangju
Paju
Cheongpyeong
Gangchon Resort
Gangjaegu Park
Hongcheon-gun
Seobongsa
Tapdongni Three-storied Stone Pagoda
Gyebangsan
Goyang-si
Uijeongbu
Namyangju-si
Daeseong-ri
CHEONGPYEONGHO
Gongjaksan
Hotel Odaesan
Seongbo Museum
Ilyeong
Palbongsan
Hongcheon Hot Spring
Hongcheon IC
Hongcheon
Suta Valley
Lee Seung-bok Memorial Hall
Bangadari Mineral Spring
Ganghwa
Goyang
GYEONGUISEON
BUKHANSAN NAT'L PARK
GYEONGCHUNSEON
Unmusan
Taegi Sanseong
Soksa IC
Jinbu IC
Gimpo
Gimpo IC
Hwajeong
Seongbuk
Namyangju
Daemyung Vivaldi Park Resort
Gangwon Folk Village
Lee Hyo-seok Literature Village
Jangpyeong IC
Nooji JC
Cheongnyangni
Guri
Deokso
Seoul
Seoul
Gimpo Airport
Seoincheon IC
Seoun JC
Yongsan
Phoenix Park Resort
Myeonon IC
Suhangsa
Yangpyeong-gun
Geummulsan
Hoengseong-gun
Hanam JC
Hanam
Yangpyeong
Seohanam IC
Bucheon
Yeongdeungpo
Yongmun
Hoengseong JC
Cheongtaesan Natural Recreation Forest
Songpa IC
Yangpyeong
Jipyeong
Hoengseong
Pyeongchang-gun
Bupyeong IC
Gwangmyeong
Yangjae IC
Namhansanseong Provincial Park
YEONGDONG EXPRESSWAY
Hyundai Sungwoo Resort
Wonju Airport
Gariwangsan
Biryong Cave
Incheon
Seongnam
Gyeongan IC
Gwacheon
Guduri
Maegok
Hansol Oak Valley
Saemal IC
Gariwangsan Natural Recreation Forest
Seochang JC
Yangji JC
Ilik JC
Anyang
Gwangju
Baekdeoksan
Nambyeongsan
Guryongsa
Siheung
Wolgot IC
Anyang
Pangyo JC
Wonju IC
Jeongseon
Manjong JC
Wonju Tourist Hotel
Chiaksan
Pyeongchang
Songhangnu
Nongok IC
Gwangju-si
Ganhyeon
Wonju
Gunpo
Uiwang
Gonjiam IC
Yeoju-gun
CHIAKSAN NAT'L PARK
Ansan JC
Buksuwon IC
Ansan
Namdaebong
Banwol IC
JUNGBU EXPRESSWAY
Icheon-si
Singal JC
Dongsuwon IC
Namwonju IC
Suwon
Suwon
Yeoju
Munmak IC
6 see P.187
Baengnyong Cave
Maesong IC
Icheon
Icheon IC
Wonju-si
Yeongwol Donggang
Gosseong Sanseong
Yangji IC
Hwaseong-si
Yongin IC
Yeoju JC
Chiaksan Natural Recreation Forest
Yeongwol Book Museum
Yeongwol-gun
Yongin
Deokpyeong IC
Hobeop JC
Beopcheonsaji
Sillim
Geumgangjeong
Hwaseong
Cheongnyeongpo
Yeongwol
Yeongwol
Yongin-si
Seojecheon IC
Jecheon
Bibong IC
Osan
Osan IC
Iljuk IC
Bongyang
Jecheon
Gosssi Cave
Daeyagul Cave
Osan
GYEONGBU EXPRESSWAY
SEOHAEAN EXPRESSWAY
Chungju-si
Gongjeon
Baran IC
Gyeonggi-do
Chungcheongbuk-do
Samgok
Seondalsan
ASANMAN
Samtan
Danyang
Cheonan JC
Anseong-si
Jincheon IC
Suanbo
Jecheon-si
Danyang-gun
Seojeong-ri
Asan
Goesan
Chungjuho
Anseong

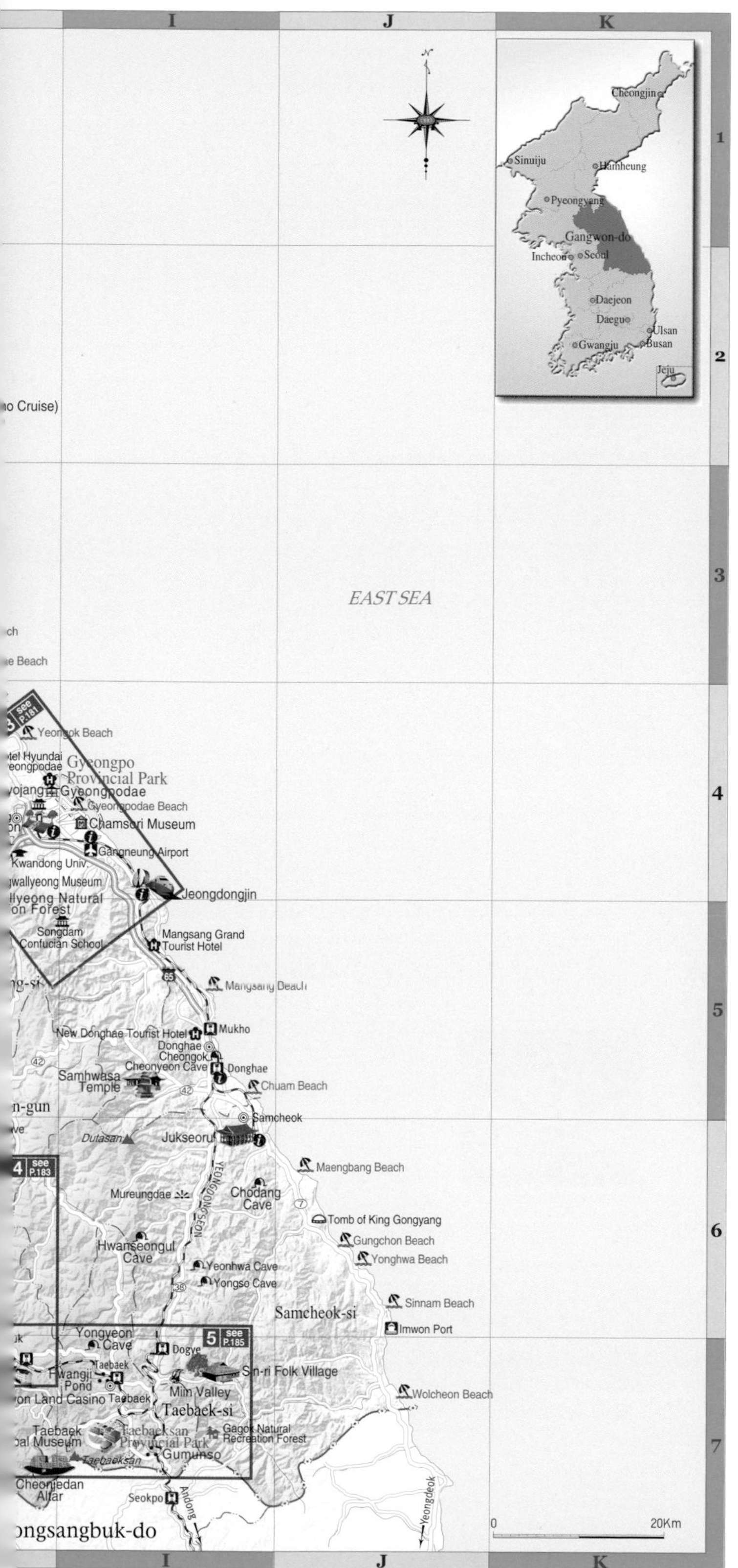

INDEX

Tourist Information

Gangwon-do Tourist Division 82-33-249-3300
Gangwon-do Tourist Information Center 82-33-244-0088
www.provin.gangwon.kr

LEGEND

- Railroad Station
- Airport
- Port
- Bus Terminal
- Tourist Information Center
- University or School
- Museum
- Prehistoric Relic Site
- Tomb
- Temple
- Site of Buddhist Artifacts
- Traditional Building
- Traditional Pavilion
- Korean War Historical Site
- Cultural Experience Area
- Falls or Valley
- Cave
- Beach
- Ski Resort
- Hot Spring or Spa
- Scenic Area
- Amusement Park
- Natural Recreation Forest
- Arboretum
- Mountain
- Stadium
- Other Tourist Attractions
- Hotel
- Condominium
- Reference Point

CHUNCHEON

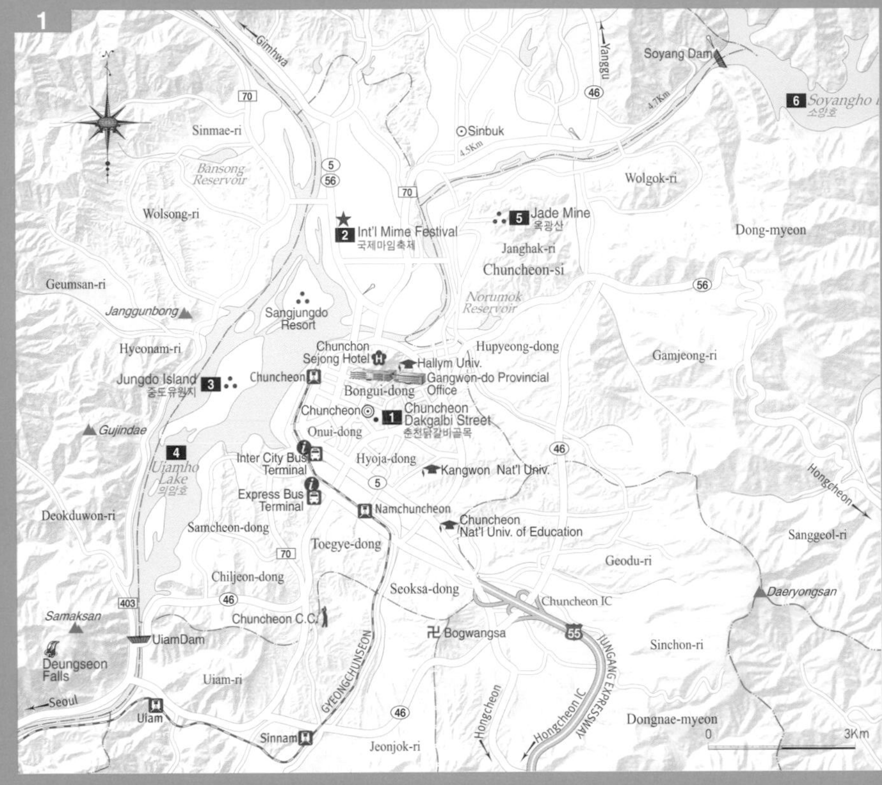

Chuncheon, often called the 'City of Lakes,' is an inviting, romantic city with several scenic lakes scattered throughout the area surrounding the city. Uiamho Lake stretches along the side of the city, while Soyangho Lake and Chuncheonho Lake are located to the north of the city. Various tourist attractions are located along the lake and visitors can enjoy a wide range of water-related activities. The city is favored by people living in metropolitan areas for weekend trips. It is not far from Seoul, the capital of Korea.

Chuncheon also hosts a variety of international cultural festivals annually, including the Chuncheon International Mime Festival, the Chuncheon International Cartoon Festival and the Chuncheon International Play Festival.

The city is also well known for its distinctive local cuisine. Chuncheon Dakgalbi and Makguksu, barbecued chicken and cold noodles, are the representative foods of the city.

Myeongdong, Dakgalbi Town

Dakgalbi

Chuncheon Dakgalbi Street 1

Chuncheon has a row of restaurants in Myeongdong where restaurants specializing in Dakgalbi are concentrated. Dakgalbi is a local food that is cooked by grilling seasoned chicken over a charcoal fire. The delicacy is popular nationwide, as it is delicious and cheap. It is called Chuncheon Dakgalbi because the dish originated in the city of Chuncheon.

Another representative food of Chuncheon is Makguksu, a cold noodle dish. The refreshingly chilled, chewy noodles are nutritious as well as low in calories.

International Mime Festival 2

International Mime Festival

In the last week of May, the International Mime Festival is held in Chuncheon. The festival, along with the International Puppet Performance Festival, are popular events in the city. Domestic mime troupes and troupes from all over the world participate in the festival, which showcases mime performances in which only non-verbal gestures and facial expressions are used.

Pond in the Jade Mine

Uiam Dam

Uiamho Mermaid Statue

Jungdo Island 3

Dolmen in Jungdo

Jungdo, 1.5km northwest of downtown Chuncheon, is an island located in the center of Uiamho Lake.

It houses some of the cultural relics of the inland area which date back to the prehistoric age, including four northern-style sarcophagus tombs and Jeokseokchong prehistoric tombs.

The island consists of large grass fields and forests, as well as a wide variety of entertainment facilities. It is an ideal place for picnics and camping.

Uiamho Lake 4

Uiamho is an artificial lake that resulted from the construction of the Uiam Dam, which was created by blocking the Sinyeongang River where the Soyanggang River and Bukhangang River converge. Chuncheon's nickname, the 'City of Lakes,' originates from Uiamho.

This lake, which lies to the west of Chuncheon, joins Chuncheonho Lake in the north and Soyangho Lake in the northeast.

Jade Mine 5

The Jade Mine, also called the Jade Cave, once yielded high-quality jade, but it has now become a tourist attraction for those people who wish to experience the 'chi,' or energy of jade.

Jade has long been thought to possess a mysterious healing power. According to 'Bonchogangmok,' a research book written by Lee Si-sin of China's Ming Dynasty in the late 16th century, jade is said to remove scars, heal muscles and chest pains, and improve the functioning of the five internal organs if taken in the form of finely crushed sesame-sized pieces.

When people enter the Jade Mine, jade pieces can be seen on both sides of the 150m cave. The mine is said to hold approximately 300,000 tons of jade.

Soyangho Lake 6

Soyangho Lake was created in October 1973 by damming the Soyanggang River. It is now the nation's largest lake. The lake is 530m wide, 123m deep, and 60km (120km long when measured in straight and curved distances, respectively.)

High-speed boat services are available for tourists along the 60km route to Inje, Yanggu, which links Mt. Seoraksan to the east coast. Cruise services are also available at Soyang Dam Wharf.

Soyangho is a favorite one-day tourist destination because it is surrounded by spectacular landscapes, such as the vista from Cheongpyeongsa Temple of the Goryeo Dynasty, and Mt. Obongsan, which is known for having rocks of unusual shapes.

Jade Accessories

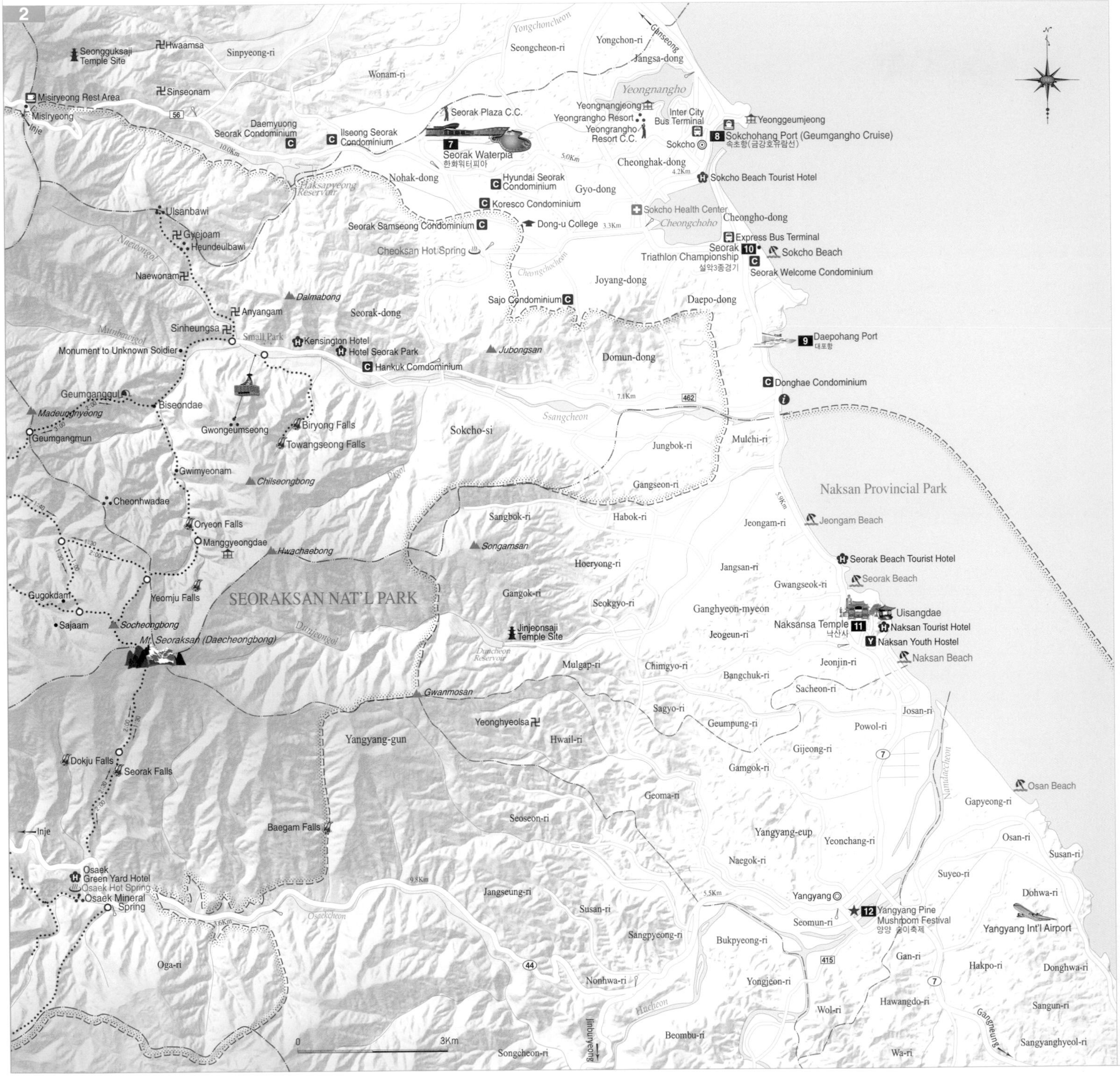

Mt. SEORAKSAN

2

Seongguksaji Temple Site
Hwaamsa
Sinpyeong-ri
Yongchoncheon
Seongcheon-ri
Yongchon-ri
Ganseong
Jangsa-dong
Wonam-ri
Sinseonam
Yeongnangho
Misiryeong Rest Area
Misiryeong
Inje
56
Seorak Plaza C.C.
Yeongnangjeong
Yeongrangho Resort
Yeongrangho Resort C.C.
Inter City Bus Terminal
Yeonggeumjeong
Daemyung Seorak Condominium
Ilseong Seorak Condominium
7 Seorak Waterpia 한화워터피아
Sokcho
8 Sokchohang Port (Geumgangho Cruise) 속초항(금강호유람선)
10.0Km
5.0Km
Cheonghak-dong
4.2Km
Haksapyeong Reservoir
Nohak-dong
Hyundai Seorak Condominium
Gyo-dong
Sokcho Beach Tourist Hotel
Koresco Condominium
Sokcho Health Center
Ulsanbawi
Gyejoam
Heundeulbawi
Seorak Samseong Condominium
Dong-u College
3.3Km
Cheongchoho
Cheongho-dong
Express Bus Terminal
Naewongol
Cheoksan Hot Spring
Seorak 10 Triathlon Championship 설악3종경기
Sokcho Beach
Seorak Welcome Condominium
Cheongchocheon
Naewonam
Joyang-dong
Dalmabong
Seorak-dong
Sajo Condominium
Daepo-dong
Anyangam
Sinheungsa
Small Park
Munbawigol
Kensington Hotel
Hotel Seorak Park
Jubongsan
Domun-dong
9 Daepohang Port 대포항
Monument to Unknown Soldier
Hankuk Comdominium
Donghae Condominium
Geumganggul
7.1Km
462
Biseondae
Madeungryeong
Ssangcheon
Geumgangmun
Gwongeumseong
Biryong Falls
Towangseong Falls
Sokcho-si
Mulchi-ri
Jungbok-ri
Gwimyeonam
Piigol
Chilseongbong
Gangseon-ri
Naksan Provincial Park
Cheonhwadae
5.0Km
Sangbok-ri
Habok-ri
Jeongam-ri
Jeongam Beach
Oryeon Falls
Manggyeongdae
Hwachaebong
Songamsan
Hoeryong-ri
Jangsan-ri
Seorak Beach Tourist Hotel
Gwangseok-ri
Seorak Beach
Gugokdam
Yeomju Falls
SEORAKSAN NAT'L PARK
Gangok-ri
Seokgyo-ri
Ganghyeon-myeon
Uisangdae
Sajaam
Socheongbong
Dunjeongol
Naksansa Temple 11 낙산사
Naksan Tourist Hotel
Mt. Seoraksan (Daecheongbong)
Jinjeonsaji Temple Site
Jeogeun-ri
Naksan Youth Hostel
Duncheon Reservoir
Mulgap-ri
Chimgyo-ri
Jeonjin-ri
Naksan Beach
Bangchuk-ri
Sacheon-ri
Gwanmosan
Sagyo-ri
Josan-ri
Yeonghyeolsa
Geumpung-ri
Powol-ri
Yangyang-gun
Hwail-ri
Gijeong-ri
7
Dokju Falls
Seorak Falls
Gamgok-ri
Namdaecheon
Osan Beach
Geoma-ri
Gapyeong-ri
Inje
Seoseon-ri
Baegam Falls
Yangyang-eup
Yeonchang-ri
Osan-ri
Susan-ri
Naegok-ri
Osaek Green Yard Hotel
Osaek Hot Spring
9.8Km
Suyeo-ri
Osaek Mineral Spring
Jangseung-ri
Dohwa-ri
5.5Km
Yangyang
12 Yangyang Pine Mushroom Festival 양양 송이축제
Osaekcheon
Susan-ri
Seomun-ri
Yangyang Int'l Airport
Sangpyeong-ri
Bukpyeong-ri
415
Gan-ri
Oga-ri
44
Hakpo-ri
Donghwa-ri
Nonhwa-ri
Yongjeon-ri
7
Hucheon
Hawangdo-ri
Sangun-ri
Wol-ri
Gangneung
Jinburyeong
0
3Km
Beombu-ri
Sangyanghyeol-ri
Songcheon-ri
Wa-ri

GANGWON

Mt. Seoraksan is known as the most beautiful mountain in South Korea. The numerous visitors to this popular mountain enjoy royal azalea blossoms in spring, the crystal-clear waters of the valleys in summer, the spectacular changing of the leaves in autumn and starkly beautiful snowscapes in winter. In 1982 Mt. Seoraksan became the first mountain in the Republic of Korea to be designated as an 'Ecosystem Preservation Area' by UNESCO.

With the Hangyeryeong Pass and Misiryeong Pass as borders, the mountain is divided into Outer Seorak in the east, Inner Seorak in the west and South Seorak in the south. Outer Seorak has craggy peaks and tremendous falls, and its features include Cheonbuldong Valley, Ulsanbawi Rock, Gwongeumseong, Geumganggul Cave, Gwimyeonam, Biryong Falls, and Towangseong Falls.

Inner Seorak displays its unparalleled beauty in the form of scenic valleys such as Baekdam Valley, Suryeomdong Valley, Gugokdam Valley, Gayadong Valley, Sibiseonnyeotang Valley, Yongajangseong, and water falls such as Daeseung Falls and Ongnyeotang in the Jangsudae area.

In Seorak-dong there are a wide range of accommodations, including deluxe hotels, tourist hotels, condominiums, inns, and lodging at private homes.

Seorak Waterpia 7

Seorak Waterpia is a 'spa theme park.' It houses not only spa facilities, which enable visitors to enjoy both exercise and entertainment, but also a broad range of water sports facilities, including a wave pool, which gives the feeling of being in the ocean, and a running-water pool, which has 70m- and 100m-long water slides.

Seorak Waterpia Wave Pool

Mt. Seoraksan in Fall

Sokchohang Port (Geumgangho Cruise) 8

The Geumgangho is a 28,000-ton cruise ship that makes the run between the city of Sokcho and Mt. Geumgangsan in North Korea.
Mt. Geumgangsan is Korea's most sacred mountain and many Koreans aspire to visit it. Previously, the mountain was inaccessible to South Koreans due to the division of the Korean Peninsula. However, access to the mountain has been recently opened through the use of cruise ship service.
The Geumgangho travels a route between Sokchohang Port in Gangwon-do and Jangjeonhang Port in North Korea.

Daepohang Port 9

Daepohang is a small port that is popular with visitors throughout the year due to the fact that tourist attractions such as Mt. Seoraksan and various accommodations are concentrated in its vicinity. The port has been transformed from a fishing village into an area which caters to the palates of visiting tourists. It is always crowded with tourists looking for the freshest and highest quality fish caught nearby.

A Lighthouse near Daepohang

Seorak Triathlon Championship 10

Sokcho hosts the Seorak Triathlon Championship at Sokcho Beach every summer.
The triathlon is a grueling athletic endurance event in which participants compete without rest in three successive events. These events include a 1.5km swim, a 40km bicycle race and a 10km run.

Naksansa Temple 11

Naksansa is the nation's only temple located along the seaside.
It was founded by the great Buddhist monk, Uisang, in the 16th year of the reign of King Munmu of the Silla Kingdom. Legend has it that the Buddhist Goddess of Mercy, Avalokitesvara, revealed to Uisang that this was the proper location for the temple as he was praying in front of a Buddha in a cave on the coast.
Inside the Naksansa Temple, there are many relics, including Uisangdae, Hongnyeonam, Hongyemun Gate and Haesugwaneumsang, a statue of Avalokitesvara, the Goddess of Mercy.

Haesugwaneumsang, Statue of Gwaneum

Hongnyeonam is a hermitage sitting like a pavilion on two huge 15m rocks. Sea waves crash incessantly between these two rock pillars. The name of Hongnyeonam (hongnyeon means red lotus flower) is based on a legend which has it that a red lotus bloomed in the sea after Uisang had prayed day and night for seven days.

Yangyang Pine Mushroom Festival 12

The Yangyang Pine Mushroom Festival is an event held in Yangyang, which is one of the country's leading sites for growing pine mushrooms. People who come to participate can enjoy the firsthand experience of picking natural pine mushrooms in the wild.
In addition to picking mushrooms, participants of the festival have a chance to sample a variety of pine mushroom cuisine, purchase local specialties and enjoy the area's traditional culture.

Pine Mushroom

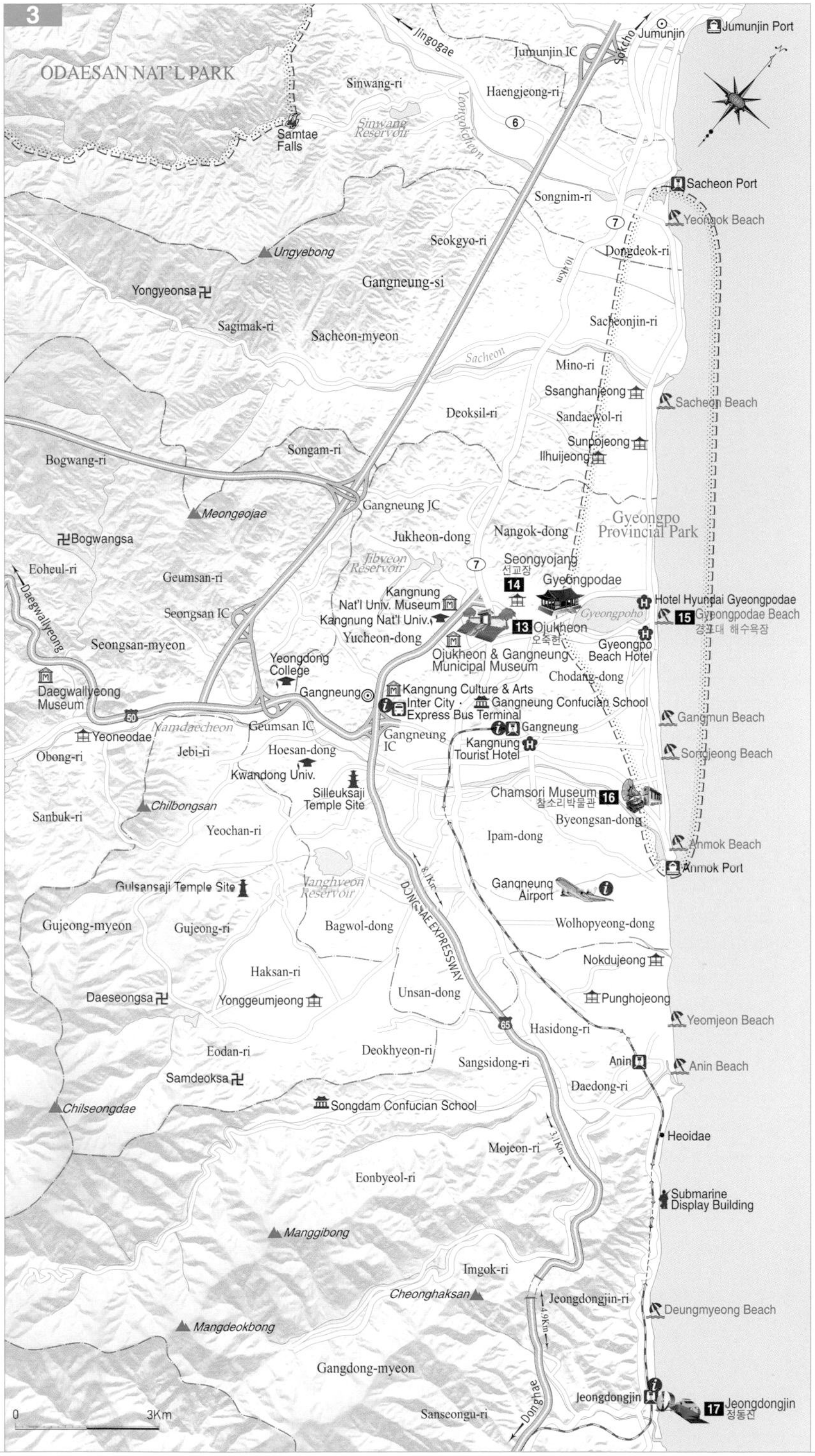

Ojukheon 13

Ojukheon is where Sin Saimdang, a woman famed for her virtues as a mother and faithful wife, and her son, Yulgok Yi Yi, a great scholar, philosopher, and statesman during the Joseon Dynasty, were born. Ojukheon got its name from the black bamboo which surrounds the residence. The residence is considered to be one of the most architecturally significant buildings of the Joseon Dynasty. Ojukheon houses the Yulgok Memorial Hall, Munseongsa Shrine, Jagyeongmun Gate and Sajumun Gate. Displayed inside the residence are calligraphy works and pictures drawn by Sin Saimdang and items used by Yulgok Yi Yi and his family.

Seongyojang 14

Seongyojang was a typical residence for the nobility during the Joseon Dynasty. It consists of Anchae (the main building), Sarangchae (Yeolhwadang: a detached building used for reception), Byeoldang (Dong Byeoldang: a detached house) and Jeonggak (Hwallaejeong: a pavilion). This combination of buildings presents a perfect structural example of the residence of the yangban, the elite nobility of the dynasty.

Seongyojang is surrounded by a picturesque landscape and serves as a valuable reference for studying not only architecture, but also the daily lifestyle and household items used during the late Joseon Dynasty. Yeolhwadang stores thousands of books, writings, and pictures, including the Yongbieocheonga (poems and songs honoring the founding of the Joseon Dynasty) and Goryeosa (the history of the Goryeo Dynasty).

Hwallaejeong

Jeongdongjin Train Station

Gyeongpodae Beach 15

6km east of Gangneung, Gyeongpodae is one of the eight scenic spots of the Gwandongpalgyeong. Just below a park is Gyeongpo Beach, with a 6km long sandy shore near the huge Gyeongpoho Lake. Thick pine tree forests add to the pictorial scenery of the beach area. It is most crowded with people in mid-summer. As the famous Mt. Seoraksan and Mt. Odaesan National Parks are also nearby, it is an ideal resort for vacationers.

Chamsori Museum 16

The Chamsori (True Sound) Museum is a private museum that displays one of the world's most unique collections of rare phonographs. These phonographs were originally collected by Son Seong-mok, an entrepreneur.

The most distinctive feature of the museum is that the exhibits are functional, although they are antiques. The museum includes a total of 1,500 exhibits, including phonographs which have been carefully repaired and are still in good operating condition. Unlike other museums which mainly focus on visual items, Chamsori Museum leaves a vivid impression on visitors through the medium of music.

A variety of sound-related items, ranging from the phonograph No.1 tinfoil invented by Thomas Edison in 1877 to the latest ultramodern laser discs, are exhibited at the museum.

Outdoor Art Gallery in Jeongdongjin

Jeongdongjin 17

Jeongdongjin, located in Gangneung-si, Gangwon-do, is a small port famous for its majestic view of the sunrise. Its romantic landscape attracts many weekend trippers. It became even more famous when it was used as a location for a popular TV drama, 'Moraesigye (The Sandglass).'

The name (Jeongdong means the central east) signifies that the site is located to the east of Hanyang, the capital where the king lived. Jeongdongjin holds a unique international distinction in the Guinness Book of World's Records as the port which has a train station located closest to the sea in the world.

Gyeongpodae Beach

4

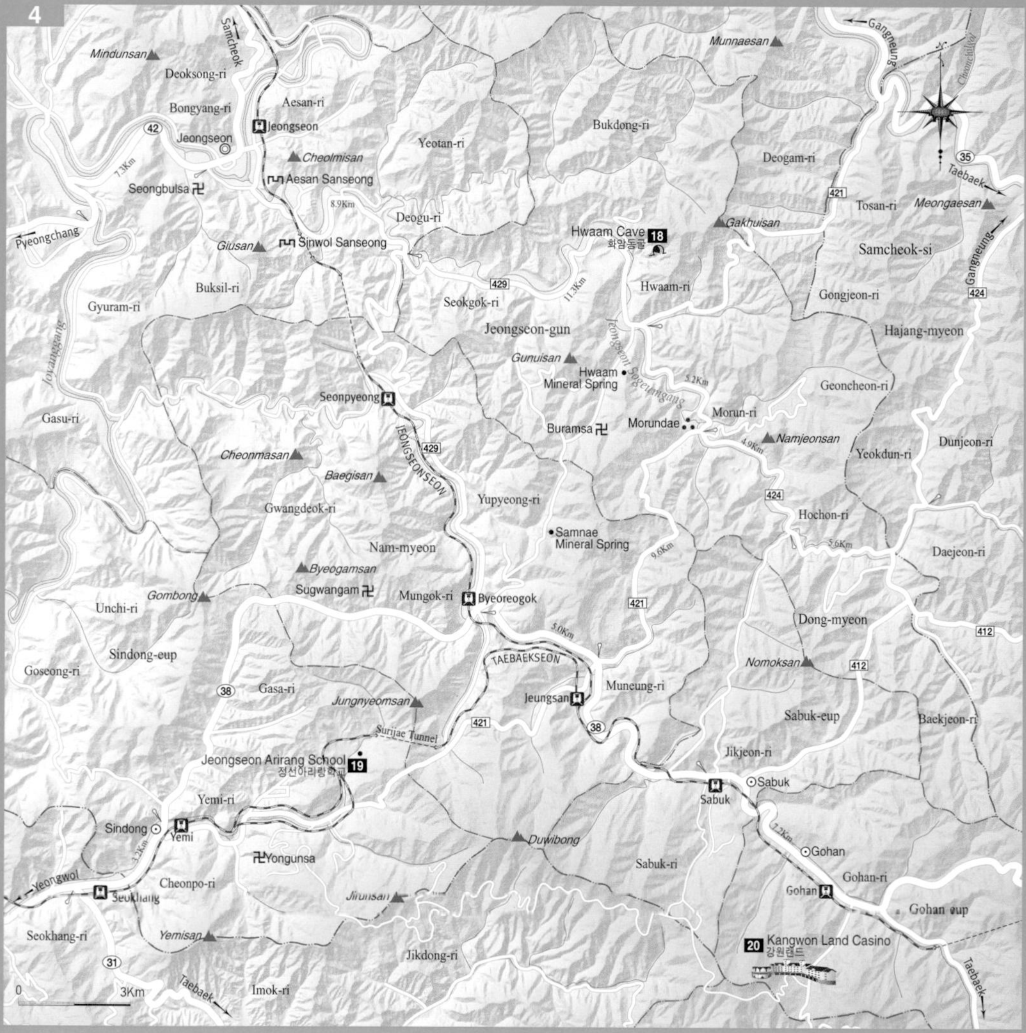

Mindunsan
Deoksong-ri
Samcheok
Bongyang-ri
Aesan-ri
Jeongseon
Jeongseon
Cheolmisan
Yeotan-ri
Bukdong-ri
Munnaesan
Gangneung
Deogam-ri
Seongbulsa
Aesan Sanseong
Taebaek
Deogu-ri
Tosan-ri
Meongaesan
Pyeongchang
Giusan
Sinwol Sanseong
Hwaam Cave 18
화암동굴
Gakhuisan
Samcheok-si
Buksil-ri
Hwaam-ri
Gongjeon-ri
Gyuram-ri
Seokgok-ri
Jeongseon-gun
Hajang-myeon
Gunuisan
Hwaam Mineral Spring
Seonpyeong
Geoncheon-ri
Gasu-ri
Buramsa
Morundae
Morun-ri
Namjeonsan
Dunjeon-ri
Cheonmasan
Yeokdun-ri
Baegisan
JEONGSEONSEON
Yupyeong-ri
Gwangdeok-ri
Hochon-ri
Samnae Mineral Spring
Nam-myeon
Daejeon-ri
Byeogamsan
Sugwangam
Mungok-ri
Byeoreogok
Unchi-ri
Gombong
Dong-myeon
Sindong-eup
TAEBAEKSEON
Nomoksan
Goseong-ri
Gasa-ri
Jeungsan
Muneung-ri
Jungnyeomsan
Sabuk-eup
Backjeon-ri
Surijae Tunnel
Jeongseon Arirang School 19
정선아리랑학교
Jikjeon-ri
Sabuk
Sabuk
Yemi-ri
Sindong
Yemi
Duwibong
Gohan
Yongunsa
Sabuk-ri
Gohan-ri
Yeongwol
Seokhang
Cheonpo-ri
Jiursan
Gohan
Gohan eup
Seokhang-ri
Yemisan
Kangwon Land Casino 20
강원랜드
Jikdong-ri
0 3Km
Taebaek
Imok-ri
Taebaek

Jeongseon-gun, located in the southeast part of Gangwon-do, is noted as the birthplace of Jeongseon Arirang, traditional folk songs which are distinctive because of their sorrowful and enchanting melodies. These songs were designated as intangible cultural properties. Auraji (meaning 'unite' or 'harmonize'), the actual area where Jeongseon Arirang originated, was so named because it is the junction where the Songcheon stream from Gujeol and the Goljicheon stream from Imgye unite.
Jeongseon boasts a spectacular stretch of scenic sites which start in Auriji and extend to the Hwaam Tourist Resort. These scenic areas include Jeongseon Sogeumgang River, Morundae and Jeongamsa Temple.
The Jeongseon Five-day Fair and Jeonseon Arirang Performance Hall will help travelers better understand and experience the traditional spirit of Korea.

Jeongseon Five-day Fair

The Jeongseon Five-day Fair is a type of traditional open-air market. In Jeongseon, the market is open only on the second and seventh day of each month.
Agricultural products, such as chili peppers, roots of bellflowers, potatoes, garlic, and other vegetables are sold directly by growers. The biggest advantage of the market is that consumers can purchase fresh products at reasonable prices directly from the farmers by cutting out any middlemen. In addition, an herb market in the vicinity of the Jeongseon Five-day Fair attracts a number of tourists wishing to buy herbal medicines, local specialties of Jeongseon. Herbs such as Hwanggi (milk vetch root), Danggwi (angelicaegigantis radix) and Cheongung (ligusticum chuanxiong hort) are available in the market.

Auraji

Performance of the Jeongseon Arirang

Night View of Kangwon Land

Hwaam Cave 18

Hwaam Cave was discovered when tunnels were being constructed for gold mines. Currently, the cave is used as a tourist attraction.
It measures 730m long and 45m high. Inside the cave is a golden-tinted stalactite wall. There are three grand stalagmites that are 7-8 m in height and 5m in circumference, as well as stones of diverse colors and shapes.
The cave also features a re-enactment of the era when miners used to dig for gold, providing visitors with an opportunity to experience first-hand the work involved in the excavation of gold.

Stone Pillars in Hwaam Cave

Jeongseon Arirang School 19

Jeongseon Arirang School, which uses the Maehwa Branch School in Jeongseon-gun as its base, was established with the goal of systematically transmitting and preserving the Jeongseon Arirang musical tradition. The school provides domestic and foreign tourists with an opportunity to personally experience Jeongseon Arirang. It has an indoor performance hall, an exhibition hall, three outdoor education areas, and an Arari practice room.
Jeongseon Arirang is regarded as the finest of traditional Korean folk song styles. It originated from poetry which was written and sung by officials loyal to the former Goryeo Dynasty (918-1392). It expresses their sorrow at the loss of the Goryeo Dynasty and their nostalgia for their hometowns and families, whom they had to leave behind when they moved to Jeongseon in the early days of the Joseon Dynasty.
Unlike other traditional Korean folk songs, which center on only one episode or legend, Jeongseon Arirang expresses the uncertainties of human existence which continuously changes according to the times. At present, the lyrics of the Jeongseon Arirang songs total more than 1,300.

Kangwon Land Casino 20

The Kangwon Land Casino is a world-class resort complex which was built at the site of an abandoned mine in Gangwon-do.
Its casino is equipped with 480 slot machines and 30 gaming tables, while a main casino, scheduled to open in 2002, will house 1,600 slot machines and 80 gaming tables.
Kangwon Land is scheduled to be developed into a family resort complex. Recreational facilities will include a ski resort, a golf driving range and a theme park.

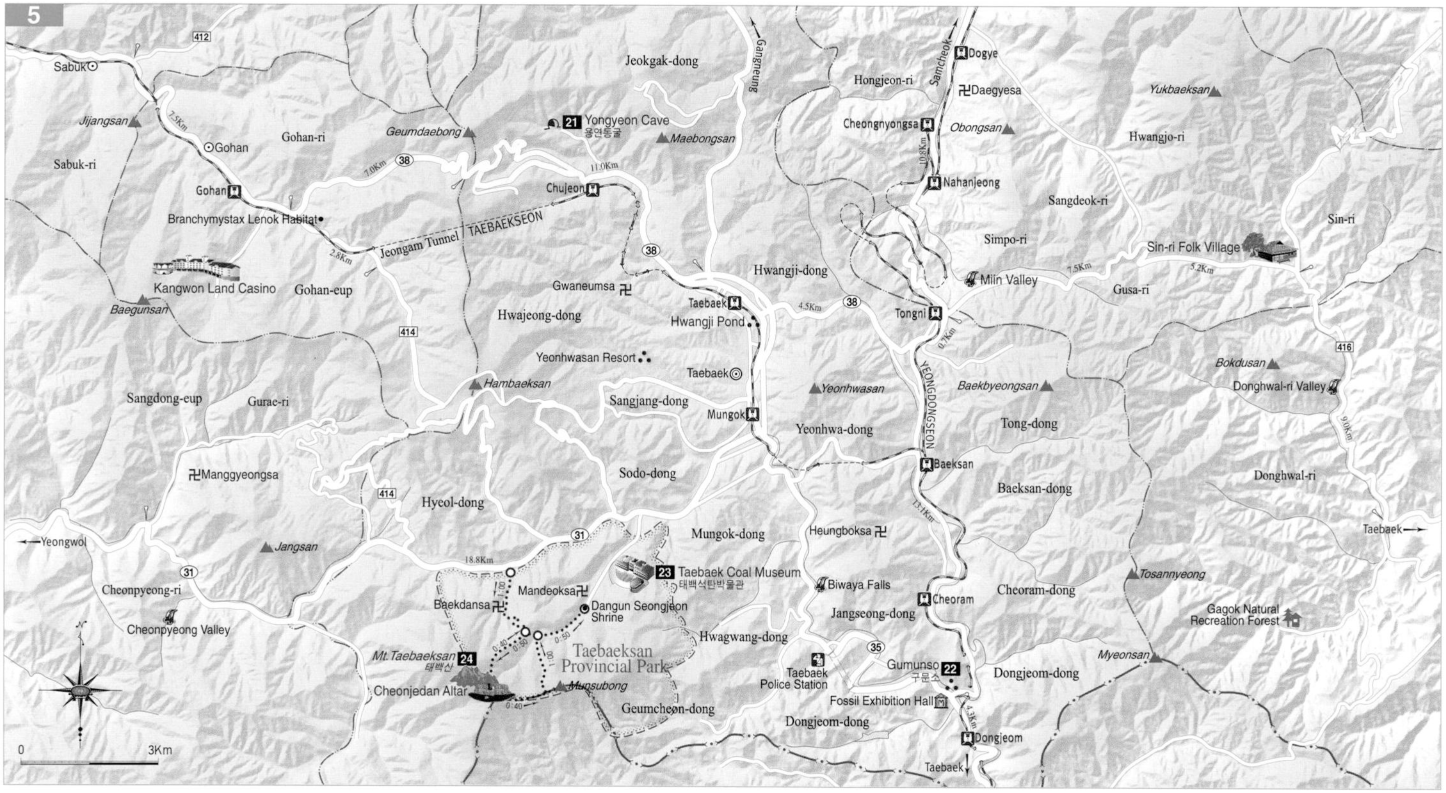

The Taebaek area, which is surrounded by Mt. Taebaeksan, is one of the most mountainous areas in Korea. Tourist attractions in this area include the Cheonjedan Altar on the summit of Mt. Taebaeksan, the Coal Museum, hundreds of ancient lime caves, a variety of famous temples and a mysterious yew tree, which is of indeterminate age.

Taebaek, the area from which the Hangang River and the Nakdonggang River originate, also contains a historical site. According to the Samguksagi (history of the Three Kingdoms), the Cheonjedan altar was where kings personally held religious services dedicated to their heavenly god. Even today, on Gaecheonjeol, Korea' s National Foundation Day, a grand ritual for the heavenly god is held at the altar here. Legend has it that on this day, Hwanung, a son of god, descended to Sindansu, Mt. Taebaeksan, and started a new town, which lay the foundation for the origins of the Korean people.

Yongyeon Cave 21

Water Fountain inYongyeon Cave

Yongyeon Cave is a lime grotto which is presumed to have been created between 150 million years and 300 million years ago.

The results of academic research have shown that the cave provides a habitat to about 12 species of animals. The cave is full of stalagmites and stalactites, and has a 30m-wide and 150m-long chamber, which presents visitors with a majestic scene.

Located in the large chamber is a rhythmic water fountain that spouts water to the beat of music, two smaller fountains and a volcano-shaped fountain.

Cheonjedan in Mt. Taebaeksan

Taebaek Coal Museum

A Natural Stone Gate in Gumunso

Gumunso 22

The Hwangjicheon Stream, from which the Nakdonggang River originates, passes through a natural arch in the rock and into the deep Gumunso Lake. The name Gumunso means 'lake with a cave.' Gumunso is a large rainbow-shaped lime grotto that is 20-30m in height and which takes up 30㎡ in floor space.

Taebaek Coal Museum 23

The Taebaek Coal Museum demonstrates the role which coal, historically one of the most important energy sources in Korea, has played over the years, as well as presenting coal-related historical facts.
Inside the museum is a special elevator that descends a 1,000m vertical coal shaft at a fast speed. In the mine gallery there are facilities in which people can experience the feeling of danger through an elevator crash simulation.

Mt. Taebaeksan 24

Mt. Taebaeksan, meaning 'great bright mountain,' is 1,567m high but is not so difficult to hike, as it has few rough or steep peaks. On the summit of Mt. Taebaeksan is the Cheonjedan, where religious services to an ancient heavenly god were held. In the Danggolgyegok Valley there is the Dangunseongjeon, where memorial services for Dangun, the mystical progenitor of the Korean people, are held every year on Gaecheonjeol, a Korean holiday commemorating the founding of the nation. Yongjeong Fountain, known for being the source of Korea's best water, are located 1,500m above sea level. Yongjeong is the highest fountain in Korea, and sacred water for religious services, which are held on Gaecheonjeol, is drawn from this fountain. Another attraction of the area is the Taebaeksan Snow Festival, which is held in late January or early February every year.

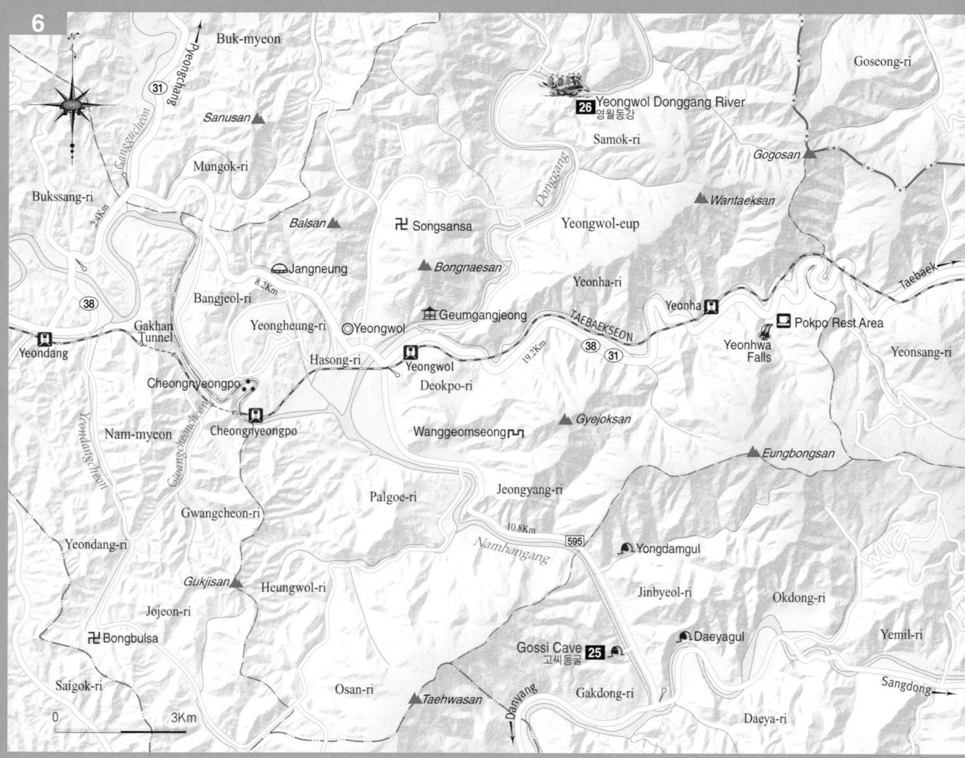

Yeongwol is in the southern part of Gangwon-do. Located here is the ancient Gossi Cave, and also numerous historical sites related to the ill-fated King Danjong, the 6th king of the Joseon Dynasty. These sites include Cheongnyeongpo, where King Danjong was exiled, Gwanpungheon, where the king took poison and died after a death penalty was imposed on him, and Jangneung, the location of the King's tomb.

Other tourist attractions include the historical sites related to Kim Sat-gat, a wandering poet during the Joseon Dynasty, the International Modern Sculpture Art Gallery, Nakhwaam Cliff, Bodeoksa Temple, Beopheungsa Temple, Jeongmyeolbogung Shrine, the Yeongwol Book Museum, and the Yeongwol Astronomical Science Hall.

Gossi Cave 25

Gossi Cave is a stalactite cave which was formed approximately 400 million years ago. It is designated as Natural Monument No. 219.

Inside the 6.3km cave are numerous stalactites, four lakes, three waterfalls and six chambers. Stalactites, stalagmites and limestone pillars in diverse hues and shapes fill the cave.

In the vicinity of the cave, there is a tourist resort with an amusement park, recreational facilities, shops selling local specialties and restaurants serving local foods.

Gossi Cave

Yeongwol Donggang River 26

Rafting along the Donggang, which flows from the Soyanggang River through Sindong-eup, is highly popular among tourists as it provides an opportunity to enjoy scenic natural surroundings and learn about the ecology of the area.

On the rafting section, which starts from Gossi Cave, tourists can enjoy both rafting and cave observation, and on the Eorayeon Valley course tourists can enjoy a breathtaking view of cliffs and canyons which have been preserved intact from ancient times.

Donggang River

CHEORWON

Within the area of Cheorwon there are numerous locations for sightseeing related to the Korean War. By taking a guided tour which includes the 2nd Tunnel, the Observatory, Woljeong-ri Station, the Baengmagoji Battlefield and the Labor Party Building, visitors can revisit the tragedy of the Korean War, which was fought here 50 years ago. Amidst the atmosphere of reconciliation and cooperation following the historic inter-Korean summit held in 2000, the sites of war in Cheorwon provide visitors with a reminder of the continued existence of the last Cold War frontier in the world.
Visitors can tour the sites accompanied by a guide after filling out an application at the War Record Management Office of the Iron Triangle Battlefield.

Seungilgyo

The 2nd Tunnel 27

The 2nd Tunnel, 108km north of Seoul, was dug by the North Korea military, who sought to use it to infiltrate South Korea. The underground tunnel cuts through solid granite 50-160m below the surface. The total distance of the tunnel is 3.5km and it stretches 1.1km to the south of the demarcation line.
The tunnel symbolizes the sharply confrontational relations between the two Koreas during the Cold War era.

Iron Triangle Battlefield 28

The Iron Triangle Battlefield, which linked Cheorwon to Gimhwa and Pyeonggang in North Korea, was a strategically key area of the central front line during the Korean War. The fiercest combat between the South and North took place here on this battleground.
Civilians were first admitted to this site in 1989, and since then it has served as a place which highlights the tragedy of the Korean War and which also contains one of the last remnants of the Cold War. The Iron Triangle Observatory allows visitors to view the DMZ (Demilitarized Zone), the Pyeonggang Highlands, North Korea's showcase villages and the Kim Il-seong goji.

Woljeong-ri Station 29

Woljeong-ri Station is the northernmost station of the Gyeongwonseon Railway. It once linked Seoul to North Korea's Wonsan, a city now adjacent to North Korea's southern boundary of the DMZ.
The remnants of train cars are now mere iron frames, along with a signboard that reads, 'The train wants to run.' This slogan expresses the pain and sorrow of the people within the divided Korean Peninsula.

Baengmagoji Battlefield 30

Baengmagoji Battlefield

Baengmagoji, along with the Iron Triangle Battlefield, is a battleground where some of the fiercest combat took place during the Korean War. The possession of the goji (hill or ground) changed hands 24 separate times and the original shape of the landscape has been altered due to the brutal bombardments. It came to be called 'Baengma (white horse) goji' because its new form resembled a prone white horse.
The Baengmagoji Monument was erected in Dongsong-eup, Cheorwon-gun, to commemorate those killed in action in defense of Baengmagoji. The Baengma Memorial Hall displays some of the guns and ammunition which were used during the fierce battles.

Labor Party Building 31

The Labor Party Building is a Soviet-style building. The North Korean communist regime constructed the building following the nation's liberation from Japanese colonial rule. For five years after its construction, the building was used as a place to decide important matters regarding the Cheorwon, Geumhwa, Pyeonggang and Pocheon areas.

Labor Party Building

Cheorwon Habitat for Migratory Birds 32

The DMZ, which has restricted civilian access for 40-50 years, symbolizes the heartbreak of the divided Korean people, but has been a boon to the preservation of the natural ecosystem. In particular, the vicinity of Saemtong Fountain has a natural environment that is a perfect habitat for wild birds.
Saemtong refers to a fountain where natural spring water wells up from the ground throughout the year by penetrating through basalt rocks. Seasonal birds that fly into Cheorwon include cranes, hooded cranes, white-naped cranes, and summer migratory birds such as herons and white herons.

Ski Resorts

Geographically, Gangwon-do is primarily a mountainous area with heavy snowfall in the winter. This has resulted in a heavy concentration of ski resorts within the province. The area has very convenient transportation networks and spectacularly scenic natural surroundings which provide an optimum environment for multi-purpose tourist resorts. Ski resorts in the province include Yongpyeong Resort, Hyundai Sungwoo Resort, Phoenix Park Resort, Daemyong Vivaldi Park Resort and Alps Resort.

Yongpyeong Resort H5

Yongpyeong Resort is widely known as the site of such prestigious international events as the 1998 and 2000 World Cup Skiing Tournaments and the 1999 Winter Asian Games. The resort is located in Pyeongchang-gun, Gangwon-do, and is situated at the foot of the 1,458m Mt. Barwangsan. The resort offers 27 different slopes, including the Rainbow Slope, a 3.7km long gondola ride and the nation's largest ski lodge.

Hyundai Sungwoo Resort F5

The Hyundai Sungwoo Resort is favored by snowboarding lovers as snowboarding is allowed on all slopes of the resort. The Hyundai Sungwoo Resort, located in Dunnae-myeon, Hoengseong -gun, has a total of 20 slopes and 9 lifts. Seven slopes out of the 20 are approved by the FIS (Federation of the International Skiing). Enthusiasts can enjoy night skiing on 14 slopes of the resort.

Alps Resort G2

Alps Resort is located in the highlands of Jinburyeong Pass, the area with the heaviest snowfall in Korea. The resort's European-style buildings exude an international atmosphere. It houses the nation's only skiing museum.
Facilities of the resort include 7 slopes, 5 lifts and 3,000 rental skis.

Daemyong Vivaldi Park Resort D5

Daemyong Vivaldi Park Resort located at Mt. Maebongsan, Hongcheon, has slopes ranging from the nation's largest beginner slope to difficult, steep slopes for advanced skiers.
Facilities include 13 slopes and 10 lifts, as well as various recreational facilities such as accomodations, a golf course and a golf range, and a sledding hill.

Pheonix Park Resort F5

Pheonix Park Resort in Mt. Taegisan, Pyeongchang-gun, is a multi-purpose mountain resort with a wide range of recreational facilities such as ski slopes, a golf driving range, a swimming pool, tennis courts and a bowling alley.
The park boasts valley-type slopes and gondolas for eight persons, 9 lifts, an internationally recognized slope exclusively for snowboarding and a large sledding hill.

Rafting

Gangwon-do provides excellent conditions for rafting with its mountainous areas and valleys and the swift currents in its rivers. In addition to rafting, people can enjoy the scenic natural surroundings of valleys and steep majestic mountains.
The most popular rafting in the province is on the Donggang River in Yeongwol, Naerincheon Stream in Inje, and Hantangang River in Cheorwon.

Hantangang River

The Cheorwon area is an ideal place to enjoy rafting, as it has a number of rapids that run through its valleys. The 13km rafting section along the Hantangang starts in Sundam Valley, and rafters can enjoy the spectacular cliffs and rocks on both sides of the river from start to finish.

Naerincheon Stream

Naerincheon, the upper tributary of the Soyanggang River, is considered one of the best places for rafting, as it has all the elements of a first class rafting site, such as its crystal clear water, high water volume, picturesque landscapes and courses for different levels of rafters.
The 16km course starts at Gungdong Resort in Buk 3-ri, Girin-myeon, Inje-gun, and ends in Bamgol, Gosa-ri, Inje-eup. This river provides an opportunity for a thrilling adventure, as it has many S-shaped bends and steeply falling rapids.

Odaesan National Park G4

Woljeongsa in Mt. Odaesan

Mt. Odaesan is a national park located at the crossroads of the Charyeong Mountains. It extends far to the west from the center of the Taebaek Mountains. The mountain consists of the highest peak, Birobong (1,563m), and neighboring peaks such as Horyeongbong, Sangwangbong and Durobong. Mt. Odaesan has an abundant forest and heavy snowfall in winter. Its peaks are not considered to be steep. The Hangang River originates from this mountain.

Mt. Odaesan is a Buddhist holy site that contains several prominent Buddhist temples from the Silla Kingdom, including the Sangwonsa Temple and Woljeongsa Temple. The area also includes a number of historical sites and cultural properties which house national treasures. The mountain' s primary attraction is the superb natural beauty provided by Sangwonsa Valley, Cheonghakcheon Valley, Guryeong Falls, Sesim Falls, Mureung Falls, Manmulsang Rocks, Sipjaso Swamp, Haksodae Hill and Songcheonyaksu, a mineral water spring.

Hwanseongul Cave I6

Hwanseongul Cave is the largest limestone cave in Asia and it is located in Daei-ri, the largest cave area in Asia. Six large caves, including the Gwaneum Cave, Jeampunghyeol Cave, Yangteomok Cave, Deokbalsegul Cave and Keunjaesegul Cave, are also in the area, which is called the 'Daei Cave Area' and is designated as a natural monument.

Hwanseongul Cave measures 6.2km in length of which 1.6km is open to the public. Hwanseongul Cave houses a central chamber that is more than 100m in width, the Okjwadae Altar, the Mallijangseong at its entrance, as well as six waterfalls of varying size.

Lee Hyo-seok Literature Village F5

Birthplace of Lee Hyo-seok

In Lee Hyo-seok Literature Village, the writer Lee Hyo-seok (pen name: Gasan) was born and raised. The village served as the setting for his short story entitled 'By the Time the Buckwheat Flower Blossoms,' which is regarded as one of the best Korean short stories. The village displays the house where Lee was born, a water mill house, Gasan Park, and Bongpyeongjangteo, the site where the Bongpyeong Market used to be.

The village hosts the annual 'Hyo-seok Cultural Festival' in late August or early September.

Sin-ri Folk Village I7

The Sin-ri Folk Village preserves the tradition of the villages of the fire-field farmers. The village has two neowajip which were built by fire-field farmers in the province. Neowajip refers to a house which has a roof covered with the finely-patched bark of oak trees, rather than the more common giwa, Korean tiles. Neowa are 70cm long, 30-40cm wide and 5cm deep. Although they does not fit perfectly with the sides of a roof, neowa are waterproof and last longer than giwa.

Neowajip, a Folk House

Chungcheongbuk-do

Chungcheongbuk-do area's rich soil was formed by a mixture of natural fertilizers deposited by the Geumgang River and granite eroded by wind and water. Thus various kinds of crops and agricultural products thrive in the area. Chungju apples are well-known for their succuleunt taste. Visitors here can enjoy spas in Suanbo, Mt. Woraksan, and the area's abundant historical sites. Chungjuho Lake and Daecheongho Lake offer a lakeside atmosphere and a wide variety of water activities.

Jikji

Jikji is the world's oldest movable metal type. It was invented 78 years before the German movable metal type created by Gutenberg. One copy of a metal type manuscript, which was printed in July of 1377 at Heungdeoksa Temple, and two copies of a woodblock manuscript printed at Chwiamsa Temple, Yeoju, survive. The Jikji consists of two volumes : the first volume contains sermons of Indian and Chinese sages, while the second volume includes hymns, sermons, discourses and letters. The 24.6 × 17.0cm Heungdeoksa manuscript is displayed at the East Asian Section of the French National Library, but only the second volume is preserved to present. The full texts of the two copies of the Chwiamsa edition are preserved at the Korean National Library and the Academy of Korean Studies, respectively.

Original Type Caster of the Jikjisimcheyojeol

Carved characters were pressed into a sand box where the type was molded.

The characters were removed from the sand box.

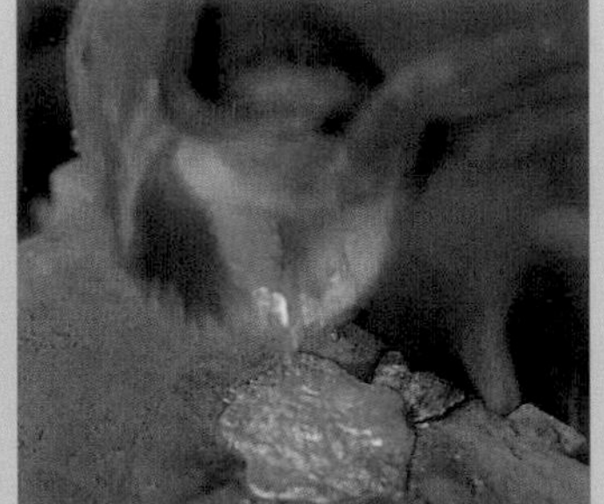

The type was cast in metal.

The mold was removed.

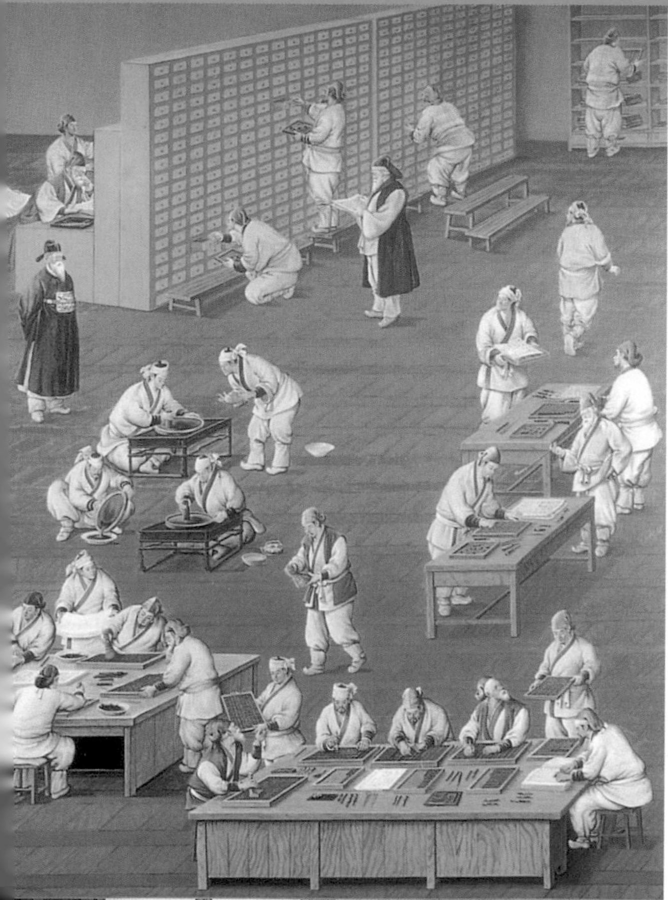

The Early Printing Museum of Cheongju

The Early Printing Museum of Cheongju is located at Heungdeoksaji Temple Site in Cheongju, where the Jikji Simche, the oldest extant book ever printed with metal type, was printed. The museum demonstrates the sophistication of ancient Korean civilization which created the first movable metal type. The museum is also a science education center and features an exhibit on the development of Korea's printing technology.

The museum has about 1,100 items on exhibit, such as ancient books, printing devices and artifacts excavated from the Heungdeoksaji Temple Site. It houses five permanent exhibition halls (Jikji and Heungdeoksa Hall, the Jikji Metal Type Workshop Hall, the Printing Device Hall, the Printing Culture Hall, and the Oriental and Western Printing Culture Hall) and one special exhibition hall.

www.jikji.or.kr

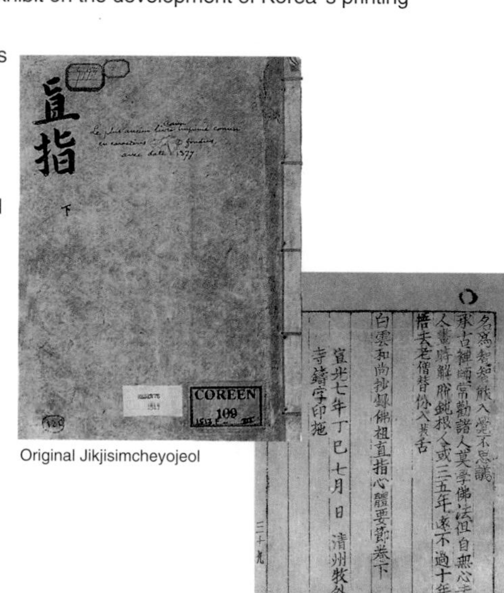

Original Jikjisimcheyojeol

Chungcheongbuk-do

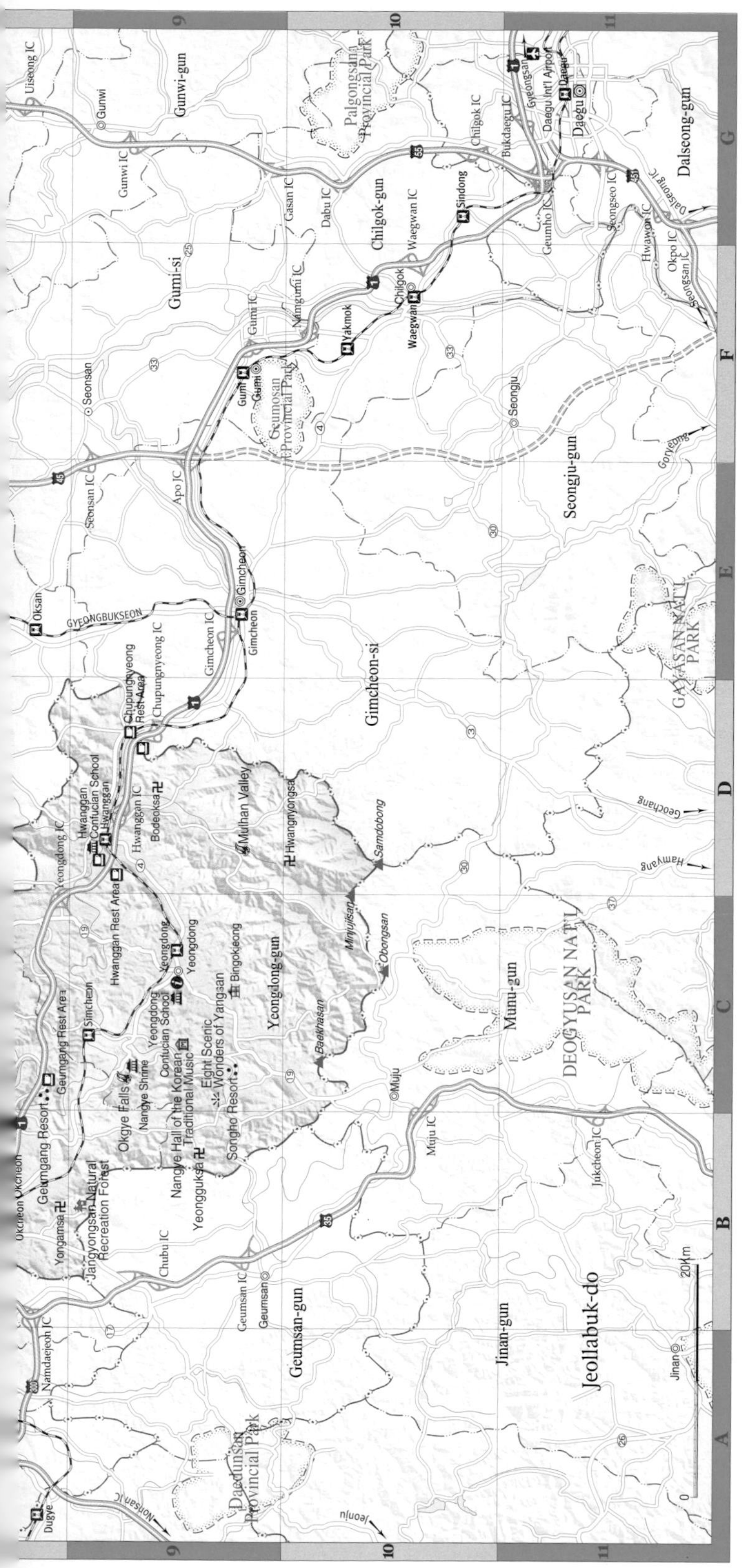

INDEX

Tourist Information

Chungcheongbuk-do Tourist Division 82-43-220-4250
Chungcheongbuk-do Tourist Information Center 82-43-233-8430
www.provin.chungbuk.kr

LEGEND

- Railroad Station
- Airport
- Rest Area
- Tourist Information Center
- Museum
- Gallery
- Fortress
- Temple
- Site of Buddhist Artifacts
- Church
- Traditional Building
- Traditional Pavilion
- Falls or Valley
- Cave
- Ski Resort
- Golf Course
- Hot Spring or Spa
- Scenic Area
- Amusement Park
- Natural Recreation Forest
- Mountain
- Other Tourist Attractions
- Hotel
- Youth Hostel
- Reference Point

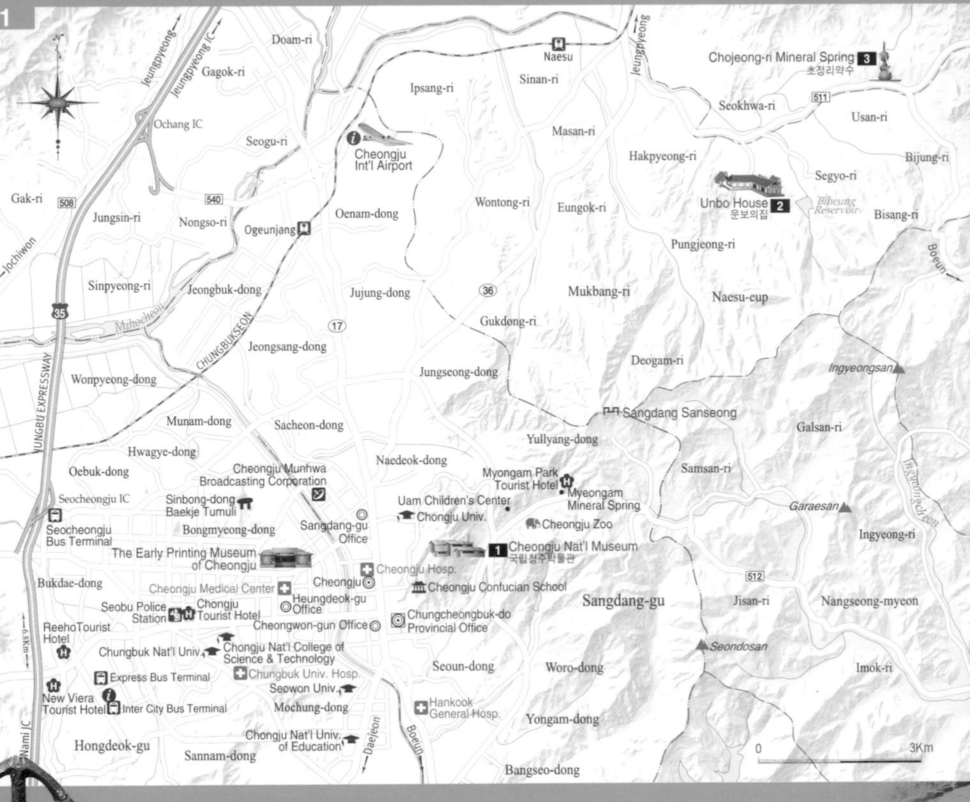

Cheongju has a reputation for being a city of education and culture, where the spirit and traditions of its ancestors are well maintained. It has tourist attractions such as the Sangdang Sanseong Fortress, Heundeoksaji Temple Site, the Early Printing Museum of Cheongju, the Cheongju National Museum, Unbo house, Chojeong-ri Mineral Spring and the Cheongju Zoo.

Cheongju National Museum 1

The Cheongju National Museum displays a variety of relics discovered in Chungcheongbuk-do. These range from the prehistoric period to the Joseon Dynasty. Of its more than 8,600 relics, 2,300 pieces are currently on display, offering visitors an opportunity to understand the history and culture of the Chungcheongbuk-do region.

There are four permanent exhibition halls: The first is the Prehistoric Hall, where relics from the Paleolithic period through the early Iron Age are displayed. The second hall is the Three Kingdoms Period Hall, where cultural assets of the Three Kingdoms Period display the characteristics of that period in Cheongju. At the third hall, one can appreciate ancient art, such as Buddhist sculptures, metal craft work and porcelain. Chinaware, white porcelain of the Joseon Dynasty and Buddhist materials, including the Sarira (Buddhist saint's bones) Case of the Bonghaksaji Temple Site are displayed in the fourth hall.

The special exhibition hall features printing-related materials, including printed materials and typesets. The museum also has an outdoor exhibition where two iron making furnaces, modeled on those which were used in ancient iron producing sites, and one small furnace, relocated from the Seokjang-ri site, are displayed. In addition, three stone tombs of the Silla Kingdom are displayed in front of the annex building of the museum.

Geumgangnyeong

Silla Kingdom Dongjegwan

Stone Triad Amitabha with Attendants and 28 other Buddhist Images (National Treasure No.106)

Unbo Gallery

Unbo House

Unbo House 2

Unbo House is where Korea's renowned painter, Kim Gi-chang (nicknamed Unbo), lived late in his life. The house contains his atelier and a display hall, where people can witness his artistic talent. This became very famous after his death and many people visit here on weekends. Nestled on the slope of a small mountain, Unbo House serves as a culture and art complex and houses the Unbo Gallery, the Pottery Exhibition Hall, a workshop and a tea shop.

Unbo Kim Gi-chang transformed himself many times as an artist. He attempted to transcend the boundary between plastic and abstract art. He is respected as a person full of artistic spirit and passion and a man of strong will who overcame a hearing defect.

Chojeong-ri Mineral Spring 3

This is one of the world's most famous mineral springs and the International Mineral Water Association has designated it as the third best spa in the world. It has more than 600-years of history, and King Sejong came here to treat an eye ailment for 60 days in 1444.

There are many mineral water spas around Chojeong. 8,500 liters of mineral water a day rise from the ground, and its content includes calcium, sodium, magnesium, and other minerals.

Using this nutrient rich water, restaurants, public baths, and other facilities have been built here, making the area an attractive tourist site.

Chojeong-ri Mineral Water Well

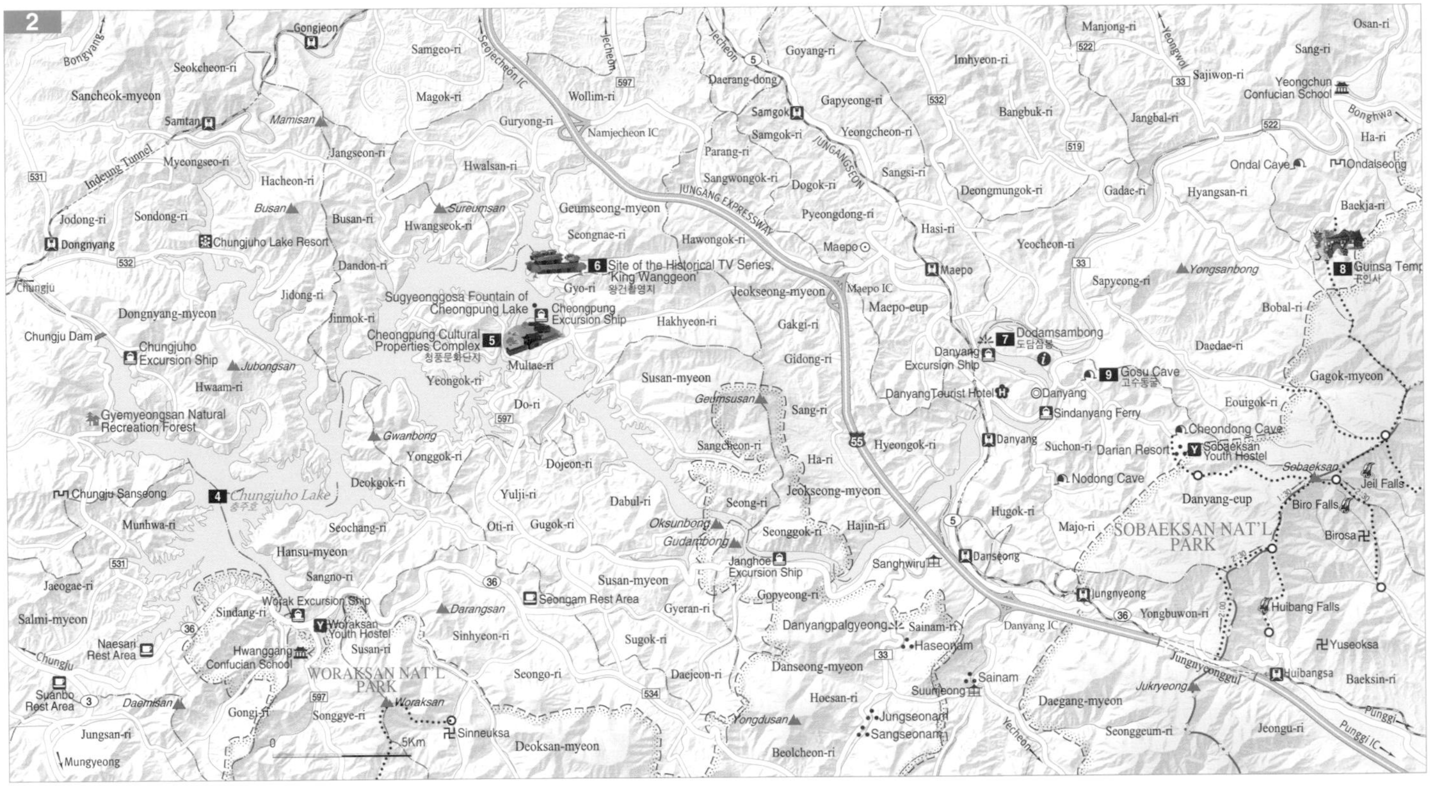

Chungjuho Lake 4

Chungjuho is the nation' s largest artificial lake. It was formed by the damming of valley waters. Numerous tourists visit the lake because of its nearby tourist attractions, which include the Cheongpung Cultural Properties Complex, Danyangpalgyeong (the eight scenic sites of Danyang), Woraksan National Park, Gosu Cave, Guinsa Temple, Suanbo Spa, and Nodong Cave.

Ferry service provides guests with an opportunity to appreciate the natural scenery unfolding on each side as the boat crosses the lake. Two kinds of boat services are available: ferry and excursion ship, both of which travel the 130-ri (one ri equals about 393m) course.

The Chungjuho Lake Resort, the country' s best lakeside resort, was established along the Chungjuho with the Ongnyeobong Peak as its backdrop. There are diverse sporting and entertainment facilities here: an archery range, tennis courts, a soccer field, a miniature golf course, an indoor table tennis hall and a swimming pool. A wide variety of water sports are also available, but the lake is enjouable year round.

Chungjuho Lake

Cheongpung Cultural Properties Complex 5

The water transportation system around scenic Namhangang River has been used since ancient times. Because of this, the culture of the region has flourished and the area is full of both cultural assets and historical significance.
A considerable share of its cultural assets was lost to water during the construction of the Chungju Dam. The remaining cultural assets, which were scattered around the area at that time, were moved to their current site, the Cheongpung Cultural Properties Complex.
The complex houses the Hanbyeongnu Pavilion, Geumnamnu Pavilion, Paryeongnu Gate, Cheongpung Confucian School and four old houses which display scenes from daily life during the Joseon Dynasty.
When visitors pass by the Paryeongnu, they

Paryeongnu

find four old homes that seem to belong in a country village. The well-established mud wall, the loom on the main wooden floor and the millstone help visitors to understand what life was like 200 years ago. Behind the ancient houses are tombs and tombstones.
Past the tomb site is the Hanbyeongnu pavillion, treasure No. 528, which was frequented by poets in ancient times. Built in 1317, the pavilion was an auxiliary structure of the administrative office building. From here one can get a full view of Chungjuho Lake. Beside the Hanbyeongnu stands Geumbyeongheon, the governor's office building. Hanbyeongnu was built before the area was promoted to a dohobu (the old administrative unit meaning a county) in 1681. The courtyard of Geumbyeongheon leads to the front gate of the compound. There are three gates of which the center gate was used

by the governor, while the other two were used by those with lower social status.
The Cheongpung Confucian School stands on a mountainside in the southwestern part of the complex. It was a local educational institute opened during the Goryeo Dynasty. It houses a main sanctuary hall, Myeongnyundang Hall, Dongmu and Seomu (east and west lecture halls), and Dongjae and Seojae (east and west student's residences). Five great Confucian sages, including Confucius himself, are enshrined in the main sanctuary hall, while Dongmu and Seomu enshrine 18 renowned Confucian scholars.

Hanbyeongnu

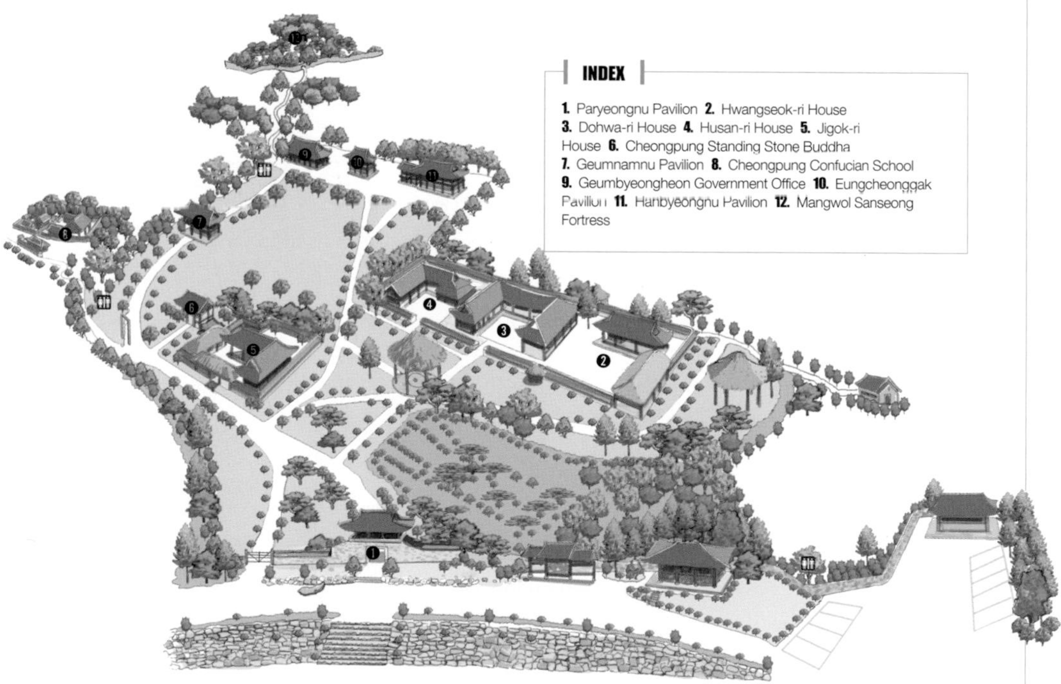

Dodamsambong

Site of the Historical TV Series 'King Wanggeon' 6

The site of the historical TV series 'King Wanggeon' is located in Jecheon-si. It is some 4km north of the Cheongpunggyo Bridge and has emerged as one of the most popular tourist sites in Korea thanks to the popularity of the series, which depicts the life of the Goryeo Dynasty's first king.
In the 39,600㎡ studio are recreations of the buildings of the Goryeo Navy and 32 houses, including many which are thatched. In addition, three navy ships, including warships which could accommodate a crew of up to 100, were recreated to duplicate the port exactly the way it was at that time.

Dodamsambong 7

Dodamsambong refers to the three peaks standing in the middle of the upper reach of the Namhangang River. Dodamsambong became well-known because Jeong Do-jeon,

Outdoor Studio of 'King Wanggeon (the founder of the Goryeo Dynasty)'

who helped to found the Joseon Dynasty, rested here. He even used Sambong (three peaks) as his pen name. At the Janggunbong stands the Samdojeong Pavilion, a hexagonal pavilion.

Guinsa Temple 8

Guinsa is the headquarters of the Cheontaejong Sect of Korean Buddhism, which has more than 140 temples across the nation. This temple is located on top of Mt. Sobaeksan, 708m above the sea level. Within

Lantern ceremony, Guinsa

its perimeter, it houses 50 buildings, including the five-storied main hall, Sambodang Hall, Seolseongdang Hall, Ingwangdang Hall, Jangmunsil Hall and Hyangjeokdang Hall.

Gosu Cave 9

Gosu Cave is a 1,300m limestone cave which was formed about 500 million years ago. It has over 120 major stalactites, stalagmites and is habitat to some 25 kinds of flora and fauna, including stinking centipedes, spiders, marsh snails and fish. Galloa insects lived within these caves some 200-300 million years ago and their fossils were discovered beneath the Golden Pillar on February 12, 1998.

Saja Bawi, a Stalactite which looks like a Lion's Head

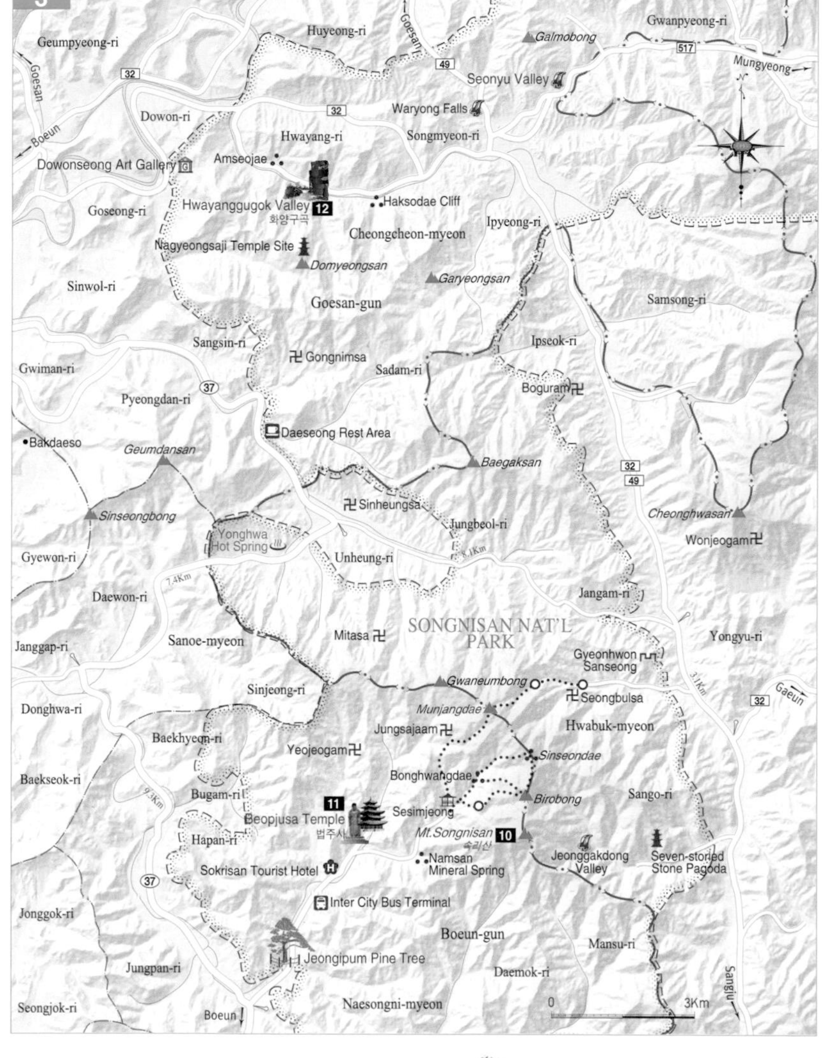

Mt. Songnisan 10

Jeongipumsong, Pine Tree
(Natural Monument No. 103)

Songni means 'retire from the world.' Designated as a national park in 1970, Mt. Songnisan is one of the most scenic areas in Korea. It is situated in the middle of the Sobaek Mountains, which stretch southwest from the Taebaek Mountains. It is distinguished by the large Beopjusa Temple, which is surrounded by Cheonhwangbong Peak, the mountain's major peak (1,057m), and other peaks. All of the peaks are more than 1,000m high and blend with deep valleys in impressive scenery. Cherry blossoms in spring, green pine trees in the summer, and colorful autumn tints welcome visitors. Located at the center of the Korean Peninsula, Songnisan National Park is easily reached from anywhere in the nation. Certain districts are designated as green zones or fire prevention areas and are subject to entry control.

Cheongdong Mireukdaebul Statue

Haksodae, One of the Hwayanggugok Scenic Spots

Hwayanggugok Valley 12

Located 32km east of Cheongju, Hwayanggugok is part of the Songnisan National Park. Song Si-yeol (pen named Uam), a great scholar of the mid Joseon Dynasty, selected nine beautiful places in Hwayang during his seclusion here. At Hwayanggugok one can enjoy crystal clear water and peaceful forested mountains.

Beopjusa Temple 11

Beopjusa was built by the monk Uisinjosa in the 14th year of the reign of King Beopheung of the Silla Kingdom, 24 years after Buddhism was introduced to Korea. There are many treasures at the temple, including Daeungjeon Hall, Sacheonwangmun Gate, the Sacheonwang Seokdeung Stone Lantern, Palsangjeon Hall, Ssangsaja Seokdeung (a stone lantern with two engraved lions) and Seogyeonji.

The most eye-catching feature at the temple is the Cheongdong Mireukdaebul (a large Buddhist statue made of bronze). The 33m-tall statue features Buddha in a gown with a bare right shoulder. At Yonghwajeon Hall, there is a gold-plated statue of a sitting Bodhisattva.

Palsangjeon is a wooden tower where Palsangdo, an eight-piece picture depicting the life of Buddha, is preserved. Tourists can observe Buddhists circling the tower on Buddha's birthday. Cultural assets of the temple include Daeungbojeon Hall, Josagak Pavilion, Iljumun Gate, Hongjeonmun Gate, Daejonggak Pavilion, Neunginjeon Hall, Sujeongam Hermitage, and Jungsajaam Hermitage.

Buddhist Monks in a Lantern Festival

Ssangsaja Seokdeung, a Stone Lantern with Two Lions (National Treasure No. 5)

Mireuksaji Temple Site

Mireuksaji Temple Site E5

Mireuksaji used to be a large temple but now only the stone foundation remains.
It is assumed, based on related relics and records, that the temple was built in the 11th century during the early Goryeo Dynasty, and was destroyed during the Mongolian invasions in the late Goryeo Dynasty. Its original name was Mireukdaewon. The Mireuksaji Temple Site has a square-shaped stone lantern, flag-pole supports, a five-storied stone pagoda and Mireuk Seokbulipsang (a standing Buddha statue). Given that these structures are scattered over a wide area, the temple is presumed to have been very large.

Suanbo Spa D5

Nestled on a slope on the northwestern part of Mt. Joryeongsan (1,017m), Suanbo Spa is a natural spa and acknowledged to have been the first spa in the nation. Even though the exact origin of the spa has been lost to time, it has a long history, especially given that it is mentioned in more than 30 ancient history books.
The hot springs of the spa come from 250m underground and maintain a temperature of 53℃. The water is slightly alkaline, with a pH of 8.3, and is rich in such beneficial minerals as potassium, sodium, fluorine and magnesium.

Open air spa

Mt. Woraksan E5

Mt. Woraksan is situated between Mt. Sobaeksan and Mt. Songnisan. It has a rough terrain, and picturesque landscape with lots of interesting rocks. It was designated as the country's 17th national park in 1984.

Mt. Woraksan

Woraksan National Park contains numerous historically significant sites, such as the Mireuksaji, Deokjusa, Silleuksa, Mireuksaji Maaebul (a Buddha statue carved into a rock), Binsinsaji Sajaseoktab (a stone lion tower), Deokju Fortress, and Silleuksa (a three-storied stone tower).

Jungangtap Pagoda D4

This 14.5m stone tower is the tallest tower among the surviving stone towers of the Silla Kingdom. It is also called the Jungang Tower because it is at the geographic center of the Silla Kingdom's territory.

Jungangtap in Jungwon Tappyeong-ri (National Treasure No. 6)

Baeronseongji, Catholic Sanctuary

Baeron Sanctuary E3

Baeron is a Catholic sanctuary which originally served as a base for the promotion of Catholicism. In 1801 the government launched a campaign of persecution against Catholicism. Hwang Sa-yeong, a Catholic martyr, wrote a report in a cave here describing the persecution which was occurring and appealing for help to the outside world. The Baeron Seminary, the first of its kind in the nation, was also located here from 1855-1866.

Father Choi Yang-eop (died in 1861), the second ordained Korean priest, after Father Kim Dae-geon, is buried here, as well as Nam Jong-sam, the first martyr killed in 1866 during the Byeonginbakhae persecution.

Munui Cultural Properties Complex B7

This complex houses ten old style buildings, including a residence for nobility and a cultural materials exhibition hall. People can view totem poles, millstones and ceremonial altars.

Inside the complex, there is a museum

Munui Cultural Properties Complex

which displays Korean traditional roof tiles that have been produced from the Baekje period to the present. Seven hundred and seventy four traditional roof tiles and 20 stone relics, including stone Buddha statues, are featured here. This place is also known as the Munui Cinema Village because it has a drive-in theater.

Taekgyeon

Taekgyeon is a traditional martial art that was practiced to safeguard the Goryeo Dynasty some 2,000 years ago. Its techniques were further developed by the late Shin Han-seung, and it became the first martial art to be designated as an important intangible cultural property.

Taekgyeon helped the Silla Kingdom unify the three kingdoms, and during the Goryeo Dynasty it was one of the test subjects in the military examination. Takegyeon provided a basis for all martial arts because it was transformed into gwonbeop (a Chinese traditional fighting technique) and judo when it was introduced to China and Japan, respectively.

The Taekgyeon Center was created for the promotion and development of this martial art. The center holds Taekgyeon matches every year and visitors can observe Taekgyeon students training.

Chungcheongnam-do

Chungcheongnam-do has two ancient cities, Gongju and Buyeo, which served consecutively as capitals of the Baekje Kingdom for more than 700 years. The sophisticated ancient cultural heritage found across the province enables people to understand more about the area' s time-honored traditions. Chungcheongnam-do has great potential to emerge as one of the most popular tourist areas when the west coast areas are more fully developed. Anmyeondo Island has already evolved into an international tourist site and a major producer of ginseng and ingredients used to make mud facial packs.

Culture and Relics in the Baekje Region

Baekje was one of the Three Kingdoms along with Goguryeo and Silla Kingdoms, and was located in the southwestern region of Korea. It was destroyed by Silla in 660.

After merging about 50 tribal states, the Baekje Kingdom emerged as the ruling power of the Hangang River basin in B.C. 18. By the time of the reign of King Goi (234-286), the administrative system which controlled the regime was fully established. However, the ever-growing power of the Goguryeo Kingdom in the north expanded downward and Baekje was forced to move its capital to Ungjin (now called Gongju) in the 1st year (475) of King Munju, and shortly afterward, to move again to Sabi (now called Buyeo), in the 16th year (538) of King Seong.

After this, Baekje's fortunes revived for a time. After recapturing territory from Goguryeo, however, its newfound national strength soon dwindled again because of excessive warfare and ambitious construction projects. In the 20th year (660) of King Uija, Baekje fell to the united forces of the Silla Kingdom and the Tang Dynasty. To this day, remnants of early Baekje era survive in the Hangang basin around Seoul. The pond of Gungnamji Palace, Nakhwaam Cliff, and numerous other historical remains are scattered around the Gongju, Buyeo, and Iksan areas and serve as a testament to the Baekje Kingdom' s age of glory.

Gilt-bronze Contemplative Bodhisattva
(National Treasure No. 83)

The move of the capital from Ungjin to Sabi led to a flowering of Baekje culture. Numerous historical remains survive from this period. While most Baekje tombs are made of stone or earth, during the Ungjin era, stone-piled tombs gave way to rectangular stone-chamber tombs, and Chinese-style brick chamber tombs were also constructed. From one of these brick chamber tombs, that of King Muryeong (501-523), a hoard of cultural treasures was excavated. They are thought to represent the quintessence of Baekje culture. In the Buyeo area, the area where six Baekje tombs are now preserved is well-known. Neungsan-ri Tomb No. 1 has four walls and a ceiling made of smoothly cut gneiss, with images of animals representing the four compass directions painted on its stone walls.

Gongsanseong Fortress

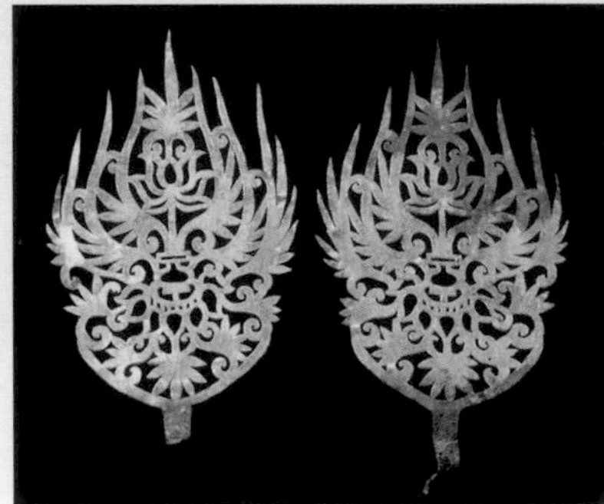

Gold Ornaments from the Diadem of the Queen
(National Treasure No.155)

Geumsan Ginseng

Ginseng Field

The quality of ginseng is strongly influenced by the environment and geography of where it is grown, as well as the season of its harvest. Geumsan is an ideal place for growing ginseng in terms of climate, as the temperature between day and night differs widely. This temperature fluctuation is of great benefit to the ginseng plants and explains why the area is recognized as the producer of the finest quality ginseng in the world.

Geumsan Ginseng, the history of which can be traced back as far as 1500, is often called 'summer ginseng' since it is harvested in early July when its efficacy as herbal medicine reaches its peak. It is then processed by late October.

As for ginseng's beneficial effects, Sinnongbonchojang (an herbal medicine book) states that it invigorates the five major internal organs, alleviates vomiting and thirst, and promotes blood circulation. In addition, the book says that when taken for an extended period, people will feel that their body has been refreshed and that they will live longer. Bonchogangmok (a Chinese encyclopedia of herbs) states that ginseng is especially good for speedy recuperation from illness, strengthening of the functions of the five internal organs and invigorating the nervous system.

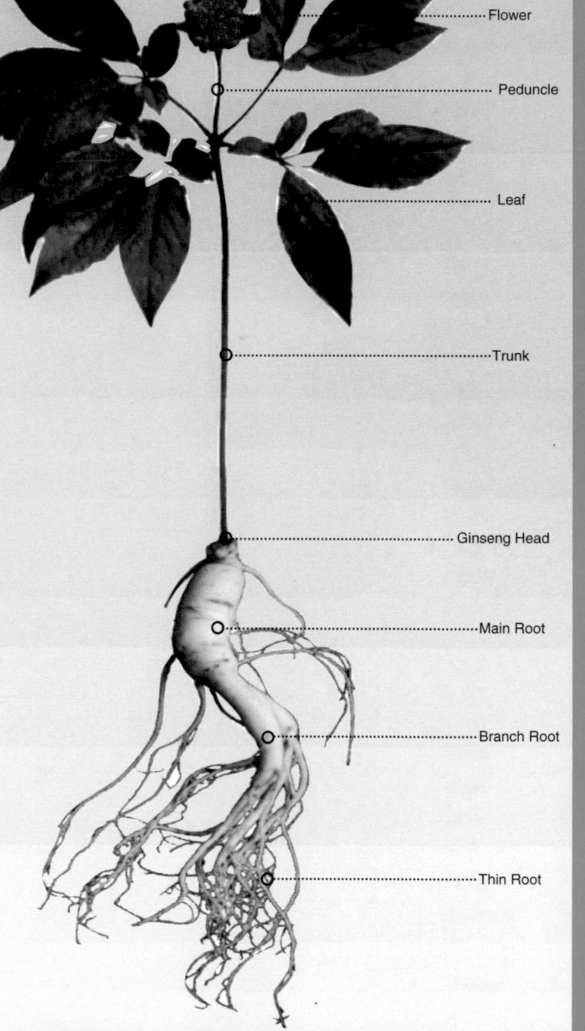

Dry Ginseng

Dried Curved Ginseng

Misam, Ginseng Rootlets

4-6 year-old Raw Ginseng

Red Ginseng that has been steamed and dried for preservation

Taegeuk Ginseng is produced from raw ginseng by submerging it in hot water and putting it through a gellatinization process.

Chungcheongnam-do

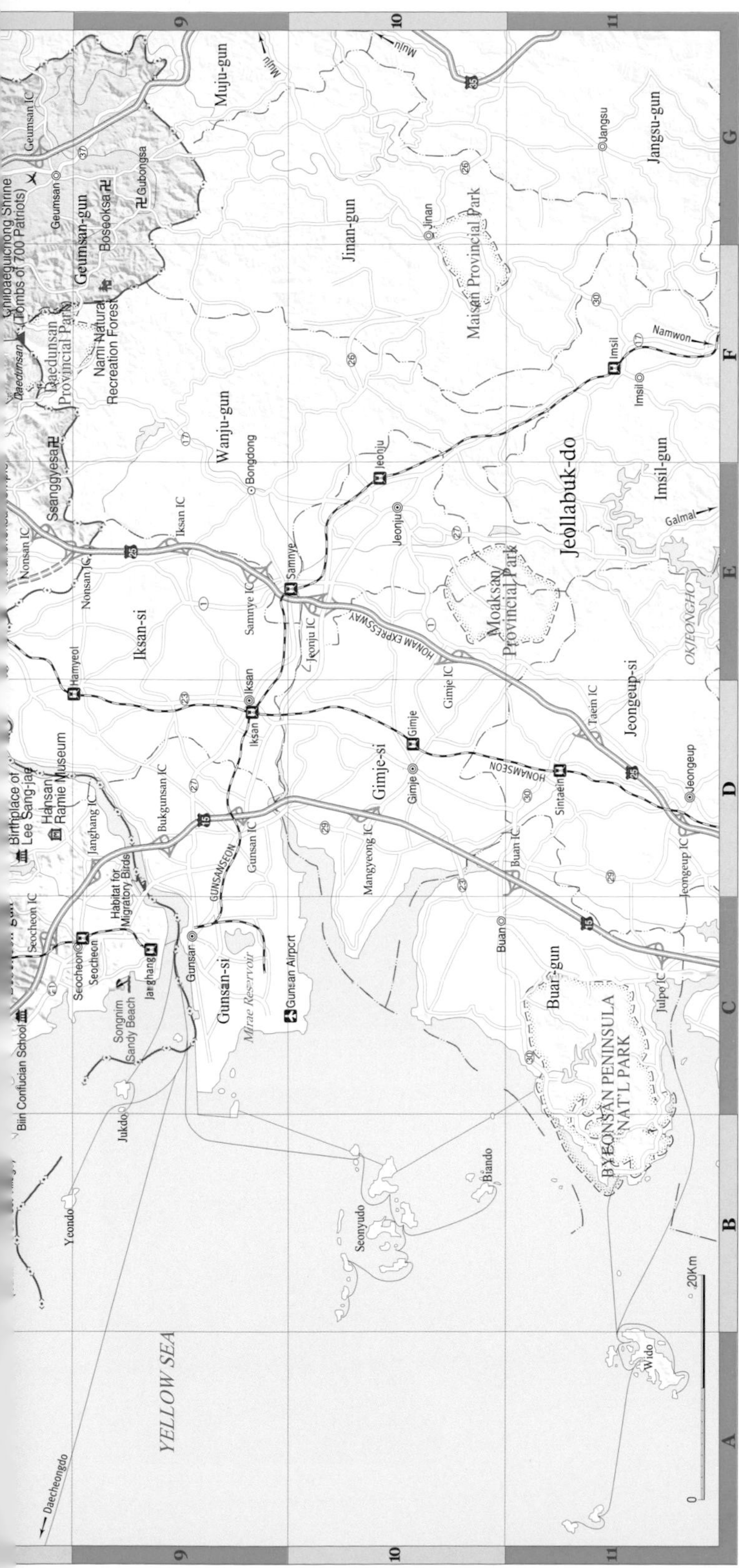

INDEX

Cultural Relics

Natural Attractions

Museums & Theaters

Places of Interest

Accommodations

Transportation

Tourist Information

Chungcheongnam-do Tourism Promotion Division 82-42-220-3332
Chungcheongnam-do Tourist Information Center 82-42-221-1905
www.provin.chungnam.kr

LEGEND

- Railroad Station
- Rest Area
- Tourist Information Center
- Museum
- Gallery
- Prehistoric Relic Site
- Tomb
- Fortress
- Temple
- Site of Buddhist Artifacts
- Church
- Traditional Building
- Traditional Pavilion
- Korean War Historical Site
- Cultural Experience Area
- Falls or Valley
- Beach
- Hot Spring or Spa
- Scenic Area
- Migratory Birds' Sanctuary
- Natural Recreation Forest
- Mountain
- Other Tourist Attractions
- Hotel
- Reference Point

Nammaetap Pagodas 2

Nammaetap (meaning brother and sister pagodas) is the name for two stone pagodas which stand at the site where Cheongnyangsa Temple used to be. The pagodas became famous because of a folk love story about a romance that was supposed to have occurred between a male member of the royal family of the Baekje Kingdom and a woman who rode on the back of a tiger.

Nammaetap, Brother and Sister Pagodas

Mt. Gyeryongsan 1

The mountain was named Gyeryong because its ridges resembles a dragon with a rooster' s crown. The mountain' s position is considered to be auspicious according to the principles of 'chi,' or the earth' s natural flow of energy. It is regarded as a mysterious place which is closely linked to those practicing shamanism.

Mt. Gyeryongsan has many rocks which were formed in unusual shapes. It has about 15 peaks, including Cheonhwangbong (845.1m), its main peak.

The mountain beckons visitors all year round: in spring, for the tunnel of cherry blossoms in front of the Donghaksa Temple, and for the fresh air of Donghaksa Valley in the summer, and for the changing foliage around Gapsa Temple and Yongmun waterfalls in autumn. The snowy landscape at Sambulbong is popular in the winter.

Gapsa Temple

Gapsa at Mt. Gyeryongsan belongs to the Yeoncheonbong sect. It is believed that the temple was built by a man named Adohwasang in the first year (420) of the reign of King Guisin.
The temple possesses numerous cultural assets, including Daeungjeon, Daejeokjeon and Cheonbuljoen Halls. Budo (sarira stupa), the ancient flagpole and its supports and Worinseokbopan (wooden typing blocks depicting Buddha's life) are also among the precious cultural items preserved at the temple.

Gongsanseong Fortress

The Gongsanseong Fortress served as the Baekje Kingdom's capital for 64 years. The rectangular shaped 2,660m-long fortress stretches some 800m from east to west and some 400m from north to south. Originally, it was a mud fortress which was built by the Baekje Kingdom but it was later rebuilt using stone during the Joseon Dynasty. In the fortress are royal palace sites presumed to be from Ungjin (Gongju's old name), two ponds of the Baekje Kingdom, Yeongeunsa (which was built in the Goryeo Dynasty), Ssangsujeong (a pavilion where King Injo rested during a rebellion), Jinnamnu (the south gate), and Gongbungnu (the north gate).
The fortress and its surrounding areas feature the peaceful Geumgang River and lush forested woods.

Changing of the Fortress Guard

Gongsanseong

CHUNGCHEONGNAM-DO

Gongju National Museum 5

The Gongju National Museum was opened in 1971 primarily to display relics excavated from the Muryeongwangneung (the royal tomb of King Muryeong). There is also a fine collection of artifacts from the period when Gongju was the capital of the Baekje Kingdom. The museum has two exhibition halls. The first exhibition hall features the relics from Muryeongwangneung and a full size replica of the tomb. This enables visitors to get a glimpse of the inside the royal tomb. The second exhibition hall displays relics which were unearthed in Chungcheongnam-do.

Currently displayed at the museum are 108 kinds of artifacts (2,906 pieces) from the royal tomb as well as 500 relics found in Gongju. Other exhibits include some 1,000 significant relics, including 14 national treasures (19 pieces).

In addition, a variety of stone images can be seen at the outdoor exhibition site.

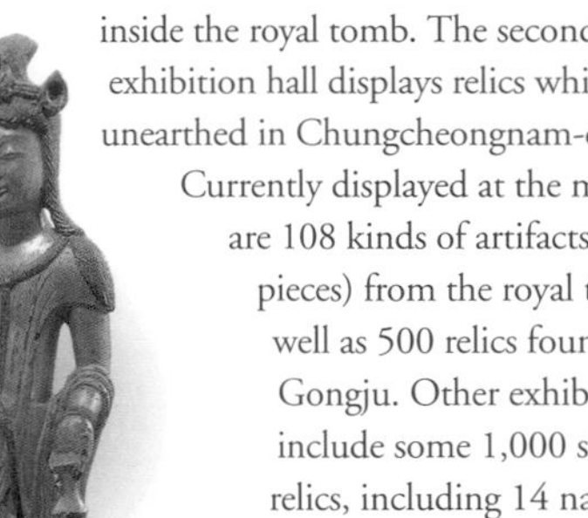

Standing Gilt-bronze Bodhisattva
(National Treasure No. 247)

Gold Hat Decoration
(National Treasure No. 154)

Gold Earings
(National Treasure No. 156)

Gold Earings
(National Treasure No. 157)

King Muryeong Royal Tomb 6

Muryeongwangneung is the royal tomb of Baekje' s 25th King Muryeong and his queen. Its arch mound, which looks like a small peak, measures 20 meters in diameter and 7.7 meters in height. It appears to have been much larger in ancient times. Muryeongwangneung is one of two brick tombs, the other being the Songsan-ri tomb No. 6, and it is an important historic site which offers priceless material for the study of the Baekje culture. Relics from the tomb were made of materials such as stone, wood, gold, silver, bronze and ceramic. It contained 2,906 artifacts. Seventeen artifacts have been designated as national treasures. The artifacts discovered in the tomb are displayed at the Gongju National Museum.

Muryeongwangneung Chamber

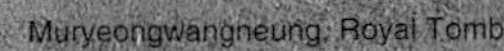

Muryeongwangneung, Royal Tomb

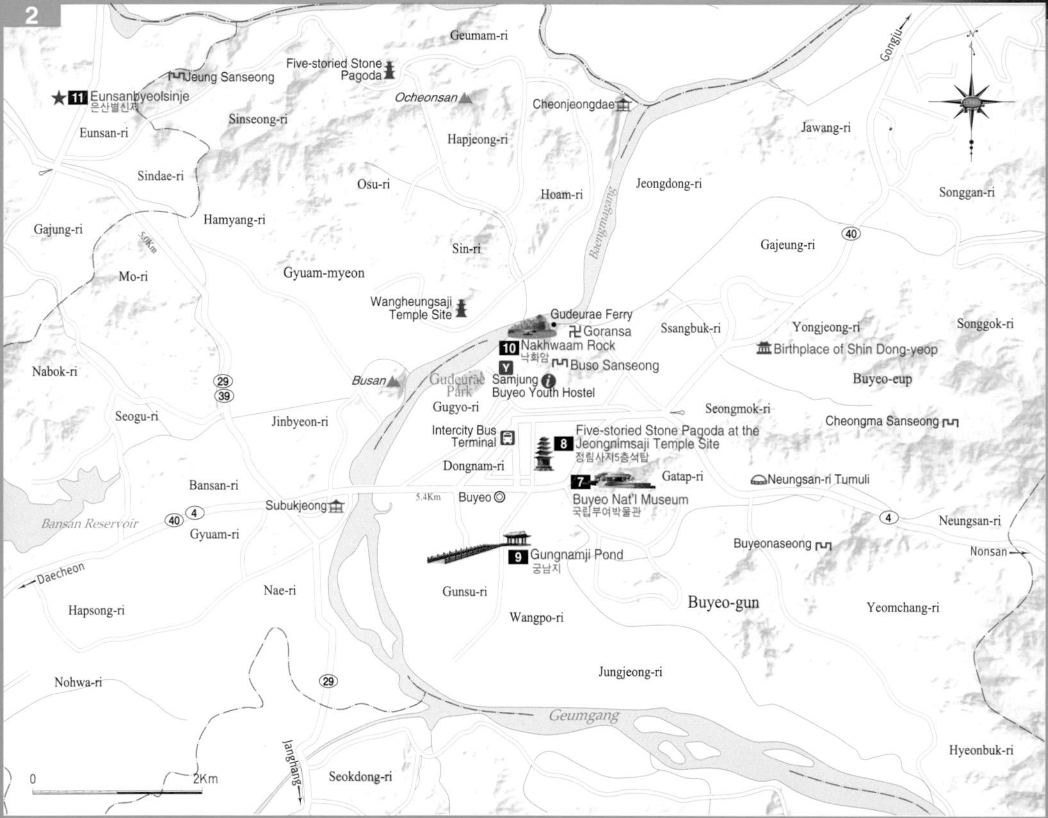

2

Geumam-ri
Jeung Sanseong
Five-storied Stone Pagoda
11 Eunsanbyeolsinje
은산별신제
Eunsan-ri
Sinseong-ri
Ocheonsan
Cheonjeongdae
Hapjeong-ri
Jawang-ri
Sindae-ri
Osu-ri
Hoam-ri
Jeongdong-ri
Songgan-ri
Gajung-ri
Hamyang-ri
Baengmagang
Gajeung-ri
Sin-ri
Mo-ri
Gyuam-myeon
Wangheungsaji Temple Site
Gudeurae Ferry
Goransa
Ssangbuk-ri
Yongjeong-ri
Songgok-ri
10 Nakhwaam Rock
낙화암
Buso Sanseong
Birthplace of Shin Dong-yeop
Nabok-ri
Busan
Gudeurae Park
Samjung
Buyeo Youth Hostel
Buyeo-eup
Seogu-ri
Jinbyeon-ri
Gugyo-ri
Seongmok-ri
Cheongma Sanseong
Intercity Bus Terminal
8 Five-storied Stone Pagoda at the Jeongnimsaji Temple Site
정림사지5층석탑
Dongnam-ri
Bansan-ri
7 Buyeo Nat'l Museum
국립부여박물관
Gatap-ri
Neungsan-ri Tumuli
Subukjeong
5.4Km
Buyeo
Bansan Reservoir
Gyuam-ri
Neungsan-ri
Buyeonaseong
Nonsan
9 Gungnamji Pond
궁남지
Daecheon
Nae-ri
Gunsu-ri
Buyeo-gun
Yeomchang-ri
Hapsong-ri
Wangpo-ri
Nohwa-ri
Jungjeong-ri
Geumgang
Hyeonbuk-ri
Janghang
Seokdong-ri
0 2Km
Gongju

Buyeo, which is rich in the Baekje Kingdom's cultural properties and spirit, is one of the most popular attractions in Korea. Buyeo was the final capital of the Baekje Kingdom before its culture perished some 1,300 years ago. The Baengmagang River runs through the center of the city, and Buyeo is loaded with a host of historic sites. The main points of interest here are the Buyeo National Museum, Gungnamji Pond, Nakhwaam Rock, and Buso Sanseong Fortress.

CHUNGCHEONGNAM-DO

Buyeo National Museum 7

The Buyeo National Museum displays an expansive collection of 9,000 artifacts. The main exhibition hall features a gilt-bronze incense burner which is regarded as an excellent example of Baekje Kingdom artistry. Other artifacts relating to Buddhism include the Geumdong Gwanseeum Bosal Ipsang (a glit-bronze standing Bodhisattva) and a stone sarira casket made during the reign of King Changmyeong. Also displayed are items which range from the prehistoric period to the late Joseon Dynasty. This group of items includes various earthenwares, bronze artifacts, roof tiles embossed with a variety of designs and metal accessories.

Buyeo National Museum

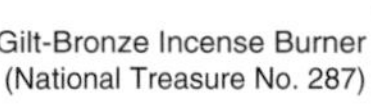

Gilt-Bronze Incense Burner (National Treasure No. 287)

Gungnamji (Historic site No. 135)

Five-storied Stone Pagoda at Jeongnimsaji Temple Site 8

The pagoda was built in the Baekje period along with the Mireuksaji stone pagoda in Iksan. The Tang Dynasty's General Sojeongbang destroyed Baekje in alliance with the Silla Kingdom. He left the writing 'Celebration Tower on Destroying Baekje' on the stone pagoda. The elegant five-storied pagoda body stands on a single, narrow and low pedestal. It is similar in structure to a wooden building and is highly valued as one of only two remaining stone pagodas from the Baekje period.

Gungnamji Pond 9

Gungnamji is Korea's oldest man-made pond. It was built by King Mu of the Baekje Kingdom. To the east of the pond are the ruins of an auxiliary palace. The pond is flanked by a well and cornerstone that appear to have belonged to the auxiliary palace. A pavilion and wooden bridge stand over the pond, and these are both surrounded by willow trees.

Five-storied Stone Pagoda at Jeongnimsaji Temple Site

Nakhwaam Rock 10

Standing high on the slope of Mt. Busosan in a jagged formation that overlooks Baengmagang River, Nakhwaam Rock is a major tourist attraction. The site is especially well-known because of the sad legend that surrounds it relating to the fall of the Baekje Kingdom. It is said that this is the spot where court maidens, who escaped the fortress where the combined invading forces of the Silla and Chinese Tang Dynasty were committing atrocities, jumped to their deaths into the Baengmagang in order to avoid the cruelties of the invading forces. The name Nakhwaam means falling flower. The name is said to derive from the sight of court maidens jumping off the rock because they resembled beautiful flowers falling. The hexagonal Baekhwajeong Pavilion stands on the cliff.

Nakhwaam & Baengmagang

Eunsanbyeolsinje 11

Eunsanbyeolsinje is a large-scale shamanistic ritual that has been designated as an important intangible asset. It is performed in the early spring every year by residents of Sindae-ri and Eunsan-ri, Eunsan-myeon. The sanctuary where the village's guardian spirits are said to be enshrined stands at the foot of a mountain at the back of Eunsan-ri village. This is where the spirit tablets of Boksinjanggun (a general) and Togeondaesa (a Buddhist monk) are enshrined. The ritual was first performed to console the souls of those who were killed for their efforts to rebuild the Baekje Kingdom. A host of interesting events are held during the six-day ritual, including brewing Jorasul (alcohol used for shaman rites), Jindaebegi (a tree-cutting ritual), Ggotbatgi (presenting paper flowers to the deities), Sangdanghaengsa (making an offering), Bonjesangdanggut (a shamanistic ritual), Hadanggut (a rite held the day after the ritual), Doksanje (a rite thanking the guardians for the successful performance of the ritual) and Jangseungje (a ritual aimed at preventing bad luck and epidemics).

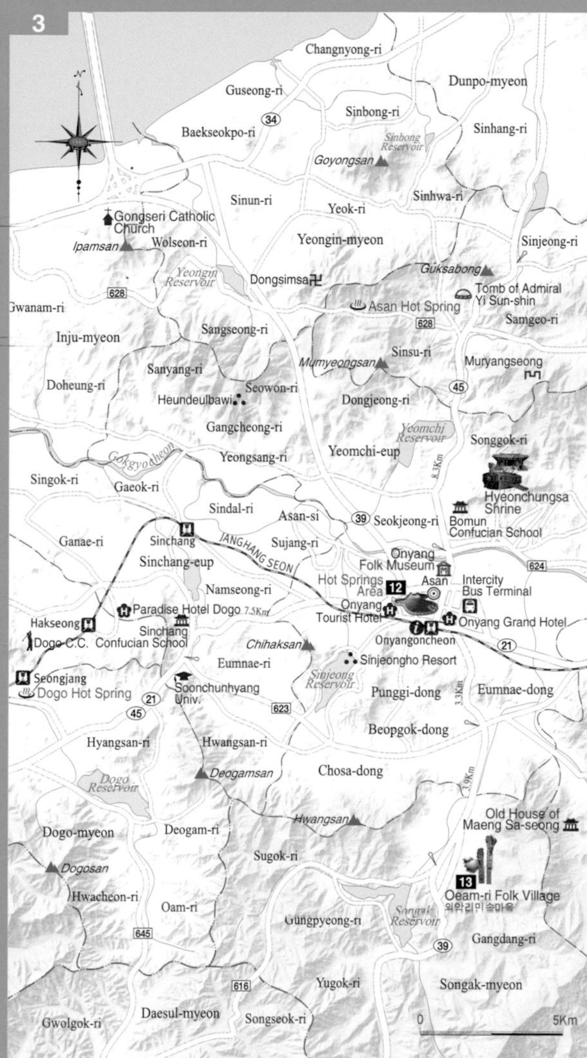

*A*san is a very popular destination for those interested in Korea's history as it holds many precious historic sites. The area has also become an all-weather spas resort. Of particular interest is Hyeonchungsa, a shrine dedicated to Admiral Yi Sun-shin of the Joseon Dynasty where people can learn of the loyalty and integrity which the nation's greatest military leader continues to inspire. Other tourist attractions, such as tombs of independence fighters, shrines and temples abound in the city. The city also contains a number of renowned hot spring spas, including the Onyang Spa, the Dogo Spa and the Asan Spa.*

Hot Springs Area 12

Spa Resort in Asan

Several nationally known spas are located in Asan. Visitors can enjoy not only saunas at the Asan, Onyang and Dogo spas, but also a forest bath where one can enjoy the rejuvenating effects of the lush forest's fresh air. These spas have a long history, some of them having been in use for almost 1,300 years. Most spas in the area have currently been transformed into resort spas.

Oeam-ri Folk Village 13

Because it has been designated as an important folk site, the Oeam-ri Folk Village is preserved and protected by the government. It is located in the foothills of Mt. Seolhwasan, and is populated mostly by the Lee clan of Yean origin, a group who settled in the area some 500 years ago.

The ancient houses which have been preserved here showcase the long history of the village. Everything in the village, ranging from the totem poles standing at its entrance to the fruit trees which are planted in the yard of each house, enables visitors to imagine what life during the Joseon Dynasty looked like.

Oeam-ri Folk Village

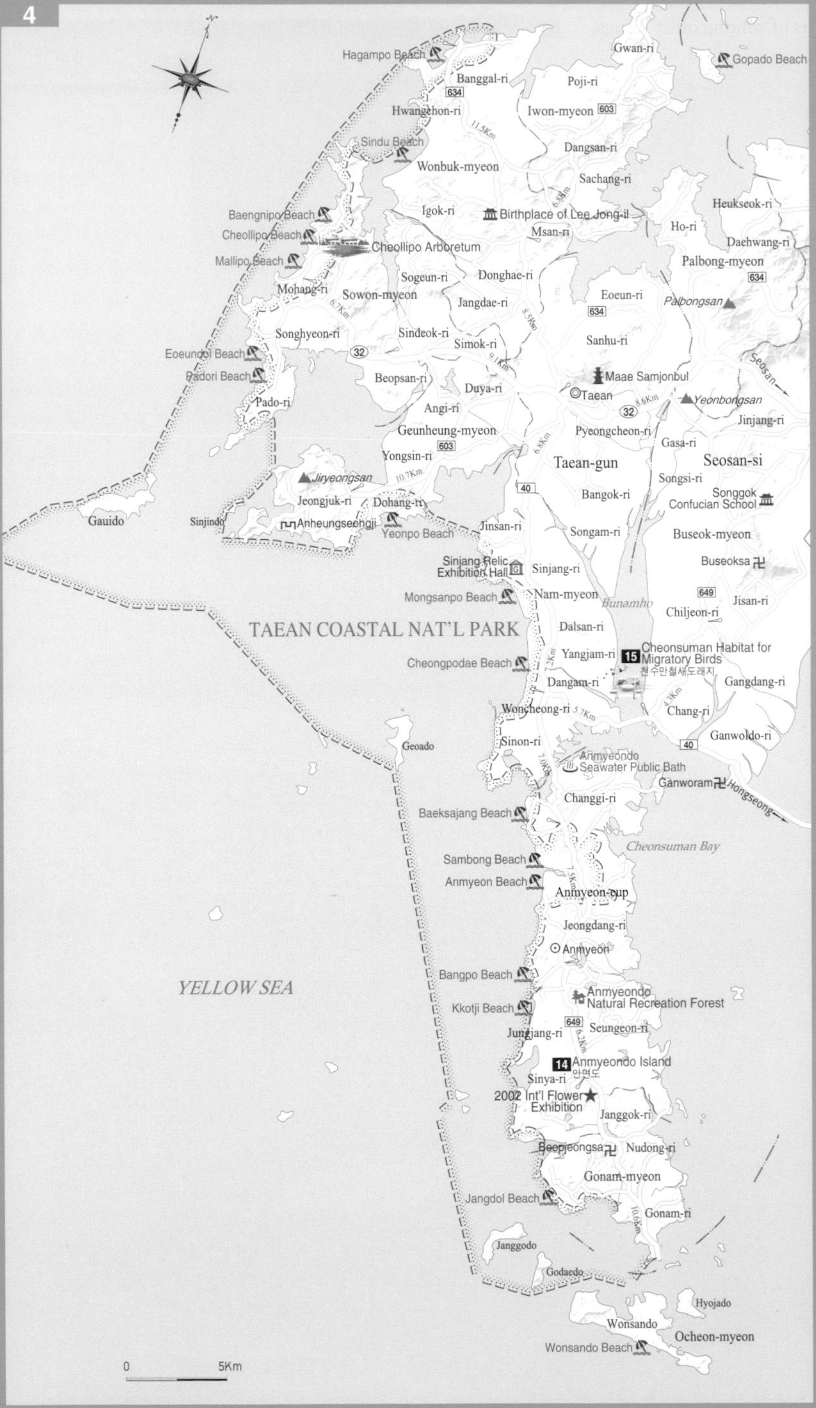

Anmyeondo Island 14

This island is linked to land by a 200m-long bridge which was built in 1970. Its coast is loaded with famous beaches. It has a softly curved coastline, silver sand, and clear water which maintains a mild temperature. The soft sand here is known for its good glass-making quality. Anmyeondo is surrounded by rocks which are shaped into interesting formations. Its uninhabited islets offer a safe habitat to sea gulls and other migratory birds.

Cheonsuman Habitat for Migratory Birds 15

Cheonsuman Bay is situated between the Seosan coast and Anmyeondo. Because of its shallow water and a large tidal range the bay was used as one of the first places for aquaculture. However, large-scale reclamation work in the central part of the bay was launched in the 1980s and reclaimed 155,000 hectares of land from the sea. Ganwolho and Bunamho were formed by the Cheonsuman sea dikes. They are fresh-water lakes where the sea water and fresh water from the river converge. With an ample amount of water vegetation, fish and shellfish, the two lakes are the area's largest habitats for seasonal birds. About 2 million birds of 111 different species can be seen here from late October to March.

Independence Hall of Korea F5

Independence Hall of Korea is a complex of buildings which houses various exhibits. These exhibits trace the nation's independence movement and the activities of patriots who fought for independence. Also shown are exhibits on the recent history of the nation's development.

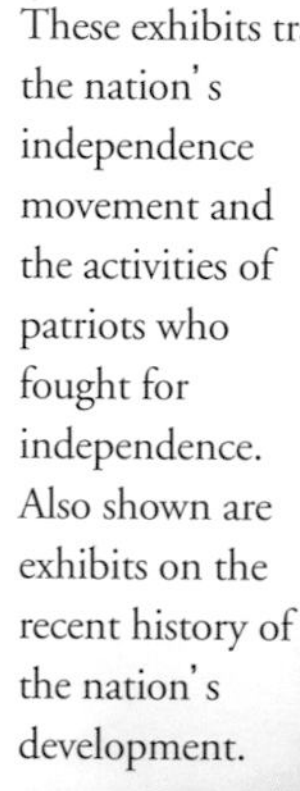

The complex consists of, among other things, Gyeoraeuijip (Grand Hall of the Nation), Gyeoraeuitap (Tower of the Korean People) and a bell which was built to express the wish for national unification.

The exhibition halls include the following: the Hall of National Heritage, the Hall of the Nationalist Movement, the Hall of Japanese Aggression, the Hall of the March First Independence Movement, the Hall of the Independence War and the Hall of the Social and Cultural Movement. The Circle Vision Theater is also a major attraction. In this theatre a 360° screen is used to show a variety of films.

Independence Hall of Korea

Gyeoraeuitap (The Tower of the Korean People)

Waemok Village (sunrise and sunset village)

Waemok Village C3

Waemonk Village is the westernmost village in Chungcheongnam-do and is the only place on the west coast where people can see both the sunrise and the sunset over the sea. Ferry boats and fishing boats are common in the area and fresh raw fish (sashimi) is served year round.

Gijisi Tug-of-War

Gijisi Tug-of-War C4

While it first began as a folk religion rite, Gijisi tug-of-war has developed into a local folk festival. Villagers are divided into two groups, the land team and the sea team.
It is believed that the year will be a bumper crop year when the land team beats the sea team and vice versa.
The rope used for this event measures 200m in length and 1.8m in diameter and over 40t of rice straw are used to make it.

Seosan Maae Samjonbul C5

On a rock cliff in a valley of Mt. Gayasan, the Standing Buddha Reborn was sculptured in the center, with standing images of Bodhisattva on the right and on the left. Widely known as 'a smile of the Baekje,' this is representative of Buddhist images carved from rock.

Maae Samjonbul in Seosan

Boryeong Mud Festival B7

In the summer when most tourists visit the area, a variety of events, including the Daecheon Beach Festival and the Mud Festival, are held. At the Mud Festival participants can experience a mud massage, mud games, mud body painting, hand printing, and many other events which use mud which has been dug from the tidal bed and purified.

The coastline of Boryeong-si, where Daecheon Beach is located, is 136km long and is rich in the type of mud which is popular for facial massages. The health benefits of the high-quality mud packs are one of the major attractions for visitors to Daecheon Beach.

Seohae Bridge D4

As part of the 353km-long west coastline highway, Seohae Bridge links Pyeongtaek-si, Gyeonggi-do to Danjing-gun, Chungcheongnam-do. It has six lanes and is 31.4m in width. The bridge is the longest of its kind in Korea and the 9th longest suspension bridge in the world. The scenery of Seohae Bridge makes a striking panoramic view.

Sudeoksa Temple C5

Sudeoksa is a temple with a long history. It is located in the foothills of the 495m-high Mt. Deoksungsan. It is believed that the temple was first built by the Buddhist monk Jimyeongbeopsa during the Baekje Kingdom and later rebuilt by renowned Buddhist monk Wonhyodaesa.

Its Daeungjeon (main hall), which was built in the 34th year of the reign of King Chungnyeol of the Goryeo Dynasty, is the oldest wooden structure in the nation and was designated as National Treasure No. 49. Iljumun (Gate), Jongnu (Bell Tower), Gwaneumbawi (Rock), Mangongtap (Pagoda) and Geumgangmun (Gate) are among the other major attractions the temple has to offer. The expansive grounds hold a three-storied stone tower built during the Silla Kingdom and the Gyeonseongam.

Buddhist Drum in Sudeoksa

Seohae Bridge

Gwanchoksa Eunjinmireuk

Gwanchoksa Eunjinmireuk E8

Gwanchoksa is a temple located on the slope of Mt. Banyasan. The temple is widely known for its Mireukbosalipsang (a stone statue of Buddha). The statue's construction began in the 19th year of the reign of King Gwangjong of the Goryeo Dynasty and was completed some 38 years later. Also known as Eunjinmireuk, the statue is 18.12m in height and 9.9m in circumference. Its coronet is 3.94m in height, and its ears measure 3.3m. It is the largest stone Buddha statue in the country. Eunjinmireuk was built according to the construction style of the Goryeo Dynasty, which ruled the area at the time.

Daecheon Beach B7

As the largest beach on the west coast, Daecheon Beach is a 3.5km strip covered with white clam shells. Daecheonhang Port is located 1km north of the beach and is known for being the center of the west coast maritime transportation network. It serves as a port for over 70 neighboring islands, including Wonsando, Sapsido and Oeyeondo. The port is also known as a great fishing site.

Muchangpo Beach C8

Once a military depot during the Joseon Dynasty, Muchangpo Beach was the first beach on the west coast to be opened to the public (1928). It is the perfect place to enjoy both swimming and the beauty of the forest, as it has a long coastline and lush pine forests surrounding the area. The best fishing location is found 1.5km off the coastline, a 6,600㎡ area which contains of numerous majestic rocks soaring out of the sea. Muchangpo is popular for its 'Miracle of Moses' phenomenon that takes place once or twice a month during spring tide. The low tide exposes land which is naturally submerged. The 'Miracle of Moses' lasts for 1 hour and 20 minutes during which people walk out on the exposed land to look for marine creatures like sea cucumbers, ascidians, trumpet shells and octopus, or to dig for thin-shelled surf clams.

'Miracle of Moses' , Muchangpo Beach

Haemi Eupseong Fortress C5

Haemi Eupseong is a stone fortress which was built in the 22nd year (1491) of the reign of King Seongjong. With three gates to the east, south and west, its 5m-high wall stretches some 1.8km, enclosing an area of more than 198,000㎡. The fortress was a holy site for the Catholic martyrs who lost their lives in the late period of the Joseon Dynasty. During the persecution campaigns against Catholicism, numerous Catholics were tortured and killed at the provincial office in the fortress. More than one thousand people were killed in 1866 alone. In the square, the site where Catholics were imprisoned and the trees where they were hung and tortured have been preserved.

Jeollabuk-do

Jeollabuk-do is located in the southwestern region of South Korea, 240km from Seoul. It is bordered on the north by Chungcheongnam-do, on the south by Jeollanam-do, on the east by Gyeonsangnam-do, and on the west by the Yellow Sea. The shortest possible route from Korea to mainland China starts in Jeollabuk-do.

Jeollabuk-do is known for its unique local foods and traditional 'sori music.' Visitors can experience these or visit some of the many historic sites the area has to offer.

The area also has a number of major national and provincial parks where people can enjoy fresh mountain air and lush flora.

Pansori

Korean Traditional Vocal Music

The Famous Pansori Singer, An Suk-seon

Pansori is a traditional singing style in which one singer tells a long story mixed with singing (Sori), words (Aniri), and gestures (Neoreumsae) to the beat of a drummer. Its origin is not exactly known, but it is presumed that Pansori came into being before King Sukjong was given the contents of Chunhyangga, a song composed by Ryu Jin-han in the 30th year of King Yeongjo of the Joseon Dynasty, or dated back to the Silla Kingdom when Pannoreum was performed.

The tempos of Pansori, which fluctuate between fast and slow depending on the situation in the story, are Jinyangjo (adagio), Jungmori, Jungjungmori (moderato), Huimori. The drummer issues exclamatory words like 'That's great!', 'Oh my god!', 'All right!' in order to tune up songs to his accompaniment.

Pansori demonstrates the spontaneous, voluntary and improvisational nature of traditional Korean art. For instance, by the time of Song Hong-rok, a famous pansori singer during the reign of King Sunjo of the Joseon Dynasty, Pansori had been verbally handed down without fixed scripts, and improvised folk songs recounting witty stories had been added to the original narrations taught by teachers because pansori values the emotions of the audience and permits a performer to change and improvise the narratives.

By the 19th century, more than 12 pansori classics were being circulated, but only five pansori classics exist today. These include 'Chunhyangjeon,' 'Simcheongjeon,' 'Heungboga,' 'Sugungga,' and 'Jeokbyeokga.'

Gochang Pansori Museum

The newly opened Pansori Museum is located in Gochang-gun, Jeollabuk-do. The museum was built to commemorate Sin Jae-hyo, a great master of pansori, and other famous female pansori performers, such as Jin Chae-seon and Gim So-hee.

The Pansori Museum preserves the cultural traditions and heritage of Gochang, the center of pansori music and from which pansori was handed down. The two-story museum shows the 200-year history of the pansori, as well as highlighting pansori singers and their achievements. The tradition of sori and other pansori-related materials from Meot-madang, Aniri-madang, Ballim-madang, and Hon-madang are each exhibited.

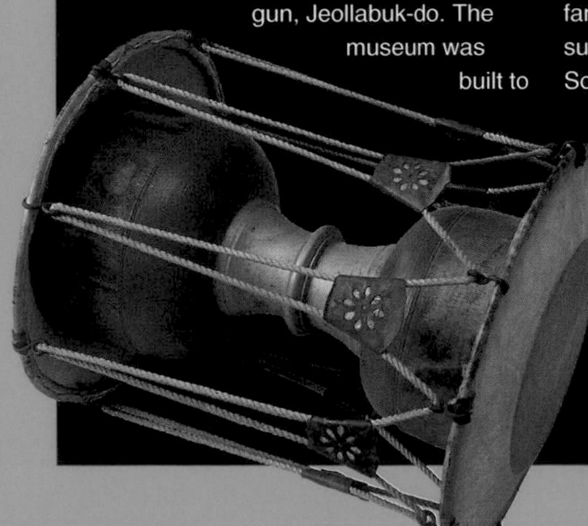
Janggu

Where to experience Pansori

The National Center for Korean Traditional Performing Arts

The National Center for Korean Traditional Performing Arts offers a traditional Korean music performance every Saturday for everyone from those new to traditional Korean music to traditional Korean music lovers. Diverse genres of music are performed, such as the Gayageum (a 12-stringed zither) Byeongchang, in which a solo musician both sings and plays the gayageum, musical instrument solo recitals, pansori, traditional Korean dances, folk songs and Samullori, the Korean traditional percussion quartet.
In addition, Pansori hanmadang, in which the audience and performers are united in creating a harmonized music through the chuimsae, is performed once a month. Five existing Pansori episodes, namely, the 'Chunhyangjeon,' 'Simcheongjeon,' 'Heungboga,' 'Sugungga,' and the 'Jeokbyeokga,' are performed.
www.ncktpa.go.kr

The Movie 'Seopyeonje'

In this movie, a male singer intentionally makes his daughter blind to train her as an expert pansori singer who can express 'han', a mixed feeling of deep sorrow and remorse unique to the Korean spirit. In the movie, sori is not merely a simple art form, but symbolizes the people's aspirations for various fundamental values which are lacking in modern society.

Jeonju Sori (musical sound) Festival

Jeonju, with its tradition of culture and art, hosts the International Sori Festival. Not only traditional Korean music is performed here but also folk music from around the world. This festival is a good opportunity to experience the uniquely beautiful Korean sori. The sori featured in the festival is divided into Korean sori, Asian sori, international sori and sori of peace. Korean sori features traditional Korean folk music, such as pansori and sanjo(a folk music style played on a solo instrument to the accompaniment of a drum).
www.jsf.or.kr

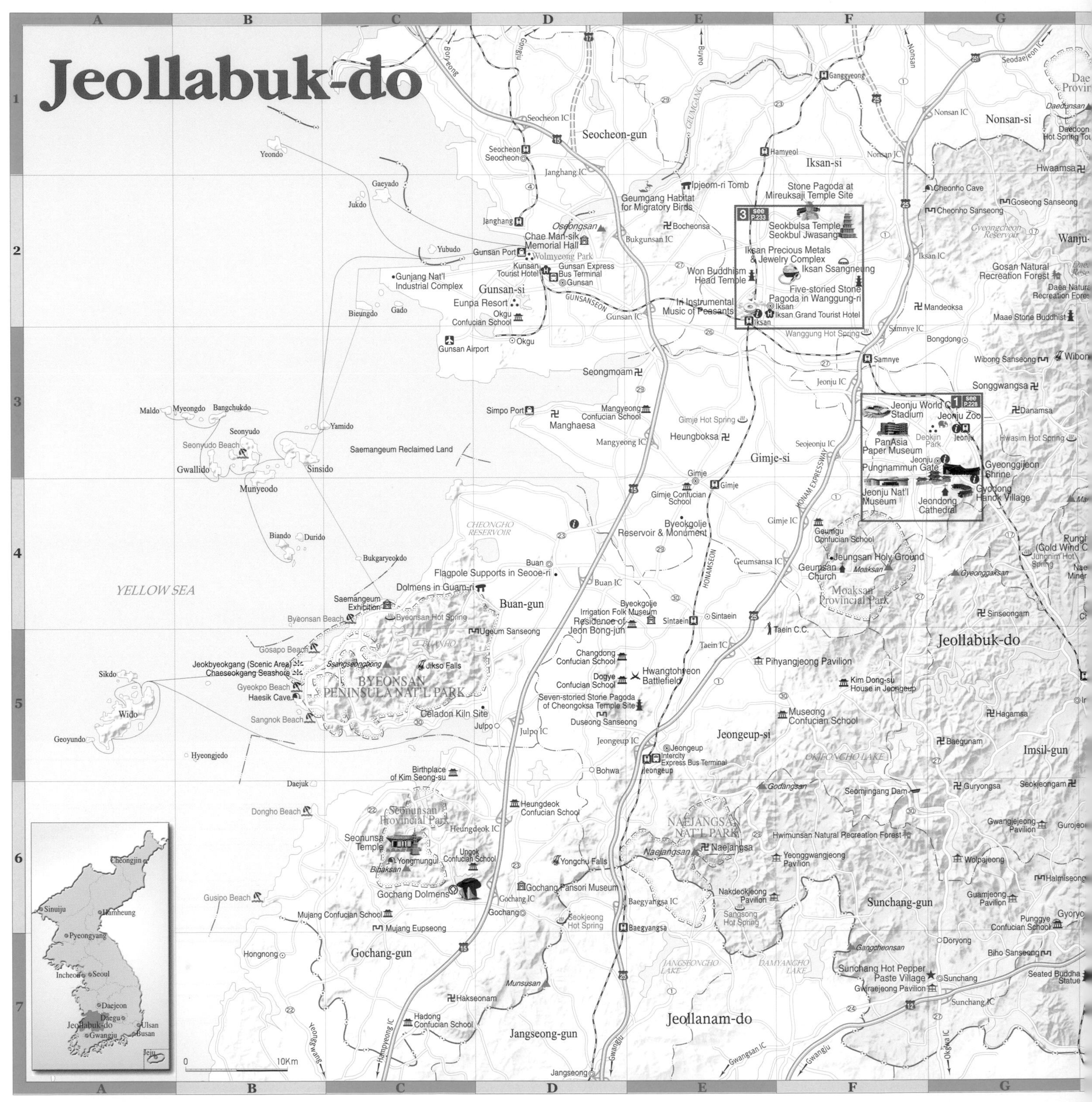
Jeollabuk-do
A
B
C
D
E
F
G
1
2
3
4
5
6
7
Seocheon IC
Seocheon-gun
Seocheon
Janghang IC
Janghang
Hamyeol
Ganggyeong
Nonsan IC
Nonsan-si
Nonsan IC
Iksan-si
Hwaamsa
Cheonho Cave
Cheonho Sanseong
Goseong Sanseong
Ipjeom-ri Tomb
Stone Pagoda at Mireuksaji Temple Site
Geumgang Habitat for Migratory Birds
Bocheonsa
Bukgunsan IC
Seokbulsa Temple Seokbul Jwasang
Iksan Precious Metals & Jewelry Complex
Iksan Ssangneung
Won Buddhism Head Temple
Five-storied Stone Pagoda in Wanggung-ri
In Instrumental Music of Peasants
Iksan
Iksan Grand Tourist Hotel
Iksan IC
Gosan Natural Recreation Forest
Mandeoksa
Maae Stone Buddhist
Yeondo
Gaeyado
Jukdo
Yubudo
Osegongsan
Chae Man-sik Memorial Hall
Gunsan Port
Wolmyeong Park
Kunsan Tourist Hotel
Gunsan Express Bus Terminal
Gunsan
Gunjang Nat'l Industrial Complex
Gunsan-si
Eunpa Resort
Okgu Confucian School
Okgu
Gunsan Airport
Bieungdo
Gado
Gunsan IC
Wanggung Hot Spring
Samnye IC
Samnye
Bongdong
Wibong Sanseong
Songgwangsa
Danamsa
Jeonju IC
Seongmoam
Simpo Port
Manghaesa
Mangyeong Confucian School
Mangyeong IC
Gimje Hot Spring
Heungboksa
Gimje-si
Seojeonju IC
Jeonju World Cup Stadium
Jeonju Zoo
PanAsia Paper Museum
Deokjin Park
Jeonju
Pungnammun Gate
Gyeonggijeon Shrine
Jeonju Nat'l Museum
Jeondong Cathedral
Gyodong Hanok Village
Hwasim Hot Spring
Maldo
Myeongdo
Bangchukdo
Yamido
Seonyudo
Seonyudo Beach
Saemangeum Reclaimed Land
Gwallido
Sinsido
Munyeodo
Gimje
Gimje Confucian School
Byeokgolje Reservoir & Monument
Gimje IC
Geumgu Confucian School
Jeungsan Holy Ground
Geumsan Church
Moaksan
Moaksan Provincial Park
Gyeonggaksan
Biando
Durido
Bukgaryeokdo
CHEONGHO RESERVOIR
Buan
Flagpole Supports in Seooe-ri
Buan IC
Geumsansa IC
HONAM EXPRESSWAY
HONAMSEON
YELLOW SEA
Dolmens in Guam-ri
Saemangeum Exhibition
Buan-gun
Byeokgolje Irrigation Folk Museum
Residence of Jeon Bong-jun
Sintaein
Byeonsan Beach
Byeonsan Hot Spring
Ugeum Sanseong
Taein C.C.
Sinseongam
Jeollabuk-do
Gosapo Beach
Jeokbyeokgang (Scenic Area)
Chaeseokgang Seashore
Ssangseonbong
Jikso Falls
Changdong Confucian School
Dogye Confucian School
Hwangtohyeon Battlefield
Taein IC
Pihyangjeong Pavilion
Kim Dong-su House in Jeongeup
Sikdo
Gyeokpo Beach
Haesik Cave
BYEONSAN PENINSULA NAT'L PARK
Seven-storied Stone Pagoda of Cheongoksa Temple Site
Wido
Celadon Kiln Site
Sangnok Beach
Julpo
Julpo IC
Duseong Sanseong
Museong Confucian School
Hagamsa
Geoyundo
Hyeongjedo
Jeongeup IC
Jeongeup
Jeongeup Intercity Express Bus Terminal
Jeongeup-si
Baegunam
Imsil-gun
OKJEONGHO LAKE
Birthplace of Kim Seong-su
Bohwa
Daejuk
Godangsan
Seomjingang Dam
Guryongsa
Seokjeongam
Dongho Beach
Heungdeok Confucian School
Seonunsan Provincial Park
Heungdeok IC
NAEJANGSAN NAT'L PARK
Hwimunsan Natural Recreation Forest
Gwangjejeong Pavilion
Seonunsa Temple
Yongmungul
Bibaksan
Ungok Confucian School
Naejangsan
Naejangsa
Yeonggwangjeong Pavilion
Wolpajeong
Halmiseong
Gochang Dolmens
Yongchu Falls
Gochang Pansori Museum
Nakdeokjeong Pavilion
Sangsong Hot Spring
Sunchang-gun
Guamjeong Pavilion
Gusipo Beach
Gochang IC
Gochang
Baegyangsa IC
Seokjeong Hot Spring
Mujang Confucian School
Mujang Eupseong
Baegyangsa
Punggye Confucian School
Gangcheonsan
Doryong
Hongnong
Gochang-gun
JANGSEONG LAKE
DAMYANG LAKE
Biho Sanseong
Sunchang Hot Pepper Paste Village
Sunchang
Seated Buddha Statue
Gwiraejeong Pavilion
Munsusan
Hakseonam
Sunchang IC
Hadong Confucian School
Jeollanam-do
Jangseong-gun
Hampyeong IC
Gwangju
Gwangsan IC
Okgwa IC
Jangseong
Cheongjin
Sinuiju
Hamheung
Pyeongyang
Incheon
Seoul
Daejeon
Daegu
Jeollabuk-do
Gwangju
Ulsan
Busan
Jeju
0
10Km
see P.233
see P.228
Boryeong
Gongju
Buyeo
Nonsan
Seodaejeon IC
Daedunsan
Daedoon Hot Spring
Gwangju

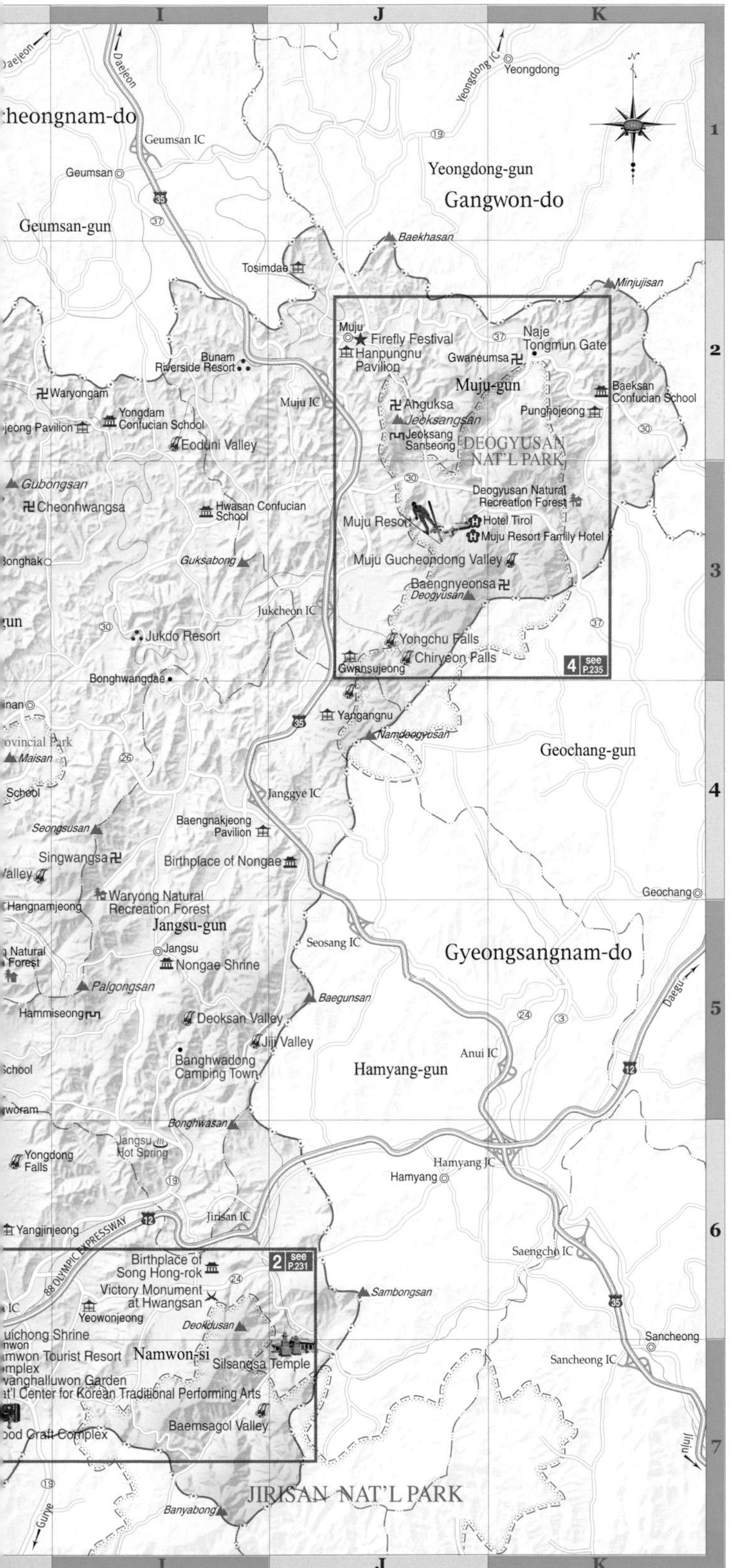

INDEX

Tourist Information

Jeollabuk-do Tourism Division 82-63-280-3335
Jeollabuk-do Tourist Information Center 82-63-288-0105
www.provin.jeonbuk.kr

LEGEND

- Railroad Station
- Airport
- Port
- Bus Terminal
- Tourist Information Center
- World Heritage Site
- Museum
- Prehistoric Relic Site
- Tomb
- Fortress
- Temple
- Site of Buddhist Artifacts
- Church
- Traditional Building
- Traditional Pavilion
- Battlefield
- Korean War Historical Site
- Cultural Experience Area
- Falls or Valley
- Cave
- Beach
- Golf Course
- Hot Spring or Spa
- Scenic Area
- Amusement Park
- Migratory Birds' Sanctuary
- Zoo
- Natural Recreation Forest
- Mountain
- Other Tourist Attractions
- Hotel
- Reference Point

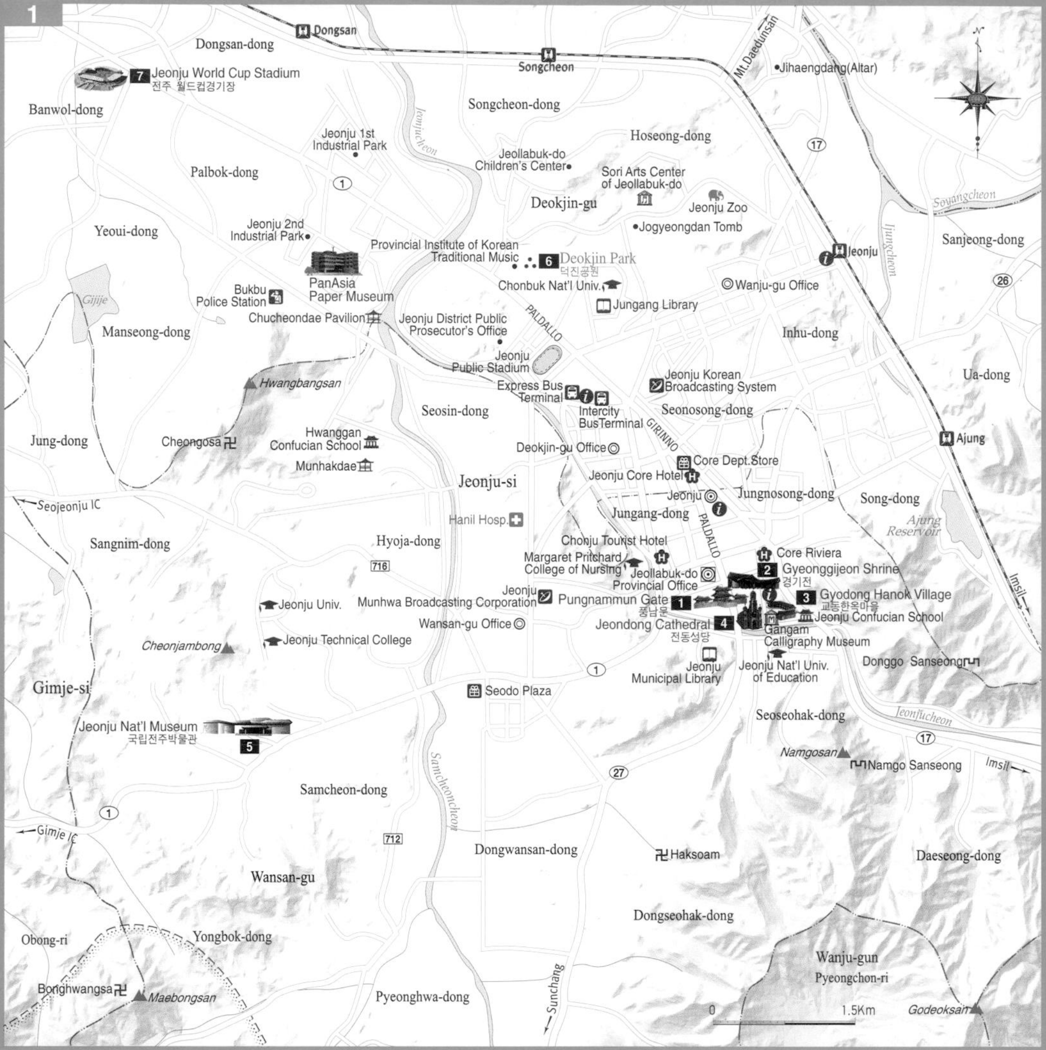

1

Dongsan
Dongsan-dong
7 Jeonju World Cup Stadium
전주 월드컵경기장
Banwol-dong
Songcheon
Songcheon-dong
Mt.Daedunsan
•Jihaengdang(Altar)
Jeonju 1st Industrial Park
Jeonjucheon
Hoseong-dong
17
Palbok-dong
Jeollabuk-do Children's Center•
Sori Arts Center of Jeollabuk-do
1
Deokjin-gu
Jeonju Zoo
Soyangcheon
Yeoui-dong
Jeonju 2nd Industrial Park•
•Jogyeongdan Tomb
Jiungcheon
Sanjeong-dong
Provincial Institute of Korean Traditional Music
6 Deokjin Park
덕진공원
Jeonju
PanAsia Paper Museum
Chonbuk Nat'l Univ.
26
Gijije
Bukbu Police Station
Wanju-gu Office
Chucheondae Pavilion
Jeonju District Public Prosecutor's Office
Jungang Library
Manseong-dong
PALDALLO
Inhu-dong
Jeonju Public Stadium
Ua-dong
Hwangbangsan
Express Bus Terminal
Jeonju Korean Broadcasting System
Seosin-dong
Intercity BusTerminal
GIRINNO
Seonosong-dong
Hwanggan Confucian School
Jung-dong
Cheongosa
Ajung
Deokjin-gu Office
Munhakdae
Core Dept.Store
Jeonju Core Hotel
Jeonju-si
Seojeonju IC
Jeonju
Jungnosong-dong
Song-dong
Jungang-dong
Hanil Hosp.
PALDALLO
Ajung Reservoir
Sangnim-dong
Hyoja-dong
Chonju Tourist Hotel
Core Riviera
Margaret Pritchard College of Nursing
716
Jeollabuk-do Provincial Office
2 Gyeonggijeon Shrine
경기전
Imsil
Jeonju Munhwa Broadcasting Corporation
Pungnammun Gate 1
풍남문
3 Gyodong Hanok Village
교동한옥마을
Jeonju Univ.
Jeonju Confucian School
Wansan-gu Office
Jeondong Cathedral 4
전동성당
Gangam Calligraphy Museum
Cheonjambong
Jeonju Technical College
Jeonju Municipal Library
Jeonju Nat'l Univ. of Education
Donggo Sanseong
1
Gimje-si
Seodo Plaza
Seoseohak-dong
Jeonjucheon
Jeonju Nat'l Museum
국립전주박물관
5
17
Namgosan
Namgo Sanseong
Imsil
27
Samcheon-dong
Samcheoncheon
1
Gimje IC
712
Dongwansan-dong
Haksoam
Daeseong-dong
Wansan-gu
Dongseohak-dong
Obong-ri
Yongbok-dong
Wanju-gun
Pyeongchon-ri
Bonghwangsa
Maebongsan
Sunchang
Pyeonghwa-dong
0
1.5Km
Godeoksan

Jeonju was the royal capital of the Hubaekje Kingdom and the birthplace of the Joseon Dynasty. The city boasts a long historical tradition, as well as a significant cultural and artistic heritage. Its local cuisine is also renowned for its distinct flavor. Major tourist attractions here include Pungnammun Gate, Gyeonggijeon Shrine, Omokdae Hill, Hanbyeongnu Pavilion, Daga Park, and Deokjin Park. Jeonju also contains cultural and art sites such as the Jeonju National Museum and the PanAsia Paper Museum. Moreover, Jeonju is host to the 'International Sori(musical sound) Festival.'

Pungnammun Gate 1

Pungnammun, which is known as the symbol of Jeonju, is the southernmost gate of the four gates which make up the Jeonju Fortress. The upper story of the gate is well-preserved and reflects the architectural style of the late Joseon Dynasty.

Gyeonggijeon

Gyeonggijeon Shrine 2

Gyeonggijeon, located 150m east from Pungnammun in Jeonju, was built in the 10th year (1410) of King Taejong's reign. It enshrines the portrait of King Taejo, who founded the Joseon Dynasty. The portrait was drawn in the 9th year (1872) of King Gojong's reign. Gyeonggijeon consists of a main building and an auxiliary building which were built for performing memorial rituals to ancestors.

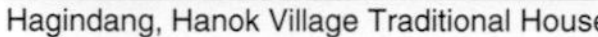
Hagindang, Hanok Village Traditional House

Jeondong Cathedral

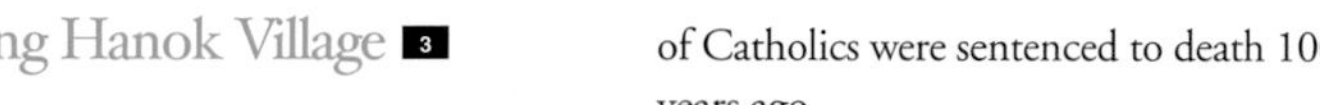

Gyodong Hanok Village 3

Hanok Village, which preserves the artistic traditions of Jeonju, is often called a place of art. The architectural beauty found in the houses is most evident in the roofs, which are covered with blackish-grey tiles. The lines of the eaves form a unique sight for those interested in traditional architecture.
The village preserves its beauty in a way which could be compared to a scene in an oriental drawing. Hagindang is a traditional building in Jeonju, the ancient capital. It is an example of how the architectural styles of the royal palaces were copied in the commoner' s houses at the time of the fall of the Joseon Dynasty. This building is a vivid model of the antique tiled-roof houses.

Jeondong Cathedral 4

Jeondong Cathedral combines Byzantine and Romanesque architectural styles and is one of the most beautiful cathedrals in Korea. Construction of the cathedral was started in June, 1891 and completed in 1914. It is located across from the Jeolla Gamyeong site, the old government building where a number of Catholics were sentenced to death 100 years ago.
Father Bodne, the first head pastor of the cathedral, purchased the land and Father Fwannel, who also designed the Myeongdong Cathedral, designed the cathedral.
Stone, which was obtained from the site where Pungnammun Fortress was demolished, was used to build the foundation platform of the cathedral. The main hall and auxiliary building are designed in a flat form and have a domed ceiling. Small bell towers are located on both sides of a central bell tower, and create a harmonious three-dimensional effect, highlighting the soaring impression of the cathedral.

Jeonju National Museum 5

The Jeonju National Museum houses a rich collection of 24,000 exhibits, of which a majority are artifacts from the prehistoric era and the Mahan and Baekje Kingdoms. These artifacts were excavated from the Jeollabuk-do area. Buddhist art works, ceramics, metal craftworks and historical ethnographic materials are also displayed in the museum. 1,100 of the relics are permanently exhibited

Jeonju National Museum

in three exhibition halls, and special exhibitions with diverse themes are held at the museum annually.

Jeonju Bibimbap

Jeonju bibimbap is the most popular local cuisine and has become the city' s specialty. It is a must for tourists visiting the city. This one-dish meal is made by mixing rice, hot pepper paste, bean sprouts, green-pea jelly and 30 different vegetables and condiments. Jeonju bibimbap is distinctive from other bibimbap dishes around the country.
The rice used in Jeonju bibimbap is cooked with ox-head meat broth and bean sprouts are steamed together with the rice.

Deokjin Park 6

Deokjin Park contains Chwihyangjeong, a pavillion surrounded by a pond built during the Goryeo Dynasty, and is a historic site (designated as a public park in 1938). Inside the park, a suspension bridge divides the park into two sections. The pond takes up two thirds of the park's area, with a boating marina located at one end.
Deokjin Pond is one of the eight scenic vistas of Jeonju, and it is one of the most popular sightseeing areas in Jeonju area because of its many lotus flowers. The fully blossomed lotus flowers in summer cover almost half of the pond.
Nowadays the park offers entertainment to visitors by holding regular performances in the outdoor performance theater, located right beside Chwihyangjeong. There are nine stone memorials in the park, including the Children's Charter, the Shin Seok-jeong Monument, the Kim Hae-gang Monument, and the General Jeong Bong-jun Statue.

Jeonju World Cup Stadium 7

Jeonju World Cup Stadium

The Jeonju World Cup Stadium will host matches to be held in Jeonju during the 2002 Korea/Japan World Cup Games. The architectural concept of the stadium is designed to emphasize the image of Jeonju as a traditional city. Its spectator stands, which divide the stadium into four sections, and its roof, were constructed to resemble Jeonju Hapjukseon, Jeonju's traditional folding fan. The ribs and curved topline of the fan are said to reflect Jeonju's open space and its desire to move forward onto the world stage and become an internationally renowned city.
The structures which uphold the roof of the stadium, mast-shaped columns with cables connected to them, symbolize the city's traditional music. The mast and the cables represent the 12-stringed gayageum, a traditional musical instrument.

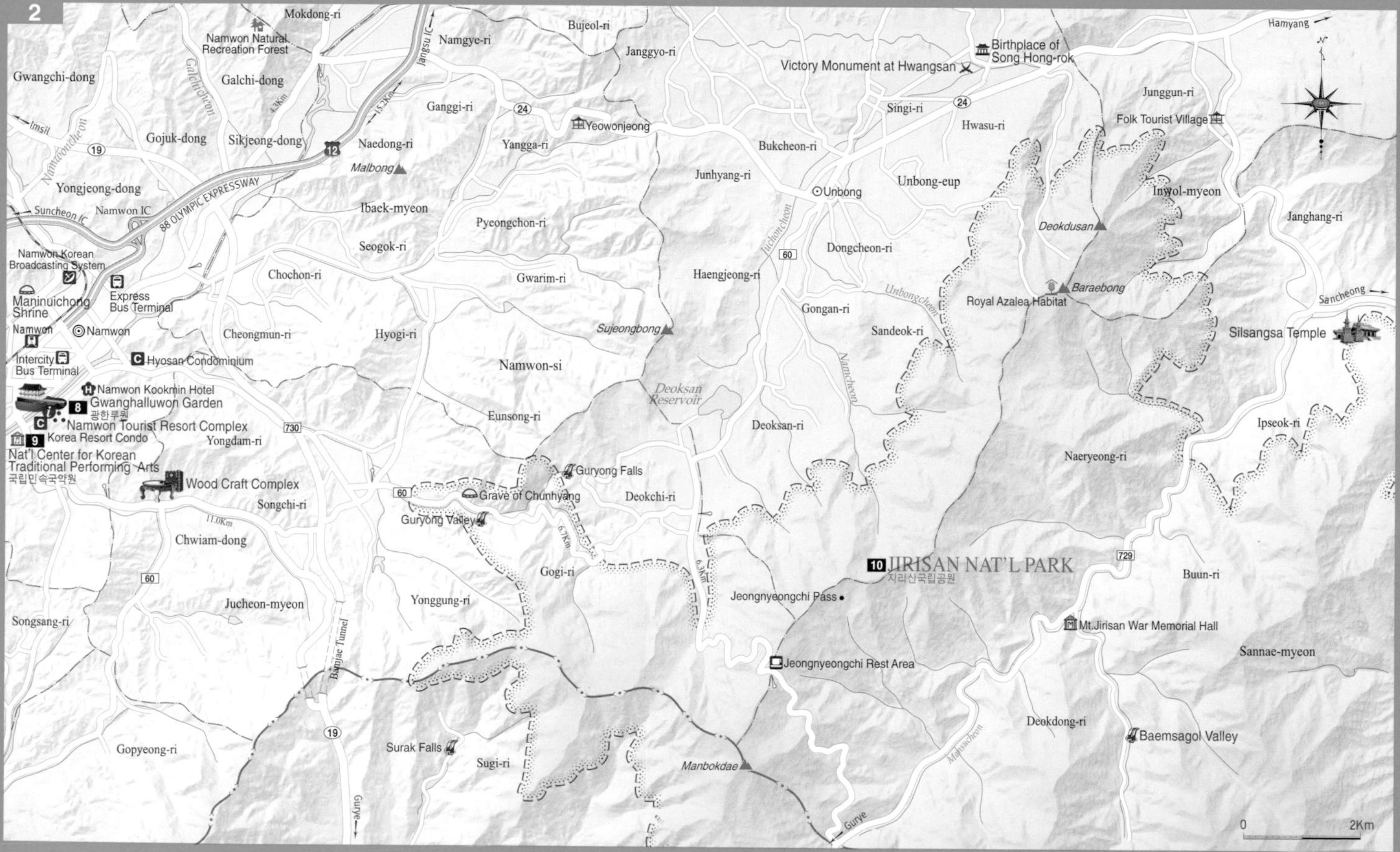

2

Mokdong-ri
Namwon Natural Recreation Forest
Galchi-dong
Gwangchi-dong
Namgye-ri
Bujeol-ri
Janggyo-ri
Victory Monument at Hwangsan
Birthplace of Song Hong-rok
Hamyang
Junggun-ri
Folk Tourist Village
Singi-ri
Hwasu-ri
Ganggi-ri
Yeowonjeong
Gojuk-dong
Sikjeong-dong
Naedong-ri
Yangga-ri
Malbong
Bukcheon-ri
Junhyang-ri
Unbong
Unbong-eup
Inwol-myeon
Janghang-ri
Yongjeong-dong
Suncheon IC
Namwon IC
88 OLYMPIC EXPRESSWAY
Ibaek-myeon
Pyeongchon-ri
Deokdusan
Seogok-ri
Dongcheon-ri
Namwon Korean Broadcasting System
Chochon-ri
Gwarim-ri
Haengjeong-ri
Baraebong
Maninuichong Shrine
Express Bus Terminal
Gongan-ri
Royal Azalea Habitat
Sancheong
Namwon
Cheongmun-ri
Hyogi-ri
Sujeongbong
Sandeok-ri
Silsangsa Temple
Intercity Bus Terminal
Hyosan Condominium
Namwon-si
Namwon Kookmin Hotel
Gwanghalluwon Garden
광한루원
Deoksan Reservoir
Eunsong-ri
Namwon Tourist Resort Complex
Korea Resort Condo
Yongdam-ri
Deoksan-ri
Ipseok-ri
Nat'l Center for Korean Traditional Performing Arts
국립민속국악원
Naeryeong-ri
Guryong Falls
Wood Craft Complex
Grave of Chunhyang
Deokchi-ri
Songchi-ri
Guryong Valley
Chwiam-dong
JIRISAN NAT'L PARK
지리산국립공원
Gogi-ri
Buun-ri
Jucheon-myeon
Jeongnyeongchi Pass
Yonggung-ri
Songsang-ri
Mt.Jirisan War Memorial Hall
Sannae-myeon
Jeongnyeongchi Rest Area
Deokdong-ri
Baemsagol Valley
Gopyeong-ri
Surak Falls
Sugi-ri
Manbokdae
Gurye
0 2Km

Namwon is widely known for 'Chunhyang' the name of a famous story based on a woman who symbolized faithfulness for Koreans. Her story is also told in 'Dongpyeonje' a well-known Korean sori, or folk song.

Namwon hosts the 'Chunhyang Festival' every May 5th, to honor the spirit of fidelity and loyalty. Events include a ceremony paying respects to Chunhyang, celebratory parties on the eve of the Chunhyang Festival, Korean traditional music, farmer's band music, a sijo (a kind of short lyric poem) competition and the Chunhyang Beauty Pageant.

The city's major tourist attractions include Gwanghalluwon Garden, which served as the setting for the novel 'Chunhyangjeon', as well as Jirisan National Park, Namwon Tourist Complex, Namwon Confucian School, Maninuichong Memorial Hall, Chunhyang Sadang Shrine, and the Hwangsandaecheopbiji (war monument site).

Mt. Jirisan

Night View of Gwanghalluwon Garden

Gwanghalluwon Garden 8

Gwanghalluwon is one of Korea' s most traditional gardens. It was constructed to symbolize the universe. With the Gwanghallu Pavilion at the center, there is also the Ojakgyo Bridge and a lake with three islets which symbolize Korea' s three sacred mountains. These mountains are Yeongju (Mt. Hallasan), Bongrae (Mt. Geumgangsan), and Bangjang (Mt. Jirisan). Legend has it that Ojakgyo is the place where Gyeonu and Jingnyeo (the Altair and Vega) meet once a year on July 7. Ojakgyo was designated as Historic Site No. 303. Originally, Gwanghallu was where Hwang Hui, a high-ranking official during the late Goryeo Dynasty, built a small pavilion called 'Gwangtongnu' . He did this so he could enjoy the beautiful surrounding landscape when he was exiled to Namwon in 1419. Later, Jeong In-ji, the governor of Buwon-gun, Hadong, was so impressed by the scenic beauty of the garden that he named the garden 'Gwanghallu.' Gwanghan means 'a palace on the moon,' where a beautiful woman named Hanga was said to live.

National Center for Korean Traditional Performing Arts

National Center for Korean Traditional Performing Arts 9

Jeonju is home to a wide variety of traditional music, including various folk songs and pansori. The city has also produced a large number of renowned traditional singers and artists. In 1992, the National Center for Korean Traditional Performing Arts was founded to reestablish, propagate and promote traditional Korean music.
The center offers regular performances, such as traditional music recitals and pansori concerts each Saturday. Namdo (Korea' s southernmost province) folk song concerts, folk dances, performances by human cultural treasures, and changgeuk (revised pansori classics with a modern touch) are also performed at the center. Special performances for tourists are regularly scheduled.

Jirisan National Park 10

Mt. Jirisan, the first national park in Korea, is a majestic and celebrated mountain which stretches across three provinces; Jeollabuk-do, Jeollanam-do and Gyeongsangbuk-do. It is the nation' s most scenic mountain and the length of its ridgeline is 40km long.
In the Jirisan area near Namwon, there are a number of spectacular natural spots. These include Banyabong, the second tallest peak in Jirisan, Baemsagol Valley, Guryong Valley and Baraebong Peak, as well as such noted temples as Silsangsa and Yeongwonsa.

Mt. Jirisan in the Winter

Silsangsa Temple

3

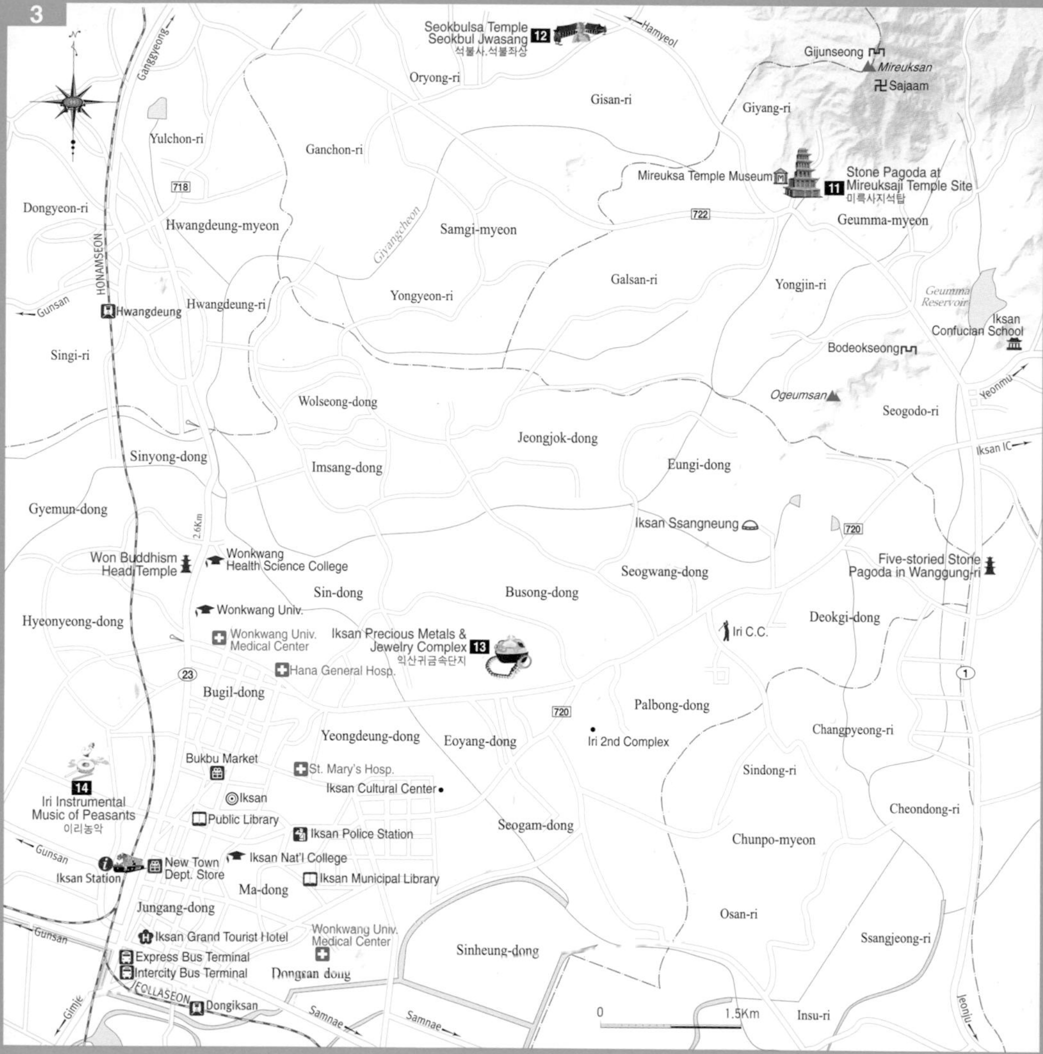

Seokbulsa Temple Seokbul Jwasang 12 석불사.석불좌상
Hamyeol
Gijunseong
Mireuksan
Sajaam
Oryong-ri
Gisan-ri
Giyang-ri
Ganggyeong
Yulchon-ri
Ganchon-ri
Mireuksa Temple Museum
Stone Pagoda at Mireuksaji Temple Site 11 미륵사지석탑
718
Dongyeon-ri
Hwangdeung-myeon
Givangcheon
Samgi-myeon
722
Geumma-myeon
HONAMSEON
Gunsan
Hwangdeung
Hwangdeung-ri
Yongyeon-ri
Galsan-ri
Yongjin-ri
Geumma Reservoir
Iksan Confucian School
Singi-ri
Bodeokseong
Ogeumsan
Yeonmu
Wolseong-dong
Seogodo-ri
Jeongjok-dong
Iksan IC
Sinyong-dong
Imsang-dong
Eungi-dong
Gyemun-dong
2.6Km
Iksan Ssangneung
720
Won Buddhism Head Temple
Wonkwang Health Science College
Seogwang-dong
Five-storied Stone Pagoda in Wanggung-ri
Sin-dong
Busong-dong
Hyeonyeong-dong
Wonkwang Univ.
Deokgi-dong
Iri C.C.
Wonkwang Univ. Medical Center
Iksan Precious Metals & Jewelry Complex 13 익산귀금속단지
23
Hana General Hosp.
1
Bugil-dong
720
Palbong-dong
Yeongdeung-dong
Eoyang-dong
Iri 2nd Complex
Changpyeong-ri
Bukbu Market
St. Mary's Hosp.
Sindong-ri
14
Iri Instrumental Music of Peasants 이리농악
Iksan
Iksan Cultural Center
Public Library
Cheondong-ri
Seogam-dong
Iksan Police Station
Chunpo-myeon
Gunsan
Iksan Station
New Town Dept. Store
Iksan Nat'l College
Ma-dong
Iksan Municipal Library
Jungang-dong
Osan-ri
Iksan Grand Tourist Hotel
Wonkwang Univ. Medical Center
Express Bus Terminal
Sinheung-dong
Ssangjeong-ri
Intercity Bus Terminal
Dongsan dong
JEOLLASEON
Gimje
Dongiksan
Samnae
Samnae
0
1.5Km
Insu-ri
Jeonju

Iksan is a town of time-honored history and culture where the traditions of ancient Koreans are vividly preserved. The city was once the capital of the Mahan and Baekje Kingdoms. It is the only place in the country to house a precious metal and jewelry processing and sales complex.

The Mahan Folk Festival, the city's major festival, is a cultural event which carries on the tradition of the ritualistic religious services which were offered to the heavens during the ancient Mahan Kingdom. Major events include the Iksangisebae(a folk play), the Iksan farmers' band competition and the Princess Seonhwa Pageant. Major tourist sites in Iksan include the Stone Pagoda at Mireuksaji Temple Site, Wanggung, a five-story stone pagoda, Hambyeokjeong Pavilion and Baesan Park.

The Stone Pagoda at Mireuksaji Temple Site 11

The Stone Pagoda at Mireuksaji, part of the Mireuksaji Temple Site, is located in the southern foothills of Mt. Mireuksan in Iksan. It was Korea's first stone pagoda, built during the reign of King Mu of the Baekje Kingdom (600-641). The pagoda is important as it illustrates the transition from the construction of wooden pagodas to stone ones. Originally, the pagoda had nine stories but only six stories survive. The southwestern portion of the pagoda was destroyed and only the northeastern portion of the six stories still retains its original shape.

According to a legend regarding the founding of Mireuksa in Samgukyusa, worship halls and pagodas were built at three different locations. Currently, only one pagoda remains.

The stone pagoda has a cross-shaped opening in its center. A huge square-shaped pillar is situated at the center of the inside of the opening. The structure's roof stone is shaped like a pyeongpan(horizontally laid wood on an architrave) and rises slightly at the four corners. The pagoda serves as the finest example of the architectural style of the Baekje Kingdom.

Mireuksaji Stone Pagoda

Seokbul Jwasang in Seokbulsa (Treasure No. 45)

Seokbulsa Temple 12

Seokbulsa Temple was built during the late Baekje Kingdom in the 7th century A.D. It was maintained until the Goryeo Dynasty in the 12th or 13th century, when it was closed but has been recently reopened.

The Seokbul Jwasang (a stone statue of a seated Buddha), a valued cultural asset, is housed in the Daeungjeon (the main hall). The statue was built during the Baekje Kingdom, around 600 A.D. It is one of the most precious statues which was created during the Three Kingdoms period. It is 1.69m in height (the tallest in Korea), or 4.48m when the measurement includes the halo.

Iksan Precious Metals & Jewelry Complex 13

The Iksan Precious Metals & Jewelry Complex, is located in the Free Trade Zone.

Iri Instrumental Music of Peasants

The complex is the only place in Korea where the processing and export of a wide variety of jewelry takes place.

The complex houses 92 resident companies and 1,600 jewelry craftsmen, who produce a broad range of accessories.

Iri Instrumental Music of Peasants 14

The Iri Farmer' s Band plays traditional Korean music which has been handed down from the Saesil Maeul (village). Of the two major types of farmer music from Jeolla Province, the Iri Farmer' s Band follows the 'Honam udo (right province type)' . This discipline was nurtured in the western portion of Jeolla Province. The Iri Farmer' s Band consists of people who learned the farmer style of music professionally in Gimje and Jeongeup.

The pangut or madangnoreum ritual consists of several parts. Notable parts of the performance include ochaejil-gut, in which the farmers move into a circling formation while skillfully beating gongs, the anbatang, in which farmers circle around while beating fast rhythms, the obangjin, in which farmers move in a spiral motion, and the hoho-gut, in which farmers circle around while shouting 'Hoho!' In the beokgu neulleum, long white streamers are attached to the top of performers' hats. These streamers make a wide arc as the leader of the performers gyrates his head and a drummer beats the drum, marking various rhythms.

4

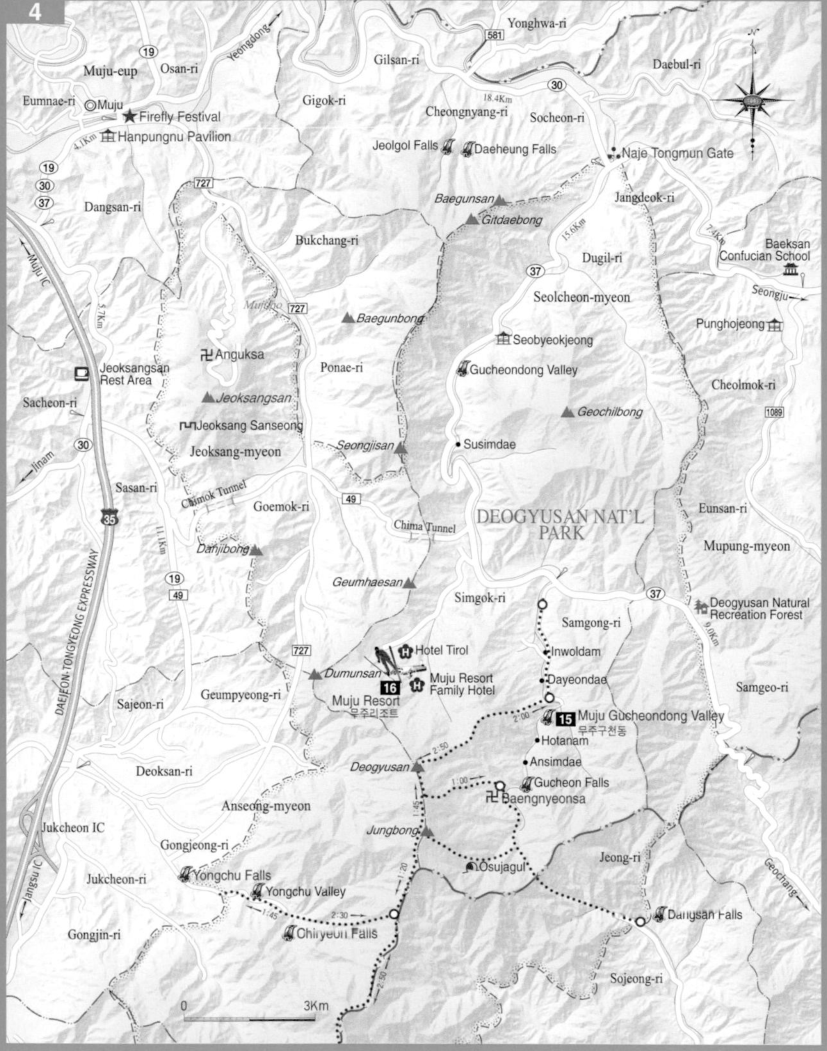

Deogyusan National Park is located in the southern part of the Sobaek Mountains. It was designated as a national park in 1975. The park harbors numerous scenic areas, including 33 scenic attractions in Muju Gucheondong Valley. These are located along a 30km ridgeline linking Najetongmun, Seolcheon-myeon, and Muju-gun to Baengnyeonsa Temple. Eleven scenic vistas in Anseong Valley are located along the ridgeline which links Yongchu Waterfall to Chiryeon Waterfall.

Historical sites such as the Najetongmun Gate, the Jeoksan Sanseong Fortress and the Hoguksaji Temple Site, as well as such famous temples as Anguksa, Baengnyeonsa, Wontongsa, and Songgyesa, are also located in the park.

Muju Gucheondong Valley 15

Gucheondong Valley

Muju Gucheondong Valley, located in Muju-gun, is a valley that stretches along the north side of Deogyusan National Park. Its thirty-three scenic vistas include Najetongmun at the entrance, Onguam, Waryongdam, Haksodae, Susimdae, Gucheon Waterfall and Yeonhwa Waterfall. In summer, the valleys are surrounded by thick forests with crystal clear brooks, ideal places to escape from the heat. Mt. Deogyusan is also well known for its colorful autumn foliage and splendid snow covered scenery in the winter.

Muju Resort 16

Muju Resort, located in the northern part of Mt. Deogyusan, is a comprehensive tourist resort with large-scale recreational, sports, entertainment and health facilities. The resort houses a broad range of recreational and sport facilities, including winter skiing facilities with 30 slopes, a highland golf course designed by Arnold Palmer, a water park, a performance hall, a mineral water pool, an amusement park and a zoo. Muju resort has a wide variety of accommodations, ranging from the world class, Alpine-style Hotel Tirol, to family hotels and budget hostels. Visitors can also enjoy diverse sports such as tennis, mountain climbing, mountain biking and horse-riding.

Sunchang Hot Pepper Paste Village G7

One of the most commonly used Korean seasonings is hot pepper paste. Sunchang is well known for its top quality hot pepper paste.

According to legend, toward the end of the Goryeo Dynasty, Yi Seong-gye was on his way to visit his master, Monk Muhak, who was living in Manilsa Temple. On his way to the temple, he stopped at a farm house and was treated to lunch made with Sunchang hot-pepper paste. He was so impressed by the taste that he ordered his subjects serve it at his table when he founded the Joseon Dynasty and became its first king. As the story circulated, Sunchang hot pepper paste became famous. Its fame and secret recipe continue to the present day.

The reddish black paste has a glossy surface, a pungent, sweet taste, and a relatively mild odor which is said to whet the appetites.

Dolmen in Gochang

Gochang Dolmens C6

In Asan-myeon, Gochang-gun, there is a group of 440 dolmens, which are megalithic funerary monuments. Since other relics of the Bronze Age were discovered in the vicinity, the dolmens are presumed to be from the family tombs of a chief who ruled the area 2,500 years ago.

The site harbors diverse types of dolmens, including the go-board type, which is also known as the southern type, the table type, which is also known as the northern type, and the capstone type. All of these dolmens are of high academic value for research.

The Gochang Dolmen Site, along with dolmen sites in Ganghwa and Hwasun, have been designated as World Heritages by UNESCO because of their high historical and cultural value.

Maisan Provincial Park H4

Mt. Maisan, which is located in Jinan, is one of the most peculiarly-shaped mountains in Korea. Along with its stone pagoda temple, Mt. Maisan holds a mysterious allure.

Mt. Maisan (the Horse Ear Mountain) was named after the two peaks of the mountain which are said to resemble the ears of a horse. The eastern peak is called 'Sutmaibong (Male)', and the western peak 'Ammaibong (Female).' On the opposite side of the peaks, situated between Sutmaibong and Ammaibong, sits Maitapsa, a temple contains unique stone pagodas created by piles of hundreds of thousands of rocks which were said to have been stacked by Yi Gap-ryong, a hermit.

Mt. Maisan is also home to such temples as Eunsusa, Geumdangsa and Buksusa.

Mt. Maisan Tapsa Temple

Geumgang Habitat

Geumgang Habitat for Migratory Birds E2

Geumgang Habitat is where the Geumgang River, which was blocked for the construction of an estuary dike, forms a lake. It has a vast reed field which provides an ideal habitat for migratory birds.

Currently, a total of 450,000 migratory birds of 101 species are estimated to visit the habitat. In winter, the habitat is visited by such rare birds as oystercatchers and Saunders' gulls, as well as swans and mallards. These species attract the attention of ornithologists and nature lovers.

Jeollanam-do

Jeollanam-do's location on the southwestern tip of the Korean Peninsula gives it abundant seashores, scenic plains, valleys and mountains. Small islets off the shore provide nice views of the sea.
In addition to the natural attractions in this area, visitors can also enjoy various temples and important historic sites. It was affected directly by Chinese culture because of its proximity to the West Sea, and many aspects of its culture were later introduced to Japan.
Jeollanam-do was the most productive agricultural area in ancient Korea and it is still well known throughout Korea for many special dishes and fresh sea food.

Boseong Tea

Boseong is home to the largest tea plantations in Korea. Almost all of Mt. Hwalseongsan in Boseong has been terraced to facilitate tea growth and the mountain looks as if green carpets have been spread out over it. Boseong has become the nation's largest producer of tea thanks to its fertile soil and high humidity, which are ideal for the cultivation of tea.

Sea fog blown in from Yulpoman Bay often shrouds the Bongsan-ri area, so the tea, always damp under the thick sea fog, is healthy and fragrant. Each of the tea plantations, including Daehan Tea Garden, Dongyang Daye, Okro Jeda, Banya Tea Garden, and Botje Tea Garden cultivates tea leaves using its own special growing methods.

Boseong Dahyangje

Dahyangje, a local tea festival, is held in Boseong-gun in May when new tea leaves are harvested. The festivities center around the traditional tea ceremony. Major events of the festival include performances by traditional bands, an exhibition of prize-winning works from a nationwide photo contest, an exhibition of potted plants, a tea-leaf picking contest, tea brewing sessions, an exhibition of tea products from around Korea, a tour of the plantations and a green tea market.

Boseong Green Tea Plantations

Goryeo Celadon

Jade, long thought of as a symbol of virtue, has been said to have a mystical significance guaranteeing riches, honor and afterlife. Because of the belief that jade provides eternal life and dispels evil, it was often used in making burial accessories. However, since jade was costly, efforts were made to create something of jade color made from earth, and this led to the birth of jade colored celadon. This bluish-green celadon became a popular material for making teacups when tea drinking culture spread across Korea.

Cheongja Sanggam Unhank Munmaebyeong, Celadon Vase with Inlaid Crane and Cloud Designs (National Treasure No. 68)

Inlaid Celadon

The technique of inlaying involves incising designs into clay and filling the recesses with other materials. For example, inside a circle inlaid with black and white slip, a crane flying upward in the sky might be engraved, while outside the circle, a crane flying downward would be engraved. By expressing the direction of the cranes in a different way, potters pursued freedom from prefabricated boundaries by transcending the limits of their horizons in all directions.

Gangjin Celadon Reference Museum

Gangjin is home to more than half of the nation's celadon kilns and many celadon relics have been excavated from here. It also houses the Gangjin Celadon Reference Museum. This museum is the nation's only museum devoted exclusively to celadon, and it aims to carry on the celadon culture in Korea through collecting, exhibiting, researching and educating visitors about Goryeo celadon. The museum is built on a site where historic relics were once excavated, and kilns used in making reproductions of Goryeo celadon can be found near the museum, providing an opportunity for tourists to learn about both past and present celadon design.

Goryeo Celadon Kiln Site

The area surrounding Daegu-myeon in Gangjin-gun is where Goryeo celadon was produced. A total of 188 kilns are reported to have existed here. These celadon kilns are presumed to have flourished from the 9th century into the 14th century.

The celadon culture was particularly advanced in Gangjin as it was able to quickly assimilate pottery techniques from China. Heightened exposure to Chinese culture was the result of an advancement in maritime transportation during the latter period of the Silla Kingdom. Other conditions, such as the climate, soil and available fuel were also favorable in Gangjin.

Hieroglyphic Celadon

When the art of making bluish-green celadon reached its apex in the early 12th century, hieroglyphic celadon, patterned after auspicious animals and plants, was produced in large quantities. Such magnificent celadon, made with a strong aesthetic sense and advanced techniques, demonstrates a harmony between delicacy and boldness.

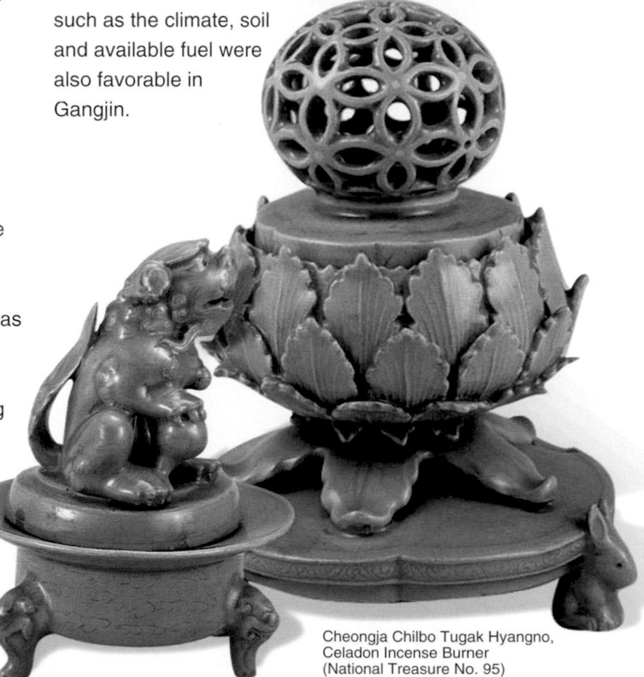

Cheongja Chilbo Tugak Hyangno, Celadon Incense Burner (National Treasure No. 95)

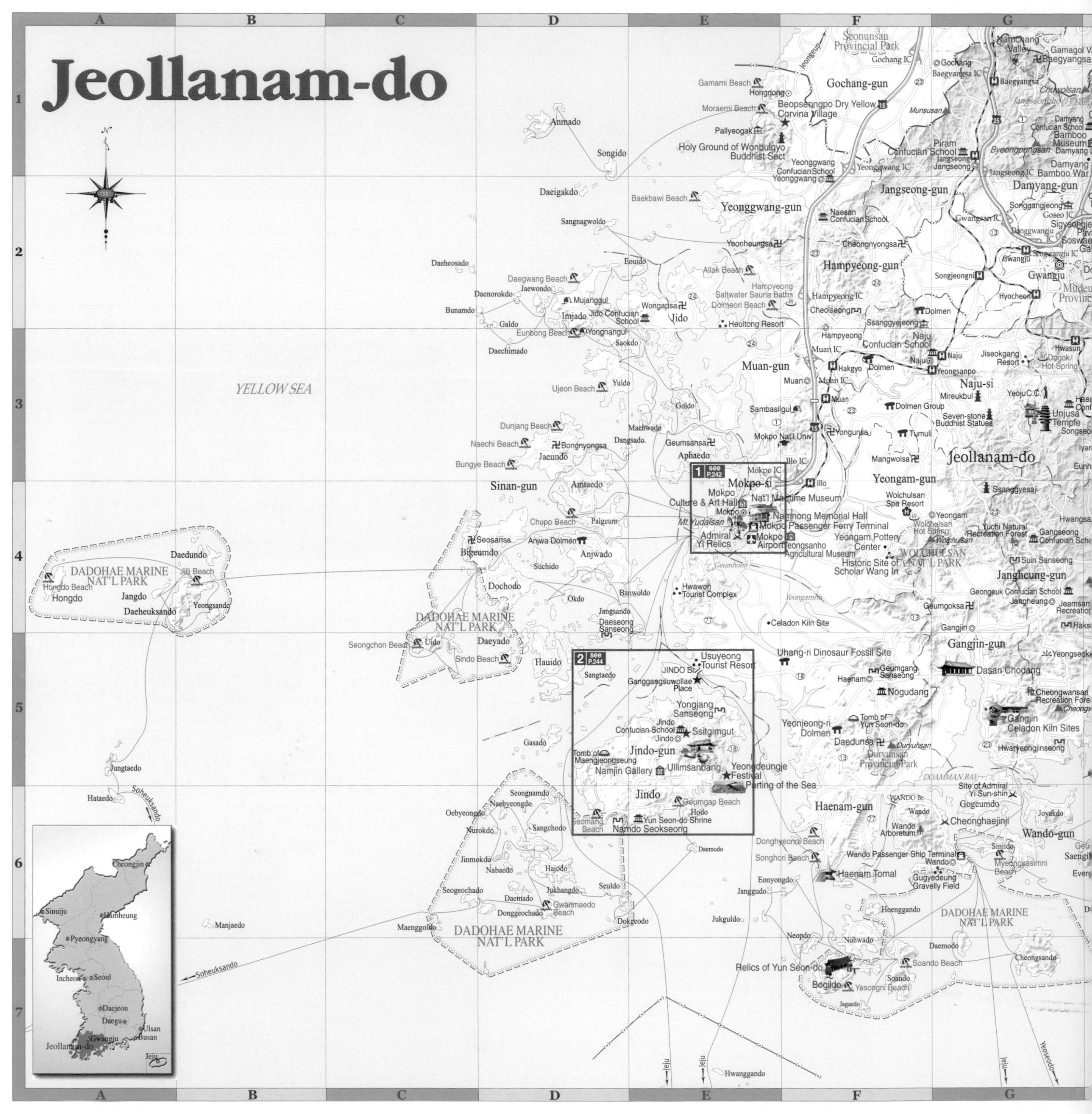

Jeollanam-do
A
B
C
D
E
F
G
1
2
3
4
5
6
7
YELLOW SEA
Seonunsan Provincial Park
Gochang IC
Gochang
Baegyangsa IC
Namchang Valley
Gamagol Valley
Baegyangsa
Gamami Beach
Hongnong
Gochang-gun
Moraemi Beach
Beopseongpo Dry Yellow Corvina Village
Pallyeogak
Holy Ground of Wonbulgyo Buddhist Sect
Yeonggwang Confucian School
Yeonggwang
Yeonggwang IC
Piram Confucian School
Jangseong
Jangseong IC
Byeongpungsan
Damyang Confucian School
Bamboo Museum
Damyang
Damyang Bamboo War
Damyang-gun
Anmado
Songido
Daeigakdo
Baekbawi Beach
Yeonggwang-gun
Naesan Confucian School
Jangseong-gun
Songgangjeong
Goseo JC
Gwangsan IC
Dongwangju IC
Sangnagwoldo
Yeonheungsa
Cheongnyongsa
Hampyeong-gun
Seogwangju IC
Gwangju
Daeheosado
Euido
Allak Beach
Songjeongni
Hyocheon
Daegwang Beach
Jaewondo
Daenorokdo
Mujanggul
Hampyeong Saltwater Sauna Baths
Dolmeori Beach
Hampyeong IC
Wongapsa
Bunamdo
Imjado
Jido Confucian School
Jido
Galdo
Eunbong Beach
Yongnangul
Heultong Resort
Cheolseongni
Dolmen
Ssanggyejeong
Hampyeong
Saokdo
Daechimado
Muan IC
Naju Confucian School
Naju
Jiseokgang Resort
Dogok Hot Spring
Hwasun
Muan-gun
Hakgyo
Dolmen
Yeongsanpo
Yuldo
Ujeon Beach
Muan
Muan IC
Naju-si
Mireukbul
Yeoju C.C.
Goldo
Sambasilgul
Dolmen Group
Seven-stone Buddhist Statues
Unjusa Temple
Dunjang Beach
Maehwado
Yongunsa
Tumuli
Naechi Beach
Bongnyongsa
Dangsado
Geumsansa
Mokpo Nat'l Univ.
Bungye Beach
Jaeundo
Aphaedo
Illo IC
Mangwolsa
Jeollanam-do
Mokpo IC
Mokpo-si
Illo
Yeongam-gun
Sinan-gun
Amtaedo
Mokpo Culture & Art Hall
Nat'l Maritime Museum
Ssanggyesaji
Wolchulsan Spa Resort
Chupo Beach
Palgeum
Mt. Yudalsan
Namnong Memorial Hall
Mokpo Passenger Ferry Terminal
Yeongam
Wolchulsan Hot Spring
Yuchi Natural Recreation Forest
Hwangsan
Seosansa
Admiral Yi Relics
Mokpo Airport
Yeongsanho Agricultural Museum
Yeongam Pottery Center
Wolchulsan
Gangseong Confucian School
Anjwa Dolmen
Bigeumdo
Daedundo
Anjwado
Historic Site of Scholar Wang In
WOLCHULSAN NAT'L PARK
Suin Sanseong
Jilli Beach
Suchido
Geumhoho
DADOHAE MARINE NAT'L PARK
Hongdo Beach
Jangheung-gun
Hongdo
Jangdo
Dochodo
Geongeuk Confucian School
Yeongsando
Okdo
Hwawon Tourist Complex
Jangheung
Daeheuksando
Banwoldo
Yeongamho
Geumgoksa
Jangsando
DADOHAE MARINE NAT'L PARK
Daeseong Sanseong
Celadon Kiln Site
Gangjin
Daeyado
Seongchon Beach
Uido
Gangjin-gun
Uhang-ri Dinosaur Fossil Site
Usuyeong Tourist Resort
Sindo Beach
Hauido
JINDO Br.
Geumgang Sanseong
Dasan Chodang
Haenam
Sangtaedo
Ganggangsuwollae Place
Nogudang
Cheongwansan Recreation Forest
Yongjang Sanseong
Jindo Confucian School
Ssitgimgut
Tomb of Yun Seon-do
Yeonjeong-ri Dolmen
Gangjin Celadon Kiln Sites
Jindo
Daedunsa
Duryunsan
Hwaryeongjinseong
Gasado
Tomb of Maengjeongseong
Jindo-gun
Duryunsan Provincial Park
Namjin Gallery
Ullimsanbang
Yeongdeungje Festival
Jungtaedo
Parting of the Sea
DOAMMAN BAY
Site of Admiral Yi Sun-shin
Hataedo
Soheuksando
Seongnamdo
Gogeumdo
Naebyeongdo
Jindo
Haenam-gun
WANDO Br.
Oebyeongdo
Geumgap Beach
Wando
Joyakdo
Hodo
Cheonghaejinji
Nurokdo
Sangchodo
Seomang Beach
Yun Seon-do Shrine
Namdo Seokseong
Wando Arboretum
Wando-gun
Donghyeonni Beach
Cheongjin
Daemodo
Sinjido
Songhori Beach
Wando Passenger Ship Terminal
Wando
Myeongsasimni Beach
Jinmokdo
Nabaedo
Hajodo
Haenam Tomal
Gugyedeung Gravelly Field
Eonyongdo
Janggudo
Seuldo
Sinuiju
Hamheung
Seogeochado
Jukhangdo
Gwanmaedo Beach
Daemado
Donggeochado
Hoenggando
DADOHAE MARINE NAT'L PARK
Dokgeodo
Jukguldo
Pyeongyang
Manjaedo
Maenggoldo
DADOHAE MARINE NAT'L PARK
Neopdo
Nohwado
Daemodo
Soheuksando
Soando Beach
Cheongsando
Incheon
Seoul
Relics of Yun Seon-do
Soando
Bogildo
Yesongni Beach
Daejeon
Jagaedo
Daegu
Ulsan
Busan
Jeollanam-do
Gwangju
Jeju
Jeju
Jeju
Hwanggando
Jeju
Yeoseodo

INDEX

Tourist Information

Jeollanam-do Dept. of Tourism Promotion 82-62-222-0101
Jeollanam-do Tourism Association 82-62-222-0242
www.provin.jeonnam.kr

LEGEND

Railroad Station	Fortress	Golf Course
Airport	Temple	Hot Spring or Spa
Port	Site of Buddhist Artifacts	Scenic Area
Tourist Information Center	Traditional Building	Natural Recreation Forest
University or School	Traditional Pavilion	Arboretum
Museum	Battlefield	Mountain
Gallery	Cultural Experience Area	Other Tourist Attractions
Theater	Falls or Valley	Hotel
Prehistoric Relic Site	Cave	Reference Point
Tomb	Beach	

1

Mokpo, a city situated on the southwestern tip of Jeollanam-do, serves as the launching point for tours of the numerous islands off the southwestern tip of the peninsula and for service to Jeju Island. Mt. Yudalsan, located in the northern part of the city, is also known as Nojeokbong Peak, and is popular for its panoramic views of the sea and sunrises and sunsets. Other major tourist attractions here include the Orchid Exhibition Hall, Samhakdo Island, the National Maritime Museum, the Namnong Memorial Hall and Yeongsanho Lake.

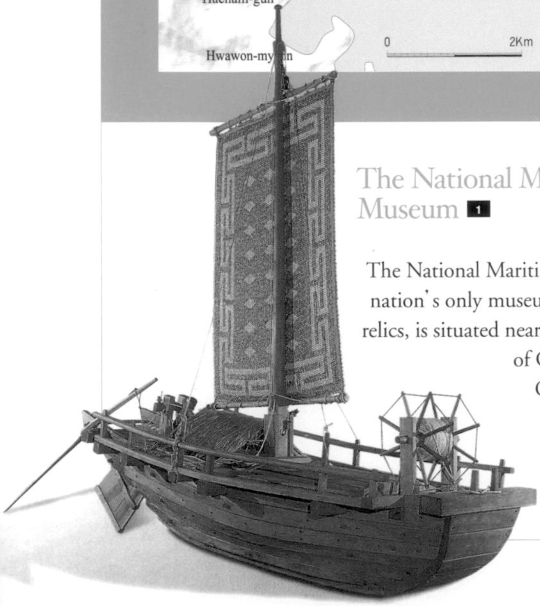

The National Maritime Museum 1

The National Maritime Museum, the nation's only museum of maritime relics, is situated near the cultural district of Gatbawi in Mokpo. On display are relics excavated from the sea off Sinan.

In the vicinity of the museum is the scenic Dadohae Sea and Gatbawi, a rock resembling the shape of a gat, a traditional Korean hat.

Over 3,000 pieces of Goryeo celadon excavated from the seas near Eodu-ri, Yaksan-myeon and Wando-gun, as well as the Wando Vessel, a wooden sea vessel from the Goryeo Dynasty are on display here. Also on display are more than 22,000 Sinan artifacts, including pottery, earthenware, metal and stone. Hyeonjachongtong, a firearm recovered from Baekdo Island in Yeocheon, as well as a variety of model vessels ranging from ancient boats to modern-day oil tankers, can also be seen. This exhibit displays the historical development of ocean-going vessels.

Wandoseon Vessel at the National Maritime Museum

Namnong Memorial Hall 2

Seonmyeonsansudo by Sochi Heo Ryeon

The Namnong Memorial Hall was established in 1985 by Namnong Heo Geon, the third owner of Ullimsanbang. His stated goal was to preserve the relics of his ancestors, maintain the tradition of Namhwa, a Chinese painting style, and to pass on cultural heritage. In Namnong Memorial Hall, works by five generations of Ullimsanbang, including Sochi Heo Ryeon (the grandfather of Namnong), are on display.

More than 300 pieces of art work, ranging from Joseon Dynasty creations to modern paintings are on exhibit. There is also ceramic ware from China and Japan, as well as 200 pieces of earthenware and pottery from the Gaya, Silla and Joseon Dynasties.

Cheonghaejin

Cheonghaejin, situated in Jangja-ri, is the site where Jang Bo-go, a famed warlord of the Silla Kingdom, settled. In Cheonghaejin, General Jang Bo-go cleared out the pirates, seized command of the three seas, and eventually contributed to Silla's maritime trade with Japan and the Tang Dynasty. Active excavation of the site for relics is currently underway. Visitors can catch a glimpse of items used in days gone by, such as bits of tile-ends, earthenware and ancestral shrines, at the Cheonghaejin Fortress.

Mt. Yudalsan 3

Yudalsan Sculpture Park

From the 228m high Mt. Yudalsan, one can look down on a panoramic view of Mokpo and the Daedohae Sea. There are many dramatic cliffs and rocks on the mountain. The Orchid Exhibition Hall, houses 180 different species of Korean and Asian orchids and 49 species of Western orchids.

At Yudalsan Sculpture Park, 78 sculptures by 64 members of the Korean Sculpture Research Association are on display.

Mokpo Passenger Ferry Terminal 4

The Mokpo Passenger Ferry Terminal is the starting point for travel to the islands in the southwestern areas. Transportation services are available here to Jejudo Island, Hongdo Island, Heuksando Island, Bigeumdo Island, and Amtaedo Island.

Mokpo Passenger Ferry Terminal

Hongdo Island

Jindo is most well known for its Jindo Dog, a pure breed originating from this island, and for the Yeongdeungje Festival. Around mid-April, people from all over Korea gather here for the festival. Major tourist attractions of Jindo include the Jindo Bridge and Ullimsanbang.
Jindo is also home to Yongjang Sanseong Fortress and Namdo Seokseong Fortress, areas where a group of military forces, called Sambyeolcho (the Three Elite Patrols), fought against the Mongolian army during the Goryeo Dynasty. The Myeongnyang Naval Victory Monument for the renowned Admiral Yi Sun-shin is located here.

Gwanmaedo

Parting of the Sea

Parting of the Sea 5

Every February and June, by the lunar calendar, an event occurs that reminds many Koreans of the biblical story of Moses' parting the Red Sea. The sea between Hoedong Village in Gogun-myeon and Modo Island parts when the water is sucked out by the outgoing tide, leaving a path 30 to 40m in width and 2.8km in length. This event became known to the outside world when Mr. Pierre Randy, the French ambassador to Korea, witnessed the sea parting in 1975 and reported it to a French newspaper.

Yeongdeungje Festival 6

Yeongdeungje is a local Jindo festival held annually when the sea parts. The origin of Yeongdeungje is derived from the legend of Grandmother Ppong, which has been passed down by word of mouth in the local villages. During the festival, traditional folk rituals and cultural performances take place, including the Ssitgimgut (an exorcism ritual), Namdo deullorae (field songs), Manga (funeral songs), and Jindo arirang. Other festivities including a Yeongdeungsal play and ceremonies dedicated to Granny Ppong also take place.

Manga Parade

Ssitgimgut

Ssitgimgut, performed in Jindo, is a shamanistic exorcism rite which prays for a dead person's easy passage to paradise by relieving any remorse (called 'han' in Korean) which he might have left in the worldly domain. Exorcisms performed in other provinces are often reminiscent of

Ssitgimgut of Jindo

Ullimsanbang

sorcery: an exorcist usually walks on drums or fodder-choppers wearing shamanistic costumes in order to convey messages from the dead. In the Jindo Ssitgimgut, however, an exorcist wears white clothing and prays to the gods with songs and dances. Designated as an important intangible cultural asset, the Jindo Ssitgimgut can be said to sublimate human being's fears of death in an artful way.

Ullimsanbang 7

Ullimsanbang is the name of the studio where the painter Sochi Heo Ryeon, a master of Chinese painting, worked in the 19th century. Ullim means the 'forest of mist'. The name of the studio is derived from the misty landscape surrounding its location, deep in the forests of Mt. Cheomchalsan. The complex consists of Ullimsanbang, a tile-roofed house and living quarters, and a newly-built memorial hall. Fronting Ullimsanbang is a square pond with floating water lily blossoms. In the center of the pond, there is a 6-meter long island, showcasing the prototypical beauty of Korean gardens. Inside the studio, replicas of paintings by three generations of the Heo family are exhibited. In the newly built memorial hall, various belongings of Heo Ryeon, including replicas of his paintings and ceramics, are exhibited.

Jindo Dog

The Jindo Dog is a native breed of Korean dog that has been designated as Natural Monument No. 53. The fur of these dogs is either yellow or white, and its ears are rigid and tilted slightly forward. Their heads are octagon-shaped and their necks are thick. They are notable for their loyalty and keen senses.

Jindo Dog, a Native Breed of Jindo Island

3

Sangbong-ri
Banwol-ri
863
Bongdu-ri
Daepo Reservoir
Suncheon
Yeosu Airport
Yeosu Nat'l Industrial Complex
Hwachi-dong
Wolha-dong
YEOCHEONSEON
Heungguksa
Yeongchwisan
Heungguksa
Homyeong-dong
Nakpo-dong
Sangam-dong
Sindeok-dong
Sindeok Beach
Deogyang
17
Deogyang-ri
Pyeongyeo-dong
Jusam-dong
859
Horangsan
Ocheon Reservoir
Mosageum Beach
Ocheon-dong
Cheonseongsan
Sora-myeon
Seokchang Inter City Bus Terminal
Seokchangseongji
22
Seonwon-dong
Yeocheon-dong
Dundeok-dong
Manseongni Beach
HALLYEO MARINE NAT'L PARK
Sagok-ri
Boksan-ri
863
Jungnim-ri
Yeocheon
17
JEOLLASEON
Maraesan
Yeosu
Yeocheon Public Stadium
Inter City Bus Terminal
Ansimsan Hot Spring
10
Yeoncheon Geobukseon Shipyard
선소
Haeundaeji
Gwangi-ri
Soho Yacht Marina
Yeosu Beach Hotel
Yeosu
SUNCHEONMAN BAY
Soho-dong
Jeongnam Literature Hall
Jinnamgwan
8
Odongdo Island
오동도
Changmu-ri
Coastal Ferry Terminal
Carferry Terminal
Bongsan-dong
Icheon-ri
Yeosu-si
Yosu Nat'l Univ.
9
DOLSAN Br.
돌산대교
Udu Beach
Guk-dong
Okjeok-ri
Yongju-ri
Hwayang-myeon
Udu-ri
Daegyeondo
Godolsanjinteo
Najin-ri
Anyangsan
Sogyeongdo
Seochon-ri
GAMAKMAN BAY
11
Swan Habitat
철새도래지
Jeollanam-do Fisheries Exhibition
Musulmok Beach
22
Imok-ri
Hwadong-ri
Geumjukdo
Woram Sanseong
17
Pyeongsa-ri
Dunjeon-ri
Gobongsan
Dolsando
Jangsu-ri
Geumbong-ri
Dolsan-eup
Jangdeung Beach
Jukpo-ri
Seodeok-ri
Bangjukpo Beach
Jobaldo
Bonghwangsan
Dunbyeongdo
Gunnae-ri
Dolsan
Baegyado
Sinbok-ri
YEOSUMAN BAY
Nangdosan
Samgyedo
Songdo
Yullim-ri
Nangdo
Hagyedo
Sanghwado
Jedo
Jabongdo
Geumseong-ri
Hyangiram
향일암
Hahwado
Geumosan
12
Sado Beach
0
5Km
Hwataedo

Yeosu-si, situated in the center of the southern tip of the Korean Peninsula, is comprised of the Yeosu peninsula and some 316 islets. Scattered across the city are over 100 mountains, including Mt. Yeongchisan (510m), the highest mountain on the Yeosu peninsula. Yeongchi was named after a mountain in India where Buddha preached. Yeosu's biggest festival is the Jinnamje Festival. This festival is held every year on May 3rd in honor of Admiral Yi Sun-shin, a national hero. Local folk customs during the festival include a procession of fishing vessels, a display of Admiral Yi's Turtle Ships and a celebration of the port opening.
Major tourist spots in Yeosu include Jasan Park, Odongdo Island, Dolsan Bridge, Jinnam Hall and Hyangiram Hermitage.

Odongdo

Odongdo Island 8

Odongdo, a key location and the terminus point of Hallyeo Marine National Park, is situated in Sujeong-dong, Yeosu-si. The island is connected to the shore by a long bulwark. Over 200 species of evergreen subtropical trees including camellia trees, fill this beautiful island.
Odongdo is famous for its camellias which begin to blossom in October and continue into April. They are unlike camellias of other provinces, which generally bloom in the spring. Towering cliffs and peculiarly shaped rocks offer a wonderful view, along with the camellias and silver magnolias. Visitors can also board tour boats and private motorboats at the pier near the entrance of Odongdo.

Swan Habitat in Pyeongsa-ri

Dolsan Bridge 9

The Dolsan Bridge, stretching from Daegyo-dong to Wudu-ri, Dolsan-eup in Yeosu, is 450m long, 11.7m wide and 62m high. Nearby, Dolsan Park commands a panoramic view of the Yeosuhang Port, the Dadohae Sea and the surrounding islands. At night, the appearance of the lighted bridge is magnificent.

Yeocheon Geobukseon (Turtle Ship) Shipyard 10

The Yeocheon Shipyard has been called the 'shipyard village' since ancient times. When naval forces were organized during the Japanese invasion of the Joseon Dynasty in 1592, the shipyard fell under the jurisdiction of Yeosu and the famous turtle ships were built here.
The turtle ship, which was the world's first ironclad ship, is the proud legacy of Korea's shipbuilding industry. The turtle ship was invented by Admiral Yi Sun-shin around the end of the 16th century. It was characterized by its strong defensive and attack features. Since the upper part of the ship was ironclad, the enemy could not jump onto it to engage in hand-to-hand combat. Also, the ironclad ship could not be destroyed by firearms used at that time. In terms of attack, it was solid and had enormous destructive power when it was rammed into another vessel. Inside, the ship was equipped with tremendous firepower.

Dolsan Bridge

Hyangiram

The Swan Habitat 11

Every winter, some 150 to 200 Whistling Swans (Natural Monument No. 201) come to the coastal area near Pyeongsa-ri, Dolsan-eup, to pass the winter. The swans are white with black beaks and are around 120 to 150cm in height. They leave for the north between late February and early March. The area is ideal for those who wish to witness wildlife in its natural habitat.

Hyangiram Hermitage 12

Hyangiram, built by the Buddhist priest Won Hyo in 644 during the reign of King Uija of the Baekje Kingdom, is one of the four most famous Buddhist hermitages in Korea. Its name means 'hermitage standing towards the sun.'
The hermitage was also the base camp for Buddhist monk soldiers who fought with Admiral Yi Sun-shin during the Japanese invasion. The main buildings of the temple, the Buddhist sanctum, the shrine and the reading room, have all been restored to their original state.
Hyangiram sits in the midst of unusually shaped rocks, camellia groves and a subtropical forest. The view of the sunrise from here is spectacular, and it attracts many tourists, even on weekdays. This is an especially popular site on New Year's Day, when visitors come from all over Korea to watch the sunrise.

Geobukseon (Turtle Ship)

SUNCHEON

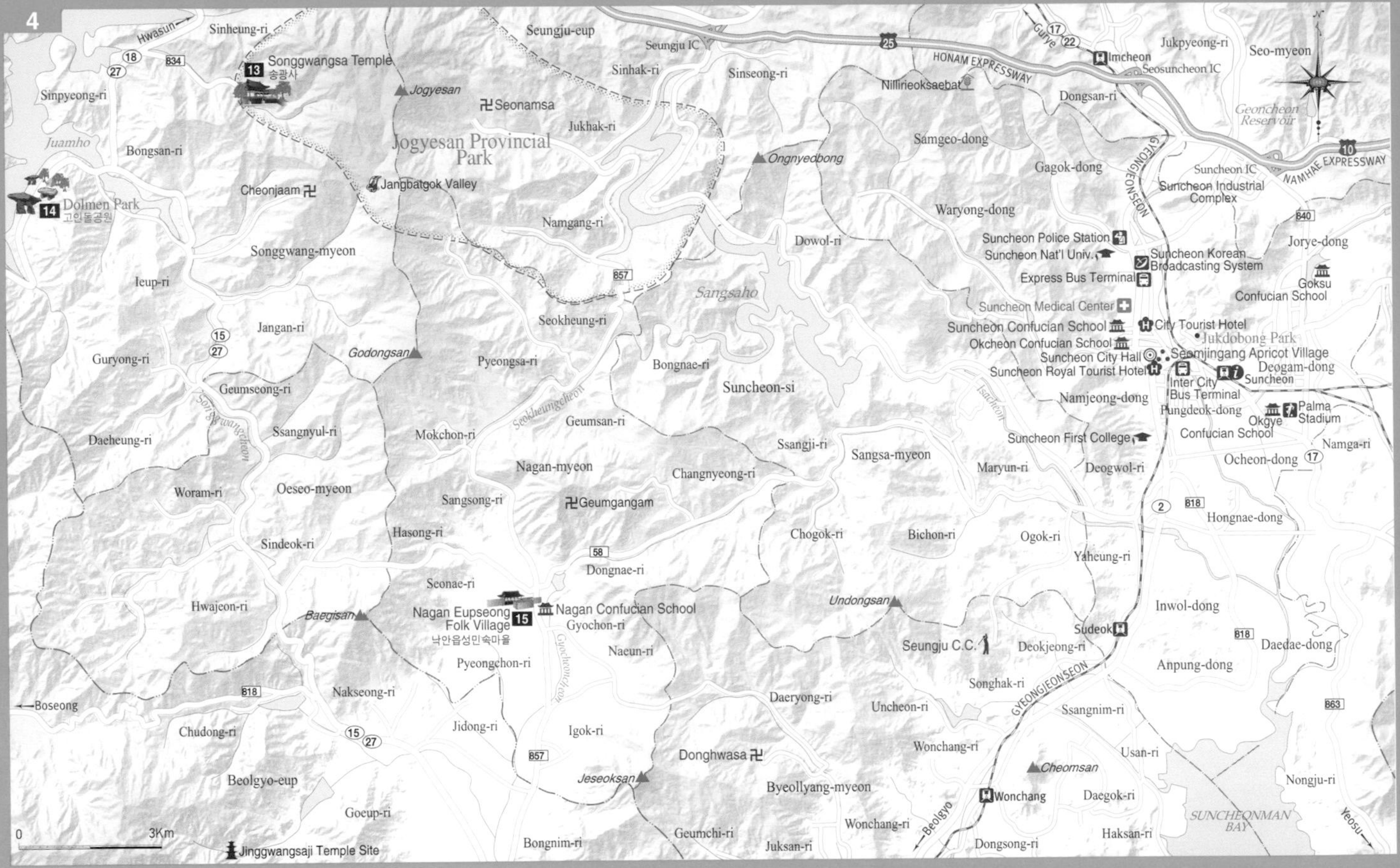

The Suncheon area has the largest number of mountains in Jeollanam-do, with 70% of its entire area being mountainous. The Seomjingang River flows through the northern part of the city. Local festivals include the Nagan Folk Cultural Festival, which is held every May in Nagan Eupseong Folk Village.

Major tourist attractions include Jogyesa and Songgwangsa Temples, Nagan Eupseong Folk Village, where residents actually live inside a fortress, Dolmen Park, where prehistoric tombs are located, Suncheon Waeseong Fortress, and Geomdan Sanseong Fortress.

Songgwangsa

Songgwangsa Temple 13

In Korea, Sambo refers to the three most precious assets of Buddhism. They are the Buddha, the teachings of Buddha and the Buddhist monks and followers. Songgwangsa, situated in the northern foothills of Mt. Jogyesan, is one of the three Sambo Shrines in Korea, along with Haeinsa Temple in Hapcheon and Tongdosa Temple in Yangsan. Songgwangsa was first built at the end of the Silla Kingdom by the Zen priest Hyerin and it was named the Gilsangsa Temple. Later, a monk named Jinul relocated the temple to its present location and it became a renowned site for spiritual exercise and Zen meditation. The temple has been home to 16 renowned monks, including Jinul and Jingak. At present, over 100 Buddhist monks reside at Songgwangsa to study Zen meditation and the Sutra (Buddhist scriptures). At the Buril International Buddhist Center, which opened here in 1972, monks from all over the world come to study Korean Buddhism.

Dolmen Park 14

Dolmen Park, situated in Songgwang-myeon, Suncheon-si, was created by relocating relics from the Stone Age here. These relics were originally scattered throughout the area, including the towns of Boseong and Hwasun, parts of which were submerged with the construction of the Juam Multipurpose Dam.

In nearby Hyosan-ri, Dogok-myeon in Hwasun, there are 237 dolmens, which are a type of prehistoric tomb. There are 311 dolmens in Daesan-ri in Chunyang-myeon. Huge dolmen caps that weigh 100 to 200t can be found in the area's quarries. The dolmens in Gochang, Hwasun and Ganghwa were designated as a UNESCO World Heritage in 2000.

Nagan Eupseong Folk Village 15

Nagan Eupseong village was built into a mud rampart during the reign of King Taejo in 1397 to counter the invasion of Japanese troops. During the reign of King Injo in 1626, the structure was rebuilt with stones, and subsequently became a castle. Unlike other fortresses in other areas, Nagan Eupseong is situated on a wide plain. It was built on naturally square stones, varying in size from one to two meters. The total length of the four-meter high fortress wall is 1,410m.

One hundred and eight households actually reside inside the fortress walls, serving as living links to the area's history. Preserved in the folk village is an inn, a monument to Admiral Im Gyeong-eop, a marketplace and various straw-thatched houses.

Dolmen Park in Suncheon-si

Nagan Eupseong Folk Village

The Stone Buddha near Unjusa

Dasan Chodang G5

Dasan Chodang, situated at the foot of Mt. Mandeoksan, is the place where Dasan Jeong Yak-yong, a noted scholar during the latter Joseon Dynasty, wrote more than 500 books during his 18-year long exile in Gangjin. In Dasan Chodang, there is a rock on which Dasan himself inscribed the word 'Jeongseok Dajo,' meaning a huge rock on which tea was boiled. There is also a pavilion named Cheonilgak, which was built on the site where Dasan relaxed and contemplated life.

Dasan Chodang

Unjusa Temple G3

Unjusa is a temple situated on the western slope of Mt. Cheontaesan. Legend has it that the monk Doseon of the Silla Kingdom, built one thousand stone Buddha images and one thousand stone pagodas overnight. At present, 93 stone Buddha images and 21 stone pagodas remain. The stone Buddha statues here range in size from a few centimeters to 10m high. The 21 pagodas are scattered around the shrine and some have a unique circular shape. The number of levels of the pagodas varies.

The Yeongam Pottery Center F4

The Yeongam Pottery Center exhibits United Silla Kingdom ceramics and teacup pieces which were excavated from kilns in Gurim-ri. Scattered in the vicinity of the center are numerous porcelain pieces and more than 10 ancient kilns, all of which are being preserved. In the pottery kilns of Gurim-ri, vessels were produced for general use, including earthenware pots with wide openings, square bottles, oil bottles and rice steamers. The nation's very first earthenware, glazed in a greenish brown and brownish luster, was produced here. Impressive in both their artistic and historic value, the glazed ceramics of Gurim are of one of the three major pottery types in Korea, along with the blue celadon of Gangjin and the white porcelain of Gwangju, Gyeonggi-do.

Yeongam Pottery Center

Hwaeomsa Temple J2

Hwaeomsa, located in Hwangjeon-ri, is a temple which was built in 544 by the Buddhist monk Yeongi, during the 22nd year of the reign of King Seong of the Baekje Kingdom. The name of the temple is derived from Hwaeomgyeong, a Buddhist scripture. The temple houses a variety of relics from the Silla Dynasty, including the Gakhwangjeon (National Treasure No. 67).

Sasaja Three-storied Stone Pagoda in Hwaeomsa

Uhang-ri Dinosaur Fossil Site

Uhang-ri Dinosaur Fossil Site F5

The dinosaur fossil site in Uhang-ri is the main tourist attraction of Haenam-gun and is the nation's first and largest site of this type. It was here that for the first time in the world footprints of pterosaurs, dinosaurs and web-footed birds were all discovered in one place. Over 100 footprints of pterosaurs have been found here, the largest number in the world and the first to be discovered in Asia. The length of the footprints, which are approximately 20 to 35cm, is the largest recorded. In addition, for the first time in Asia, the footprints of ancient sea crabs were discovered here. It was also here that dinosaur fossils were first discovered in Korea.

Uhang-ri is also knwon as a sedimentary site, which is valuable in geological terms. The depth of the sedimentary rocks runs 400m deep, and because there have been no major crustal movements, the geological features and fossils remain intact. The site has been featured in acclaimed academic publications such as 'Nature.'

The Relics of Yun Seon-do F7

Yun Seon-do was a civil minister and a poet during the mid Joseon Dynasty. Upon hearing that the king had surrendered to the Chinese during the invasion of Joseon in 1636, he was so grieved that he left for Jejudo Island. On his way to the island, however, he was so taken aback by the scenic beauty of Bogildo Island that he decided to settle there.

Yun stayed on Bogildo for 13 years and wrote such noted literary pieces as 'Eobusasisa.' The names of the rocks and mountain peaks on the island, given by Yun personally, are still in use.

Across from Nakseoje, Yun dug a pond and built a house, naming it 'Goksudang.' Across from that house, on the mountainside, he built another house, which he called 'Dongcheonseoksil.' In the northeastern part of the valley, Yun built 'Seyeonjeong,' where he enjoyed reading in natural surroundings.

The Historic Site of Scholar Wang In F4

This historic site in Seonggi-dong houses items used by Scholar Wang In, who introduced the Baekje culture to Japan during Baekje Kingdom. Items here include the Seongcheon, where he drank water, and the Yuheobi Monument, which was erected beside his birthplace in Seonggi-dong. Also, on Mt. Wolchulsan is the Chaekgul Cave, where Wang stored his books, and Munsanjae and Yangsajae, where Wang In's followers taught eager young students after his departure to Japan. On March of every year, a ceremony is held in commemoration of Wang In.

Relics of Yun Seon-do

Wang In Cultural Festival

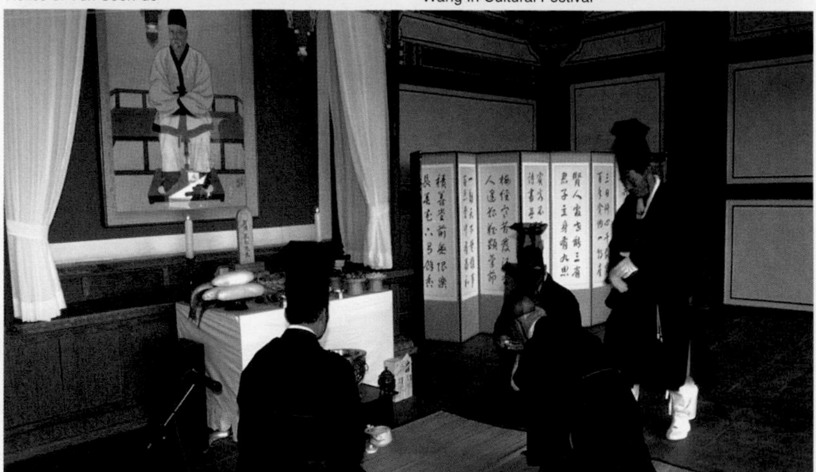
Reinactment of the Wang In Ceremony

Haenam Tomal F6

Haenam Tomal, literally meaning 'the end of the land,' is located in Haenam, at the edge of the Korean Peninsula. When the sea route to Bogildo was opened in 1980, Haenam became nationally known as the 'village at the end of the land.' When 'the end of the land' is expressed in Chinese characters, it is pronounced 'tomal.' Tomal Monument and Tomal Tower were believed to have been named accordingly. From the observatory tower located in the village, islets in the Dadohae Sea and the indigo blue Namhae Sea come into full view.

Apricot Village

Damyang Bamboo Ware H1

Damyang is the nation's largest grower of bamboo trees because the climate and the soil of the area are ideal for its cultivation.

Bamboo Ware

Bamboo products made of Damyang bamboo are strong, sturdy and smooth and are said to be among the best in the world. Products made here include mats, car seats, baskets, and other accessories. Damyang is also home to the world's largest bamboo museum.

The Seomjingang Apricot Village J3

Seomjin Village in Sinwon-ri is also known as Apricot Village. It lies between Mt. Jirisan and Mt. Baegunsan. A wide plain of more than 132,000㎡ is filled with apricot trees. The view of more than 100,000 apricot trees blooming every spring is breathtaking. The villagers of Seomjin began to grow apricot trees over three decades ago. The idea was initiated by Mrs. Hong Sang-ri of the Cheongmaesil Apricot Farm, who planted the apricot trees in an old chestnut tree orchard. At present, of approximately 70 households in the village, 60 or more of them grow apricot trees. The flowers begin to bloom in early March and an apricot festival is held in mid-March.

Haenam Tomal (Land's End)

Gyeongsangbuk-do

Gyeongsangbuk-do is the heartland of Korean traditional culture. The Buddhist culture of the Silla Kingdom, the mysterious Gaya culture and the patrician Confucian culture are all well preserved here. The area is also rich in such natural attractions as scenic mountains, deep hidden valleys and the blue East Sea, to name just a few.

Due to the bountiful historical, natural and cultural attractions, this region has long been a major tourist destination in Korea.

Bulguksa (World Heritage Designated by UNESCO)

Bulguksa Temple

Bulguksa is located in the foothills of Mt. Tohamsan. Construction was first begun by the famed mayor, Kim Dae-seong, during the 10th year (751) of the reign of King Gyeongdeok of the Silla Kingdom, and ended in the 10th year (774) of King Hyegong's reign.

Bulguksa epitomizes the spirit of Silla's artistry and represents the apex of Korea's Buddhist culture and art.

In the terraced courtyard are two great pagodas, one being the Dabotap and the other being the three-storied Seokgatap. In addition, there are the Cheongungyo and Baegungyo, two double-level bridges which lead to the Jahamun Gate, and Yeonhwagyo and Chilbogyo, which are stone bridge stairways leading to Geungnakjeon Hall. These cultural properties showcase the excellent craftsmanship of the Silla people and their talent with stonework.

A number of the cultural heritages found in Bulguksa, including the Amitayeorae Jwasang (Seated gilt-bronze Amitabha Buddha) housed in Geungnakjeon and the Birojanabul Jwasang (Seated gilt-bronze Vairocana Buddha) in Birojeon Hall, are reminders of the well developed and sophisticated Buddhist culture that existed at the time. Because of its unparalleled artistic and cultural value, Bulguksa was registered as one of the World Heritages by UNESCO in December 1995, along with the Seokguram Grotto.

Dabotap

Seokguram Grotto

Located high on the ridges of Mt. Tohamsan, the construction of Seokguram was first begun by the famed mayor, Kim Dae-seong, during the 10th year (751) of the reign of King Gyeongdeok of the Silla Kingdom. It was completed in the 10th year (774) of the reign of King Hyegong. Inside an artificial stone grotto created with white granite is a central Buddha figure, flanked by other icons of the Bosal (Bodhisattvas), Disciples, Yeoksa (guardian deities) and Cheonwang (the heavenly king) figures. Originally, there were a total of 40 sculptured Buddhist figures. Currently 38 figures remain.

In the Seokguram Grotto, a corridor connects a rectangular room with the main rotunda. The rotunda's arch ceiling was built using 360 huge granite blocks, an architectural technique unprecedented in the world.

Seokguram is a masterpiece which was built during the peak of Silla's Buddhist artistry, and its beauty is all the more striking given that it harmoniously combined elements of architecture, mathematics, geometry, religion and art. It was registered as a UNESCO World Heritage in December 1995, jointly with Bulguksa.

Gyeongsangbuk-do

2 see P.262
3 see P.265
4 see P.267

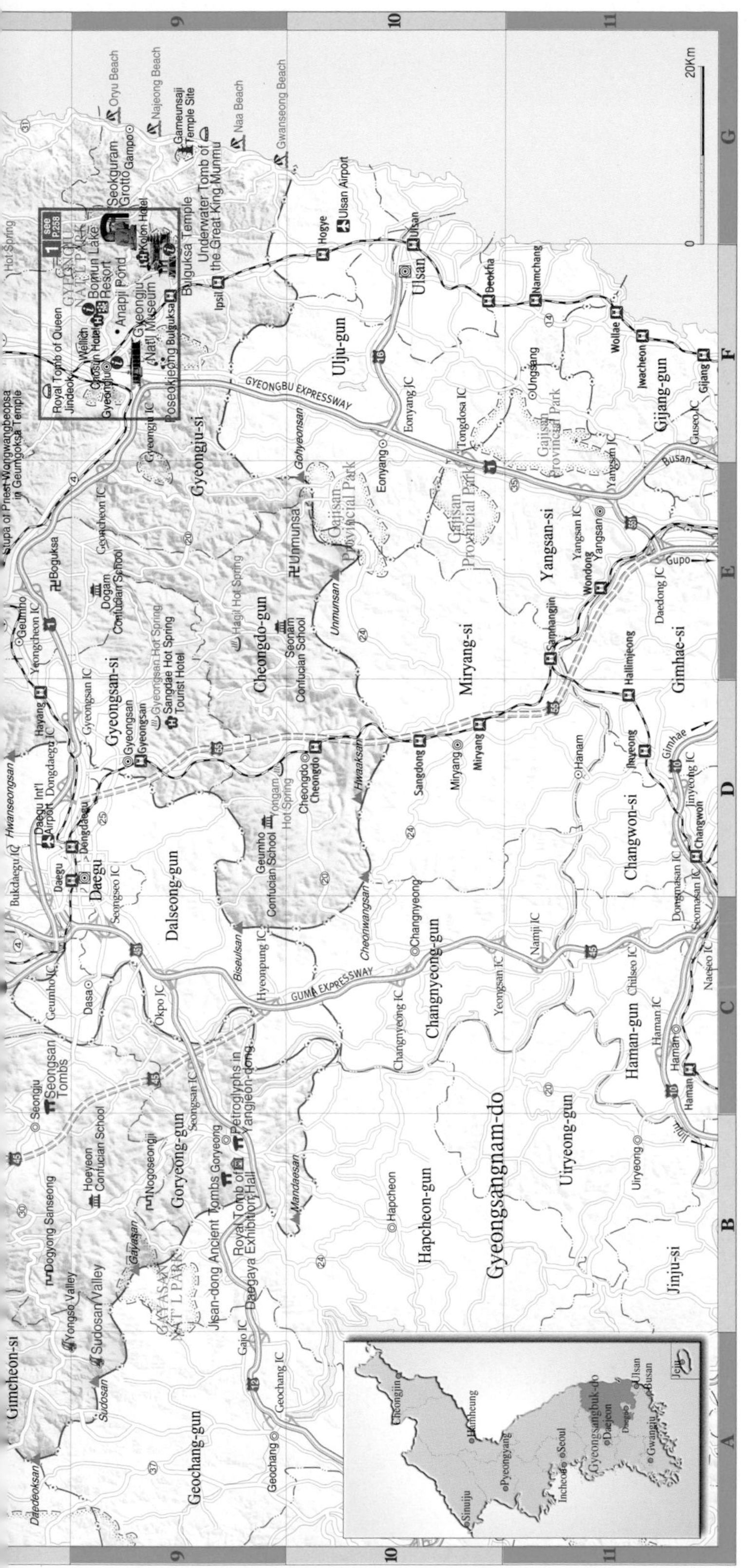

INDEX

Tourist Information

Gyeongsangbuk-do Tourism Promotion Department 82-53-950-3331
www.provin.gyeongbuk.kr

LEGEND

- Railroad Station
- Airport
- Tourist Information Center
- Museum
- Prehistoric Relic Site
- Tomb
- Fortress
- Temple
- Site of Buddhist Artifacts
- Traditional Building
- Traditional Pavilion
- Korean War Historical Site
- Falls or Valley
- Cave
- Beach
- Hot Spring or Spa
- Scenic Area
- Amusement Park
- Natural Recreation Forest
- Arboretum
- Botanical Garden
- Mountain
- Other Tourist Attractions
- Hotel
- Department Store or Market
- Reference Point

1

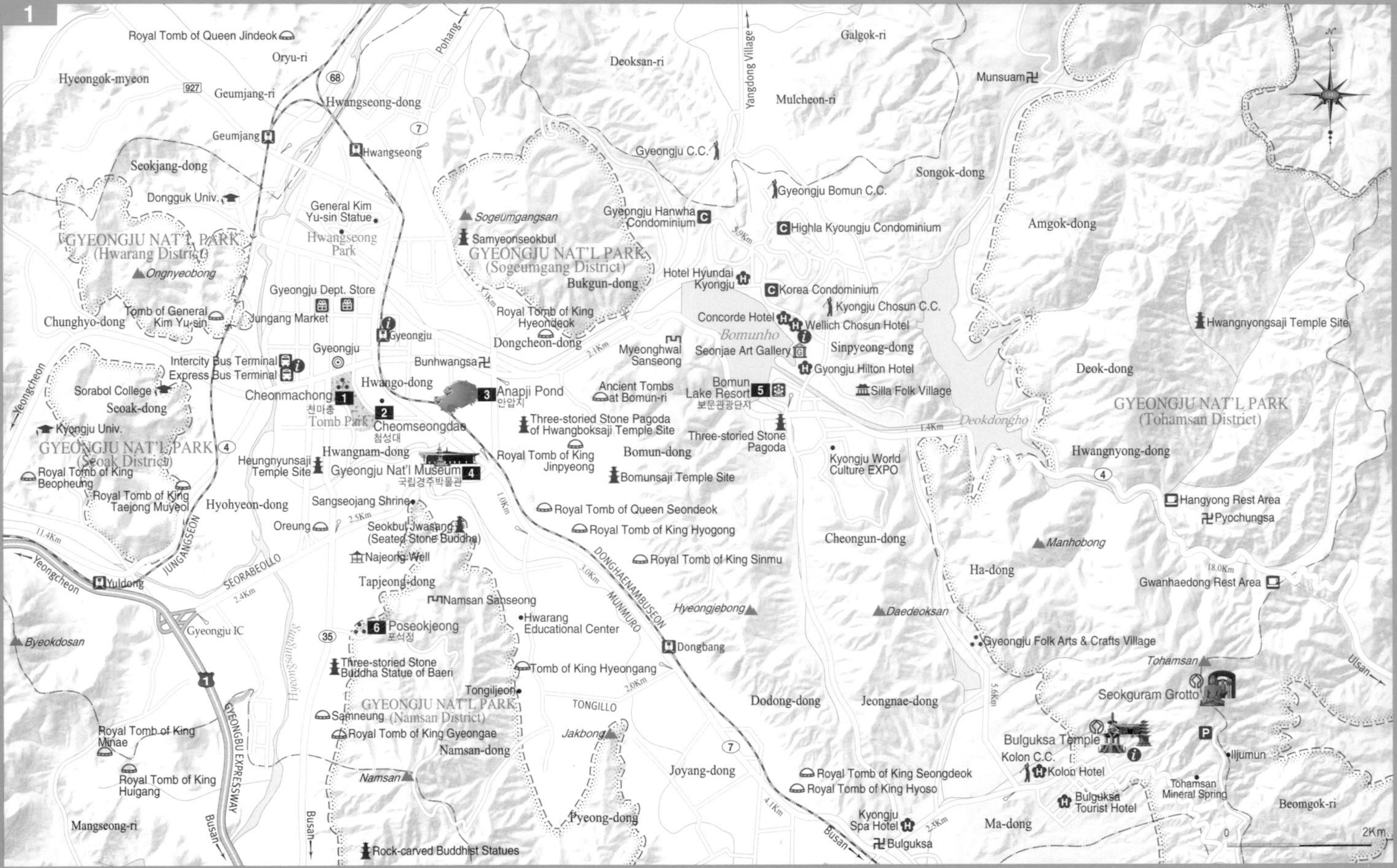

Royal Tomb of Queen Jindeok
Oryu-ri
Hyeongok-myeon
Geumjang-ri
Hwangseong-dong
Geumjang
Hwangseong
Pohang
Deoksan-ri
Yangdong Village
Galgok-ri
Mulcheon-ri
Munsuam
Gyeongju C.C.
Songok-dong
Gyeongju Bomun C.C.
Seokjang-dong
Dongguk Univ.
General Kim Yu-sin Statue
Hwangseong Park
Sogeumgangsan
Samyeonseokbul
GYEONGJU NAT'L PARK (Sogeumgang District)
Gyeongju Hanwha Condominium
Highla Kyoungju Condominium
Amgok-dong
GYEONGJU NAT'L PARK (Hwarang District)
Ongnyeobong
Gyeongju Dept. Store
Bukgun-dong
Hotel Hyundai Kyongju
Korea Condominium
Kyongju Chosun C.C.
Chunghyo-dong
Tomb of General Kim Yu-sin
Jungang Market
Royal Tomb of King Hyeondeok
Concorde Hotel
Wellich Chosun Hotel
Hwangnyongsaji Temple Site
Gyeongju
Dongcheon-dong
Bomunho
Seonjae Art Gallery
Sinpyeong-dong
Intercity Bus Terminal
Express Bus Terminal
Bunhwangsa
Myeonghwal Sanseong
Gyongju Hilton Hotel
Deok-dong
Yeongcheon
Sorabol College
Cheonmachong 1
Hwango-dong
Anapji Pond 3
안압지
Ancient Tombs at Bomun-ri
Bomun Lake Resort 5
보문관광단지
Silla Folk Village
GYEONGJU NAT'L PARK (Tohamsan District)
Seoak-dong
천마총
Tomb Park
Cheomseongdae 2
첨성대
Three-storied Stone Pagoda of Hwangboksaji Temple Site
Deokdongho
Kyongju Univ.
GYEONGJU NAT'L PARK (Seoak District)
Hwangnam-dong
Three-storied Stone Pagoda
Bomun-dong
Hwangnyong-dong
Royal Tomb of King Beopheung
Heungnyunsaji Temple Site
Gyeongju Nat'l Museum 4
국립경주박물관
Royal Tomb of King Jinpyeong
Kyongju World Culture EXPO
Royal Tomb of King Taejong Muyeol
Hyohyeon-dong
Sangseojang Shrine
Bomunsaji Temple Site
Hangyong Rest Area
Pyochungsa
Oreung
Seokbul Jwasang (Seated Stone Buddha)
Royal Tomb of Queen Seondeok
Royal Tomb of King Hyogong
Cheongun-dong
Manhobong
Najeong Well
Royal Tomb of King Sinmu
Ha-dong
Yuldong
SEORABEOLLO
JUNGANGSEON
Tapjeong-dong
DONGHAENAMBUSEON
Gwanhaedong Rest Area
Namsan Sanseong
Hwarang Educational Center
Hyeongjebong
Daedeoksan
Byeokdosan
Gyeongju IC
Poseokjeong 6
포석정
MUNMURO
Dongbang
Gyeongju Folk Arts & Crafts Village
Three-storied Stone Buddha Statue of Baeri
Tomb of King Hyeongang
Tohamsan
Tongiljeon
TONGILLO
Ulsan
Seokguram Grotto
GYEONGJU NAT'L PARK (Namsan District)
Dodong-dong
Jeongnae-dong
Samneung
Royal Tomb of King Gyeongae
Royal Tomb of King Minae
Jakbong
Namsan-dong
Bulguksa Temple
Kolon C.C.
Iljumun
Joyang-dong
GYEONGBU EXPRESSWAY
Kolon Hotel
Royal Tomb of King Huigang
Namsan
Royal Tomb of King Seongdeok
Royal Tomb of King Hyoso
Tohamsan Mineral Spring
Bulguksa Tourist Hotel
Beomgok-ri
Pyeong-dong
Kyongju Spa Hotel
Ma-dong
Mangseong-ri
Busan
Bulguksa
Rock-carved Buddhist Statues
0 2Km

Great Tomb Park in Gyeongju

As capital of Silla for almost 1,000 years, Gyeongju preserves much of the remarkable and fascinating culture of the Silla Kingdom. Since evidence of its historical and cultural heritage is evident throughout the city, the city itself serves as one huge museum. Popular tourist attractions are Bulguksa, Seokguram Grotto, Cheonmachong and Anapji Pond. Along with Bulguksa and Seokguram, the Gyeongju Historical District has been designated as a World Heritage site by UNESCO.

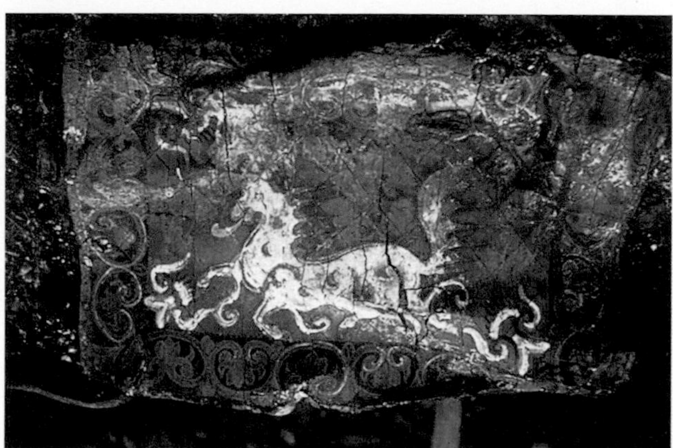

Cheonmado (Painting of a Flying Horse)

Anapji Pond

Cheonmachong 1

Cheonmachong was first excavated in 1973. It is a grave mound which was constructed using a wooden chamber covered with stones and earth. This type of grave mound was typical of the Silla Kingdom. The mound has a 50-meter diameter, while its height is 12.7 meters. A total of 11,500 artifacts were unearthed from the mound. Including ornaments, weaponry, equestrian equipment and pottery. Among the excavated artifacts, the most significant archeological find was a painting of a galloping or flying horse, which was discovered on a jangni. A jangni was used as a saddle guard and covered the abdominal area of a horse on both sides. It was used as both protection and as a kind of ornament. The flying horse was painted on layers of birch bark. This painting was the tomb' s greatest discovery because it was the first and the only Silla painting ever to be found. It was also this discovery that gave this tomb the name Cheonmachong, which means the heavenly horse tomb. The inside of the tomb is now open to the public after having been extensively restored.

Cheomseongdae 2

Cheomseongdae is an astronomical observatory built during the reign of Queen Seondeok of Silla. It is known to be the oldest existing observatory in the East. It was very scientifically constructed, and each stone used in the observatory bears a symbolic meaning.

The total number of stones used was 361.5, the exact number of days in the lunar calendar year. On the lip of these circular stones lies a rectangular stone tier positioned to form a square. There are a total of 28 stone tiers, which symbolize the 28 major stars. There are twelve tiers of stones leading to the window which is placed half way up on the observatory, and another twelve tiers above this window, symbolizing 24 seasonal divisions. The rectangular stones on the top are calibrated to the standards of Silla' s meridian, and each corner of the stones points to one of the four directions: north, south, east and west. The window in the middle of the stone tiers is positioned to face the true south.

Anapji Pond 3

Anapji was first constructed during the 14th year (674) of the reign of King Munmu, immediately after Silla unified the Three Kingdoms. Three small islands are at the center of a huge pond, imitating Samsindo, imaginary islands which are believed to be in the East Sea and a minature 12-peak mountain is located to the north and east, imitating Wu-shan Mountain in China. Plants and flowers were brought from around Korea and placed in this scenic garden, along with a number of rare animals. Anapji is the most revered garden and pond that exists from the Silla era.

Imhaejeon Hall, the terrace adjacent to the pond, and other annexes, were used during national celebration days and when lavish performances were presented for important guests. Anapji was carefully designed to evoke the feeling of standing on the edge of a wide sea, not a small pond. The rim of the pond was intentionally curved to prevent onlookers from getting a full view of the entire pond.

Cheomseongdae
Astronomical Observatory

Gyeongju National Museum 4

Gyeongju National Museum offers an opportunity to view 1,000 years of Silla culture at a single location. The museum, open year round, houses 80,000 artifacts excavated in Gyeongju and its vicinity. Over 2,500 artifacts date back to the prehistoric era and others in the display highlight the influence of Buddhist culture.

Gold Cap Excavated from Cheonmachong (National Treasure No. 189)

Gold Bracelet from the North Mound of Tumulus No. 98 (Treasure No. 623)

Gold Crown from Cheonmachong (National Treasure No.188)

Divine Bell of King Seongdeok

Bomun Lake Resort 5

The Bomun Lake Resort is a resort complex stretching over an area of 10.65 million square meters and is located alongside the 1.65 million square meter Lake Bomun. The resort boasts deluxe hotels, a golf course, souvenir shops, shopping centers, theme parks and other entertainment facilities. There is also an international convention hall and banquet rooms, making it possible to host international conferences, seminars, exhibitions, concerts and other diverse events. In the spring, a tunnel created by the blossoms of cherry trees provides a perfect path for a nice leisurely walk.

During the peak season, which runs from April into November, traditional dance and music performances are featured on an outdoor stage.

General View of Bomun Lake Resort

Poseokjeong 6

Poseokjeong is the place where kings and high-ranking government officials enjoyed themselves by setting a cup of wine afloat in a cool stream of water which ran through the irregular stone channels. They would then take turns attempting to compose verses before the cup reached a specified individual.

INDEX

1. Allakjeong **2.** Ihyangjeong
3. Ganghakdang **4.** Simsujeong
5. Yihuitaegaok **6.** Yidonggigaok
7. Yiwonyonggaok **8.** Yiwonyongbong
9. Wolseongsondongmanssigaok
10. Nakseondang **11.** Suunjeong
12. Daeseongheon **13.** Mucheomdang
14. Sujoldang **15.** Hyangdan
16. Gwangajeong

Hyangdan House

Yangdong Village

Yangdong Village preserves the traditional culture and character of the Joseon Dynasty and is the nation's largest aristocratic (yangban) village. This village was initially formed by the families of the Wolseong Son clan and the Yeogang Yi clan.

Yangdong Village serves as an outdoor exhibition center for traditional architecture. It displays a wide variety of diverse and distinctive traditional architectural structures from the mid-late Joseon Dynasty. There are several buildings in this village designated as important cultural properties including Mucheomdang (Treasure No. 411), Hyangdan (Treasure No. 412) and Gwangajeong (Treasure No. 442).

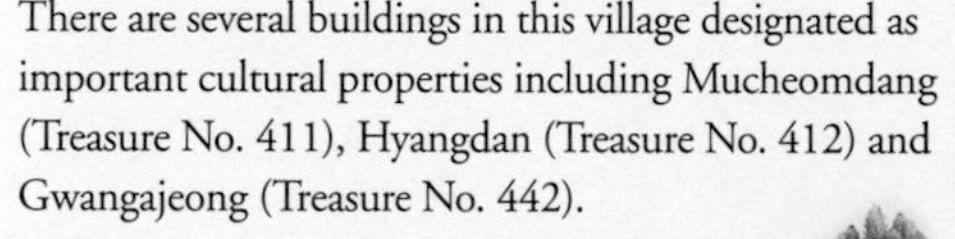

Mucheomdang

Gwangajeong Pavilion

2

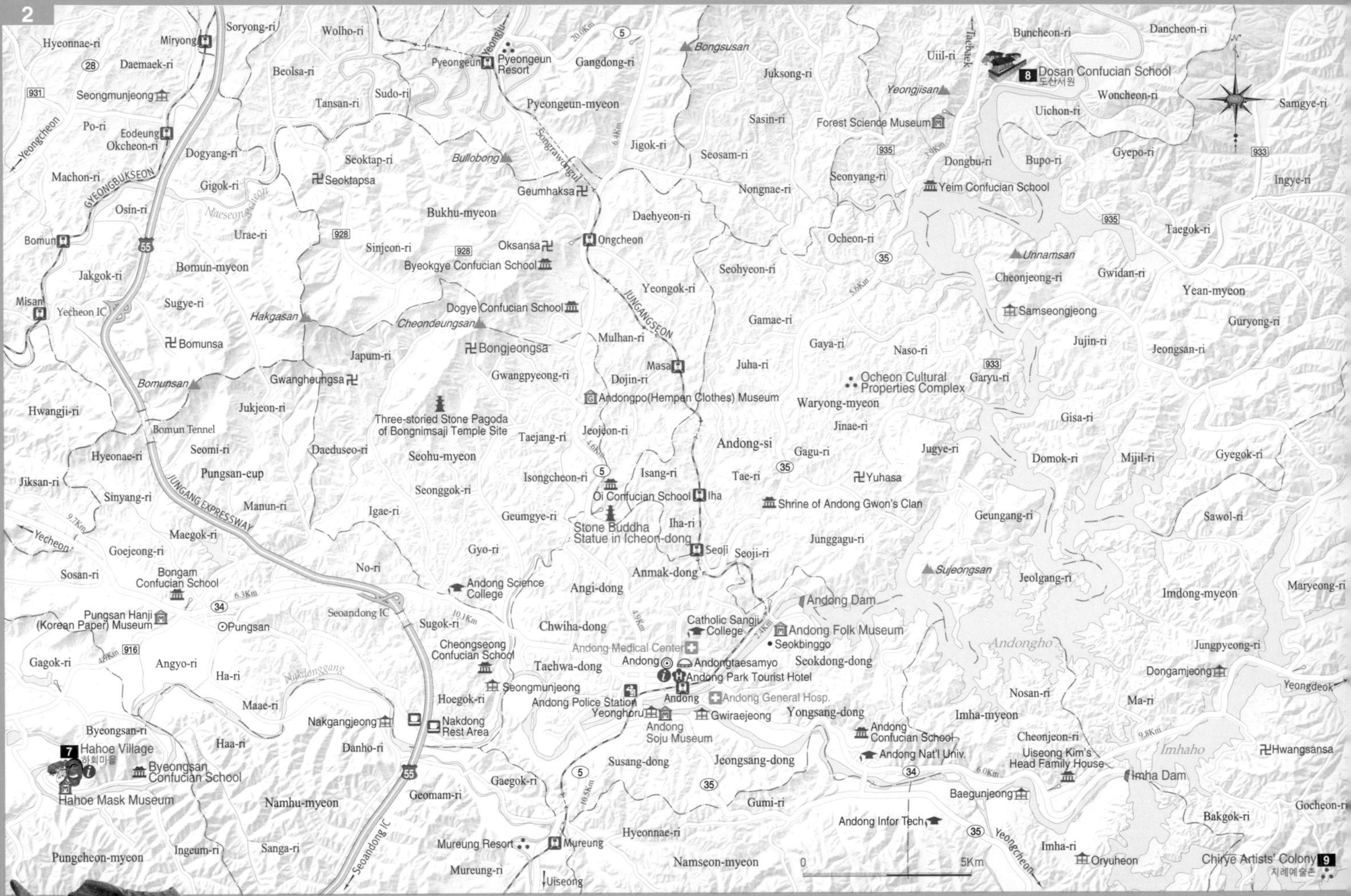

Andong is the best place to experience Confucianist traditions and cultural heritage in Korea. Confucianism was prevalent during the Joseon Dynasty and some of the good examples of its influence include Dosan Confucian School, Byeongsan Confucian School and Hahoe Village.

Major cultural events held at Andong are Hahoe Byeolsingut Tallori (shamanistic rituals), Chajeon Nori (folk war games), Notdari Balgi (folk dances), Jeojeon Nonmaegi (farmers' songs sung during the weeding of rice fields), and art festivals which include Dosanbyeolsi (poetry compositions), traditional music performances and other exhibitions.

Special local products include Andong Soju (a locally brewed liquor made of rice), traditional Hahoe masks, Andong apples, beef, and Andong hemp clothes.

Namchontaek

Hahoe Village 7

Hahoe Village is the most well known folk village in Korea. This village was named Hahoe (meaning the returning river) after the Nakdonggang, which flows eastward but changes its direction to envelop the village in the shape of an 'S'.

Hahoe Village was a collective residential area inhabited by family of the Pungsan Ryu clan. It preserves a great number of traditional houses significant enough to have been designated as cultural properties. The village became even more prominent after it was visited by Queen Elizabeth II during her state trip to Korea.

Hahoe Byeolsingut Tallori

Hahoe Byeolsingut Tallori is a mask ritual, performed at Hahoe Village, that originated with the peasants in the mid 12th century. Byeolsingut proceeds in the order of Gangsin (descending god), Yeongsin (welcoming god), Osin (entertaining god) and Songsin (bidding farewell to god). The Tallori refers to the Osin section in which people wanted to drive away evil spirits and bring luck by entertaining the gods. The contents of the Tallori are satirical, often poking fun at the ruling aristocrats and scholars and exposing the corruption of the Buddhist religion and the corrupt acts of the Buddhist monks.

Hahoe Byeolsingut Tallori humorously depicts the difficulties and problems that the peasants of the time experienced.

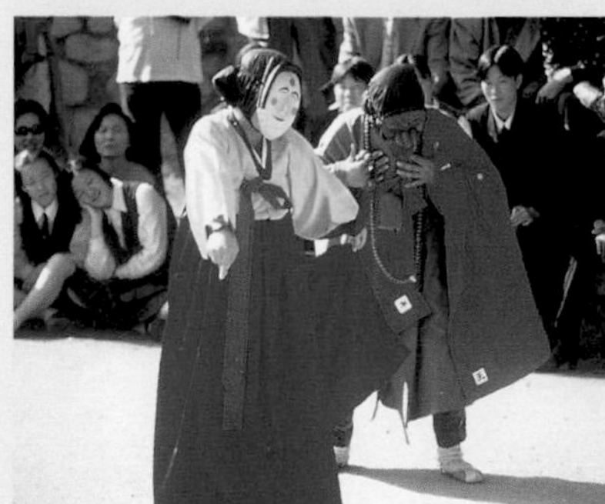
Hahoe Byeolsingut Tallori

Hahoe Masks

Legend has it that the wooden masks used in the performances of the Hahoe Byeolsingut Talnori were first manufactured by Heo Doryeong (an unmarried young man). The masks are made of the wood of black alder. Currently, 11 varieties of the Hahoe masks are collectively designated as National Treasure No. 121.

Hahoe masks convey an impression of Koreans' unique facial structure and expressions. Though fixed, the faces of Hahoe masks display a variety of emotions, such as happiness, anger, sadness and frustration.

Hahoe Village

Aerial Hahoe Village

Dosan Confucian School

Dosan Confucian School 8

Portrait of Toegye Yi Hwang

The Dosan Confucian School is an ancient school where the great Confucian scholar Toegye Yi Hwang educated his disciples during the mid Joseon Dynasty. Toegye taught at Dosan Confucian School for ten years, beginning in 1557. At that time, there were only two structures, the Dosan Seodang (the lecture hall) where he gave lectures to students, and Nongun Jeongsa (the study room). However, Confucian scholars built the Sadang Shrine, Jeongyodang Hall, and Dongjae and Seojae (the east and west students' residences) as a memorial to Toegye in 1574. In the following year, Dosan Confucian School became a government-sponsored Confucian academy and it received an official nameplate proclaiming it 'Dosan Seowon.' The nameplate was inscribed by Han Seok-bong, the most famous calligrapher of the time. The Dosan Confucian School is a very meaningful place historically, but it is also noted for its scenic landscape with lush pine forests, ancient trees, and the tranquil Andongho lake.

Chirye Artists' Colony 9

Chirye Artists' Colony was established when the residence of the head of the family of the the Kim clan and the Jisan Seodang (the lecture room) were about to be submerged as the result of a water development project. They were relocated to their current site and made into an artists' village. Field trips for experiencing the average peasant's life at the time and the rigors of studying Confucianism at the center are the focus of field trips to the colony.

The Colony resembles a serene oriental painting with its numerous 350 year-old houses and peaceful scenery.

Traditional Korean House in Chirye Artists' Colony

The village runs programs such as traditional art camps, cultural and historic relics programs, and other educational programs.

Andong Soju

It is presumed that soju, a locally brewed liquor made of rice, was first introduced to Korea around the end of the Goryeo Dynasty. Until the end of the Joseon Dynasty, soju brewed at Andong, Gaeseong and Jeju Island was popular. Andong Soju is still produced by a distilling technique which was passed on by generations who have lived in the Andong region. Andong Soju is made from top-quality rice grown in the fertile land of the region and is known for its refined aroma and taste.

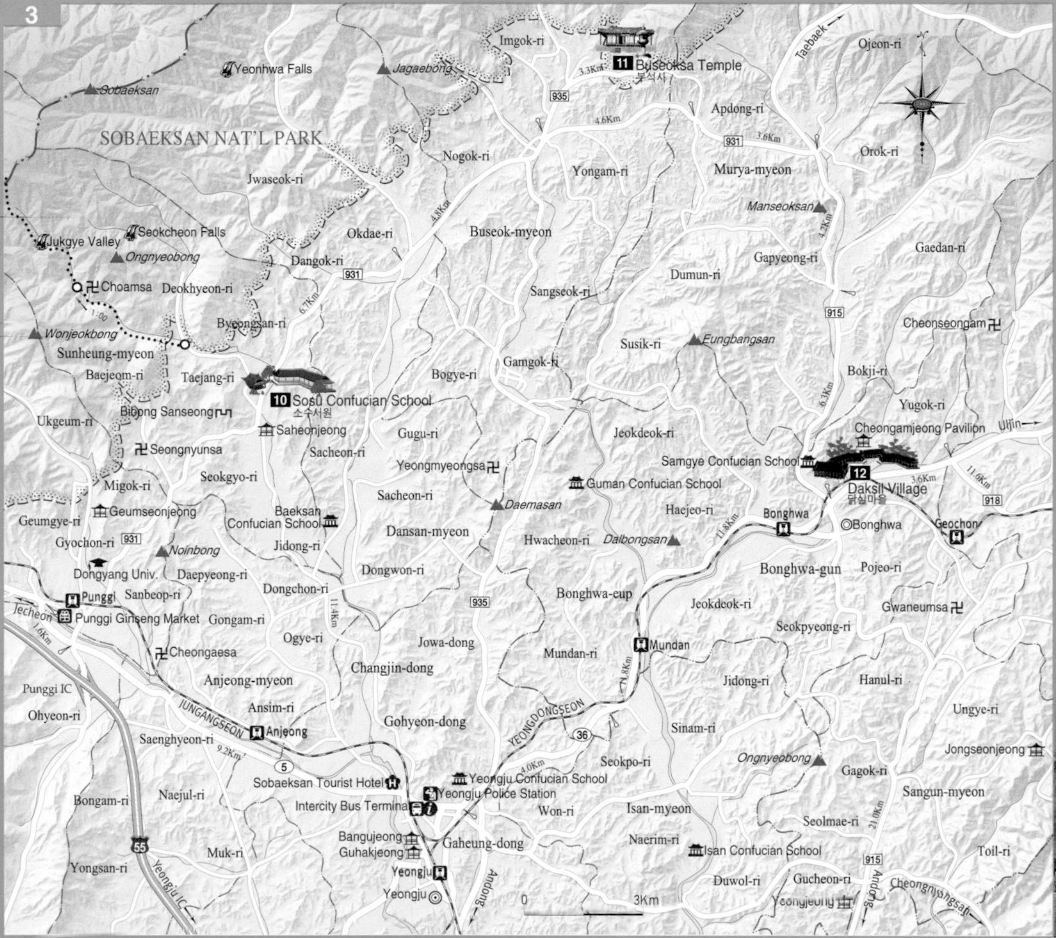

3

Yeongju, located in the northernmost part of Gyeongsangbuk-do, has well preserved its Confucian culture.
There are many historically important attractions in Yeongju, including the Sosu Confucian School and Buseoksa Temple, which houses Muryangsujeon Hall, a significant building in Korea's architectural history. Other attractions include Huibangsa Temple, Birosa Temple, Huibang Waterfall, Jukgye Gugok (the nine valleys) and Sobaeksan National Park. The most famous local product is Punggi Ginseng.

Sosu Confucian School in Yeongju

Sosu Confucian School 10

Sosu Confucian School is the first Confucian school ever authorized by the government. It was the birthplace of Hoeheon Anhyang, a notable Confucian scholar in the late Goryeo Dynasty. Ju Se-bung erected the school during the 37th year (1542) of King Jungjong's reign in memory of Anhyang, who also served as the Mayor of Punggi-gun. Anhyang held high public offices and dedicated himself to teaching upon retirement. He was the first Neo-Confucianism scholar in Korea, and he exercised great influence over junior scholars.
Inside the Sosu Confucian School are the Ganghakdang (the lecture hall), Munseonggongmyo (shrine), Jikbangjae/Ilsinjae (the student dormitories), Jangseogak (the archives), Jeonsacheong Hall and Hakgujae/Jirakjae (study halls). There are also portraits of Anhyang and Ju Se-bung, and a painting of Confucius and his disciples.

Muryangsujeon in Buseoksa (National Treasure No. 18)

Buseoksa Temple 11

Buseoksa is a temple which was built by the great monk Uisangdaesa during the Silla Kingdom. Buseoksa houses five national treasures and four other treasures, including the Muryangsujeon Hall, the oldest wooden structure in Korea, a stone lantern stand, Josadang Shrine, Sojoyeorae Jwasang (a seated clay Buddha statue), and mural paintings in the Josadang.

Muryangsujeon is not only known for its ancient history but also for its superb architectural artistry. The graceful and flexible contours of the columns of Muryangsujeon come from the fact that the diameter of each column's bottom is 44 cm while that of the column's head is 34 cm.

Sojoyeorae Jwasang

From the entrance to Anyang Gate, there are 108 stone steps representing 108 agonies believed by Buddhists to exist in life.

A path lined with ginkgo trees and a scenic view from the Anyangnu Pavilion also draw visitors to Buseoksa.

Daksil Village 12

The configuration of the grounds of this village is said to resemble a hen brooding on eggs, hence the name Daksil (a hen's nest). The village boasts a long history, as evidenced by some of the houses which date back to 500 years ago.

Daksil Snacks (Hangwa)

Daksil is especially famous for its tasty snacks. They are made from old recipes which have been handed down by the head family of the village over the years. Daksil snacks (hangwa) are beautifully decorated with chija (gardenia seed), heugimja (black sesame) and other natural colorings and have an assortment of tastes and scents.

Punggi Ginseng

Punggi Ginseng is grown in the rich soil at the foot of Mt. Sobaeksan. It has a strong aroma and high content of gin-saponin. Punggi Ginseng is presumed to have been widely used since the time of the Silla Kingdom. Ginseng was first cultivated in Punggi-gun during the reign of King Jungjong of the Joseon Dynasty. At the time, Ju Se-bung, the mayor of Punggi-gun, studied the soil and climate of the part of the county where a large number of wild ginseng plants grew naturally. He concluded that the conditions in the county were ideal for cultivating ginseng and started to grow it by using the seeds of wild ginseng.

Bonghwa Songi (pine mushroom) Festival

Bonghwa-gun is a mountainous region full of craggy peaks and hills of the Taebaek Mountain Range. The county has rich forest resources, such as songi (pine mushrooms) and edible wild greens. It hosts the Songi Festival every fall when pine mushrooms are harvested.

The festival includes the songi picking contest, a display of traditional foods, the songi cooking contest and traditional music performances.

Visitors can pick wild songi and taste a wide variety of foods containing the distinctive aroma and subtle flavor of pine mushrooms during the festival.

4

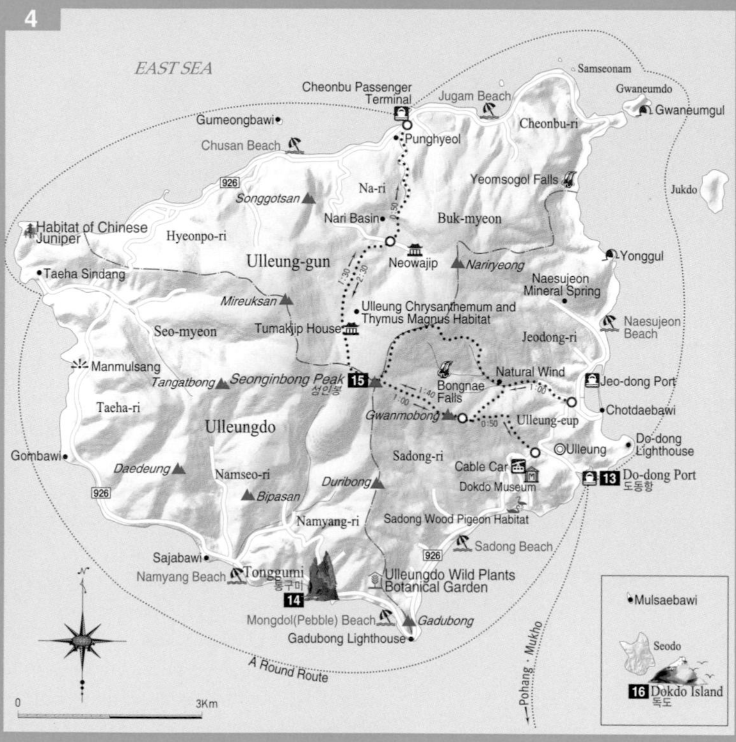

Ulleungdo is an island created by two volcanic eruptions approximately 6,000 years ago. Seonginbong Peak, which rises 984 meters above sea level, is located in the center of the island. Nari Basin is situated on the northern slope of Seonginbong and is the only place on the island that is relatively flat.

Rocks along the sea coast have odd shapes which have been naturally sculpted by rain, wind and waves, creating surreal imagery. An easy hike offers a great view of thick forests at Seonginbong and the scenic Bongnae Waterfall.

Dokdo Island

Squid Hanging to Dry

Do-dong Port 13

Do-dong Port is the main port of Ulleungdo. It is the starting point for both hiking trips into the island and excursion ships off the coast.

Tonggumi 14

Tonggumi is the name of a cliff located behind the village of Namyang-ri on Ulleungdo. A great number of Chinese juniper trees grow right out of the cracks of the Tonggumi. In the past, large, old Chinese juniper trees were found all over the island but these days they are rare due to logging. Tonggumi, the natural growth area for Chinese juniper trees, is no exception to this unfortunate trend.

Tonggumi is considered important because it is thought to be the first place where Chinese juniper trees were grown.

Seonginbong Peak 15

This peak got the name Seongin because the mountain here resembles the shape of a sacred person. It is shrouded in fog for more than 300 days a year on average, creating an ethereal atmosphere. At the summit is a rock that looks like an altar. Hiking the trail from Do-dong Port up to Gwanmobong Peak takes about three hours and a panoramic view of Ulleungdo awaits visitors.

Dokdo Island 16

Dokdo is an isolated island in the eastern reaches of the nation's territory. It is located 92 km southeast of Ulleungdo Island and consists of 34 rock islands and reefs, including Dongdo and Seodo (the east and west islands), Gajae (crayfish) Rock, Gumeong (hole) Rock and Jine (centipede) Rock.

It is home to many sea birds which have been designated as natural monuments, such as black-tailed gull, the Swinhoe's storm petrel and the puffinus tenuirostris. A multitude of sea life, such as squid and yellow-tail tuna, form the basis for a prosperous fishery industry.

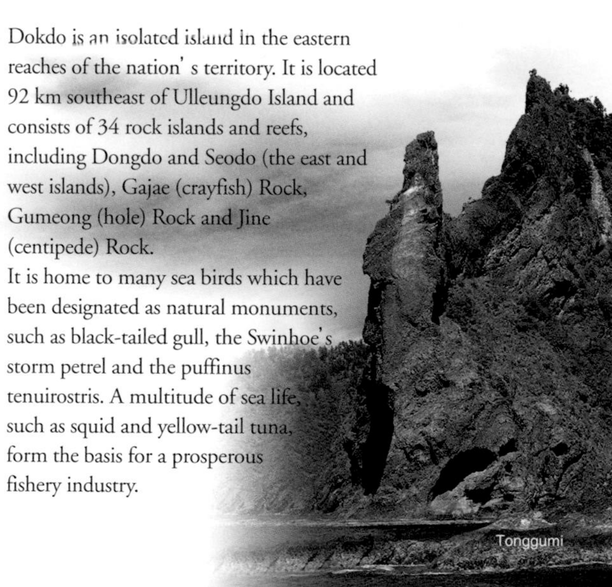
Tonggumi

Cheongdo Bullfighting Festival

Cheongdo Bullfighting Festival

The Cheongdo Bullfighting Festival is the nation' s largest bullfighting contest. This traditional folk festival is held every March. The festival has developed into an international event with a wide variety of events, such as a competition between Korean and foreign bulls and a rodeo by U.S. servicemen stationed in Korea.
Bullfighting in Korea started as a form of amusement among cow herders but was eventually further developed into a match for honor between villages or clans, and ultimately it turned into this exciting festival.

Jisan-dong Ancient Tombs B9

Goryeong-eup was the capital of the Great Gaya, a dynasty which prospered for 520 years (A.D. 42-562). Two hundred old tumuli built during this period are located along the southeastern ridge of Mt. Jusan. The largest tumulus in the area is presumed to be the Geumnimwangneung (the tomb of King Geumnim) and other large tombs are also presumed to be royal.
A number of artifacts have been discovered in the area, ranging from gold, silver, and jade ornaments, such as those contained in a gilt-bronze crown, to weaponry, such as armor and large swords and equestrian equipment like stirrups and saddle guards. These items reflect the highly-advanced civilization of the Great Gaya Kingdom. Tomb No. 44 is the nation' s first confirmed 'sunjang' tombs (a burial system where the living, including servants, are buried with their dead master). The tumulus serves as an important research reference in verifying the burial system, as it houses a main stone chamber in the center and auxiliary chambers in the south and the west, surrounded by 32 small stone coffins which were used to inter the living.
The Royal Tombs of the Great Gaya Exhibition Hall, which is located at the foot of Mt. Jusan, displays the unique aspects of the sunjang burial system and has exhibitions on the history of the Great Gaya Kingdom.

Jikjisa Temple A7

Jikjisa, located at the foot of Mt. Hwangaksan, is the most popular temple of the city of Gimcheon. The temple was founded by the monk Adohwasang in the second year (418) of the reign of King Nulji of the Silla Kingdom. Jikjisa houses the Samyeonggak, a shrine that preserves the portrait of the great monk Samyeongdaesa. Cheonbuljeon Hall, located at Jikjisa, contains the Cheonbulsang, 1,000 Buddhist statues which were fashioned from jade stone by the monk Gyeongjamdaesa.
In addition, such well-preserved treasures as a three-storied stone pagoda, a temple bell, Buddhist statues and paintings are scattered around the compound. The recently opened Seongbo Museum displays Buddhist-related exhibits which were obtained from branch temples managed by the Jikjisa monks.

Gaya Period Gold Crown
(National Treasure No.138)

Royal Tombs of the Great Gaya Exhibition Hall

Gyeongsangnam-do

Gyeongsangnam-do is home to numerous relics from the Gaya and Silla cultures. The province is also dotted with popular tourist attractions. Jirisan and Gayasan National Parks have an ancient beauty and Haeinsa Temple and Tongdosa Temple allow visitors the chance to visit two of the three largest temples in Korea. Bugok Hot Springs and the picturesque Mt. Geumsan are some of the other popular attractions in the province.

The Tripitaka Koreana

During the reign of King Gojong, Daejangdogam, the office in charge of making the Tripitaka Koreana, was established. It took 16 years of labor to complete the carving of the Tripitaka Koreana which was made as an entreaty to Buddha to protect the Goryeo nation from the Mongolian invasions. It survives today as evidence of Korea's ancient culture.

The Tripitaka is also called the Goryeo Tripitaka, as it was carved during the Goryeo Dynasty, and the Palman (eighty-thousand) Tripitaka, because it has around 80,000 wooden printing blocks containing 84,000 Buddhist texts. There is not a single mistake in the entire collection of the Tripitaka Koreana.

The carving of the Tripitaka Koreana was a tedious process. First, birch trees were cut and soaked in sea water for three years. After this, the trees were cut into pieces, and the wooden blocks were boiled in salt water and then dried. Next, the wooden blocks had to go through a planing process to smooth their surfaces. After all of these procedures, the characters of the Buddhist sutras were carved in the blocks.

Janggyeonggak is the storage complex that houses the Goryeo Palman Tripitaka. It is on a hill behind Daejeokgwangjeon (the main hall) and has two long buildings to the north and south which are identical, as well as two shorter structures to the east and west.

The depository was built during the 19th year (1488) of King Seongjong's reign. It attracts the attention of visitors due to its preserved state, which is thought to be more remarkable than its architectural style. Janggyeonggak uses a simple architectural style in which large blocks of wood are assembled void of any extraneous decorations.

The four buildings here have survived fires on numerous occasions and are believed by some to be protected by a mysterious power. The wooden blocks also remain free from damage that could have easily been caused by insects.

A close look at the depository reveals that it was meticulously constructed, taking into careful account factors such as the size and layout of windows on both sides, climate control, ventilation, humidity and ease of moving around inside the building.

Storehouse for the Tripitaka Koreana Tablets

The windows of the depository were designed with consideration to the geographical features of the surrounding mountain. Because of this, drainage, ventilation and humidity pose noproblems. For instance, the lower part of the windows that face the south is wider than the upper part, whereas the windows in the north are the opposite. This is just one feature that helps controll the climate in the building.

Janggyeonggak, the Storehouse for the Tripitaka Koreana Tablets (National Treasure No.52)

Haeinsa Temple

At Daejeokgwangjeon, the main hall of Haeinsa, one can study Buddha's teachings. The original building was constructed in 802, while the present building was built in 1817.

In Zen Buddhism meditation, one controls one's breathing, body and mind, casting off earthly desires and passions and looking deep within oneself. Visitors to the temple will have an opportunity to gain a sense of serenity by participating in meditation programs offered here. These programs include study sessions on Buddhist texts, special lectures, and hermitage pilgrimages. Visitors can also taste temple foods.

Buddhist Monks in front of Janggyeonggak

The Inner Gate of Janggyeonggak

Buddhist Mass in Haeinsa

Gyeongsangnam-do

INDEX

Tourist Information

Gyeongsangnam-do Tourism Promotion Division 82-55-279-3332
Gyeongsangnam-do Tourist Information Center 82-55-279-3336
www.provin.gyeongnam.kr

LEGEND

- Railroad Station
- Airport
- Port
- Bus Terminal
- Rest Area
- Tourist Information Center
- Museum
- Gallery
- World Cultural Heritage Site
- Prehistoric Relic Site
- Tomb
- Fortress
- Temple
- Site of Buddhist Artifacts
- Traditional Building
- Traditional Pavilion
- Battlefield
- Falls or Valley
- Cave
- Beach
- Golf Course
- Hot Spring or Spa
- Scenic Area
- Amusement Park
- Migratory Birds' Sanctuary
- Natural Recreation Forest
- Botanical Garden
- Mountain
- Other Tourist Attractions
- Hotel
- Reference Point

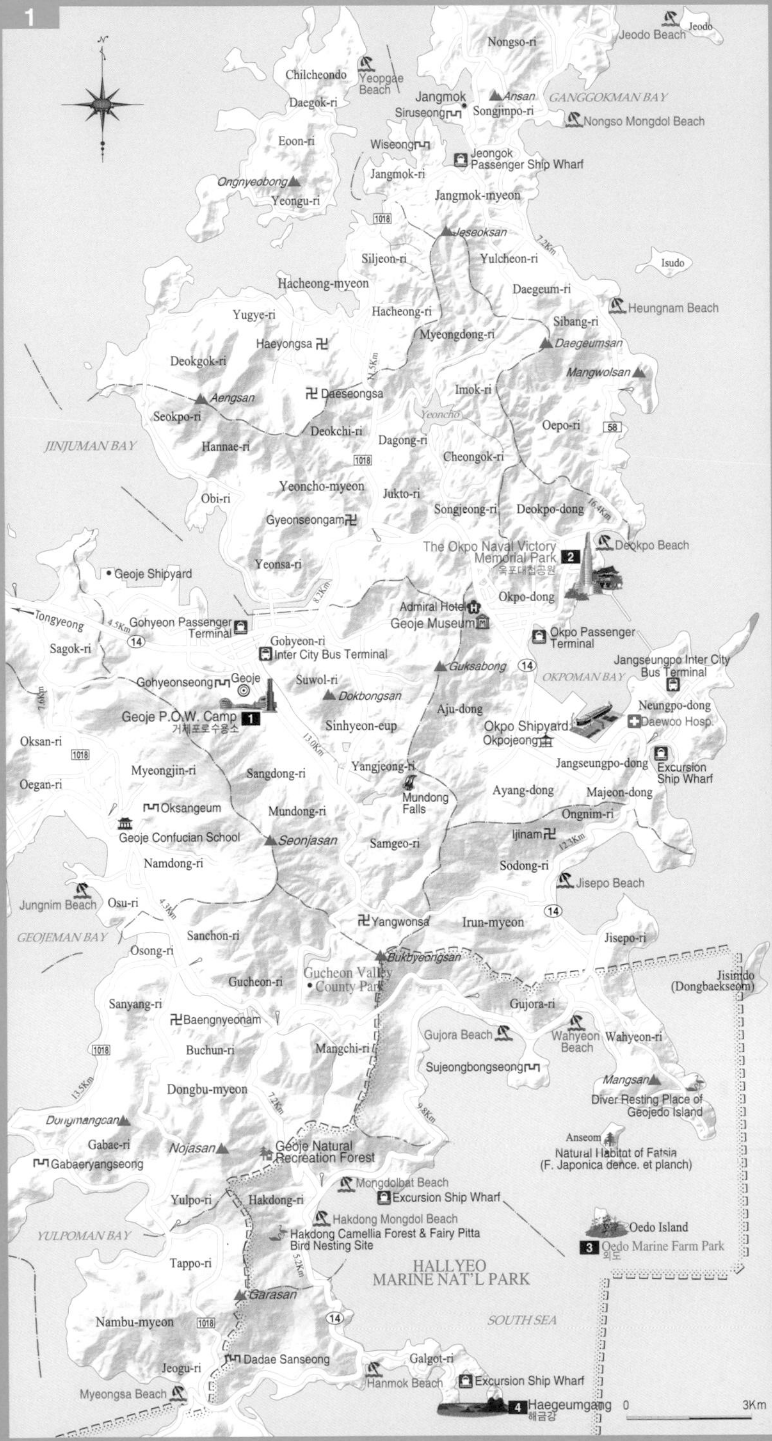

Geojedo boasts a beautiful coastal landscape. It has a distinctive local culture and is home to a number of historic relics and cultural heritages from different eras. In times of national crisis, Geojedo always weathered the difficulties by protecting itself with a tightly knit military culture and society. In particular, during the period between the Japanese invasion and the late Joseon Dynasty, it served as a strategic point of military importance. It also became known during the Korean War as the location of camps for prisoners of war.
Geojedo has many oceanside tourist attractions, including sandy beaches, black pebble beaches, camellia flowers, pine forests and a rocky coast line.

Geoje P.O.W. Camp 1

Remains of a Geoje P.O.W. Camp

The Geoje P.O.W. Camp, located in Geoje-si, was first set up when the Korean War broke out. From November 1950, P.O.W. Camps were centered around the Gohyeon, Sangdong, Yongsan, Yang, Suwol, Haemyeong, and Jeosan districts. The camps accommodated a total of 170,000 prisoners of war, including 150,000 North Korean P.O.W.s and 20,000 Chinese P.O.W.s. Three hundred of them are believed to have been women.
When the armistice agreement was signed on July 27, 1953, the camp was closed and the P.O.W.s were repatriated to North Korea through the truce village of Panmunjeom. The remnants of the camps were scattered, and in 1995, a five-year long restoration project for the camps was started and included the construction of a memorial building.
The major facilities of the memorial include an exhibition hall, ten rebuilt camps, a symbolic statue, a memorial monument and an exhibition room for various kinds of weaponry and equipment.

Oedo Marine Farm Park

Okpo Naval Victory Memorial Park 2

Okpo Naval Victory Memorial Park was created next to Okpoman Bay to commemorate the Okpo Naval War, during which Admiral Chungmugong Yi Sun-shin defeated Japanese invaders.
Inside the park stands a memorial and visitors get an unobstructed view of Okpoman Bay from the Okporu Pavilion.
The monument is 30m in height and is shaped to symbolize a crane wing formation, a war vessel, and a huge legendary mountain. There is an altar in the park resembling the shape of '忠,' a Chinese character meaning patriotism. Articles related to Admiral Yi, such as paintings of naval warfare, are on display in the Okporu exhibition hall.

Okpo Naval Victory Memorial Park monument

Oedo Marine Farm Park 3

Oedo is an island located 20 minutes by ferry from Gujorahang Port. About 30 years ago, an individual bought the island and established a horticultural farm. Currently, camellia fields carpet much of the island. A wide variety of subtropical plants, such as palm trees and cactuses, as well as rare plants, such as blue gum trees, sparitium and mahonia, draw tourists. The island 's forest is filled with indigenous trees including camellia japonica, bamboo and silver magnolias. Birds like the Japanese white-eye, the kingfisher, and various others nest in the forest.
Inside the park lies a path lined with chamaecyparis obtusa trees leading to Venus Park. Visitors can unwind here on an observatory deck and take in the panoramic view of the Haegeumgang landscape. Other attractions within the park include a sculpture display and an outdoor stage.

Haegeumgang 4

Haegeumgang refers to the area from Galgot Cape, located approximately 500m to the south of the village of Galgot, to a small rock island called Galdo. Haeguemgang is known for its rock formations. The area used to be called Galgotdo Island, but the name was changed because the island is reminiscent of the Haegeumgang area of Mt. Geumgangsan in North Korea. The highest peak on the island, Mt. Najasan, stretches high into the sky, and sea cliffs and caves are added attractions.
A tour of Haegeumgang is possible only by boat. Each rock here has a name which symbolizes its shape, for example, Seonnyeobawi (Goddess Rock), Sajabawi (Lion Rock), and Mireukbawi (Maitreya Bodhisattva Rock). Geunebawi where a 1,000-year old pine tree grows and Sajabawi are popular for their good view of the sunrise and sunset.

TONGYEONG

2

Masan
Dongdal-ri
Geoje
8.0Km
BUKSANMAN BAY
Hwasam-ri
Inter City Bus Terminal
Tongyeong Police Station
Tongyeong
Myeongjeong-dong
Sebyeonggwan
Mangilbong
Cheonamsan
Docheon-dong
Chungmu Beach
Gyeongsang Nat'l Univ. College of Marine Science
Nammangsan Park
Yeonan Ferry Teminal
Chungmu Br.
Undersea Tunnel
Tongyeong Br.
Donam Tourist Complex
도남관광지
Tongyeong Mother-of-Pearl Lacquerware Festival
Chungmu Marina Condominium
Punghwa-ri
Misu-dong
Bongpyeong-dong
Yeongun-ri
Obido
Nampyeong-ri
Mireukdo
Yonghwasan
Sanyang-eup
Daegaksa
Sanyang
Mireukdo Special Tourism Area
Sinjeon-ri
Dangposeong
Institute of Fisheries Sciences
Yeonhwa-ri
Sanyang Beach Road
Gollido
Dara Park
Minam-ri
TONGYEONGMAN BAY
HALLYEO MARINE NAT'L PARK
Jeodo
Hangnimdo
Manjido
Yeondaedo
Shell Mound
Ogokdo
SOUTH SEA
0 3Km
Pyewangseong
Haksan-ri
Simok-ri
Sanbang-ri
Dundeok-myeon
Bohyeonsa
Suryeok-ri
Bangha-ri
Hadun-ri
Hwado
Sorokdo
Eogu-ri
Beopdong-ri
Sandaldo
Yeomho-ri
Bisando
Hansan Naval Victory Memerial Tower
Seojwado
Songdo
Jeseungdang Shrine
Changjwa-ri
Dueok-ri
Vestiges of Admiral Yi Sun-shin
Hansando Island
한산도
Mangsan
Haso-ri
Chubong-ri
Bongammongdol Beach
Hansanam
Hansan-myeon
Yongchodo
Yongho-ri
Natural Habitat of Fatsia
Bijindo
Jukdo
Bijin Beach
Bijin-ri
Seonyudae

Tongyeong-si, located in the center of Hallyeo Marine National Park, is a beautiful port city. It is known for its picturesque landscape and mild temperatures. Tongyeong-si has tourist attractions such as the Hallyeo Marine National Park, Donam Tourist Complex, the Jeseungdang Shrine, and Maemuldo Island.

View from A Submarine Porthole, Tongyeong

Tongyeong Najeonchilgi Festival

Tongyeong Najeonchilg (mother-of-pearl lacquer ware)

Tongyeong city dates back some 400 years. Tongyeong' s najeonchilgi (mother-of-pearl lacquer ware) is popular both at home and abroad.

Najeonchilgi refers to the technique used to attach the rainbow-hued inner shells of abalones onto blocks of lacquered wood in a variety of inscribed drawings and patterns. The fame of Tongyeong najeonchilgi owes much to the quality of the abalone, clam and trumpet shells which are found in the region.

The Tongyeong Najeonchilgi Festival is an event which is designed to promote traditional mother-of-pearl lacquer ware.

During the festival, visitors can look at 400-year old mother-of-pearl lacquer ware when visiting the exhibition hall (which is named Najeonchilgi, 400 years of Tradition). They can also participate in making Najeonchilgi and learn about Tongyeong' s unique craftsmanship by observing demonstrations of the najeonchilgi manufacturing process.

Donam Tourist Complex 5

Donam Tourist Complex lies at the center of Hallyeo Marine National Park and is noted for its natural scenery. It is a multi-purpose complex that operates marine sports facilities, a yacht clubhouse, condominiums and a sports center.

It is also the starting point for a cruise to Hallyeo Marine National Park. The cruise course includes such attractions as Jeseungdang where Admiral Yi Sunshin is enshrined on Hansando Island, Haegeumgang of Geoje, and the island of Maemuldo.

Visitors can enjoy a wide variety of water sports, including motor boats, sailing, water skiing, jet skiing, para-sailing, wind surfing and scuba diving.

Hansando Island 6

Hansando has a scenic coast and is where Admiral Yi Sun-shin waged the Great Hansan War against Japanese invaders. For seven years, starting in 1592, Hansando played a pivotal role in protecting the southwest part of Korea, the bread basket of the country. Hansando hosts the Great Hansan War Commemorative Festival each year in Tongyeong-si. It is a cultural festival celebrating Korea's victory in the Great Hansan War, the technical achievements in naval warfare which took place at this time, and the feats of Admiral Yi Sun-shin. During the festival, war victory dance performances, a ritual to pray for abundant fish, Tongyeong Ogwangdae (a folk play performed with five masks), contests, and other exhibitions are featured.

· Hansandaecheopdo, a picture of a battle during the Great Hansan War against Japanese invaders (top)
· Jeseungdang Shrine in Hansando (bottom)

Hallyeo Marine National Park

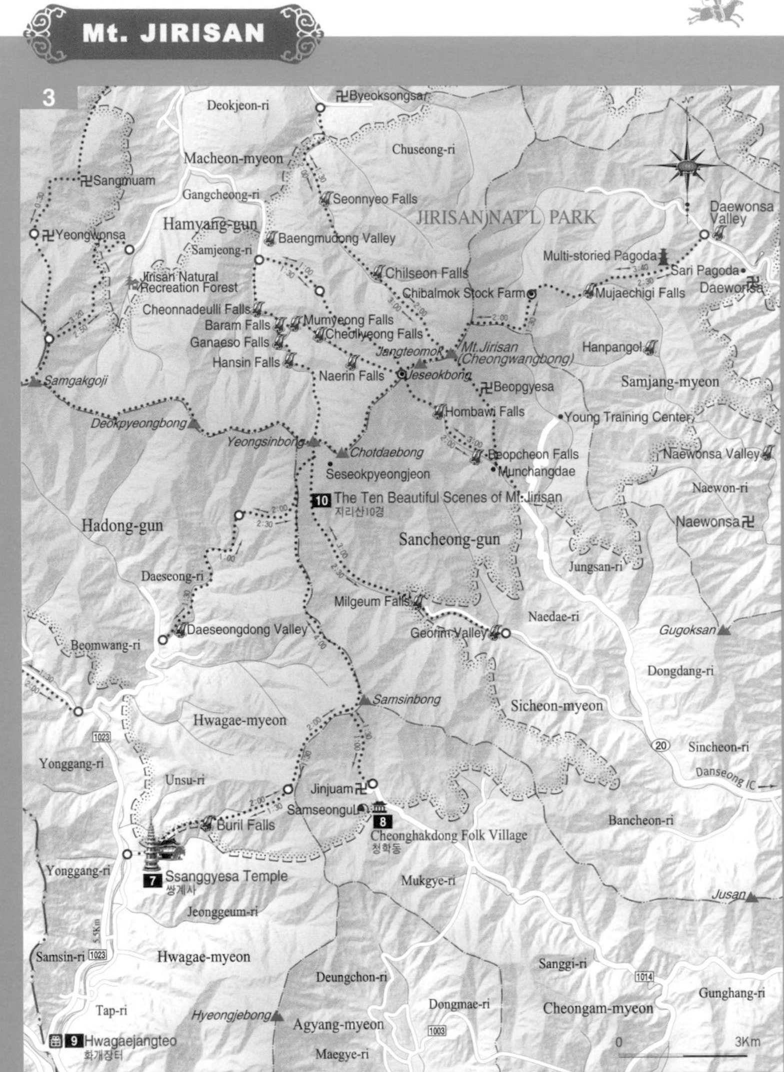

Mt. Jirisan

Mt. Jirisan has been said to be one of the Samsinsan (the three mountains where God lives), along with Mt. Geumgangsan and Mt. Hallasan. People also believed that Mt. Jirisan had the special power to make a fool into a wise man. 'Jiri' means wisdom in Chinese characters.

Mt. Jirisan consists of ten jagged peaks, which include Cheonwangbong Peak, the second highest peak in South Korea, Banyabong Peak and Nogodan Peak. There are also ten waterfalls. Mt. Jirisan is home to a number of Buddhist temples and hermitages, including Hwaeomsa Temple and Ssanggyesa Temple.

Ssanggyesa Temple 7

Ssanggyesa in Mt. Jirisan

Ssanggyesa, located in the southern part of Mt. Jirisan, is the main temple of the Joggye Order of Buddhists. It was constructed by the Buddhist monk, Sambeop, a disciple of Uisang, in 723 during the Silla Kingdom.

Major cultural assets of the temple include a stone monument dedicated to the Buddhist monk Jingamguksa, a stupa, a pagoda enshrining Yukjodaesa, Buddhist texts and Palsangdo, which are eight Buddhist paintings describing the eight stages of Buddha's life.

In the courtyard of Guksaam Hermitage, located 500m from Ssanggyesa, stands Sacheonwangsu (meaning the Four Divas Tree). Legend has it that the cane which was used by Jingamguksa turned into Sacheonwangsu, an elm tree. The Buriram Hermitage, where the great Buddhist monks Wonhyo and Uisang of the Silla Kingdom meditated, is also located here. The hermitage's name, Buril, is derived from the posthumous name of the monk Bojoguksa.

Cheonghakdong Folk Village 8

Cheonghakdong Folk Village is a residential area where people honoring the philosophy of Confucianism live together and wear traditional clothing. Houses here still have thatched roofs. Unmarried men and women of the village grow their hair in braids, while older men wear a gat, Korea's traditional hat. This

attire was worn in the old days.
Instead of attending regular schools, children in Cheonghakdong go to the village seodang (a private Confucian school) to receive a traditional education. Villagers make their living by growing herbs, picking wild vegetables and raising bees and livestock.

Cheonghakdong Folk Village

Hwagaejangteo 9

Hwagaejangteo obtained its fame because it was home to one of the most popular traditional market places in Korea. It is located where Jeollanam-do meets Gyeongsangnam-do. Before Korea was liberated from Japanese occupation, Hwagaejangteo was the busiest market in Korea.
The market is open once every five days, just as other Korean traditional markets are. Farmers living arouand Mt. Jirisan bring their goods, such as bracken and potatoes, and sell them in the market, while people from inland regions sell products like rye. Peddlers travelling across the country sell household products, and residents of Yeosu, Gwangyang, Namhae, Samcheonpo, Chungmu and Geoje all travel here by boat to sell foods from the sea.

Ten Beautiful Scenes of Mt. Jirisan 10

The ten most well-known sites at Jirisan are collectively called the 'ten beautiful scenes of Mt. Jirisan.'

Sea of clouds at Nogodan

First scene: Sea of Clouds at Nogodan
A picturesque sea of clouds which can be seen from Nogodan, the highest peak in western Jirisan.

Second scene: Jikjeon Autumn Foliage
Beginning in mid-October every year, Piagol Valley, the largest deciduous forest at Jirisan, turns into a kaleidoscope of autumn foliage of various colors.

Third scene: Banya Sunset
When dark shadows hang over the northwestern ridge line of Simwon Valley at dusk, a view of the setting sun is visible.

Fourth scene: The Bright Moon of Byeokso
The bright moon lighting the forest in Byeokso Valley creates a graceful and surreal image.

Fifth scene: Seseok Royal Azalea Blossoms
From late May to early June, pink royal azalea blossoms carpet a vast area of the Seseok highlands.

Sixth scene: Buril Falls
Thunderous cascades of water come crashing down on the rocks in the rugged valley behind Ssanggyesa.

Seventh scene: The Mysterious Scenery of Yeonha
Flowers go into full bloom throughout the four seasons on Yeonhabong Peak, which is located between Seseok and Jangteomok Valley. Rocks of odd formations and covered with thousands of years of moss, creating a mysterious scenery.

Eighth scene: Cheonwang Sunrise
At the summit of Cheonwangbong, one can enjoy an unblocked view in all directions. This is especially impressive at dawn, when the sunrise begins to fill the sky.

Ninth scene: Chilseon Valley
A crystal-clear stream runs through a forest in Chilseon Valley, giving the valley a quiet serenity.

Tenth scene: The Blue Water of Seomjingang River
The blue water of the Seomjingang, which originates from Jinan and Jangsu of Jeollabuk-do and flows into the South Sea, is known for its distinctive coloring.

Geumgang Gyedan in Tongdosa

Tongdosa Temple I3

Tongdosa is a huge Buddhist temple compound located in the southern part of Mt. Yeongchwisan. It contains Buddha's sariras and is known as one of the three temples which preserves Buddhist treasures. It is also one of the three largest temples in Korea. The Buddhist monk Jajangyulsa went to China during the Tang Dynasty to learn and meditate and brought back with him Buddha's sariras and built the temple in 646. What differentiates the temple from others is the fact that the main hall, Daeungjeon (National Treasure No. 290), does not have any Buddhist statues. An altar located behind Daeungjeon, houses the sariras of Buddha. Within the temple compound, there are 35 buildings. In the vicinity of the temple are 17 hermitages and a forest. The forest is so thick with trees that one cannot see the sky when inside it. Also housed here is Treasure No. 334, Eunipsahyangno, a bronze incense burner inlaid with silver, and Treasure No. 74, Gukjangsaeng Seokpyo, an old stone boundary marker (gukjangsaeng means a marker erected by the order of the government).

International Formula 3 Korea Grand Prix H4

International motor races are one of the three biggest sporting events in the world, together with the Olympics and the World Cup games. The International Formula 3 Korea Grand Prix car race held in Changwon is a race of cars below the 2,000cc-level.
The Changwon main track is a road circuit that utilizes roads that are used by the general public. As the shape of the Changwon track looks like a monkey wrench, it is also called the monkey wrench track. This is an appropriate symbol for Changwon, the cradle of the nation's mechanical industry. The total length of the track is 3,044m and its width varies from around 10-16 meters. Major facilities here include a four-story control tower, a starting arch and spectator stands which can accommodate up to 7,000. Guard rails are installed around the entire raceway to protect spectators.

Royal Tomb of King Kim Su-ro H4

Royal tomb of King Kim Su-ro

King Kim Su-ro was the founder of both the Geumgwan Gaya Kingdom and the Kim clan of Gimhae. His tomb is called Napneung. The tomb is a circular mound, 5m in circumference. The surrounding 59,400㎡ area has been formed into a royal tomb park. Inside the park is Sungseonjeon, which contains ancestral tablets, Anhyanggak Pavilion, Jeonsacheong Hall, Jegigo (a warehouse), the Napneung Front Gate, the Sungjae/Dongjae/Seojae residences, Sindobigak (a monument house), Hongsalmun Gate and Sunghwamun Gate, and stone monuments such as Sindobi.

Earthenware
(Treasure No.637)

Jillye Pottery Village H4

The Jillye Pottery Village, located at Gimhae-si, produces buncheong ware, a popular Korean ceramic.
Most of the ceramics produced here are very similar to those which were used by the people of the Gaya Kingdom. These pieces are all categorized as buncheong ware. The village' s ceramics have a longer tradition than the ones manufactured at other enclaves of ceramic making.
Every October at the Gimhae Pottery Festival, visitors can buy Gaya earthenware reproductions, various kinds of buncheong ware, and modern ceramics. Visitors can also manufacture their own ceramics, build fires in kilns and participate in ceramics classes.

Gimhae National Museum H4

Gimhae National Museum was established in order to better people' s understanding of the Gaya culture. Here artifacts have been collected and displayed to highlight the cultural trends of the Gaya culture in different eras. The exterior of the building is decorated with black bricks which are reminiscent of iron ore and charcoal, in an effort to symbolize Gaya' s image as an iron kingdom.
The museum features artifacts dating back to the prehistoric times relics from Byeonhan, a state preceding Gaya, and artifacts of Geumgwan Gaya (based in Gimhae), a populous region of the former Gaya civilization. The Gaya display shows the accomplishments of Gaya cultre and chagnes it underwent.

Junam Reservoir H3

Junam Reservoir provides a nesting area for all kinds of migratory birds that return there every winter. It is home too hundreds of thousands of various migratory birds, such as mallards, baikal teals, bean geese and common teals, as well as birds which have been designated as natural monuments, including whistling swans, white-naped cranes and Eurasian white spoonbills.
A swamp covering an area of 5.94 million ㎡, has two reservoirs and an island covered with naturally grown reeds making it ideal for the birds. All year round the reservoir contains water and the water' s surface does not freeze over so migratory birds are able to find abundant food there.

Junam Reservoir

Upo Swamp

Upo Swamp F2

Upo Swamp was formed around 140 million years ago. Unique creatures of all kinds live in the swamp, which is the largest natural swamp in Korea.
The swamp covers an area of 2.31 million m² and it consists of four wetlands: Upo, Mokpo, Sajipo and Jjokjibeol.
Upo Swamp is of significance to the natural ecosystem because it offers habitats for a total of 342 kinds of animals and plants. It is home to wetland plants such as euryale ferox, sweet flag calamus and trapa japonica. Resident and migratory birds alike are found at the swamp. In total, there are 62 kinds of birds, and the number of winter migratory birds is steadily increasing in number.
The government designated Upo Swamp as an ecosystem preservation area in 1997 and registered it in the Ramsar Convention (an international convention on wetlands) in 1998.

Dinosaur Footprints at Deongmyeong-ri E6

Deongmyeong-ri, Goryeong-gun became famous for its fossils of extinct animals and plants dating back to the Cretaceous Period of the Mesozoic era.
Footprints of dinosaurs and various other fossils were found here, offering valuable data for the study of dinosaur habitats on the Korean Peninsula.
The stratum along the coast was created during the Cretaceous Period of the Mesozoic era, approximately 100 million years ago. Along the 4-km coastline, more than 1,900 dinosaur footprints have been found and this place is recognized as having

some of the most important dinosaur footprint fossils along with areas in Brazil and Canada.

Galchon Mask Museum F5

The Galchon Mask Museum features all types of masks from every region, masks used in mask dances, picture masks, letter masks and naturally formed masks.

Jeju-do

Jeju-do is an island with beautiful natural settings and a unique traditional culture. It is the premier tourist destination in Korea because of its natural beauty and semitropical climate. Scenic beaches, waterfalls, cliffs and caves throughout the island allow visitors numerous ways to enjoy their leisure time here. Mt. Hallasan, a national park which is comprised of an extinct volcano cone, is especially popular with hikers. There are various hotels and golf courses to further enhance the enjoyment of the island's laid back atmosphere.

Jeju Island has also served as a venue for several historical peace summits.

Hallasan National Park

Baengnokdam

Mt. Hallasan, which rises above the center of Jeju-do, is the highest mountain in South Korea. It has a number of spectacular peaks and slopes. Mt. Hallasan is regarded as one of the most sacred mountains in Korea. The 1,950m high mountain is also home to a rich variety of flora and fauna. It has been designated as Natural Monument No. 182-1, and its vegetation is highly valued in academic study.

Mt. Hallasan has numerous natural tourist attractions, including Baengnokdam Crater at the summit of the mountain, Yeongsilgiam Slope, Wanggwanneung (the mountain's crown rock) and Eorimok Valley.

Baengnokdam Crater

Baengnokdam is a volcanic crater on the summit of Mt. Hallasan. The name Baengnokdam (meaning White Deer Lake) originated from a legend that mountain gods riding on white deer descended to the lake and drank water from it. Deer can be seen grazing on the grassy fields of the Baengnokdam basin.

Yeongsilgiam (the Jagged Slope)

Yeongsilgiam, located 3km southwest of the top of Mt. Hallasan, is a steep and jagged slope. The name Yeongsil (God's Chamber) originated from a legend which has it that mountain gods lived in the area which looks like a stone chamber amid the rocks. The rocky slope is surrounded by a lush primeval forest as well as rare flowers and vegetation.

Wanggwanneung (the Crown Rock)

To the north of Baengnokdam is Tamna Valley, which shows a different face of Mt. Hallasan. The northern part of the crater is surrounded by strange-looking peaks like Jangumok, Wanggwanneung, Samgakbong (Triangular Peak), Keundurewat and Seonnyeobawi (Nymph Rock), which rise out of a forest of Korean firs.

Wanggwanneung, located across from the valley of Samgakbong Peak, is a crown-shaped rock that soars high into the sky. The name is derived from the fact that at twilight, the rocky area becomes tinged with golden hues, resembling that of a golden crown.

Eorimok Valley

The Eorimok Valley overlooks the crater walls of Baengnokdam, the symbol of Mt. Hallasan, and Chetmang Oreum and Eoseungsaengak. Roe deer running across the grasslands and rare plants such as azaleas and evergreens can be seen in the valley.

Trails of Mt. Hallasan

There are several hiking trails at Mt. Hallasan, each trail having its own unique charm.
Major trails include the two most popular courses, Yeongsil Trail, Eorimok Trail, and also Seongpanak Trail, Gwaneumsa Trail, Eoseungsaeng Trail and Donneko Trail.
A number of the trails are sometimes restricted due to a plan to conserve the natural environment of Mt. Hallasan.
Hiking information on each trail is as follows:

Eorimok Trail

The Eorimok Trail is located in the northwestern part of Mt. Hallasan. Under the plan to provide relief to the summit area of Mt. Hallasan, which has been implemented since July 1994, climbing is permitted only up to Utse Oreum Shelter, 1,700m above sea level. It takes about two hours to reach the peak and the distance is 4.7km.

Eoseungsaengak Trail

Eoseungsaengak is a path frequented by visitors who enjoy light hiking. On a clear day, people can enjoy an unobstructed view of Chujado Island, Biyangdo Island and Seongsan Ilchulbong Peak. The distance to the peak is 1.3km and it takes about 30 minutes to hike each way.

Yeongsil Trail

The Yeongsil Trail, located in the southwestern part of Mt. Hallasan, is the shortest trail to the rock formations of Yeongsilgiam. In addition, trees around the trail turn bright colors in the fall. As in the case of the Eorimok Trail, the nature relief plan to protect the summit area restricts climbing above the Utse Oreum Shelter. It takes about one and a half hours to get there and the trail distance is 3.7km.

Seongpanak Trail

The Seongpanak Trail, located in the eastern part of Mt. Hallasan, is a gentle and easy trail. As hiking to the summit area will be restricted until February, 2003, mountaineering is permitted only up to the Jindallaebat Shelter, 1,500m above sea level. During the months of December, January and February, hiking to the summit is permitted, however.
This hike takes about three hours one way and the distance is 7.3km.

Gwaneumsa Trail

Because it winds through a number of valleys with magnificent scenery, the Gwaneumsa Trail is thought to display the essence of Mt. Hallasan. Hiking in the summit area is restricted until February, 2003 and mountaineering is permitted only up to Yongjingak, located 1,500m above sea level. However, during December, January and February, hiking to the summit here is also permitted.
The full trail takes about three and a half hours one way and the distance is 6.7km.

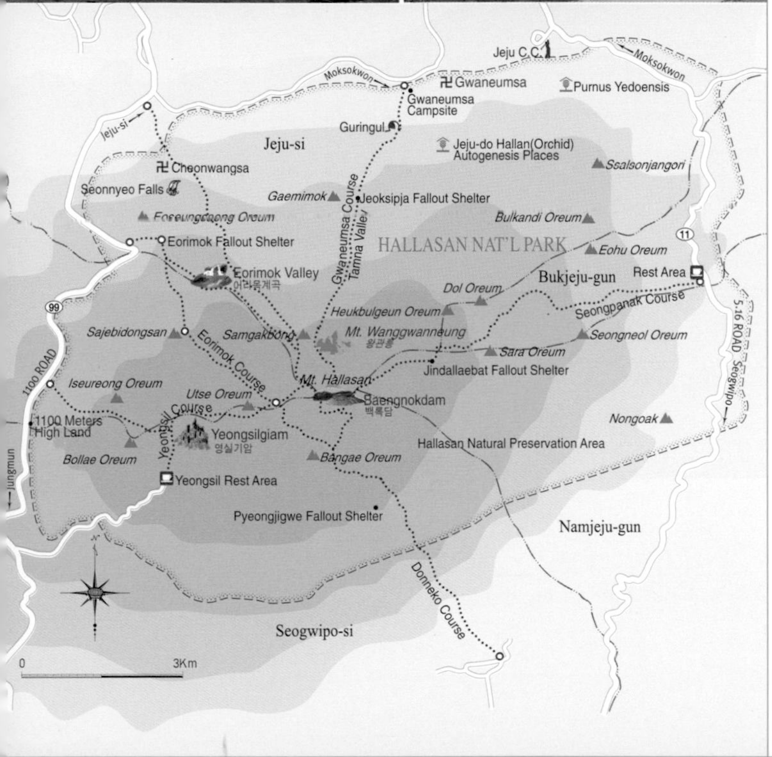

Flora and Fauna of Mt. Hallasan

Mt. Hallasan is widely known as a natural habitat for a wide variety of plants. Approximately 160 species of plants grow in the area and many of them are endemic plants which grow exclusively on the mountain. Prefixes such as 'Halla' and 'Jeju' are attached to the names of these plants and some examples of them include the Halla-Somdari, the Halla-Gaeseungma, the Halla-Jangguchae and the Jeju-Hwanggi. The animals on Mt. Hallasan are mostly subspecies or varieties, slightly different from the original species in other places due to Jeju-do's geographical isolation from the mainland. Moreover, because Mt. Hallasan has different temperature zones, animals of both the frigid and tropical varieties coexist on the mountain.

Mt. Hallasan is inhabited by such mammals as roe deer, Jeju weasels, badgers and Jeju striped field mice. Roe deer, the biggest mammal on Mt. Hallasan, were once on the verge of extinction, but now they can be seen all across the mountain as the result of a stringent protection policy.

Mt. Hallasan is also inhabited by 160 species of birds. The most numerous birds include eagle owls, long-eared owls, short-eared owls, scops owls, collared scops owls, brown hawk owls and Korean wood owls, all of which belong to the strigidae family.

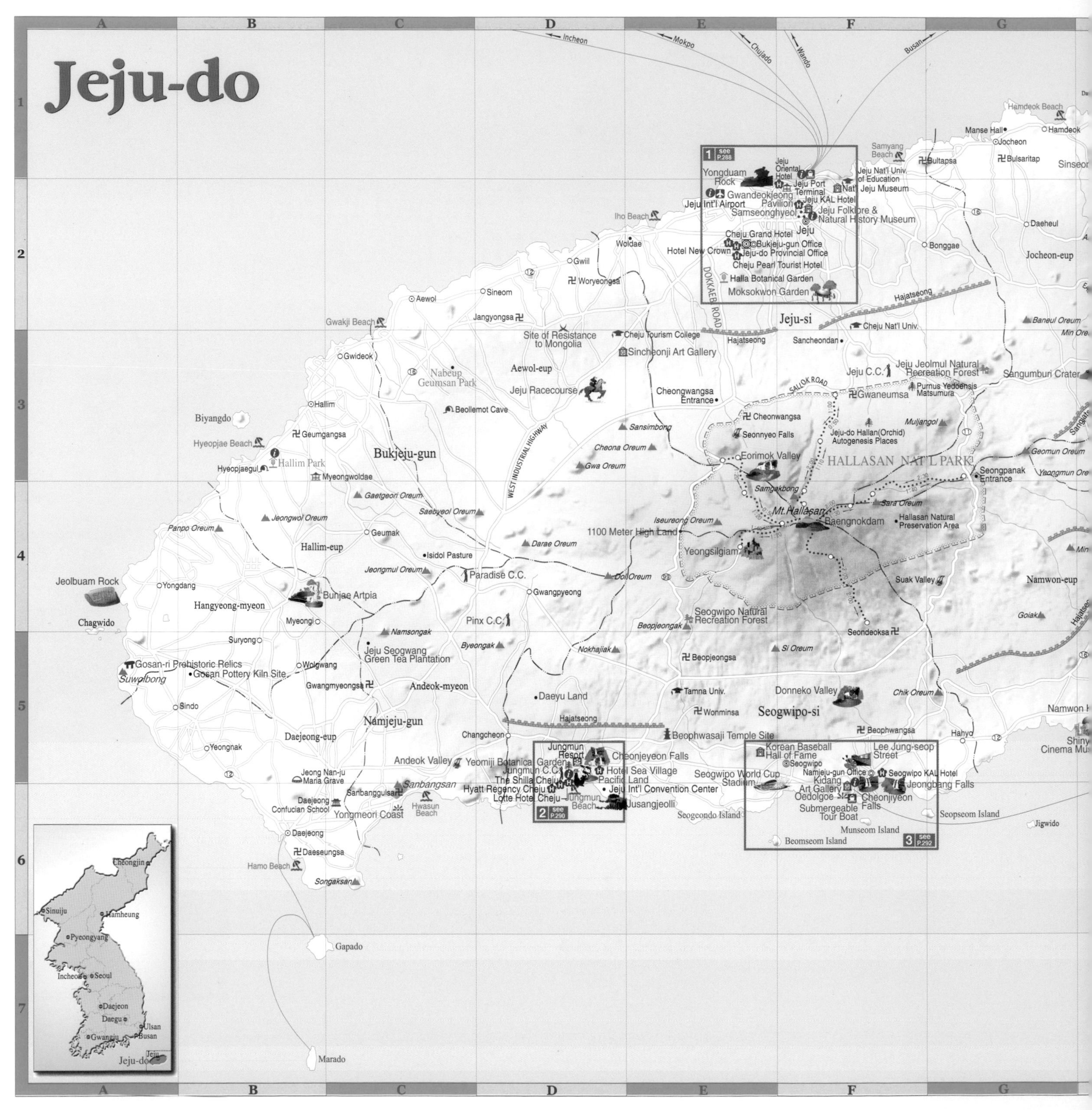

Jeju-do
A
B
C
D
E
F
G
1
2
3
4
5
6
7
Incheon
Mokpo
Chujado
Wando
Busan
Hamdeok Beach
Manse Hall
Hamdeok
Jocheon
Samyang Beach
Bultapsa
Bulsaritap
1 see P.288
Yongduam Rock
Jeju Oriental Hotel
Jeju Port Terminal
Gwandeokjeong Pavilion
Jeju Int'l Airport
Samseonghyeol
Jeju KAL Hotel
Jeju Nat'l Univ. of Education
Nat'l Jeju Museum
Jeju Folklore & Natural History Museum
Jeju
Iho Beach
Daeheul
Woldae
Cheju Grand Hotel
Bukjeju-gun Office
Jeju-do Provincial Office
Hotel New Crown
Cheju Pearl Tourist Hotel
Halla Botanical Garden
Moksokwon Garden
Bonggae
Jocheon-eup
Gwill
Woryeongsa
Sineom
Aewol
DOKKAEBI ROAD
Hajatseong
Jeju-si
Cheju Nat'l Univ.
Baneul Oreum
Min Oreum
Jangyongsa
Gwakji Beach
Site of Resistance to Mongolia
Cheju Tourism College
Sincheonji Art Gallery
Sancheondan
Gwideok
Nabeup Geumsan Park
Aewol-eup
Jeju Racecourse
Jeju C.C.
Jeju Jeolmul Natural Recreation Forest
Sangumburi Crater
Purnus Yedoensis Matsumura
SALLOK ROAD
Cheongwangsa Entrance
Gwaneumsa
Biyangdo
Hallim
Beollemot Cave
Cheonwangsa
Muljangol
Geumgangsa
Sansimbong
Seonnyeo Falls
Jeju-do Hallan(Orchid) Autogenesis Places
Hyeopjae Beach
WEST INDUSTRIAL HIGHWAY
Cheona Oreum
Geomun Oreum
Hyeopjaegul
Hallim Park
Bukjeju-gun
Gwa Oreum
Eorimok Valley
HALLASAN NAT'L PARK
Myeongwoldae
Seongpanak Entrance
Yeongmun Oreum
Gaetgeori Oreum
Samgakbong
Saebyeol Oreum
Sara Oreum
Jeongwol Oreum
Mt.Hallasan
Baengnokdam
Hallasan Natural Preservation Area
Panpo Oreum
Iseureong Oreum
Geumak
1100 Meter High Land
Hallim-eup
Darae Oreum
Yeongsilgiam
Isidol Pasture
Jeongmul Oreum
Paradise C.C.
Jeolbuam Rock
Yongdang
Doll Oreum
Suak Valley
Namwon-eup
Bunjae Artpia
Gwangpyeong
Hangyeong-myeon
Chagwido
Myeongi
Pinx C.C.
Seogwipo Natural Recreation Forest
Goiak
Beopjeongak
Namsongak
Seondeoksa
Suryong
Byeongak
Nokhajiak
Si Oreum
Jeju Seogwang Green Tea Plantation
Gosan-ri Prehistoric Relics
Wolgwang
Beopjeongsa
Suwolbong
Gosan Pottery Kiln Site
Gwangmyeongsa
Andeok-myeon
Tamna Univ.
Donneko Valley
Chik Oreum
Daeyu Land
Sindo
Wonminsa
Seogwipo-si
Namwon
Hajatseong
Namjeju-gun
Beophwangsa
Daejeong-eup
Changcheon
Beophwasaji Temple Site
Hahyo
Shiny Cinema
Yeongnak
Jungmun Resort
Cheonjeyeon Falls
Korean Baseball Hall of Fame
Lee Jung-seop Street
Seogwipo
Andeok Valley
Yeomiji Botanical Garden
Jungmun C.C.
Hotel Sea Village
Jeong Nan-ju Maria Grave
The Shilla Cheju
Pacific Land
Seogwipo World Cup Stadium
Namjeju-gun Office
Seogwipo KAL Hotel
Sanbangsan
Kidang Art Gallery
Jeongbang Falls
Hyatt Regency Cheju
Jeju Int'l Convention Center
Oedolgoe
Cheonjiyeon Falls
Daejeong Confucian School
Sanbanggulsa
Lotte Hotel Cheju
Jungmun Beach
Jusangjeolli
Hwasun Beach
Yongmeori Coast
2 see P.290
Seogeondo Island
Submergeable Tour Boat
Seopseom Island
Jigwido
Daejeong
Munseom Island
Beomseom Island
3 see P.292
Daeseungsa
Hamo Beach
Songaksan
Cheongjin
Sinuiju
Hamheung
Pyeongyang
Gapado
Incheon
Seoul
Daejeon
Daegu
Ulsan
Gwangju
Busan
Jeju
Jeju-do
Marado

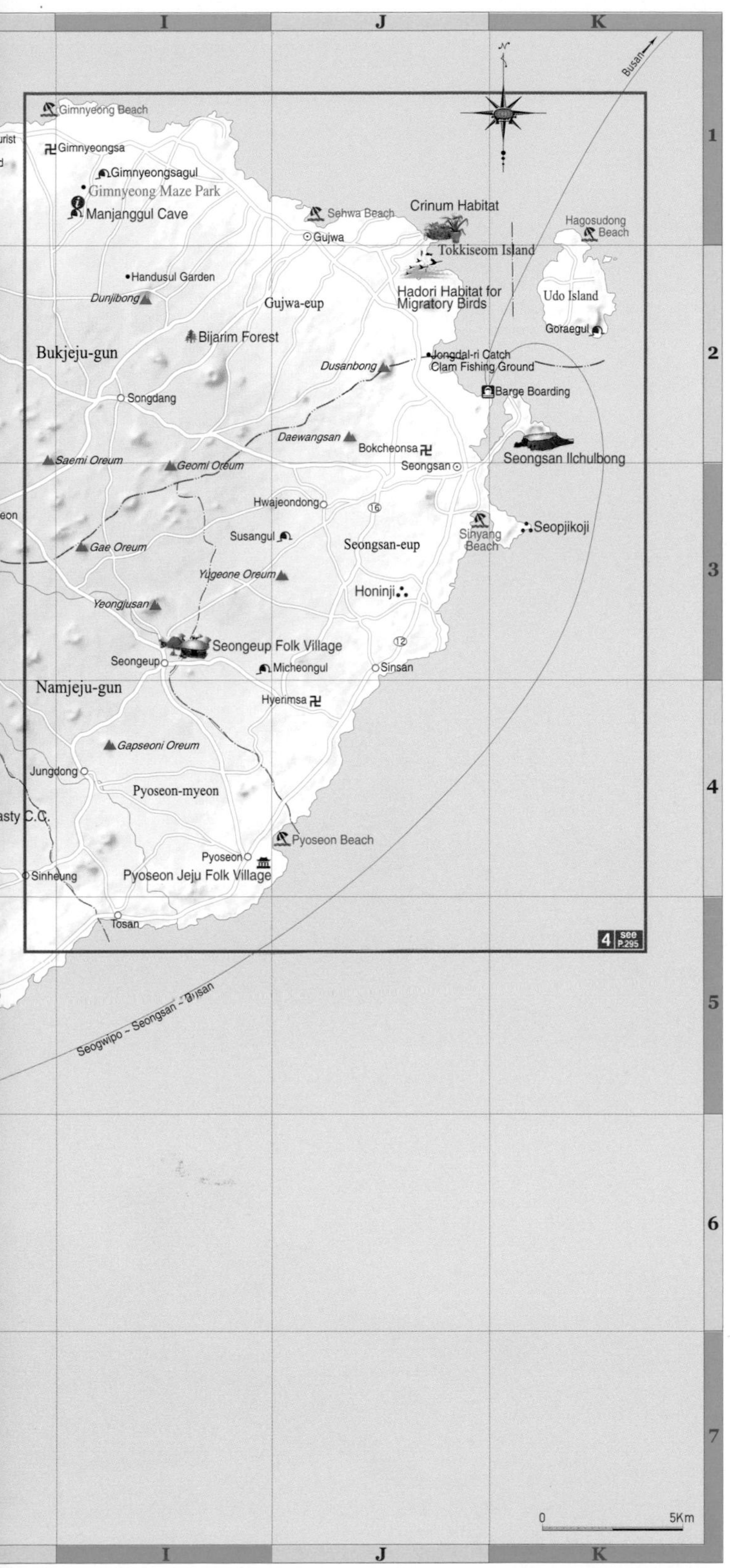

4 See P.295

INDEX

Tourist Information

Jeju-do Dept. of Tourism Promotion 82-64-710-3310
www.jeju.go.kr

LEGEND

- Airport
- Port
- Tourist Information Center
- University or School
- Museum
- Gallery
- Prehistoric Relic Site
- Tomb
- Temple
- Traditional Building
- Traditional Pavilion
- Battlefield
- Cultural Experience Area
- Falls or Valley
- Cave
- Beach
- Golf Course
- Scenic Area
- Amusement Park
- Natural Recreation Forest
- Arboretum
- Botanical Garden
- Mountain
- Stadium
- Other Tourist Attractions
- Hotel
- Reference Point

1

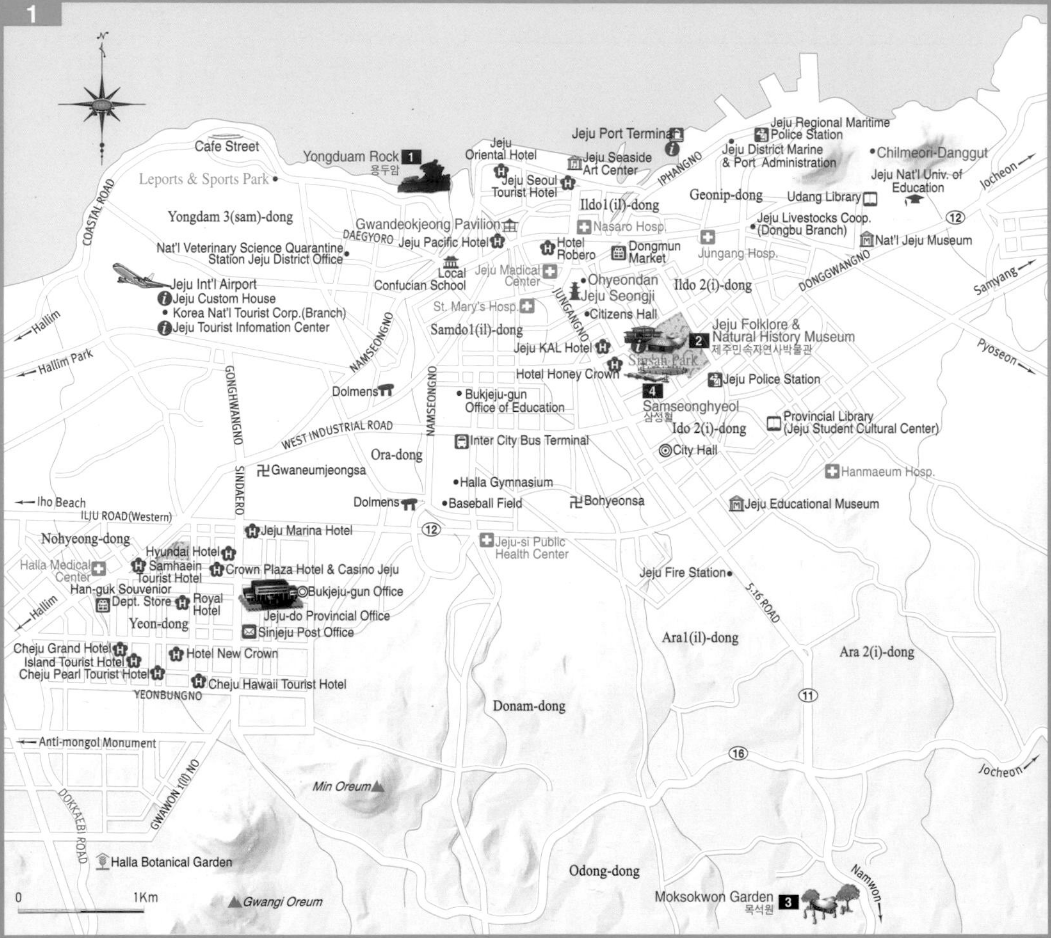

Cafe Street
Leports & Sports Park
Yongduam Rock 1
용두암
Jeju Oriental Hotel
Jeju Seoul Tourist Hotel
Jeju Seaside Art Center
Jeju Port Terminal
Jeju Regional Maritime Police Station
Jeju District Marine & Port Administration
Chilmeori-Danggut
Jeju Nat'l Univ. of Education
IPHANGNO
Ildo1(il)-dong
Geonip-dong
Udang Library
Jeju Livestocks Coop. (Dongbu Branch)
Nat'l Jeju Museum
COASTAL ROAD
Yongdam 3(sam)-dong
Gwandeokjeong Pavilion
DAEGYORO
Jeju Pacific Hotel
Nasaro Hosp.
Jungang Hosp.
Hotel Robero
Dongmun Market
Nat'l Veterinary Science Quarantine Station Jeju District Office
Local Confucian School
Jeju Medical Center
Ohyeondan
Jeju Seongji
Citizens Hall
Ildo 2(i)-dong
DONGGWANGNO
Jeju Int'l Airport
Jeju Custom House
Korea Nat'l Tourist Corp.(Branch)
Jeju Tourist Infomation Center
St. Mary's Hosp.
Samdo1(il)-dong
JUNGANGNO
Jeju Folklore & Natural History Museum 2
제주민속자연사박물관
Jeju KAL Hotel
Sinsan Park
Hotel Honey Crown
Jeju Police Station
Hallim
Hallim Park
NAMSEONGNO
GONGHWANGNO
Dolmens
Bukjeju-gun Office of Education
Samseonghyeol 4
삼성혈
Ido 2(i)-dong
Provincial Library (Jeju Student Cultural Center)
WEST INDUSTRIAL ROAD
Inter City Bus Terminal
Ora-dong
City Hall
Gwaneumjeongsa
Halla Gymnasium
Hanmaeum Hosp.
Iho Beach
IlJU ROAD(Western)
SINDAERO
Dolmens
Baseball Field
Bohyeonsa
Jeju Educational Museum
Nohyeong-dong
Jeju Marina Hotel
Hyundai Hotel
Halla Medical Center
Samhaein Tourist Hotel
Crown Plaza Hotel & Casino Jeju
Jeju-si Public Health Center
Han-guk Souvenior Dept. Store
Royal Hotel
Bukjeju-gun Office
Jeju Fire Station
5·16 ROAD
Yeon-dong
Jeju-do Provincial Office
Sinjeju Post Office
Ara1(il)-dong
Ara 2(i)-dong
Cheju Grand Hotel
Island Tourist Hotel
Cheju Pearl Tourist Hotel
Hotel New Crown
Cheju Hawaii Tourist Hotel
YEONBUNGNO
Donam-dong
Anti-mongol Monument
GWAWON 1(il) NO
DOKKAEBI ROAD
Min Oreum
Halla Botanical Garden
Gwangi Oreum
Odong-dong
Moksokwon Garden 3
목석원
Jocheon
Samyang
Pyoseon
Namwon
0 1Km

Jeju-si is the hub of tourism around Jeju-do. It houses the Jeju Airport, ferry terminals and a bus terminal with routes to every part of Jeju-do.
The city is divided into the traditional old district and the newly-developed district. Various natural resources and cultural properties are scattered across the city.
Major tourist attractions include the Samseonghyeol Hole, Gwanateo (the site of ancient government buildings), the Jeju Folklore and Natural History Museum, Yongduam Rock and Moksokwon Garden.

Yongduam Rock 1

Yongduam (Dragon Head Rock) is located on the northern coast of Jeju-si and is 10m-high. The name was given because the rock has been eroded over time to resemble the head of a dragon. The site is adjacent to the downtown area of Jeju-si and is popular with tourists.
Legend has it that once a dragon stole a jade bead from the mountain god of Mt. Hallasan. The mountain spirit was so enraged that he shot the dragon with an arrow. The dragon's body was submerged under the water, but his head reared up towards the sky and was turned to stone.

Jeju Folklore and Natural History Museum 2

This museum can be regarded as Jeju-do in miniature as it displays a collection of the island's plant and animal life, as well as folklore relics. The Natural History Exhibition Hall features geographical and petrological artifacts, marine organisms, plants, insects, birds and mammals that are native to Jeju-do. The Folklore Exhibition Hall displays the lifestyle of the Jeju people and has three exhibition rooms dedicated to showing visitors the housing, clothing and livelihoods unique to this area.

Moksokwon Garden 3

Jeju-do, with its abundant stones, has numerous stone-related tales which have been handed down from ancient times. Moksokwon is a park where these tales are visualized through the use of stones and tree roots.
Around 1,000 roots of trees and about 500 human-shaped stones are displayed among the natural items in this garden.
The most famous exhibit at Moksokwon is 'The Life of Gapdori,' in which a series of stone tableaux are said to represent the youth, mid-life and old age of Gapdori and Gapsuni, characters from an ancient tale.

Samseonghyeol

Samseonghyeol Hole 4

Samseonghyeol Hole is a site from where three progenitors named Go-eulla, Yang-eulla and Bu-eulla, all of whom founded Tamna, an old name of Jeju-do, are believed to have emerged. Moisture from rain and snow do not penetrate the hole and the surrounding trees face the hole at an angle, as if they were bowing to the three founders.
In Samseonghyeol, 500-year-old pine trees, camphor trees, crape-myrtles, an evergreen arbor create a lush wooded area in the downtown section of the city.
The site is designated as Historical Site No. 134.

Jeju Country Club

Jeju Country Club, located in Jeju-si, overlooks majestic Mt. Hallasan and Jeju-si. It is a popular course and its 18 holes are surrounded by a beautiful natural landscape.

Jungmun Tourist Complex is a large-scale comprehensive tourist resort located along the coast of Jungmun-dong, at the west end of Seogwipo-si. This complex provides accommodation facilities for more than 5,000 guests, and includes golf courses, beaches, a marine park, a botanical garden, shopping centers and recreational facilities.

Jungmun Country Club 5

Jungmun Country Club is an 18-hole golf course located within the Jungmun Tourist Complex. It is the nation's only golf course which is situated on a coastline. Deluxe hotels are located in its vicinity and it is frequented by foreigners.

This golf course is the nation's longest at 6,820m. It has 88 bunkers and four water hazards and is open for play all year around. Golfers are often fooled by an optical illusion on the No. 8 hole, where they confuse the height of the putting green and fairway.

Yeomiji Botanical Garden 6

Yeomiji Botanical Garden contains 2,000 varieties of plants. More than 1,700 species of trees and flowering plants are also planted outside of the botanical garden. Traditional Korean gardens, as well as those of Japanese, Italian and French design, are displayed in the area.

A tourist train with 60 seats runs between the botanical garden and the gardens of different countries. A 38m high observation tower at the center of the greenhouse allows people to see as far as Marado Island, Korea's southernmost island, on clear days.

Pacific Land 7

Pacific Land, which is situated inside the Jungmun Tourist Complex, is a world-class marine park and family leisure center that can be enjoyed by all family members. Performances involving dolphins, sea lions and penguins are offered at the park.

The Dolphin Performance Hall consists of a large pool and seating for up to 2,000 spectators, a mini-aquarium where tropical fish are displayed, and several restaurants.

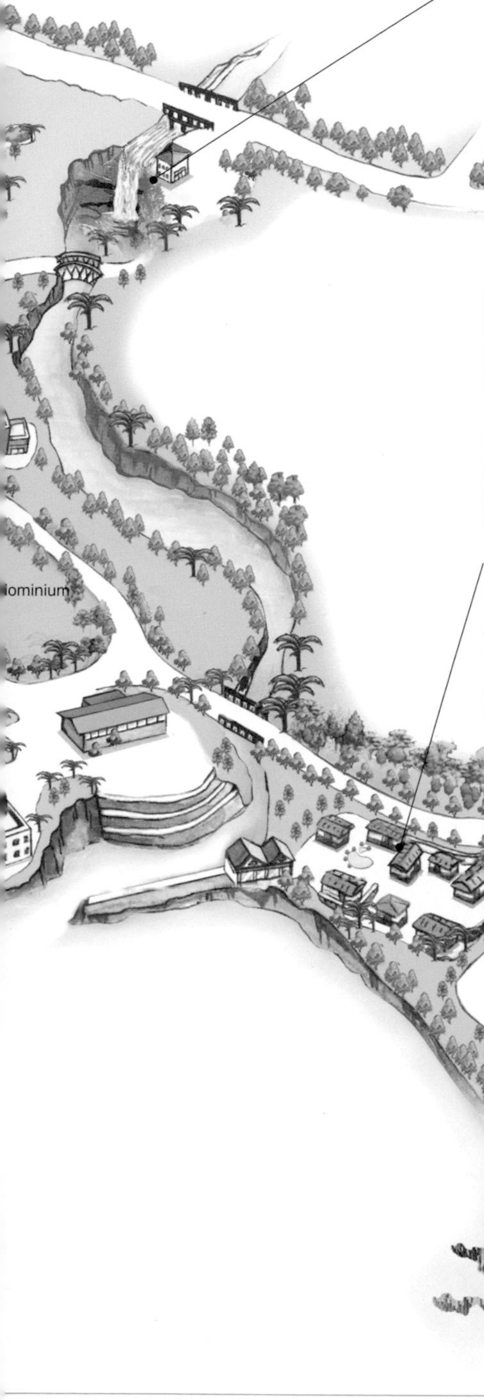

Cheonjeyeon Falls 8

This spectacular three-layered fall cascading from the high cliffs is surrounded by sub-tropical vegetation. The first fall cascades from a 22m high cliff into a 21m deep pond. The water continues over two more falls until it reaches the sea. In the valley of Cheonjeyeon, there is an arched bridge named 'Seonimgyo,' on which the graceful seven nymphs are carved, and a pavilion called 'Cheonjeru' is located across the bridge. The falls are surrounded by natural sub-tropical vegetation and are designated as one of the protected areas in Jeju-do.

Sea Village 9

The Sea Village, which has traditional thatched houses commonly seen in Jeju, is actually a villa-style lodge. With its thatched roof, stone walls, wooden fence, palm trees and various types of vegetation in the garden, the area is very peaceful and quaint.

Unlike its traditional outer appearance, the interior of the building is decorated in a modern style. The building overlooks Korea's southernmost island, Marado.

ominium

Jeju Convention Center

Jusangjeolli 10

Jusangjeolli, located along the eastern coast of Jungmun Tourist Complex, is one of Seogwipo's unique natural resources. A series of hexagonal stone columns, which formed through the earth's crustal movements, rise high above the 1.4km coastline. The waves below the cliffs surge as high as 10m.

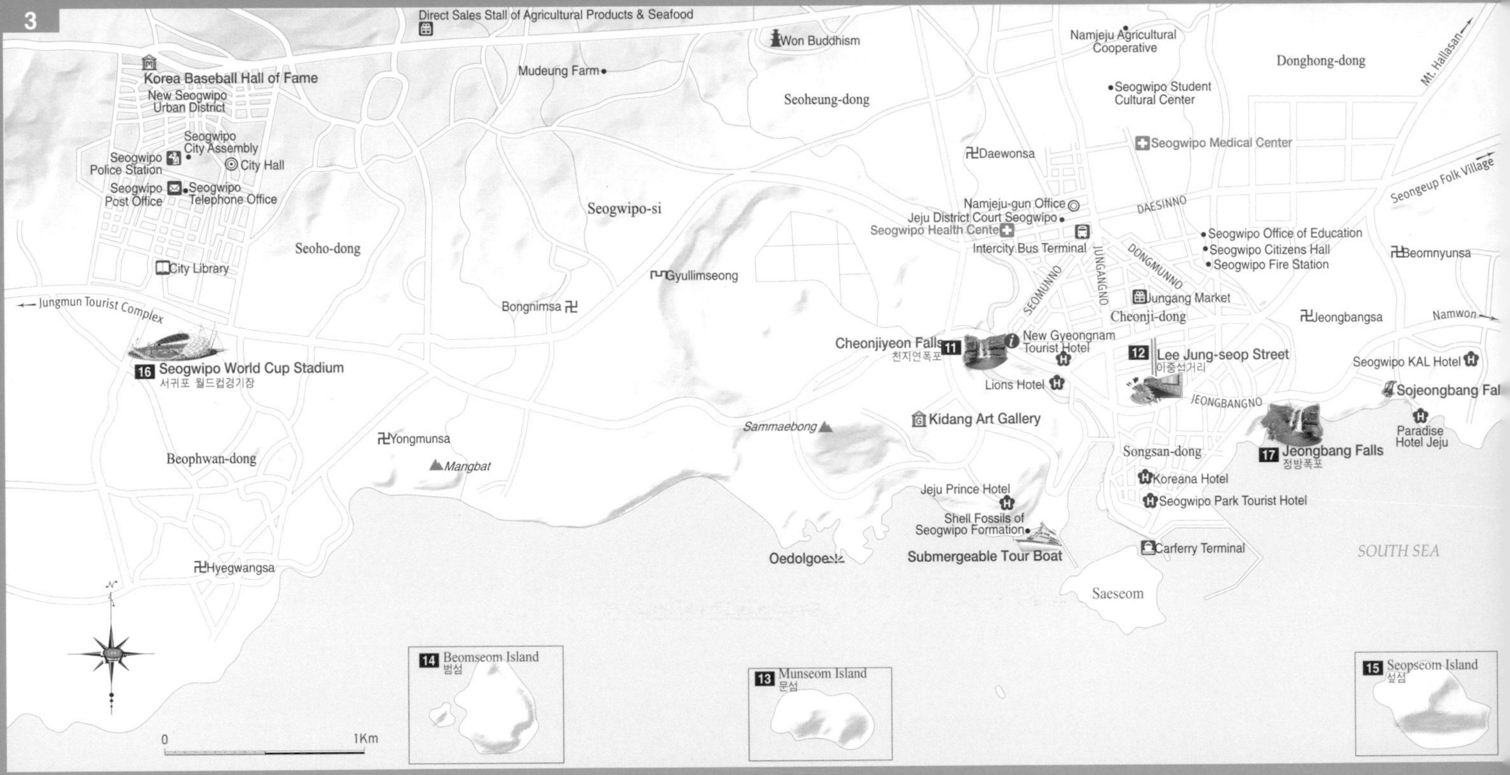

3

Direct Sales Stall of Agricultural Products & Seafood
Won Buddhism
Namjeju Agricultural Cooperative
Donghong-dong
Mt. Hallasan
Korea Baseball Hall of Fame
Mudeung Farm
Seoheung-dong
Seogwipo Student Cultural Center
New Seogwipo Urban District
Seogwipo City Assembly
Seogwipo Police Station
City Hall
Daewonsa
Seogwipo Medical Center
Seogwipo Post Office
Seogwipo Telephone Office
Seogwipo-si
Namjeju-gun Office
Jeju District Court Seogwipo
Seogwipo Health Center
DAESINNO
Seongeup Folk Village
Intercity Bus Terminal
Seogwipo Office of Education
Seogwipo Citizens Hall
Seogwipo Fire Station
Beomnyunsa
Seoho-dong
City Library
Gyullimseong
SEOMUNNO
JUNGANGNO
DONGMUNNO
Jungang Market
Jungmun Tourist Complex
Bongnimsa
Cheonji-dong
Jeongbangsa
Namwon
Cheonjiyeon Falls 11 천지연폭포
New Gyeongnam Tourist Hotel
12 Lee Jung-seop Street 이중섭거리
Seogwipo KAL Hotel
16 Seogwipo World Cup Stadium 서귀포 월드컵경기장
Lions Hotel
Sojeongbang Fal
JEONGBANGNO
Sammaebong
Kidang Art Gallery
Paradise Hotel Jeju
Yongmunsa
Songsan-dong
17 Jeongbang Falls 정방폭포
Beophwan-dong
Mangbat
Koreana Hotel
Jeju Prince Hotel
Seogwipo Park Tourist Hotel
Shell Fossils of Seogwipo Formation
Carferry Terminal
SOUTH SEA
Hyegwangsa
Oedolgoe
Submergeable Tour Boat
Saeseom
14 Beomseom Island 범섬
13 Munseom Island 문섬
15 Seopseom Island 섶섬
0 1Km

Seogwipo, located to the south of Mt. Hallasan, is a city situated in the center of Jeju' s southern area.
The city's most popular folk custom is 'Geolgung,' a kind of traditional Korean farmers' folk music ceremony in which people visit every house of the village and perform a 'Gut,' a shamanistic ritual aimed at exorcising evil spirits and bringing good luck. This ceremony occurs in the month of January according to the lunar calendar.
Major tourist attractions in Sogwipo-si include Cheonjiyeon Falls, Donneko Valley, Beomseom Island and Munseom Island. Jungmun Tourist Complex, is located in the vicinity.
The area around the city leads the nation in the production of mandarin oranges, accounting for more than 60% of the mandarin orange harvest on Jeju-do.

Cheonjiyeon Falls 11

Cheonjiyeon Falls

The falls cascading from the cliffs are a popular attraction. Additionally, the neighboring valley is considered one of the most scenic valleys in Jeju-do. The valley is full of verdant sub-tropical vegetation, such as various evergreens and ferns.
The water from the falls passes through a pond surrounded by tropical plants and on into the sea. The path linking Seogwipohang Port to Cheonjiyeon Falls provides a romantic setting, as gardenia flowers, large cherry trees, royal azaleas and reeds along the path create an intoxicating atmosphere.

Lee Jung-seop Street 12

Lee Jung-seop was an ill-fated painter of profound genius who made great contributions to the development of Korean art. Lee Jung-seop Street is the area where Lee and his family fled and stayed during the Korean War. In a tiny room shared by four family members, he painted such immortal

'White Ox' by Lee Jung-seop

masterpieces as 'Fantasy of Seogwipo,' 'A Crab and a Child' and 'Fish.'
The street houses the thatched house where Lee resided and worked during his lifetime and a gallery where visitors can view his paintings.
The municipal authorities of Seogwipo-si have restored Lee's house and designated the area near the house as 'Lee Jung-seop Street.' Every October, the month of his death, the 'Lee Jung-seop Art Festival' is held on the street in commemoration of his artistic spirit.

Munseom Island 13

Legend has it that once upon a time, a hunter on Mt. Hallasan brushed the belly of the Emperor of Heaven with his bow by mistake. The angry Emperor snatched off the peak of Mt. Hallasan and hurled it so forcefully that its scattered pieces became the islets of Munseom and Beomseom in the waters off Seogwipo. There is abundant marine life around the island, such as red sea bream, parrot fish, black sea bream and grunts, making Munseom a good place for fishing.

Fishing in the Sea

Beomseom Island 14

Beomseom (Tiger Island), located 30 minutes from Seogwipo by boat, got its name because its shape resembles a crouching tiger. The island is made of latite rock, on which vertical jusangjeolli (a series of rocky columns) have developed. Caves formed by sea water erosion can be found all over the island. Spring water wells up in the flat southern areas and in the northern areas, and Pittosporum tobira trees, chestnut trees and sea pine trees form a verdant evergreen forest. Ten rare species of trees, including Bakdalmokseo, a subtropical plant, grow indigenously on the island.

Seopseom Island 15

Seopseom, located 3km southwest of Seogwipo-si, is an uninhabited island where 180 species of rare plants can be found. 'Pachoiryeop' (a type of bracken plant, Asplenium anti uum Makino), is found only on this island. The waters surrounding the island are abundant in various types of sea life, such as parrot fish, red and black sea bream, dageumbari (nippon spinosis), bleekers and baengeodom.

Seogwipo World Cup Stadium 16

The facilities of Seogwipo World Cup Stadium were constructed using the shape of the Baengnokdam (Crater) as the model. There has been much praise for the design, with the chief of the FIFA 2002 World Cup Organizing Committee once remarking that Seogwipo Stadium would be the most beautiful soccer stadium in the world when completed.

www.2002seogwipo.com

Jeongbang Falls 17

Jeongbang Falls are the only falls in Korea which fall directly into the sea. The 23m-high falls cascade from black cliffs with a thunderous roar. When the falling water is reflected by sunlight, its refracted colors create a shimmering rainbow.

The cliffs of Jeongbang Falls have a legend related to the origin of the name of Seogwipo. Once upon a time, a man named Seobul travelled around the world in search of the elixir of life under orders from the Chinese Emperor Jinsi. He visited the falls area but failed to find the secret fountain of youth. He was so touched by the beauty of the falls, however, that he engraved the Chinese characters '徐佛過此' on the cliff to signify that he had passed through the site. The name Seogwi (meaning 'west' and 'return') was given to the area, as Seobul returned to the west.

4

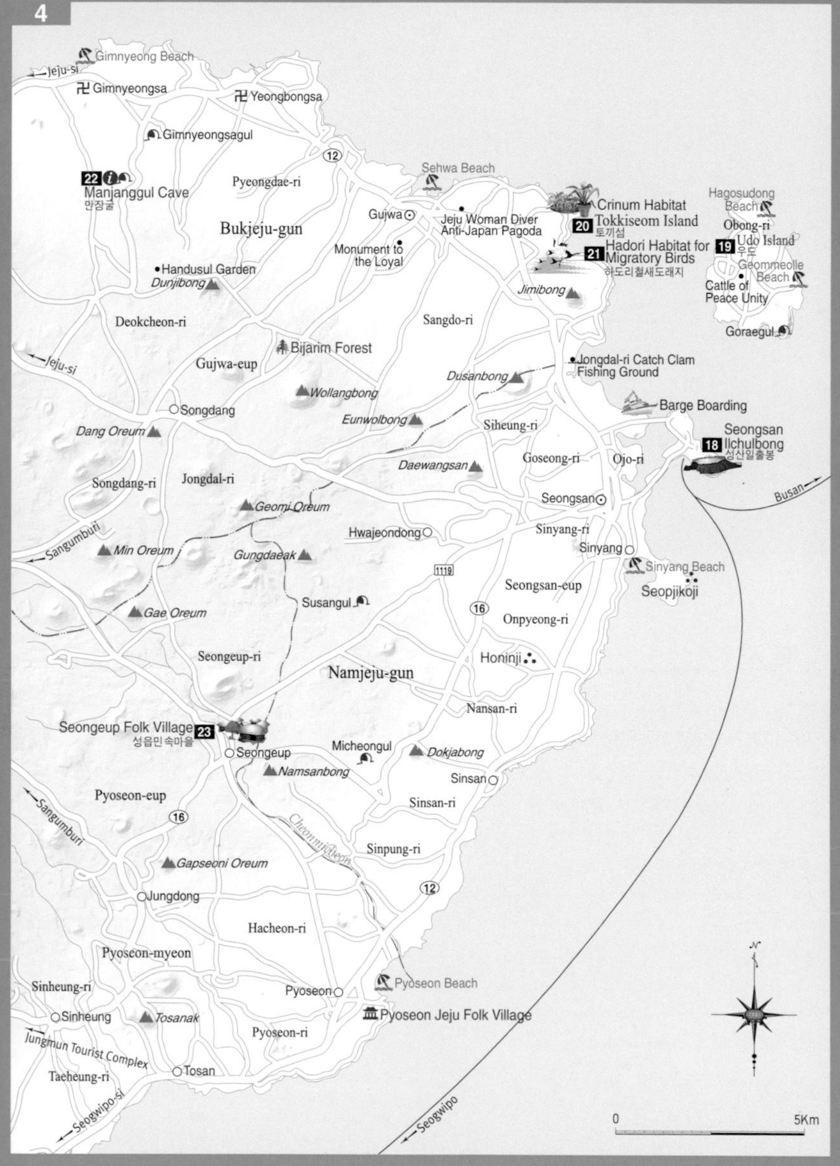

The eastern area of Jeju-do contains two folk villages, Seongsan Ilchulbong (Sunrise Peak), one of the most popular places to visit on Jeju-do, and Manjanggul, the world' s longest lava cave. In addition, Tokkiseom Island, which is the only native habitat for Crinum, an evergreen perennial plant, and Sangumburi, a volcanic crater, share this area with numerous local beaches.

Seongsan Ilchulbong 18

Seongsan Ilchulbong, Sunrise Peak

Seongsan Peninsula, whose three sides are surrounded by the sea, is 48km east from Jeju-si. The peninsula contains the 182m peak, Seongsan Ilchulbong, which offers the most spectacular view of the sunrise in Jeju-do.

The peak was formed even before the island of Jeju-do was created. Its southeastern and northern outer walls are craggy cliffs which have been eroded by sea water. Only the northwestern side of the peak has a grassy ridge line, and this leads to Seongsan Village. Visitors can reach the peak' s summit by hiking along a well-prepared path.

Udo Island 19

Udo Coral Beach

Udo (Cow Island) was named because its shape looks like a cow lying down. It is a 15 minute ride from Seongsanhang Port by boat. Surrounded by scenic landscapes, the island harbors eight beautiful vistas, and is most known for its soft, bright white sand.

Gwangdaekoji is a cave in the southern part of Udo. When the sun shines through the cave entrance, it is reflected on the ceiling, and the image looks like a rising moon. The cave is ranked first among the eight beautiful sites of Udo.

The white lighthouse on the top of Udobong Peak is also a popular site.

Crinum, a Native Flower in Tokkiseom

Hadori Habitat for Migratory Birds

Tokkiseom Island 20

Tokkiseom is a small island 50m off shore from Guldongpogu, Hado-ri. In the summer, white flowers of Crinum, a type of narcissus, cover the entire island, making it resemble a rabbit with white fur. That is how the name of Tokkiseom originated.

The island has a sandy beach and a whinstone hill. When the tide ebbs, people can reach the island from the mainland by foot.

When the tide rises, the sandy beach and the hill are divided, and the island is separated from the land again.

Tokkiseom is the only place in the world where the Crinum asiaticum grows. This plant is a perennial evergreen which belongs to the narcissus family. It grows up to 60-70cm. New leaves sprout from its branches in the spring and its white flowers bloom continuously from late July.

Hadori Habitat for Migratory Birds 21

Located at the foot of Jimibong Peak, Hado-ri, Gujwa-eup is a vast area of reed beds which migratory birds inhabit between the months of September and December. These birds include such rare species as white storks and black-faced spoonbills, as well as white herons and wild ducks.

The habitat is a destination for many migratory birds because of its abundant food sources.

Migratory birds, such as European wigeons, spotbill ducks, pintails, gadwalls, green-winged teals, white herons and mallards, visit the habitat en masse. Moreover, migratory birds which are designated as natural monuments, such as white storks, spoonbills, black-faced spoonbills and ospreys, as well as rare birds like black-winged stilts and avocets, can also be seen at the habitat. This attracts much attention from algologists and other nature lovers.

Haenyeo (Women Divers)

Haenyeo at work

Haenyeo refers to the women who dive to gather seafood from the ocean floor. The number of Haenyeo plunged following Korean industrialization and urbanization. Still, some middle-aged women divers continue to do this work. These women dive without using any diving equipment, staying under water for up to two minutes at a time. They mainly collect turbines, abalones, ascidians and sea cucumbers. Travellers can purchase fresh seafood collected by the divers at major tourist attractions or atroadside stalls.

Seongeup Folk Village

Manjagngul, the Longest Lava-Tube System in the World

Manjanggul Cave 22

Manjanggul is a 13,422m lava-tube, which is the longest known lava-tube system in the world.
Annual temperatures inside the tube range from 11℃ to 21℃, making it cool throughout the year.
Manjanggul is home to rare flora and fauna, so it serves as a valuable research site. Inside the cave, there are lava stalactites that hang from the ceiling, lava stalagmites that rise from the ground, and lava pillars which touch both the ceiling and ground and were created by the meeting of a stalactite and a stalagmite.

Seongeup Folk Village 23

The Seongeup Folk Village, located 8km north from Pyeoseon-ri, is situated at the foot of Mt. Hallasan. Between 1410 and 1914, Jeju-do was divided into three hyeon (prefectures), and this town was the capital of the Jeongui-hyeon. The village still preserves houses which were typical of the commoners in Jeju-do.
It has been designated as a national folk village because a number of tangible and intangible cultural assets are preserved in the village. Tangible cultural assets located here include old houses, Confucian schools, old government buildings, dolhareubang, millstones, fortress sites, and tombstones. Intangible cultural assets include the folk songs which circulated in the mountainous area, folk games, local native foods, folk craft skills, and the distinctive Jeju dialect.

Water Pot which Commoners Used in the Past

Pyoseon Jeju Folk Village (right)
Bunjae Artpia (below)

Bunjae Artpia B4

Bunjae Artpia, which is the first bunjae park in Korea, displays a hundred different types of rare trees, which range in age from 30 years to 250 years old. It has a number of stone walls unique to Jeju, ponds, stone bridges, palm trees and an artificial waterfall.

Sangumburi Crater H3

Sangumburi, located 26km southeast from Jeju-si, is a crater that measures 650m in diameter, 100m in depth and 2,070m in circumference. The cratert is a reasure trove of plants and is home to over 420 species of plants, including subtropical, temperate and alpine species.
Sangumburi Crater has been designated as Natural Monument No. 263. Besides its large variety of plants, the area offers numerous other things to see. The sea of culalia flowers in autumn and farms on the grasslands in the vicinity create a romantic setting.

Sangumburi Crater

Pyoseon Jeju Folk Village I4

Jeju Folk Village vividly recreates the unique lifestyle and traditional culture of Jeju-do during the 19th century. On the 462,000㎡ site is a recreated mountain village and a fishing village. There is also a botanical garden, a market place, an exhibition hall (displaying fishing tools), an outdoor exhibition area, a place for shamanistic rites, old historical government buildings and the House of Intangible Cultural Assets.
Traditional cultural performances which originated in Jeju-do, such as Jeju folk songs, Haenyeo dances, mask dances, and ogomu, a traditional dance, are performed twice a day at the Folk Performance Hall. In addition, certified craftsmen demonstrate their time-honored techniques while crafting such items as wood, bamboo and textiles. Through video and audio materials, Jeju' s cultural assets can be experienced at the House of Intangible Cultural Assets. Prominent cultural assets include local legends, folk songs and Jeju' s provincial dialect.

Subtropical Botanical Garden in Hallim Park (left)
Jeju Sculpture Park (above)

Hallim Park B3

Hallim Park is a theme park which is surrounded by a host of palm trees and a forest of pine trees.
The park houses the Subtropical Botanical Garden, which has 2,000 species of rare sub-tropical plants that are native to Jeju, and also Bunjaewon, which contains hundreds of bunjae works, as well as a folk village in which traditional Korean thatched houses have been recreated.
The most eye-catching sites in Hallim Park are Hyeopjaegul Cave and Ssangyonggul. They are caves which were transformed by lava into golden stalactite caves. They make up two of the world' s three most mysterious caves, and draw keen attention from the speleology community.

Mt. Sanbangsan

Mt. Sanbangsan C6

Unlike other mountains in Jeju-do, Mt. Sanbangsan doesn' t have a crater. Half way up the mountain is Sanbanggulsa, a temple built during the Goryeo Dynasty. This temple provides a panoramic view of Hyeongjeseom (Brother Island), Gapado Island, Marado Island and the Yongmeori Coast.
The rock-wall vegetation area in Mt. Sanbangsan was designated as Natural Monument No. 376 in February, 1986.

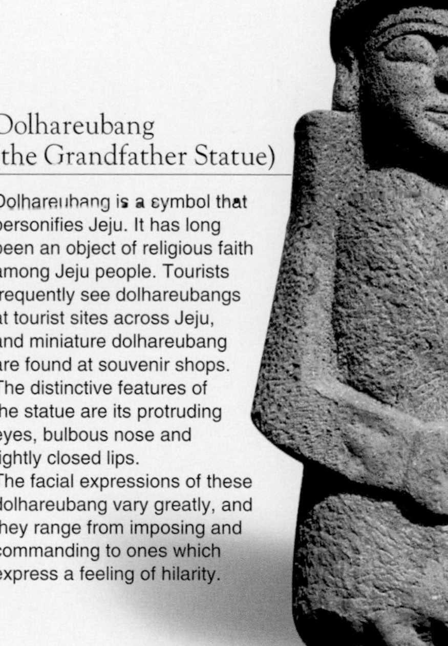

Dolhareubang (the Grandfather Statue)

Dolhareubang is a symbol that personifies Jeju. It has long been an object of religious faith among Jeju people. Tourists frequently see dolhareubangs at tourist sites across Jeju, and miniature dolhareubang are found at souvenir shops. The distinctive features of the statue are its protruding eyes, bulbous nose and tightly closed lips.
The facial expressions of these dolhareubang vary greatly, and they range from imposing and commanding to ones which express a feeling of hilarity.

Marado Island B7

Marado, Korea's southernmost island, is about a 50 minute ride by boat from Moseulpohang Port. Its cliffs and rock formations form a magnificent view. The total length of Marado's coastline is 4.2km. The total time needed to tour the island on foot is around 1 hour. This island has a lighthouse which is indicated on international mariner charts. The Marado Lighthouse and and Marabungyo are sites which many visitors find worth visiting.

Marado Island

Donneko Valley F5

Donneko is one of the area' s most popular summer resort destinations. Crystal-clear water originating from Mt. Hallasan flows through here and sub-tropical evergreens cover both sides of the valley. Donneko Resort is widely known as a place where Jeju residents come to indulge in water recreation. A waterfall in the valley adds more beauty to the already scenic site. In Donneko, where Mt. Hallasan can be most vividly seen, there are various facilities, such as a youth camp and camping areas, making it popular with backpackers. Tent rental is also available.

Marado Lighthouse

Rape Flower Blossom Festival

When spring comes in Jeju-do, yellow rape flowers blossom in the fields all around the island. The Rape Flower Blossom Festival is held every year between the middle of April and the beginning of May. Celebrity performances, talent shows, food festivals, photo contests and various other events are held during this time.

Donneko Valley

Attractions by Theme

Korean Food

A diverse array of foods and dishes can be found throughout Korea.
Korea was once primarily an agricultural nation, and Koreans have cultivated rice as their staple food since ancient times. These days Korean cuisine is characterized by a wide variety of meat and fish dishes along with wild greens and vegetables. Various fermented and preserved foods, such as kimchi (fermented spicy cabbage), jeotgal (matured seafood with salt) and doenjang (fermented soy bean paste) are notable for their specific flavor and high nutritional value.
The prominent feature of a Korean table setting is that all dishes are served at the same time. Traditionally, the number of side dishes varied from 3 for the lower classes to 12 for royal family members.
Table arrangements can vary depending on whether a noodle dish or meat is served. Formal rules have developed for table setting, demonstrating the attention people pay to food and dining.
Compared to neighboring China and Japan, a spoon is used more often in Korea, especially when soups are served.

Kinds of Traditional Korean Food

1 Bap (steamed rice) and Juk (porridge)

Boiled rice is the staple of Korean cuisine. Most people use a white sticky rice, which sometimes has beans, chestnuts, sorghum, red beans, barley or other cereals added for flavor and nutrition.
Juk is thought of as a highly nutritious light food. Many varieties of juk exist, for example, juk made of rice, red beans, pumpkin, abalone, ginseng, pine nuts, vegetables, chicken, mushrooms and bean sprouts.

2 Guk (soup)

Soup is an essential dish when rice is served. Ingredients of different soups include vegetables, meat, fish, shellfish, seaweed, and beef bones.

3 Jjigae (stew)

Jjigae is a similar to guk but is thicker and hardier. The most famous jjigae is made from fermented soy bean paste. Jjigae is usually spicy and served piping hot in a heated stone bowl.

4 Dubu Jeongol (casserole)

Jeongol is often eaten in the evening. It is cooked in a steaming pot and contains noodles, mushrooms, small octopuses, cow intestines, vegetables, and other ingredients. The dubu (tofu) is sliced, coated with starch and pan-fried. Seasoned ground beef is then stuffed inside the dubu and it is tied with watercress. In a casserole pan, vegetables and dubu are arranged and boiled with soy sauce flavored broth.

5 Jjim and Jorim (simmered meat or fish)

Jjim and jorim are similar dishes which are prepared with vegetables and soaked in soy bean sauce, then slowly boiled together over a low flame.

6 Namul (vegetables or wild greens)

Namul is made from slightly boiled or fried vegetables and wild greens mixed with salt, soy sauce, sesame salt, sesame oil, garlic, onions, and other spices.

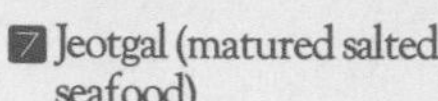

7 Jeotgal (matured salted seafood)

Jeotgal is a very salty food made of naturally fermented fish, shellfish, shrimp, oysters, fish roe, intestines and other ingredients.

8 Gui (broiled/barbecued dishes)

When cooking gui, marinated meats are barbecued over a charcoal fire. The most popular meats of this type are bulgogi and galbi. There are also many fish dishes which are cooked this way.

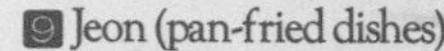

9 Jeon (pan-fried dishes)

Jeon is a kind of pancake made from mushrooms, pumpkin, slices of dried fish, oysters, unripe red peppers, meat or other ingredients which are mixed with salt and black pepper, dipped in flour and egg and fried in oil.

10 Mandu (dumpling)

Mandu is wheat or buck wheat noodles stuffed with beef, mushrooms, stir-fried zucchini, and mungbean sprouts. Pork, chicken, or fish is sometimes used instead of beef.

Royal Cuisine of the Joseon Dynasty

The style of serving royal dishes developed during Korea's history and royal foods such as sinseollo (a fancy hot pot) and gujeolpan (a nine-sectioned dish) were served according to strict rules. Well-trained court ladies prepared them from the agricultural produce and seafood that had been presented to the king from all corners of Korea.

Royal court foods were not much different in taste from those outside the court because the two societies influenced each other.

Sinseollo

Sinseollo is a colorful party dish. Strips of beef, pan-fried liver and tripe, mushrooms, carrots, and sliced sheets of egg yolks and whites fried separately, are placed in layers in a spoke fashion. They are garnished with meatballs, walnuts and ginkgo nuts and boiled in meat broth.

Gujeolpan

This nine-sectioned dish is served with wine. Eight different foods are arranged in a circle, with crepes in the middle. The eight foods include carrots, cucumbers, watercress, mushrooms, egg yolks and whites, beef, and other items. They are wrapped in a crepe to form a bite-sized morsel.

Tangpyeongchae

Tangpyeongchae is seasoned mung-bean starch jelly with vegetables. The name of the dish reflects the strong yearning for pacification (tang-pyeong) during the King Jeongjo era of the Joseon Dynasty.

Special Foods

Since ancient times, Koreans have prepared special foods to celebrate the change of seasons and to wish for the good health and prosperity of family members. Seasonal foods include 'five-grain rice,' which has nine different seasoned vegetables and is made for Daeboreum, the first full moon festival, surichwi tteok, a Korean rice cake made from rice flour and flavored with mugwort, which is made for the Dano Festival on the fifth day of the fifth month on the lunar calendar, and songpyeon, crescent-shaped rice cakes which are made for Chuseok, the harvest moon festival. The preparation of these foods, along with other traditional customs, originated with religious rites based on the practices of shamanism.

New Year's Day

On the morning of New Year's Day, family members perform memorial services to their ancestors and eat tteokguk (rice cake soup). Tteokguk has long been an important food for New Year's Day because Koreans believe that a person gains a year in age by eating tteokguk. Tteokguk is cooked by boiling thinly-sliced, plain white rice cakes in beef broth and adding freshly chopped spring onions.

Birthdays

Traditionally, birthdays were celebrated by eating a variety of foods with one's family. Recently, there has been an increasing tendency to serve a birthday cake or to eat out to celebrate the occasion.
One of the most popular traditional foods eaten on birthdays is miyeok-guk, a seaweed soup.

Chuseok (harvest moon festival)

Chuseok falls on the 15th day of the eighth month on the lunar calendar, is also called Hangawi or Jungchujeol. It is one of the two most celebrated traditional holidays in Korea, along with New Year's Day. One of the favorite foods eaten during Chuseok is songpyeon, a crescent-shaped rice cake. It is made by kneading newly harvested rice flour into dumplings and stuffing the dumplings with green beans, beans or sesame seeds.

Dongji

Dongji is the shortest day and longest night of the year. Koreans celebrate by making red bean porridge with small round rice cakes.
They often sprinkle the porridge around the house and nearby large trees because of the belief that the red color of the porridge will scare away evil spirits.

Jeongwol Daeboreum

On Jeongwol Daeboreum (the first full moon day), which falls on the 15th day of the first month on the lunar calendar, many people pray for a bountiful harvest in the new year. Koreans eat bureom, or nuts such as walnuts and peanuts, to guard themselves against getting boils in the new year.
A special 'five-grain rice' is also eaten on this day. This rice is a combination of glutinous rice, non-glutionous rice, red beans, beans, millet and sorghum.

Sambok (three hottest days)

Sambok refers to the three hottest days in summer, starting with Chobok (at the beginning of the summer), Jungbok (in the middle of the summer), and Malbok (at the end of the summer). People drink wine and eat foods believed to ward off heat on these days.
One of the most popular foods eaten during the Sambok days is samgyetang, a nutritious food made by stuffing a chicken with rice, ginseng, chestnuts, jujubes, pine nuts, gingko nuts, and garlic and boiling it until it creates a soup.

Traditional Snacks

Traditional snacks include tteok (rice cakes) and confections made from a variety of nuts and grains. Rice cakes are an important part of all holidays and appear on tables prepared for ancestral memorial rites. Tteok can be made from non-glutinous grain, flavored with red beans, sesame seeds, or azalea flowers. Koreans enjoy a number of confections made of rice flour and flavored with combinations of honey, wheat gluten, sesame oil, and sugar. The confections are kneaded, shaped or pressed into molds, then either cooked in hot oil or steamed.

Sujeonggwa

This beverage is cinnamon flavored dried persimmon punch. It is a sweet and spicy and can be served warm or chilled.

Sikhye

This sweet beverage is made of steamed rice fermented with malt water. Ginger juice and citron honey are sometimes added.

Jeungpyeon (steamed rice cake)

Rice flour is kneaded with makgeolli (crude rice wine), fermented, topped with dried jujube, cockscomb's leaf, black sesame, and mushroom, and then steamed. It is sliced into squares or diamonds to produce jeungpyeon.

Yaksik

This is a glutinous rice cake mixed with honey, dried jujube, and chestnuts.

Hangwa

Hangwa is a fruit-shaped confection. Types of hangwa are yumilgwa, which contains sesame oil and honey, gangjeong (sweet fried rice cookies with nut or grain powder), sanja (smaller fried cookies coated mainly in glutinous rice powder), dasik (small molded cookies), jeongwa (candied vegetable roots and seeds) and yeot (wheat gluten). Like tteok, hangwa is an important food in ceremonies such as ancestral memorial rites, weddings and banquets.

Gangjeong

Gangjeong is a cookie made of fried rice, sesame or nuts.

Injeolmi (pounded rice cakes)

Injeolmi was first served at ancestral memorial rites during the Goryeo Dynasty. These rice cakes differ in shape according to the region in which they were made. In the southern provinces, injeolmi is cut into small, delicate shapes, while in the northern provinces it is cut into larger and more appetizing shapes. Injeolmi used for ceremonies is rolled into one long piece and placed on a table without being cut.

Hwajeon

Hwajeon is a flower pancake. There are two methods of making hwajeon. One is by kneading glutinous rice flour into small, round shapes and pan-frying them with flower petals arranged on top. The other method, which was used mainly in the royal court, is kneading the rice flour into a dough and then pressing it flat and arranging flower petals on top of it. The dough is then pressed into hwajeon molds and fried. Various flowers, such as azaleas, roses, pear flowers, and chrysanthemums, are used in making hwajeon.

Traditional Regional Foods

Korean foods vary considerably by region, reflecting variations in the area's natural surroundings. The most diverse varieties of foods were developed in ancient capitals or regional centers, while more plain local foods for commoners were developed in the rural areas.

As with traditional foods, traditional liquor differs greatly by region due to the different ingredients used. Each region has its own distinctive liquor.

Songjeolju

Japchae

Bulgogi

Seoul

Because of its long status as the capital of Korea, Seoul has a wide range of foods which use ingredients from every corner of the country.

Major cuisines here include sinseollo (a casserole-like dish), neobiani (broiled seasoned beef), jeonbokcho (a dish of chopped abalone boiled in soy sauce) and honghapcho (a dish of chopped mussels boiled in soy sauce). Seoul's traditional alcoholic drinks include Songjeolju and Haesamju.

Sogokju

Olgaengi-guk

Danhobak-juk

Chungcheong-do

Traditional foods in Chungcheong-do are cooked with little seasoning, emphasizing the natural taste of their ingredients. Popular foods here include ogolgye-tang (black chicken soup), olgaengi-guk (shell-fish soup), bammuk (chestnut jelly), insameo-juk (ginseng porridge) and daeha-gui (roasted lobster). Traditional spirits of the region include Myeoncheon Dugyeonju, Sogokju (grain wine), Sinseonju and Baegilju.

Seoul

Incheon

GYEONGGI

CHUNGCHEON

JEOLLA-DO

Gwangju

Jeolla-do

Jeolla-do food is perhaps most well-known in Korea. The foods here have relatively strong seasonings and are served in generous portions. Popular local foods include Jeonju bibimbap (cooked rice mixed with meat and seasoned vegetables), baekhap-juk (seafood porridge), jeonbok-juk (abalone porridge) and hongeo-jjim (steamed thornback). Traditional spirits of the region include igangju (a wine flavored with pears and ginseng), Chunhyangju, Bokbunjaju and Songhwa Baegilju.

Jeonju Bibimbap

Hongeo-jjim

Igangju

GANGWON-DO

Ulleungdo

Dokdo

GYEONGSANG-DO

Daegu

Ulsan

Busan

JEJU-DO

Gyeonggi-do

The food from Gyeonggi-do is simple yet diverse. Seasoning is not heavily used, and foods are generally neither too spicy nor bland.
Popular foods from this region include Suwon galbi (roasted ribs), seollong-tang (beef bone and tripe soup), yeongyangbap (rice cooked with nutritious vegetables) and janggukbap (rice soup). Traditional alcoholic beverages of the region include Munbaeju (wine made from hulled millet and sorghum), Ongmiju, Gyemyeongju and Pocheon makgeolli (rice wine).

Suwon Galbi

Naengitojang-guk

Munbaeju

Makguksu

Gamja-jeon

Ojingeo Bulgogi

Gangwon-do

Foods from Gangwon-do are simple but appetizing. In the mountainous areas of the region, many dishes use potatoes and wild vegetables, while in the coastal areas, major ingredients include anchovies and clams. Popular foods here include Chuncheon dakgalbi (grilled chicken), ojingeo bulgogi (grilled squid) and memil makguksu (buckwheat noodles). Traditional spirits of the region include deodeoksul (wine made from plant roots) and corn wine.

Gyeongsang-do

The foods found in Gyeongsang-do are relatively spicy and use strong seasonings. People in the region enjoy grilled and dried fish, as well as guksu (noodles) and kalguksu (home-made noodles). Popular foods of the region include Andong heotjesabap (rice served at ancestral memorial rites), Nakdonggang ingeo-jjim (steamed carp) and Masan agu-jjim (steamed angler). Traditional spirits of the region include the popular Andong soju (a distilled liquor) and Gyeongju beopju (wine made of rice and medicinal herbs).

Heotjesabap

Mideodeok-jjim

Andong Soju & Gyeongju Beopju

Jeju-do

The primary ingredients of Jeju-do foods consist of seafood and seaweed. These foods are usually seasoned with doenjang (soy bean paste). Dishes made from sea bream, such as okdom and jaridom, are popular here and various kinds of fish are often cooked into soups or porridges.
Common foods include grilled sea bream, jarimulhoe (a type of raw fish) and grilled black pork. Major traditional spirits include local wines made from millet and omegisul.

Dom Hoe

Obunjagi-jjim

Experiencing Korean Food

A large part of the enjoyment of traveling around Korea is sampling the variety of foods. Another way to enrich ones' travel experience in Korea and have a first-hand experience of the culture is to learn to cook Korean food. Travelers can experience making foods such as kimchi, japchae (sweet potato noodles with various vegetables), buchimgae (Korean pancakes) and boggeumbap (fried rice).
Various organizations offer cooking classes. In addition to providing an opportunity to make Korean foods, these organizations offer visitors programs where they can learn traditional tea drinking etiquette, calligraphy, painting and how to wear traditional Korean attire. Fees for programs generally range from 60,000 won to 150,000 won per person.

1 Yejiwon Cultural Institute

Tel: 82-2-2253-2211
How to Get There: It's a 15-minute walk from Exit 6 of Dongguk University Station on Metro Line 3. In the Jayu Center across from the National Theater.

2 Insitute of Korean Royal Cuisine

Tel: 82-2-3673-1122
How to Get There: Take maeul (village) bus No.1 from Exit 2 of Anguk Metro Station on Metro Line 3.

3 Han Bok-sun's Cooking Institute

Tel: 82-2-592-3783
How to Get There: It's a 7-minute walk from Exit 4 of Seoul National Univ. of Education Station on Metro Line 2 or 3.

4 Han's Institute of Culinary Arts

Tel: 82-2-742-3567
How to Get There: It's a 5-minute walk from Exit 4 of Jongno 3-ga Station on Metro Line 1, 3 or 5.

5 Jeon Jeong-won Korean Cooking Studio

Tel: 82-2-535-1432
How to Get There: Take maeul (village) bus No.02-3 from Exit 1 of Bangbae Station on Metro Line 2 to the 'car center' across the street.

Kimchi

Kimchi, which is made from fermented Chinese cabbage, radish and cucumbers, is an essential part of Korean cuisine. The ingredients are salted and seasoned with pepper, onions, garlic, ginger, jeotgal and other spices. The result is a spicy and highly nutritious food, although the taste and flavor of kimchi varies depending on factors like ingredients, temperature, fermentation and recipes.
Kimchi provides beneficial vitamins and helps strengthen the immune system and activate digestion. It is also believed to prevent geriatric ailments such as enlarged intestines, arteriosclerosis, and anemia.

1 Kkakdugi (cubed radish kimchi)

Kkakdugi is made from cubed radishes which are mixed with red pepper powder, garlic, ginger, fermented shrimp sauce and other spices. It has a sourish-sweetish hot taste.

2 Nabak Kimchi (water kimchi made from sliced radish)

This watery kimchi is made of salted radish squares with red pepper powder, scallions, garlic, ginger and other spices.

3 Yeolmu Kimchi (young radish kimchi)

Yeolmu kimchi is a type of kimchi eaten in the summer. It is made of tender young radishes which are spiced with red pepper powder, onions, scallions and other ingredients.

4 Tongbaechu Kimchi (Chinese cabbage kimchi)

Tongbaechu kimchi is the most common kind of kimchi. The taste of this type of kimchi differs depending on the region and family recipes. It is made of entire heads of Chinese cabbage which are salted and stuffed with sliced radish, red pepper powder, garlic, ginger and other spices.

5 Dongchimi (radish kimchi in water)

Dongchimi is a relatively plain kind of kimchi made of whole radishes that are salted and immersed in water. Dongchimi and its brine are often eaten in the winter with buckwheat and acorn jelly, or with broiled and barbecued potatoes. Because it is a fermented product, cold dongchimi brine stimulates digestion.

6 Chonggak Kimchi (pickled young radishes)

Chonggak kimchi, which is made from long radishes with leaves, reminds many people of the braided style of hair that bachelors wore long ago in Korea. Radishes are cut into 2-4 parts and cooked with their leaves in the preparation of this kimchi.

7 Oisobagi Kimchi (cucumber kimchi)

Oisobagi kimchi is made of cucumbers and scallions arranged in a ring shape. Although preparing it is very time consuming and it cannot be preserved for a long time, its taste and shape make oisobagi a favorite for many people.

Hanbok
Traditional Clothing

Women's hanbok is comprised of a wrap-around skirt and a jacket. It is often called chima-jeogori, chima being the Korean word for skirt and jeogori the word for jacket. Men's hanbok consists of a short jacket and pants, called baji, that are roomy and bound at the ankles. Both ensembles may be topped by a long coat of a similar cut called durumagi.
Hanbok worn today are patterned after those worn during the Confucian-oriented Joseon Dynasty (1392-1910). Yangban, a hereditary aristocratic class based on scholarship and official position rather than on wealth, wore brightly colored hanbok of plain and patterned silk in cold weather and closely woven ramie cloth or other high-grade, light-weight materials in warm weather. Commoners, on the other hand, were restricted by law as well as finances to bleached hemp and cotton and could only wear white, pale pink, light green, gray or charcoal colors.

Royal Clothes

The early Joseon Dynasty kings made neo-Confucianism the ruling ideology. Its emphasis on formality and etiquette dictated the style of dress for the royal family and the aristocrats and commoners for all types of occasions including weddings and funerals. Integrity in men and chastity in women became the foremost social values and was reflected in the were people dressed.

King and Queen's Ceremonial Robes

Beauty of Hanbok

The beauty of hanbok lies in the harmony between its colors and its bold, simple lines.
Most jeogori have a snap or small tie ribbons on the inside to hold them closed. The long ribbons of the jacket are tied to form the otgoreum. The 'otgoreum' is very important because it is one of three things by which the beauty and quality of hanbok is judged. The other two are the curve of the sleeves, 'baerae' and the way the 'git,' a band of fabric that trims the collar and front of the jeogori, is terminated. The ends of the git are generally squared off and a removable white collar called the dongjeong is placed over the git.
The regular pleats of the chima stretch downward from the high waist and increase in width as they reach the lower end of the traditional skirt, creating a sense of gracefulness.

Gat (Men's hat)

Durumagi

The durumagi is a traditional overcoat worn on special occasions over the traditional jacket and pants.

Baji

Baji refers to the lower part of the men' s hanbok. Compared to western style pants, it does not fit tightly. The roomy nature of the cloth is due to a design aimed at making the cloth ideal for sitting on the floor.

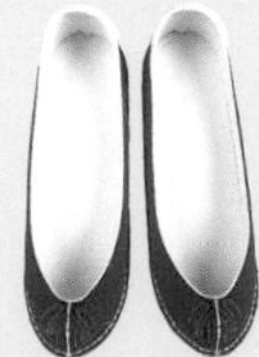

Kkotsin

The kkotsin refers to silk shoes on which flower patterns are embroidered. They play an important role in completing the graceful line of the lower rim of the chima.

Men' s Hanbok

Women' s Hanbok

Patterns

Traditional patterns graceful lines and color combinations enhance the beauty of hanbok. Plant, animal, or other natural patterns are added to the rim of chima, the areas surrounding the outer collar, womens' jackets, and the shoulders of the wonsam.

Kinds of Hanbok

The various kinds of hanbok are classified according to the social status, class, gender, and age of those who wear them. Today, hanbok is worn mostly on special occasions, and is divided into categories based on its function. These include, but are not limited to, weddings, 61st birthdays, first birthdays, and holidays.

Jeogori

The jeogori makes up the upper part of hanbok. Men' s jeogori are larger and simplistic while women' s jeogori are rather short and characterized by curved lines and delicate decorations.

Dongjeong

The dongjeong refers to a white-collar attached along the rim of the neckline. It contrasts and harmonizes with the overall curve of the neck.

Otgoreum (Cloth Strings)

The otgoreum is a women' s ornamental piece which hangs vertically across the front of the chima (women's skirt).

Baerae (Jeogori Sleeve)

The baerae refers to the lower lines of the sleeve of either the jeogori (traditional jacket), or the magoja (outer jacket). It features a circular line which is naturally curved, similar to the line of the eaves of a traditional Korean house.

Chima

The chima is the women' s outer skirt. There are different kinds of chima: single-layered, double-layered, and quilted. Pul-chima refers to a chima with a separated back, whereas a tong-chima has a seamed back.

Beoseon

The beoseon corresponds to a pair of contemporary socks. Although the shape of the beoseon does not reflect any difference in the gender of its users, men' s beoseon are characterized by a straight seam.

Myeongjeol Hanbok

Koreans traditionally show their respect to their parents early in the morning on the first day of the New Year by bowing deeply. Customarily, both parents and children wore hanbok. Children's hanbok usually consists of a rainbow-striped jeogori (jacket) and either a chima (girls' skirt) or a baji (boys' pants).

Dol Hanbok

The first birthday of a child, the dol, is traditionally celebrated with wishes for longevity and health. Children wear the dol-hanbok or dol-ot on this special day. A boy usually wears a pinkish jeogori (jacket) with a long blue goreum (cloth strings). Girls usually wear a rainbow-striped jeogori for special occasions. Currently, the trend is for girls to wear a dangui, a kind of ceremonial coat.

Hoegabyeon Hanbok

Hoegabyeon is when children throw a party to celebrate the 61st birthday of either parent and wish for their longevity. Men who turn 61 wear a geumgwanchobok, while women wear a dangui, a kind of ceremonial dress for special occasions.

Hollyebok (Wedding Hanbok)

Unlike hanbok for daily use, hanbok worn as a traditional wedding costume is marked by its bright appearance. The bridegroom wears the baji (pants), the jeogori (a jacket), the jokki (a vest), the magoja (an overcoat), and the durumagi (an overall coat). The bride wears a green chima (a skirt), a yellow jeogori (a short jacket), and a wonsam (a bride's long overcoat). Her hair is prepared using a jokduri (a special head ornament).

Saenghwal Hanbok

The use of traditional hanbok follows complex rules, and requires meticulous attention. Because of this, a simplified version of hanbok has been introduced for daily use which incorporates simplicity and convenience. An increasing number of people want to express their individuality by wearing something that combines traditional beauty and modern simplicity. The modern version comes in a wide variety of styles and fabrics.

Hollyebok

Jangsingu

Jokduri

The jokduri is a black headpiece which is worn by women in ceremonies. It is made of silk, shaped like a cylinder that is round at the bottom and hexagonal at the top. Inside it is hollow so it can be placed on top of carefully combed hair.

Norigae

Of the many traditional accessories, the norigae is the most commonly used. Dangling from the chest line down to the chima (a traditional skirt), it features a finished knot ornament. It signifies a wish for wealth, rank, male children and longevity. It can also conceal a container of either aromatic materials or a silver dagger for self-defense.

Gwijumeoni

Also called the bokjumeoni, this small purse-like accessory originated as a good luck charm. Domestic and foreign silk are the favorite material on which exquisite embroideries are added.

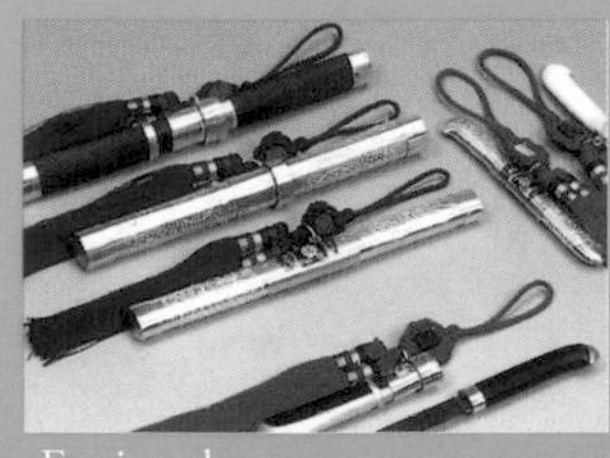

Eunjangdo

The eunjangdo is a traditional accessory that combines practicality and art. The Sanggam Eunjangdo is produced by a technique developed in Sanggam. It is supposed to be possible to check the owner's health by the change in the metal's color.

Tteoljam and Cheopji

The tteoljam, also called the tteolcheolbanja, is a special hairpin which was usually worn by queens or women from the upper class. When wearing a eoyeo-meori (a woman's ceremonial wig) or a keun-meori (a woman's formal hairdo), women usually place the tteoljam in the center of their hair line. A cheopji is an ornamental hairpin fixed to the center of the hair line, where a woman's hair is combed up in a chignon.

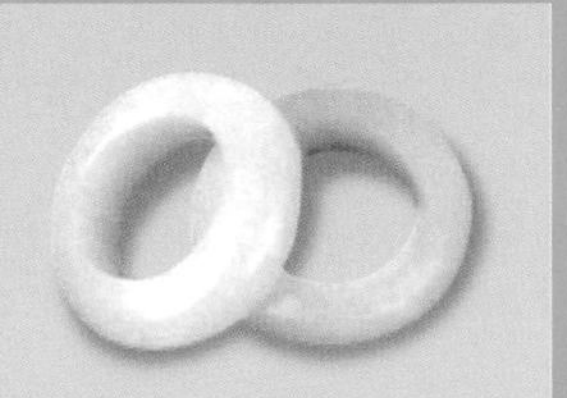

Banji (Ring)

The banji is an accessory that signifies a married couple's commitment and devotion, as well as the woman's virtuousness. Married women used to wear this item at all times. A banji can be made of a variety of materials, such as gold, silver, chilbo, amber, jade and green jade.

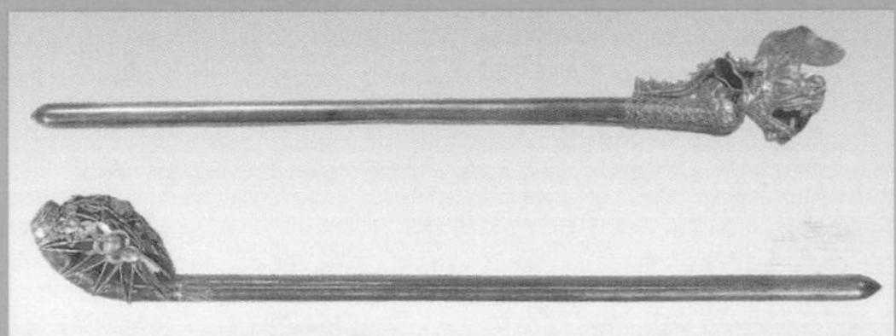

Binyeo

The most popular hairstyle used when wearing hanbok is ollinmeori, or swept-up hair. In addition to holding up hair, hair pins also have a significant ornamental value. The binyeo is made from various precious materials such as gold, silver, auspicious wood, coral and jade. In the past, the social status of the wearer was signified by the material used for ornaments and the dress's length. Royal women wore a binyeo with dragon or phoenix carved on it, whereas ordinary women wore one with a bamboo tree and ume flowers carved on it.

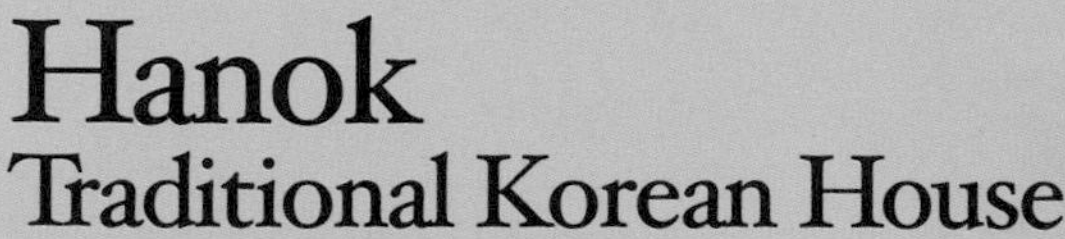

Hanok
Traditional Korean House

A traditional Korean house is called 'Hanok'. Hanok sought to create a living space based on the coexistence of nature and humans. Accordingly, the natural aspects of a traditional Korean houses range from the structure's inner layout to the building materials which were used.
Another unique feature of traditional houses is their special design for cooling the interior in the summer and heating the interior in the winter. Since Korea has such hot summers and cold winters, the 'ondol gudeul,' a floor- based heating system and 'daecheong,' a cool wooden-floor style hall were devised long ago to help Koreans survive the frigid winters and to make the sweltering and humid summers bearable. These primitive types of heating and air-conditioning were so efficient that they are still in use in many homes today.

Principles of Positioning Hanok

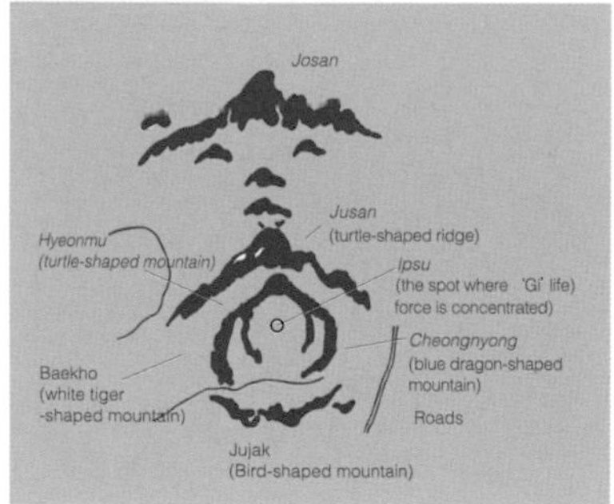

Traditional houses in Korea have been heavily influenced by the natural environment. The location of a house was selected according to the tenets of the ancient art of geomancy, also known as Feng Shui, which determined a site's natural energy forces based on its geographic features. The philosophy of 'baesanimsu,' which stipulated that houses should face water and have mountains in their background was also a strong consideration.

Layout of Hanok

The internal layout of a traditional house was based on Confucian ideas so there were separate residences based on class, sex and age. Living quarters were divided into a high-, mid- and low sections through the use of separate buildings or the erection of small walls. The higher section consisted of the anchae (the main building) and the sarangchae (the men's sitting room) was used by the elite yangban class. The lower section, which was located closest to the main gate, served as living quarters for the servants. The mid section was attached to the jungmun (the inner gate) and was used by middle-class household managers.

Composition of Hanok

A yangban residence had various types of living quarters for its residents. The living quarters consisted of the sarangchae, the building reserved for the head of the house hold to reside and receive guests in, the haengnangchae, which were servants' living quarters, the anchae, the inner living quarters for the head woman of the household, her children and other women, and the sadangchae, the shrine to honor the spirits of family ancestors. Each section was separated by walls with gates, such as the jungmun, which allow access to other sections of the house.

The main gate of the soseuldaemun is connected directly to the sarangchae, but the anchae was hidden behind the jungmun (the inner gate) so that it couldn't be seen from the outside. The shrine was surrounded by a separate set of walls, an indication of its sacredness.

Giwa (Korean tiles) and Roofs

Giwa was a criterion for distinguishing nobles from commoners. They were used to build yangban houses. The roof shapes of yangban houses included the soseul jibung (a combination of a paljak jibung and a gabled roof), the paljak jibung (a 八-shaped roof), the ujingak jibung (a hipped roof) and the matbae jibung (a gabled roof).

Sarangchae

Soseuldaemun

Soseuldaemun

A soseuldaemun is a large main gate with a high upper roof. It indicated the social class of the house owner and served as a symbol of yangban homes.

Sarang Daecheong

Sarang Daecheong (wooden-floored halls of the sarangchae)

The daecheong of a high class residence is a space which connects rooms. Sarang Daecheong served as a place for social functions, receiving guests and for dining in the summer. Both sides of the hall were usually decorated with sabang tables that had celadon ceramics and antiques on them.

Sarangbang

Sarangbang

In traditional yangban houses, the sarangbang was the main room of the sarangchae, where the head of the household lived and received guests in addition to taking meals, reading, contemplating, and engaging in artistic activities.

Anchae

Jungmun

Saetdam and Jungmun (small walls and inner gate)

The traditional yangban residence was divided into the 'inner' quarters used by women and the 'outer' quarters used by men. The sections were divided by erecting small walls in a large courtyard or using separate living quarters, and people accessed the other sections through a jungmun.

Latticed doors

Anbang

Anbang

The anbang was the center of the residence, where the head woman of the household ran various aspects of the household, especially those relating to clothing and food. It mostly contained various types of wardrobes and chests that stored clothes and bedcloths. It also contained other furniture, small household items and folding screens.

Andaecheong

Andaecheong

The andaecheong consisted of the anbang and the geonneonbang, where the head woman of the household and any daughter-in-laws lived. It was furnished with a wooden rice chest, cupboards, a table used for ancestral memorial services, a small table with an incense burner, chairs, and candlesticks.

Kitchen

During this time, the kitchen was either attached to the anbang, the women's living space, or built separately.
The kitchen floor was generally built 75cm-90cm lower than other rooms, which had an 'ondol' heating system. In this heating system, flat stones underneath the floor (called gudeul) were heated by warm air that flows from the kitchen fireplaces through the ducts which were built under the rooms.

Jangdokdae

The jangdokdae is a terrace where small and large onggi (crockery and clay ware) were placed to store and ferment various foods. The jangdokdae was situated in a clean area near the kitchen. This placement was chosen because it could get plenty of sunshine and ventilation to preserve foods and maintain freshness.

Sadang

A sadang is a shrine where ancestral tablets were preserved. It was located in the innermost area of the residence, where it was thought to receive the energy of nearby mountains. Usually memorial tablets of family ancestors from the previous four generations were kept in the shrine.

Traditional Houses by Region

Traditional Korean houses varied sightly by region. The differences were the result of adaptation to the region's natural environment. Local construction materials were used and houses were designed according to regional climatic forces, such as strong winds and heavy snow, which were common in certain areas. Houses in the central and southern provinces were mainly thatched roof houses made of straw, while in Jeju-do, most of the houses were thatched roof houses made of stone and straw ropes. Both Ulleungdo and Gangwon-do contained the neowajip style house, a shingled house which was made from oak trees. The Ulleungdo area also had tumakjip houses, which were constructed from logs and mud. Houses of commoners also had different shapes according to their region. For instance, houses in the northern area were 'ㅁ' shaped while houses in the southern and middle areas were '11' and 'ㄱ' shaped.

Commoner' s house in central Korea

Commoner' s house in southern Korea

Commoner' s house in northern Korea

Jeju-do Thatched-Roof Houses

On Jeju-do, where strong winds and typhoons frequently occur, houses were mainly built with stone and straw, and straw ropes were used to secure the roof and prevent it from being blown away by winds. Unlike other regions, the walls here were made with both mud and stones.

Neowajip

Gangwon-do Neowajip

Neowajip, a wooden shingled type of house, is a traditional house which was found in the region of Gangwon-do. In the mostly mountainous province, it was difficult to grow rice, so houses were made of logs, which were easily found in the vicinity. Neowajip houses were roofed with shingles made of oak tiles sliced directly from the trees.

Tumakjip

Ulleungdo Tumakjip (log cabin)

Tumakjip houses, also called gwiteuljip, were built by settlers on Ulleungdo. These houses were constructed by overlapping logs and filling the gaps with mud. The outside of the structure was covered with udegi and woven eulalias to block the wind.

Thatched-roof house

Ecotour

Demilitarized Zone
Sokcho
Dongducheon
Chuncheon
Paju
Gangneung
Seongmodo
Gimpo
Namyangju
Gangwon-do
Ganghwado
Seoul
Cheonyeon
Donghae
Incheon
Samcheok
Yeongheungdo
Anyang
Gwangju
Eungamgul
Hwaam
Chodangul
Hwanseongul
Yeonhwagul
Wonju
Baengnyong
Yongyeongul
Hwaseong
Suwon
Icheon
Taebaek
Gossi
Gyeonggi-do
Ondal
Cheondong
Pyeongtaek
Chungju
Gosu
Seongnyugul
Nodong
Jeombongsan Eollaeji Flower
Asan
Cheonan
Seosan
Yeongju
Chungcheongbuk-do
Anmyeondo
Cheongju
Cheongseokgul
Chungcheongnam-do
Andong
Gongju
Sangju
Boryeong
Daejeon
Gyeongsangbuk-do
Chunjangdae
Cheonho
Gimcheon
Gumi
Gunsan
Pohang
Iksan
Muju Firefly Habitat
Yeongcheon
Daegu
Jinbong Peninsula
Gimje
Jeonju
Gyeongsan
Gyeongju
Jeollabuk-do
Jeongeup
Ulsan
Miryang
Yonggul
Namwon
Gyeongsangnam-do
Yangsan
Changwon
Gwangju
Cheonyeon
Jinju
Masan
Gimhae
Busan
Jinhae
Naju
Gwangyang
Donghwacheonyeon
Suncheon
Sacheon
Geoje
Mokpo
Tongyeong
Jeollanam-do
Yeosu

Ulleungdo
Gwaneumgul
Dokdo

LEGEND
Tideland
Cave
Marsh Area
Migratory Sanctuary

Gimnyeongsagul
Billaemot
Jeju
Hyeopjaegul
Manjanggul
Hwangeumgul
Jeju-do
Ssangyonggul
Sanbanggul
Seogwipo
Marado

Tectonic movements in ancient times left severe twists and bends in the topography of the Korean Peninsula, giving rise to numerous mountains, rivers, and valleys. Various caves, wetlands, and reservoirs in all shapes and sizes are also scattered throughout the country. These natural and geological endowments, combined with diverse natural resources, make Korea an interesting destination for ecotours.
The nation's topography, which is characterized by higher elevations in the east and lower elevations in the west, has gentle coastlines in the west and long, rugged coastlines in the east. On the west coast, a number of muddy tidal pools along banks of inlets make up a unique coastal and ecological system. The southern coast has beautiful coastal scenery thanks to its many islands and irregular coastline.
Various plants that are rarely seen in other parts of Korea are found thriving in major swamps found throughout the country.
Natural caves are rich in stalagmitic pillars, stalagmites, and stalactites.
Those who want to experience an ecology tour of Korea can explore caves, visit ecological systems in the wetlands along the inlet banks, watch birds and observe a wide range of indigenous animals and plants.

Wetlands

The southwestern coast of Korea is ranked among the top five wetland areas in the world. This distinction comes not only from the wetland's large size, but also from the ecological diversity it offers. Thanks to a rich clay content, these wetlands boast a powerful purification capability, which is 15 to 200 times stronger than that found in the wetlands of Great Britain. Korea's wetlands are located along migratory bird routes. Korean wetlands offer a natural haven for spoonbills, snipes, white herons and yellow-pecked spoonbills gather, while paper bubbles, fiddler crabs, and razor clams make the area their permanent home. Therefore, efforts to preserve the wetlands and protect migratory birds are underway.

Major wetland areas in Korea can be found in Janghwa-ri and Yeocha-ri, on Jebudo Island, Seongmodo Island (all in Gyeonggi-do) in Boryeong, along the coast of the Taean Peninsula in Chungcheongnam-do, and in Beolgyo in Jeollanam-do.

Alpheus Brevicristatus

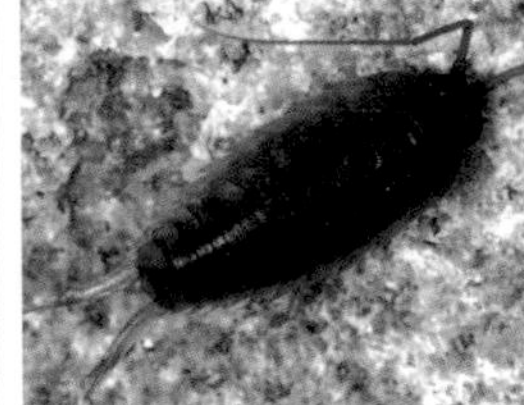

Sea Slater

Shells

Crab

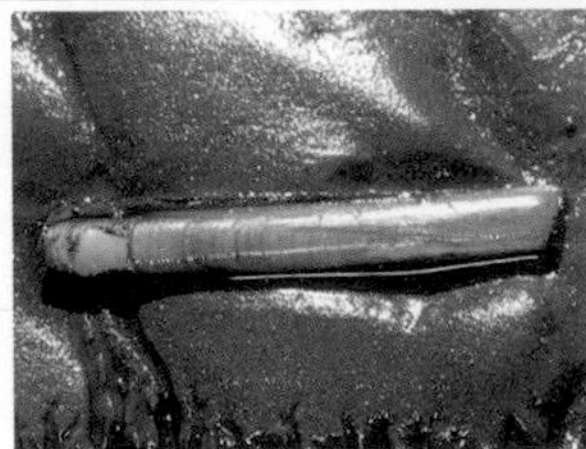

Razor Clam

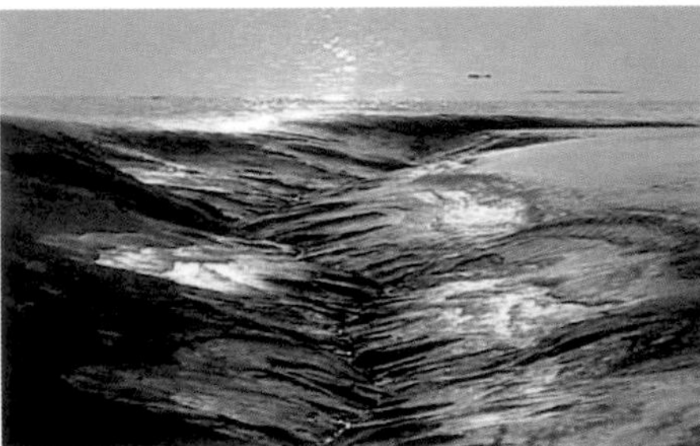

Janghwa-ri, Wetlands in Ganghwado

The wetlands in Janghwa-ri, found west of Ganghwado Island, are reputed to be a treasure trove of coastal life forms. Mollusca such as paper bubbles and crustaceans such as pebble crabs abound. One can also find button shells, shrimp, mudskippers, large-eyed spotted herring, gray mullets, and blue crabs. The area is also a major habitat for rare or endangered species, such as Chinese egrets, spoonbills, and spotted Nordmanns greenshanks.

Muchangpo Wetlands in Chungcheongnam-do

Located in Boryeong, Chungcheongnam-do, the wetlands in Muchangpo are famous for a natural parting of water which occurs twice a year, leaving a path to walk on. Visitors can catch various marine creatures such as sea cucumbers, sea squirts, turban shells, and octopuses, or dig for thin-shelled surf clams here.

Beolgyo Wetlands in Jeollanam-do

The wetland area in Beolgyo, which is situated at the southeastern tip of Boseong-gun, has a reputation as one of the cleanest areas of this type in Korea. Its uncontaminated wet lands are home to ark clams, black clams, thin-shelled surf clams and octopuses, among other creatures. The area also serves as an important feeding ground for migratory birds, thanks to the many coastal life forms that inhabit it.

Red Maiden of Mujechi Swamp

Wilfordian Lychnis of Yong Swamp

Marsh Flower of Upo Swamp

Hanabusaya Asiatica Nakai of Yong Swamp

James Gentian of Yong Swamp

Dogtooth Violet of Mujechi Swamp

Swamps

Swamps all over the world have a facinating variety of life forms. As home to a wide range of invertebrate animals, fish and birds, swamps form the backbone of the natural ecological systems on our planet. Rich in unique ecological resources, swamps are an ideal destination for ecology tours.

Asian Euryale of Mujechi Swamp

Upo Swamp

Having emerged 140 million years ago at the time of the formation of the Korean Peninsula, the Upo Swamp, the largest naturally formed swamp in Korea, has since sustained a diverse array of living creatures. Currently, a total of 342 kinds of plants and animals live in the Upo Swamp, including such birds as little grebes, white herons, common herons and whistling swans. Upo Swamp was registered with the Ramsa Convention on Wetlands of International Importance as a waterfowl habitat (a treaty to protect areas visited regularly by migratory birds) in March 1998. The swamp has beautiful scenery thanks to various plants thriving here, including plant species unique to this area, namely, prickly water lilies, together with sweet flags, peltiformis floating hearts and great duckreeds.

Mujechi Swamp

Mujechi Swamp, the largest high moor in Korea, literally serves as a natural history museum where almost all of the swampy flora that can be found in Korea exist.

It has played an important role in the study of the natural ecology of the Korean Peninsula. Taking up as much as 180,000 square meters, the swamp is reported to host over three hundred plant species and over 50 kinds of insects. Among the many plants found here are the Mujechi Orchid, which lives exclusively in the area, morning-star lilies, hypericum laxum koidz, damp parnassia, adder tongue lilies and sundews.

Yong Swamp of Mt. Daeamsan

Yong (Dragon) Swamp is located on Mt. Daeamsan, which straddles Yanggu-gun and Inje-gun in Gangwon-do. As typical high moor, it maintains a very unique ecological system. The composition of the swamp is unique; it has one large swamp and two smaller swamps. A total of 191 species of plants make their home here, including hanabusaya asiatica nakai, a globally rare species, trientalis europaea L., james gentians and wilfordian lychnises. Its ecological significance, however, is not confined to being a habitat for flora alone; as many as 224 different insect species, including ectinohoplia obducta, also prosper here.

Caves

Caves in Korea are divided primarily into lime grottos and volcanic caves. While lime grottos are found throughout the Korean Peninsula, lava caves are found in limited areas, particularly on Jeju Island.

Representative lime grottos include the Gossi Cave, the Hwanseon Cave, the Gosu Cave, the Nodong Cave, the Ondal Cave and the Seongnyu Cave. The lava counterparts of these caves include the Hyeopjae Cave, the Manjang Cave and the Billemot Pond Cave.

Caves have various features which are rarely seen in other geographical settings. Features of cave ceilings include soda straws, stalactites, and curtain-shaped stalactites. Formations on cave floors and cave walls include stone pillars, stalagmites, stalactites, cave coral and line flowers. Samcheok-si in Gangwon-do is Korea's most popular cave tour destination, with the Hwanseon and the Gwaneum Caves serving as the nation's most well known caves.

Stalagmitic Pillar in Cheongok Cave

Hwaam Cave

Gosu Cave

Known as the most beautiful lime cave in Korea, Gosu Cave was formed over 450 million years ago. It contains many stalactites and stalagmites, which are naturally carved in grotesque, intriguing shapes as the result of active erosion and a large quantity of flowing underground water. Rich in speleothem, it is virtually an integrated exhibition hall of all imaginable cave resources.

Seongnyu Cave

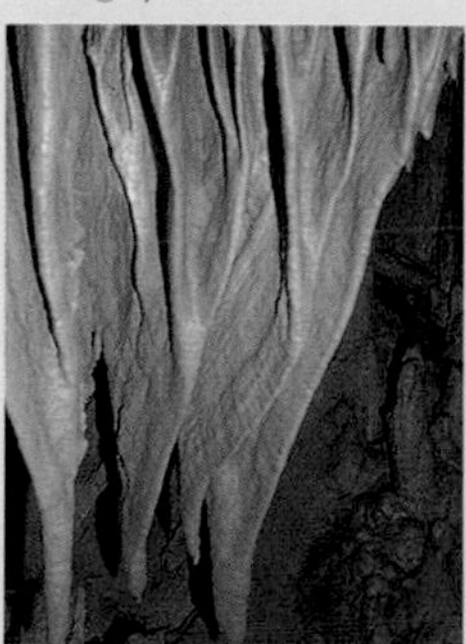

Seongnyu lime cave stretches over 472m. A seemingly endless line of stalactites and stalagmites stand inside the cave, which is comprised of 12 small caverns and five small ponds. Cavern No. 11 has three naturally-formed Buddha shapes that stand in a queue. Cavern No. 12 has stalactites and stalagmites that look like gemstones.

Hwanseon Cave

The Hwanseon Cave, the largest lime cave on the entire Asian continent, extends over 6.2km. The area open to the public is about 1.6km long and has two small caverns and six branch caves.
There are a large number of spleothem and extraordinary stalactites. One can observe the life cycle of a cave in this place: its generation, growth, and degradation.

Nodong Cave

Nodong Cave, presumed to have been formed about five hundred million years ago, is the nation's largest vertical cave. This cave is slanted approximately 40 to 50°. The central part is divided into five branch caves. A hole inside the cave lets in sunlight, so the cave was dubbed the Ilgwang (Sunlight) Cave.

Manjang Cave

The Manjang Cave is the world's largest known lava cave. It is five meters in width, and varies from five to 10m in height, and is 13,422m in length. It is presumed that the cave was created about 2.5 million years ago by lava that flowed from the volcano that is now Mt. Hallasan on Jeju Island.
A naturally formed stone turtle, which looks like a carved sculpture, and the world's largest lava pillar are located here.

Billemot Cave

The Billemot Cave is a 12,425m-long lava cave which is not open to the general public. It is labyrinth-like, with a large number of branch caves. Features of the Billemot Cave include a large lava stalagmite and a silicic pillar. The lava stalagmite was deemed the world's second tallest at 68cm. The silicic pillar, which is 28cm high, was formed as a result of silicification. It is exceptionally rare for a silicic pillar to form inside a lava cave.

Migratory Bird Routes

Located in the northeastern part of Asia, which is an integral part of the migration path of birds that move between Southeast Asia and Siberia, Korea abounds in locations regularly visited by migratory birds. As a consequence, the large numbers of migratory birds make Korea an ideal country for bird watching. Birds seen here include globally endangered cranes, spoonbills and yellow-pecked Chinese egrets.

Migratory birds can be found at the Demilitarized Zone, Ganghwado Island, Cheonsuman Bay, Geumgang River Estuary, Suncheonman Bay, Eulsukdo Island and Junam Reservoir.

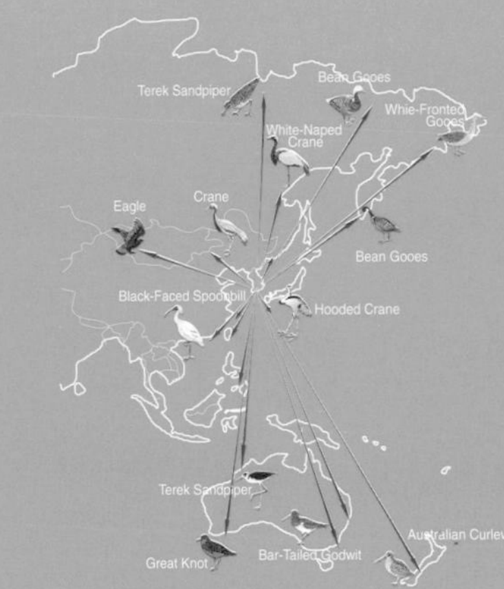

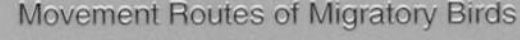

Movement Routes of Migratory Birds

Spoonbills

Sacred Ibis

Black-headed Stork

Chinese Egrets

Geumgang River

Located on the border between Chungcheongnam-do and Jeollabuk-do, this location is visited regularly by migratory birds. During winter, Eurasian oystercatchers and saunder gulls, both globally rare species, as well as whistling swans and wild ducks, can be seen in the area.

Nakdonggang River

Located to the southwest of Busan, Korea's second largest city, this location is a perfect environment for migratory birds with its sand dunes, tidelands, and reed fields, all formed as a result of repetitive flows and ebbs of tides from the Nakdonggang River. In local reed fields, visitors can watch wild ducks, pinitails, bean geese, white-fronted geese, common black-headed gulls and herring gulls seek out food.

Suncheonman Bay

Straddling the Yeocheon and Goheung Peninsulas in Jeollanam-do, this location is famous for its huge wetland area. This wetland area, which is visible during low tide, covers several million ㎡, and is home to a well-developed reed field. It has been reputed to be among the world's most important natural ecological areas. In winter, birds such as hooded cranes, saunders gulls, wild ducks, teal and common shellducks can be seen. Suncheonman Bay is particularly significant as a winter-spot for hooded cranes, the species designated as Korea's Natural Monument No. 228.

Cirsium Setidens Nakai

Keumgang Fairy Bells

Leotopodium Soreanum Nakai

Demilitarized Zone

The Demilitarized Zone is designated as a Natural Monument by both South and North Korea. Because entrance to the zone has been strictly controlled since the end of the Korean War, the area's natural ecological system has remained mostly unaltered and pristine. It has attracted enthusiastic attention from a variety of nature lovers. Today, the area is a habitat for diverse fauna and flora, fish and birds, as well as many rare protected species. Fish in the area include rare species such as the Manchurian trout, sparlings, Korean dotty barbells, Korean landlocked masu salmon, Korean splendid dace, Geumgang minnows and silurus microdorsalis, all thriving in the cold-water region of the DMZ. No plant species has been transplanted here, either from other areas in Korea or from abroad, so indigenous plants thrive and remain autogeneous. As a consequence, several special tree and herb communities have formed and grow in certain high areas along the Civilian Control Line and in the forests of the DMZ. Many rare species of birds have made their home in the DMZ. The area is also regularly visited by migratory birds. The barren land in Jangdan, on the western front line, is noted for attracting migratory birds.

DMZ

Manchurian Trout

Otter

Goral

Flying Squirrel

Large Spotted Butterfly

Cyprinid Fish

Hooded Crane

Eagle

Hedgehog

Raccoon

Museums

One of the principle ways to explore the nuances of Korean culture is to visit the many unique Korean museums scattered all across the nation. They offer a glimpse of the distinctive culture and ancient traditions of Korea. It is worthwhile to visit a number of theme museums and view their collections of unique and curious items.
When travelling around Korea, these unique museums can serve as some of the most rewarding ways to garner a better understanding of the diversity of Korean folklore and culture.
www.korea-museum.go.kr

Seoul

The Royal Museum

The Royal Museum displays artifacts which were used at royal palaces during the Joseon Dynasty. There are musical instruments and other artifacts which reflect the politics, economy, science, national ceremonies, palace architecture and royal court ceremonies of the time. Royal seals, kings' books, royal handicrafts, court attire and dress ornaments, paintings and models of various palaces are also displayed in the museum.

The Bank of Korea Museum

The construction of the main building of the Bank of Korea, where this museum is located, was built 1912, during the Daehan period. The structure has an eclectic Renaissance style and is designated as Historic Site No. 280.
The museum consists of four areas which illustrate

the purpose and functions of the Bank of Korea. There are displays explaining currency production and policies on consumer prices, currency and credit. Currencies from Korea and countries around the world are also on display.

Lotte World Folk Museum

Lotte World Folk Museum is an educational facility designed to introduce Korean history and culture. The museum uses images, pictures, dioramas and miniatures to vividly recreate the culture and lifestyle of ancient Korea. A total of 80 scenes set in 1/8 scale depict royal palaces, lifestyles of the nobility and commoners, and traditional festivals and rites.

Ihwajang

Ihwajang is a private residence that belonged to Lee Seung-man, the first President of the Republic of Korea. It depicts his frugal lifestyle and the history of the founding of the republic. Major items exhibited here include his clothing (some of which was darned several times), scrapbooks of magazine articles, old kitchen cupboards, brassware, and wardrobes which were made of paper boxes. Visitors can also view former president Lee's reception room, bedroom, study and kitchen.

Museum of Korean Traditional Music

The Museum of Korean Traditional Music features exhibits on the history of gugak (a traditional Korean style of music), musical instruments and books on gugak, audio-visual materials and relics of deceased gugak artists. The museum is located inside the National Center for Korean Traditional Performing Arts and houses a gugak library and a shop that sells items related to traditional Korean music. In addition, the museum offers a gugak course, where people can learn this style of traditional Korean music. On Saturdays a gugak concert is performed.

Onggi Folk Museum

The Onggi (Korean pottery) Folk Museum features 3,000 onggi pieces, ranging from the time of the Goguryeo Kingdom to the Joseon Dynasty. There are 10,000 folk items located here, including mortars and stone wash basins. Onggi is household pottery which is used either to store grains such as rice and barley, or to ferment foods such as kimchi and jeotgal (pickled seafood). Onggi has qualities which not only prevent foods from spoiling by allowing air to penetrate the pottery, but which also facilitate fermentation by maintaining optimal temperatures.

Ho-Am Art Museum

The Ho-Am Art Museum consists of a main building modeled after a traditional house and the Huiwon, a traditional garden. The museum is home to diverse ceramic artifacts, ranging from the ingenuitive Goryeo celadon and aesthetic Buncheong ware to the refined white porcelain of the Joseon Dynasty. Also exhibited are other invaluable art works, such as rare Goryeo Buddhist paintings, landscape paintings, paintings of the four gracious plants (plum, orchid, chrysanthemum and bamboo).

Latin American Cultural Center and Museum

The Latin American Cultural Center and Museum features a comprehensive collection of artifacts from the ancient Maya and Inca Civilizations, as well as a number that are from other parts of Latin America. These items vividly reflect the history, culture and lifestyle of each Latin American country. Among the items displayed are ceremonial knives which are believed to have been used to cut out human hearts during religious rituals 1,300 years ago, jade necklaces from Mexico, Costa Rican tools which were used to grind grains, and a variety of wooden, stone and earthenware. Also on display are paintings, ceramics and Mexican masks with varied facial expressions.

Euro Decorative Art Museum

The Euro Decorative Art Museum is a museum dedicated to exhibiting, preserving and researching decorative art works from Western Europe. Decorative art is a formative type of art designed to adorn human housing and surroundings. This art genre expresses the human desire to beautify their surroundings. Major exhibits here include yellow wax dolls, armor and headpieces of medieval knights, small statues of English knights, French ceramic dolls, Venetian masks, glass from Italy, collages and hangers from Germany and posters from the Cannes Film Festival.

Gangwon-do

Yanggu Prehistoric Museum

The Prehistoric Museum features relics of the Stone Age excavated at Sangmuryong-ri, Yanggu-eup, dolmens from Godae-ri and Gongsu-ri, as well as stoneware and earthenware from the Bronze Age excavated from Hyeon-ri, Haean-myeon.

Joseon Folk Art Museum

The Joseon Folk Art Museum is located in the Gimsatgat Valley in Yeongwol, Gangwon-do. It features exhibits of the Joseon Minhwa. Minhwa is a traditional painting which expresses the joys and sorrows of people's lives. These paintings were done by amateur painters in the 17～18th century.

Minhwa comes in various types, such as 'Hojakdo' which depicts a tiger and a magpie, 'Sansuhwa' which depicts a natural scenes, 'Hwahwedo' which depicts flowers such as the peony and the lotus, 'Hwajodo' which depicts flowers and birds, 'Yeongsuhwa' which depicts imaginary animals such as dragons or a mythical unicorn-lions.

Yeongwol Book Museum

The Yeongwol Book Museum was created by reconstructing a closed school. It is the nation's first book museum, housing a large collection of old and rare books. The museum collects, stores, displays and researches materials related to the culture of books, helping to establish an appreciation of books and a heightened awareness of their importance.

Chungcheong-do

Korean Old Architecture Museum

This architecture museum was established to contribute to the study and preservation of Korea's traditional architecture. It features traditional houses of scholar-officials (from the literati and aristocrat classes), houses of commoners, three-room thatched houses, a training center and examples of Chinese and Japanese houses.

Major items on display include a number of scale reproductions of such national treasures as Gaeksamun Gate in Gangneung, Guksajeon Hall of Songgwangsa Temple, Muryangsujeon Hall of Buseoksa Temple, Geungnakjeon Hall of Bongjeongsa Temple, Daeungjeon (the main hall) of Sudeoksa Temple, Namdaemun (South Gate) in Seoul, Yaksajeon Hall of Gwangnyongsa Temple.

Gongju Folk Drama Museum

The Gongju Folk Drama Museum specializes in a wide variety of Korean folk arts. It displays dolls used as folk puppets, masks, musical instruments and shamanism materials. Traditional farm tools are also on exhibit and the museum hosts a multitude of folk-related events.

Onyang Folk Museum

The Onyang Folk Museum, Korea's first folk museum, houses about 17,000 artifacts that display the creativity of ancient Korea. The museum illustrates life in old Korea, traditional agriculture, hand-weaving and hunting techniques, folk crafts and has a special exhibition hall which displays minhwa, colorful decorative paintings drawn by anonymous artists.

Jeolla-do

Dongjin Irrigation Folk Museum

The Dongjin Irrigation Folk Museum features a vast collection of old document, farming and household tools and sold irrigational items including the mujawi (a water pump), which was used to move water from lower areas to higher areas, the matdure (a water scoop) and a yongdure (a large, scooped wooden bowl). Over 1,200 farming tools and household items are alse displayed.

Gunsan
Iksan
PanAsia Paper Museum
Jeonju Gangam Calligraphy Museum
Jeonju
Jeonju Nat'l Museum
Dongjin Irrigation Folk Museum
Jeolla-do
Gochang Pansori Museum
Damyang Bambo Museum
Gwangju
Naju
Naju Pear Museum
Mokpo
Nat'l Maritime Museum
Yeosu

PanAsia Paper Museum

The PanAsia Paper Museum provides visitors with an opportunity to enhance their understanding of the history of paper in Korea and throughout the world. The first exhibition hall features displays on the pre-paper era, the birth of paper and its dissemination, and the effects of paper on civilization. The second hall features a program in which visitors can participate in the craft of paper folding, with instructions given by computer. Visitors can also take part in paper-making programs in a section of the hall dedicated to hanji reproductions. There is also an exhibit here on the future of paper.

Damyang Bamboo Museum

The Damyang Bamboo Museum has a wide collection of bamboo products and information on bamboo's history. The exhibition room features household items such as fine-tooth bamboo combs and hair pins used by women in olden days, as well as kitchen utensils like bamboo baskets, winnowing baskets and various other bamboo-related products. In the special exhibition hall, there are bamboo swords and musical instruments like the tungso (a bamboo flute). Bamboo products produced in Damyang, an area famous for its high quality bamboo, are displayed and sold in front of the museum.

Gyeongsang-do

Hahoe Mask Museum

The Hahoe Mask Museum houses intangible cultural assets such as Korean masks used in mask drama performances and masks from about 30 countries around the world, such as Papua New Guinea, Mexico, China, Indonesia, and New Zealand.

Taejeong Folk Museum

The Taejeong Folk Museum is the only museum in the world specializing in feldspar ornaments. Inside the museum, the ceiling and both sides of the stairway leading to the exhibition halls are dotted with various kinds of feldspar ornaments. The exhibition hall on the second floor exhibits all types of letter-shaped

feldspar embellishments, as well as those which have shapes resembling flowers and animals such as butterflies, the Chinese phoenix, deer and cranes. Feldspar mosaic pictures here also depict the Chinese phoenix, playful fish, tigers and the Taegeuk (the symbol of yin and yang in the Orient).

Tongdosa Temple Seongbo Museum

Tongdosa Seongbo (Sacred Art) Museum is the only

Korean museum which specializes in Buddhist paintings, and boasts a total of 30,000 artifacts of various types, from prehistoric times to modern times.

The museum has a collection of more than 600 Buddhist paintings in various genres, ranging from draft paintings to an oversized painting with a total length of 15 meters. The Tongdosa Seongbo Museum is recognized for having the largest number of Buddhist paintings anywhere in the world.

Jeju-do

Jeju Teddy Bear Museum

The Jeju Teddy Bear Museum is the place where teddy bears of all kinds, from across the world during the past century, are on exhibit. It houses a historical display and art galleries, a museum shop, and an outdoor garden where visitors can admire an unobstructed view of Jungmun Beach. Teddy bear exhibits depicting the history of this beloved doll, from the 1900s to the present along with antique teddy bears. The art gallery exhibits teddy bears made by internationally renowned artists and cartoon characters loved by children.

Jungmun Fishing Village Museum

The Jungmun Fishing Village Museum is a fishing

village called Beritnae, meaning 'the village of falling stars,' which has been remodelled to resemble its original form. About 20 households remain in this fishing village, which has a history of hundreds of years. About 3,000 pieces of farming and fishing tools, which illustrate the work done in the daily lives of fishermen, are on display in the museum, along with various household items.

Sinyoung Cinema Museum

In the entrance to the museum, visitors can see the portraits of 150 Korean actors and actresses who have made significant contributions to the development of Korean cinema from the 1920s to the present. The museum is a sort of hall of fame for the Korean cinema community.

The Cinema History Exhibition Hall features visual presentations that depict the birth of cinema and world cinema history, as well as various trends in the history of Korean cinema. It enables visitors to enhance their understanding of Korean movies by allowing them to operate motion picture equipment from the 19th century. The museum is equipped with numerous facilities, such as an information search area, a cinema simulation room, a character shop, a snack bar and an outdoor cafe.

Jeju
Jeju Folk Museum
Jeju Folklore and Natural History Museum
Mokseokwon Garden
Jeju-do
Seongup Folk Village
Bunjae Artpia
Pyoseon Jeju Folklore Village
Sinyoung Cinema Museum
Seogwipo
Jeju Teddy Bear Museum
Jungmun Fishing Village Museum

Experiencing Korean Culture

When it comes to experiencing culture, visitors to Korea have many options available. Those interested in experiencing Korean cuisine can participate in kimchi making, tea making and cooking Korean food. Music lovers can try their hand at playing various traditional Korean musical instruments, including the ones used by a samullori (a percussion quartet). Those who have an interest in fashion may try on a variety of Korean modern clothing, as well as different styles of the hanbok (Korea's traditional attire). A wide range of interesting cultural programs and festivals also provide visitors with a closeup look at Korea.

Music & Dance

Traditional Music

Traditional Korean music can be broadly divided into jeongak, which was originally court music with an intellectual emphasis, and minsogak, which is folk music that is full of emotional expression. The former was closely related to the culture of the royal family and the upper class literati, while the latter belonged more to the common people in the lower strata of society.
The first general characteristic of Korean music to note is its slower tempo. Most court music moves at a slow pace, sometimes so slow that a single beat can take up to three seconds. As a result, the mood of this music is static, meditative, and reposeful. The reason for this stately tempo is related to Koreans' concept of the importance of the breath.

Traditional Dance

Traditional dance can be broadly divided into court dance and folk dance. Court dance includes jeongjaemu, dances performed at banquets, and ilmu, the line dances performed in Confucian rituals. Jeongjaemu is subdivided into native hyangak jeongjae and Tang-derived dangak jeongjae. Hyangak jeongjae and dangak jeongjae can be distinguished by the manner in which the dancers enter and exit, the calls that mark the beginning and end of a dance, the presence or absence of a spoken greeting, and the content of the sung lyrics. Ilmu can be further divided into a civil dance, munmu, and a military dance, mumu.

Traditional Musical Instruments

Korean wind instruments include the cylindrical oboe (piri), the metal-bell shawm (taepyeongso), the transverse flute (daegeum), and the end blown flute (danso). String instruments include the twelve-stringed zither (gayageum), the six-stringed zither (geomungo), the seven-stringed bowed zither (ajaeng) and the two-stringed fiddle (haegeum). Percussion instruments include the handheld gong (kkwaenggwari), the hanging gong (jing), the barrel drum (buk), the hourglass drum (janggu), the clapper (bak), bell chimes (pyeonjong), and stone chimes (pyeongyeong).

Places to experience traditional Korean music

National Theater of Korea

The National Theater of Korea was established to contribute to the creative development of local arts through a multitude of cultural and art performances held throughout the year. By staging both regular and special performances, the National Theater of Korea brings the general public closer to traditional culture and art. Under the motto of 'Reaching out to the Public,' it conducts provincial tours as well.
The programs available in the theater include regular performances, special performances, Saturday cultural performances, unabridged pansori performances (traditional vocal music), Sunday stage productions, etc.

The National Center for Korean Traditional Performing Arts

The National Center for Korean Traditional Performing Arts hosts regular gugak performances featuring all genres of traditional music and dance, as well as specially designed monthly performances that harmonize traditional and modern styles.
It offers courses for visitors to enable them to learn and experience Korean dance and the best known traditional musical instruments such as the gayageum (12-stringed zither) and the janggu (hour-glass drum). By giving visitors an opportunity to perform on instruments and in dances, the center helps deepen people's understanding of traditional Korean performing arts and develop a sense of familiarity and affinity for Korea.

Chongdong Theater's Gugak Performances

Chongdong Theater classifies traditional Korean performing arts into four categories: dance, pungmul (percussion instrumental music), instrumental and sori (vocals). Chongdong Theater presents both court and folk music and introduces audiences to the true spirit of the traditional Korean performing arts by offering programs that consist of seven performances in all four categories. The performances include the fan dance, sanjo ensemble (scattered melodies in literal translation, meaning a popular folk music style played on a solo instrument to the accompaniment of a drum), salpuri (exorcist dance), pansori (Korea's narrative solo opera), hwagwanmu (flower crown dance), and gayageum byeongchang (a music genre in which a performer plays gayageum while singing).
Japanese and English interpretation services are available along with the 'duitpuri,' an after-show session in which performers and audiences mingle.

Unhyeongung Palace

Unhyeongung was the private residence of the Regent Heungseon Daewongun, who ruled the Joseon Dynasty in its final days. Designated as a historic site, the palace offers various performing art programs every week. This palace was the place where King Gojong, the son of Heungseon Daewongun, and his queen consort Myeongseong Hwanghu, held their national wedding ceremony. Every Saturday and Sunday, a wedding ceremony in the traditional sadaebu style (the literati and aristocrats of the Joseon Dynasty) is reenacted for the benefit of tourists.
Unhyeongung also presents various educational programs designed to preserve and pass on Korea's unique sense of decorum. Major contents of the educational programs include lectures on traditional manners, traditional musical instruments, the art of tea-making, folk games, etc.

Seoul Nori Madang (open-air stage for various folk performances)

Seoul Nori Madang hosts gugak performances that feature traditional vocals and dramatic presentations, as well as special monthly performances that combine traditional and modern themes.
Educational courses that teach traditional dance and how to play traditional musical instruments such as the gayageum (12-stringed zither) and the janggu (hour-glass drum) are offered to visitors.
Performances are given from April to October on Saturdays and Sundays.

Korean Life

Visitors who are eager to find out what the daily life within an average Korean home is like are encouraged to visit Korean households that invite people from foreign contries into their homes. There are also special agencies that operate cultural experience programs for foroigners.

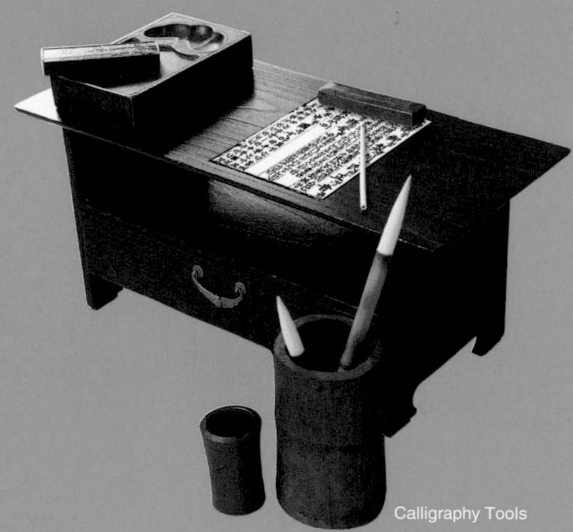

Calligraphy Tools

Son's Home

Son's Home is a private residence where visitors can experience genuine Korean culture. Those who visit Son's Home can feel the essence of Korean life by participating in kimchi-making with the mother of the Son family or learn how to play the jang-gu attired in hanbok (traditional Korean clothes) or paint 'sagunja' (the four gracious plants that symbolize the high integrity of the scholar/aristocrat, the plum, orchid, crysanthemum and bamboo) with a meok (black Chinese ink sticks) and an ink stand. The attraction of Son's Home lies in the fact that visitors can have the opportunity to experience Korean life by spending time with an average Korean family.

Son's Home provides programs which allow people to experience traditional tea-making, kimchi-making, sagunja painting, wearing hanbok, playing traditional musical instruments, playing folk games and trying typical Korean dishes.

Yoo's Family

Yoo' s Family maintains a traditional large-scale family structure where four generations live together. In a traditional house, visitors can experience Korean culture with the Yoo family, who offer Korean cultural activity courses and Korean food making courses.

Traditional Wedding

Korea House

The Korea House is a complex which was established with the aim of introducing visitors to the traditional culture and customs of Korea. Catering to both Korean and foreign visitors, it presents various programs that showcase some aspects of the unique style and culture of Korea, including a sampling of traditional court cuisine, folk performances and traditional wedding ceremonies.

Traditional wedding ceremony reenactments which follow the customs of Seoul and the surrounding Gyeonggi-do have become a popular attraction for both Korean people and foreigners. Folk performances are presented by skilled dance and gugak performing troupes and translation services are available in both Japanese and English.

Yejiwon

Yejiwon operates various educational programs to teach the proper decorum required in family and society. It is an instructive venue, especially for foreigners who wish to learn Korea's traditional etiquette and sensibilities. Those who enroll in Yejiwon's programs can experience the ceremony of traditional tea-making and try on hanbok.

Buddhist Culture

Lotus Lantern Festival on Buddha's Birthday

During the Lotus Lantern Festival, which is held on Buddha's Birthday (8th of April, on the lunar calendar), people put up lotus lanterns in which their long-held wishes are contained. The festival has a long history and is one of the country's major celebrations. Starting with the lighting ceremony in front of Seoul City Hall, a wide variety of events are held, including exhibitions of traditional lanterns in all sorts of colors and shapes, street festivals where folk games are played and Buddhist culture is represented, lantern parades of tens of thousands of people, and a Buddhist memorial service on Jongno and Ujeonggungno streets in honor of the

Yeongsanje

departed.

Yeongsanje Ceremony of Bongwonsa Temple

Yeongsanje is a grandiose Buddhist ceremony which reenacts the Seokgamoni, Buddha's historical sermon of the Lotus Sutra on the Yeongchuisan. This ritual is very meaningful in that it is said to awaken both the living and the dead, leading them to nirvana. During the ceremony, Buddhist music and dances are performed. For example, such musical instruments as the hojeok (a kind of trumpet), the chwita (a kind of small drum) and the beopgo (a drum made of calf leather) are played and butterfly dances are performed. While watching the ceremony, spectators can enjoy traditional Buddhist foods consisting of wild vegetables, green-pea jelly curds and rice cakes.

Jogyesa Temple

The information center for foreigners operated by Jogyesa provides visitors to the temple with an opportunity to be introduced to the true spirit of Korean Buddhism and to learn about the history and structure of Jogyesa. In addition, the temple runs a number of programs which are designed to give foreigners a chance to experience Korean Buddhism. The programs include meditation practice, tea-making, introduction of Korean Buddhism and a two-hour long tour of the temple compound.

Hwagyesa Temple

The International Zen Center of Hwagyesa teaches Korean Zen Buddhism to foreign monks and offers English Buddhist services and English language programs for the general public. A wide variety of other activities are also carried out by the temple.

Tongdosa Temple

The International Department of the Busan Propagation Center of Tongdosa provides a systematic program for foreigners to survey Korea's history and culture, especially Buddhist culture. Lectures on Korea's traditional culture, seasonal folk

Oriental Medicine

Oriental medicine considers illness to be the result of an imbalance in the forces generated within one' s body, a view which differs from that of Western medicine. It treats an illness by strengthening the weakened immune system and restoring the harmony of overall body functions, rather than using chemical based medicines and surgery.

Oriental pharmacy

An Oriental pharmacy is full of a variety of aromatic and bitter roots, bark, flowers, leaves and seeds from a wide range of plants. A pharmacy even includes some animal products. These are usually mixed in a formula and dispensed as liquid remedies.
These herbal medicines have little or no side effects, and they have proved effective in curing diseases for thousands of years. Another common treatment is acupuncture, in which sharp, thin needles are inserted either into the skin or deep into the flesh. The major effect of this is the stimulation of the meridians, the channels in the body through which the vital force called 'chi' flows. There are 360 cardinal points along the meridians, which relate directly to the body's internal functions. Stimulating these points with a needle and sometimes electrical pulses or finger pressure, can improve the balance and flow of 'chi' and help restore physical strength. Sometimes, bunches of dried mugwort are applied to the cardinal points on the meridians instead and slowly burned down. This pinpointed heat has a therapeutic effect and is called moxibustion.

Hand Therapy

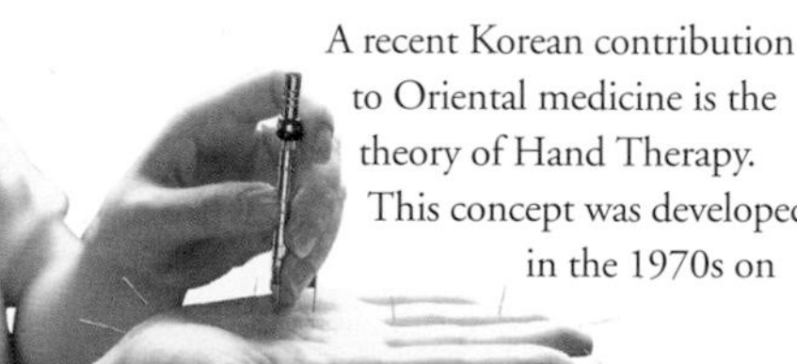

A recent Korean contribution to Oriental medicine is the theory of Hand Therapy. This concept was developed in the 1970s on the principle that the hand can be a microcosm of the entire body, and that most of the 360 basic acupuncture points can be mapped out on the palm, the back of the hand and the fingers.
Lecture and experience programs of 2 hours, a half-day, and 16 hours are taught at the Koryo Hand Therapy Institute, in English or Japanese, at the request of travel agencies and organizations.
Koryo Hand Therapy Institute 82-2-2231-8012
www.koryohand.com

Hanjeungmak

Hanjeungmak is a kind of sauna with a history of almost 600 years in Korea. It serves as an excellent way of relaxing the body, promoting metabolism and alleviating neuralgia and muscular fatigue. The 'mak' in hanjeungmak means a dome-shaped steamroom made of stone and heated underneath by a pine fire. When the stones are hot, water is thrown on them to create steam. One enters this room after a shower and sweats for about 5 minutes. This rids the body of toxic matter and other waste substances.

Oriental Medical Centers and Clinics Catering to Foreigners

Nam Seoul Oriental Medical Clinic 82-2-577-0142
Oriental Medicine Department of National Medical Center 82-2-2265-9131
Oriental Medicine Center of Kyung Hee University 82-2-958-9100
Seoul Oriental Medicine Center of Kyong-won University 82-2-425-3456
Kangnam CHA Oriental Hospitals 82-2-3468-3584/5
Hye Dang Oriental Medical Hospital 82-2-335-1010
Conmaeul Oriental Hospital & Medical Clinic 82-2-3475-7000
Dr. Jou' s Oriental Hospital & Medical Clinic 82-2-3411-8835
In-Dang Oriental Medicinal Clinic 82-2-557-3906
Karam Clinic 82-2-855-3696
Kang Seo Oriental Medical Clinic 82-2-3662-7986
Kka Chi Oriental Clinic 82-2-698-5816

Herbal Medicine Markets

Gyeongdong Herbal Medicine Market in Seoul 82-2-969-4793/4
Jecheon Herb Market 82-43-646-2320
Yakjeon Alley 82-53-253-4729

Taekwondo

Taekwondo, Korea's traditional martial art, is an internationally recognized sport which has become popular across the world. It is aimed at training not only one's mind and body, but also at building one's character. It is a high-level martial art which focuses on self defense rather than on attacking. It was designated as a demonstration sport during the 1988 Seoul Olympic Games and adopted as a medal sport during the 2000 Sydney Olympic Games. There are many programs designed to give people a chance to experience Taekwondo. Taekwondo watching, and one-day or three-day package programs in which participants can learn the varying skills and techniques of Taekwondo are offered. Those who are interested in participating in these programs can apply through travel agencies.

Hoki Taekwondo

The Hoki Taekwondo cultural experience program consists of courses on Taekwondo etiquette, Taekwondo demonstrations, basic movements of Taekwondo, self-defense techniques, board breaking and Taekwondo form. After the completion of the program, a graduation ceremony is held for participants. People can choose from two types of one-day programs: a four-hour and a six-hour course. During the program, lunch is provided, along with mementoes that include a Taekwondo uniform and a black belt, an honorary membership card and a certificate of graduation.

Festivals & Events

Korea abounds with festivals as diverse as the changes which occurred throughout its long history. These festivals are held at all the times of the year on a nationwide basis.
The central and local governments have put forth an effort to preserve precious cultural properties and promote various local festivals, as an attempt to maintain the parts of the Korean identity which are rooted in these various cultural fields.
Visitors can experience traditional Korean culture through these festivals.
The festivals are divided into several types, including natural festivals, cultural festivals, traditional festivals and sports festivals.

1. *Korean Traditional Drink & Cake Festival (March)*
2. *Goyang World Flower Exhibition (April)*
3. *Chunseol Da-hyang Festival (May)*
4. *Boseong Da-hyang Festival (May)*
5. *Hadong Mountain Dew Tea Cultural Festival (May)*
6. *World Festival for Island Cultures (May)*
7. *Hansan Ramie Fabric Cultural Festival (May)*
8. *Gwangju Biennale (March)*
9. *Wangin Culture Festival (April)*
10. *Daegu Textile & Fashion Festival (April)*
11. *Naval Port Festival (April)*
12. *Jeonju Daesaseup Nori (May)*
13. *Chunhyang Festival (May)*
14. *Jindo Yeongdeung Festival (May)*
15. *Daegu Yangnyeongsi Festival (May)*
16. *Cheongdo Korea Bullfighting Festival (May)*
17. *Sudalrae Festival (May)*

18. *Mt. Sobaeksan Royal Azalea Festival (June)*
19. *Boryeong Mud Festival (July)*
20. *World Ceramic Exposition (August)*
21. *Gangjin Celadon Porcelain Cultural Festival (August)*
22. *Hyo-seok Culture Festival (August)*
23. *Muju Firefly Festival (August)*
24. *The Gangneung Dano Festival (June)*
25. *Chuncheon International Mime Festival (June)*
26. *Daejeon Science Festival (August)*
27. *Goseong Dinosaur World Festival (August)*
28. *Busan Sea Festival (August)*
29. *Tongyeong Najeon Lacquer ware Festival (September)*
30. *Geumsan Ginseng Festival (September)*
31. *Bonghwa Pine Mushroom Festival (September)*
32. *Yangyang Pine Mushroom Festival (September)*
33. *Mt. Mindungsan Eulalia Festival (October)*
34. *Mt. Naejangsan Autumn Tints Festival (October)*
35. *Gwangju Kimchi Festival (October)*
36. *Gimhae Ceramic Ware Festival (October)*
37. *Namdo Food Festival (October)*
38. *Iksan Jewelry Festival (October)*
39. *Punggi Ginseng Festival (October)*
40. *Gyeongju World Culture Expo (September)*
41. *Jeongseon Arirang Festival (October)*
42. *Yeongdong Nangye Festival (October)*
43. *Jeonju Sori (Musical Sound) Festival (October)*
44. *Andong International Mask Dance Festival (October)*
45. *Busan Jagalchi Festival (October)*
46. *Pusan International Film Festival (October)*
47. *Chungju World Martial Arts Festival (October)*
48. *Ganghwado Cultural Festival (October)*
49. *International Formula 3 Korea Super Prix (November)*

50. *Daegwallyeong Snow Festival (January)*
51. *Mt. Hallasan Snowflake Festival (January)*
52. *The Polar Bear Swimming Competition (January)*

53. *Sugyeonggosa Fountain of Cheongpung Lake*

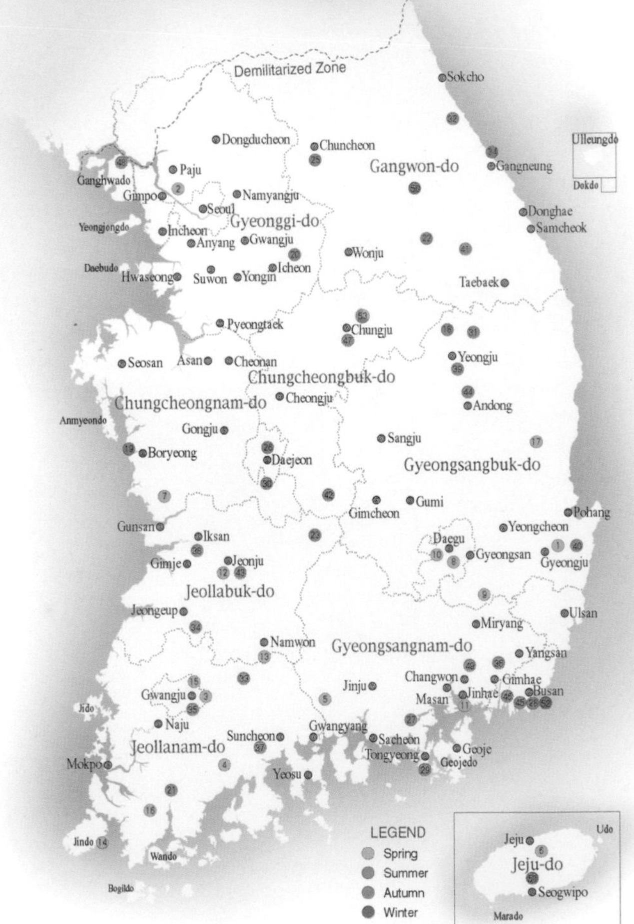

Festivals Related to Nature

Muju Firefly Festival

The Muju Firefly Festival was initiated to better preserve the environment in which everyone lives. These little insects serve as reminders of reckless development, urbanization and industrialization and the need to restore the environment back to its original state. The purpose of this festival is to create an awareness of the importance of maintaining the environment and making the world a better place to live. Many programs are planned during the festival, including main events, traditional performances and games.

Goyang World Flower Exhibition

The Goyang World Flower Exhibition is a festival which is themed the 'Harmony between Flowers and Human Beings.' Its main venue is Ilsan Lake Park in Gyeonggi-do.
Participating buyers from overseas and persons from the horticultural industry are in attendance, and the exhibition includes a trade fair which contributes to promoting commerce, mutual friendship and exchanges of information within the floral trade.
There are many special exhibition halls in Ilsan Lake Park, including the World Hall, the Domestic Hall, the Potted Plant Hall, the Native Plant Hall, the Theme Garden and the National Flower Garden of Korea. Various beautiful flowers are on display in each exhibition hall.

Mt. Naejangsan Maple Festival

The Mt. Naejangsan Maple Festival is held on Mt. Naejangsan, an area noted for the beauty of its maple trees. The festival is held when the maple leaf colors are at their brightest. 13 kinds of maple trees are scattered across the ridges and gorges of the mountain.
A number of events occur at the festival, including a maple fair, a drive-in theater and traditional performances.

Mt. Hallasan Snowflake Festival

The Mt. Hallasan Snowflake Festival is held in the last week of January every year.
Mt. Hallasan captivates visitors with its breathtaking beauty in each of the four seasons. During the winter, pure white snowflakes cling to the trees and provide spellbinding scenery.
With the crystal white Mt. Hallasan as a backdrop, the festival kicks off with events that include sledding, games and trekking.

Jinhae Cherry Blossom Festival

The Jinhae Cherry Blossom Festival is held in Jinhae-si, Gyeongsangnam-do.
Jinhae is a city known for both its naval port and its cherry blossoms. This festival is held from the end of March to early April, centering around the birthday of Admiral Yi Sun-shin who fought and defeated the Japanese invasion during the Joseon Dynasty. The festival originated to honor the memory of the patriotism of Admiral Yi Sun-shin and to promote local culture and art.
This festival begins with a ritual ceremony in memory of Admiral Yi Sun-shin and is followed by various events, including an opening ceremony, a lantern festival with 10,000 lights, a parade and folk performances.
This festival also offers visitors a chance to see the naval academy, the Jinhae Museum, a turtle boat and a naval vessel in Jangcheonhang Port.

Muju Firefly Festival

Goyang World Flower Exhibition

Maple Leaf Tunnel of Mt. Naejangsan

Festivals Related to Local Culture

Gwangju Kimchi Festival

Ingredients of Kimchi

Bossam Kimchi

The Gwangju Kimchi Festival is a unique cultural festival which attracts domestic and foreign tourists and promotes the kimchi industry.
The festival holds a variety of cultural events, such as traditional instrument performances, traditional Korean narrative songs, a kimchi concert, a visitors' song contest, a pavilion exhibit on the history of kimchi, a display of various types of kimchi and foods made from kimchi and a kimchi-making contest for diplomats and international visitors.

World Festival for Island Cultures

The World Festival for Island Cultures is held on Jeju Island. It is the only festival celebrating island culture in the world. Islands have historically been isolated from each other and from main land cultures, and as a result, they have developed unique cultures.
People representing about 30 islands and 900 performers from all parts of the world participate together in this event to share their own cultures and to build friendship. The festival begins with a ritual service and an opening ceremony, which is followed by various events, including folk performances by participating islanders, a beauty pageant, a painting contest, an air show, and a exhibition of artwork. Wind-surfing, paragliding, scuba diving and mountain biking can also be enjoyed on Jeju while the festival takes place.

Gangjin Celadon Porcelain Cultural Festival

Gangjin is the home of Goryeo celadon, which flourished for over 500 years during the Goryeo Dynasty.
The Gangjin Celadon Porcelain Cultural festival is an effort to pass on the Goryeo celadon culture to the next generation and develop it further.
Visitors have a chance to make celadon works of their own here and be entertained with a number of folk performances. Other events awaiting tourists include a pottery exhibition, a requiem service for deceased anonymous potters and a performance of southern folk songs.

Porcelain Kiln

Korean Traditional Drink and Cake Festival

The Korean Traditional Drink and Cake Festival is held in Gyeongju-si, Gyeongsangbuk-do.
On display are exotic home-brewed liquors and hand made rice cakes, historical and regional specialties and traditional confectionaries.

Making Hangwa

Traditional Korean beverages and rice cakes can be sampled for free. Varied culinary contests are open to all, and visitors can work a rice mallet, slice up long rice-cake bars, or decorate glutinous rice pancakes with azalea flower petals.

Andong International Mask Dance Festival

The mask dance festival is held in Hahoe Village, Andong-si, the home of Korean Confucianism. Here the traditional Korean lifestyle has remained intact to a significant degree.
The festival provides a good opportunity to view Korean mask dances, as well as mask dances from other parts of the world. Visitors to the festival can also make their own masks, learn folk dancing and view cultural exhibitions.
This festival's events include an international mask dance performance, an Andong folk festival, a Korean puppet show, a Hahoe Village festival, mask dance lessons, an exhibition of mask dance paintings, mask making and totem pole carving.

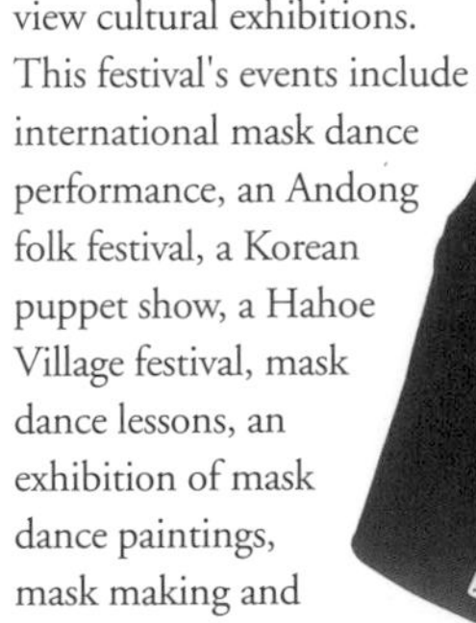

Andong Mask Dance

Gyeongju World Culture Expo

Gyeongju World Culture Expo

Gyeongju is a historical city which has developed and transferred indigenous ideas from the Silla culture into the present.
This expo is an exciting event where visitors can appreciate the value of world cultural heritage.
The Gyeongju World Culture Expo is held bi-annually. It will open not only the era of a new renaissance, but also play a crucial role in establishing Gyeongju as a center of world culture.

Gangneung Dano Festival

The Gangneung Dano Festival is held in the Danojang (Market) in Gangwon-do for five days, starting on the fifth day of the fifth month on the lunar calendar.
The Gangneung Danoje, or Dano Festival, is one of the oldest seasonal folk festivals in this area. It is still a major folk festival for the region because of its accurate depictions of the area's traditional culture.

Ritual Ceremony in Gangneung Danoje

Jindo Yeongdeung Festival

The sea waters between Jindo Island and Modo Islet part annually at low tide in the 3rd lunar month, opening a sea road 2.8km long and 40m wide. The Jindo Yeongdeung Festival is held at this time every year.
The festival hosts a variety of cultural activities, such as the hundred boat parade, the ganggangsuwollae (a circle dance performed by girls or women), the yeongdeungsalpuri (a shaman rite to exorcise evil spirits), the dasiraegi (a mourner's ceremony performed the night before a burial), the namdo deullorae (farming songs of the Jindo region), the namdo manga (a pall-bearers dirge) and Jindo dog show.

Chunhyang Festival

The Chunhyang Festival is held each year at the Gwanghalluwon Garden in Namwon-si, Jeollabuk-do, on the fifth of May.
Gwanghallu was the rendezvous spot for Seong Chun-hyang and Yi Mong-ryong, romantic characters in an old novel whose names have become a synonym for 'lovers.'
With much fanfare, this festival brings together tourists from all quarters to enjoy local culture and art including Pansori Chunhyang-jeon, the lengthy epic solo song describing the life of Chunhyang.
Many other events also take place during the festival, including a ceremony paying respects at Chunhyang's tomb, a costume parade depicting Chunhyang's life story, a national folk music performance, a Chunhyang pansori performance, a national archery contest and the Chunhyang Beauty Contest.
The Chunhyang Beauty Contest, with its contestants adorned in traditional Korean attire, is the climax of the festival.

Chunhyang Festival

Festivals Related to Sports

Cheongdo Bullfighting Festival

The Cheongdo Bullfighting Festival is held annually in Cheongdo-gun, Gyeongsangbuk-do, in May. This festival has a long and unique history. Cattle have played diverse roles in Korea's agrarian society. Korean bullfighting dates back to ancient times and the type exhibited at the Cheongdo Bullfighting Festival is like the original version. Korean bullfighting involves neither a stadium full of people nor a toreador's fancy maneuvers with a cape and sword. It is bull-to-bull combat, held on special occasions and the animals are not seriously injured. Traditional activities like seesawing, kite flying and other folk merriment also occur during this festival.
Events include a bullfighting tournament which is divided into separate weight classes, a Korea-Japan goodwill bullfighting match, a Korean bull rodeo contest, a Cheong-do bullfighting photograph contest and exhibition, a heifer contest and a traditional market.

Polar Bear Swimming Competition

The Polar Bear Swimming Competition is held in January as one of the first events of the new year. Participants plunge into the sea and swim 80 meters before emerging from the water.
This festival has been held since 1988. It has contributed to making winter swimming popular and has been increasing popularity in recent years.

Festivals Related to Local Products

Yangyang Pine Mushroom Festival

The Yangyang Pine Mushroom Festival is held on the edge of the Namdaecheon (Stream) in Yangyang-gun, Gangwon-do, in October of every year. This festival originated in 1997.
In addition to picking mushrooms, participants may stay at a pine mushroom farm, receive instruction in distinguishing

Picking Mushrooms

Yangyang pine mushrooms, cook with pine mushrooms and witness a ceremony performed for the mountain gods.

Geumsan Ginseng Festival

The Geumsan Ginseng Festival is held in Geumsan-gun, Chungcheongnam-do. It is a popular local festival in this region. Geumsan is the home of Goryeo ginseng and the largest ginseng market in the world. 80% of the nation's supply of ginseng is produced here.
This festival features various products made from Geumsan ginseng and offers visitors the chance to purchase ginseng and other medicinal herbs at low prices.
Visitors can also participate in the ginseng harvest.

The festival's main events include an international ginseng exhibition, international folk performances, medicinal herb dicing and souvenir ginseng bottle making.

Daegu Textile & Fashion Festival

Daegu has established itself as the center of Korea's textile industry. For this reason, Daegu holds the Daegu Textile & Fashion Festival every year. This festival is a part of the Milano Project, which aims to make Daegu internationally known for its textiles & fashions. During the same period, the city government invites overseas buyers to visit in order to promote the export of local textile products.
Events during the festival include a sewing competition, an international design exhibition, a traditional Korean costume (hanbok) exhibition and a traditional embroidery exhibition.

Fashion Show in the Daegu Textile & Fashion Festival

Korea-Japan Bullfighting Match

Shopping

There are various items in Korea, which can be purchased as souvenirs, such as ceramic, embroidery, macrame, doll, papercrafts, hanbok, woodcraft, Najeon lacquer ware, etc.
These souvenir items can be purchased at duty free shops, department stores, souvenir shops, traditional markets, etc.

The Tax Refund System

Foreign tourists can purchase duty-free goods in Korea. The goods must be exported within 3 months of the date of purchase. To purchase duty-free goods, tourists must follow the procedure below. When tourists purchase a minimum of 50,000 Korean won (about 40 US dollars) of goods in an affiliated store, they will receive a refund check. Their refund slip must be presented together with their goods at the customs desk at the Incheon International Airport before leaving Korea, and their refund slip must be validated by a customs stamp. Refund slips can be cashed in at the Refund Service Operator Desk in the airport. If tourists don't have time to visit the Refund Service Operator Desk in the airport, they can also mail their validated Global Refund Checks. In this case, tourists will be sent a bank check or their credit card account will be credited for the amount. A handling fee will be deducted from the refunded taxes.

Korea Pass Card

The Korea Pass Card (KPC) is a card which can function as a mass transit ticket, a telephone card, or a credit card. It may only be purchased by tourists traveling in Korea. It can be used to pay for items purchased in most businesses that accept major credit cards, including hotels, duty-free shops, and shopping centers. Discounts from 5% to 20% are available when using the KPC at participating stores. This card can also be used to pay for transportation, such as buses, deluxe taxis (with stickers indicating a KPC logo), subways, airlines and trains. It may even be used for making local and international telephone calls. The cards are available in denominations of 100,000 won, 200,000 won and 500,000 won. They can be purchased at the Incheon International Airport and at the customer center in Myeongdong. In case there are funds remaining on the card, the card owner may receive a refund by handing in the card at its place of purchase. Questions or complaints about the card can be directed to the 'KPC Service Center.' This telephone number is found on the card and in its accompanying information booklet.

www.koreapasscard.com

Hwanghak-dong Flea Market
Dongdaemun Market
Sewoon Plaza
Gyeongdong Market
Jangan-dong Antique Market
Namdaemun Market
Myeongdong
Itaewon
Yongsan Electronics Market
Apgujeong Rodeo Street

Major Shopping Places in Seoul

Duty Free Shops

Name	Address	Tel
Duty-Free Korea (Incheon International Airport)	2172-1, Unseo-dong, Jung-gu, Incheon	82-32-743-2000
Hotel Lotte	Lotte Department Store Duty Free Shop (10th floor), Sogong-dong, Jung-gu, Seoul	82-2-759-7586~8
SKM Duty-Free Shop (COEX INTERCON SHOP)	COEX Inter Continental Seoul, 159, Samseong-dong, Gangnam-gu, Seoul	82-2-3484-9600
Dongwha Duty-Free Shop	211-1, Sejongno, Jongno-gu, Seoul	82-2-399-3000
SKM Duty-Free Shop (Sheraton Walker Hill)	Sheraton Walker Hill Hotel, Gwangjang-dong, Gwangjin-gu, Seoul	82-2-458-6760
Hotel Shilla Duty-Free Shop	202, Jangchung-dong 2(i)-ga, Jung-gu, Seoul	82-2-2230-3662
Lotte Department Store (Main Store)	1, Sogong-dong, Jung-gu, Seoul	82-2-771-2500
Lotte World Shopping Mall	40-1, Jamsil-dong, Songpa-gu, Seoul	82-2-411-2500
Galleria Department Store	515, Apgujeong, Gangnam-gu, Seoul	82-2-3449-4114
Midopa Department Store	123, Namdaemunno 2 (i)-ga, Jung-gu, Seoul	82-2-754-2222
Hyundai Department Store	429, Apgujeong, Gangnam-gu, Seoul	82-2-549-2233

Purchasing Souvenirs

Ceramics

Foreign tourists can purchase inexpensive ceramic items at any ceramic shop in Korea, including cups, plates, porcelain, and decorative ceramics. For expensive ceramics with artistic value, tourists must visit specialized ceramic stores or a ceramic village.

Hyungbae

Hyungbae are embroidered patches which were worn on the breast and on the back of the official uniforms of the king, the prince, and civil and military officials during the Joseon Dynasty. An embroidery featuring two tigers was used for military official's uniforms.

Sewing Workboxes

These workboxes have been used by Korean women for a long time. They are used to hold pins, spools of thread, thimbles and other sewing implements.

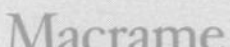

Macrame

Korean macrame items are personal ornaments which make great souvenirs. They can be purchased in Insa-dong, at Namdaemun Market, and at specialized hanbok stores.

Ornamental Silver Knife

This is an accessory for women which was traditionally kept in a pocket or worn around the neck. It was used for decorative purposes as well as for self-defense.

Embroidery

Embroidery is made up of patterns of letters and drawings which are sewn into silk fabrics. These designs are used as material for clothing, sewing workboxes, wrapping cloths, etc.

These traditional items are both popular and inexpensive. They are available in numerous souvenir shops.

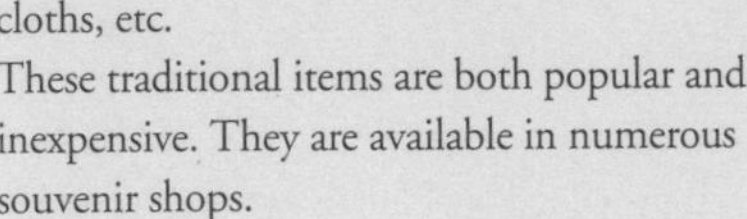

Najeon Lacquerware (Lacquerware inlaid with Mother-of-pearl)

Najeon lacquerware refers to items that have been produced by first lacquering a material like wood or bamboo, then attaching bright shells in elaborate patterns before applying a final finishing coat of lacquer.

The Tongyeong area is the main producer of Najeon lacquerware in Korea.

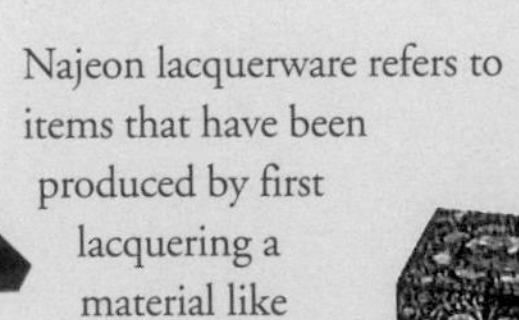

Hwagak Crafts (Hornwork)

Hwagak crafts are crafts which were produced for use by the royal family traditionally. They are made from cow horns.

Woodcrafts

Korean woodcrafts have a long artistic tradition. These woodcrafts vary from small decorative items to large furniture. They can be purchased at antique shops and at tourist souvenir shops.

Folding Fans

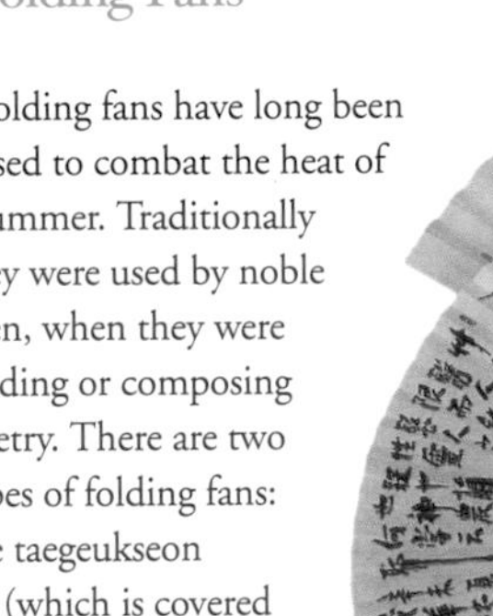

Folding fans have long been used to combat the heat of summer. Traditionally they were used by noble men, when they were reading or composing poetry. There are two types of folding fans: the taegeukseon (which is covered with taegeuk patterns) and the hapjukseon (which is covered with oriental paintings). The hapjukseon is especially popular because of its antique looking oriental paintings.

Papercrafts

Hanji, a kind of traditional Korean paper made from mulberry bark, is characterized by its durability, luster, and absorption. Papercrafts made from this traditional Korean paper have a splendid color. Papercrafts are considered a valued asset to Korea's arts. They can be bought in ornamental boxes at folk souvenir shops in Insa-dong.

Dolls

Dolls with traditional costumes are usually found in folk souvenir shops, and are one of Korea's most popular souvenirs. The majority of these dolls are attired in traditional Korean wedding clothing.

Ginseng

Ginseng, which is a specialty of Korea known worldwide, comes in a number of varieties. Hongsam, which is a type of steamed and dried ginseng, is especially popular among visitors to Korea.

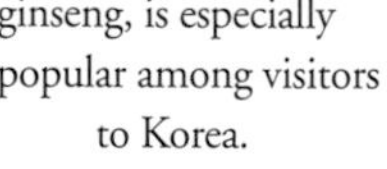

Gim

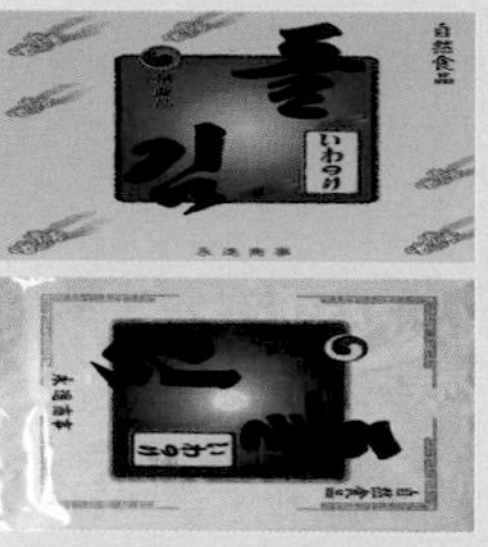

Gim, a very popular food item, is dried, seasoned sea weed. It is packed in small containers for convenient carrying.
It can be purchased at department stores, souvenir shops, and traditional markets.

Kimchi

Kimchi is one of the most popular kinds of traditional Korean food. Visitors can find it at department stores or duty-free shops.
There are also various kinds of vacuum-packed kimchi for carrying convenience.

Leather Goods

Leather products in a multitude of colors and designs are also available. Leather coats and jackets are relatively inexpensive, as are other leather goods, such as shoes, bags, belts, and purses.

Electronic Merchandise

Electronic merchandise is available at department stores, electronic goods stores and electronic markets. Stores have fixed prices, but discounts ranging from 10% to 30% may be obtained by shopping prudently at electronics markets like the one located in Yongsan.
Buyers from overseas are advised to check their devise's electronic voltage requirements. 220v is the voltage primarily used in Korea.

Hanbok

Hanbok has been the Korean people's unique traditional clothing for centuries.
Like much of Korea's art, hanbok is characterized by subtle curves, flowing lines and plenty of blank spaces. These clothes can be purchased at hanbok stores.

Handbags

Visitors can buy handbags that reflect a broad range of refinement and elegance. Both world famous brands and high quality Korean brands are available to shoppers.

Clothing

Visitors to Korea can buy high quality suits made from a broad range of materials and colors, including beautiful silks, at surprisingly low prices. These items can be found at traditional markets, such as Namdaemun market and Dongdaemun Market, and at department stores.

Special Products

Korea has various special products which are produced in each region. Special products include things like ceramics, amethysts, Hwamunseok, woodcrafts, ginseng, pine mushrooms and other items too numerous to mention.

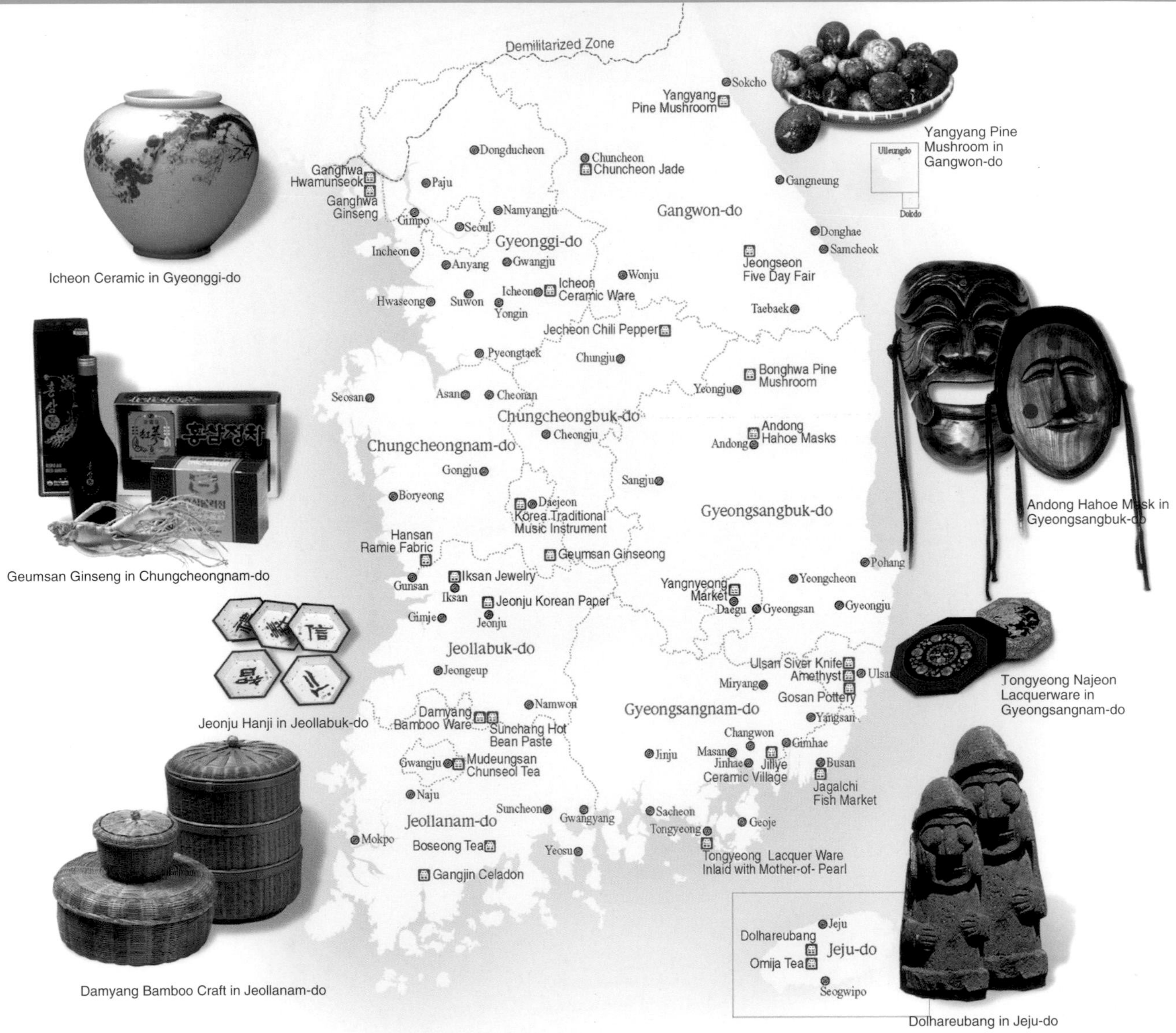

Demilitarized Zone
Sokcho
Yangyang Pine Mushroom
Ganghwa Hwamunseok
Ganghwa Ginseng
Dongducheon
Chuncheon
Chuncheon Jade
Paju
Gangneung
Gangwon-do
Gimpo
Seoul
Namyangju
Gyeonggi-do
Incheon
Donghae
Samcheok
Anyang
Gwangju
Wonju
Jeongseon Five Day Fair
Hwaseong
Suwon
Icheon
Icheon Ceramic Ware
Yongin
Taebaek
Jecheon Chili Pepper
Pyeongtaek
Chungju
Bonghwa Pine Mushroom
Seosan
Asan
Cheonan
Yeongju
Chungcheongbuk-do
Andong Hahoe Masks
Andong
Chungcheongnam-do
Cheongju
Gongju
Sangju
Boryeong
Daejeon
Korea Traditional Music Instrument
Gyeongsangbuk-do
Hansan Ramie Fabric
Geumsan Ginseong
Pohang
Gunsan
Iksan Jewelry
Iksan
Yangnyeong Market
Yeongcheon
Jeonju Korean Paper
Daegu
Gyeongsan
Gyeongju
Gimje
Jeonju
Jeollabuk-do
Ulsan Siver Knife
Amethyst
Ulsan
Jeongeup
Miryang
Gosan Pottery
Namwon
Gyeongsangnam-do
Damyang Bamboo Ware
Sunchang Hot Bean Paste
Yangsan
Changwon
Gimhae
Gwangju
Mudeungsan Chunseol Tea
Jinju
Masan
Jinhae
Jillye Ceramic Village
Busan
Jagalchi Fish Market
Naju
Suncheon
Gwangyang
Sacheon
Jeollanam-do
Tongyeong
Geoje
Mokpo
Boseong Tea
Yeosu
Tongyeong Lacquer Ware Inlaid with Mother-of- Pearl
Gangjin Celadon
Ulleungdo
Dokdo
Jeju
Dolhareubang
Jeju-do
Omija Tea
Seogwipo

Icheon Ceramic in Gyeonggi-do

Geumsan Ginseng in Chungcheongnam-do

Jeonju Hanji in Jeollabuk-do

Damyang Bamboo Craft in Jeollanam-do

Yangyang Pine Mushroom in Gangwon-do

Andong Hahoe Mask in Gyeongsangbuk-do

Tongyeong Najeon Lacquerware in Gyeongsangnam-do

Dolhareubang in Jeju-do

Appendix

ACCOMMODATIONS

SUPER DELUXE HOTELS

Ⓡ: Room Ⓛ: Location

COEX Inter-continental Seoul — SEOUL

159, Samseong-dong, Gangnam-gu
Tel. 82-2-3452-2500 Fax 82-2-3430-8000
http://seoul.interconti.com/coeic/
Facilities: Restaurants & Bar, Lounge, Health Club, Business Center, Banquet & Meeting Room
Ⓡ: 654 Ⓛ: P 234 A4

Grand Inter-Continental Seoul — SEOUL

159-8, Samseong-dong, Gangnam-gu
Tel. 82-2-555-5656 Fax 82-2-559-7990
http://seoul.interconti.com/seoic/
Facilities: Restaurants(Korean, Chineses, Japanese, French, Australian, Italian), Bars, Fitness Center, Sauna, Swimming Pool, Lobby Lounge, Cafe, Night Club, Business Center, Banquet & Meeting Room
Ⓡ: 654 Ⓛ: P 234 A4

Hotel Amiga — SEOUL

7-248, Nonhyeon-dong, Gangnam-gu
Tel 82-2-3440-8000 Fax 82-2-3440-8200
http://www.amiga.co.kr
Facilities: Coffee Shop, Restaurants (Korean, Chinese, Japanese, Continental Buffet)
Amiga Club, Business Center, Meeting Room & Banquet Hall
Ⓡ: 654 Ⓛ: P 234 A4

Renaissance Seoul Hotel — SEOUL

676,Yeoksam-dong,Gangnam-gu
Tel 82-2-555-0501 Fax 82-2-553-8118
http://www.renaissance-seoul.com
Facilities: 15 Restaurants and Lounges, Diamond Ballroom, Fitness Center
Ⓡ: 654 Ⓛ: P 234 A4

The Ritz-Carlton Hotel Seoul — SEOUL

602-Yeoksam-dong, Gangnam-gu
Tel 82-2-3451-8000 Fax 82-2-556-8855
http://www.ritz.co.kr
Facilities: Restaurants(Korean, Western, Japanese), Coffee Shop, Lobby Lounge, Bar, Night Club, Grill, Fitness Club (Indoor Swimming Pool, Sauna, Aerobics, Indoor Golf Range, Banquet Halls
Ⓡ: 654 Ⓛ: P 234 A4

Sheraton Walker Hill — SEOUL

San 21, Gwangjang-dong, Gwangjin-gu
Tel 82-2-453-0121 Fax 82-2-452-6867
http://www.walkerhill.co.kr
Facilities: Coffee Shop, Restaurants (Korean, Chinese, Japanese, French, Italian), Buffet, Delicatessen, Health Club, 17 Meeting rooms, Casino, Duty Free Shop, Gallery, Shopping Arcade
Ⓡ: 654 Ⓛ: P 234 A4

The Swiss Grand Hotel — SEOUL

201-1, Hongeun-dong, Seodaemun-gu
Tel 82-2-3216-5656 Fax 82-2-3216-7799
http://www.swissgrand.co.kr
Facilities: Restaurants (Korean, Chinese, Japanese, Continental), Buffet, Bars, Fitness Center, Swimming Pool, Shopping Arcade, Swiss Beauty Clinic, Meeting & Banquet Hall
Ⓡ: 654 Ⓛ: P 234 A4

JW Marriott Hotel Seoul — SEOUL

19-3, Banpo-dong, Seocho-gu
Tel 82-2-6282-6262 Fax 82-2-6282-6263
http://marriotthotels.com/
Facilities: 5 Restaurants, Duty Free Shop, Fitness Center
Ⓡ: 654 Ⓛ: P 234 A4

Hotel Lotte World — SEOUL

40-1, Jamsil-dong, Songpa-gu
Tel 82-2-419-7000 Fax 82-2-417-3655
http://www.hotel.lotte.co.kr
Facilities: 10 Restaurants and Bars, 6 Meeting Rooms (Including an International Convention Center), Executive Floors, Sauna, Indoor Golf Range, Swimming Pool, Largest Duty Free Shop in East Asia
Ⓡ: 654 Ⓛ: P 234 A4

Grand Hyatt Seoul — SEOUL

747-7, Hannam-dong, Yongsan-gu
Tel 82-2-797-1234 Fax 82-2-798-6953
http://www.seoul.hyatt.com
Facilities: Restaurants and Bars, Banquet & Convention Center, Fitness Center (Indoor and Outdoor Swimming Pools, Tennis Courts, Squash Courts, Gymnasium, Aerobics, Men's and Ladies' Sauna, Business Center, Acade
Ⓡ: 654 Ⓛ: P 234 A4

Hotel Lotte — SEOUL

1, Sogong-dong, Jung-gu
Tel 82-2-771-1000 Fax 82-2-752-3758
http://www.hotel.lotte.co.kr
Facilities: 17 Restaurants and Bars, 15 International Meeting Halls, Banquet Rooms, Executive Floors, Fitness Center, Sauna, Duty Free Shop
Ⓡ: 654 Ⓛ: P 234 A4

Radisson Seoul Plaza Hotel — SEOUL

23, Taepyeongno 2-ga, Jung-gu
Tel 82-2-771-2200 Fax 82-2-755-8897
http://www.seoulplaza.co.kr
Facilities: Restaurants (Korean, Chinese, Italian, French), Banquet Hall, Business Center, Club Plaza Lounge, Lobby Lounge, Coffee Shop, Fitness Club, Shopping Arcade, Grand Wedding Plaza, Flower Shop
Ⓡ: 654 Ⓛ: P 234 A4

Seoul Hilton — SEOUL

395, Namdaemunno 5-ga, Jung-gu
Tel 82-2-753-7788 Fax 82-2-754-2510
E-mail selhitw@Bora.dacom.co.kr
http://www.hilton.com
Facilities: Restaurants (Korean, Chinese, Japanese, French, Italian), Buffet, Delicatessen, Health Club, Arcade, Business Center
Ⓡ: 654 Ⓛ: P 234 A4

The Shilla — SEOUL

202, Jangchung-dong 2-ga, Jung-gu
Tel 82-2-2233-3131 Fax 82-2-2233-5073
http://seoul.shilla.net
Facilities: Shopping Arcade, Travel Agency, Duty Free Shop, Business Center, Restaurants (Korean, Chinese, Italian, French), Fitness Center
Ⓡ: 654 Ⓛ: P 234 A4

The Westin Chosun Hotel — SEOUL

87-1, Sogong-dong, Jung-gu
Tel 82-2-771-0500 Fax 82-2-753-6370
http://www.westinchosun.co.kr
Facilities: Restaurants (Korea, Chinese, Japanese, Continental, Italian), Business Center, Gift Shop, Executive Club, Irish Pub & Sports Bar, Sauna, Swimming Pool, Aerobics, Barbershop, Beauty Salon, Meeting & Banquet Room
Ⓡ: 654 Ⓛ: P 234 A4

Haeundae Grand Hotel — BUSAN

651-2, Woo 1-dong, Haeundae-gu
Tel 82-51-7400-114 Fax 82-51-7400-141
http://www.grandhotel.co.kr
Facilities: Coffee Shop, Restaurants (Korean, Chinese, Japanese), Pub, Restaurant, Buffet, Italian Restaurant, Lobby Lounge, Cocktail Bar, Night Club
Ⓡ: 654 Ⓛ: P 234 A4

Hotel Lotte Pusan — BUSAN

503-15, Bujeon-dong, Busanjin-gu
Tel 82-51-810-1000 Fax 82-51-810-5110
http://www.hotel.lotte.co.kr
Facilities: 14 Restaurants and Bars, Health Club, Swimming Pool, Indoor Golf/Mini Golf Course, Men & Women's Sauna, Squash, 11 Banquet Halls, Meeting Rooms & Wedding Halls, Executive Floor, Lounge
Ⓡ: 654 Ⓛ: P 234 A4

Paradise Hotel & Casino Pusan — BUSAN

1405-16, Jung-dong, Haeundae-gu
Tel 82-51-743-1234 Fax 82-51-743-1250
http://www.busanmarriott.co.kr
Facilities: Business Center, Regency Club, 7 Restaurants, Coffee Shop, Meeting & Banquet Hall
Ⓡ: 654 Ⓛ: P 234 A4

Busan Marriott Hotel
BUSAN

1405-16, Jung-dong, Haeundae-gu
Tel 82-51-743-1234 Fax 82-51-743-1250
http://www.busanmarriott.co.kr
Facilities: Business Center, Regency Club, 3 Restaurants, Pub, Meeting & Banquet Hall
Ⓡ: 654 Ⓛ: P 234 A4

The Westin Chosun Beach Hotel
BUSAN

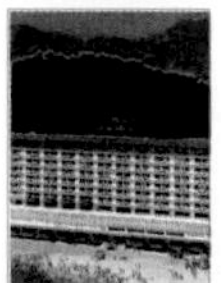

737, Woo 1-dong, Haeundae-gu
Tel 82-51-742-7411 Fax 82-51-742-1313
http://www.chosunbeach.co.kr
Facilities: Tongbaek, Lobby Lounge, Restaurants (Japanese, Korean, Western), Junior Ballroom, Private Dining Room, Grand Ballroom, Pub
Ⓡ: 654 Ⓛ: P 234 A4

Hotel Concorde
GYEONGBUK

410, Sinpyeong-dong, Gyeongju-si

Tel 82-54-745-7000 Fax 82-54-745-7010
http://www.concorde.co.kr
Facilities: Restaurants (Japanese, Korean, Western), Buffet, Lounge, Night Club, Swimming Pool, Spring Water Sauna, Banquet Hall
Ⓡ: 654 Ⓛ: P 234 A4

Hotel Hyundai
GYEONGBUK

477-2, Sinpyeong-dong, Gyeongju-si
Tel 82-54-748-2233 Fax 82-54-748-8111
http:// www.hyundaihotel.com
Facilities: Restaurants (Korean, Chinese, Japanese, Western), Lobby Lounge, Coffee Shop, Outdoor · Indoor Swimming Pool, Bowling Alley, Hot Spring Sauna, Banquet Hall
Ⓡ: 654 Ⓛ: P 234 A4

Kolon Hotel
GYEONGBUK

111-1, Ma-dong, Gyeongju-si
Tel 82-54-746-9001 Fax 82-54-746-6331
http://www.kolonhotel.co.kr
Facilities: Restaurants & Bars, Hot Spring Bath & Sauna, Golf Course & Driving Range, Convention Facilities, Night Club, Shopping Arcade, Laundry, Swimming Pool, Barbershop
Ⓡ: 654 Ⓛ: P 234 A4

Wellich Chosun Hotel
GYEONGBUK

410-2, Sinpyeong-dong, Gyeongju-si
Tel 82-54-745-7701 Fax 82-54-740-8349
Facilities: Restaurants (Korean, Japanese, Western), Bar, Coffee Lounge, Swimming Pool, Spa, Sauna, Tennis Courts, Business Center, Shopping Arcade, Karaoke, Banquet Hall
Ⓡ: 654 Ⓛ: P 234 A4

Kyongju Hilton
GYEONGBUK

370, Sinpyeong-dong, Gyeongju-si
Tel 82-54-745-7788 Fax 82-54-745-7799
Facilities: Restaurants (Koeran, Chinese, Japanese, Western), Buffet, Sky Lounge, Lobby Lounge, Coffee Shop, Sauna, Swimming Pool, Health Club, Squash,Tennis Courts, Museum, Casino, Nammoon Duty Free Shop, Arcade
Ⓡ: 654 Ⓛ: P 234 A4

Hotel Green Villa Cheju
JEJU

2812-10, Saekdal-dong, Seogwipo-si
Tel 82-64-738-3800 Fax 82-64-738-9990
http://www.greenvilla.co.kr
Facilities: Coffee Shop,Restaurants (Korean, Japanese, Western), Lobby Lounge, Cocktail Bar, Karaoke, Outdoor Swimming Pool, Terrace, Banquet Hall
Ⓡ: 654 Ⓛ: P 234 A4

Hyatt Regency Cheju
JEJU

3039-1, Saekdal-dong, Seogwipo-si
Tel 82-64-733-1234 Fax 82-64-732-2039
http://www.hyattcheju.com
Facilities: Casino, Shopping Arcade, Restaurants (Korean, Japanese, Western), Coffee Shop, Bakery, Disco, Cocktail Bar, Regency Lounge, Singing Room, Sauna, Swimming Pool, Tennis Court, Game Room for Children, Banquet Hall
Ⓡ: 654 Ⓛ: P 234 A4

Lotte Hotel Cheju
JEJU

2812-4, Saekdal-dong, Seogwipo-si
Tel 82-64-731-1000 Fax 82-64-731-4117
http://www.hotel.lotte.co.kr
Facilities: 7 Restaurants and Bars, 5 Banquet Rooms, Duty Free Shop, Casino, Fitness Center, Sauna, Tennis Court, Indoor · Outdoor Swimming Pools
Ⓡ: 654 Ⓛ: P 234 A4

Paradise Hotel Cheju
JEJU

511, Topyeong-dong, Seogwipo-si
Tel 82-64-763-2100 Fax 82-64-732-9355
http://paradisehotelcheju.co.kr
Facilities: Restaurants (Korean, Western), Coffee Shop, Bar, Karaoke, Health Club, Sauna, Beauty Salon, Outdoor Swimming Pool, Gift Shop, Fashion Store, Banquet Hall
Ⓡ: 654 Ⓛ: P 234 A4

The Shilla Cheju
JEJU

3039-3, Saekdal-dong, Seogwipo-si
Tel 82-64-738-4466 Fax 82-64-735-5414
http://cheju.shilla.net
Facilities: Coffee Shop, Restaurants (Korean, Japanese, Western), Lobby Lounge, Disco Club, Bar, Karaoke, Outdoor · Indoor Swimming Pool, Racquetball Court, Tennis Court , Bowling Alley, Sauna, Banquet Hall
Ⓡ: 654 Ⓛ: P 234 A4

Cheju Grand Hotel
JEJU

263-15, Yeon-dong, Jeju-si
Tel 82-64-747-5000 Fax 82-64-742-3150
http://www.grand.co.kr
Facilities: Restaurants (Korean, Japanese), Sky Restaurant, Coffee Shop, Main Bar, Lobby Lounge, Night Club, Bakery Shop, Business Center, Country Club, Casino, Sauna, Outdoor Swimming Pool, Health Club, Banquet Halls
Ⓡ: 654 Ⓛ: P 234 A4

Cheju KAL Hotel
JEJU

1691-9, Ido 1-dong, Jeju-si
Tel 82-64-724-2001 Fax 82-64-720-6515
Facilities: Restaurants (Korean, Chinese, Japanese), Coffeeshop, Lobby Lounge, Main Bar, Bakery, Karaoke, Night Club, Sky Lounge, Swimming Pool, Health Club, Sauna, Aerobic Room, Souvenir Shop, Sports Shop, Banquet Hall
Ⓡ: 654 Ⓛ: P 234 A4

Cheju Oriental Hotel
JEJU

1197, Samdo 2-dong, Jeju-si
Tel 82-64-752-8222 Fax 82-64-752-9777
Facilities: Restaurants (Korean, Japanese, Western), Shopping Center, Casino, Coffee Shop, Bar, Lobby Lounge, Men's Sauna, Barbershop, Beauty Salon, Bowling Alley, Banquet Hall
Ⓡ: 654 Ⓛ: P 234 A4

Crowne Plaza Hotel Jeju
JEJU

291-30, Yeon-dong, Jeju-si
Tel 82-64-741-8000 Fax 82-64-746-4111
Facilities: Restaurants (Korean, Chinese, Japanes, Westerne), Lobby Lounge, Main Bar, Crowne Plaza Casino, Las Vegas Style Show, Indoor Swimming Pool, Health Club, Banquet Hall, Karaoke Bar, Beauty Clinic, Barbershop
Ⓡ: 654 Ⓛ: P 234 A4

World Inn

World Inn is the name of the World Cup accommodation service in Korea. Each accommodation facility of World Inn has been designated by the area's regional government.
The World Inn Reservation Service provides visitors with comfortable and cheap lodging while they stay in Korea. Reservations can be made through the internet (www.worldinn.com) or the call center (82-2-3279-5690). Visitors need to make reservations at least 2 weeks prior to their preferred check-in date.

DELUXE HOTELS

Remark

Ⓒ: Chinese Restaurant Ⓚ: Korean Restaurant Ⓙ: Japanese Restaurant Ⓦ: Western Restaurant Ⓑ: Buffet Restaurant Ⓘ: Italian Restaurant

Hotel Name	Rms	Address	Tel	Fax	Homepage	Restaurant	Business center	Entertainment	Leisure & Sports	Convention	Banquet Hall
Seoul											
Hotel Ellelui	124	129, Cheongdam-dong, Gangnam-gu	82-2-514-3535	82-2-548-2500	www.ellelui.co.kr	ⓀⓌ	○		Leisure & Sports		○
Hotel New World	222	112-5, Samseong-dong, Gangnam-gu	82-2-557-0111	82-2-557-0141		ⒸⓀⒿⒷ	○		Fitness Center		○
Hotel Riviera	163	5307, Cheongdam-dong, Gangnam-gu	82-2-541-3111	82-2-546-6111	www.hotelriviera.co.kr	ⒸⒿⒷ		Night Club, Karaoke	Saunas, Fitness Club (Gymnasium, Indoor Swimming Pool, Indoor Golf Range, Aerobics		○
Novotel Ambassaor Kangnam Seoul	336	603, Yeoksam-dong, Gangnam-gu	82-2-567-1101	82-2-564-4573	www.ambatel.com	ⓀⒿⓌⒷ	○				○
Novotel Ambassaor Toksan Seoul	230	1030-1, Doksan 4-dong, Geumcheon-gu	82-2-838-1101	82-2-854-4799	www.ambatel.com	ⓀⓌ	○	Pub, Restaurant			○
Holiday Inn Seoul	362	169-1, Dohwa-dong, Mapo-gu	82-2-717-9441	82-2-715-9441	www.holiday-inn.co.kr	ⒸⒿⒾ	○		Sauna, Health Club		○
Seoul Palace Hotel	283	63-1, Banpo-dong, Seocho-gu	82-2-532-5000	82-2-532-0399	www.seoulpalace.co.kr	Ⓚ	○		Health Club, Sauna,		○
Seoul TEMF Hotel	237	202, Yangjae-dong, Seocho-gu	82-2-571-8100	82-2-571-7055	www.temf.co.kr	ⓀⒿⓌⒷ		Movie Theater, Drive-In Theater	Sports Center, Indoor Golf Course,		
Hotel Capital	287	22-76, Itaewon-dong, Yongsan-gu	82-2-792-1122,3322	82-2-797-4244		ⓀⒿ			Sauna, Health Club, Aerobic Room		○
Olympia Hotel Seoul	270	108-2, Pyeongchang-dong, Jongno-gu	82-2-2287-6000	82-2-2287-6103	www.olympia.co.kr	ⒿⓌⒷ	○				○
Hotel President	303	188-3, Euljiro 1-ga, Jung-gu	82-2-753-3131	82-2-752-7417	www.hotelpresident.co.kr	ⒿⒷ				○	
Hotel Sofitel Ambassador	432	186-54, Jangchung-dong 2-ga, Jung-gu	82-2-2275-1101	82-2-2272-0773	www.ambatel.com	ⒸⒿⒷ		Pub	Leisure & Sports		○
Koreana Hotel	344	61-1, Taepyeongno 1-ga, Jung-gu	82-2-730-9911-20	82-2-730-9025	www.koreanahotel.com	ⒸⓀⒿⓌ					○
Sejong Hotel Seoul	235	61-3, Chungmuro 2-ga, Jung-gu	82-2-773-6000	82-2-755-4906	www.sejong.co.kr	ⓀⒿⒷ		Pub	Health Club, Sauna		○
Seoul Royal Hotel	307	6, Myeong-dong 1-ga, Jung-gu	82-2-771-4500	82-2-756-1119	www.seoulroyal.co.kr	ⒿⓌⒷ		Night Club	Leisure & Sports		○
Tower Hotel	218	San 5-5, Jangchung-dong 2-ga, Jung-gu	82-2-2236-2121	82-2-2235-0276	www.towerhotel.co.kr	ⒸⓀⓌ			Outdoor Swimming Pool, Sauna, Health Club, Outdoor Golf Range, Tennis Courts, Jogging Course	○	○
Busan											
Hotel Paragon	132	617-809 , Gwaebeop-dong, Sasang-gu	82-51-328-2001	82-51-328-2009	www.hotelparagon.com	ⓀⒿⓌⒷ		Room saloon			○
Commodore Hotel	326	743-80, Yeongju-dong, Jung-gu	82-51-466-9101	82-51-462-9101	www.commodore.co.kr	ⒸⓀⒿⓌⒷ		Cocktail Bar, Discotheque, Karaoke	Indoor Swimming Pool, Sauna, Health Club		
Hotel Sorabol	162	37-1, Daechang-dong 1-ga, Jung-gu	82-51-463-3511	82-51-463-3510	www.sorabolhotel.co.kr	ⓀⒿⓌ					
Daegue											
Taegu Prince Hotel	117	1824-2, Daemyeong 2-dong, Nam-gu	82-53-628-1001	82-53-628-2833	www.princehotel.co.kr	ⒸⓀⒿⓌ		Night Club	Sauna		○
Taegu Grand Tourist Hotel	111	563-1, Beomeo-dong, Suseong-gu	82-53-742-0001	82-53-742-0002	www.taegugrand.co.kr	ⒸⓀⒿⓌⒷ		Night Club	Sauna		○
Taegu Park Hotel	133	San 98-1, Manchon-dong, Suseong-gu	82-53-952-0088	82-53-952-0808	www.ibtaegupark.co.kr	ⒸⓀⒿⓌ		Night Club	Swimming Pool, Health Club		○
Incheon											
Hotel Songdo Beach	197	812, Dongchun 1-dong, Yeonsu-gu	82-32-832-2000	82-32-832-1325	www.songdobeach.co.kr	ⓀⒿⓌ		Bar	Sauna, Health Center		○
Hotel Olympos & Casino	175	3-2, Hang-dong 1-ga, Jung-gu	82-32-762-5181	82-32-763-5281	www.olympos.co.kr	ⓀⒿⓌ		Casino, Night Club, Karaoke, Room Salon	Sauna		○
Gwangju											
Mundeung Park Hotel	110	San 63-1, Jisan-dong, Dong-gu	82-62-226-0011~30	82-62-226-6020	www.hotelmudeung.co.kr	ⒸⓀⒿⒷ		Night Club, Room Salon	Sauna, Bowling Alley, Health Club, Aerobic Room		○

Hotel Name	Rms	Address	Tel	Fax	Homepage	Restaurant	Business center	Entertainment	Leisure & Sports	Convention	Banquet Hall
Daejeon											
Hotel Lotte Daejeon	69	382, Doryong-dong, Yuseong-gu	82-42-865-7000	82-42-862-0059	www.hotel.lotte.co.kr	ⓀⒿⓌ			Sauna, Bowling Lanes		○
Hotel Riviera	174	444-5, Bongmyeong-dong, Yuseong-gu	82-42-823-2111	82-42-822-5250	www.hotelriviera.co.kr	ⒸⓀⒿⓌ		Pub, Restaurant, Night Club	Saunas, Spa Club, Fitness Club, Outdoor Swimming Pool, Indoor Swimming Pool, Aerobics		○
Yousoung Hotel	191	480, Bongmyeong-dong, Yuseong-gu	82-42-822-0811	82-42-822-0041		ⒸⓀⓌ		Night Club, Room Salon	Sauna, Swimming Pool, HealthClub, Aerobic Room,Bowling Lanes		
Ulsan											
Hotel Hyundai Ulsan	283	283, Jeonha-dong, Dong-gu	82-52-251-2233	82-52-232-7170	www. hotelhyundai. com	ⓀⒿⒾ			Swimming Pool, Men' s Sauna, Health Center		
Koreana Hotel	175	255-3, Seongnam-dong, Jung-gu	82-52-244-1911-15	82-52-244-1665	www.koreanahotel.co.kr	ⓀⒿ		Cocktail Bar, Night Club	Sauna		○
Gangwon-do											
Hotel Hyundai Kyongpodae	92	274-1,Gangmun-dong, Gangneung-si	82-33-644-2181	82-2-236-5012	www.hyundaihotel.com	ⓀⓌ			Tennis Court		○
Hotel Sorak Park	121	74-3, Seorak-dong, Sokcho-si	82-33-636-7711	82-33-636-7724	www.hotelsorakpark.com	ⓀⓌ		Casino, Night Club, Karaoke, Singing Room, Billiards	Sauna	○	○
Kensington Hotel Sorak	120	106-1 Seorak-dong, Soksho-si	82-33-636-7131	82-33-635-4011	www.kensington.co.kr	ⓀⒿⓌ		Karaoke, Internet Room	Tennis Court, Golf Putting		
Dragon Valley Hotel	191	130, Yongsan-ri, Doam-myeon, Pyeongchang-gun	82-33-335-5757	82-33-335-5769	www.yongpyong.co.kr	ⓀⓌ		Health Club, Swimming Pool, Squash Room		○	○
Hotel Odaesan	306	221-1, Ganpyeong-ri, Jinbu-myeon, Pyeongchang-gun	82-33-330-5000	82-33-330-5123	www.hotelodaesan.co.kr	ⓀⒿⓌ		Pub, Restaurant			○
Phoenix Park The Hotel	141	1095, Myeonon-ri, Bongpyeong-myon, Pyeongchang-gun	82-33-333-6000	82-33-330-6508	www.phoenixpark.co.kr	ⓀⓌ		Game Room, Karaoke	Swimming Pool, Sauna, Ski Slope, Country Club, MTB Track		
Gyeonggi-do											
Hotel Castle	81	144-4, Uman-dong, Paldal-gu, Suwon-si	82-31-211-6666	82-31-212-8811		ⓀⒿⒷ		Night Club	Men' s Sauna		○
Hotel Miranda	160	408-1, Anheung-dong, Icheon-si	82-31-633-2001	82-31-633-2030		ⓀⓌ		Night Club, Pub, Restaurant			
Jeollabuk-do											
Hotel Tirol	118	San 60-4, Simgok-ri, Seolcheon-myeon, Muju-gun	82-63-320-7200	82-63-322-9267		ⓀⓌ					○
Chonju Core Hotel	111	627-3, Seonosong-dong, Deokjin-gu, Jeonju-si	82-63-285-1100	82-63-285-5707		ⒸⓀⓌ		Night Club	Sauna		○
Core Riviera Hotel	166	26-5, 3-ga, Pungnam-dong, Wansan-gu, Jeonju-si	82-63-232-7000	82-63-232-7100	www.hotelriviera.co.kr	ⒸⒿⒷ		Bar, Game Room			
Chungcheongnam-do											
Onyang Grand Hotel	157	300-28, Oncheon-dong, Asan-si	82-41-543-9711	82-41-543-9729	www.grand-hotel.co.kr	ⓀⓌ		Karaoke, Night Club	Sauna, Indoor Swimming Pool Karaoke, Game Room, Billiard Room, Bowling Alley		○
Gyeongsangbuk-do											
Kyongju TEMF Hotel	270	150-2, Shinpyeong-dong, Gyeongju-si	82-54-745-8100	82-54-748-8563	www.temf.co.kr	ⓀⓌ					
Hotel Cygnus	120	145-21, Yongheung-dong, Buk-gu, Pohang-si	82-54-275-2000	82-54-275-2218	www.hanwharesort.co.kr	ⓀⒿⒷ			Sauna, Health Club		○
Gyeongsangnam-do											
Dongbang Tourist Hotel	125	803-4, Okbong-dong, Jinju-si	82-55-743-0131	82-55-742-6789		Ⓚ		Karaoke	Men's Sauna		○
Hotel International	121	97-4, Jungang-dong, Changwon-si	82-55-281-1001	82-55-284-2000	www.hotelinternational.co.kr	ⓀⓌⒷ		Night Club	Sauna		○
Jeju-do											
Cheju Prince Hotel	170	731-3, Seohong-dong, Seogwipo-si	82-64-732-9911	82-64-732-9900		ⓀⓌ		Karaoke	Men's Sauna, Beauty Salon, Barber Shop, Outdoor · Indoor Swimming Pool		○
Seogwipo KAL Hotel	221	486-3, Topyeong-dong, Seogwipo-si	82-64-733-2001	82-64-733-9377	www.kalhotel.co.kr	ⓀⒿⓌ		Night Club	Tennis Court, Indoor · Outdoor Swimming Pool, Indoor Golf, Sauna, Gateball Court		○
Cheju Pacific Hotel	177	159-1, Yongdam 1-dong, Jeju-si	82-64-758-2500	82-64-758-2521		ⓀⒿⓌ		Karaoke	Sauna		○
Royal Hotel	108	272-34, Yeon-dong, Jeju-si	82-64-743-2222	82-64-748-0074		ⓀⒿⓌ		Night Club, Room Salon, Bar	Sauna		○

TRANSPORTATIONS

BUS

The city bus systems differ slightly from city to city in Korea, but most cities have local and express buses.

They are numbered but since their signs are only in Korean, finding the right bus may be confusing to a first-time visitor. It is advisable to request assistance to find the bus stop and bus number needed.

Buses are numbered according to their specific routes. It is best to know the bus routing and number in advance. Visitor may get assistance from the hotel front desk to find out where the bus stops are and which bus number people need to take.

Visitors may also contact the Bus Route Information Center (Tel. 82-2-414-5005).

Bus fare can be paid with either coins or a bus card available at booths near bus stops.

Local City Bus

Local buses are the most common means of transportation in Seoul. They are frequent, reliable, and inexpensive. Seoul's bus network serves every area of the city. The adult fare is 600 won regardless of distance.

City Coach Bus

City coach buses and the new deluxe city express buses, called 'Jwaseok' buses in Korean, are more comfortable. The fares for the city coach buses and the new deluxe city express buses are 1,200 and 1,300 won respectively.

Alirport Limousine Bus

Luxury limousine buses and non-stop coach buses provide fast, convenient and economical means of transportation from Incheon Airport to downtown Seoul and the surrounding metropolitan area. Bus fares are 10,000 won and 5,500 won for the limousine buses and coaches, respectively.

A total of 21 bus lines (15 limousines and 6 non-stop coaches) are in operation to downtown Seoul and five to Incheon (1 limousine, 1 non-stop coach, 2 ordinary coach buses and 1 city bus).

The first bus leaves the airport at 4:30 A.M., and the last one leaves the airport at 11:00 P.M.

Transportation Card

The Transportation Card or coins can be used to pay bus fares. The Transportation Card is a pay-per-ride card with 2 % added value and can also be used to pay metro fares. 10,000, and 20,000 won bus cards are sold and recharged at kiosks or news stands near the bus stop. A 1,500 won deposit is required when purchasing a Transportation Card, which is refunded when the card is returned.

When a passenger gets on a bus, he or she needs to place the transportation card on the card reader beside the driver to pay the bus fare. The card reader displays how much money is left on the card. If a person wants to pay for the fares of more than one person, he needs to tell the driver how many people he wants to pay for and place the card on the card reader as many times as the number of the people.

TAXI

Taxis are safe, plentiful and inexpensive in Korea. There are three kinds of taxis; regular, deluxe and jumbo.

The last two offer a higher standard of service compared to the first, but are more expensive.

There are taxi stands in most city areas and taxis can also be hailed on the streets. Certain taxis can be requested by phone, though the fare for these special call taxis is somewhat higher than regular taxis. An increasing number of taxi drivers speak some English.

Vacant taxis have their roof indicator lamps on.

Regular Taxi

The taxi fare system is based on both the distance and the time taken. Fares are 1,600 won for the first 2km and 100 won for each 168m afterwards. Fares increase 20% between midnight and 4 a.m.

Deluxe Taxi

Deluxe taxis are black with a yellow sign on the top and the words 'Deluxe Taxi' written on the sides. They offer more passenger space and a high standard of service. Fares are 4,000 won for the first 3km and 200 won for each additional 205m or 50 seconds (if the speed drops below 15km per hour). Receipts are available. There is no late-night surcharge. Deluxe taxis can be taken at stands located at hotels, airports, train stations, bus terminals, and on major city streets.

Jumbo Taxi

Jumbo taxis are black mini-vans. They offer space for up to 8 passengers at a time and a high standard of service, including a taxi call service and a simultaneous interpretation phone service. Fares are 4,000 won for the first 3km and 200 won for each additional 205m or 50 seconds (if the speed drops below 15km per hour). Receipts are available. There is no late-night surcharge. Jumbo taxis can be taken at stands located at hotels, airports, train and bus stations and on major city streets.

Free Interpretation Service

A special interpretation service is provided in all taxis on a request basis. Three way simultaneous communication is possible between the passenger, driver and interpreter in English, Japanese and Chinese, through a wireless phone installed in the taxi. If passengers need information, call 82-17-200-3000

METRO

Eight Metro lines and a surface line of the government-run Korean National Railroad (KNR) serve Seoulites and visitors. Seoul Metro lines link the farthest parts of Seoul and its satellite cities through lines of various colors and numerous transfer stations.
On average, Metro trains operate at intervals of 2.5 to 3 minutes during the morning and evening rush hours and 4 to 6 minutes during the non-rush hours.
A basic fare for a single journey within Seoul is 600 won (zone 1) or 700 won (zone 2). Special fares apply for the Korean National Railroad Line (KNR section) depending on distance travelled. Tickets can be bought at coin-operated vending machines or at bill-operated machines. Transportation card, that are also good for bus fares are now accepted for fare.

RAILROAD

Train service in Korea is provided and operated by the Korean National Railroad (KORAIL). Tourists can use this fast, safe and reliable service at very reasonable prices. Trains are operated by strict schedules, and there are no delays or traffic jams, so travellers can get to their destination on time dependably. KORAIL's routes cover all of the country, and there are three kinds of trains in operation: the Super-Express Saemaeul-ho, the Express Mugunghwa-ho, and the Limited Express Tongil-ho.

Super-Express: Saemaeul-ho

This train provides various services for passengers: dining room, clean and spacious seats, the fastest traveling times, pay-phones, and tables for notebook computers. Many business people prefer the Super-Express Saemaeul-ho. The train is divided into first- and second-class sections and is more expensive than other trains.

Express: Mugunghwa-ho

Most passengers prefer Mugunghwa-ho when going from one city to another. It provides very clean and comfortable service. The train is divided into first- and second-class sections. It is cheaper than Saemaeul but travel time may be slightly longer.

Seoul Station

Everyday about 90,000 people use the gateway to the nation's capital, Seoul Station. The station was opened first in 1910 as Gyeongseong Station, and its name was changed to the current Seoul Station in 1946. In 1988, the station was expanded to include a shopping arcade. A train museum depicts the history of trains in Korea, and there is a cultural center that holds exhibitions. This station is the starting point of the Gyeongbuseon and Honamseon Routes which connect Seoul to Busan and Mokpo, respectively.

Cheongnyangni Station

This station was opened in 1914 and was officially named Cheongnyangni in 1942. The station building was remodeled in 1959. It averages 36,000 passengers per day and 32 round trip trains are operated out of this station. It is the beginning point of the Gyeongchunseon, Jungangseon, Taebaekseon and Yeongdongseon Routes, which connect Seoul to the East Coast and several national parks.

KR Pass

A KR Pass can be purchased from a sales representative abroad in the form of a voucher. This needs to be exchanged for a KR Pass at a designated station in Korea. With this ticket, visitors can take any train run by the Korean National Railroad Administration (except the subway) within a certain period of time, without any restriction on the train sections or the number of rides.

Railroad Information

	Gyeongbuseon (Seoul-Busan)						Honamseon (Seoul-Mokpo)				
Seoul	Suwon	Daejeon	Gimcheon	Gumi	Dongdaegu	Busan	Seodaejeon	Iksan	Jeongeup	Songjeong-ri	Mokpo
Suwon	41.5km										
Daejeon		166.8km									
Gimcheon			254.6km								
Gumi				277.5km							
Dongdaegu					327.1km						
Busan						444.3km					
Seodaejeon							167.9km				
Iksan								250.1km			
Jeongeup									293.6km		
Songjeong-ri										347.9km	
Mokpo											418.5km

Three types of KR Pass are available: Normal Pass, Saver Pass, and Youth Pass.

Normal Pass: This is an ordinary ticket for adults and children.

Saver Pass: This is for a group of 2~5 persons with the same schedule.

Youth Pass: This is for youth (13~25 years old).

Voucher Purchasing:

Travel agencies in foreign countries sell vouchers. The price is based on the exchange rate at the time of purchase.

Purchasers must specify the date that they want to start using the pass; it can be any date within 60 days of purchase.

KR PASS Fare

Class	Normal		Saver	Youth	Remark
	Adult	Child	2~5person	13-25age	
Tickets for 3 days	48	24	44	39	* When using the SAVER PASS, adult rates are charged for youth or children included.
Tickets for 5 days	72	36	65	58	
Tickets for 7 days	91	46	82	73	
Tickets for 10 days	106	53	96	84	

Unit: US ($)

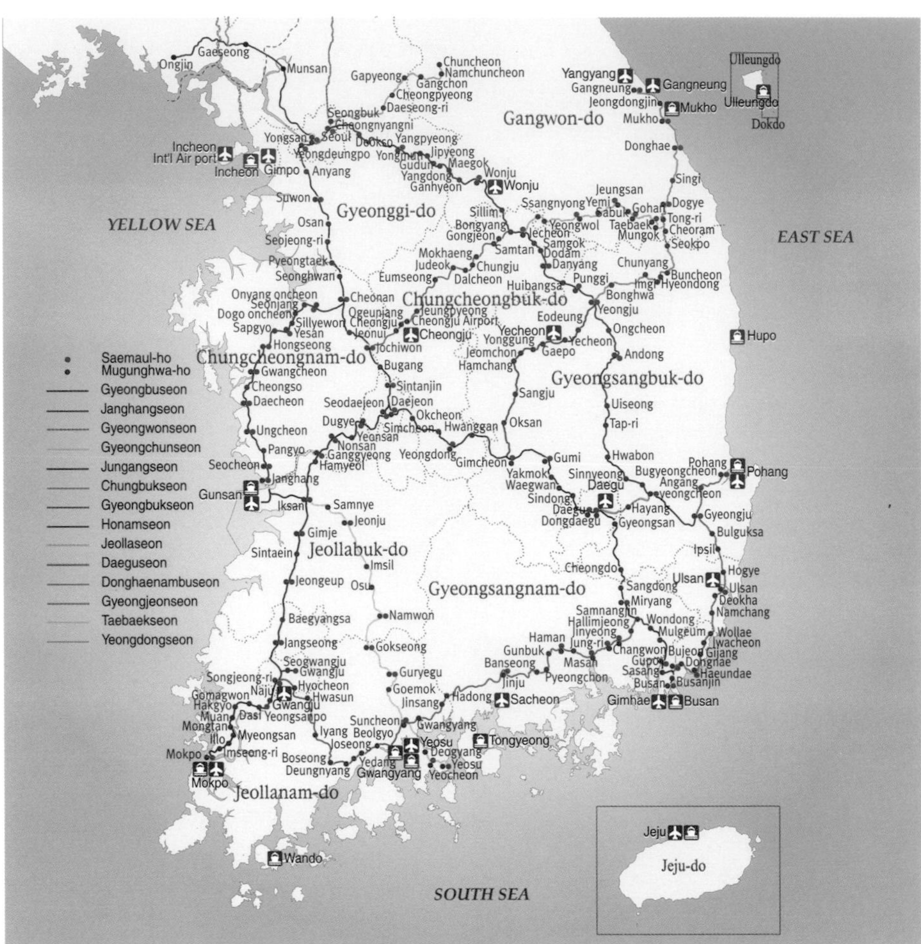

RENTAL CAR

Rental cars are available for those visitors who choose to drive in Korea. Rental car charges range from 55,000 to 460,000 won per day. Cars are driven on the right side of the road and most road signs are written in Korean and English. Due to the high traffic density and complex road systems, it is probably advisable to hire a driver along with the car, especially in large cities. Visitors who wish to hire a chauffeur-driven car must be prepared to pay for the driver' s meals and hotel expenses as well.

For further details, call the Korea Car Rental Union; 82-2-525-9077/8

Visitors must meet the following requirements to rent a car:

Have more than 1 year's driving experience

Have an international driver' s license

Be over 21 years of age

Possess a valid passport

Major Car Rental Companies in Korea

City	Name	Tel
Seoul	Geumho(Hertz)	82-2-797-8000
	VIP(Avis)	82-2-3663-2847
	Han Gang	82-2-2247-0022
	Jaeil	82-2-733-8887
	Joy	82-2-710-5445
	Korea Express	82-2-719-7295
	Sambo	82-2-591-9977
	Samjee	82-2-362-3233
	Saehan	82-2-896-0031
Busan	Hanguk	82-51-205-3240
	New Busan	82-51-469-2222
	Noksaek Gomduri	82-51-704-0057
Daegu	Yeong-il	82-53-952-1001
	Geukdong	82-53-743-0008
Incheon	Kyeong In	82-32-525-4444
	New Incheon	82-32-882-0106
	Paldo	82-32-864-8686
Gwangju	Line	82-62-671-9933
	Green	82-62-361-1006
	Hyundae	82-62-373-0089
Daejeon	Donghwa	82-42-631-4902
	Chungnam	82-42-585-5801
	Gana	82-42-254-2266
Ulsan	Geumgang	82-52-287-9000
Gyeongju	Gyeongju	82-54-741-6666
Jeju	Jeju	82-64-743-3301
	Dong-a	82-64-743-1515
	Green	82-64-743-2000
	Halla	82-64-755-5000
	Hanseong	82-64-747-2100
	Seongsan	82-64-746-3230
	Beomhan	82-64-748-4001
	Seokgwang	82-64-748-2800
	Wooli	82-64-752-9600

USEFUL INFORMATION

1330 Travel Phone Service

By dialing 1330, tourists can reach English, Japanese or Chinese-speaking tour advisors who will provide infomation on attractions, accommodations, transportation and festivals.

The phone service is available from 09:00 to 18:00 (09:00-20:00 in Seoul) every day throughout the year. With a cellular phone visitors have to dial the area code before entering 1330 (if visitors want to call a particular region, they should use that area code).

Please refer to the area codes as follows: Seoul 02, Incheon 032, Daejeon 042, Busan 051, Ulsan 052, Daegu 053, Gwangju 062, Gyeonggi-do 031, Gangwon-do 033, Chungcheongnam-do 041, Chungcheongbuk-do 043, Gyeongsangnam-do 055, Gyeongsangbuk-do 054, Jeollanam-do 061, Jeollabuk-do 063, Jeju-do 064.

If calling to Korea from abroad, dial 82 (country code) + area code (without 0) + 1330.

www.tour2korea.com

The websites below are provided by the Korean government for overseas visitors in Korea. They can help make reservations for mid-range or low-priced hotels, and provide useful information for tourists.

Tourist Information Center

Information and assistance are readily available at KNTO's Tourist Information Center (TIC) or at information counters at the three international airports or major tourist sites. Information counters provide city maps, brochures and useful information on tours, monthly events and shows, shopping, dining, and accommodations. KNTO's TIC is open every day from 09:00 to 21:00.

Business Hours

Government offices are open between the hours of 09:00 and 18:00 from March to October and between 09:00 and 17:00 from November to February. On Saturday, hours are 09:00 to 17:00. Most private businesses open from 08:30 to 22:00. Banks are an exception. Their business hours are from 09:30 to 16:30 on weekdays, and from 09:30 to 13:30 on Saturday.

Foreign diplomatic missions in Seoul are usually open from 09:00 to 17:00 on weekdays and are closed on Saturday and Sunday.

Regional Harbor Information

Area	Address	Tel
Incheon Harbor	88, Hang-dong 7-ga, Jung-gu, Incheon-si	82-32-888-8052
Boryeong Harbor	950, Sinheuk-dong, Boryeong-si, Chungcheongnam-do	82-41-934-8772
Gunsan Harbor	1-8, Jangmi-dong, Gunsan-si, Jeollabuk-do	82-63-442-0116
Mokpo Harbor	6-10, Hang-dong, Mokpo-si, Jeollanam-do	82-61-243-0116
Wando Harbor	1255, Hangdong-ri, Wando-gun, Jeollanam-do	82-61-552-0116
Yeosu Harbor	682, Gyo-dong, Yeosu-si, Jeollanam-do	82-61-663-0116
Tongyeong Harbor	316, Seoho-dong, Tongyeong-si, Gyeongsangnam-do	82-55-642-0116
Masan Harbor	6, Wolpo-dong 2-ga, Happo-gu, Masan-si, Gyeongsangnam-do	82-55-245-0116
Busan Harbor	16, Jungang-dong 5-ga, Jung-gu, Busan-si	82-51-469-0117
Pohang Harbor	58-54, Hanggu-dong, Pohang-si, Gyeongsangbuk-do	82-54-242-5111
Jeju Harbor	918-30, Geonip-dong, Jeju-si, Jeju-do	82-64-757-0117

Flight Information

Seoul	Busan	Jeju	Gwangju	Daegu	Sokcho	Yeosu	Ulsan	Pohang	Jinju	Mokpo	Gunsan	Yecheon	Gangneung
Busan	60min												
Jeju		65min											
Gwangju			55min										
Daegu				50min									
Sokcho					50min								
Yeosu						60min							
Ulsan							60min						
Pohang								50min					
Jinju									60min				
Mokpo										60min			
Gunsan											50min		
Yecheon												50min	
Gangneung													50min

Tourist Information Center

City	Name of Information Center	Tel
Seoul	- KNTO Tourist Information Center . Incheon Int'l Airport - Seoul Tourist Information Center . Itaewon . Myeong-dong . Dongdaemun Market . Namdaemun Market . Deoksugung . Seoul Express Bus Terminal . Seoul Metropolitan Rapid Transit Infonet	82-2-757-0086 82-32-743-2600~3 82-2-731-6337 82-2-794-2490 82-2-757-0088 82-2-2236-9135 82-2-752-1913 82-2-756-0045 82-2-537-9198 82-2-735-5678
Busan	- Gimhae Int'l Airport - Busan Railroad Station - Busan Int'l Ferry Terminal - Busan Information Service Center for Foreigners	82-51-973-1100 82-51-441-6565 82-51-465-3471 82-51-462-2256
Gyeongju	- Gyeongju Railroad Station - Bulguksa Temple - Gyeongju Express Bus Terminal	82-54-772-3843 82-54-746-4747 82-54-772-9289
Jeju	- Jeju Int'l Airport - Jeju Harbor Passenger Terminal - Jungmun Tourist Center	82-64-742-8866 82-64-758-7181 82-64-738-8550

Major department stores are open from 10:30 to 19:30, including Sunday, but smaller shops tend to be open earlier and close later every day of the week.

Lost & Found

In the event of misplaced or lost property, contact the Lost and Found Center of the Seoul Metropolitan Police Bureau:
http://www.lost114.com
11F (1104), Aju Bldg. Yeoksam-dong, Gangnam-gu, Seoul
Tel: 82-2-5544-182, Fax: 82-2-5540-182

Tourist Complaint Center

Overseas visitors to Korea who experience any inconvenience or who simply want to offer some suggestions should call or write the Tourist Complaint Center, operated by the Korea National Tourism Organization:
K.P.O. Box 1879, Seoul 100-180,
Korea Tel: 82-2-735-0101 Fax: 82-2-777-0102
e-mail: tourcom@www.knto.or.kr

Automated Teller Machines

Travellers who carry internationally recognized credit cards can withdraw cash from their accounts or get a cash advance at most automated teller machines (ATMs) installed at major hotels, department stores, subway stations and tourist attractions.
In addition, travelers holding any ATM card with a Cirrus or Plus logo can withdraw cash from their checking and savings accounts.

Internet Homepage Information

Name	Home-page
KNTO	http://www.knto.or.kr http://www.visitkorea.or.kr
Seoul Metropolitan City	http://www.metro.seoul.kr
Busan Metropolitan City	http://www.metro.busan.kr
Daegu Metropolitan City	http://www.daegu.go.kr
Incheon Metropolitan City	http://www.inpia.net http://www.metro.incheon.kr
Daejeon Metropolitan City	http://www.metro.daejeon.kr
Gwangju Metropolitan City	http://www.metro.gwangju.kr
Ulsan Metropolitan City	http://www.metro.ulsan.kr
Gyeonggi-do	http://www.provin.gyeonggi.kr
Gangwon-do	http://www.provin.gangwon.kr
Chungcheongbuk-do	http://www.provin.chungbuk.kr
Chungcheongnam-do	http://www.provin.chungnam.kr
Jeollabuk-do	http://www.provin.jeonbuk.kr
Jeollanam-do	http://www.provin.jeonnam.kr
Gyeongsangbuk-do	http://www.provin.gyeongbuk.kr
Gyeongsangnam-do	http://www.provin.gyeongnam.kr
Jeju-do	http://www.provin.jeju.kr

Emergency Service

Dial 112 for the police and 119 for the fire department.
A hotel front desk or hotel manager can arrange for a doctor or an ambulance. If you need a doctor on the street, ask a policeman or passerby for assistance. Police boxes can be found on every major street. In addition, International SOS Korea (Tel: 82-2-790-7561) provides a 24-hour emergency service for foreigners, acting as a link between the patient and Korean hospitals for a fee.

Electricity

In Korea, outlets for both 110 and 220 volts 60 cycle are available, although hotels usually have only 220 volt outlets. Always check the power supply before using your equipment.

Tax

Value added tax (VAT) is levied on most goods and services at a standard rate of 10% and is included in the retail price.
In tourist hotels, this 10% tax applies to rooms, meals and other services and is added to the bill.

Tipping

Tipping is not customary in Korea. A 10% service charge is added to your bill at all tourist hotels.

Telephone Calls

There are three types of public telephones in Korea: coin-operated telephones, card telephones, card phones and credit card phones. A local call costs 50 won for three minutes. Intercity calls cost more. Coin phones return coins which are unused, but they do not return change for partially used 100 won coins.
Card telephones can be used to make international calls as well as local and intercity calls. Telephone cards come in 2,000, 3,000, 5,000, and 10,000 won denominations and are on sale in shops near telephone boxes and in banks. There are also credit card phones, which visitors can use with major credit cards.
To make an international call, first dial the international dialing code (001 or 002 or 008), depending on the service provider used, then the country code, area code, and finally the individual number.
International calls or collect calls can also be made through an operator by dialing 00799. For more information on operator-assisted calls, dial 00794.
Korea's regional codes are as follows: Seoul 02, Incheon 032, Daejeon 042, Busan 051, Ulsan 052, Daegu 053, Gwangju 062, Gyeonggi-do 031, Gangwon-do 033, Chungcheongnam-do 041, Chungcheongbuk-do 043, Gyeongsangnam-do 055, Gyeongsangbuk-do 054, Jeollanam-do 061, Jeollabuk-do 063, Jeju-do 064.

Telephone Service

Tourist Information 1330
Tourist Complaint Center 82-2-735-0101
Police 112
Fire and Ambulance 119
Medical Emergencies 13399
Local Directory Assistance 114
Long Distance Directory Assistance Area Code+114
International Calls 00794
International Telegram Services 00795
Operator-assisted Calls 00799
Exchange Rate Information 82-2729-0528

Currency

The unit of Korean currency is the won. Currency is divided into coins and notes.
Coin denominations are 1, 5, 10, 50, 100 and 500 won, but 1 won and 5 won coins are rarely used.
Notes are 1,000 won, 5,000 won and 10,000 won.
Bank checks in 100,000 won denominations can be

used, but when you use a bank check, you must show your I.D. card or passport.

Credit Cards

Credit cards, including VISA, American Express, Diners Club, Master Card and JCB, are accepted at major hotels, department stores, and restaurants.
VISA Tel: 82-2-524-9827
Master Card Tel: 82-2-730-1221
Diners Club Tel: 82-2-222-6100
American Express Tel: 82-2-552-7600
JCB Tel: 82-2-755-4977

Money Exchange

Foreign bank notes and traveler' s checks can be converted into Korean won at foreign exchange banks and other authorized money changers. The exchange rate is subject to market fluctuations.
The Exchange Rate ARS Service Tel: 82-2-3709-8000 (code No. 351)
Thomas Cook Tel: 82-2-733-6601
American Express Tel: 82-2-399-2904

Medical Service

- **Samsung Medical Center**
  50, Irwon-dong, Gangnam-gu, Seoul
  Tel: 82-2-3410-2114
  International Clinic (English is spoken)
  Tel: 82-2-3410-0200
- **Severance Hospital**
  134, Shinchon-dong, Seodaemun-gu, Seoul
  Tel: 82-2-361-5114
  International Clinic (English is spoken)
  Tel: 82-2-361-6540
- **Asan Medical Center (Chungang Hosp.)**
  388-1, Pungnap-dong, Songpa-gu, Seoul
  Tel: 82-2-224-3114
  International Clinic (English is spoken)
  Tel: 82-2-224-5001
- **Kangbuk Samsung Hospital International Clinic**
  Seodaemun-gu, Seoul
  Tel: 82-2-723-2911
- **Hannam-dong International Clinic**
  Hannam-dong, Seoul
  Tel: 82-2-790-0857
- **AMI Women' s Clinic**
  Apgujeong-dong, Seoul
  Tel: 82-2-516-0808
- **Chiropractic Clinic**
  Apgujeong-dong, Seoul
  Tel: 82-2-3443-0527
- **Seoul Foreign Clinic**
  Oksu-dong, Seoul
  Tel: 82-2-796-1871
- **Samsung Cheil Hospital**
  Tel: 82-2-2262-7071
- **Yeoui St. Mary' s Hospital**
  Yeongdeungpo-gu, Seoul
  Tel: 82-2-789-1114
- **Kangnam St. Mary' s Hospital**
  Gangnam-gu, Seoul
  Tel: 82-2-590-1114
- **Cha General Hospital**
  Tele: 82-2-558-1112
- **Soonchunhyang Hospital**
  Tel: 82-2-709-9881
- **Seoul National Univ. Hospital**
  Telephone : 82-2-760-2890

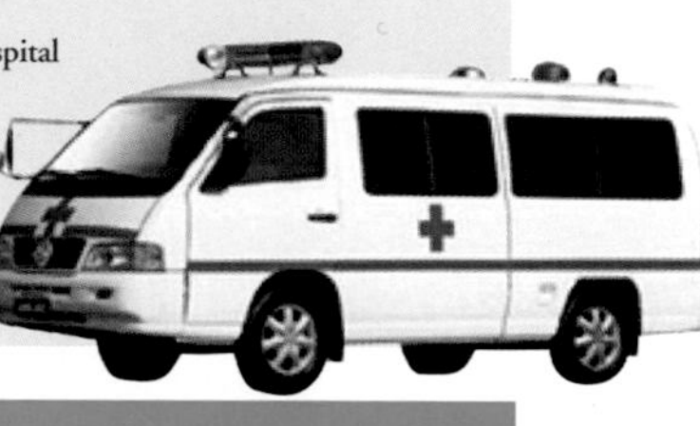

Foreign Diplomatic Missions in Korea

Country	Address	Tel
Australia Embassy	P.O. box. 562, 11F Gyobo Bldg., 1-1, Jongno 1-ga, Jongno-gu, Seoul	82-2-730-6490
Austria Embassy	P.O. box. 1099, 1913F Gyobo Bldg., Jongno 1-ga, Jongno-gu, Seoul	82-2-732-9071/2
Belgium Embassy	1-94, Dongbinggo-dong, Yongsan-gu, Seoul	82-2-749-0381~3
Brazil Embassy	3F Geumjeong Bldg., 192-11, Euljiro 1-ga, Jung-gu, Seoul	82-2-756-3170
Britain Embassy	4, Jeong-dong, Jung-gu, Seoul	82-2-735-7341/3
Canada Embassy	9F Kolon Bldg., 45, Mugyo-dong, Jung-gu, Seoul	82-2-3455-6000
China Embassy	83, Myeong-dong 2-ga, Jung gu, Seoul	82-2-319-5101
Denmark Embassy	5F Namseong Bldg., 26-199, Itaewon-dong, Yongsan-gu, Seoul	82-2-795-4187/9
France Embassy	30, Hap-dong, Seodaemun-gu, Seoul	82-2-312-3272
Germany Embassy	308-5, Dongbinggo-dong, Yongsan-gu, Seoul	82-2-748-4114
Indonesia Embassy	55, Yeouido-dong, Yeongdeungpo-gu, Seoul	82-2-783-5675
Italy Embassy	1-398, Hannam-dong, Yongsan-gu, Seoul	82-2-796-0491/5
Japan Consular Missions	1147-11, Choryang-dong, Dong-gu, Busan	82-51-465-5101/6
Japan Embassy	18-11, Junghak-dong, Jongno-gu, Seoul	82-2-2170-5200
Libya Embassy	4-5, Hannam-dong, Yongsan-gu, Seoul	82-2-797-6001~6
Malaysia Embassy	4-1, Hannam-dong, Yongsan-gu, Seoul	82-2-794-7205,0349
New Zealand Embassy	19F Kyobo Bldg., Jongno 1-ga, Jongno-gu, Seoul	82-2-730-7794
Norway Embassy	124-12, Itaewon-dong, Yongsan-gu, Seoul	82-2-795-6850/1
Philippines Embassy	9F Diplomatic Center, 1376-1, Seocho 2-dong, Seocho-gu, Seoul	82-2-577-6147
Portugal Embassy	2F Wonseo Bldg., Wonseo-dong, Jongno-gu, Seoul	82-2-3675-2254~5
Russia Consulate	8F Korea Exchange Bank Bldg., 89-1, Jungang-dong, Jung-gu, Busan	82-51-441-9904/5
Russia Embassy	1001-13, Daechi-dong,Gangnam-gu, Seoul	82-2-552-7094/7096
Singapore Embassy	19F Taepyeongno Bldg., Taepyeongno 2-ga, Jung-gu, Seoul	82-2-774-2464~7
Spain Embassy	726-52, Hannam-dong, Yongsan-gu, Seoul	82-2-794-3581~2
Sweden Embassy	12F Hanhyo Bldg., 136, Seorin-dong, Jongno-gu, Seoul	82-2-738-0846,1149
Switzerland Embassy	P.O. box. 2900, 32-10, Songwol-dong, Jongno-gu, Seoul	82-2-739-9511~4
Thailand Embassy	653-7, Hannam-dong, Yongsan-gu, Seoul	82-2-795-3098
United States (of America) Embassy	82, Sejongno, Jongno-gu, Seoul	82-2-397-4114
Vatican Embassy	2, Gungjeong-dong, Jongno-gu, Seoul	82-2-736-5725

National Holidays

New Year's Day (January 1)
People exchange New Year' s greetings and cards on this day. It is not considered as important as the Lunar New Year' s Day.

Lunar New Year's Day (Lunar January 1)
This is the most significant Korean holiday and lasts for three days. People wear traditional dress and pay tribute to their ancestors. They also wish their relatives and friends good luck in the new year. Rice cake soup is served for breakfast, after which families gather and play traditional games.

Independence Movement Day (March 1)
This holiday celebrates the independence movement against Japanese colonial rule in 1919.

Buddha's Birthday (Lunar April 8)
This day celebrates the birth of Buddha. The night before, a street parade with multi-colored lanterns is held and colorful lanterns are lit in temples.

Children's Day (May 5)
This is a day for children as they can spend time picnicking with their parents and receive gifts.

Memorial Day (June 6)
This day pays tribute to those who sacrificed their lives for the country.

Constitution Day (July 17)
This day remembers the establishment of the Korean constitution in 1948.

Liberation Day (August 15)
This day celebrates Korea's liberation from Japanese rule which lasted 36 years. Many commemorative events take place throughout the country, including parades and fireworks.

Chuseok-Thanksgiving Day (Lunar August 15)
Together with the Lunar New Year's Day, Chuseok is one of the most important traditional holidays, and is also celebrated for three days.

National Foundation Day (October 3)
This is the day when Dangun is said to have founded Korea in 2333 B.C.

Christmas (December 25)
As in other countries of the world, the birth of Christ is celebrated on this day.

USEFUL KOREAN PHRASES

GREETING AND COMMON COURTESY

Good-Bye	안녕히 가세요. (Annyeonghi gaseyo.)
How do you do?	처음 뵙겠어요. (Cheoeum boepgetseoyo.)
Yes, No.	예, 아니오. (Ye, Aniyo.)
Good Morning / Good afternoon / Good evening	안녕하세요. (Annyeonghaseyo.)
Thank you.	감사합니다. (Gamsahamnida.)
You are welcome.	천만에요. (Cheonmaneyo.)
I' m glad to meet you.	만나서 반가워요. (Mannaseo bangawoyo.)
Excuse me.	실례합니다. (Sillehamnida.)
Please!	부탁합니다. (Butakhamnida.)
My name is ( ).	제 이름은 ( )라고 합니다. (Je ireumun ( ) rago hamnida.)

SHOPPING

How much is it?	얼마에요? (Eolmaeyo?)
That' s too expensive!	너무 비싸요.(Neomu bissayo).
Do you have cheaper one?	조금 싼 것은 없습니까? (Jogeum ssan geoseun upseumnigga?)
May I have change please?	잔돈으로 바꿔 주세요. (Jandoneuro baggwo juseyo.)

EATING OUT

May I have a menu, please?	메뉴 좀 보여주세요. (Menu jom boyeojuseyo.)
What do you call this in Korean?	이것을 한국말로 뭐라고 합니까? (Igeoseul han-gungmallo mworago hamnigga?)
What' s your specialty here?	이 집에서 잘하는 음식이 무엇이죠? (Ijipeseo jal-haneun eumsigi mueosijo?)
Please make it mild.	맵지 않게 해주세요. (Maepjianke haejuseyo.)
Please take all the meat out	고기를 전부 빼 주세요. (Gogineun jeonbu bbaejuseyo.)
Where is the toilet?	화장실이 어디에 있습니까. (Hwajangsili eodie isseumnigga?)
Please bring me the bill.	계산서를 주세요. (Gyesanseoreul juseyo.)
Do you take traveler's checks?	여행자 수표를 받습니까? (Yeohaengja supyoreul batseomnigga?)

ACCOMMODATION

Do you have any vacancy?	빈 방 있어요? (Bin bang isseoyo?)
May I have a quiet room?	조용한 방을 부탁합니다. (Joyonghan bangeul butakhamnida.)
How much do I have to pay for one night?	1박에 얼마입니까? (Ilbage eolma imnigga?)
With private bath, please.	욕실 있는 방 주세요. (Yoksil inneunbang juseyo.)
Do you have anything cheaper?	더 싼 방은 없습니까?. (Deo ssan bangeun eopseumnigga?)
I want to stay one more night.	하루 더 묵고 싶습니다. (Haru deo muggo sipseumnida.)
Can I have my clothes washed?	세탁서비스 됩니까? (Setak seobis deomnigga?)
Could you clean my room, please?	방 청소 좀 해주세요. (Bang cheongso jom hae juseyo.)

TRANSPORTATION

How can I get to ( ) ?	( ) 에 어떻게 가면 됩니까? (( )e eoddeoke gamyeon doemnigga?)
Does this ( ) go to the ( ) ?	이 ( ) 은/는 ( )에 갑니까? (I ( ) eun/neun ( )e gamnigga?)
Where can I take a taxi?	택시는 어디에서 탑니까? (Taeksineun eodieseo tamnigga?)
I want to get off here.	여기에 내려 주세요 (Yeogie naeryeo juseyeo.)
How long does it take to get to...?	... 까지 시간이 얼마나 걸립니까? (... ggaji sigani eolmana geollimnigga?)
How much do I pay you to go ...?	... 까지 가는데 얼마입니까? (... ggaji ganeunde eolmaimnigga?)
Where can I catch the bus to ...?	... 행 버스는 어디에서 탑니까? (... haeng beoseuneun eodieseo tamnigga?)

INDEX

Cultural Relics

Example: Anapji Pond (P.259) 257F9
The name of tourism resource (The page of explanation) The page of the map, The grid

Natural Attractions

Museums & Theaters

Places of Interest

Explore Korea
Essence of Culture and Tourism

Published by the Ministry of Culture and Tourism (MCT), Republic of Korea

Publisher
Namkung Jin (Minister, Ministry of Culture and Tourism)

Project Overseer & Managing Editor
Yangwoo Park (Director General, Tourism Bureau, MCT)

Assistant Project Overseers
Chan Kim (Director, Tourism Policy Division, MCT)
Geunho Kim (Deputy Director, Tourism Policy Division, MCT)
Jinsuk Oh (Staff, Tourism Policy Division, MCT)

Editorial Director
Dr. Youn-taek Lee (President, Korea Tourism Research Institute)

Project Managers (Researching, Planning & Editing)
Dr. Seokho Lee, Dr. Chulwon Kim (Senior Researchers, Korea Tourism Research Institute)

Researching, Planning & Editing Assistants
Sookhyun Jung, Minjeong Seong,
Haemin Jung (Researchers, Korea Tourism Research Institute)
Brandon Butler (English Editor)

Map Producing / Designing / Printing Associates
Eungyong Bae (Director), Seungho Lee (Map Engineer), Seonghan Kim (Designer)
Hyundae Mapping Co.
82-2-335-1717

Copyright © 2002 The Ministry of Culture and Tourism, Korea,

All rights reserved. No part of this publication may be reproduced, stored in a retrieval system, or transmitted in any form or by electronic, mechanical, photocopying, recording or otherwise, without the prior written permission of the publisher and copyright owner.

The contents of this edition are believed correct at the time of printing. Nevertheless the publisher can accept no responsibility for errors or omissions, changes in the detail given or for any expense or loss thereby caused.

Printed in Korea

The Atlas is based on topographical maps of the National Geography Institute, such as 1:5,000, 1:25,000, 1:50,000, 1:250,000 scale map. The Atlas is approved by the Korean Association of Surveying and Mapping. (No. 2002-83, April 6, 2002)

ISBN 89-7820-077-X 00910